The fifty-plus extant manuscripts of *Piers Plowman* have always posed a puzzle to editors and readers. This book is an account of the editions of the poem which have appeared since 1550, when it was first published by the Protestant reformer Robert Crowley. It examines the circumstances in which the editions were produced, the lives and intellectual motivations of the editors, and the relationship between one edition and the next. Dr Brewer places the work of W. W. Skeat at the centre of *Piers Plowman* editing, showing how he towered above his predecessors and determined the path subsequently taken by editors of the poem (for example, in his dismissal of the Z-Text), and presents new biographical information about this extraordinary man. She also tells the story, pieced together from hitherto unpublished letters and papers, of the almost unknown edition of *Piers Plowman* embarked upon by R. W. Chambers in 1909, with the blessing of Skeat, a project that was on the point of foundering when it was inherited by George Kane over forty years later. Nearly fifty years on, Kane's Athlone edition of the poem is about to reach completion, while much additional editorial work on the poem has changed the face of *Piers Plowman* editing. By placing such work in its historical and textual context, Dr Brewer sheds new light on attempts to crack one of the major editorial conundrums in medieval studies.

CAMBRIDGE STUDIES IN MEDIEVAL LITERATURE 28

Editing *Piers Plowman*

CAMBRIDGE STUDIES IN MEDIEVAL LITERATURE

General Editor: Professor Alastair Minnis, Professor of Medieval
Literature, University of York

Editorial Board
Professor Piero Boitani (Professor of English, Rome)
Professor Patrick Boyde, FBA (Serena Professor of Italian, Cambridge)
Professor John Burrow, FBA (Winterstoke Professor of English, Bristol)
Professor Alan Deyermond, FBA (Professor of Hispanic Studies, London)
Professor Peter Dronke, FBA (Professor of Medieval Latin Literature, Cambridge)
Dr Tony Hunt (St Peter's College, Oxford)
Professor Nigel Palmer (Professor of German Medieval and Linguistic Studies,
Oxford)
Professor Winthrop Wetherbee (Professor of English, Cornell)

This series of critical books seeks to cover the whole area of literature written in the
major medieval languages – the main European vernaculars, and medieval Latin and
Greek – during the period *c.* 1100–*c.* 1500. Its chief aim is to publish and stimulate
fresh scholarship and criticism on medieval literature, special emphasis being placed
on understanding major works of poetry, prose and drama in relation to the
contemporary culture and learning which fostered them.

Recent titles in the series

A complete list of titles in the series is given at the end of this volume.

Editing *Piers Plowman*
The evolution of the text

CHARLOTTE BREWER

Hertford College, Oxford

CAMBRIDGE
UNIVERSITY PRESS

Published by the Press Syndicate of the University of Cambridge
The Pitt Building, Trumpington Street, Cambridge CB2 1RP
40 West 20th Street, New York, NY 10011–4211, USA
10 Stamford Road, Oakleigh, Melbourne 3166, Australia

© Cambridge University Press 1996

First published 1996

Printed in Great Britain at the University Press, Cambridge

A catalogue record for this book is available from the British Library

Library of Congress cataloguing in publication data
Brewer, Charlotte, 1956–
Editing Piers Plowman: the evolution of the text / Charlotte Brewer.
p. cm. – (Cambridge studies in medieval literature: 28)
Includes bibliographical references and index.
ISBN 0 521 34250 3 (hardback)
1. Langland, William, 1330?–1400? Piers the Plowman – Criticism, Textual.
2. Christian poetry, English (Middle) – Criticism, Textual.
3. Langland, William, 1330?–1400? – Manuscripts.
4. Manuscripts, English (Middle) – Editing.
I. Title. II. Series.
PR2017.T48B74 1996
821'.1–dc20 95–26694 CIP

ISBN 0 521 34250 3 hardback

For Chris

Then his friends would borrow his rough-drafts which were not on loose sheets, but in regular quires, and probably loosely (or well) bound. And his friends would copy them out (& a nice mess they sometimes made): & if any of them liked to add lines on his own account, there was nothing to prevent him. I believe we are utterly misled by modern notions, & clean forget how *casual* our ancestors were. How did *they* know that they were anything more than ephemeral productions? They looked upon them much more as we should regard a modern 'leading article'. They copied them because they wanted to *read them over again*! *not* because they wished to perpetuate them. They never regarded posterity one bit. What – as the famous remark runs – had posterity done for *them*?

W. W. Skeat (1909)

Have you ever produced a definitive edition of Langland? ... I have. I've just finished producing one. It has queer psychological effects. You begin to wonder if you're mad.

Edmund Crispin, Buried For Pleasure (1958).
(With thanks to David Benson)

Contents

Contents

Acknowledgements

I am very grateful to the Warden and Fellows of All Souls College, Oxford, for electing me to a Fellowship during the tenure of which I carried out much of the research for this book. I am also grateful to Hertford College and the University of Oxford, whose generous provision of maternity leave has later cushioned the effect of producing three children while writing. In this respect I especially thank the former Principal of Hertford, Sir Christopher Zeeman, who has been (there is no other word for it) magnificent. Thanks are also due to the Council of the Early English Text Society, the libraries of University College, London and King's College, London, the Director of Administration at the University of London, the Syndics of Cambridge University Library, and the Principal and Fellows of Newnham College, for permission to quote from material in their possession, and to the *Yearbook of Langland Studies* for permission to reproduce material in chapter 20 originally published as an article in that journal.

It goes without saying that it would have been impossible to conduct my research without the majestic editions of *Piers Plowman* by George Kane and E. T. Donaldson, with their display of the variant readings of the A- and B-MSS. I have also found the annotated bibliography of the poem by Vincent DiMarco, 'a monument of bibliographical scholarship' as Derek Pearsall has justly described it, an inestimable aid at almost every stage in research and writing.

I owe a signal debt to Randolph Quirk, who told me of the existence of the Chambers archive in the library of University College, London. I owe another to E. G. Stanley, who has been exceptionally generous with his time and advice, reading through an early draft of the entire book, making numerous suggestions and corrections, and saving me from some embarrassing errors. And I owe most of all to A. G. Rigg, for introducing me to the demanding pleasures of *Piers Plowman* textual scholarship. One of the enjoyable by-products of writing this book has been the stimulating and productive conversations I have had with Robert Adams about the text of *Piers Plowman*; I look forward to many more. I should also like to thank George Kane, for information and correction most generously given in a long conversation in September 1993 and in a subsequent letter, A. V. C. Schmidt, for kindly letting me see a copy of the proofs of his second Everyman edition of the B-Text of *Piers Plowman*, and A. G. Mitchell, for looking over, and giving me permission to publish, extracts from letters he wrote nearly fifty years ago, now lodged at University College, London and with the Early English Text Society.

A number of other people have given me extremely helpful suggestions and responses, although in some cases so long ago they may themselves have forgotten about them: A. S. G. Edwards, who during several conversations came up with fruitful recommendations for avenues of inquiry, Malcolm Godden, who also discovered the material in the EETS archives relating to the projected Chambers edition of *Piers Plowman*, S. S. Hussey, Derek Pearsall, David Fowler, John Pickles, C. David Benson, and especially my uncle Derek Brewer, who has warmly dispensed much advice and encouragement from an early stage in my research. James Simpson responded heroically to a late call for help, and gave me some invaluable feedback and corrections. T. C. Skeat has been most generous to me, as has K. M. Elisabeth Murray, who allowed me to read through the Skeat–Murray correspondence in her possession and to print an extract from one of Skeat's letter's to Furnivall (of which a transcription was kindly sent me by William Schipper). Celia Sisam very helpfully supplied me with details of her father Kenneth Sisam's correspondence and gave me permission to quote from it. I also thank Katharina Brett, of Cambridge University Press, for cheerfully tolerating so lengthy and delayed a volume. Without the contributions of all the above the book would have many more errors than it doubtless still contains.

On the domestic front, Lynn and Paul Hancock, Maria Brown, and especially Jocelyn Lewry have given my family and me superbly staunch support, for which I am eternally grateful. But my greatest debt, more than I can possibly express, is to my husband Chris Goodall, for his loyal and unflagging encouragement, his astonishingly resilient enthusiasm, his constructive criticism, and in particular his hounding me to completion.

Abbreviations

BJRL	*Bulletin of the John Rylands University Library of Manchester.*
CUL	Cambridge University Library.
DNB	*Dictionary of National Biography.* Ed. Leslie Stephen and Sidney Lee. 22 vols. Oxford, 1921–2.
DNB 1912–21	*Dictionary of National Biography.* Ed. H. W. C. Davis and J. R. H. Weaver. Oxford, 1927.
EETS	Early English Text Society.
JEGP	*Journal of English and Germanic Philology.*
Kane	George Kane, ed., *Piers Plowman: The A Version.* London, 1960.
Kane-Donaldson	George Kane and E. T. Donaldson, eds., *Piers Plowman: The B Version.* London, 1975.
Knott-Fowler	T. A. Knott and David Fowler, eds., *Piers Plowman. A Critical Edition of the A Version.* Baltimore, 1952.
MÆ	*Medium Ævum*
MED	*The Middle English Dictionary*
MLN	*Modern Language Notes*
MLR	*Modern Language Review*
MP	*Modern Philology*
NED	*The New English Dictionary* (subsequently *The Oxford English Dictionary*)
NM	*Neuphilologische Mitteilungen*
NLH	*New Literary History*
N&Q	*Notes & Queries*
Pearsall	Derek Pearsall, ed., *Piers Plowman, by William Langland. An Edition of the C-Text.* London, 1978.
PBA	*Proceedings of the British Academy*

Abbreviations

PMLA	*Publications of the Modern Language Association of America*
RES	*Review of English Studies*
Rigg-Brewer	A. G. Rigg and Charlotte Brewer, eds., *Piers Plowman: The Z Version*. Toronto, 1983.
SAC	*Studies in the Age of Chaucer*
Salter-Pearsall	Elizabeth Salter and Derek Pearsall, eds., *Piers Plowman. Selections from the C-Text*. London, 1967.
SB	*Studies in Bibliography*
Schmidt	A. V. C. Schmidt, ed., *William Langland, The Vision of Piers Plowman. A Critical Edition of the B-Text*. Second edition, 1995.
SEL	*Studies in English Literature*
Skeat, *A-Text*	W. W. Skeat, ed., *The Vision of William concerning Piers Plowman ... The 'Vernon' Text; or Text A*. EETS OS 28. London, 1867.
Skeat, *B-Text*	W. W. Skeat, ed., *The Vision of William concerning Piers Plowman ... The 'Crowley' Text; or Text B*. EETS OS 38. London, 1869.
Skeat, *C-Text*	W. W. Skeat, ed., *The Vision of William concerning Piers Plowman ... The 'Whitaker' Text; or Text C*. EETS OS 54. London, 1873.
Skeat, *Parallel-Text*	W. W. Skeat, ed., *The Vision of William concerning Piers Plowman in Three Parallel Texts ... 2 vols*. Oxford, 1886.
SN	*Studia Neophilologica*
St Phil	*Studies in Philology*
STC	*A Short-Title Catalogue of Books Printed in England, Scotland and Ireland, and of English Books Printed Abroad, 1475–1640*. Compiled by A. W. Pollard and G. R. Redgrave. London, 1926; revised edition K. Pantzner *et al.*, 1976.
TPS	*Transactions of the Philological Society*
YES	*Yearbook of English Studies*
YLS	*Yearbook of Langland Studies*

Note on the texts

Unless otherwise indicated, references to *Piers Plowman* are to the following editions:

Z-Text: Rigg, A. G., and Brewer, Charlotte, eds., *Piers Plowman: The Z Version*. Toronto, 1983 (Rigg-Brewer).

A-Text: Kane, George, ed., *Piers Plowman: The A Version*. London, 1960 (Kane)

B-Text: Schmidt, A. V. C., ed., *William Langland, The Vision of Piers Plowman. A Critical Edition of the B-Text*. Second edition, London and New York, 1995 (Schmidt).

C-Text: Pearsall, Derek, ed., *Piers Plowman, by William Langland. An Edition of the C-Text*. London, 1978 (Pearsall).

Introduction

This book is about the editing of *Piers Plowman*. The poem survives in over fifty manuscripts, all of which differ from each other to a greater or lesser extent. Most of them fall, very roughly, into three main narrative shapes, which have traditionally been called A, B, and C. Others can be squeezed into these three categories only with great difficulty. It is generally supposed that the various versions stem ultimately from a single author, William Langland, who wrote and then revised his poem several times towards the end of the fourteenth century.

The job of the editor is a tricky one. He or she must scrutinise and analyse the scribally preserved evidence of Langland's words and produce for the modern reader something that approximates to a satisfactory reproduction of them. Even this brief description begs many questions. Should the editor aim to penetrate the veil of scribal corruption (for all scribes introduce errors into their texts as they transcribe them), and by some means or other divine exactly what the author originally wrote? Or should he or she be content to produce something approximating to what Langland's contemporary audience would have read? To what extent do the differences between the manuscripts reflect authorial revision, and to what extent scribal corruption? Is it possible that the author produced more than the three traditionally identified versions of his poem, either wholesale rewritings or interim revisions? Or are the rogue manuscripts of the poem (to explain which the last suggestion has been invoked) attributable instead to extensive scribal rewriting of the work, for purposes it is now impossible to reconstruct? And if scribes *did* interest themselves in extensive rewriting, should one then treat them as authors in their own right? Certainly one might treat them as editors. Scribes, or their supervisors, intervened crucially in the transmission of *Piers Plowman*. They were in charge of lay-out, and

1

so divided the poem into paragraphs; they rubricated particular words and phrases and thus gave them greater prominence; they may well have been responsible for the organisational titles (Dowel, Dobet, and Dobest etc.) carving the poem into sections which affect the way it is read and understood; and of course they chose exemplars from which to copy the poem. Some of them compared different versions of the poem and transferred readings from one copy to another. All of them made mistakes as they transcribed, for it is impossible to copy out so many lines without a good deal of error. Many of them, consciously or unconsciously, changed the dialect of their original, and substituted words or phrases for a variety of reasons, ranging from the wish to censor to illegibility in the manuscript from which they copied.

There is a book to be written on the editing of *Piers Plowman* by its scribes. This is not it. Instead, this book begins with the first printed edition, published in 1550 by Robert Crowley, and surveys the following editions (or editings, or editorial discussions) of the poem up to and beyond the great Athlone Press editions this century by George Kane and E. Talbot Donaldson. During the course of the survey, I attempt to investigate some of the questions on editing mentioned above.

Each editor after Crowley has approached the poem with the (often express) intention of dislodging the work of his or her predecessor. Many have been able to claim new evidence, and nearly all have come up with fresh interpretations of existing evidence and with improved (or at least different) applications of editorial theory. Despite this appearance of linear development, some of the decisions or assumptions made by previous editors have been incorporated without question into the thinking of the next generation. This is almost certainly because the chaos of manuscripts and variants of the poem presents too complicated an entity to deal with. It is necessary to start with an arbitrarily chosen structure in order to organize the material into a form which can then be productively analysed. Some editors have chosen a single manuscript, others the three-version hypothesis first adopted by Skeat. These structures have had an important impact on the way we see the poem. Thus for many readers, Skeat's text of B, closely based on the Laud manuscript, is *the* version of the B-Text; for many more, Skeat's division of the work into three authorial versions, and three only, is a 'fact', subject only to frivolous questioning.

Editorial manoeuvres of this sort were not made in a vacuum. They reflect the thinking of the time on the nature of poetic composition, authorial revision, and scribal transmission of texts. Consequently the editions vary substantially from each other, both in the texts of the poem they present to the reader and in the additional apparatus – introductions, notes, glossaries etc. – they include to facilitate reading the poem. No single edition can claim exclusive authority; there is no such thing as a disinterested editor. This is true despite the peculiarly fascinating characteristic of *Piers Plowman* textual criticism which becomes evident from Skeat's work onwards: its frequent employ-ment of a vocabulary and diction which mimics that of the empirical sciences, and reaches its splendid apotheosis in the writings of George Kane. Yet – as Kane has been the first to acknowledge – textual criticism, despite the type of mind it tends to attract (ruthlessly logical), is quintessentially an art, in the exercise of which human judgement at every stage supervenes. In the case of *Piers Plowman*, a poem with an enormous number of manuscript variants, to choose between the surviving manuscript readings (or to reject them as unsatisfactory, and instead conjecture what the author wrote) is an act of literary criticism, even literary creation, based on a succession of undemonstrable hypotheses, whose result (the edited text) can never be tested in the way that scientific theories can, except in the unlikely event of the discovery of the author's holograph(s). The editor is inextricably combined with the text he or she produces, despite the paraphernalia of rigorously objective discussion that accompanies editions of *Piers Plowman*. I have written this book with the aim of revealing how close is the link between editor and text, and conse-quently how disingenuous must be any claims to dispassionate editing.

PART I

The early phase

I

Crowley

The history of the publication of *Piers Plowman* begins with the three quarto editions of Robert Crowley. All three were printed in the year 1550, as a result, presumably, of popular demand; and this success with the public makes Crowley unique among the editors of the poem. Crowley's work performs a very different function from that of subsequent editions. He attempts to make the poem mesh with current issues in a way unparalleled by later editors, for whom the poem has become more of a historical curiosity. For Crowley it is part of a vibrant and directly relevant past, which can explain or at least shed light on current events. His address to the reader, and his marginal annotations on the text of the poem, reveal that he saw the poem as making a significant contribution to current religious and political issues. At the same time, he shows an antiquarian interest in uncovering as much as he can about the author and the circumstances under which the poem was written.

From its first reception, *Piers Plowman* was allied with Catholic or anti-Catholic reforms of one sort or another. Contemporary records report that the name 'Piers Plowman' was used as a rallying cry in the so-called Peasants' Revolt of 1381, and this misunderstanding of Langland as a radical revolutionary heralded the sixteenth-century interpretation of him as a crypto-proto-Protestant.[1] Langland many times throughout his poem calls for reform of a corrupt society, particularly of its clerical elements, but always in terms that implicitly

---

[1] It is possible that 'Piers Plowman' was a traditional name existing independently of the poem, but the letter from John Ball (under the pseudonym of John Sheep) to the poor men of Essex makes it clear that Ball, one of the leaders of the rebellion, had read the poem and used its terms to incite revolt. Elsewhere (the *Dieulacres Abbey Chronicle*; see Clarke and Galbraith, 'The Deposition of Richard II', 164–5), *Per Plowman* is referred to as a real person, one of the leaders of the revolt. See Anne Hudson, '*Piers Plowman* and the Peasants' Revolt', and 'The Legacy of *Piers Plowman*', 251–2, together with the references there cited. Both these articles and that of John Bowers ('*Piers Plowman* and the Police') provide important information on the early reception and influence of *Piers Plowman*.

or explicitly reinforce traditional social and religious structures. But sixteenth-century reformers assumed that *Piers Plowman* was written by a Wycliffite supporter whose aims could therefore be seen as precursors of their own; in fact, the antiquarian John Bale appears originally to have ascribed the poem to Wyclif himself, although he subsequently revised that opinion.[2]

In the years following the poem's original dissemination, the figure of Piers the Ploughman had taken on a specific social and political dimension apparently independent of its literary antecedents in Langland's poem and in Chaucer's *Canterbury Tales* (though his first appearance subsequent to his treatment by Langland is in *Pierce the Ploughman's Crede*, composed probably shortly after 1393, which shows unmistakable familiarity with the earlier poem).[3] Chaucer, who may have read *Piers Plowman*, includes a ploughman among his pilgrims – a hard-working, godly fellow, brother to the saintly parson – but does not give him a tale.[4] This deficiency was made up during the course of the next two centuries, with not one but two apocryphal Plowman's tales being fathered upon the dead poet by writers whose aims seem to have been very different from Chaucer's.[5] The first, a poem by Hoccleve on the miracle of the Virgin and the Sleeveless Garment, which was provided with a spurious 'Prologe of the Ploughman' so as to fit it into one of the manuscript versions of the *Canterbury Tales*, says nothing about its supposed teller.[6] The second is a debate poem between a griffin and a pelican, which presents through the mouth (or rather, beak) of the pelican an extreme attack

---

[2] As noted by Vincent DiMarco and Anne Hudson; see DiMarco, *Piers Plowman: A Reference Guide*, references cited for Bale, 1548 and 1557 (4, 6); Hudson, 'The Legacy of *Piers Plowman*, 261. Bale's autograph notebook, written some time after 1546, also attributes the poem to (Robert) Langland; see p. 11 below. Various modern critics have considered the question of the poem's Wycliffite or Lollard sympathies and concluded, in the words of David Lawton, that 'the issue is really that Lollards had Langlandian sympathies' ('Lollardy and the *Piers Plowman* Tradition', 793). See also Pamela Gradon, 'Langland and the Ideology of Dissent', Anne Hudson, 'The Legacy of *Piers Plowman*', Christina von Nolcken, '*Piers Plowman*, the Wycliffites, and *Pierce the Plowman's Creed*', Robert Adams, 'Langland's Theology', John Bowers, '*Piers Plowman* and the Police'.

[3] As do the three other main poems in the *Piers Plowman* tradition, *Richard the Redeless*, *Mum and the Sothsegger*, and *The Crowned King*, all written between 1393 and 1415, and recently edited by Helen Barr. See Barr, *The Piers Plowman Tradition*, 5–8, Hudson, 'The Legacy of *Piers Plowman*, 255–6, and references there cited.

[4] *Riverside Chaucer*, ed. L. D. Benson, I (A) 529–41. On the relation between Chaucer's and Langland's Prologues to their respective works, see Helen Cooper, 'Langland's and Chaucer's Prologues'.

[5] See Andrew Wawn, 'The Genesis of the *Plowman's Tale*', and 'Chaucer, *The Plowman's Tale* and Reformation Propaganda'.

[6] See *A New Ploughman's Tale*, ed. A. Beatty, 12.

on church corruption, in terms clearly linked with Wycliffite anti-papal doctrine.[7] It is apparent from this poem that the ploughman is identified with anti-papal sympathies, and this is how he figures in most of the other sixteenth-century works of popular complaint in which he appears.[8] Three printed works have titles mentioning Piers Ploughman: *I playne Piers which cannot flatter*, *A godly dyalogue and dysputacyon betwene Pyers plowman and a popysh preest*, and *Pyers plowmans exhortation vnto the lordes*.[9] All three use Piers as spokesman for the author, the voice of reason, moral and religious enlightenment, and social concern, complaining about such things as the Catholic doctrine of transubstantiation, the clergy, the problems caused by the absorption of formerly monastic land and personnel into the community, and rapacious landlords. The author of *The Praier and Complaynte of the Ploweman*,[10] a work with similar concerns printed in the 1530s but claiming an early fourteenth-century origin, makes almost no reference to the occupation of his composition's supposed narrator, but presumably felt that such a title would attract readers sympathetic to his concerns.

It is an open question whether such representations of the ploughman are, necessarily, conscious allusions to Langland's poem. Instead, the figure of the ploughman as honest labourer may have been proverbial, even before Langland used him; indeed, such a figure may have been the source for Chaucer's ploughman in the first instance, although it is of course tempting to believe that he was influenced by the portrait painted by his contemporary.[11] More primary research in the period is required. Certainly there is evidence that Langland's poem was actively read, if only by a very small number of people, in the first half of the sixteenth century, before the publication of Crowley's edition; for four manuscript copies survive

[7] The association with a ploughman in this tale is less tenuous, although to be found only in sixteenth-century additions to the original fifteenth-century material. The text has been edited most recently by Andrew Wawn in his unpublished University of Birmingham doctoral dissertation (1969), and is printed by Skeat in *Chaucerian and Other Pieces*, Supplement to *Complete Works of Geoffrey Chaucer*, vol. VII, 147–90.

[8] Not all portraits of the ploughman were complimentary or associated him with reforming views; see further Hudson, 'The Legacy of *Piers Plowman*', 260.

[9] Respectively STC 19903a, 19903, and 19905. The revised STC dates all three as about 1550 (the same date as Crowley's edition of *Piers Plowman*). For summary and discussion, see Helen C. White, *Social Criticism in Popular Religious Literature of the Sixteenth Century*, 28–34, and Hudson, 'The Legacy of *Piers Plowman*', 258–60.

[10] STC 20036, 20036.5.

[11] See Hudson, 'The Legacy of *Piers Plowman*', 257–60; also Robert L. Kelly, 'Hugh Latimer as Piers Plowman', and Helen Cooper, 'Langland's and Chaucer's Prologues'.

from this period, of each of the three different versions, while many other manuscripts have sixteenth-century annotations.[12] But even if Langland's poem was not widely known in the years before Crowley's edition, it is clear that the ploughman figure had significant and powerful connotations of religious and social reform; and this must go some way towards explaining the success of his publishing venture.

Crowley was an interesting character who managed to combine in one person several different careers, 'by turns a pamphleteer, stationer, poet, and clergyman'.[13] During the reign of Edward VI (1547–53), previous restrictions on Protestant writings were relaxed, and it became possible to publish Protestant literature without fear of reprisal.[14] Crowley's stationery business seems to have acted as a conduit for controversial works aligned with Protestant reforms,[15] and it is in this political context that it is appropriate to view his publication of *Piers Plowman*. Crowley himself published a significant body of satirical, anti-papist writing, some of which recalls Langland in its designation of merchants and lawyers as objects of satire and in its use of type characters and allegorical personifications.[16]

Crowley prefaces his edition of *Piers Plowman* with an address to the reader which makes clear his interest in the poem's religious, historical and political relevance to his own times. He describes the period of composition of the poem as one in which

> it pleased God to open the eyes of many to se hys truth, geuing

[12] The sixteenth-century manuscripts are Digby 145, copied by Adrian Fortescue in 1531–2, an A/C conjoint version; the former Sion College manuscript (now Takamiya 23), and CUL Gg.4.31, both B versions; and BL Royal 18.B.XVII, a C version. See also George Russell, 'Some Early Responses to the C-Version of *Piers Plowman*', '"As They Read It"'. The approving comments on the poem made by the reformer Stephen Batman, chaplain to Matthew Parker and one-time owner of MS Digby 171, are quoted below (p. 168 n. 20). A garbled quotation from two of the most famous passages in the poem, the prophecies in B Passus VI and X, is to be found in British Library MS Sloane 2578; see Sharon L. Jansen, 'Politics, Protest, and a New *Piers Plowman* Fragment'. Both these passages are referred to in the address to the reader Crowley printed at the front of his edition, so the fragment need not be evidence that the writer independently read the poem.

[13] In the words of John N. King, in 'Robert Crowley: A Tudor Gospelling Poet'; see also his 'Robert Crowley's Editions of *Piers Plowman*'. Much of the material in these two articles is recapitulated and expanded in his book, *English Reformation Literature*. See also David Norbrook, *Poetry and Politics in the English Renaissance*, e.g. 50–5.

[14] It may have been in order to avoid this earlier censorship that the work which passed as one of Chaucer's *Canterbury Tales*, the *Plowman's Tale*, had been given its title and attribution, thus acquiring a veneer of respectability.

[15] See King, 'Robert Crowley: A Tudor Gospelling Poet', 222.

[16] For the characteristics of Crowley's own writings, see the collection in *The Select Works of Robert Crowley*, ed. J. M. Cowper, and King, *English Reformation Literature*, 339–57.

them boldenes of herte, to open their mouthes and crye oute agaynste the worckes of darckenes, as did Iohn wicklefe, who also in those dayes translated the holye Bible into the Englishe tonge, and this writer who in reportynge certaine visions and dreames, that he fayned him selfe to haue dreamed: doeth moste christianlye enstruct the weake, and sharply rebuke the obstinate blynde. There is no maner of vice, that reigneth in anye estate of men, which this wryter hath not godly, learnedlye, and wittilye, rebuked.[17]

Crowley is particularly interested in the passage in B Passus X, 'concerning the suppression of the Abbaies: the scripture there alledged, declareth it to be gathered of the iuste iudgement of god, whoe wyll not suffer abomination to raigne vnpunished'. This passage evidently seemed to foretell, and sanction, Henry VIII's dissolution of the monasteries (1536–9), since it tells how 'a king' shall come and 'confesse yow religiouses,/And bete yow, as the Bible telleth, for brekynge of youre rule,/And amende monyals, monkes and chanons,/ And puten hem to hir penaunce' (B Passus X 316–19). Crowley finishes by warning his reader of the moral nature of the poem: 'Loke not upon this boke therfor, to talke of wonders paste or to come, but to amende thyne owne wille, which thou shalt fynd here most charitably rebuked. The spirite of god gyue the grace to walke in the waye of truthe, to Gods glory, & thyne owne soules healthe.'

Crowley also treated his task as editor with some seriousness. He opens his address to the reader with an immediate statement of his antiquarian interests in the source of the poem:

Beynge desyerous to knowe the name of the Autoure of this most worthy worke (gentle reader) and the tyme of the writynge of the same: I did not onely gather togyther suche aunciente copies as I could come by, but also consult such men as I knew to be more exercised in the study of antiquities, then I my selfe haue ben. And by some of them I haue learned that the Autour was named Roberte langelande, a Shropshere man borne in Cleybirie, aboute viii. myles from Maluerne hilles.

Crowley almost certainly derived his information about the author of the poem from John Bale, whose *Index of British and Other Writers* (written some time after 1546) records four times that *Piers Plowman* was written by a Robert Langland, who lived in Cleobury Mortimer,

---

[17] I quote these and other lines from the printer's address to the reader as found in the first edition (there are minor differences of spelling and punctuation in the three editions). Abbreviations have been silently expanded.

about eight miles from the Malvern Hills.[18] Crowley further pursued his antiquarian and historical interest in the poem by trying to ascertain the date of composition:

> For the time when it was written: it chaunced me to se an auncient copye, in the later ende wherof was noted, that the same copye was written in the yere of oure Lorde .M.iiii.C. and nyne, which was before thys presente yere, an hundred and xli. yeres.

This fifteenth-century manuscript has probably perished; at any rate, it has so far not turned up. But it is interesting that Crowley felt it worthwhile and important to search out other copies of the poem to see whether they yielded additional information. Crowley puts this information together with that provided by lines in B Passus XIII (269–70), referring to a year of dearth, which his manuscript gave as 1350, occurring during the time that Chichester was mayor of London.[19] (As it happens, the manuscripts disagree on the date, some giving it as 'a thousand and three hundred, twice thirty and ten', some ' ... twice *twenty* and ten'; Chichester's dates identify the former date as the correct one.) Consequently, Crowley feels he 'may be bolde to reporte' that the poem was composed *after* 1350 (or, correctly, 1370) and *before* 1409.

Crowley's concern for searching out separate versions of the poem indicates a sense of editorial responsibility. On the other hand, like the scribes before him, and like all sixteenth-century reprinters of Middle English works, Crowley had little notion of the integrity of any particular text or manuscript, or of how relations between them might constitute a sort of puzzle holding the key to what the author originally wrote. While he is interested in who the author was, and

---

[18] Bale's manuscript was published in 1902 (reissued 1990) as *Index Britanniae Scriptorum ... John Bale's Index of British and Other Writers*. See 383, 509, and 510, and DiMarco's comments, *Piers Plowman*, 4. Bale seems to have puzzled over the first line of the poem, which normally reads 'In a somer seson, whan softe was the sonne', variously noting the readings *sonday* for *seson*, and *warme, sote, set* and *hot* (*caleret*) for *softe* (*softe* itself he does not record, although it is overwhelmingly attested in the manuscripts; see p. 28 n. 33 below). Crowley prints *season* and *sette*. James Simpson has pointed out to me that *Piers Plowman* appears to be uniquely represented in Bale's Index in the respect that its *incipit* is not translated into Latin, unlike that of other vernacular works. The attribution to Robert rather than William Langland has been variously explained; for further details and for discussion of the part this confusion over names played in the *Piers Plowman* multiple authorship controversy, see George Kane, *Piers Plowman: The Evidence for Authorship*, 37ff.; also R. W. Chambers, 'Robert or William Longland'. As Skeat comments, *B-Text*, xxxii n. 1, 'the distance from Cleobury Mortimer to the Malvern Hills [is] a rather long "eight miles"'; Kane (*The Evidence for Authorship*, 40) suggests that viii is a scribal error for xviii or xxiii.

[19] The reference was noted by John Bale in *Scriptorum Illustrium ... Catalogus*, 474.

when he wrote, and in comparing (to a limited extent) different manuscripts with each other, he has no notion of absolute faithfulness to a text, and no interest in indicating the source of his manuscript variants. Indeed, several of the extant copies of the three editions are found to combine quires from one edition with quires from another, producing a bibliographical nightmare.[20]

The quality of Crowley's text was later to be called in question by Tyrwhitt, the eighteenth-century editor of Chaucer, who believed the edition 'was printed from so faulty and imperfect a MS. that the author, whoever he was, would find it difficult to recognize his own work'. On the other hand, Thomas Wright, the nineteenth-century editor of *Piers Plowman* immediately preceding W. W. Skeat, remarked on the 'excellence' of Crowley's manuscript.[21] The discrepancy between these judgements can be explained, Skeat himself (surely rightly) suggests, by recognizing that 'the "faultiness and imperfection" which Tyrwhitt justly attributes to Crowley's edition are the result of his inability, in numerous instances, to read the text correctly ... the frequent blunders are Crowley's own, and his MS. must have been extremely-good, even better at times, I venture to think, than the one which Mr Wright has printed' (*B-Text*, p. xxxvi).

Crowley based the text of his first edition on a manuscript of the B version, now lost, which he emended in various places. From a comparison of the readings of Crowley's text with those of the extant B-MSS, it can be deduced that it was closely related to three B-MSS: Trinity College Cambridge B. 15. 17 (W), Huntington 128 (Hm, Hm[2]), and the Sion College manuscript (S; a sixteenth-century version of the poem, extensively modernised, now Takamiya 23).[22] The second edition was reset and based on a different B-MS, also lost; Crowley seems to have conflated its text with readings from the first impression. The third edition may have incorporated readings from yet a third manuscript.[23] Crowley's researches went further than the

---

[20] Presumably the second and third editions were printed within a short time of each other, and when the copies were bound up the two redactions were not always distinguished. See Kane-Donaldson, 6–8, Skeat, *B-Text*, xxxiv–xxxv n. 1, and William R. Crawford, 'Robert Crowley's Editions of Piers Plowman' (unpublished Yale University dissertation, 1957). Hoyt N. Duggan reports that Carter Hailey of the University of Virginia is working on a bibliographic survey of the sixteenth-century Crowley printed editions in preparation for an electronic edition ('The *Piers Plowman* Electronic Archive', n. 20).

[21] See pp. 32 and 59 below.

[22] See Kane-Donaldson, 6–7 and 38ff., 42ff., 49ff. For a description of the former Sion manuscript, which contains 'some 2,700 peculiar unoriginal variants', see Kane-Donaldson 15.

[23] See Kane-Donaldson, 7 and 19 n. 13.

B-Text. Later on in his address he tells us that a couple of lines in the early part of the poem, which have the character of a prophecy, are 'lyke to be a thinge added of some other man than the fyrste autour. For diuerse copies haue it diuerslye.' This must be the first suggestion that more than one author was responsible for the variations between the various versions of the poem, an idea that was to take off in the early twentieth century. Crowley continues,

> For where the copie that I folowe hath thus.
>
> And when you se the sunne amisse, & two monkes heades
> And a mayde haue the maistrye, and multiplie by eyght.[24]
>
> Some other haue.
>
> Three shyppes and a shefe, wyth an eight folowynge
> Shall brynge bale and battell, on both half the mone.

The first set of lines comes from a riddlingly prophetic passage at the end of B Passus VI (325–6). But the second set is found only in the C-Text equivalent to the B lines (C Passus VIII 350–1), so that Crowley must have had access to a C-MS. The strange thing is that he should have noticed only this trifling difference between the C-MS and his own B-MS, for many far more striking differences exist. By the time he came to print the second and third impressions, Crowley seems to have read further afield in *Piers Plowman* manuscripts, although, once again, with extreme selectivity. Thus the two later impressions insert a number of lines in the Prologue not found in any extant B-MS, which correspond to a passage in the A-Text which is substantially rewritten in B.[25] Presumably Crowley compared his A-MS with his first B edition at this point, and discovered that the former contained extra lines which he felt merited inclusion. Had he carried out this operation over other portions of the text, he would have found numerous examples of lines in A which were omitted in B; but there is no sign that he did so. The two later editions also insert four separate lines which are otherwise found in some B-MSS of a different family from

---

24 *you*] Crowley's manuscript would have had the nominative form of the second person singular pronoun, *ye* rather than *you*, and he prints *ye* in his text. *two*] Crowley's second edition reads *thre* here; but both first and second editions read *two* in the passage as it stands in the text. *eyght*] In the text itself, Crowley's first edition reads *eight*, but the two subsequent ones read *hight*. All these points are noted by Skeat, *B-Text*, xxxiv.

25 See the account provided by Skeat in his *B-Text*, 389–90. Unfortunately there are no distinctive variants in Crowley's version of the A lines (Pro 90–5) which would link his A-MS with any now extant.

the one that formed his copy text.[26] This is puzzling, to say the least. Crowley must have had access to at least four manuscripts of the poem: two (or possibly three) B-MSS, from different families, on which he based his texts, and both an A- and a C-MS. One would have thought that, at the very least, the differing length of the A, B, and C versions would have made an impression on him and encouraged him to explore further the differences between them. But this seems not to have been the case.[27] So instead of systematic checking of the various manuscripts, line by line and word by word, to identify precisely how and where they differed from each other, Crowley seems only to have compared manuscripts sporadically. (It was not until three centuries later that editors would consider it customary, if not obligatory, to read through and check thoroughly all the versions of a work before producing a critical edition, Tyrwhitt's 1775–8 edition of the *Canterbury Tales* being an exception.)[28]

Crowley gives the reader no indication as to precisely how his text is composed of elements from different sources. There is nothing that corresponds to the modern critical apparatus, identifying which words in the text are derived from which manuscripts. Crowley does, however, provide various editorial aids. His initial address explains to an unfamiliar audience the convention of alliterative poetry: 'He wrote altogyther in miter: but not after the maner of our rimers that write nowe adayes (for his verses ende not alike) but the nature of hys miter is, to haue thre wordes at the leaste in euery verse whiche beginne with some one letter.' (He also comments, with justice, that the 'sence' of the poem is 'somewhat darcke', though 'not so harde, but that it may be vnderstande of suche as wil not sticke to breake the shelle of the nutte for the kernelles sake'.) And he silently modernises many of the Middle English grammatical forms and words in the text, so as to make the poem more palatable to a sixteenth-century reader. Thus he replaces thorns and yoghs with equivalent modern spelling, removes the 'y' prefix from past participles of verbs (substituting *graunted* for *ygraunted, blessed* for *yblessed* e.g., at B Passus VII 8, 13), occasionally

---

26 After Passus XVIII 295 (shared with GYOC²CBHt), after Passus V 269 (shared with YOC²CBHt), after Passus V 330 (shared with YOC²CBHt), and after Passus VI 47(a) (shared with YOC²CBHt). See Kane-Donaldson, 224; I quote their line numbers. Skeat (*B-Text*, 399) notes the second of these lines.

27 Thomas Wright similarly noted only minor differences between an A- and a B-MS; see below, p. 61.

28 Crowley's sporadic collations of other manuscripts may be compared with Caxton's reworking of his first edition of *The Canterbury Tales*, although the latter tinkered more intensively with his text. See Beverley Boyd, 'William Caxton', 25–7.

alters syntax to conform with more modern word-order, occasionally replaces Middle English words likely to strike his readership as archaic or even incomprehensible (thus he substitutes *sette* for *softe* in the first line of the poem, a change that was to provoke a good deal of later discussion),[29] and reduces the number of verbal inflections.[30] In making these sorts of changes he was presumably concerned to reinforce the reader's impression of the direct topicality and political urgency of the issues that the poem addresses. Archaism was all very well for poets like Spenser, a self-conscious heir to Chaucer who went out of his way to introduce into his writing just the sorts of grammatical and lexical forms that Crowley removes, in pursuit of a different linguistic and political agenda. Crowley, by contrast, published *Piers Plowman* in order to make a direct and intelligible contribution to current theological and political controversy, and he needed therefore to reduce the opacity of its language.

The contemporary relevance of the poem to a sixteenth-century readership was reinforced by another editorial aid provided by Crowley, marginal comments on the text. In the two subsequent editions these comments were greatly expanded, suggesting that Crowley warmed to his editorial task as his familiarity with the poem increased; and he also expanded the prefatory matter at the beginning of the volume with a summary, passus by passus, of the main events of the poem.[31]

Crowley uses his marginalia to draw the reader's attention to particular aspects of the poem, and to interpret these in the light of current concerns. Thus against a passage in Passus B III where Lady Meed indicates her willingness to give a dishonest friar money in

[29]   In this he may have followed Bale (see n. 18 above), although Skeat (see below, p. 147 n. 27) thought that the *sette* of Crowley's text was a misreading of his manuscript's *softe*. For eighteenth-century discussion of this crux, see p. 28 below.

[30]   Examples abound; see eg. the replacement of 'þyn' with 'your' at Passus VII 73, 'Forþi' with 'Therfore' at Passus VII 82, 'ensamples' with 'examples' at Passus VII 128, 'sholdest' with 'shold' at Passus VII 135, 'shullen' with 'shall' at Passus VII 163. J. R. Thorne and Marie-Claire Uhart note that 'while spelling and grammar *are* pervasively modernized, one of the notable features of Crowley's texts is the extent to which he preserves "difficult" vocabulary' ('Robert Crowley's *Piers Plowman*', 249).

[31]   It is notable that the summary of Passus VIII identifies 'Pierce' with the dreamer, a curious mistake frequently made by readers of the poem; cf. Anne Middleton, 'The Critical Heritage', 4–5, who regards the attribution of Piers' name to the authorial presence found throughout the work as indicative of a reading of the poem as the product of 'a single voice, loosely identified as the poet'. Some of the first editions also contain the passus-by-passus summary, together with a second title page from one of the two later editions. This is true of the copy originally belonging to Pepys, for example, now in Magdalene College, Cambridge (reprinted in a facsimile edition in 1976), and also of Rawlinson 4°271 (Bodleian Library).

exchange for absolution, Crowley prints in the margin, 'The fruites of Popishe penaunce', commenting on the potential corruptibility of the practice of confession discontinued under the new Protestant regime. Many other of Crowley's marginal notes indicate a similarly Protestant orientation. Writing in the aftermath of the dissolution of the monasteries, he is clearly very excited by the warning uttered by Reason in Passus B V (45–7) that 'religion' would, unless it 'held its rule', be harmed by the king 'and his conseil', and comments, 'The suppression of Abbayes. Good counsell'.[32] He writes 'True pilgrimage' beside further remarks by Reason in the same speech (B Passus V 56–7) about the preferability of seeking St Truth in your heart, rather than on pilgrimage jaunts abroad.[33] And he warns, somewhat irrelevantly, that 'The Byshop shal answere for many' in response to Repentance's advice to Covetousness later in the passus (B V 291–3) to return stolen or borrowed goods to the bishop if he does not know the person to whom they properly belong.[34] Other examples of Crowley's comments are 'Note howe he scorneth the auctority of Popes Math. vi' (against B Passus VII 172–3, where the dreamer casts aspersions on the power of papal indulgences);[35] and 'Wo be to you þat turn the tithes to priuate use' (against B Passus IX 67–8, where the allegorical personification Wit argues that the Church should provide for members of the community unable to do so for themselves).[36] Most famously, as indicated in his Preface to the reader, he highlights the condemnation of contemporary monastic behaviour in B Passus X, noting in the margin 'Reade thys', and lower down, 'The suppression of Abbayes'.[37] Evidently he regarded the passage as accurately prophesying the dissolution of the monasteries, and the mention of the Abbot of Abingdon in particular as liable to suffer from the action of the monarch ('And thanne shal the Abbot of Abyngdoun and al his issue for evere/ Have a knok of a kyng, and incurable the wounde'; B Passus X 325–6) must have seemed especially significant, given the extreme wealth and power of this foundation. To modern eyes the prediction may also appear uncanny, but as the nineteenth-century editor Skeat notes, the views expressed here by the allegorical personification Clergy were straightforwardly in step with 'prevalent views as to the supreme power of the king'.[38]

---

[32] Douce L. 205, fol. xxi^r.　　[33] *Ibid.*, fol. xvi^r.　　[34] *Ibid.*, fol. xxv^v.
[35] *Ibid.*, fol. xxxix^r.　　[36] *Ibid.*, fol. xlii^v.　　[37] *Ibid.*, fol. l^v.
[38] *The Vision of William concerning Piers Plowman . . . Notes to Texts A, B, and C*, 96, note to C Passus VI 169; cf. Pearsall 106, note to C Passus V 168–71.

Despite the clear polemical orientation of these annotations, it is perhaps a little strong to say (as does King) that Crowley 'kidnapped' the poem in an attempt to 'interpret it as reformist propaganda'.[39] Certainly there is evidence that not all Crowley's readers were persuaded by his commentary. A surviving copy of his second edition was owned by one Andrew Bostock in 1613, seemingly an educated Catholic, who annotated his version with comments on Crowley's marginalia. He corrects a number of Crowley's remarks, for example by writing 'Not the fruits but abuse of Penaunce' beside Crowley's 'The fruites of Popishe penaunce' noted above, and by pointing out that Crowley's summary of the argument of Passus V, 'That Abbayes should be suppressed', is 'false, for the Author speaks against abuses onely'. More significantly, he adds a substantial note in the margin of Crowley's address to the reader explaining that 'Wickliffe was a corrupter of the truth', and in response to Crowley's comment that Langland 'scorneth the auctority of Popes' writes a lengthy refutation:

> No Catholick Doctor can be shewd to have writ or ever taught that the Pope hath potest to pardon without any penanc or obligation to live well. The Popes Bulls or pardons are for remitting of Canonical penancs, or temporal punishment, which remains to be sufferd after the sin as far as it incurrd eternal damnation is forgiven by the Sacrament of penance. And these pardons or Indulgences ever suppose a fit disposition in the persones to whom they are applied. And that must be a sincere resolution of forsaking evill and of doing good. And the Author must not be understood to scorn the Authority of the Cheif Pastor, as the Heretical margin, wold

---

[39] *English Reformation Literature*, 322, 332. One of the pieces of evidence King presents to support this view is 'Crowley's most sweeping alteration', 'his complete omission of a thirteen-line passage in praise of the Gregorian rule and monastic ideal' at B Passus X 291–302. As noted by Thorne and Uhart, this passage is in fact found in only two B-MSS, R and F, which together form a separate line of transmission of the B-Text. It is extremely unlikely that the passage appeared in the B-MS Crowley used as his copy-text, and hence it will not have been deliberately omitted by him. See Skeat, *B-Text*, 406–7, Kane-Donaldson 63–9. King also claims that 'the Roman Catholic doctrine of purgatory was deleted by altering "and many a prisone fram purgatorie thorw his preyeres he delyvereth" (B XV 345) to "and mani prisoners by his praier he pulith from paine"'. But many times elsewhere Crowley lets stand references to purgatory (e.g. at Passus II 104, VI 44, VII 11, VII 104, IX 77, etc.). The other two pieces of evidence King mentions in the same place (*English Reformation Literature*, 330–1) stand: they are the substitution of the name of Christ for that of Mary at Passus VII 197, and the removal of a reference to transubstantiation at Passus XII 85 (see discussions by Skeat in *B-Text*, 403 and 409). Presumably both changes were introduced to remove any offence to Protestant readers. See also Skeat's notes to Passus XIII 259 and XV 176 in *B-Text*, 411 and 414).

suggest, but to reprove those who trust, or presume upon such pardons whilst they live vitiously.[40]

It is clear that Crowley was interested in the religious, satiric and political content of the poem. As a reader of his edition, Andrew Bostock was able to detach the editor from the poem – the heretical margin from the text – and come up with a different interpretation, one that completely undermined Crowley's own. Later editors have had different aims in view in presenting the poem to a contemporary public, aims in general much less bold and much less easy to infer from their respective editions. Crowley's concern with the poem has more in common with that of the rebels of 1381: both were using *Piers Plowman* for its political relevance to their own immediate ends. They made no or little attempt to interpret the poem on its own terms.

[40] Douce L 205, fol. xxxixʳ. See further King, *English Reformation Literature*, 338–9.

2

Percy, Warton, Tyrwhitt, Ritson

Crowley's edition was inaccurately reprinted by one Owen Rogers in 1561, which indicates that the success of the previous printing still promised a financial reward eleven years later. Rogers based his text on Crowley's third edition, and he rearranged the prefatory material, prefixing the appropriate portion of Crowley's summary of the poem before each individual passus. He also appended a copy of *Pierce the Ploughman's Crede*, presumably in the mistaken belief that both poems were by the same author.[1] But *Piers Plowman* then languished unprinted for over two hundred years. It was not that the poem went completely unnoticed, or even unread. Michael Drayton paraphrased some of the final vision in his *Legend of Thomas Cromwell* (1607);[2] Milton refers to the 'vision and Creed of Pierce Plowman' and possibly drew on some of its material in *Paradise Lost* (1667);[3] while Dryden in 1700 evidently knew enough of the poem to be able to confuse it with the apocryphal *Plowman's Tale*.[4] A selection of extracts from the poem survives in a seventeenth-century collection made by Richard James, the antiquary and librarian to Sir Robert Bruce Cotton.[5] The more famous antiquary, Thomas Hearne,

---

[1] See Skeat, *B-Text*, xxxv–vi, and DiMarco, *Piers Plowman: A Reference Guide*, 7.
[2] Cf. Skeat, *The Vision of William concerning Piers Plowman ... Notes to Texts A, B, and C*, 455–7, and *The Vision of William concerning Piers Plowman ... General Preface, Notes, and Indexes*, 868. See also DiMarco, *Piers Plowman*, 13.
[3] Cf. *The Vision of William concerning Piers Plowman ... General Preface, Notes, and Indexes*, 869; also DiMarco, *Piers Plowman*, 14.
[4] See the quotation from his *Fables Ancient and Modern* in DiMarco, *Piers Plowman*, 17.
[5] See Bodleian Library MS James 2, 149–59 (first foliation). The manuscript was written about 1620–34, and contains a number of excerpts of historical material, e.g. from the letters of Thomas à Beckett, Capgrave's *Legend*, the works of William of St Amour (see Falconer Madan, H. H. E. Craster, and N. Denholm-Young, eds., *A Summary Catalogue of the Western Manuscripts in the Bodleian Library*, no. 3839). On James, see *DNB* vol. X, 655–6. The *Piers Plowman* section is in part a paraphrase. James' copy of the text contains some unique variants and may have been derived, at least in part, from one of Crowley's editions, with which it shares some variant readings. It includes some of the lines from B Passus X on the impending downfall of the monasteries, presumably of interest to James on account of

who had seen at least two manuscripts of the poem, and owned at least one copy of Roger's edition and two copies of Crowley's, wrote on the flyleaves of both of the latter some interesting and perceptive speculations on the poem's author and date, suggesting there and elsewhere that the poem had been revised both by the author and by an additional person (1724 and 1725).[6] A collection of poetry published in 1737 by Elizabeth Cooper, under the title *The Muses Library; or a Series of English Poetry from the Saxons, to the Reign of Charles II*, included some lines from Langland 'as the first *English* poet we can meet with, who employ'd his Muse for the Refinement of Manners, and, in the Rudeness of his Lines, we plainly discover the Rudeness of the Age he wrote in'.[7] And Arthur Sherbo has provided important evidence of further eighteenth-century interest in *Piers Plowman*, for example that Samuel Pegge, in an article published in the *Gentleman's Magazine* of 1755, was the first to discriminate between Crowley's three editions of *Piers Plowman*, and that in 1787, Holt White in the same journal called for a new edition of the poem: 'Is there no Tyrrwhit [*sic*] left to rescue the father of English blank verse from his present wretched plight, and place him by the side of Chaucer, the father of our rhyme?'[8] These examples are a selection from a number of references made by writers and scholars during the two centuries following Crowley's edition.[9]

his strong Protestant views. Cf. also Chambers and Grattan, 'The Text of "Piers Plowman"' (1931), 50 n. 3.

6   Hearne had been lent a B-MS of *Piers Plowman*, now Rawlinson 38, by Peter Le Neve, and had used Cotton Caligula A. XI, which also contained a 'mixed' version of *Piers Plowman*, for his edition of Robert of Gloucester's *Chronicle*. His two copies of Crowley, both formerly belonging to William Fulman, are now in the Bodleian and British Libraries. Hearne noted on the volume now Bodley 4° Rawl. 123 that he possessed a copy of Roger's as well as Crowley's edition, and wrote 'This is certain that this work of Pierce Plowman's Visions hath been much altered at different times... the work seems to have undergone the same changes [sc., two sets of revision, by the author and by someone else] with Robert of Gloucester.' He wrote exactly the same on his other Crowley copy, as recorded by DiMarco (who does not note the same inscription on the Bodley copy), 'Eighteenth-Century Suspicions Regarding the Authorship of *Piers Plowman*', 125. See further 124–7, and also DiMarco, *Piers Plowman*, 20–2, for Hearne's views recorded elsewhere on *Piers Plowman*, and cf. Eric Dahl, 'Diverse Copies Have It Diverselye', 59–63.

7   xi. Cooper prints three excerpts taken from one of Crowley's third editions: lines on Meed's proposed marriage to False (Passus II), on the Deadly Sins (Passus V), and on the downfall of the Barn of Unity (Passus XX).

8   See Arthur Sherbo, 'Samuel Pegge, Thomas Holt White, and *Piers Plowman*'. Holt White also proposed an emendation to Crowley's text, namely *dright* for *bryht* at B Passus XIII 269. Skeat thought that Holt White's article, signed only T. H. W., was written by Whitaker; see *C-Text*, lxvi n. 1.

9   A virtually comprehensive list can be found in DiMarco, *Piers Plowman*; cf. A. S. G. Edwards, 'Piers Plowman in the Seventeenth Century'. See also Skeat, *The Vision of William concerning Piers Plowman ... General Preface, Notes, and Indexes*, 863–74 and

Hearne (1678–1765) was one of the most industrious and exact of the early excavators of medieval documents, and published over forty volumes of learned print. He came from a long line of English antiquaries who were fascinated by ancient documents, and devoted their lives to discovering and acquiring manuscripts and writing learned histories.[10] This antiquarian interest was subject to considerable suspicion and contempt by others; Pope, for example, remorselessly pilloried the dullness of learned pedants in the *Dunciad* (selecting Hearne for special mention: 'To future ages may thy dulness last / As thou preserv'st the dulness of the past').[11] Dr Johnson took a similar view, ridiculing the mindless amassment of old books by narrow-minded antiquaries.[12] In the later eighteenth century, this antiquarian interest in the past underwent a change in character. It became more popular, and it became more literary. Many readers turned to the literature of previous centuries to be delighted by its wild, imaginative, and refreshingly simple qualities, and simultaneously instructed in the life and times of their forefathers. This had an effect both on reading habits and on literary practice, and the new poetic movement signalled by the publication of Wordsworth's *Lyrical Ballads* in 1798 is in part a reflection of the increased interest in the language and literature of the past in both Britain and Europe which was to become characteristic of the Romantic movement. Looking back on the preceding century in 1831, Thomas Carlyle described how 'Manuscripts, that had for ages lain dormant ... issued from their archives into public view; books that had circulated only in mean guise for the amusement of the people, [became] important, not to one or two virtuosos, but to the general body of the learned.'[13] Prominent among these enthusiasts were Richard Hurd, Thomas Percy, Thomas Warton, Joseph Ritson, George Ellis, and (in the next century) Walter Scott, all of whom

Whitaker, *Visio Willi* de Petro Plouhman, xlii–xlviii. Elsewhere ('Godwin on Langland'), DiMarco illustrates some of the ways in which references to *Piers Plowman* were repeated from one commentator or critic to another, often without acknowledgement.

[10] On Hearne, one of the few accurate scholars before Tyrwhitt, see David Douglas, *English Scholars*, 178–94; Anne Hudson, 'Robert of Gloucester and the Antiquaries'.

[11] See *Dunciad Variorum*, III, 181–6.

[12] See the references quoted by H. R. Steeves, *Learned Societies and English Literary Scholarship*, 88–9, including Dr Johnson's later admission that 'Percy's attention to poetry [viz. in his *Reliques*] has given grace and splendour to his studies of antiquity. A mere antiquarian is a rugged being.'

[13] Quoted by Arthur Johnston in his excellent account of the study of medieval romance in the eighteenth century, *Enchanted Ground*, 22. Carlyle is giving an account of the situation in Germany, in a review of editions of the *NibelungenLied* by Lachmann and others.

were influential in bringing medieval literature, previously obscure, before a more general readership.[14]

For our purposes, Percy and Warton are the most interesting of these men. Both published important editions of medieval poetry which, in rather different ways, raised the public profile of early English literature. Bishop Percy's *Reliques of Ancient Poetry*, which achieved considerable notoriety, initiated an important debate about the methods of editing medieval texts, while Warton's *History of English Poetry* was the first work since Crowley to print substantial portions of the text of *Piers Plowman*.

Percy's pioneering role was well recognised by his intellectual successor and later advocate Frederick Furnivall (founder of the *Early English Text Society*) in his own edition of Percy's *Reliques*: 'No common man was the grocer's son, though no one could call him great. He led the van of the army that Wordsworth afterwards commanded, and which has won us back to nature and truth. He opened to us the road into the Early English home in which we have spent so many happy hours ...'[15] The *Reliques* were purportedly an edition of ballad-type poems found in a medieval manuscript. These did not, of course, include *Piers Plowman*, but Percy's edition is nevertheless worth a glance in relation to the treatment and reception of the poem, since it contained an Appendix on the metre of *Piers Plowman* which must have been the first introduction for many readers to the nature and content of the work.[16] The *Reliques* are also an enormously influential document in the history of Middle English editing, which brought to light many issues still under debate today.

Percy's account of his discovery of the manuscript which gave him the material for his *Reliques* is well known; apparently he saved it – in a mutilated form – from housemaids using it as fire-kindling in the house of Humphrey Pitt.[17] He published its contents in 1765. But although the collection met with immediate popular success, it made its editor notorious for editorial inaccuracy and invention. Percy's Preface declared that the editor had 'endeavoured to be as faithful as the imperfect state of his materials would admit'; but the notion of fidelity in relation to reproduction of original texts is one that is

---

[14] Each of these men is given a chapter in Johnston, *Enchanted Ground*.

[15] Hales and Furnivall, *Bishop Percy's Folio MS* , vol. I, xx.

[16] The metre had been previously (?1760–61) discussed by Thomas Gray in 'Metrum: Observations on English Metre' (*The Works of Thomas Gray*, vol. II, 37–9), who had quoted the beginning of B Passus II and referred to Crowley's remarks on metre.

[17] Hales and Furnivall, *Bishop Percy's Folio MS*, vol. I, xii.

dangerously subjective. The Folio manuscript which Percy transcribed had suffered badly from Pitt's housemaids, and the text itself had originally been copied from corrupt exemplars. To correct what appeared to him evident errors (or as he subsequently put it, 'miserable trash or nonsense'),[18] and to make good the numerous lacunae, Percy introduced quite sweeping changes, rewriting stanzas whose wording or sentiments offended him, and in many cases composing entirely new material.[19] For this he was hounded by Joseph Ritson, a fellow antiquary whose own scholarly editions were far less popular, and who devoted considerable energy to the exposure of Percy's editorial heinousness in an extensive campaign.[20] In response to this criticism, Percy added an extra paragraph to the Preface of the fourth edition of the *Reliques*, which explained his editorial policy. The 'old copies' from which the manuscript was compiled

> were often so defective or corrupted, that a scrupulous adherence to their wretched readings would only have exhibited unintelligible nonsense, or such poor meagre stuff, as neither came from the Bard, nor was worthy the press; when, by a few slight corrections or additions, a most beautiful or interesting sense hath started forth, and this so naturally and easily, that the Editor could seldom prevail upon himself to indulge the vanity of making a formal claim to the improvement; but must plead guilty to the charge of concealing his own share in the amendments under some such general title, as a 'Modern Copy', or the like ... His object was to please both the judicious Antiquary, and the Reader of Taste; and he hath endeavoured to gratify both without offending either.[21]

The reactions to Percy's work continue to be relevant in textual criticism, since they touch on fundamental questions of authorial intention and editorial responsibility. Ritson took the harshest possible view of Percy's editorial policy, accusing him of fabricating the Folio manuscript's very existence, and certainly of 'preferr[ing] his ingenuity to his fidelity'.[22] But as Arthur Johnston comments,

---

18   *Reliques*, 4th edition, vol. I, xii.
19   See W. J. Bate, 'Percy's Use of His Folio-Manuscript'. See also Gillian Rogers, 'The Percy Folio Manuscript Revisited'.
20   See Hales and Furnivall, *Bishop Percy's Folio MS*, vol. I, xvii–xix n. 2, xix–xx n. 1 for quotation of some of the documents. Ritson asserted that 'no confidence can be placed' in Percy's collection, and exclaimed that 'secretly to suppress the original text, and insert his own fabrications for the sake of provideing more refine'd entertainment for readers of taste and genius, is no proof of either judgement, candour, or integrity'.
21   *Reliques*, 4th edition, vol. I, xvi–xvii.
22   Quoted Hales and Furnivall, *Bishop Percy's Folio MS*, vol. I, xvii n. 2.

> Percy's attitude towards the poems in his manuscript is not unlike that of Pope towards the text of Shakespeare. It could never have been the intention of the Bard to perpetrate such crudities; the transmission of the text has, we know, resulted in corruption and debasement; the editor is therefore in the position of the literary executor, unwilling to allow his friend's work to appear in the rough state in which accident has allowed it to survive. There is much to be said for this attitude.[23]

These remarks can certainly find support in modern editorial scholarship, although we would cavil at the scale of emendation in which Percy indulged. A large number of practising editors and textual theorists would attach considerable, even overriding, importance to editorial judgement, erudition, and expertise, and argue (implicitly or explicitly) that editors have a responsibility to the original author to make the material they transmit intelligible and acceptable to a contemporary audience. Such has been the view of the two most outstanding editors of *Piers Plowman*, George Kane and E. T. Donaldson, although their work is characterised by a breathtaking rigour and thorough acquaintaince with their manuscript sources far removed from the intellectual and scholarly competence of a Percy.[24] The problem is, that literary tastes vary from period to period (and from individual to individual), so that what will seem acceptable or unacceptable, in the way of emendation, to one generation may seem the reverse to the next. Some editors will make many alterations to the material preserved in their manuscripts in the more-or-less confident belief that they are reproducing either what their author wrote in the first place, or what he or she intended to write. Other scholars will regard this as undue interference with original evidence. The resulting editorial crux is one that we shall return to again and again during the course of this book.

Ironically enough, the immediate effect of Percy's *Reliques* was to create a context where such editorial panache was quite unacceptable. The furious reaction of Ritson to Percy's editorial licence was a fearsome example to any editor contemplating bold and unfettered

---

[23] *Enchanted Ground*, 81. Pope was, of course, perfectly aware of the liberties that editors took with texts; cf. the comments on conjectural emendation at the beginning of *Dunciad Variorum* II (p. 96), quoted by Robert Adams, 'Editing *Piers Plowman B*', 31.

[24] See e.g. Kane, 'Conjectural Emendation'. His views are shared by George Russell, editor of the forthcoming Athlone edition of the C-Text; see 'Editorial Theory and Practice in Middle English Texts'.

conjectural emendation, however dull and corrupt the original.[25] Thus Percy's friend Walter Scott is able to write in 1802 with a secure assumption of editorial consensus:

> It is no doubt highly desirable that the text of antient poetry should be given untouched and uncorrupted. But this is a point which did not occur to the editor of the *Reliques* in 1765, whose object it was to win the favour of the public, at a period when the great difficulty was not how to secure the very words of the old ballads, but how to arrest attention upon the subject at all.[26]

Such a non-interventionist attitude characterises much nineteenth-century editing of medieval texts. The aim of the editors is to get their material into print, and they are not much concerned with fine understanding of lexical or metrical detail (indeed the state of philological learning did not allow for this). Nor, on the whole, are they concerned with detecting scribal error and reconstructing an authorial original which was possibly rather different from the corrupt manuscripts preserving their texts. Where *Piers Plowman* is concerned, the sort of creative editorial spirit which informed Percy's intentions, if not his actions, is not to be found for another two hundred years.

The long-term effect of Percy's *Reliques* was thus twofold. First, it established an editorial norm of minimal intervention with the original text. And secondly, it secured the place of medieval literature in both scholarly and popular affection. Percy's work contributed significantly towards the increased value that was put upon medieval literature in the fifty-odd years following the publication of the *Reliques* – and indeed still further, well into the nineteenth century and beyond (hence Furnivall's admiration for his example). When his edition was first published, one of the typically unfavourable responses Percy met with was that of Dr Johnson's friend William Warburton, who commented that 'antiquarianism was to true letters what specious funguses are to the oak'.[27] Forty-odd years later the tide had turned, and as Malone wrote to Percy in 1809, 'the whole world is to be "bespread with the dust of antiquity" and what was formerly thought a good subject of ridicule, is now quite the

---

25 The exposure of Macpherson's creativity created a similar uproar; see Fiona Stafford, *The Sublime Savage.*

26 Quoted by Bate, 'Percy's Use of his Folio-Manuscript', 337.

27 Quoted by J. Pickford in his 'Life of Bishop Percy' (Hales and Furnivall, *Bishop Percy's Folio MS*, vol. I, xxxviii).

fashion'.[28] The importance of this shift in literary taste cannot be overestimated; as we shall see in chapter 4, it stimulated a flood of publication of medieval works largely ignored over the previous three centuries. *Piers Plowman* was a significant beneficiary, achieving not one but two separate editions in less than thirty years.

Two of the poems in Percy's Folio manuscript, *Death and Life* and *Scottish Feilde*, are written in the same alliterative metre as *Piers Plowman*, i.e. without rhyme or a fixed number of syllables, but instead a long line of varying length with four main stresses, the first three of which begin with the same sound. Percy's substantial metrical appendix (entitled 'On The Metre of Pierce Plowman's Visions')[29] was designed to explain the origin of this metre in order to set the two poems in some sort of a context. Briefly, he shows with quotations from Old Norse and from Anglo-Saxon (taken from Hickes' *Thesaurus*, 1705) what was indeed the case, that alliterative metre had certainly not been invented by Langland. In fact, of course, Langland was writing in a Middle English alliterative tradition which was by his time well established; these poems were, however, as yet largely unknown to Percy and to many of his contemporaries.[30] Percy goes on to provide a brief account of *Piers Plowman* in the following terms:

> There are some readers, whom it may gratify to mention, that these VISIONS OF PIERCE (i.e. Peter) the PLOWMAN, are attributed to Robert Langland, a secular priest, born at Mortimer's Cleobury in Shropshire, and fellow of Oriel College in Oxford, who flourished in the reigns of Edward III. and Richard II. and published his poem a few years after 1350. It consists of xx PASSUS or Breaks ... exhibiting a series of visions, which he pretends happened to him on Malvern hills in Worcestershire. The author excells in strong allegoric painting, and has with great humour, spirit and fancy censured most of the vices incident to the several professions of life; but he particularly inveighs against the corruptions of the clergy, and the absurdities of superstition. (*Reliques*, vol. II, pp. 261–2)

Apart from the final mention of 'the absurdities of superstition', this is a decent account of the poem. Percy would have had ample opportunity to read it; he tells us that he wrote the appendix with four different editions of *Piers Plowman* 'now before me', three by Crowley and one by Rogers.

---

[28] Quoted by Johnston, *Enchanted Ground*, 50.   [29] Vol. II, 260–70.
[30] Thomas Warton later printed some examples in his *History of English Poetry*; see vol. I, 309–17.

Percy's friend Thomas Warton took a considerably more detailed interest in *Piers Plowman*. He first notes its existence in a parenthetic comment attached to his *Observations on the Faerie Queene of Spenser* (1754), which while appreciative of the poem complains about Langland's choice of alliteration as opposed to rhyme.[31] His rather testy remarks clearly indicate the difficulty experienced by eighteenth-century readers with alliterative poetry, especially when coupled with a dialect considerably less accessible than that of Chaucer.[32]

Warton relies on Bale for biographical information about the poet, and he uses Bale's Latin translation of the first line of the poem, 'In aestivo tempore cum Sol CALERET', as grounds for suggesting that a reading to be found in Crowley's edition should be emended. Crowley's text (all three editions) opens 'In a somer season when sette was the sunne'; and Warton rightly points out (in the first detailed discussion of a textual crux in the poem) the implied contradiction between a summer morning and a setting sun. Instead, he urges, we should read 'hotte', in line with Bale's 'caleret'. This crux continued to fascinate him – presumably because it was the first line of the poem – and in his second edition of the *Observations* (1762, vol. II, p. 216), he returns to the discussion, favouring the variant 'softe', which he had in the interim discovered in three Bodleian MSS (which he names as Laud F. 22, Digby 102, and Digby 108),[33] on the grounds that it 'preserves the alliteration' while escaping the internal contradiction of 'sette'.[34] He also reports in his second edition that his

---

[31] *Observations*, 1st edition, 88–90.

[32] A. S. G. Edwards provides evidence of comparable seventeenth-century difficulty with *Piers Plowman*'s alliterative style; see '*Piers Plowman* in the Seventeenth Century'.

[33] The first and third of these shelf-marks must be errors; the two Laud manuscripts of *Piers Plowman* are Laud Misc. 581 (a B-MS) and Laud Misc. 656 (a C-MS); the three Digby MSS of *Piers Plowman* are Digby 171, 102 (both C-MSS) and 145 (a conjoint A/C-MS). All the extant manuscripts of the poem would appear to read *softe* for Crowley's *set*, apart from the B-MS Hm 128 (which also reads *set*) and three A-MSS which substitute a different b-half of the line altogether (see Kane, 175).

[34] For Bale's records of the first line, see p. 12 n. 18 above. Percy wrote to Warton in June 1761 to comment on a pre-publication version of the second edition of *Observations*, discussing the variants *soft, set* and *hot* and plumping for *hot* – without, however, giving any very convincing argument. See David Nichol Smith and Cleanth Brooks, eds., *The Percy Letters*, vol. III, 12–16. Puzzlingly, in his *Reliques*, published in 1765 (vol II, 261) Percy notes in his essay 'On the Metre of Pierce Plowman's Visions' that he 'would read *hot* with Mr Warton, rather than either "soft" as in MSS, or 'set' as in PCC', as if Warton had not favoured the variant *soft*. Ritson's later discussion of this textual crux is (to begin with, at any rate) an excellent example of scholarly discrimination between variants: see his *Bibliographia Poetica*, 404–6. The discussions in Warton's second edition of *Observations* are missed by the indefatigable and normally infallible DiMarco (*Piers Plowman*).

28

friend Edward Lye (author of the Anglo-Saxon and Gothic dictionary) had put forward to him the emendation previously suggested by Holt White (see p. 21 n. 8 above), namely *dryghte* for *bryghte* in B Passus XIII 269. Despite this evidence of rather obsessive interest in the detail of the poem, Warton's familiarity with it should perhaps not be overestimated; he appeared to believe, for example, that Piers Plowman and the narrator were one and the same person.[35]

Several years later Warton printed considerable swathes of the poem in his far more ambitious *History of English Poetry* (3 vols., 1774–81),[36] a work as pioneering as Percy's *Reliques* and received with comparable enthusiasm.[37] Percy had wanted his collection of medieval poetry to 'shew the gradation of our language, exhibit the progress of popular opinions, display the peculiar manners and custom of former ages, or throw light on our earlier classical poets' (vol. I, p. ix); likewise Warton formulates a precise and indeed portentous motive for reading and publishing medieval works: this is now understood as being that of a highly civilised society seeking to discover its own origins. These motives should be contrasted with the more disinterested antiquarianism of (for example) Thomas Hearne; the difference between the two attitudes is identified by Brian Stock : 'With the Enlightenment, the antiquarian, who studied the Middle Ages without necessarily imposing a pattern on it, yielded to the ideologist, who, taking as his primary concern his own place in history, sought in the past a justification and an assurance.'[38] Thus Warton's Preface begins with this explanation for the printing of his anthology:

> In an age advanced to the highest degree of refinement, that species of curiosity commences, which is busied in contemplating the progress of social life, in displaying the gradations of science, and in tracing the transitions from barbarism to civility. (vol. I, p. i)

Study of our past literature, Warton felt, was morally and socially instructive, and secured our hold on and understanding of the civilised qualities of our own culture. In particular, a history of poetry 'must be more especially productive of entertainment and utility'. On these various counts, clearly, Langland's *Piers Plowman* deserved

---

35 *Observations*, 2nd edition 213–17. Crowley thought the same; see p. 16 n. 31 above.
36 A fourth volume was begun but never completed.
37 It was six times re-issued in the next century.
38 'The Middle Ages as Subject and Object', 538. Cf. Johnston's account of Warton, *Enchanted Ground*, 100–19.

admission to the canon; as a poem with artistic quality, as a record of social complaint and customs, and as an early example of the favourite eighteenth-century genre, satire.

Again following Bale, Warton names the poet as 'Robert Longlande ... a secular priest, and a fellow of Oriel college, in Oxford' (vol. I, p. 266). Warton evidently approves of Langland's subject matter and treatment; in a description partly cribbed from Percy, he describes the poem as 'a satire on the vices of almost every profession: but particularly on the corruptions of the clergy, and the absurdities of superstition. These are ridiculed with much humour and spirit, couched in a strong vein of allegorical invention.' But he has not grown any fonder of Langland's chosen method of versification, describing his rejection of 'the rising and rapid improvements of the English language': 'this imposed constraint of seeking identical in-itials, and the affectation of obsolete English, by demanding a constant and necessary departure from the natural and obvious forms of expression, while it circumscribed our author's genius, contributed also to render his manner extremely perplexed, and to disgust the reader with obscurities'. These remarks suggest that Warton believed that the differences between Langland's language and that of, say, Chaucer, were an indication of Langland's affectation and preciosity rather than a reflection of dialectal variation.

Warton quotes substantial sections from the poem, totalling about 500 lines in all, to illustrate Langland's 'imagination' and to give the reader examples of 'striking specimens of our author's allegorical satire, [which also] contain much sense and observation of life, with some strokes of poetry'. These include a long passage from the *Visio*, extracts from the confessions of the Deadly Sins, and another from the ploughing of the half-acre, all apparently taken from one of the second impressions of Crowley's edition.[39] Warton gives no indica-tion that he is aware of differences between Crowley's various editions (unlike Pegge before him in 1755, and Ritson later in 1793–4). He makes almost no mention of the manuscripts of the poem, but it is clear he knew of some (presumably the three in Bodley alluded to in his *Observations*), for in his comment on the B Passus X prophecy of the king who will bring the religious to rule (quoted in vol. I, p. 282, n. 'o'), he remarks that he had 'imagined it was foisted into the copies, in the reign of king Henry Eighth. But it is in

---

[39] Judging from the characteristic variants as listed in Kane-Donaldson's critical apparatus.

manuscripts of this poem earlier than 1400.' His provision of the text with an apparatus is a new step in *Piers Plowman* editing.[40] Most of its entries are glosses of individual words (as *hire deys*: their table, *gorge*: throat); but some provide more far-ranging comment. For example, Warton believes that the conversation between Lady Meed and the friar in B Passus III was 'plainly copied by Chaucer' in his *Summoner's Tale*, who added 'new strokes of humour', and he draws the reader's attention to a similar passage in *Pierce the Ploughman's Crede*.[41] Given the paucity of published medieval works, it is not surprising that Warton was unaware that satirical accounts of friars attempting to extract money from parishioners are commonplace in the contemporary literature.

Other of Warton's annotations provide lengthy historical discussions of details in the text, with many citations of sources or parallels to his remarks, illustrating remarkable erudition and curiosity, albeit contributing only slightly to contextual understanding of the poem. (An exception is his identification of the chivalric images predominating in B Passus XVIII; see vol. I, p. 282 n. 'o'). The general effect is of an editor intent on assimilating the references in the poem into his existing knowlege of the literature and history of the period, rather as one might put together a jigsaw. Any correspondence is seen as significant, although to a modern eye, with the benefit of the vast quantity of published work from the period now available, it seems unnecessary to claim that (for example) Lady Mede and her friar are a source for Chaucer's *Summoner's Tale*.[42]

Warton's later editor, Richard Price, whose editing of the *Piers Plowman* section in the *History* we shall examine in more detail below, defends Warton's magpie bundle of references to bits and pieces of history and literature. He points out that, as indicated in Warton's Preface, he felt that his projected *History* was 'to be made a channel for conveying information on the state of manners and customs among our feudal ancestry, the literature and arts of England and occasionally of Europe at large'. Consequently, his commentary was rich in incidentals designed to illuminate the culture from which his chosen examples of literature had sprung: 'a commentary was

---

40   Though a sixteenth-century annotator had provided a list of glosses to his manuscript of the B-Text; cf. below, p. 40 n. 4.

41   Vol. I, 278; Warton refers to the friars as 'monks'.

42   DiMarco demonstrates that Warton borrowed a few of his editorial comments, unacknowledged, from Elizabeth Cooper's anthology mentioned above; see 'Godwin on Langland', 126.

indisputably necessary, not a mere gloss upon words, but things, a luminous exposition of whatever had changed its character, or grown obsolete in the lapse of time, and which, as it unfolded to the reader's view the forgotten customs of the day, assisted him to live and feel in the spirit of the poet's age'.[43]

The next scholarly discussion of the poem, its manuscripts, and its author is to be found in Thomas Tyrwhitt's distinguished edition of the *Canterbury Tales* (1775–8). Tyrwhitt 'deserves to be considered as the founder of modern Chaucer editing',[44] and his edition stands out for the respect and deference it accords the manuscripts.[45] Tyrwhitt described how, 'In order to make the proper use of these MSS. to unravel the confusions of their orthography, and to judge between a great number of various readings, it was necessary to inquire into the state of our language and versification at the time when Chaucer wrote'; and he discusses *Piers Plowman* as a contrasting example of contemporary use of language, noting in addition,

> The Visions *of* [i.e. *concerning*][46] Pierce Plowman are generally ascribed to one *Robert Langland*; but the best MSS. I have seen, make the christian name of the author *William*, without mentioning his surname. So in MS. *Cotton.* Vesp. B. xvi. at the end of p. 1. is this rubric. 'Hic incipit secundus passus de visione *Willelmi* de petro plouhman.' And in ver. 5. of p. 2. instead of, '*And sayde*; sonne, *slepest thou?*' The MS has, '*And sayde*; Wille, *slepest thou?*' See also the account of MS. *Harl.* 2376 in the Harleian Catalogue. I cannot help observing, that these Visions have been printed from so faulty and imperfect a MS. that the author, whoever he was, would find it difficult to recognize his own work.[47]

This last reference was presumably to the edition of Crowley (or its later reprinting by Rogers). Both Tyrwhitt's named manuscripts, Cotton and Harley, are C-MSS: and if, as would appear from his remarks, Tyrwhitt had read the Cotton manuscript with some care, this would explain why he regarded the Crowley text as manifestly defective and unsatisfactory. Crowley's text was based on a B-MS,

---

[43] Richard Price, *The History of English Poetry ... by Thomas Warton ... A New Edition Carefully Revised With Numerous Additional Notes ...* vol. I, 13.

[44] In the words of B. A. Windeatt ('Thomas Tyrwhitt', 118).

[45] As indicated by the first sentence of the Preface to his edition of the *Canterbury Tales*, quoted below, p. 54.

[46] This annotation indicates that Tyrwhitt sought to avoid any confusion of the narrator with the figure of Piers Plowman; cf. p. 16 n. 31 above.

[47] *The Canterbury Tales of Chaucer*, vol. IV, 74–5 n. 57.

and Tyrwhitt would doubtless have observed that it lacked or apparently misrepresented passages found in Cotton. He would have concluded that the more complete text was the superior and original one.

Joseph Ritson, the sour-natured antiquary whose fearsome passion for accuracy of transcription had so harried Percy, was the next scholar to record his investigations of *Piers Plowman*.[48] As we have seen, Ritson was an important figure in the history of Middle English editing, since his strictures on other editors went some way towards elucidating principles of editing so far unformulated, in particular the need to distinguish clearly between material original to the manuscripts and editorial intervention.[49] In 1793–4 he published *The English Anthology*, in three octavo volumes, in which he presented a selection of English poetry designed to feature all poets 'of eminence or merit' who had written between the beginning of the sixteenth century and the end of the eighteenth. Only Chaucer and Langland are included from before this period, 'the nicety of the present age being ill disposed to make the necessary allowances for the uncouth diction and homely sentiments of former times' (*Advertisement*, vol. I, p. v). Ritson seems also to have felt that, if he included other medieval works, he would attract the same sort of critical opprobrium which he himself had heaped upon Percy and Warton (see pp. v–vi). From Chaucer he prints the Prologue to the *Canterbury Tales*, and follows this with an extract from Passus V of Crowley's text of *Piers Plowman* (vol. III, pp. 35–58). Presumably Ritson chose this portion of the poem, from the confessions of the Deadly Sins, as containing some of the poem's most vivid and dramatic poetry.[50]

Ritson has read Bale and Tyrwhitt, and presents some of their comments on the poem and its author in a judiciously worded footnote. He is aware that there are manuscripts in existence which differ from the printed copies, and he repeats Tyrwhitt's argument

---

[48] On Ritson's life, see Bertrand H. Bronson, *Joseph Ritson*. Ritson had similarly pursued Warton; see e.g. his *Observations* on Warton's *History*, and Price's account of the dispute in his edition of Warton's *History*, 19–24. Tyrwhitt escaped the peculiarly virulent abuse directed at the other two scholars; though see e.g. the caustic remarks in Ritson, ed., *Ancient Engleish Metrical Romances*, vol. I, lxxx, ccxxiv.

[49] See A. S. G. Edwards, 'Observations on the History of Middle English Editing', 44, who points out that Ritson's practice did not always match his precepts, and cf. Bronson, *Joseph Ritson*, e.g. vol. I, 376.

[50] This printing of and reference to the poem is also unnoticed by DiMarco (*Piers Plowman*); he does, however, note Ritson's earlier mentions of the poem in his *Observations* on Warton's *History of English Poetry* (32). Ritson prints B Passus V 1–441.

that the author's name may have been William not Robert – with the reservation that the name William (as in the title, '*Visio* WILLELMI *de Petro Ploughman*') may have been deliberately chosen by the author as 'a personification of the mental faculty', and hence have been mistakenly applied to the poet. He is thus the first critic to make a distinction between the poet and the narrator. Ritson goes on to describe the poem very briefly: it is 'a kind of religious allegorical satire; in which Piers the ploughman, the principal personage, appears to be put for the pattern of Christian perfection, and seems once or twice to stand for J. C. himself'. He also refers to *Piers Plowman*'s popularity about the time of the Reformation 'from his having lashed the vices of the clergy with a just severity, and foretold (as was thought) the destruction of the monasteries by Henry VIII'.

The English Anthology is conceived on a much less ambitious scale than Warton's *History of English Poetry*, and so it is not surprising that, unlike Warton, Ritson gives no explanatory literary or historical help with the various references in the text. Neither does he introduce or summarise the portion of the poem he prints; in fact the only additional information he supplies is textual, and even that is exiguous. He tells us that he has printed an extract 'From the first edition, 1550; compared with the second in the same year'; which indicates that he has worked out, if not as clearly as Pegge in 1755, that Crowley's various editions read differently. He marks departures from the text of Crowley's first edition by enclosing the relevant word or phrase in inverted commas, and recording in a note at the foot of the page the alternative reading. The implication of this practice is that the reading incorporated in Ritson's text is that of Crowley's second edition, while the reading given in the footnote is that of his first. This is sometimes, but not always, true. In several instances Ritson introduces his own editorial emendation into the text without indicating that it is such, meantime recording the reading of the *first* edition of Crowley in the footnote.[51] Another implication of Ritson's annotation practice is that *all* departures from Crowley's first edition are recorded in the footnotes; but again this is not so.[52]

Ritson continued to read and think about the poem. In 1802, he published a biographical catalogue of English writers, in which he

---

[51] As at lines 226 (Ritson wrongly gives the line reference in his footnote as 228), 308, 313, 315, 317, 321 (Ritson's numbering).
[52] For example, differences between Crowley's first and second editions are not noted at Passus V 32, 36, and 43.

discussed what was known of Robert, or William, Langland and his poem.[53] He again notes the difference between the printed copies and the manuscripts, and prefers William as the author's first name. But he has now made a significant stride forward, and become the first critic to make a distinction between manuscripts and versions.[54] He appears to have sought out at least nine manuscripts in London, Cambridge, and Oxford, and subjected them to a 'thorough and attentive investigation', as a result of which he was able to make a better analysis than Tyrwhitt of 'the comparative merits of the printed copy, respecting the faultyness and imperfection whereof Mr. Tyrwhitt may have been somewhat too hastey in his judgement'.

Five of his nine manuscripts, he tells us, together with 'others', unnamed, conform pretty much, give or take a few variations, to the version printed by Crowley, thus constituting one 'edition', while the remaining four, also with additional 'others', constitute a second.[55] What Ritson had done was to read the first few lines of his various manuscripts, some of which begin as A-MSS and some as C-MSS, and compare them with Crowley's text. Since A-MSS and B-MSS do not diverge widely for the first seventy-odd lines of the Prologue, he assumed that the Crowley text and the A-MSS represented one version, sharply differing from that found in the C-MSS. Of course, had he persevered with his comparative reading, he would have found that Crowley and the A-MSS also differed sharply from each other. Ritson goes on to make the same suggestion of authorial revision as Hearne earlier, commenting that

> the subsequent variations, throughout the poem, are still more considerable; so that it appears highly probable that the author had revised his original work, and given, as it were, a new edition; and it may be possible for a good judge of ancient poetry, possessed of a sufficient stock of critical acumen, to determine which was the first, and which the second. No MS., however, of this celebrated and really excellent composition examined by the present annotator, has

---

[53] *Bibliographia Poetica*; see 26–31 on 'Langelande Robert'.

[54] A point made by E. T. Donaldson, *Piers Plowman: The C-Text and Its Poet*, 4.

[55] The named MSS are firstly Harley 3954 (which starts off as an A-MS, H³), Harley 875 (another A-MS, H), Harley 6041 (a conjoint A/C-MS, H²), the Vernon MS (an A-MS, V) and the Lincoln's Inn MS (another A-MS, L); and secondly Vespasian B XVI (a C-MS, M), Caligula A II 18 B XVI (presumably Cotton Caligula A XI, a conjoint CAB MS which starts off with C Pro–Passus II, and has the sigil Cot for its portion of B and O for its portion of C), Harley 2376 (a C-MS, N), and finally 'Mr Douce's' MS (i.e. Douce 104, the C-MS D). To illustrate the differences between the two 'editions' these manuscripts supposedly comprise, Ritson printed the first ten lines of the Prologue.

been found deserveing, either for accuracy or for antiquity, to be preferred to that or those whence the printed copy appears to be taken.

Ritson's forbearance in making a judgement on relations between the versions is admirable, and his discussion is more scholarly and acute than that so far accorded to the problem of manuscripts and variants (as evidenced, for example, in his discussion of the favourite crux *soft/ set/hot* in the first line of the poem).[56] Indeed, it was not to be matched until the arrival of Walter Skeat on the editing scene, sixty-odd years later. Certainly his scholarship compares well with that of William Godwin, who in the following year included a fairly substantial, although almost wholly derivative, account of *Piers Plowman* and its poet in his *Life of Geoffrey Chaucer*.[57] Nevertheless, despite his severe strictures on the shortcomings of other editors of medieval works, Ritson did not read the manuscripts in full by the time he published his final account of them. Otherwise he would have swiftly observed the differences between the manuscripts of the A and B versions.[58]

[56] See *Bibliographia Poetica*, 404–6. He decides in favour of *soft*, although he offers an unfortunate etymology for the word.

[57] See William Godwin, *Life of Geoffrey Chaucer*, vol. II, 406–20; also DiMarco, 'Godwin on Langland'.

[58] There is evidence that he did so some time after his account was published. As Vincent DiMarco observes, 'That Ritson at one time strongly suspected a third text is clear from a manuscript entry in his own hand, quoted by Donaldson [*Piers Plowman: The C-Text and Its Poet*, 4–5]: "The differences as well between the printed copies on the one hand and most if not all the MSS. on the other, as between the MSS. themselves is very remarkable. Of the latter indeed there appears to be two sets, of which the one has scarcely 5 lines togr. in common with the other"' ('Eighteenth-Century Suspicions', 129).

3

Whitaker and Price

In 1813, after a gap of over two hundred and fifty years, the second major edition of the poem was published in an impressive black-letter folio edition. Its editor, Thomas Dunham Whitaker (1759–1821), was a Lancastrian vicar, one of whose claims to fame was a fascination with trees (he planted a forest and had his coffin fashioned from a particularly notable specimen), and whose other published output, apart from an edition of *Pierce the Ploughman's Crede* prepared from the 1553 edition, comprised distinguished works of topography.[1] Whitaker's volume is far closer to what we would now recognise as a scholarly edition of the poem. The difference between his attitude to his edition and that of Percy and Warton is clear: there has been a signal shift in literary sensibilities in the last forty years. Whitaker feels no need to argue for the importance of medieval literature generally, either for its own sake or for its illumination of the editor's contemporary society. He shows a more detailed knowledge and grasp of the historical circumstances in which the poem was composed, and his orientation is more literary than that of his predecessors.

In his substantial Introductory Discourse, Whitaker sets out to explain what he regards as the principal literary characteristics of *Piers Plowman* – the predominance of satire on the one hand, and allegory on the other – in terms of the historical circumstances of both poet and poem. He sees the reign of Edward III, during which the poem was at least partly composed, as a time of corruption and decline, and hence an effective instigator of satirical literature. The writings of Chaucer and Langland are a response to their age, the one poet

---

[1] His works on Whalley and Craven display a magnificent range and depth of erudition. See *An History of the Original Parish of Whalley and Honour of Clitheroe* and *The History and Antiquities of the Deanery of Craven*. For biographical information, see *DNB*, vol. XXI, 19–20, and the additional information supplied by Skeat, *C-Text*, lxiii–lxvi, who draws on J. Gough Nichols, 'Biographical Memoirs of Thomas Dunham Whitaker', prefixed to the fourth edition of Whitaker's *History of Whalley*.

enlarging the minds, the other improving the moral feelings, of their contemporaries. Langland's adoption of an allegorical mode ('the most insipid for the most part and tedious of all vehicles') was necessitated by his 'subordinate station in the church', which exposed 'this free reprover of the higher ranks' to the punitive discipline of both the ecclesiastical and the civil authorities (p. iv). While appreciative of Langland's 'sarcastic and ironical vein of wit, his knowledge of low life, his solemnity on some occasions, his gaiety on others, his striking personifications, dark allusions, and rapid transitions', Whitaker's praise is not undiluted. He points out that the attractiveness of allegory as a vehicle for the poet's message spelt its own undoing. Allegory allowed Langland to cloak his criticisms of contemporary culture, so that he himself might escape censure and punishment, but at the same time it made his writing more obscure and less powerful. Clearly Whitaker disliked the promiscuous and sometimes chaotic mix of allegorical and literal levels in *Piers Plowman*. What it is now fashionable for us to regard as bold and creative exploitation of allegorical convention struck the nineteenth-century clergyman as ill-judged, haphazard, and indecorous.

Whitaker thinks that the same reason that dictated the choice of allegory – the need for obscurity, in order to protect the author from reprisal for his boldness in speaking out – was responsible for the mystery surrounding his identity. He correctly points out that most of the attributions of authorship can be traced back to Bale, and carry no more than Bale's single authority. So we have to turn to the poem itself for information about the poet: 'this ... is prima facie evidence, and must be allowed, until there is something to rebut it' (p. v). Whitaker is untroubled by any notion of an author's deliberate creation of a poetic persona bearing no necessary relation to his or her historical self, and interprets his *prima facie* evidence freely:

> ... wherever born or bred, and by whatever name distinguished, the author of these Visions was an observer and a reflector of no common powers. I can conceive him (like his own visionary William) to have been sometimes occupied in contemplative wanderings on the Malvern Hills, and dozing away a summer's noon among the bushes, while his waking thoughts were distorted into all the misshapen forms created by a dreaming fancy. Sometimes I can descry him taking his staff, and roaming far and wide in search of manners and characters; mingling with men of every accessible rank, and storing his memory with hints for future use. I next pursue him

Whitaker and Price

to his study, sedate and thoughtful, yet wildly inventive, digesting the first rude drafts of his Visions; and in successive transcriptions, as judgment matured, or invention declined, or as his observations were more extended, expanding or contracting, improving and sometimes perhaps debasing his original text.[2]

It is difficult not to believe that this portrait owes a great deal to the poet of the *Lyrical Ballads* and the *Prelude*. Like Wordsworth, Langland mingles with men of low degree, and like Wordsworth, he retires to his study to recollect emotion in tranquillity and to write and rewrite. Whitaker's suggestion that the author might revise his poem to ill effect is a significant statement in the history of editing the poem. Whitaker did not begin to tackle the textual problems of the poem, and so his speculations on the poet's methods of composition were not hampered by any view on the origins of the poem as indicated by the relationships between the extant manuscripts. Thus it is easy for him to imagine the poet producing successive revisions of possibly inferior quality. Such a notion is almost intolerable to editors who try to discriminate between different textual variants on the assumption that the author will have been responsible for the best of the readings, and mistranscribing copyists for the rest. If not only scribes but also, on occasion, authors themselves, are capable of replacing good writing with less good, then this mainstay of editorial discrimination falls by the board. We shall see below the relevance of these remarks for much recent editing of *Piers Plowman*.

After pronouncing on the dialect of the poem (which he believed to be of the 'midland counties' – in fact the dialect varies with scribe and manuscript; Whitaker's manuscript was written by a scribe from the Gloucestershire-Monmouthshire border),[3] Whitaker moves to a discussion of the origins of alliterative verse. Like his predecessors, he found the choice of alliterative metre over syllabic and rhymed verse one greatly in need of explanation and justification, and he suggests that Langland may have 'disdained to adopt' Chaucer's 'courtly improvements', being 'too deeply enamoured of the old Saxon models, whose spirit he had early imbibed, to be much delighted with the uniform recurrence of rhyme, or the restraints imposed by regular versification'.

Whitaker further discusses at some length the question which had

---

2   *Visio Willi de Petro Plouhman*, v–vi.
3   The manuscript was lent to him by Heber, subsequently became Phillipps 8231 and is now Huntington 137. See Samuels, 'Dialect and Grammar', 206–7.

preoccupied Bostock in his reading of Crowley's edition: the degree to which the author was a proto-Protestant. He deals sensibly with this, pointing out that the fact 'that he believed and taught almost all the fundamental doctrines of Christianity has no tendency to prove him a Wickliffite or Lollard. The best and soundest members of the church of Rome have done the same' (p. xviii).

These remarks implicitly correct Crowley's view of the poem. Whitaker goes on to inform us that his predecessor's edition was 'printed from a MS. of late date and little authority, in which the division of the passus's is extremely confused, and the whole distribution of the work perplexed'. Whitaker's judgement, like Tyrwhitt's before him, is presumably coloured by comparison of his own manuscript with Crowley's text. Crowley based his text on a manuscript of the B-Text, while Whitaker used a manuscript of the C-Text; Whitaker must have been struck by the differences in length and passus organisation, together with some substantial changes between B and C in the body of the text. Not unusually in the history of editing, differences between manuscripts are explained by the assumption that two (or more) equivalent versions of the same text cannot both (or all) be right. Only one can be attributed to the author, and the other(s) exist as the result of error in transmitting the original text. It would be natural for Whitaker to believe in the superiority of his text over that of his rival editor; hence his attempt to discredit the previous printed edition.

Even with the aid of better manuscript sources, though, he has to confess that the poem presents its readers with significant problems: 'The work is altogether the most obscure in the English language, both with respect to phraseology, to the immediate connection of the author's ideas, and to the leading divisions in the subject' (p. xix). To help the unfortunate reader overcome these obstacles he provides a glossary, an on-the-page commentary, notes, and a full-length summary of the poem, passus by passus (pp. xix–xxx).[4] The last item, which takes up a substantial proportion of his Introductory Discourse, indicates that Whitaker felt that a prime duty of an editor of the poem was to spell out its narrative line (to the extent that it could be said to have one), interpreting the poem so as to entice and hold the reader's interest and to counteract the offputting impression given

[4] Whitaker was not the first to provide a glossary to the poem; a short list of glosses had been written by a sixteenth-century annotator to one of the B-MSS of the poem, Ll. 4. 14 (C²), reprinted by Skeat, *B-Text*, 421–4, with comments 424–6.

by the unfamiliar language and convoluted expession. (We should not despise the reader for needing this amount of help; some present day translations of the poem also provide passus-by-passus summaries, and are similarly found useful by readers seeking initial orientation.[5]) But like most summaries of the poem, Whitaker's flattens the poetic and also dramatic texture. He gives no impression of the way in which Langland weaves between chaotically – or creatively – coexisting allegorical levels, nor of the poem's other poetic qualities, for example the characteristically startling and dense imagery, often expressed through bold word-play and pun. Nor does he alert the reader to such highly charged episodes as the harrowing of hell, merely summarising this passage as 'the whole history of the passion'. Owing to such suppression, compression, and omission, he is able to trace a coherent line through the poem and thus present it as a rational and intellectually manageable whole. Similarly, the Commentary which accompanies the text is a loose expository paraphrase, collapsing its rich ambiguities and density of expression into a flat and deadpan narrative.

Whitaker was certainly not insensitive to the characteristics of Langland's writing which his summaries iron out. He calls Langland the 'first English satirist', who had 'an acute moral sense, with a vehement indignation against the abuses of public and the vices of private life; to this was added a keen sarcastic humour, and a faculty of depicting the manners of low life with an exactness and felicity, which have never been surpassed, but by the great satirist of the present day' (by whom, he says, he means George Crabbe). Nevertheless he regrets Langland's 'acquaintance with schoolmen', which led to unnecessary obscurity, and his 'ignorance of classical antiquity', which led to an unpolished style. 'He often sinks into imbecility, and not unfrequently spins out his thread of allegory into mere tenuity.' Here too Whitaker reflects the literary tastes of his age, as he does in his admiration of Langland's occasional 'wildness of imagination, which might have been illustrated by the pencil of Fuseli', and his 'sublimity (more especially when inspired by the great mysteries of revelation) which has not been surpassed by Cowper' (p. xxxvii).

Whitaker winds up his introduction with a discussion of the so-called prediction of the dissolution of the monasteries, which he finds almost as interesting as did Crowley, and warns the reader that his

---

[5]   See J. F. Goodridge, *Langland: Piers the Ploughman*, and A. V. C. Schmidt, *William Langland: Piers Plowman*.

editorial annotation falls short in several respects, e.g. in tracing references to the schoolmen and 'in elucidating some ridiculous stories of those times, alluded to by the author'. The Introductory Discourse is followed by a useful section quoting references by subsequent writers to *Piers Plowman*.

Whitaker's discussion of the manuscripts is far more satisfactory than any account given by Crowley. This is to be expected, given the increased sophistication in textual scholarship in the intervening period. He consulted three manuscripts: two (now Hm 114 and 137) belonging to his friend Richard Heber, to whom he dedicated his edition,[6] and one in Oriel College Oxford.[7] He took one of the Heber manuscripts, Hm 137, as his base-text, although well aware that this manuscript differed considerably both from Hm 114 and from the text to be found in Crowley and the Oriel manuscript. To allow the reader to form some idea of the extent of variation between manuscripts and versions, Whitaker printed parallel texts of the portrait of Wrath found in all three of the manuscripts known to him and in one of the impressions of Crowley.[8]

The interesting question, of course, was why there should exist such major discrepancies between the various versions. Whitaker ruled out scribal variation as a sufficient explanation: 'All these varieties ... bear marks, not of the same spirit and genius only, but of the same peculiar and original manner, so that it is scarcely to be conceived that they are interpolations of successive transcribers.' At the same time, though, 'it may be confidently affirmed, that the text of no ancient work whatever contains so many various readings, or differs so widely from itself' (p. xxxiii). Whitaker made this remarkable statement – which has powerful resonances beyond the purely textual – on the basis of limited knowledge, but (excepting the textual

---

[6] Heber (1773–1833) was a distinguished antiquary and a noted bibliomaniac whose books have been estimated to amount to well over 146,827 volumes at his death and filled eight houses to overflowing (*DNB*, vol. IX, 358). See A. N. L. Munby, *Phillipps Studies*, vol. III, 73–5. Heber owned three *Piers Plowman* manuscripts, all of which passed after his death into the hands of Sir Thomas Phillips. The third, which Whitaker seems not to have consulted (*pace* Skeat) became Phillipps 9056 and is now BL Add. 34779 (P²). See Skeat, *C-Text*, xlix–l.

[7] MS Oriel College Oxford 79. Whitaker knew of the existence of the British Museum MS Cotton Vesp. B XVI (a C-Text) but never saw it; he was unable to obtain a transcription and was 'prevented by many engagements from visiting London during the progress of this work' (xl).

[8] xxxiv–xxxv. The quotation from Oriel was so inaccurate that Skeat reprinted it to set the record straight. See p. 144 below.

tradition of the Bible) it may well be true. Whitaker tries to explain why such variation should have arisen:

> we are at liberty to suppose that the first edition of his work appeared when he was a young man, and that he lived and continued in the habit of transcribing until extreme old age. But a man of *his* genius would not submit to the drudgery of mere transcription; his invention and judgment would always be at work; new abuses, and therefore new objects of satire, would emerge from time to time. (p. xxxiii)

Moreover, as time passed and his vocabulary came to be perceived as archaic, he might change it for the sake of greater intelligibility – although, Whitaker concedes, his transcribers might in that respect 'use some freedoms': 'for while we deny them invention to add, we may at least allow them skill to translate'.

In accordance with the theory that the author simplified as he rewrote, Whitaker took his own base-manuscript, Hm 137, to be an early authorial version of the poem. He believed that the 'Saxon words and idioms' with which it abounded were removed in 'succeeding transcriptions', along with 'many original passages, which the greater maturity of the author's judgment induced him to expunge; in short, it bears every mark of being the first but vigorous effort of a young poet' (p. xxxi).[9] As with Whitaker's consideration of the possibility that Langland may have debased his visions as he rewrote them, this remark smacks of an open-minded and exploratory view, which later editors find themselves unable to afford. The notion that C, the longest version of the poem, could possibly have been composed first, has seemed untenable to all textual commentators on the poem; although it has very recently been argued that B might have preceded A.[10]

Whitaker made a pretty incompetent job of reading his manuscript, for which successive textual critics have taken him to task. Skeat produces a frank but charitable explanation:

> The marks of an evident anxiety to represent the MS. with extreme exactness are indeed most apparent on every page; how then are we

---

[9] Whitaker adduced as another reason for adopting the manuscript the fact that he liked the dialect, and recognised it as in many respects similar to 'that Semi-Saxon jargon, in the midst of which he [Whitaker] was brought up, and which ... he continues to hear daily spoken on the confines of Lancashire, and the west riding of the county of York' (xxxii); cf. p. 56 n. 19 below.

[10] See further below, pp. 429–30.

to account for the most frequent amazing variations from the true text of the old scribe? Only, I believe, by the old observation that the eye only sees what it has been *trained* to see. It is clear that, as a scholar, he frequently misunderstood his author; and that, as a transcriber, he often failed in deciphering the not very difficult characters in which the manuscript is written. The two causes together are sufficient to account for such mistakes as, despite all his care, are certainly to be found in his edition.[11]

Whitaker's glossing skills were also embarrassingly variable. His notes give a good indication of the difficulties he had with his text. Sometimes he is quite candid about them: for example, on the notorious grammatical passage in Passus III, he comments: 'the sense is so slender, and the allusions so poor, that the later copies have very properly omitted it. I have retained it merely from respect to the original text, and have picked my way through its obscurities as well as I was able', and he punctuates his notes at this stage with remarks such as 'I am quite at a loss as to the meaning of the word, or the passage' (Notes, p. 3). Whitaker does his best to explain some of the more recondite references in the poem, but acknowledges that 'on subjects of so much uncertainty, the Editor is aware that the reader will sometimes differ from him; in fact, the notes will prove that he has, on a review of what had already been printed, not unfrequently differed from himself'.[12]

As we have seen, Whitaker had access to MS Hm 114 and to the Oriel manuscript. To begin with, he compared the two manuscripts – together with the text printed in Crowley – fairly regularly with his base-manuscript, and he commented in his Notes on differences which seemed to him significant.[13] But his enthusiasm for comparing

[11] *Parallel-Text*, vol. II, lxxxi . Richard Price and Thomas Wright also have more or less harsh comments to make on Whitaker's incompetence or ignorance of Middle English, examples of which can be found throughout the glossary and notes. Skeat describes the edition and its limitations in his own edition of C (*C-Text*, li–lxiii), and provides a useful account of Whitaker's errors of transcription and misjudgement in his *C-Text*, Critical Notes, 449–66. Very occasionally, Whitaker makes a valuable contribution to textual interpretation of the poem. Thus at Passus IX 90 (Skeat's numbering) he suggests (Notes, 7) that *worchyng* in the line 'By here warnyng and worchyng worch þow þer-after' should be replaced by *wording*. Skeat comments, 'This is an excellent suggestion, and I have no doubt that it is correct. My only reason for not introducing it into the text is that all the MSS. agree in the mistake' (*C-Text*, 456). Pearsall – presumably independently – comes to the same conclusion as Whitaker, and does introduce *wordynge* into his text, noting that the reading is not found in any of the MSS (XIPU) that he consulted to form his text (see critical apparatus to Pearsall, VIII, 90).

[12] For an example, see his comment on Notes, 2 (on p. 28 line iii of his text).

[13] Thus he notes that the last line of Hm 137's Passus II (I 204 in Pearsall's text) is inferior to

the various versions dwindled as he made his way through the poem; the last such comment appears on C Passus XIII 5, where he prints Hm 137's text but rightly labels it 'absurd' and prefers that of Hm 114.[14] Evidently the labour involved in finding his way round the various manuscripts became less and less welcome.

Whitaker's text was not on the whole well received. It was thought to be too expensive, and the black letter print, together perhaps with Whitaker's retention of thorns and yoghs, rendered it inaccessible to the casual reader. Isaac D'Israeli gave Whitaker his *coup de grâce* in a form which usefully distinguished between the quality of the poem and of the editor, leaving the door open for an improved shot from a different hand. 'For the general reader,' he wrote in his *Amenities of Literature* (1841),

> I fear that 'the Visions of Piers Ploughman' must remain a sealed book. The last edition of Dr. WHITAKER, the most magnificent and frightful volume that was ever beheld in black letter, was edited by one whose delicacy of taste unfitted him for this homely task: the plain freedom of the vigorous language is sometimes castrated, with a faulty paraphrase and a slender glossary; and passages are slurred over with an annihilating &c. Much was expected from this splendid edition; the subscription price was quadrupled, and on its publication every one would rid himself of the mutilated author. The editor has not assisted his reader through his barbarous text interspersed with Saxon characters and abbreviations, and the difficulties of an obscure and elliptical phraseology in a very antiquated language. Should ever a new edition appear, the perusal would be facilitated by printing with the white letter.[15]

The cheated public had to wait only a few years before some portions, at least, of the poem received more intelligible and expert treatment. The next editor was Richard Price, who subjected these excerpts to remarkably scholarly scrutiny in his edition of Thomas Warton's *History of English Poetry*, published in 1824. Price decided to investigate more fully the text provided by Warton, which as we have seen was taken from Crowley's second edition. He makes use of a number of different manuscripts and versions in addition to

---

the equivalent line in Hm 114, which reads as B at this point (I 209). The B-Text line makes a better link with the start of the next passus (Notes, 2, on p. 23 of his text).

[14] See Notes, 10, commenting on p. 215 line 7 of his text. The line is 'ʒut ret me that Abraham and Iob weren wonder ryche'; Hm 137 reads *that* for *ret*.

[15] D'Israeli, *Amenities of Literature*, vol. I, 303–4.

Warton's text: two B-MSS (Cotton Caligula A XI and Harley 3954), Whitaker's edition of C, two C-MSS (Vespasian B XVI – known to but not seen by Whitaker – and Harley 2376), and two A-MSS (Harley 875 and Harley 6041).[16]

Between them these represent a bewilderingly various array of texts. As we have seen, both Crowley's and Whitaker's editions are somewhat inaccurate representations of the manuscripts they purportedly transcribed. Neither of the two B-MSS Price consulted are straightforward texts of B, for Cotton Caligula A XI begins with a C-Text, switches to an A-Text part-way through Passus II, and continues from Passus III to XX as a B-Text; while Harley 3954 begins as a B-Text of the poem and switches part-way through Passus V to an A-Text. The two C-MSS are less confusing as they simply present single texts of C. But the two A-MSS are again far from straightforward; the first, Harley 875, is physically defective throughout its length and stops part-way through Passus VIII, while the second, Harley 6041, is a conjoint AC manuscript, beginning with an A-Text but switching to a C-Text after A Passus XI.

Price made a remarkable job of what must have seemed very confusing material. For the texts of the excerpts in the body of the *History*, he swapped Warton's Crowley text for the Cotton Caligula manuscript (which throughout these excerpts reads as a B-Text), and recorded Crowley's variants in a critical apparatus. Then in an Appendix (vol. II, pp. 481–510) he printed parallel passages from Whitaker's edition, which had of course not been available to Warton, and corrected the text as he thought necessary by substituting readings from the other C-MSS, recording their variants as before in his critical apparatus. Presumably he was interested in the different readings provided by different authorities, and thought his readers would share his interest.

Price also provided his readers with a brief discussion of the texts of the poem. He reports Whitaker's view that his edition of the poem (C) represented the original version written by the author, while Crowley's edition (B) represented a later, revised version, and comments that it 'is not to be admitted without considerable hesitation'. For the two Harleian manuscripts (875 and 6041) indicate that

---

[16] He also refers to 'the Oxford MS' in a context which makes it virtually certain that he means the Oriel College MS known to Whitaker. See Price, *History*, vol. II, 482; Whitaker, *Visio Willi de Petro Plouhman*, xxxii–iii.

another and a third version was once in circulation; and if the first draught of the poem be still in existence, it is here perhaps we must look for it. For this the narrative is considerably shortened, many episodes of a decidedly episodic cast – such as the tale of the cat and ratons, and the character of Wrath – are wholly omitted; others, which in the later versions are given with considerable detail of circumstance, are here but slightly sketched; and though evidently the text book of Dr. Whitaker's and Crowley's versions, it may be said to agree with neither, but to alternate between the ancient and modern printed copies. (vol. II, pp. 482–3)

The reader is invited to 'form his own opinion' from the twenty-five-odd lines ending the Prologue of Harley 6041, which Price prints with variants from Harley 875. The version of the Prologue found in these two manuscripts, like that of the other A-MSS, is substantially different from the equivalent passages in B and C, omitting as it does the belling-of-the-cat episode.

This is the first time that a commentator on the poem identifies the existence of three separate versions. Price evidently read the manuscripts with considerably greater care and attention than his predecessors. Not carefully enough, however; for he makes no mention of the fact that Harley 6041, his proto-text of the poem, ceased to differ from the C-MSS after the end of A Passus XI, nor does he seem to have been aware that Harley 3954, the A-Text/B-Text conjoint manuscript, changed its character after Passus V.[17]

It is distinctly ungenerous to cavil at these shortcomings given Price's notable gains on the work of his predecessors. Instead, let us turn to the quality of his editing. The first of Warton's excerpts was a thirteen-line stretch from the Prologue. Price prints the equivalent lines from Harley 3954, and substitutes a superior reading from Crowley's text at B Pro 21, which restores alliteration (he prints the manuscript reading in the critical apparatus).[18] 'On further inspection', he tells us in a footnote, he found Harley 3954 to be 'not only ... incomplete, but essentially varying from the printed copy of Crowley'. So he switched to the Cotton B-MS, which, he accurately observed, 'has a different commencement from Crowley's edition' (as

[17] So in his note to B Passus X 38 he notes that Harley 3954 reads a completely different line (in his view superior) to that of Cotton and Crowley, without at the same time acknowledging that its (A) text elsewhere differs substantially. It seems likely that his consultation of the Harley manuscripts was sporadic only.
[18] Vol. II, 102; the line is 'In settynge and sowynge swonken ful harde'. Harley 3954 reads *trauelyd* for Crowley's *swonken*; the latter reading is shared with all the other manuscripts.

noted above, it begins as a C-Text, switches briefly to a version of A, and then continues with a B-Text from Passus III to the end of the poem). Price has in fact replaced Warton's Crowley text with the Cotton text in the excerpts he prints, although Cotton's 'erroneous or doubtful readings – more especially such as offended against the alliteration – have been removed to the notes below, and those of Crowley's edition substituted in their stead'. And he describes Crowley's manuscript as 'a very excellent one … the printed copy has conferred nearly as many favours upon the present text as have been gleaned from the Cotton manuscript'.[19] It is true that most of Price's emendations of the Cotton manuscript are made on grounds of alliteration. His collations are on the whole thorough and accurate, although occasionally he lets slip unrecorded some of the significant Crowley variants.[20] Price also provides occasional shrewd comments on the text, weighing up rival variants with due awareness of the difficulty of determining the probable original.[21] Similarly judicious comments are to be found in the introduction and critical apparatus to the C-Text extracts published in the Appendix. Price recognises that his substitution in the main part of the *History* of a manuscript copy for the Crowley extracts Warton had originally printed might have raised objections, and that 'a difference of opinion might arise as to the value and importance of the respective texts'. Hence 'it was thought adviseable to meet the difficulty in the shape of compromise, by giving the corresponding passages from Dr Whitaker's edition in an Appendix'. This act of generosity puts the reader in the position of making an independent judgement on the respective qualities and characteristics of the two versions. Price was clearly aware that

---

[19]   Vol. II, 102–3.

[20]   As is evident from a comparison of the variants recorded in the critical apparatus with the text chosen to displace them, see eg. at Passus VIII 40 (Kane–Donaldson 39), *ground] world* Crowley; Passus VIII 43 (Kane–Donaldson 42) Crowley omission of text. He also occasionally puts square brackets around what is in fact a Cotton reading, e.g. at VIII 32 (Kane–Donaldson 31), perhaps as an additional signal to the reader that there is significant variation in the text. Elsewhere he adopts Crowley's text on the grounds of sense (e.g. Passus VIII 77; Kane–Donaldson 76). Price also at one point adopts a reading from Whitaker's text; see B Passus X 182 (Kane–Donaldson 185), Price vol. II, 114.

[21]   So at B Passus VIII 32 (Kane–Donaldson 31), 'Maketh the man many tyme to falle and to stonde', Price (vol. II, 104) discusses the virtues of the variants *and* and *than,* choosing Cotton's reading *than* for his text but recognising the possibility that *and* might be the original, and also citing the 'better' reading of Whitaker's text (at C Passus X 35), *if.* Cf. also his comments (vol. II, 108) at Passus IX 39 (Kane–Donaldson 40), on the merits of 'if he hadde a pen' (Cotton) as opposed to 'if he had no pen' (Crowley) where he again favours Cotton over Crowley (thus, incidentally, siding with Kane–Donaldson against Schmidt), but recognizes the possible originality of the alternative reading.

Whitaker's manuscript was flawed, and moreover misread by its editor, and believed that the texts found in the British Library copies provided valuable additional evidence as to the original readings of the poem.[22] His aim in printing the parallel passages from Whitaker's edition, along with variant readings from the British Library manuscripts, was to illuminate 'the means by which we may one day obtain an authentic text of our earliest English satirist' (vol. II, p. 486).

Altogether, this is an extraordinary piece of work. It reveals a scholarly thoroughness and concern for accuracy, even in cases of minutiæ, now considered indispensable in editing but then a rarity (with the exact Ritson regarded an eccentric), as Whitaker's example makes all too clear. Price also demonstrates a clear-headed recognition of the imponderables of editing, as for example the difficulty of deciding between variants of indeterminate merit. As we shall see, such rigour and judgement are largely uncharacteristic of nineteenth-century Middle English editing.

[22] See vol. II, 484. Price's critical apparatus repeatedly takes issue with Whitaker's glossing and interpretation of his text.

4

Wright

The publications of Whitaker and Price, however different in scope and quality, were characteristic of their time. The general interest in medieval literature which Percy's *Reliques* both answered to, and in its turn strengthened, bore fruit in the nineteenth-century explosion of literary book societies, whose main purpose was to publish unedited manuscripts. 1812, the year before Whitaker's edition appeared, saw the establishment of the Roxburghe Club, a highly exclusive society which took pride in restricting access to its own ranks and originally limiting the number of copies of each volume published.[1] In the following years, a number of other societies, often with the same members, followed suit, producing a host of important first editions of early English works; for example the Bannatyne Club (founded in 1823, with Walter Scott as its first president, which in 1839 published a landmark in Middle English editing, Madden's anthology of the *Gawain* poems), the Maitland Club, founded in 1828, the Surtees Society (1834) and the Ælfric Society (1842). The Camden Society (1838) counted Thomas Wright, the future editor of *Piers Plowman*, as one of its founder members, including his famous *Political Songs* among its first publications, and the Percy Society (1840), of which he was also a founder member, published along with many other works Wright's new edition of the *Canterbury Tales* (1847–51).[2]

In the March 1848 issue of the *Quarterly Review*, a long unsigned review article entitled 'Antiquarian Book Clubs' (pp. 309–42) castigated some of these societies for deliberately making their publications scarce and difficult to come by, and criticised manuscript owners for sitting on their treasures and effectively barring scholarly access.[3] The

[1]   See Nicolas Barker, *The Publications of the Roxburghe Club*.
[2]   See further H. R. Steeves, *Learned Societies and English Literary Scholarship*.
[3]   Sir Thomas Phillipps, the owner of three *Piers Plowman* manuscripts, is excepted as an

author, Richard Garnett,[4] also subjected the book society publications themselves to scornful and searching scrutiny, suggesting that in some circumstances material was better left unpublished than given such unworthy reproduction, and excepting only Sir Frederic Madden's recent publication of Laȝamon's *Brut*.

Garnett (1789–1850) was a friend of John Mitchell Kemble (1807–57), the distinguished Anglo-Saxon scholar who did much to raise editing standards in England.[5] He was an accomplished philologist, unusually well read in German scholarship, and also assistant keeper of printed books at the British Museum, where he worked under Madden (another friend of Kemble). Earlier in his career, in 1815, he had been appointed curate at Blackburn, at which time the vicar was Dr Thomas Whitaker. Garnett perhaps formed some of his ideas about editing texts as a result of contact with that gentleman; it is hard to believe that he would have judged Whitaker's *Piers Plowman* lightly, although no record survives of his opinion of his vicar's editorial skills.[6] Certainly Garnett's judgement on Madden's qualities as editor is entirely reasonable. Most unusually, Madden appreciated the necessity for accurate representation of the text, in particular indicating to the reader what was editorial and what original to the manuscript, as the Introduction to his *Gawain* anthology indicates:

> The poems here taken from original manuscripts are printed with a scrupulous regard for accuracy, and the abbreviations left as written, but, for the convenience of the reader, a list of these is annexed, and the words are written at length in the Glossary and Notes. The truth is, that editors of our old poetry have, with few exceptions, paid too little attention to the old system of writing used by the early scribes, and the consequence is, that but a small portion of all that has been published will bear collation with the originals. (p. xlv)

As a gifted palaeologist, Madden knew what he was talking about and could deliver what he promised.[7] His scholarship and editorial

generous lender of his material (313n.). This was unusual praise; cf. A. N. L. Munby, *Phillipps Studies*, and *Portrait of an Obsession*.

4   The article is reprinted in *The Philological Essays of the Late Rev. Richard Garnett*, 111–46.

5   One of Kemble's letters to Garnett is quoted in *The Philological Essays of the Late Rev. Richard Garnett*, pages xi–xii. On Kemble, see pp. 67–8 below.

6   Garnett refers to Whitaker's edition of *Piers Plowman* without comment in 'Antiquarian Book Clubs', 334. His son records that Whitaker requested Garnett to preach his funeral sermon; see *The Philological Essays of the Late Rev. Richard Garnett*, iii. For an account of Garnett's life, see the memoir prefixed to this volume (i–vxi) and *DNB*, vol. vii, 885–6.

7   A. S. G. Edwards assigns the *Gawain* anthology a crucial place in the history of Middle English editing, suggesting that it might be seen as 'the first completely scrupulous edition of Middle English works... In Madden's work we see merged the components of a genuine

methods were exceptional, however, and the consistency and self-consciousness of his editorial method were not to be matched in English editing for many years, and certainly not in the next edition of *Piers Plowman*.

Among the other books reviewed by Garnett were several medieval works edited by John Orchard Halliwell (later Halliwell-Phillipps)[8] and Thomas Wright under the auspices of the Camden Society, and these came in for remorseless criticism. Wright was singled out for special treatment:

> Mr Wright ... one of the chief working members of Camden and some other societies, has employed himself during a pretty long period with the literature of the middle ages, and has considerable practice in extracting and editing MSS. reliques of various sorts. On the strength of this he has in a manner constituted himself editor in general in Anglo-Saxon, Anglo-Norman, Middle-English, and Middle-Latin, and seems to be regarded by a certain clique as a supreme authority in all departments of archaeology. He has indeed some requisites for making himself useful in a field where industrious workmen are greatly needed. But his activity is so counterbalanced by want of scholarship and acumen, that he can never be more than a third or fourth rate personage, bearing about the same relationship to a scientific philologist and antiquarian that a law-stationer does to a barrister, or a country druggist to a physician. (p. 319)

Such pillorying seems very harsh; but Wright's efforts were understandably perceived to be disgraceful in comparison with those of Madden. Thomas Wright (1810–77) was a noted antiquary whose rate of publication was phenomenal. While still an undergraduate at Trinity College, Cambridge, he contributed antiquarian articles to various publications and became yet another of the friends of John Mitchell Kemble. It was there he formed a lifelong friendship with

---

critical edition: accuracy, collation, emendation, a systematic procedure for indicating emendations of whatever size, as well as the necessary supporting explanatory materials' ('Observations on the History of Middle English Editing', 45). Madden's edition of *Laȝamon* was similarly scrupulous (see his description of editorial policy in vol.1, xxxviii; his accuracy is confirmed by the work's recent editors, G. L. Brook and R. F. Leslie, in EETS 250, x), as was his joint edition (with Josiah Forshall) of the Wycliffite Bible (see their description of editorial policy in vol. I, Preface, xxxiv, including e.g. an account of the switch of copy-text for the General Prologue). For a further account of his achievements, see R. W. Ackerman, 'Sir Frederick Madden and Medieval Scholarship', and 'Madden's Gawain Anthology'.

8 He changed his name in order to inherit the estate of Sir Thomas Phillipps (whose estranged son-in-law he was). See A. N. L. Munby, *Portrait of an Obsession*, 99–112.

Halliwell, a younger undergraduate, with whom he collaborated constantly in later years. Wright was enormously prolific in a wide range of subjects, of broadly antiquarian historical and literary interest, and often in collaboration with other scholars. Many of his books are still useful, but he is now chiefly remembered for his editions of two of the major works of the late fourteenth century, *Piers Plowman* (1842), and *The Canterbury Tales* (1847–51). As Sidney Lee wrote of him, 'Much of his work was hastily executed, and errors abound, but his enthusiasm and industry were inexhaustible... Nearly all his philological books are defaced by errors of transcription and extraordinary misinterpretations of Latin and early English and early French words and phrases. But as a pioneer in the study of Anglo Saxon and medieval literature and British archaeology he deserves grateful remembrance.'[9]

Wright first staked his claim to *Piers Plowman* in an article published in the *Gentleman's Magazine* in April 1834, at the tender age of twenty-four. Previous editors, he said, had been interested in the poem's anti-Catholicism, and 'knew nothing of, and cared little for, the critical accuracy of the text which came from their presses'.[10] For a more faithful account of the poem, consequently, a modern editor had to turn to the manuscripts, of which fortunately there were plenty.

Wright's awareness of so many different manuscript versions meant that he was the first editor of *Piers Plowman* to be in a position to produce what we would now think of as a critical text. Most of the editions of Middle English poems which had so far appeared existed in one or two manuscripts only, so that the editor's task in establishing the text was not especially exacting: he had to be able to read the manuscript, and come to a decision about whether to retain the original reading or emend it. As we have seen, the range of editorial accuracy and method varied greatly from one practitioner to another, with the scrupulous regard for the accurate representation of editorial processes shown by Madden on the one hand and the cavalier invention of Percy on the other. *Piers Plowman* was different, as was *The Canterbury Tales*: both works existed in significantly large numbers of manuscripts, owing to their extraordinary popularity in the century following their composition, which had resulted in the

---

[9] *DNB*, vol. XXII, 1045–48.
[10] It appears Wright believed that the poem had been edited by others than Crowley, Rogers, and Whitaker; see the second paragraph on p. 388.

poems being copied out many times over. Hence the editor had to make decisions between manuscripts and manuscript variants.

The Canterbury Tales had a peculiar history. First published by Caxton, successive editors had come across more and more manuscripts, and produced a sort of hodge-podge text, part derived from their immediate predecessor, part made up of readings which they introduced into this 'vulgate' text by unsystematic collation of the manuscripts known to them. By the late eighteenth century attitudes towards editing had somewhat changed, and Tyrwhitt was the first editor to attempt something more explicitly rigorous, claiming in the opening sentences of the Preface to his edition (1775), that

> The first object of this publication was to give the text of *The Canterbury Tales* as correct as the Mss. within the reach of the Editor would enable him to make it. The Editor therefore has proceeded as if his author had never been published before. He has formed his text throughout from the Mss. and has paid little regard to the readings of any edition ...

This suggests an eclectic method of editing, choosing readings for their intrinsic value from now one manuscript and now another.[11] Tyrwhitt's text was certainly known to Wright, who published his own edition of *The Canterbury Tales* a mere five years after his *Piers Plowman*, in 1847. There he rejected eclectic collation as a viable method of editing, describing it as 'the most absurd plan which it is possible to conceive' (vol. I, xxxiii). Instead he suggested that the proper way to deal with a large number of manuscript sources was to go for what is now often referred to as 'best-text' editing: choosing what seems to be the best manuscript witness as a base text, and introducing emendations into this as required, usually taken from the other manuscripts.[12] But Wright's collation of other *Canterbury Tales* manuscripts seems to have been perfunctory, to say the least, and he remarks that 'In general, I have reaped little general advantage from collating a number of manuscripts.'[13]

[11] Tyrwhitt's collation papers tell a different story. Acccording to B. A. Windeatt, they 'reveal that Tyrwhitt worked by "cannibalizing" a copy of the edition of 1687 of Speght, taking out its pages and using them as the "base" against which his manuscripts were collated' ('Thomas Tyrwhitt', 123).

[12] '... to form a satisfactory text of Chaucer, we must give up the printed editions, and fall back on the manuscripts; and ... instead of bundling them together [as, in his view, Tyrwhitt had done] we must pick out one best manuscript which at the same time is one of those nearest to Chaucer's time' (vol. I, xxxv).

[13] Vol. I, xxxvii. For an account of his edition of the *Canterbury Tales*, see Thomas Ross, 'Thomas Wright', and compare Thomas R. Lounsbury, *Studies in Chaucer*, vol.I, 313–24.

Wright's general approach with *Piers Plowman* seems to have been very similar. Only one manuscript could be adopted as a text, he states in his *Gentleman's Magazine* article, since to use several, thus forming 'a mixed text out of manuscripts written at different periods and in different counties, would be to bring into the world a monster, a language which could never have existed'.[14] However, 'in a very few instances, where there is an evident error of the copyist, and where some other manuscripts of authority supply an equally certain correction', their testimony may be incorporated into the text. Wright cooks his own goose by prefacing a devastating account of Whitaker's edition with the stipulation that a modern editor should 'collat[e] all the other manuscripts to which he has access, and ... giv[e], wherever they are important, a rather copious list of their variations, both in words and orthography'. No such collation or lists are to be found in the edition he himself produced eight years later; and as we shall see, he made only minimal comparison of his manuscript with the others to which he had access.

The *Gentleman's Magazine* article makes it clear that Wright is well aware of the existence of manuscript versions of the poem very different from Whitaker's text, but he makes no mention at this stage of different authorial revisions. He simply quotes some parallel passages to 'show the great superiority' of his favoured manuscript, the B-Text in his old college, Trinity (B. 15. 17, hereafter referred to as 'W'), over that of Whitaker (the C-MS P, formerly Phillipps 8231 and now Hm 137). No compelling reasons are offered for this judgement, although he later wrote that the W was in his view 'the best and oldest manuscript now in existence. It is a fine folio manuscript, on vellum, written in a large hand, undoubtedly contemporary with the author of the poem, and in remarkably pure English, with ornamented initial letters.'[15] None of these attributes, of course, other than the date, make the manuscript likely to be more authoritative than any other.[16] Wright tells us that so far (i.e., by 1834) he has

---

Wright took a similar view of the editing of *The Chester Mystery Cycle*, considering a full collation of the five cyclic manuscripts 'not worth the effort', in the words of the Cycle's recent editors Lumiansky and Mills. See their *The Chester Mystery Cycle*, EETS SS 3, xxvii, and cf. Wright, *The Chester Plays*, vol. I, xx–xxi.

[14] Modern exponents of a correspondingly eclectic method of editing (of whatever variety) have escaped giving birth to monsters by adapting their various readings to conform in dialect and spelling to the pattern found in one particular manuscript; cf. e.g. Knott–Fowler, Kane, and Kane–Donaldson.

[15] *The Vision and the Creed of Piers Ploughman*, vol. I, xlviii.

[16] Kane–Donaldson date W as fourteenth/fifteenth century (13).

'collated' (his word, but he seems to mean something closer to 'glanced at') only a few of the other manuscripts: the second *Piers Plowman* manusript in Trinity College (R. 3. 14, henceforward 'T'), whose orthography but not whose text he distinguishes from that of W – in fact it is a conjoint AC version – and five manuscripts in Cambridge University Library (Dd. 1. 117, Ll. 4. 14, Gg. 4. 31, Dd. 3. 13, and Ff. 5. 35); of these seven, only the last two give Whitaker's text, 'all the rest agreeing, with hardly a variation, in the text given in [W]'. This is an accurate assessment, except for the fact that, as already mentioned, T is certainly not a B-Text. Probably Wright diagnosed it by reading the first few lines only, making the same mistake as Ritson had done earlier.

Wright published his own text, with Introduction, Notes and Glossary, in 1842, following it with a 'second and revised edition' in 1856[17] (it should be noted that the supposed edition of 1832, referred to by Kane, seems to be a bibliographical fiction).[18] His description of the poem's qualities gives some idea of why he thought it was worth editing. On the one hand, he felt it was 'peculiarly a national work', 'the most remarkable monument of the public spirit of our forefathers in the middle, or as they are often termed, dark ages'; and on the other, that it was 'a pure specimen of the English language, at a period when it had sustained few of the corruptions which have disfigured it since we have had writers of "grammars"; and in it we may study with advantage many of the difficulties of the language which these writers have misunderstood'.[19]

He has little more to say about the language of the poem, perhaps, as we shall see, because he had some considerable trouble under-

---

17   He included with both editions an edition of *Pierce the Ploughman's Crede*, as the title makes clear: *The Vision and Creed of Piers Plowman*. Wright's second edition, of 1856, seems to be the same as the first throughout the Introduction and text, although the material has been reset. Skeat noted that the second edition contains 'eighteen errors in the text from which the first edition is free' ('First Editions', 480), listing them in his *B-Text*, xxxvii–xxxviii. The Notes contain a very few extra items, e.g. on lines 5412 and 5415, where Wright supplies an additional biblical reference and explains medieval beliefs on the circumstances of Cain's conception (see second edition, vol. II, 533). The Glossary is changed in very minor details; e.g. *bigirdle* is omitted from, but *rather* is added to, the second edition. All the following page references are to the first edition.

18   See Kane, 'The Text', 176–7; DiMarco, *Piers Plowman*, 41.

19   Introduction, xxxiii. Garnett similarly approved of Laȝamon's *Brut*, as edited by Madden, on account of its linguistic qualities (he felt it was particularly interesting since it bore witness to a transitional stage between Old and Middle English, 'Semi-Saxon', a language of which Herbert Coleridge produced a dictionary in 1862); while Skeat, as we shall see (e.g. p. 93 below), devoted his life to the study of Old and Middle English texts very largely because of his fascination for their philological forms.

standing it; but the poem's historical importance is a matter that much concerns him. His Introduction set the scene for the appearance of *Piers Plowman* by sketching out a 'stirring picture; its dark side is the increasing corruption of the popish church' and the oppression of the commons by the ruling classes; 'its bright side, the general spread of popular intelligence, and the firm stand made by the commons in defence of their liberties, and in their determination to obtain a redress of grievances' (p. ix). Wright dates the poem to 1362, on the basis of the 'southwestern wind' identified by Tyrwhitt.[20] He believes the author of *Piers Plowman* to have been a monk, although he adduces no evidence in support of this notion, and envisages him 'contributing by his satirical pen towards producing a reform among his countrymen' (p. xxvi). He also reports Madden's apparently recent discovery of the entry on the flyleaf of one of the Trinity College, Dublin manuscripts of the poem to the effect that the author was called William Langland and was the son of one Stacy de Rokayle. Notwithstanding, Wright feels that the traditional attribution to Robert Langland should stand until more convincingly overthrown.[21] Wright had recently published his collection for the Camden Society of *The Political Songs of England*, mostly Latin satires on just the subjects he has described as being exposed to the whiplash of the satirist's pen in *Piers Plowman*, and not surprisingly he regards these works as in effect an introduction to the English poem.[22] However, our author 'makes his attacks less directly, under an allegorical clothing' inherited from the *Roman de la Rose*, the thirteenth-century French dream poem that spawned vast numbers of allegorical offspring in both England and France. These references show that Wright, as one would expect from his published work, had read far more widely in the period than had Whitaker.

Wright goes on to describe *Piers Plowman* as 'in fact, rather a succession of dreams, than one simple vision', and follows both his predecessors, Crowley and Whitaker, in giving a passus-by-passus summary of the poem. It is as unsatisfactory as all such summaries must be, but does rather better than Whitaker in giving some

---

[20] He is so fond of this date as to reject the reference to 1370, the date of the mayoralty of Chichester, referred to in B Passus XIII 269–70. As Skeat later comments, 'Mr Wright's difficulty arose from supposing that the poem was written *all at once*; whereas Langland almost expressly states the contrary (Text B. xiii. 3)' (*A-Text*, xxxii–iii n. 2).

[21] x n. 3. On the ascription, see Kane, *Piers Plowman: The Evidence for Authorship*, 26ff.

[22] See xv. Wright comments that 'The [English] Poem on the Evil Times of Edward II... contains within a small compass all [Langland's] chief points of accusations against the different orders of society'; see *Political Songs*, 323–45.

impression of the allegorical layers of the poem. Wright also gives his readers the customary disquisition on alliterative verse.[23]

As already indicated, Wright's edition does not live up to the standards he himself set the future editor of the poem in his 1834 discussion of the manuscripts. But he makes some interesting observations: for example that the 'great number' of extant copies of the poem are a proof of its 'ancient popularity', and that 'the circumstance that the manuscripts are seldom executed in a superior style of writing, and scarcely ever ornamented with painted initial letters, may perhaps be taken as a proof that they were not written for the higher classes of society' (p. xxvii).[24] He also quotes the letter written by John Ball as evidence of the poem's popular appeal and political significance.[25]

Wright has come across more manuscripts since 1834, and seems to have known of thirty-odd in total: 'at least eight in the British Museum ... ten or twelve in the Cambridge Libraries ... they are not less numerous at Oxford' (pp. xxxix–xl). But he has evidently not read them in full, for he identifies only the two categories (in effect the B- and C-Texts) he referred to earlier, and to illustrate them quotes two of the same parallel passages he had printed in the *Gentleman's Magazine* article published eight years previously. But he now puts forward more definite views of the relationship between the two versions. Noting that 'there are in the second text [i.e. Whitaker's] many considerable additions, omissions, and transpositions', he remarks,

> It would not be easy to account for the existence of two texts differing so much; but it is my impression that the first [Crowley's text] was the one published by the author, and that the variations were made by some other person, who was perhaps induced by his own political sentiments to modify passages, and was gradually led on to publish a revision of the whole. It is certain that in some parts of Text II [i.e. the C-Text] the strong sentiments or expressions of the first text are softened down;

and Wright quotes parallel passages from the B- and C-Text versions of the Prologue, on the respective powers of King and Commons, to instance this.[26] This suggestion of dual authorship – adumbrated, as

23 xxxiv–xxxix.
24 On this point see J. A. Burrow, 'The Audience of *Piers Plowman*', Anne Middleton, 'The Audience and Public of "Piers Plowman"', A. I. Doyle, 'Remarks on Surviving Manuscripts of *Piers Plowman*'.
25 See above, p. 7 n. 1.
26 xl–xli. The lines are B Pro 112–22 and C Pro 139–46 ('Thanne kam ther a kyng ...'); B gives

we have seen, by Crowley and also Hearne – was to be enthusiasti-
cally seized by J. M. Manly at the start of the next century; meanwhile
it lay virtually unnoticed.[27] 'In general', Wright concluded, 'the first
text [i.e. B, as represented in his own manuscript W] is the best,
whether we look at the mode in which the sentiments are stated, or at
the poetry and language' (p. xlii); and he mocks Whitaker for
adopting a manuscript which he (wrongly) believed to represent an
early draft by the author, a draft which contained, as Whitaker
himself conceded, ' "many original passages which the greater maturity of the author's judgment induced him to expunge" '.[28]

In keeping with these comments, Wright delivered a number of
further blows to his unfortunate predecessor and immediate compe-
titor. In summary, Whitaker's edition was too large,[29] too expensive,
inaccurate and imperfect. The editor had access to only three manuscripts, and did not choose the best even of those, selecting his copy
text, as we have already seen, partly on the grounds that its dialect
reminded him of that with which he had been familiar since
boyhood.[30] By contrast, Crowley's edition, published sufficiently
long ago to be less of a rival, is praised for being based on 'an excellent
manuscript; the printer has changed the orthography at will, and has
evidently altered a word at times, but on the whole this printed text
differs very little from the one we now publish' (p. xliv).

Such unforgiving criticism of Whitaker might be thought to have
enjoined on Wright a high degree of editorial care and thoroughness
in producing his own *Piers Plowman*. But he himself seems to have
recognised his failure to live up to expectations, pleading 'other
employments' to explain the various deficiencies of his edition. He
claims to have reproduced manuscript W in 'as popular a form as is
consistent with philological correctness'; which in practice meant that
he modernised the spelling (removing yoghs and thorns, as had
Crowley before him but not Whitaker) and made very minor
changes such as introducing a hyphen after the initial *y* of a past
participle. He also printed the text in half lines rather than whole

---

the Commons far greater responsibility than C. Wright quotes from his own and from
Whitaker's text.

[27] See pp. 14 and 21 above.   [28] xliii; cf. p. 43 above.

[29] Wright tells us 'it is not generally known that Dr Whitaker projected an edition of the same
text and paraphrase which are given in his 4to edition, in 8vo, with Roman type instead of
black-letter. After a few sheets had been composed, the design was abandoned, as it is said,
in favour of the larger form' (xlvi).

[30] Wright wrongly identifies Whitaker's copy-manuscript as BL Add. 10574, a conjoint CAB-
Text formerly belonging to Dr Adam Clarke, not (as Wright states, xlv, xlv n. 24) Heber.

lines, on the unconvincing grounds that this better represented the alliterative pattern. It is sometimes difficult to distinguish between deliberate change and unintentional error in his text; Skeat lists about forty misprints.[31] As might be expected, these led to problems in Wright's Glossary, the editor being forced to come up with explanations for non-existent Middle English words. The Glossary was nevertheless an improvement on Whitaker's, although it was in turn to be greatly surpassed by that of Skeat, which included many more words.[32]

Wright's Notes, he says, were intended for the general reader, and were added as they 'occurred to him in the course of editing the text'; 'they might have been enlarged and rendered more complete, if he had been master of sufficient leisure to enable him to undertake extensive researches'. This is a fair account of his annotating principles: large tracts of the poem remain without comment, and Wright seems to have selected lines or words for discussion almost at random, or only if prompted to disagree with another authority.[33]

He claims to record in his Notes the important variations of the Whitaker text, together with a few readings from T (as we have seen, an A-MS), and if this claim were true he would have made a significant contribution indeed to the study of the poem, for it would have been impossible to miss the extent and nature of the differences between the three texts witnessed by his three sources, Whitaker's C-Text, his own MS's B-Text, and T's A-Text. And from his impressive account in the Introduction of the various manuscripts known to him, one might indeed have hoped that Wright would have read more than just these three. But he seems to have consulted only T while actually putting together his text, presumably because of its

---

31 *B-Text*, xxxvii–xxxviii.

32 E.g. *abedde, afelde, alay,* etc. Skeat's glossing is more exhaustive and more accurate. Examples of words wrongly or insufficiently glossed in Wright are *abosten,* which he defines as *to assault;* cf. Skeat's glossing of the lemma *abosted* as 'boasted against, defied in a bragging manner' (B Passus VI 156, Skeat's numbering); *ofgon,* which Wright defines as 'to derive (?)'; cf. Skeat's *agon,* 'obtain' (Passus IX 106); *luft,* which Wright defines as 'fellow, person'; cf. Skeat's 'worthless fellow, weak creature, wretch' (Passus IV 62), etc. Wright also misreads his manuscript, as for example at Pro 74, where *'bonched* hem with his breuet', describing the pardoner striking his congregation with his letter of indulgence, is read as *'bouched ...'* and the corresponding word *bouchen* glossed as 'to stop people's mouths(?)' Wright would have been misled by Crowley here, all three of whose editions read 'bouchid'.

33 For example, he devotes over half a page (vol. II, 508–9) to the reference 'whit wyn of Oseye and reed wyn of Gascoigne', part of the taverners' street cry at the end of the Prologue, in order to take issue with Richard Price's theory that the correct reading was 'weyte [i.e. wheat] of Gascoyne', as found in a corrector's hand in MS Harley 875.

ready accessibility in the same library (Trinity College Cambridge) as his base manuscript W.

Moreover, it is impossible that he read T with any thoroughness. The Notes do occasionally record the differences of T (the A-MS) from W (the B-MS), e.g. at Pro 34 and 74, where there is a one-word difference, at Pro 216, after which T adds an additional six lines (corresponding, as it happens, to the B lines 87–94 which Wright has already printed, although he does not notice the similarity), and at Pro 231, which line Wright explains is missing from W and therefore adopted from T (it is also found in Crowley's text and in most of the other B-MSS, as Wright might easily have discovered). These are the only points in the Prologue stated as differing in the two Trinity manuscripts; but in fact the differences are far more extensive, as a glance at Skeat's Parallel-Text edition of the A, B and C versions will demonstrate. Wright's consultation of the second Trinity manuscript must have been extraordinarily cursory for him not to have observed this. Further comparisons with T are noted in the same manner up to Passus XIII 63, and then disappear. They remain bafflingly inconsistent. Occasionally Wright records variations of a few lines rather than just one word (see e.g. vol. II, pp. 539–40), but he shows no sign of noticing the wholesale differences between the two manuscripts, nor of the fact that T changes its character at the end of Passus XI and is completed with a C-Text continuation, thus bringing it into line with Whitaker's text.

Wright is better at picking up the differences between his and Whitaker's text. He quotes long chunks from the latter in his notes, including the so-called autobiographical passage in C Passus V and the passage on beggars in C Passus IX (which he describes as 'very curious, and well worthy to be preserved'). The comparisons are by no means exhaustive, however. Wright occasionally admits this, as when he states that 'throughout this part of the poem, Whitaker's text differs very much in words and phraseology from the one now printed, but it would take up too much space to point out all these variations' (vol. II, p. 561). And he is the first commentator to notice that the differences between B and C are substantially less in the last two passus of the poem (vol. II, p. 565).

All this is rather tantalising. If Wright had spent an extra ten minutes here and there on his manuscripts, one feels, he might have registered their characteristics more accurately and fully, and made a substantial contribution to textual understanding of the poem.[34] But his methods were sometimes unbelievably slapdash, as illustrated by his reference to Price's edition of Warton mentioned above (n. 33). Here he quotes Price's note on the wine of Gascony under the impression that the text Price is annotating is taken from MS Cotton Vesp. B XVI. This manuscript is mentioned a couple of pages earlier by Price, but there is no excuse for Wright's mistaking it as the source of the text he alludes to, which as Price perfectly clearly states is taken from Harley 6041 – it is in fact the short excerpt which Price prints in order to illustrate his hypothesis that the two Harleian manuscripts (875 and 6041) represent a third, and earliest, text of the poem. Had Wright read Price more carefully, and registered the significance of this hypothesis, he might have had the distinction of being the first editor to sort out the relations between the three major versions of the poems, A, B, and C. This prize was instead reserved for W. W. Skeat.[35]

[34] Lounsbury takes Wright to task for just such perfunctory performance of his editorial duties: 'As an editor, he was of the most exasperating kind ... He seemed to be unaware of the fact that there was no compulsion resting upon him to assume any particular editorial duty; and to be equally unaware, after having assumed it, that there was any moral obligation resting upon him to perform it thoroughly' (*Studies in Chaucer*, vol. I, 314–15).

[35] For Skeat's relationship with Wright, see p. 152 n. 40 below.

PART II
The late nineteenth century

5

The Early English Text Society and its editorial context

THE NEW PHILOLOGY

Thomas Wright's edition of *Piers Plowman* fell considerably short of the promise it appeared to offer. By the mid nineteenth century, as indicated by the criticism directed by Richard Garnett at Wright's earlier efforts, expectations of editing standards had in some respects risen. But they seem rarely to have been met. Sir Frederick Madden's editions of the *Gawain* poems and Laȝamon's *Brut* stand out as exceptions. Both Madden and Garnett were well aware of contemporary developments in European, particularly German scholarship, which gave them a head start over many of their fellow philologists. It is worth taking some time to survey the state of editing theory and practice in England during this period, in particular the work of the Early English Text Society, so as to set the achievement of the next editor of *Piers Plowman*, W. W. Skeat, in its proper context.

English scholarship throughout the nineteenth century lagged far behind German, in a wide range of disciplines but particularly in Germanic Philology and in Old English and classical studies. According to A. E. Housman, the period after 1825 was the time when 'our own great period of scholarship, begun in 1691 by Bentley's *Epistola ad Millium*, had ended', and English classical scholars, 'having turned their backs on Europe and science and the past, sat down to banquet on mutual approbation, to produce the Classical Museum and the Bibliotheca Classica, and to perish without a name'. E. J. Kenney adds, 'It was an age when a Fellow of Trinity, the college of Bentley and Porson, could write in all seriousness that "Hermann and Lachmann deserved to be called scholars, and wanted nothing to give a perfect finish to those accomplishments for which nature had so well qualified them, except

65

the advantages of an English education, and the competition of an English University." "[1]

The rise of medieval manuscript studies in Germany is a complex phenomenon beyond the scope of the present book.[2] It is linked with a number of disparate elements – for example the epistemological shift between eighteenth- and nineteenth-century study of language, which was marked by a move away from a philosophical towards a more historical approach, the rise of nationalism, and the consequent interest in the literature and language of Germany's past. Time and again, the romantic German writers insist on the identity between the spirit of a nation and its tongue.[3] But access to the language of the past, to Germany's national heritage, could only be through its language: and that meant turning to manuscripts.

The philologist and medievalist Jacob Grimm (1785–1863) is a symbolic figure in the development of the historical, scientific method of linguistic studies in Germany: on the one hand gathering folktales with his brother Wilhelm to illustrate Germany's native culture; on the other making revolutionary contributions to philology in his grammar and their dictionary.[4] The connection between philology and the close study of manuscripts is self-evident; E. J. Kenney prints as an epigraph to his book on editing, *The Classical Text*, a quotation from Alphonse Dain (1964): 'On n'oubliera pas ... que tous les progrès de la philologie ont été faits autour du problème de l'édition des textes.'

England was unreceptive to this intellectual revolution. Outside the University of London, modern languages were not studied, so there was no place in Oxford and Cambridge for the 'new philology', as it was called ('Neuphilologie' being the philology of modern (European) languages, as opposed to 'Altphilologie'). Oxford had had an Anglo-Saxon chair since 1795, owing to a bequest from Rawlinson in 1755, which provided that each incumbent of the chair was to hold it for five years at a time. But by 1830, only three of the incumbents had

---

[1]   E. J. Kenney, *The Classical Text*, 116, quoting Housman's *Preface to Manilius*, and J. W. Donaldson's *Classical Scholarship and Classical Learning* (1856).

[2]   A brief account and references to further sources can be found in Hans Aarsleff, *The Study of Language in England*. Cf. also W. K. Ferguson, *The Renaissance in Medieval Thought*, 113–26.

[3]   See e.g. Aarsleff, *The Study of Language*, 129 n. 49 (Leibniz), 144 (Condillac), 147 (Reid), 148 (Herder).

[4]   Grimm perceived the link clearly: 'Das einladende studium mittelhochdeutscher poesie führte mich zuerst auf grammatische untersuchungen' (quoted by Aarsleff, *The Study of Language*, 166). Cf. Allen Frantzen, *Desire for Origins*, 68–72; Peter Ganz, *Jacob Grimm's Conception of German Studies*.

actually published on Anglo-Saxon.[5] Cambridge had no chair until 1877, when James Bosworth's will provided £10,000 for this purpose (W. W. Skeat was its first incumbent in 1878); Bosworth himself, the editor of the Anglo-Saxon dictionary, had held the Oxford Rawlinson chair from 1858–76.[6]

The difficulty of penetrating the academic establishment is illustrated by the experience of John Mitchell Kemble, one of the most distinguished Anglo-Saxon scholars of the century.[7] Kemble was a member of the famous acting family, who studied philology in Germany after taking his degree at Cambridge. He became a close friend of Grimm's, and returned to England with the aim of continuing his academic work on language and texts and introducing the new discipline into academic circles in England. In 1833 and 1834 Kemble published reviews in the *Gentleman's Magazine* of Benjamin Thorpe's edition of Caedmon and his *Analecta Anglo-Saxonica* (a selection of Anglo-Saxon works). Kemble was on the whole approving of Thorpe's work, but bitterly criticised the scholarship of the Anglo-Saxon professors at 'one of our universities' (clearly Oxford). 'Had it not been for the industry of Danes and Germans, and those who drew from the well-heads of their learning, we might still be where we were, with idle texts, idle grammars, idle dictionaries, and the consequences of all these – idle and ignorant scholars.' Instead of setting themselves to learning the language properly, Kemble continued, English Saxonists had 'begun by editing books they could not hope to understand', with appalling results.

A particularly furious debate on the scentific principles of new philology ensued (both Madden and Thomas Wright, Kemble's friends, participated on the side of German scholarship).[8] Kemble praised the successful results of applying systematic analysis to philological forms: 'It is strange, and not a matter of pride or pleasure to Englishmen, that a Dane and a German should have put us in the right road; that Rask and Grimm, without even an opportunity of

[5]   James Ingram (1803–8), John Josias Conybeare (1808–12), and Thomas Silver (1817–22). See Georgian R. Tashjian *et al*, eds., *Richard Rawlinson*, 83–103, and cf. Aarsleff, *The Study of Language*, 170ff.

[6]   For information on Bosworth's endowment of the Anglo-Saxon chair at Cambridge, see W. W. Skeat, *A Student's Pastime*, lxviii.

[7]   See Aarsleff, *The Study of Language*, 191–210, and Bruce Dickins, 'John Mitchell Kemble and Old English Scholarship'. As stated above, Kemble was a friend and correspondent of Richard Garnett, another learned autodidact who operated outside the university system.

[8]   *Gentleman's Magazine*, vol. 103–vol. 5, 1833–35. See Aarsleff, *The Study of Language*, 195–205, for further references and discussion.

seeing Anglo-Saxon MSS. should, from their knowledge of the tongue, have corrected the printed works, and that the MSS. should nearly always confirm their readings ... ',[9] while his opponents, displaying what others recognised to be a failure to understand the basic principles of Grimm's work, poured virulent scorn on German scholarship in general, talking of Grimm's 'sound iron-bound system' (a phrase Kemble had used in the Preface to his edition of *Beowulf*) and on Kemble himself in particular. Kemble was never appointed to a university position, nevertheless his editorial and philological work, together with that of Benjamin Thorpe, was crucially important in establishing better texts of Old English works based on improved understanding of the language.[10]

The philological work by such men as Grimm and the Danish scholar Rask was matched by a revolution in the theory of editing texts; indeed, the one was frequently referred to as 'scientific' philology (the scholarly standards of which discipline, as we have seen, Richard Garnett cruelly reproached Thomas Wright for failing to attain), the other as 'scientific' editing. The work of Lachmann (1793–1851) and others on the continent had established a new method of editing (commonly referred to as recension), whereby the editor reconstructed the archetype of the existing manuscripts of a work by comparing the witnesses reading by reading, establishing a genealogical tree based on the identification of shared error. Lachmann's work was the object of much critical discussion in Germany and France, but it had little impact in England.[11] As we have already observed, there was a new surge of interest in England's medieval literature during the course of the nineteenth century, as seen preeminently in the numerous publications of editions of texts from original manuscripts. But there was little corresponding interest in and discussion of the proper way to edit texts, and virtually no recognition among Old and Middle English scholars of the implications of

[9]   Vol. 103 (1833), 329.
[10]   Kemble's experience of the academic establishment was to be matched by that of Henry Sweet; see further below.
[11]   A standard exposition of Lachmann's theories can be found in the *Princeton Encyclopedia of Poetry and Poetics*, ed. Alex J. Preminger, Frank J. Warnke, and O. B. Hardison, Jr., 'Textual Criticism', 849–53. See E. J. Kenney, *The Classical Text*, 102–10, 130–42, for an account of the origins and influence of Lachmann's work and its place in the history of textual scholarship. See also Aarsleff, 'Scholarship and Ideology', and for a description of Lachmann's non-recensionist method in editing the *Niebelungenlied*, Lee Patterson, 'The Logic of Textual Criticism', 82–5. For Lachmann's influence in France, see Alfred Foulet and Mary Blakely Speer, *On Editing Old French Texts*, 8–39; and see Aarsleff, *The Study of Language*, 178–9, for the progress of German scholarship in Scotland.

Lachmann's work for editing medieval vernacular texts. Additionally, however, English scholars seem to have had a distrust and ignorance of systems of editing, just as they had a distrust and ignorance of the systematic rules established by the new philology.[12] We have seen how haphazard and *ad hoc* were the editorial endeavours of Whitaker and Wright; and many of the texts published by the various book clubs in the first half of the century, and by the Early English Text Society in the second half, have similar characteristics.

In general, there was a very varied acceptance and knowledge of what discoveries in Germany entailed for home-grown attitudes towards scholarship. As early as 1835, the battle was in some circles declared to be won; for example an article on English lexicography by Richard Garnett, the fierce critic of Thomas Wright, opens with a defence of philology and compares its introduction into the educational establishment with the science of geology.[13] But in the case of both geology and philology, there were more discoveries to be made, and a long way to go before their revolutionary effect would be universally understood.

FURNIVALL AND THE EETS

Garnett was a founder member of and active contributor to the Philological Society, which was established by a number of amateur and professional philologists in 1842.[14] This Society has an important rôle in the history of Middle English editing, since one of its offspring was the Early English Text Society, under whose auspices W. W. Skeat's great edition of *Piers Plowman* first appeared. In November

---

[12] See e.g. Richard Garnett's remarks on the English distrust of systems of knowledge based on empirical study as opposed to unsubstantiated premise, *The Philological Essays of the Late Rev. Richard Garnett*, 6–7; and cf. the remarks of Henry Sweet quoted below p. 80.

[13] 'It would have been equally easy to ask fifty or sixty years ago – and would at that time have sounded just as plausibly – what can be the use of comparing unsightly fragments of bone that have been mouldering in the earth for centuries? But now, after the brilliant discoveries of Cuvier and Buckland, no man could propose such a question without exposing himself to the laughter and contempt of every man of science. Sciolists are very apt to despise what they do not understand; but they who are properly qualified to appreciate the matter know that philology is neither a useless nor a trivial pursuit, – that, when treated in an enlightened and philosophical spirit, it is worthy of all the exertions of the subtlest as well as the most comprehensive intellect. The knowledge of words is, in its full and true acceptation, the knowledge of things, and a scientific acquaintance with a language cannot fail to throw some light on the origin, history, and condition of those who speak or spoke it.' See *Philological Essays*, 1–40 (2); also quoted by Aarsleff, *The Study of Language*, 210.

[14] See Aarsleff, *The Study of Language*, 211ff., on the early days of the Society together with its members and characteristics, and also William Benzie, *Dr. F. J. Furnivall*, 77–9.

1857, Richard Chenevix Trench, then Dean of Westminster, later Archbishop of Dublin, delivered two enormously influential papers to the Philological Society on 'Some Deficiencies in our English Dictionaries', which set out desiderata for a new historical dictionary based on illustrative quotations drawn from past literature, selected so as to show the development through time of the vocabulary of English in its entirety. The Society decided to take on this great and revolutionary project, and many years later it was published as the *New English Dictionary* (1884–1928).[15]

Frederick J. Furnivall (1825–1910) was involved in the Dictionary from the start, and played a lifelong and complex role in its compilation and eventual fruition.[16] Furnivall's energy and drive were phenomenal. In addition to his longstanding work for the Dictionary and the Early English Text Society, he presided over the Chaucer Society, the Wyclif Society, the Ballad Society, the Shakspere Society, the Shelley Society and the Browning Society. Throughout his life, he also devoted an enormous amount of time to the London Working Men's College, and still found it possible to spend Sundays skulling down the Thames with London shopgirls.[17]

Furnivall had been a member of the Philological Society since 1847, and acted with his usual indefatigable energy as its Honorary Secretary from 1853 up to three weeks before his death in 1910.[18] In 1862, when putting together the papers delivered to the Society in 1858 for publication, he was unable to persuade one of the speakers to deliver his copy. Furnivall leapt into the breach (complaining, good-humouredly, that as an 'unhappy Official', he had no option but 'to write Papers himself, or copy MSS. to fill the volume that his refractory friends have left vacant'). He filled up the 1858 volume's spare space with a selection of 'Lives of the Saints' transcribed from MS Harley 2277, together with a 'few songs' from a transcription of part of the famous Vernon manuscript.[19]

---

[15] First known as the *Philological Society's Dictionary*, and subsequently as the *Oxford English Dictionary*. Trench had been at Cambridge at the same time as Kemble (they were both Trinity Apostles) and was a close friend.

[16] He was for seventeen years its editor; see K. M. Elisabeth Murray, *Caught in the Web of Words*, e.g. 137ff.

[17] On Furnivall's remarkable and colourful life, see John Munro, ed., *Frederick James Furnivall*; Derek Brewer, 'Furnivall & the Old Chaucer Society'; William Benzie, *Dr. F. J. Furnivall: Victorian Scholar-Adventurer*; Renate Haas, 'The Social Functions of F. J. Furnivall's Medievalism'.

[18] See Benzie, *Dr. F. J. Furnivall*, 78.

[19] See *TPS* 1858, Preface i-vi. He had consulted Sir Frederic Madden for advice on which of the unpublished Middle English manuscripts best deserved to be brought to light (the letter

Furnivall's ingenious substitution of material, so he later describes, encouraged Dr Richard Morris, a very active Middle English scholar of the time,[20] to follow suit and edit a number of other works, as did also two other scholars. Morris, however, had to find foreign publishers for his work since 'there was no journal or Society in England to print them'. This, said Furnivall, '*did* seem to me a shame, and that if people only knew it, they'd stop it'. Furnivall evidently did his best to make people know it, and 'the result was the getting-up of the Early English Text Society, which, to say the least of it, has done some worthy work for our Language and Literature'.[21]

It is more usual to attribute the foundation of the Early English Text Society to the needs of the Philological Society's Dictionary.[22] Material for this was to be provided by getting members to read through as many printed books as possible, recording quotations illustrating the use of words from the Anglo-Saxon period to the present. In this respect the *Oxford English Dictionary* (as it subsequently became) broke tradition with all previous English dictionaries, none of which had attempted to provide such a formidable quantity and variety of information. It was early realised that 'many poems and other pieces, a collation of which would be invaluable for such a work as this, still lie hid in MS.' – especially from the early English period;[23] and the Early English Text Society undoubtedly provided superlatively helpful fodder for the lexicographers, both dictionary staff and

survives as British Library, Egerton MS 2847; see Benzie, *Dr. F. J. Furnivall*, 80). For Madden's views on Furnivall and the EETS, see below, p. 85.

[20] And much regarded by both Furnivall and Skeat; see for example Furnivall's remarks in *TPS* 1873–4, 237–41, and Skeat, *A Student's Pastime*, xxiii–xxv. In 1867, Morris reprinted an excerpt from the Vernon manuscript's version of *Piers Plowman*; see below, p. 116 n. 7.

[21] I have amalgamated two accounts given by Furnivall of the founding of EETS. One appears in a begging letter to EETS subscribers, dated 10 June 1867 and issued (apparently) with the Society's Annual Report for that year; the other forms part of Furnivall's report on Early English for the Philological Society President's annual address for 1873, printed in *TPS* 1873, 236. See also *TPS* 1852, p. 1 of the Preface to '*Early English Poems and Lives of Saints*, ... Copied and edited ... by Frederick J. Furnivall'. The Society published three more editions of early English works: the *Liber Cure Cocorum*, edited by Morris, in 1862; the *Pricke of Conscience*, also edited by Morris, in 1863; and in 1864 the Middle English version of *Castel of Loue*, translated from Grosseteste, edited by R. F. Weymouth. The Society's lack of funds, however, prevented it from continuing to publish these texts (see e.g. the letter from Furnivall to Bradshaw on this, dated 24 December 1863, CUL Add. 2591: 2123), and the EETS was accordingly established in 1864 to carry on the work independently.

[22] See, for example, Skeat in *The Student's Pastime*: 'It will now readily be understood that the foundation of the Early English Text Society was the first outcome of the desire of the Philological Society to provide for the publication of the *New English Dictionary*' (xxvii), and again in John Munro, ed., *Frederick James Furnivall*, 177; or R. W. Chambers, *Man's Unconquerable Mind*, 353–4.

[23] Trench, *Proposal for the Publication of A New English Dictionary*, 7.

amateurs, to work on, since its aim was to do precisely that – publish work hitherto available only to the few English scholars who were able to read early manuscripts and had access to the major library (or private) manuscript collections.

The Annual Reports of EETS (written by Furnivall), issued to subscribers along with the editions for the year, display an interesting duality in their attitudes to the texts published. From the outset, the Society was desperately in need of funds, and it made its appeals – both to existing members who had failed to deliver their subscriptions on time, and to potential new members – on the grounds of the cultural and patriotic significance of the enterprise of editing early English texts. It is this that is stressed on the one hand, and the usefulness of the Society in clarifying philological problems on the other; for as Furnivall repeats several times, the EETS Committee's first resolve was to print 'the whole of the Early English Romances relating to ARTHUR and his Knights'; its second 'to illustrate the Dialects, and the increase in the Vocabulary, of the English tongue'.[24]

In the *Third Annual Report* of the EETS Committee (January 1867), Furnivall described the Society's aims as 'the bringing to light the whole of the hidden springs of the noble Literature that England calls its own' (p. 4). Perhaps the fullest statement of the Society's attitude towards England's past literature occurred in the *Report of the Committee* of January 1868, where Furnivall urged upon the Society 'the determination not to rest till Englishmen shall be able to say of their Early Literature, what the Germans can now say of theirs, "every work of it's printed and every word of it's glossed". England must no longer be content to lag behind' (p. 1). He went on to comment upon the foundation of the Anglo-Saxon Professorship at Cambridge by a member of the Society, the Reverend Professor James Bosworth – the chair to which W. W. Skeat was unanimously elected as first holder. The creation of the Cambridge chair, he declared,

---

[24] See e.g. the *Second Annual Report* of the Committee, January 1866. Of the first ten works published by the Society, five were of Arthurian texts and one (an edition of a work by Hume, *Of the Orthographie and Congruitie of the Britan Tongue*, EETS 5) on philology; cf. EETS nos. 2, 4, 6, 8, 10. Furnivall's fascination with Arthurian literature is characteristic of the period; cf. Beverly Taylor and Elisabeth Brewer, *The Return of King Arthur*. In relation to the emphasis on philology, cf. Skeat's remarks on the value of studying English literature at school, quoted below, p. 92, and Sweet's Preface to Alfred's *Pastoral Care*, ix, where he describes the text as 'of exclusively philological interest'. What is striking to modern eyes is the absence of any reference to assessment (or appreciation) of the content and style of the works to be edited.

will rescue that seat of learning from the disgrace it has hitherto laboured under, that the University of Spenser, Ben Jonson, Bacon, Milton, Wordsworth, Byron, Macaulay, and Tennyson, has had no recognised teacher of their mother tongue. Well has Professor Seeley[25] said, 'Classical Studies may make a man intellectual, but the study of the native literature has a moral effect as well. *It is the true ground and foundation of patriotism* ... We too are a great historic nation; we too have "titles manifold" ... I call that man uncivilized who is not connected with the past through the state in which he lives, and sympathy with the great men who have lived in it.' (p. 6)

Such remarks set the EETS in a clear line of descent from Thomas Warton's *History of English Poetry*: the study of a nation's earlier literature is a key to the understanding of that nation's true identity and historical destiny. *Piers Plowman*, with its wealth of social detail, and its uplifting search for spiritual truth, was an obvious candidate for publication and was among the very first editions to be produced by the Society. No doubt Furnivall also favoured *Piers Plowman* for its satirical treatment of social and ecclesiastical hierarchies, which fitted well with his reformist beliefs: as Derek Pearsall has commented,

> The late nineteenth century saw *Piers Plowman*, as a document of social history, flower into a prophecy of the constitutional reforms which led to 'modern democracy', a passionate rebuke to tyranny and a cry from the heart of England for reform. Piers Plowman becomes the symbol of the idealised English labourer, the people's Christ who walked English fields and inspired men to throw off the shackles of a corrupt Church and State.[26]

Pearsall goes on to note that one of the consequences of this 'historical fantasy' was the publication of a series of school textbooks in the following century called 'The Piers Plowman Histories', 'each volume of which was prefaced with the story of Langland's dreamer roaming the Malvern Hills and envisioning a time when English people would be freed from oppression and would be truly part of a democratic commonwealth'.[27] It is significant, therefore, that *Piers Plowman* had

25 Sir John Seeley was Professor of Modern History at Cambridge and a friend of W. W. Skeat; see below, p. 102.

26 *An Annotated Critical Bibliography*, x. See also Haas, 'The Social Functions of F. J. Furnivall's Medievalism', 320–1. As Pearsall points out, the articles of J. J. Jusserand present classic statements of this view of the poem; cf. 'Piers Plowman, the Work of One or of Five', 272–3.

27 For the nineteenth-century hankering after the 'English way of life', see Martin J. Wiener, *English Culture and the Decline of the Industrial Spirit*, ch. 2.

been one of the main texts chosen by the EETS for its work in schools; Skeat's student edition of 1869 (an offshoot from his work for EETS) was in regular use from its first publication onwards, and the Society makes frequent reports of its examinations based on this and other texts in schools and colleges.[28]

THE CRITICISMS OF HENRY SWEET

The work of the EETS substantially improved the quality of edited texts. But the patriotism that fuelled the Society may also have contributed towards the insularity of the work its editors produced. In 1877, the President of its parent Philological Society, Henry Sweet, had some tart things to say about the universities and about the state of English philology, illustrating how remote was English scholarship, and in particular English editorial work, from its European equivalent. For the greater part of his active academic life Sweet 'enjoyed neither an official position nor a settled endowment', as his *DNB* entry (written by C. T. Onions) puts it, despite being 'the chief founder of modern phonetics' and 'the greatest philologist that this country has produced'.[29] His estrangement from established academic institutions was due in part, no doubt, to his subject, but also to his notorious bad humour, which was well attested by his contemporaries. He was born in 1845, and first came across German philological method at the university of Heidelberg in 1864, where he studied before going up to Balliol in 1869. Until 1901, when a readership in phonetics was created for him at his old university, he worked away outside the universities, publishing works of quite fundamental importance in Anglo-Saxon and phonetics – among them his famous Anglo-Saxon reader (1876), many times reprinted and still in print today.

In his annual address to the Philological Society, reporting on the year's work, Sweet devoted considerable space to an admonitory discussion of 'The Characteristics of English Work' – by which he

---

[28] See e.g. *Third Annual Report*, January 1869, 2. EETS set special examination papers in English for some of the public schools, including questions on *Piers Plowman*. Most of the exam questions are philological rather than literary; for example, asking for explanation of such constructions as 'I went *me* to reste', 'I behelde *an heigh* to the sonne', thanne *gan* I to meten'. As noted above, the terms of the EETS annual reports recall Skeat's remarks on the study of English literature at school; in both cases, the detailed statements the writers make on the value of literature suggest that they believe this to reside largely in increased knowledge and understanding of linguistic forms, rather than analysis of the stylistic or literary qualities of the works as we should understand them nowadays.
[29] *DNB 1912–21*, 519–20.

meant the characteristics of English scholarship. England had 'contributed its fair share', he felt, 'considering the disadvantages under which philological research labours in this country'. In phonology (his own field) and dialectology, 'we take a decided lead', while in historical philology,

> our energies are mainly devoted to publishing our rich stores of MSS., and making them generally accessible in a reliable form [he is thinking here, evidently, of the Philological Society's offshoot EETS]. We have, in fact, to make up for the sloth of our fathers and grandfathers, and, indeed, were it not for the energy and public spirit of some of the founders of this Society, our MSS. treasures might still be mouldering in musty oblivion, unless, indeed, the zeal and industry of German students of our early language and literature had shamed us into action.[30]

'The two best features of our editing', Sweet continues, 'are minute accuracy and fullness of material. Hence our parallel-text editions, of which the Six-text Canterbury Tales, published by the Chaucer Society [and spear-headed by Furnivall], is a noble example.'[31] Sweet mentions three of his own editions as additional examples, and remarks that 'The Germans are also beginning to see the advantage of a plan which makes the reader independent of possible editorial vagaries, besides supplying inexhaustible material for special investigations of every kind.'

Sweet was choosing his words carefully. Having softened up his audience with a measure of praise, he proceeds to quote from a recent review of the editions of the EETS by the German philologist Julius Zupitza, who was later to produce a study of the mutual relations and comparative value of the numerous manuscripts of the *Canterbury Tales*:[32]

> The editors are, with very few exceptions, dilettantes. Many of them have very vague ideas of philological method, of the treatment of the text, especially when it is preserved in several MSS., of what is essential and what not in reproducing a MS., or of the plan of a glossary, etc. ... Many of the better class of editors, who are quite competent to turn out good work, do not always take enough time

---

[30] *TPS* 1877–9, 10.
[31] On this project, see further below, p. 84.
[32] *Specimens of All The Accessible Unprinted Manuscripts of the Canterbury Tales*, Parts I–III, published for the Chaucer Society in 1892–3. Furnivall and Koch completed the six remaining parts after Zupitza's death, and published them in 1897–1902.

about it. It really looks sometimes as if the copy of the MS. made by some clerk or other went straight to the printer, and that the editor cleared off the whole business of editing during the process of correcting the proofs, so that gross blunders are almost inevitable.

'The truth of these criticisms', Sweet comments, 'cannot be denied.' 'How is it', he goes on to ask, 'that while the principles of text-criticism have been firmly established for the last thirty years in other Teutonic countries, we at the present day have hardly advanced beyond the mere mechanical reproduction of MS. texts?'[33] Zupitza placed the blame for England's sorry comparative performance firmly and squarely on Oxford and Cambridge, which did not 'afford young men desirous of studying their mother-tongue the opportunity of devoting themselves especially to it'. What was needed was 'first a change in the examination system [he means, presumably, the syllabus], and then the appointment of competent professors'. Sweet thoroughly endorses this analysis, pointing out, with feeling induced by personal experience, that 'most of us – indeed, nearly all of us – are by force of circumstances compelled to work in a dilettante style: we cannot expect much from a philologist whose whole working day consists, perhaps, of an hour snatched from other labours'. And he continues with a powerful indictment of the present system and strong appeal for change as follows:

> Where, again, are we to get our training? We are left to pick it up at random, often quite late in life ... How different are the circumstances of the foreign student! He starts young with a thorough training, and with the certainty of full opportunity of devoting himself to his subject for the rest of his life. An undergraduate of an English University who were to announce to the Head of his College his intention of devoting himself to English philology would be regarded as a dangerous lunatic – to be repressed by any means. If he persisted, in the face of ridicule and opposition of every kind, he would be branded with the terrible epithet of 'specialist,' no matter how wide his range of culture, and that by men who only escape the epithet themselves by not possessing a scientific knowledge of any subject whatever.

[33] The force of Sweet's criticisms of EETS editors is somewhat modified by the story Furnivall told Henry Bradshaw in a letter of 18 January 1868: 'The master of the Charterhouse School said the other day to a boy, "What is this Early English Text Society? I've never heard of it in England, but I see it in every German book I take up now. Ask your father if he can tell me anything about it?" 1 to the German!' (quoted Benzie, *Dr. F. J. Furnivall*, 132). On the other hand, the anecdote supports Sweet's point about general English ignorance of the values held dear by German scholarship.

When philology in England is once put on the same footing as in other countries, when young students, instead of being all forced indiscriminately into a few antiquated grooves of study, hopelessly narrowed by a rigid, iron-bound examination system, from which few emerge without intellectual deterioration, have free choice of subjects and competent professors to be trained under, together with the opportunity of devoting themselves to their work in future, we may confidently look to a brilliant future for English philology.[34]

The reference to the 'iron-bound' examination system is a clear echo of the insult thrown at Kemble in the *Gentleman's Magazine* controversy described above, with its reference to Grimm's system by the same phrase. Sweet evidently feels that the debate is far from over.

The next year (1878), he continues his complaint against English attitudes towards and comparative performance in philology, especially those found in the universities. He properly salutes Skeat, now the first holder of the new Bosworth Professorship of Old English at Cambridge:

We, if any, ought to be able to appreciate his extraordinary energy, accuracy, and disinterested zeal in forwarding the interests of English philology and literature. His appointment will infuse new life into Old English studies, raising their prestige at our universities, and, let us hope, will incite many of our younger generation to tread in his footsteps.[35]

Even more interestingly for our purposes, he launches into a further critique of the state of English philology that sheds helpful light on current views and practices concerning the editing of texts. He deplores the absence of knowledge (or assimilation) of German research on comparative grammar – particularly the work of Rask and Grimm – and says that this dilettanteist ignorance gives rise to what 'may be termed the *mechanical* view of language, [which] is based on the assumption that language, unlike all other natural phenomena, including even the most complex evolutions of social life, is not governed by general laws; but consists merely of a mass of disconnected details'. His analysis of the application of this '*mechanical* view' to textual criticism is worth quoting in full, for its echoing of the editorial debate initiated, as we saw above, by the publication of

[34] For similar sentiments, cf. Sweet's Preface to *The Oldest English Texts*, v–vi.
[35] *TPS* 1877–9, 376. In his previous address, he had marked Skeat out as the obvious incumbent of the new chair (*TPS* 1877–9, 4).

Percy's *Reliques*, for the light it sheds on the editing policies of Furnivall and Skeat, and for twentieth-century attitudes to the editing of *Piers Plowman*:

> In a milder shape mechanical philology assumes the form of a slavish and undeviating adherence to MS. readings. To a certain extent this tendency is a healthy reaction against the slovenly inaccuracy and wanton tampering with the MS. evidence, which characterized the older school of editors. We now assume, and rightly, that the first business of an editor is to lay the evidence of the MSS. themselves before the reader in an accurate and unadulterated form. Therein we are all of one mind, but while the scientific philologist regards the written letters of the scribe simply as a means to an end, namely, the recovery of the original text and the actual forms of the language, both of which the MSS. always represent more or less inaccurately, our mechanical friend resents any attempts of the kind as high treason to the scribe, who, he argues, must understand what he was writing better than any modern editor. To this it may be answered that many of them did not understand what they were writing half so well as a thoroughly competent editor.[36]

This is a refined discussion of the issues first raised by Percy's tampering with the evidence of his manuscript. It is valuable to consider here partly because it is so unusual to come across any explicit recognition in this period of the different theories and practices of editing in English, partly because it rehearses clearly and straightforwardly views and issues which are still in question today, and still as far from being satisfactorily resolved. Sweet's insistence on the superiority of the modern editor to the medieval scribe was a recapitulation, presumably conscious, of the terms of a debate initiated by Kemble in his edition of *Beowulf* (1833), where he had stated much the same: 'A modern edition, made by a person really conversant with the language he illustrates, will in all probability be much more like the original than the MS. copy, which, even in the earliest times, was made by an ignorant or indolent

---

[36] *TPS* 1877–9, 413. It should be pointed out that Sweet had taken a different view on editorial responsibility in the Preface to his edition of Alfred's *Pastoral Care* (1871): 'All alteration in the text of a MS., however plausible and clever, is nothing else but a sophistication of the evidence at its fountain-head: however imperfect the information conveyed by the old scribe may be, it is still the only information that we have, and, as such, ought to be made generally accessible in a reliable form' (viii). He was in general, despite his Presidential strictures, a conservative editor, and a careful one (although he also confesses in this Preface that he did not use the best manuscript because he did not have the time).

transcriber.'[37] The point was to be made again many years later, in 1946, by Kenneth Sisam, in a plea for more adventurous editing of Old English texts, and less slavish adherence to the corrupt witness of late manuscripts copied by fallible scribes.[38] As we shall see in a later chapter, Sisam's words were quoted with approval by two of the present-day editors of the Athlone edition of *Piers Plowman*, George Kane and George Russell, and taken as licence for extensive alteration, on conjectural grounds, of the manuscript evidence of the poem;[39] yet they were also to be strongly resisted by Eric Stanley, one of the recent occupants of Skeat's sister-chair at Cambridge, the Rawlinson-Bosworth Professorship, in 1984: 'we in our subject have to remember with constant humility that though perhaps, not certainly, most scribes may not have been the equals in Old English of the best Old English poets, every one of them, sleepy and careless as he may have been at times, knew his living Old English better than the best modern editor of Old English verse'.[40] As will be common knowledge to readers of this book, the dispute as to the proper nature and degree of editorial interpretation of manuscript evidence continues unabated today (not least as a response to the path-breaking edition of Kane and Donaldson), both in *Piers Plowman* studies and elsewhere.[41]

To return to the late nineteenth century: Furnivall, as we shall see, was a chief exponent of the 'mechanical school' mocked by Sweet, while Skeat's various editions of *Piers Plowman* approached more to Sweet's desired standards, in that he produced texts assembled by comparing more than one manuscript, which he was not afraid – on a small number of occasions – to emend. But his method of emendation was to substitute, for unsatisfactory readings in his base manuscript, readings found in other manuscripts of the poem, not to import into his text his own conjectural emendations, completely unsupported by manuscript evidence. In this respect, as in others, he was a far more conservative editor of the poem than his descendants Kane and Donaldson.

---

[37] See Kemble, ed., *Beowulf*, xxiii–xxiv.

[38] E.g.: 'there would be a real gain if conjecture, instead of being reserved for the useful if disheartening task of dealing with obvious or desperate faults, were restored to its true functions, which include probing as well as healing'. See 'Notes on Old English Poetry', 268.

[39] See pp. 339 and 339 n. 26 below.   [40] 'Unideal Editing of Old English Verse', 257.

[41] Cf. (for example) the remarks made by Siegfried Wenzel in 1990: '*Piers* is not an isolated case; the field of editing all major poetic texts in Middle English is in great turmoil ... In fact the principles for editing a medieval text continue to be subjected to intense debate and probing theoretical questions' ('Reflections on the (New) Philology', 13–14). See further below, pp. 428–9.

Sweet roots the English tendency towards mechanical philology – mindless reproduction of the manuscript evidence, regardless of manifest scribal error – in laziness: 'Whatever may be said of the worthlessness of the results of modern philology, it cannot be denied that their application to a special language postulates an enormous amount of hard labour and patient training, and any amount of critical sagacity. The mechanical philologist escapes all this' (p. 416). And Sweet observes that 'the inability to grasp general principles is, indeed, one of the marked characteristics of English philologists' – although he stresses, as before, that all these evils are 'not due to any defect in the English character, but simply to want of systematic training ... We want universities, we want endowment ... we want competent teachers.'[42]

So far, Sweet has been concerned with editing as regards philology. But not surprisingly, the 'inability to grasp general principles' leads him on to textual criticism proper:

> Another of our deficiencies is the almost universal ignorance of the principles of text-criticism. There is really no reason why we Englishmen should confine ourselves to the mechanical reproduction of MSS., or, still worse, to the construction of texts on radically false principles, and leave the interesting and important work of genuine critical reconstruction entirely to our German brethren ....
>
> There is, of course, no reason why we should not at the same time keep up our present method, from which, indeed, foreign scholars still have much to learn. (p. 417)

EDITING THEORY AND PRACTICE: NICHOL, FURNIVALL, BRADSHAW, SKEAT

Sweet excepts one writer from his sweeping criticisms of the ignorance of English editors. 'I wish', he says, 'that all would-be editors would carefully read our member Mr Nicol's paper on 'M. G. Paris's

---

[42] It was France's 'enlightened system of public education', Sweet believed, that made their version of EETS, the Société d'Anciens Textes Français (founded in 1875 by Gaston Paris and Paul Meyer), 'as regards Text-criticism ... far ahead of the English'. The French were able to combine 'faithful reproduction of the MS. texts with sound critical method, which so favourably characterizes the present school of French philology' (*TPS* 1877–9, 6). Furnivall claimed in 1868 that 'the [proposed] collection of Early French Texts, undertaken by MM. Paul Meyer and Gaston Paris, is ... mainly due to the [EET] Society's example' (*Report of the Committee*, 1868, 1). Paris' pupil Bédier was of course later to repudiate the Lachmannian method adopted by his teacher; see further Foulet and Speer, *On Editing Old French Texts*, 19ff.

Method of Editing in his *Vie de St Alexis*' ... They will there find the falseness of some of the apparently most self-evident axioms of ordinary editing briefly and clearly demonstrated' (p. 417). The member he refers to was in fact his cousin, Henry Nicol, whom Gaston Paris described as 'presque le seul qui, en Angleterre, fît de l'Anglo-normand une étude vraiment scientifique'.[43] He died tragically young from consumption. The explanation for his superior knowledge of 'text-criticism' is evidently that he was an Englishman working on French medieval texts, and hence abreast with French medieval scholarship.[44]

This was far more in touch with developments in Germany than was English scholarship. Gaston Paris (1839–1903), and Paul Meyer (1840–1917), were enthusiastic followers of Lachman's so-called scientific method of editing, and waged an energetic campaign to promulgate it among French editors.[45] Paris' edition of the *Alexis* was an important ingredient in this campaign, with a 138–page preface strongly arguing the merits of genealogical editing, and justifying the editor's reconstruction of a hypothetical original version of the poem – extremely hypothetical, in fact, given that its language was that of 'la bonne langue française telle qu'elle devait se parler et s'écrire au milieu du XIe siècle', no examples of which had been preserved in any literary manuscript.[46] Paris judged the date of his reconstructed version to be 1040, yet used as his sole evidence for the reconstruction four manuscripts of the twelfth and thirteenth centuries.

In the paper referred to by Sweet, delivered to the Philological Society in 1873,[47] Nicol gives a judicious account of the genealogical method, and with it an interesting sketch of the state of editing on either side of the Channel. 'In this country', he says, 'a healthy reaction against careless and doctored texts makes us apt to think that in publishing a faithful transcript of the best MS. or MSS. of a work, we do wonders; on the Continent, the importance of such a transcript

---

43 Quoted in Nicol's obituary notice in *TPS* 1882–4, 2–3. See also Alexander Ellis' remarks in *TPS* 1880–1, 254–5, and K. M. E. Murray's references in *Caught in the Web of Words*, especially 114. See also n. 49 below.

44 Ellis lists his published articles in *TPS* 1880–1, 255 n. 1, and notes that 'his principal work on Old French Pronunciation is unfortunately left incomplete'.

45 See Foulet and Speer, *On Editing Old French Texts*, 8ff. Both men were involved with the EETS, Meyer editing with Furnivall *Caxton's Englishing of Alain Chartier's Curial* for the Society in 1888, and Paris acting as one of the Society's advisers (he is thus recorded on the endpapers of editions in the early 1890s).

46 Foulet and Speer, *On Editing Old French Texts*, 12.

47 'M. G. Paris's Method of Editing in his *Vie de Saint Alexis*'.

seems to me often much underrated' (p. 343); and he goes on to lament the absence of any genealogical classification of the manuscripts of Chaucer (such as was later produced by Zupitza), despite the Chaucer Society's six-text edition. Nicol's view is that English editors have simply not caught up with developments in Europe – developments now some several decades old, and are practising a method of editing, which, while it has its advantages in representing original manuscript evidence accurately, is simply insufficiently sophisticated and perhaps positively misleading.

For our purposes, it is significant that the editor he chooses to criticise by name is Walter Skeat. I shall reproduce his remarks in full:

> I may be allowed to express the hope that in the concluding part of his most careful and valuable edition of *Piers Plowman*,[48] Mr. Skeat will, in spite of his numerous other labours, find time to give a genealogical table of the forty or fifty known MSS. of the work. The question is here complicated by the facts that the author himself sent out his poem in three different shapes, possibly in intermediate ones; and that the scribes of some of the existing MSS. appear to have copied from different originals in different parts of their work. But I do not doubt that with the various copies, extracts, etc. in his possession, Mr. Skeat will be able to mark an approximately accurate classification, and thus test the truth of the proposition he apparently assumes, that if two or three of the best MSS. give a reading good in itself, we may, without consulting the others, infer it to be the author's. (pp. 339–40)[49]

This significant comment is the only informed piece of textual criticism of Skeat's work that I have been able to find before 1909: as we shall see, Nicol was utterly unusual in perceiving that Skeat relied on the evidence of only a few manuscripts for each of his editions of A, B and C.[50]

Skeat's ideas on editing seem to fall somewhere between those of the 'mechanical' school castigated by Sweet and those of the genealogical school (whose work for the EETS is later instanced by the

---

[48] Skeat had by this time published editions of A (1867) and B (1869). C appeared in the year that Nicol's paper was given, 1873, and Part IV (Notes etc.) in 1877 and 1885.

[49] Skeat may well have been in the audience when this paper was delivered to the Philological Society. The two men evidently knew each other; Skeat in the Preface to his *Etymological Dictionary* acknowledges the help of 'the late Mr. Henry Nicol, whose knowledge of early English phonology was almost unrivalled' (xi).

[50] Skeat had, in fact, attempted a rough classification of the manuscripts of B and of C, but these were eminently unsatisfactory, and it is possible that Nicol had understood that this was the case. See below, pp. 138–40 and 163–4.

editions of Lydgate by the German scholars Schick and Glauning).[51]
It is hard to find any overt comment or discussion by him on editing,
whether theory or practice, and much of what he thought has to be
inferred from his actual editions. Some sense of the context of his
editing may be arrived at by looking at the views of his friend and
colleague Furnivall, which are easier to ascertain. As already stated,
Furnivall falls fairly and squarely into the 'mechanical' school of
editing condemned by Sweet, whose remarks in his Presidential
address to the Philological Society must have had some *ad hominem*
application, especially considering that Furnivall would almost certainly have been sitting in his audience.[52]

Furnivall's motive for setting up the great Chaucer Society in 1868
was 'to do honour to CHAUCER, and to let the lovers and students of
him see how far the best unprinted Manuscripts of his works differed
from the printed texts';[53] and this makes it clear that he was one of
those who was healthily reacting 'against the slovenly inaccuracy and
wanton tampering with the MS. evidence, which characterized the
older school of editors'.[54] Of course, where Chaucer was concerned,
it was an entirely reasonable aim to reproduce the manuscripts as they
stood, given the unduly creative intervention of previous editors.[55]
Writing on Furnivall's contribution to Chaucerian editing, Donald
Baker comments, 'As an *editor* ... his work cannot really be
evaluated, for he never, in a sense, *edited* anything. He printed, but
how fully, how gloriously, he printed!'[56] A major part of his life was
devoted to getting as many Middle English manuscripts into print as
possible, and the methods by which they might be further analysed
seem not to have greatly interested him.[57] Apparently he once said, 'I

[51] See J. Schick, *Lydgate's Temple of Glas*, ch. III, 'Genealogy of the Texts' (xxx–xlix); Otto
Glauning, *Lydgate's Minor Poems*, section 3, 'Genealogy and Criticism of the Texts'
(xvii–xix).

[52] Furnivall attended almost every meeting of the Philological Society; cf. Brewer, 'Furnivall &
the Old Chaucer Society'.

[53] Quoted from the foreword printed on the inside of the front cover of each of the Chaucer
Society editions. The Chaucer Society was established independently from the EETS
because 'the hands of [EETS] were too full to undertake an edition of Chaucer', since it had
already, 'by Mr Skeat's generous help, undertaken to do justice to Chaucer's great
contemporary – above him in moral height, below him in poetic power – William, the
author of *The Vision of Piers Plowman*, by an edition of the three versions of his chief
work, executed with Mr Skeat's well-proved ability, fullness, and care' (*A Temporary
Preface to the Six-Text Edition of Chaucer's Canterbury Tales*, Part I, 3).

[54] Sweet in *TPS* 1878–9, 413, quoted above.

[55] On the earlier editors of Chaucer, see Paul Ruggiers, ed., *Editing Chaucer*, 1–156.

[56] 'Frederick James Furnivall', 168–9.

[57] That is not to say, of course, that he was not interested in evaluating the quality of different
readings, as his deliberations over Chaucer manuscripts make clear; see *A Temporary*

never cared a bit for philology; my chief aim has been throughout to illustrate the social condition of the English people of the past.' As William Benzie comments, although this remark 'tends to separate Skeat the scholar from Furnivall the social historian at the outset, it must be emphasized that it was the impulse generated by Furnivall's dynamic energy that drove Skeat and other scholars to achieve what they did'.[58]

Furnivall's editorial method, if it can be called one, aroused strongly conflicting feelings in his contemporaries. Some saw him as heroic. Alexander Ellis' Presidential address to the Philological Society in 1873 heaps glowing praise on his

> magnificent Six-Text Edition of Chaucer, still in progress, which I regard as entirely [Furnivall's] own in conception and execution. Mr. Furnivall has in this work inaugurated a new era in philology. No one will henceforth be satisfied with collations of important works. An editor may patch up a text to shew his own particular views, and defend them in elaborate comments. But students, who wish to know what the works are like, will now require the lively counterfeits of their oldest existent forms placed side by side for actual comparison with one another and each part with its whole; not a mosaic presentment of disaccordant patches. This is what Mr. Furnivall has done for our first English poet, mostly with his own hand, entirely by his own thought ... [59]

This praise accords with the judgement of the *Pall Mall Gazette* in 1871, which saw Furnivall's enterprise as essentially historical, revealing the 'facts', i.e. the *verba ipsissima* of the manuscripts, which were alone valid, and with which historians would now be able to rout the poorly based conjecture which had governed our knowledge of early English literature hitherto: 'Literary inquiries, just as much as scientific, must be based on exact knowledge of facts; and from this point of view we can hardly praise too much the labours of the Chaucer Society.'[60] The Early English Text Society editions were

Preface, 5ff. Furnivall's Chaucer Society printed the texts of Chaucer over a period of thirty-four years (1868–1902), with, as Baker points out ('Furnivall', 158), 'the great majority being copied, printed and proofed in an amazingly short period of eight years (1868–76)'.

[58] Benzie, *Dr. F. J. Furnivall*, 7 (quoting John Munro, ed., *Frederick James Furnivall*, 43), 124.

[59] *TPS* 1873–4, 245. This recognition of the importance of the testimony provided by the original manuscripts is matched today in the flurry of publications of facsimile editions of manuscripts such as those produced by Boydell and Brewer and the Scolar Press.

[60] Quoted by Benzie, *Dr. F. J. Furnivall*, 170, cf. 139: 'In this "the heyday of scientific and conscientious recovery of England's literary past," Furnivall and many other philologists were only mildly interested in questions of evaluation and criticism. They were concerned

similarly seen by some as performing an outstandingly useful function. Its subscribers were, as observed by a reviewer in the *Gentleman's Magazine*, able to buy 'seven pages of old English for a penny', and 'ought to be numbered, not by hundreds, but by thousands, in order that all our early English MSS. that are of any value ... may be printed as soon as possible ... this Society deserves all support, partly because the work which it is doing is a work that ought to be done, but principally because the editors are so painstaking, and are doing their work so well.'[61]

Other critics were less favourable, for example Sir Frederic Madden. In his journal, now preserved in the Bodleian Library, Madden wrote scornful reports of the editorial qualities of Furnivall and his '*collaborateurs*', and interestingly contrasts Furnivall with Skeat:

> I never saw Mr. Skeat in my life but from the whole tenor of his correspondence I feel a great respect for him.[62] As to that jackanapes Mr. Furnivall, I think it is a matter of great regret that he should be allowed to edit any works of the [EETS] Society. His style of writing is thoroughly disgusting, and his ignorance is on a par with his bad taste.[63]

And this establishment view of Furnivall as a maverick and unscholarly outsider is confirmed by a letter Skeat wrote to the editor of the *Oxford English Dictionary*, J. A. H. Murray, in November 1877: 'Somehow, he isn't believed in at the Universities ... It has arisen from his odd prefaces, etc., & modes of expression.'[64]

What was it, then, about Furnivall's scholarship and his prefaces that aroused offence? A good example is one of his early productions, *Political, Religious and Love Poems* (1866), the fifteenth in the EETS series. In it he engagingly admits

> Of the pieces now issued some have been printed elsewhere, and of most, perhaps better texts exist; but the time that it takes to ascertain

---

with the restoration and rehabilitation of their texts, and any scruples about literary value that had obviously bothered Bishop Percy were easily answered: scientific method demanded authenticity, and literary value *was* the authentic primitive purity of the text.' Cf. *ibid.*, 271–2.

[61] No. 23, new series, November 1867.

[62] The two men had corresponded over Skeat's forthcoming EETS edition of *Havelok* (1868), a work previously edited by Madden for the Roxburghe Club.

[63] Quoted by Benzie, *Dr. F. J. Furnivall*, 130–1. Madden later refers to Furnivall as 'that coxcomb' (*ibid.*, 132).

[64] Murray, *Caught in the Web of Words*, 148.

whether a poem has been printed or not, which is the best MS. of it, and in what points the versions differ, &c., &c., is so great, that after some experience I find the shortest way for a man much engaged in other work, but wishing to give some time to the [Early English Text] Society, is to make himself a foolometer and book-possessor-ometer for the majority of his fellow-members, and print whatever he either does not know, or cannot get at easily, leaving others with more leisure to print the best texts. *He* wants *some* text, and that at once. (p. x)[65]

An interesting feature of the edition is that it prints two parallel texts of the poem *The Complaynt of Criste*, taken from two different versions. The original reason for this was that Furnivall set up in type one of the versions before coming across the second, a superior text in an earlier manuscript. He then had to decide, as he tells us, whether or not to cancel the first version. He concluded that it should be retained, 'as an instructive instance to readers in general, and a caution to careless people like myself, of how one of those scribes to whom we owe almost all our knowledge of our forefathers' minds, had chanced to go astray ... "the errors of Manuscripts are sacred, and must be preserved"' (pp. xviii–xix). The result is peculiarly Furnival-lian. It is indeed very interesting to compare the two versions as an instance of the effect of scribal corruption on the transmission of a text. On the other hand, Furnivall's acknowledgement of the *ad hoc* way in which his printing of the two came about tends to undermine confidence in the theoretical justification for the exercise. It is exactly the sort of editorial behaviour which earned the condemnation of Zupitza reported above (p. 75). Certainly the edition infuriated Henry Bradshaw, who, as Furnivall cheerfully reports, wrote an account of the collection for the *Saturday Review* in which he called it 'a pig-stye'.[66]

Bradshaw's views on editing were very different from those of Furnivall. He roundly attacked several of the EETS editions, and

---

[65] Furnivall's Prefaces are full of such outrageously chatty addresses to the reader. For a particularly egregious example, see sections 5 and 6 of his foreword to Capgrave's *Life of St Katharine of Alexandria*, ed. Carl Horstmann, EETS OS 100 (1893), xxix–xxxi.

[66] Bradshaw is named as the reviewer only in the second edition of 1903; Furnivall describes him as a 'learned and much-esteemed friend – who (unluckily for us) devotes his spare energy to denouncing the Committee in general and me in particular, instead of editing texts for us all'. This is a reference both to Bradshaw's long-running criticism of Furnivall's editing practices (which began as early as 1865; see e.g. CUL Add. 2591: 252) and to Furnivall's continued attempts to persuade Bradshaw into print (see their correspondence in the Bradshaw letters, e.g. CUL Add. 2591: 609, 632).

poured scorn on Furnivall's aim to reproduce, in type, as near as possible facsimile representations of the manuscripts. 'You now perhaps see what I mean by the remarkable absence of literary editorial power w^h the Society's work displays. A great deal of care about marginal notes, italic abbreviations, &c &c &c &c &c &c but not a feather's weight of care for the substance of the matter.' Later in the same letter he says, 'And what I insist on is that until some of you [viz. EETS editors] begin to *edit* books there is no chance for any of us learning anything.'[67]

Bradshaw (as the rest of the letter makes clear) believed that one should correct manuscripts ruthlessly, and that there were 'a thousand' instances where 'you cannot trust the best MSS. for spelling rightly'. While editors such as Furnivall reproduced the often corrupt language of the manuscripts without any correction or intervention, the progress of scholarship and knowledge about the language in its earlier stages was retarded (one should remember that Bradshaw had more experience of Latin manuscripts, and there, as with Middle High German and Old French, it was a tradition to regularise spelling).

Furnivall would not be persuaded, however, that his idea of reproducing manuscripts to enable close comparison of different versions was not an excellent one. In hot response to Bradshaw at a later stage in their correspondence, he writes 'You are the *only* man who has not seen the immense advantage of the 6–Text [Chaucer Society project] over separate texts ...'[68] Despite their differences, Furnivall spent a good deal of his time trying to persuade the elusive though extremely knowledgeable Bradshaw to commit himself to publishing some small fraction of his unrivalled knowledge of Chaucer (as it turned out, an almost fruitless task, although Bradshaw

---

[67] CUL 2591: 384a.

[68] CUL Add. 2592: 257. The letter is dated 21 December 1870. Furnivall had paid a handsome tribute to Bradshaw in the Temporary Preface to his *Six-Text* edition of Chaucer, 9.

[69] For some of his thinking, see Donald C. Baker's transcription of correspondence between him and Furnivall in 'The Evolution of Henry Bradshaw's Idea of the Order of *The Canterbury Tales*', also Baker's article 'Frederick James Furnivall', and A. S. G. Edwards, 'Walter W. Skeat'. The Bradshaw letters in CUL bear frequent witness to the despair of correspondents trying to elicit responses of one sort or another from him; one contemporary remarked on 'the strange contradictions of Bradshaw's character, in which astonishing powers of industry went hand in hand with a monumental capacity for sloth'; another described him as 'expiating with bewildering energy the guilt of a pathological sloth'. See J. C. T. Oates, 'Young Henry Bradshaw', 279 and 281. The standard biography of Bradshaw is G. W. Prothero, *A Memoir of Henry Bradshaw* (1888); see also David McKitterick, *A History of Cambridge University Press*, 658–764.

thought long and deeply about the problems of Chaucer editing).[69]
On 8 February 1871 Furnivall wrote to him, 'Don't be absurd.
You're the man to *edit* Chaucer, if only you will. I'm the man to print
the texts, if only you'll add your notes of MSS. to mine, or tell me
what books to look in to find out the MSS.'[70]

Although it is virtually impossible – or at least so I have found – to
turn up any explicit statement by Furnivall of his views on editing
that fully acknowledges his position relative to those of others, it is
almost certainly wrong to underestimate his theoretical sophistication.
It seems baffling now to read through the letters and published
remarks of many Middle English scholars of the late-nineteenth
century and find almost no reference to the sorts of theoretical
discussion going on in Europe. However, a letter from Paul Meyer
(see above, p. 81 and note 45) to Furnivall of 22 February 1868
certainly assumes a perfectly clear understanding of the term 'critical
text' as it had now begun to be understood in France and Germany;
viz. a text based on a thorough knowledge of the manuscripts and
their genetic relationships. Meyer is apparently answering a query by
Furnivall about the manuscripts of Machaut in the Sorbonne –
Machaut's poem 'Dit du Lion' had evidently struck Furnivall as a
possible source for or translation of the mysterious poem by Chaucer,
mentioned as his in the Retractions at the end of the *Canterbury Tales*
but unknown both then and now. Meyer replies, 'Quatre mss.
contiennent le Dit du Lion, je vous en ferai bien volontiers un texte
(un texte critique! of course [*sic*]) pour votre nouvelle société.'[71]
Furnivall's reply is not, unfortunately, preserved.

It seems simplest, and most obvious, to think that he saw his task as
bringing manuscripts to light, and/or getting them into print. It
would then be for others to make of the original material what they
would. This must be the view underlying his words to Bradshaw
quoted above, and it also appears fairly clearly in his remarks on
Bishop Percy:

> By the bishop's own showing, he altered his manuscripts at discre-
> tion ... By the way of justification the bishop tells his readers that
> 'his object was to please both the judicious antiquary and the reader

---

[70] Quoted by Benzie, *Dr. F. J. Furnivall*, 165.
[71] CUL Add. 2591: 495. On 25 March of the same year Meyer writes again, summarising the
content of Machaut's *Dit du Lion*, and saying, evidently with some regret, 'Vous voyez
qu'il n'y a là dedans rien de commun avec le *Songe* de Chaucer ... Vous auriez sans doute
jugé qu'il était inutile au but de la *Chaucer Society* de faire imprimer le Dit du Lion ...'
(CUL Add. 2591: 566).

of taste; and he hath endeavoured to gratify both without offending either.' Now 'in a polished age like the present' as Percy described his own time, a judicious antiquary (unlike Ritson) might possibly be pleased with such treatment of manuscripts as the bishop's was; but in an age which (like our Victorian) has thank Heaven, lost that kind of polish, a judicious antiquary would get judiciously furious at such tampering with a text, and demand imperatively the very words of the manuscript. After their production he might listen to any retouching and additions of editions, clever or foolish, but not before.[72]

Skeat's attitude was not the same, however. It is clear from his account of his introduction to editing (quoted below, p. 97) that his primary orientation was decidedly empirical. Furnivall threw him in at the deep end with the manuscript of *Lancelot of the Laik*, and he seems to have learned to swim through determination, incessant hard work, and the exercise of his somewhat sceptical native intelligence. Bradshaw's influence on him is difficult to fathom.[73] As Edwards remarks, their almost daily contact meant that there was little need for them to write, and so no substantial epistolary record survives of their relationship. But it is hard to imagine that there was not a clash between the perfectionist Bradshaw and the pragmatist Skeat, although Skeat himself, in a letter written to Bradshaw shortly after his election to the Elrington-Bosworth Anglo-Saxon Professorship, acknowledges Bradshaw's tutelage of him fulsomely.[74]

As Bradshaw's acolyte (to start off with, anyhow) Skeat might be expected to take a different view of editing from Furnivall. And such is certainly indicated by an important letter from Skeat which Furnivall prints in the *Fourth Report* of the Chaucer Society, published in January 1872.[75] Skeat had just completed editing Chaucer's *Astrolabe* for EETS, and in his report to Chaucer Society subscribers, Furnivall explains his decision to issue this edition to them as well as to EETS subscribers. This was done, he says,

> In accordance with the advice of Mr Skeat, who knows more about the manuscripts of Chaucer's Astrolabe than anybody else ... Mr Skeat, in advising this issue, says in a recent note to me:

[72] Quoted Benzie, *Dr. F. J. Furnivall*, 137–8, from the *Gentlemen's Magazine* of January 1867. Furnivall edited Percy's Folio Manuscript with John W. Hales. For Percy's editing, see pp. 23–7 above.
[73] See Baker, 'Frederick James Furnivall', for Furnivall's relationship with Bradshaw.
[74] Quoted by Edwards, 'Walter W. Skeat', 178.
[75] It is wrongly entitled *Third Report*.

What *more* do you want than my edition? It rests on 5 or 6 MSS. throughout, and is a sort of 'multum in parvo'. Were you to print 2 MSS. at length, it would take more paper, and the result would be that the public would get far less information for their money. Even the best MS., the Cambridge one, is only good so far as the *corrections* go. The last few sections, not corrected, contain several sentences which are mere nonsense. The *Astrolabe* is a quite different matter to Chaucer's other works. In Boethius, for example, a MS. consists of sense more or less all the way through; but the MSS. of the *Astrolabe* frequently scorn sense. You can only get at it by collation; and in no other way. If you want to shew the public how my edition is made up, you would have to print 4 or 5 MSS. and then would know less about the matter after all. If, again, it is urged that every letter (nonsense or not) ought to be printed, I reply, that my edition accounts for every single letter in the two best Cambridge and Bodley MSS. – and prints much of the St John's MS. *verbatim* besides. In my opinion, even if all or six MSS. of the Astrolabe are printed *litteratim* hereafter, there is no reason why Subscribers to the Chaucer Society should not have my edition as well.[76]

These remarks suggest Skeat was completely out of tune with the founding aims of the Chaucer Society, which were to print the manuscripts as they stood in order to correct the vagaries of previous editorial interpretation of Chaucer. It may well have been his experience of *Piers Plowman* manuscripts which had convinced him that this was a waste of time (by now he had edited A and B, and C was shortly to appear in 1873). Skeat's letter also communicates his no-nonsense pragmatic attitude towards scribal evidence and his untroubled faith in his ability to 'get at' the sense 'by collation': by this he means, not the establishment of a text through analysis of the genealogical relationships between all the extant manuscripts, but a commonsensical comparison of a few alternative readings. This breezy self-confidence, coupled with a sure sense of what his audience wanted to read (an edited – but not over-edited – text), is at the heart of his editorial method.

[76] Furnivall comments, 'I had of course intended to print parallel texts of the Astrolabe [he knew of eighteen] as well as Chaucer's other works, but as Mr Skeat knows the facts of the case, and I do not, I feel bound by his opinion till any one shows cause why it is wrong. If any one can, then we will print some more of the MSS' (5–6).

6

Skeat: introduction

Furnivall needed a large band of editors to fuel his project of bringing as many unpublished medieval English works to light as possible. Several of his victims were novices, none more so than W. W. Skeat (1835–1911), the man who was to become one of the most distinguished and industrious of editors produced by the late nineteenth century. Skeat was the first person to publish an edition of *Piers Plowman* which, by the standards of today, properly substantiates its claim to be full and scholarly. Like his predecessors, he was interested in the poem as a social document, but his slant on it was markedly different. From the beginning, he saw the issue of editing the poem as one of coming to terms as fully as possible with the manuscripts, and he seems to have believed that explicating the poem from a historical and literary point of view was necessarily subsequent to establishing the text. Today, of course, it is often accepted that the two processes are inextricably interlinked: editing is itself an interpretation of a text; nevertheless, Skeat's position is a substantial advance on that of his predecessors.

It is difficult to find out very much about Skeat, despite his extraordinarily prolific output of publications and editions, many of which contributed vitally to the state of knowledge of Middle and Old English texts. He expressed the strong wish that no biography should be written, and his family destroyed his papers after his death.[1] The result is that little biographical material has ever been published on Skeat, other than the entry (by Kenneth Sisam) in the *Dictionary of National Biography*.[2] The best source on Skeat's life is

---

[1] Skeat's grandson, Theodore Cressy Skeat (b. 1907), Keeper of Manuscripts and Egerton Librarian at the British Museum (1961–72), remembers his mother telling him that after W. W. Skeat's death, his two sons 'spent weeks tearing up old letters'. He also reports that 'my grandfather certainly was most anxious that no biography of him should be published, and my father religiously obeyed this so far as he was able' (letter to the author).

[2] *DNB 1912–21*, 495–6.

in fact to be found in his own writings, in the chatty but tantalisingly elliptic Introduction to *A Student's Pastime*, a selection made by Skeat himself of his many articles (he calls them 'scattered utterances') published in 1896. Skeat was born on 21 November 1835. He was educated at various schools, and at one of them (King's College School, in the Strand) was taught by the distinguished philologist and editor, the Reverend Oswald Cockayne, author of an Anglo-Saxon dictionary and editor of Ælfric's *Lives of the Saints*, who no doubt influenced the young Skeat's future bent.[3] But it was at the Sir Roger Cholmeley's School at Highgate that Skeat first 'gained some notion of the excellence of English literature', apparently as a result of being made to translate 'occasional scraps' of it into Greek and Latin verse. English literature, he says,

> was then considered as a thing altogether apart from our ordinary curriculum, and only to be seriously regarded when in the privacy of our own homes during holiday. And what an astounding fact this now seems to me! If we really possess, as many think, one of the finest literatures in the world, why are not boys informed of its value, and why are they not shown how to approach it with profit to themselves? All we knew of its etymology was that many English words are derived from Latin and Greek; but I doubt if even our masters could have told us the history of such common words as *home* or *ransom*.
>
> But there were some gleams of light accorded us, which were by no means devoid of benefit. There was a school library, and one of its possessions was a glorious copy of Spenser. He must have felt rather solitary, from the dearth of fellow-poets around him; but doubtless, the isolation has long been remedied. (pp. ix–x)

Despite these strictures, Skeat traced his love for early writers to one of his lesson-books, Mrs Markham's *History of England*, which contained a series of 'Conversations' (between Mrs Markham and her three children) appended to the various historical chapters. The 'Conversation' on the reign of Richard II mentioned Chaucer as 'the father of English poetry', and quoted a few modernised lines from *The Knight's Tale*. Next, Skeat tells us, the 'good lady' turned to Langland,

---

[3] Cockayne published several editions for EETS, and kept in touch with Skeat in later life. They would have met regularly through the Philological Society. A letter from Skeat to Cockayne dated 20 January 1859 survives among the Skeat papers at King's College, London.

"who wrote a very severe satire against persons of all professions, called the *Vision of Piers Plowman*, which, for all the insight it gives into the manners of the times, is a very valuable relic." Asked, if it is as difficult to understand as Chaucer's poetry, she replies: "You will find it more so." She then gives some idea of what is meant by "alliterative" poetry, and selects for our instruction the following extract:

> I found there
> A hall for a high king, a household to holden,
> With broad boards abouten, y-benched well clean;
> With windows of glass wrought as a church,
> And chambers with chimneys, and chapels gay.

(As Skeat points out, this is not in fact from *Piers Plowman*, but from *Pierce the Ploughman's Crede*, the fifteenth-century poem by a different author who uses Langland's character of the ploughman.)[4] 'Young as I then was', Skeat continues,

these quotations haunted me; and I well remember making an internal resolution that, if ever I lived to grow up, I would desire better acquaintance with the originals, little dreaming that it would be my good fortune to edit both of the works which the extracts represent...

Nor was this all. The words 'holden' and 'abouten' and 'y-benched' seemed so quaint, that their forms irresistibly invited further consideration. Why and when did people say 'abouten,' and what did they mean by the prefix *y-* in 'y-benched'? These were problems to be seriously considered; they could not be beyond human discovery, and discovered some day they must be!

Hence it was that, throughout my college life, classics, mathematics, and theology were my more serious studies, whilst Chaucer, and Spenser, and Shakespeare were an unfailing resource in many an hour of leisure. My future was, as I then supposed, to be spent in the obscurity of a country curacy, and our great writers could be safely depended on for affording excellent companionship on a rainy day. (pp. xiv–xv)

It is noteworthy that although Skeat deprecates the absence of English literature from the standard school curriculum, what he in fact mentions as especially interesting about this literature are its philological forms – the linguistic, rather than literary aspects of

---

4   Cf. Barr, *The Piers Plowman Tradition*, 70, lines 203–9; Mrs Markham, *A History of England*, 164–5.

English. One of Skeat's obituarists, A. J. Wyatt, records the view that 'with his liking for literature he combined a curious lack of the "sense of literary values"'.[5] Whatever this means, it would almost certainly be wrong to imagine that Skeat was insensitive to the non- or supra-philological aspects of literature. The idea 'that words contained their own poetry, that a language was itself far greater than the great works composed in it, was a nineteenth-century view';[6] Archbishop Trench, author of two highly popular books on language as well as initiator of the *Oxford English Dictionary*, took up Emerson's term 'fossil poetry': 'Many a single word also is itself a concentrated poem, having stores of poetical thought and imagery laid up in it.'[7] Skeat himself stoutly resisted the notion that philologists were insensible of or uncaring about the aesthetic and affective aspects of literature; or, as he put it, that 'a critical examination of the language is likely to interfere with the romantic element'. 'Why are we to be debarred from examining a poet's language because his words are sweet and his descriptions entrancing? That is only one more reason for weighing every word that he uses.' 'The philologist', he felt, ' ... has the larger view [i.e. in comparison with the literary critic], and can see the value both of the language and of the ideas.'[8] This rigorous approach to literary studies, with its emphasis on fact rather than feeling, was influential in elevating English studies to the status of a university subject; Skeat worked for many years to improve the academic status of English literature in schools and universities. His introductions and annotations to his editions do not often parade literary insight, but they exhibit a remarkable range and depth of historical knowledge of the periods in which the works were written, reflecting wide and curious reading. His philological interests found their best expression in his *Etymological Dictionary* (1882–4), which was a standard work for many years.

Skeat went up to read mathematics[9] at Christ's College, Cambridge in 1854, became a Fellow in 1860, and in the same year took up orders, married (thus losing his Fellowship), and became curate of

---

5   Quoted by Arthur Sherbo in 'Walter William Skeat in the *Cambridge Review*' (112).
6   In the words of James Milroy, *The Language of Gerard Manley Hopkins*, 61.
7   *On the Study of Words*, eighth edition, 4–5.
8   *A Student's Pastime*, xiii.
9   The link between mathematics and philology may seem slight, but it is one paralleled in the career of the mathematician Gauss, who studied philology in his youth, and the medievalist Joseph Wright, who apparently said that 'Everybody who would be a philologist must have done mathematics, or be capable of doing mathematics'; quoted by C. H. Firth, 'Joseph Wright', 6.

East Dereham in Norfolk. Here, he says, 'the first two years of my married life were happily spent', and he acquired 'a good deal of the Norfolk dialect'.[10] Very little evidence survives of Skeat's short career as a curate, although there is a rather tart observation in the diaries of Benjamin Armstrong, his vicar at the time, for 17 April 1861: 'In the evening to the Institute to hear Skeat read some of Hood's poems. I wish he would be so lively in the pulpit as he is on these occasions.'[11] Armstrong records attending another lecture by Skeat 'on the origin of the English language', on 27 February of the same year; it is this lecture that Skeat came to regard as the origin of his later career: 'it was received with some favour, and, with a few alterations, appeared in all the glory of print. This little pamphlet of forty pages, now (happily) no longer procurable, was the beginning of a long series of works on the same subject.'[12] It argued the importance of a knowledge of Anglo-Saxon, then much neglected, as a basis for English grammar and etymology.

Skeat's subsequent move to Godalming had at first disastrous consequences:

> The neighbourhood was beautiful, but the climate proved unsuitable; and at last an alarming attack, of a diptheric character, totally unfitted me for clerical work and rendered a long rest absolutely necessary; and I thus found myself, in the end of 1863, at the age of twenty-eight, in the desolate condition of finding my chosen career brought to a sudden end, without any future course, and even without much prospect of ever again rendering any help to my fellow-creatures, which (I can truly say) has always been my object as regards this present world. (p. xx)

He therefore returned to Cambridge and took up a lectureship in mathematics at his old college. The fact that no more is heard of illness in Skeat's long and exceptionally hard-working career may indicate that his throat infection was of psychosomatic origin. At any rate, despite what he says about his 'desolate condition', it is difficult to see that hard work in a country parish would be preferable to a leisurely life in Cambridge. Earning money was not a concern for

---

10   *A Student's Pastime*, xvi. Cf. Skeat's reference to his knowledge of Norfolk mores at p. 171 below.

11   Herbert B. J. Armstrong, ed., *Armstrong's Norfolk Diary*, 91. Unfortunately the references to Skeat are scanty; cf. *A Norfolk Diary. Passages from the Diary of the Rev. Benjamin John Armstrong*, 75. I am grateful to Dr John Pickles for alerting me to the existence of Armstong's diaries.

12   *Armstrong's Norfolk Diary*, 90; *A Student's Pastime*, xvi.

Skeat at any time in his life. He was well supported by his father, who lavished gifts on his only surviving son.[13] This parental support was crucial to his career, since it gave him the independence he needed to pursue his English studies in complete financial security, an occupation for which he received no direct support until he was elected to the Cambridge chair in Anglo-Saxon in 1878.[14] It also allowed him to maintain his large family in comfort. He had two sons and four daughters, and his family life is said to have been 'evenly happy and full'. Evidently it did not obstruct his phenomenally prolific published output.

It was in the year following Skeat's return to Cambridge, 1864, that the remarkable F. J. Furnivall set up the Early English Text Society. As we have seen, his purpose was to provide good published texts of a wide range of Middle and Old English works, partly at least so that these in turn could be searched through and culled for words by the lexicographers attached to the Philological Society's project for a *New English Dictionary* (later to become the *Oxford English Dictionary*). At the time that Skeat returned to Cambridge, Furnivall 'began to cast about for more editors'. 'My name,' says Skeat, 'was mentioned to him as that of one who was fond of Early English and had some leisure' (evidently Skeat's mathematics job took up little serious time),[15] and Furnivall asked him to re-edit *Lancelot of the Laik* (formerly edited for the Maitland Club in 1839), a poem which Skeat describes, not unfairly, as 'of no great value'. Furnivall's invitation was to have momentous consequences for the editing of Middle English texts. With typical high-handedness and optimism, he over-ruled Skeat's objection that he was unable to read a manuscript 'on the grounds, first, that the sole MS. was always at hand in the

---

[13] This information comes from T. C. Skeat, who possesses his grandfather's account books for the period 1835–67. These record regular and substantial presents and payments.

[14] Skeat acknowledges his father's help towards the end of his General Preface to the final volume of his great EETS edition of *Piers Plowman* (*Piers Plowman: The Vision of William Concerning Piers Plowman. General Preface, Notes and Index*, lxvi).

[15] It would not have been customary for gentlemen at rich colleges to spend much time with their tutors. The Skeat–Furnivall collection at King's College, London preserves three sheets of paper on which are written out solutions to various mathematical problems, apparently by one Andrew Moir (his name is written at the head of the first sheet) – presumably a student of Skeat's. On the reverse side of the first sheet Skeat has jotted 'Lincoln's Inn' – a reference to the *Piers Plowman* A-Text MS; on the reverse side of the other two sheets occur transcriptions of equivalent passages from 'Wright's Text. p. 5. l. 123', 'Whitaker's Text. p. 4.', 'MS. Vesp. B. XVI.', and 'MS. Calig. A. XI.'. Skeat must have been trying to work out the relationship between these four very different versions of *Piers Plowman*, which suggests that the transcriptions were written out soon after undertaking to edit the poem. See below, pp. 106ff.

Cambridge University Library; and secondly, that I could learn'. Skeat wrote back to him on 29 October 1864, in terms that again betray his essentially philological interest in Middle English:

> Dear Sir,
> I have today received your letter relative to the editing of some of the E.E. Text Soc[iety] books. -
> As mine would be a first attempt, I shall be glad to adopt your suggestion of re-editing *Sir Lancelot*. I shall be glad to make the attempt, being interested in the *language* in which the old romances are written.
> It would be a great kindness if you would introduce my name to Mr Bradshaw's notice, that he might know who I was, should I call on him.

'Mr Bradshaw' was of course Henry Bradshaw, the librarian of the University Library. The letter was passed on to him by Furnivall, who underlined the last paragraph and scribbled at the top 'My dear Bradshaw, Please help W. Skeat if he should come and ask you any questions'; it now survives as one of the many letters in the Bradshaw collection in the Cambridge University Library.[16] Writing thirty-two years later, Skeat describes how, 'to this day', he could 'remember the smile of amused satisfaction with which the MS. was brought me by our justly celebrated librarian, Henry Bradshaw by name, of King's College' – aware, presumably, of Skeat's tiro status and the likelihood that he would be 'quite extinguished' by the difficult hand in which the Scottish fifteenth-century manuscript (CUL Kk. 1. 5) is written. 'Indeed, after puzzling over the first page for a couple of hours, I was not conscious of having advanced beyond some twenty lines; and so retreated for that time' (p. xxv). The presence of Bradshaw, however, meant that 'there was a teacher at hand such as few men have ever had'. Bradshaw's experience and knowledge of manuscripts were renowned, and his encounter with Skeat on this occasion led to a long and fruitful partnership between the two men.[17]

Skeat must have worked hard in his leisure hours, for his edition of *Lancelot* appeared with remarkable swiftness in the following year, 1865. He had evidently progressed fast and well under Bradshaw's guiding hand, for he was able to announce in his preface that the earlier Maitland Club edition contained 'some strange errors', which

---

[16] CUL Add. 2591: 240.
[17] See *A Student's Pastime*, xxvi, and A. S. G. Edwards, 'Walter W. Skeat', 177–9, on the relationship between the two men; also pp. 86–9 above.

indicated that it must have been printed from a faulty transcript which the editor had failed subsequently to check with the original. Skeat's audacity in thus overturning the existing editorial authority seems to have caused something of a stir, creating, in his own words, 'quite a nine-days' wonder'.[18] His edition showed, Skeat says, 'that the editors for the Early English Text Society really aimed at a reasonable accuracy'; and far more importantly for our purposes, the favourable response received by the edition resulted in Skeat's taking on a bigger and much more significant project, the editing of *Piers Plowman*. This took him nearly twenty years from start to finish, and gave him the idea, he says, of 'endeavouring to print or reprint, in due course, all the Early English poems that have come down to us in the form of alliterative verse without rime'. Typically, it was their philological characteristics that interested him quite as much as their literary content: 'nearly all of these poems are of considerable service to the lexicographer owing to the abundance in them of unusual, dialectal, and obsolescent words. By the difficulties which they thus frequently present I was especially attracted.'

Some of these editions appeared while he was still working on *Piers Plowman*, along with quantities of other works: several individual Canterbury Tales, various glossaries and books on etymology, a new edition of Ælfric's *Lives of the Saints*, and editions of *The Kingis Quair*, Shakespeare's Plutarch, and *The Two Noble Kinsmen*, to mention a very few.[19] For many of these editions, as he acknowledges in their introductions, he used diligent and accurate amanuenses. Later, in 1894, Skeat brought out his six volume *Complete Works of Geoffrey Chaucer*. This was a less revolutionary edition than his *Piers Plowman*, since it relied heavily on previous work by Furnivall and others, but was nevertheless to hold an important place in Chaucer studies.[20]

---

[18] The first version of his revised edition of *Lancelot* got short shrift from James Murray, however. Murray had for some years acted 'in a general advisory capacity' for EETS, 'and in 1870 Furnivall asked him to pass Skeat's proofs for a revised edition of his *Lancelot de Laik*. James was very outspoken and Skeat protested, "I really think, however that you are in almost too great a hurry to fasten on me the name of 'ignorant' ... I think ... that I *may* claim to know *something* ... of the *older* Lowland & Northumberland language ..." But he owned that his remarks on dialect in the original edition were "as weak as anything I ever wrote", and said that he had made most of the corrections James had suggested.' Quoted from K. M. Elisabeth Murray, *Caught in the Web of Words*, 97.

[19] Skeat prints a bibliography of his works in *A Student's Pastime* (lxxviii–lxxxiv).

[20] It is given full, if less than wholly generous, appraisal by A. S. G. Edwards, in 'Walter W. Skeat'. Modern editors have relied extensively on Skeat's work; L. D. Benson, for example, insisted that the *Riverside Chaucer* edition took Skeat as a major reference point for its explanatory notes.

Skeat's attitude towards his work was characterised by remarkable robustness, as we shall see. He worked with extraordinary rapidity, and had a ceaseless flow of projects on the go. As his friend of forty years, A. L. Mayhew said of him, 'he was always planning some literary task, for before he had finished one work, he had either begun another, or had another in prospect',[21] and he inevitably made some mistakes for which subsequent scholars have criticised him. In the preface to the first edition of his *Etymological Dictionary* he explains that he usually gave three hours to a difficult word: 'During that time I made the best I could of it and then let it go.' Presumably this attitude accounts both for his extraordinary productivity and for his occasional errors of fact or judgement: unlike many academics, he was goal-oriented. He was also unremittingly industrious:

> I have frequently been asked how I managed to turn out so much work, and to edit so many texts. The answer is, simply, that it was done by devoting to them nearly all my spare time, and that of spare time I had abundance, having not much else to do. It is astonishing how much can be done by steady work at the same subject for many hours a day, and by continuing the same during most months in the year. It is also necessary to be enthusiastic, working with an ever-present hope of doing something to increase our knowledge in every available direction. Then the merest drudgery becomes a sincere pleasure; and, if any one would learn what drudgery means, let him make glossaries, and *verify the references*.[22]

Undoubtedly Skeat was driven by his desire to demonstrate that 'our old literature' was 'not ... a compilation of unintelligible monstrosities of forms', but represented 'modes of speech which were actually in the mouths of men in the olden times'.[23] He wrote to his wife with great excitement of an old watchmaker he met in Cleobury Mortimer (since Bale, traditionally regarded as Langland's home), to whom some friends had lent Skeat's student edition of *Piers Plowman* (1869):

> The old gentleman had begged to be allowed to buy it – however, they gave it him. He had *no difficulty* (!!) in reading it, because it was so like the talk of the place. He had read & reread it – indeed, the book was well-thumbed, & knew bits by heart – & could only

---

21   *A Glossary of Tudor and Stuart Words*, v.
22   *A Student's Pastime*, liii-iv. The injunction to 'verify your references, sir!' Skeat took from M. J. Routh; see *Quarterly Review* 146 (1878), 30.
23   See *TPS* 1873–4, 245.

say that it was 'glorious' – he knew no other word for it. It was not merely the language that took his fancy – tho' that was partly it. For example, he said – 'the book says – "if they live*n* as they sholde*n*." & that is *how we talk*; we say live*n*, we don't say *live*, & we say *sholden*' (which to my surprise he pronounced in the Old English (Ellis's) manner, viz. *shoalden* – riming with *golden*). 'That's how we say it'-said he – 'But it isn't that as I like best; it's the wording of it – isn't it glorious? – how it goes on to shew that Reason & Meed couldn't get on together', &c. &c. You may be sure it was most amusing to me to hear him go on ... It really is valuable evidence, for it shews that the peculiar allegorical form of the poem – to us rather dull – is, to the half-educated poor, just the *very thing* they enjoy thoroughly. It was also very instructive to find that a man like this can read, without any difficulty, a book which educated (!) Englishmen think is difficult. He gets some old people together sometimes, & expounds it all, & it is a source of great pleasure to them. In fact, as he emphatically declared, the book was worth more than its weight in gold to him for the pleasure it afforded. This let me see how it was that, in olden times, it had such a run among the peasantry. Altogether, I learnt a good deal by my visit, & it was a great success.[24]

In 1873 the President of the Philological Society, Alexander Ellis (to whose pronunciation scheme Skeat refers in this letter), announced in his Annual Address that 'the Rev. W. W. Skeat, a Member of our Council, to whom our own and the Early English Text Society are so deeply indebted for long, laborious, and accurate work, has started, and with his usual promptitude and vigour actually set on foot, an English Dialect Society'. This prospered, and prepared the ground for Joseph Wright's *English Dialect Dictionary* (1896–1905). The *Etymological Dictionary* of 1882–4 was another massive and important work entirely characteristic of Skeat's aims; much of his surviving correspondence consists of postcards to a variety of different correspondents explaining the etymology of various words, and Kenneth Sisam describes how Skeat 'would take part in a fireside conversation, all the while sorting glossary slips as tranquilly as a woman does her knitting'. Commenting on 'the breadth of his knowledge and the sureness of his combinative power as an English philologist', the President of the British Academy (of which Skeat was a founder member) remarked,

---

[24] Letter dated 11 September 1874, in the possession of T. C. Skeat.

Any one with knowledge who compares the fourth edition of the *Dictionary* with the original edition will find reason for admiring, among Skeat's distinctive qualities as a scholar, his rare capacity for growing with his subject. While he successfully sought to keep pace with the steadily expanding work in the science of etymology, which was being carried out both in this country and abroad, he had when necessary the courage to admit that his decisions in certain points demanded revision, and thus at the same time gave proof of the true scholar's humility, for which those honoured him most who knew him best.[25]

Certainly Skeat's correspondence with his friend J. A. H. Murray, Furnivall's successor as editor of the *OED*, gives ample proof of his generosity and openness as well as his willingness to admit error. Having initially advised Murray against the 'Big Dictionary' project as impracticable – perhaps characteristically rejecting the idea of such a risky if heroic venture – Skeat constantly encouraged his friend once Murray had embarked on it, urging him to resist depression and describing himself by contrast as 'buoyant as a cork'.[26]

By 1878 he was regarded as an obvious choice as the first occupant of the newly founded Elrington and Bosworth chair in Anglo-Saxon at Cambridge, to which he was subsequently elected. The Skeat Family Album charmingly records the tension at the Skeat household at the hour of the election, in a transcript of a letter from Mrs Skeat to her brother Reginald written on 23 May 1878.

> I think I told you about the election for the Professorship being fixed for Wed. May 15. Well! the long expected day at length arrived. The election was fixed for 2.30. After our early dinner we felt in strange suspense, wondering when the news would reach us & by what means. Walter occupied himself in the garden, putting up the tennis net & I busied myself in the house. The children were all in the garden with their father. As for poor Rosine [the French nurse], she was so excited that she could not eat any dinner & she placed herself near the window on the lookout for the first comer. Just at half past three she saw a tall man walking up the drive,

25 Presidential Address by Dr A. W. Ward, read 30 October 1912, announcing Skeat's death; *PBA* 5, 23–5.
26 See K. M. Elisabeth Murray, *Caught in the Web of Words*, 140, 145, 148. Skeat helped Murray financially by giving him a mortgage (much of the correspondence between the two men, now preserved in the Murray Papers, accompanies payment or receipt notes), and marked his completion of the various stages of the dictionary with witty light verse (see *ibid.*, 273–4, 297). K. M. Elisabeth Murray characterises Skeat as 'a gentle, generous, optimistic man … extraordinarily humble … always grateful for help and correction and apologetic about his mistakes' (85–6).

presently he rang the bell, she rushed to open the door & then flew to Walter, who came quietly in and read on a paper wh. the man (the University Marshal) gave him, written by the V.C. [Vice Chancellor], that he (W.) was the happy man! *Unanimously elected.* Then the Marshal retired and we embraced all round in great glee & jumped about like so many mad creatures, except Walter who was very quiet, and almost as if stunned.

But he soon aroused himself & called Bertha [his eldest daughter] & they went to the station to telegraph to Mama & two of his friends. We actually got a telegram back the same evening ... All expressed themselves very delighted & said they had been quite excited. Before W. returned from the station Professors Seeley & Cowell [colleagues of Skeat's at Christ's] came in and Prof. S. shook hands most kindly with me, congratulating me as Die Frau Professorinn! wh. I thought a very pleasing and graceful compliment. [27]

Some time after this Skeat became 'the first Cambridge Professor who ventured to trust himself to a bicycle', and according to his *Times* obituary

> was probably better known to the general public of Cambridge, both town and gown, than any of the other professors, both by repute and by sight ... by repute – though strangers by an odd anagram, sometimes called him Professor Keats – because of the widespread fame of his Dictionary; by sight, because in fine weather he almost invariably walked the mile and a half from his house [he lived at 2 Salisbury Villas] to the Divinity Schools, where he lectured, in a peculiar ambling trot, with his silk gown caught up behind him with one arm. His white beard at once attracted attention, and it never seemed rude to watch him because he always appeared oblivious of passers-by. [28]

Skeat did not find it easy to attract much interest in Old English from Cambridge undergraduates; one of his articles in the *Cambridge Review* advertises his services in a way that suggests they were not often taken up: 'I cannot but think that such lectures [Skeat delivered thirty or forty a year] could be turned to good account by students; nevertheless, from various causes unknown to me, the attendance is very scanty', [29] and the *Times* writer points out that 'The majority of the students of English at Cambridge are women, and they did not attend his lectures. There were always a number of men, some of

---

[27] The Skeat Family Album is now in the possession of T. C. Skeat.
[28] *The Times*, 8 October 1912.
[29] Quoted by Sherbo, 'Walter William Skeat', 116.

whom said the Professor's lectures were the one thing connected with their studies they would most reluctantly have missed'; nevertheless the fact that undergraduates did not require any familiarity with Anglo-Saxon in order to pass university examinations must have acted as a disincentive to larger audiences. (The same writer says that he 'once heard [Skeat] give a lecture on English etymology in a Baptist schoolroom and hold a half-educated audience for an hour and a half'.) The obituaries agree on his academic teaching skills. 'Skeat was not an ideal Professor. While his own contributions to learning were of the highest value, he seemed to care little about inspiring others to follow him in the same field. His relation to Professor Israel Gollancz, possibly his most distinguished pupil, is a notable exception; but on the whole it must be admitted that his own teaching-work was less valuable than his research.' The failure to build up a circle of disciples is perhaps explained by A. J. Wyatt: 'Though many of his pupils felt for him an almost chivalric admiration, there was hardly one whom he drew to himself with the bond of personal affection.'[30]

All the obituaries stress his extraordinary energy, though not necessarily in wholly complimentary terms. 'Mentally and physically – he was an expert skater –' wrote Wyatt,

> he seemed to be fashioned out of springs, or like a clock wound up to go for centuries. Nothing daunted him, nothing hindered him for long – his own mistakes as little as anything else ... Holidays and recreation were an irrelevancy to him, to be tolerated only because without them the springs lost their rebound, not for their own sake. This student's pastime was books ... He was not a great original genius; he was a great populariser (in the best sense) in a field of knowledge almost unexplored by his countrymen before. He was not a great teacher ... Yet his lectures were eagerly followed by the fit though few ... His judgment did not appear to be founded upon great principles; he was apt to reverse a decision. Though the great contrast between him and his forerunners is that he brought scientific method into his researches, to the last his genius refused to be fettered by scientific method and rule.[31]

The reference to his knowledge and experience in 'scientific' method echoes the *Times*' judgement that 'his mind had not the scientific cast of the true philologist ... Wherever strict scientific method was required he would have failed.' The point is especially significant,

[30] *Ibid.*, 112.   [31] *Ibid.*, 111–12.

since it captures nicely Skeat's extraordinarily sound instinct but his frequent lack of system – in collating manuscripts of *Piers Plowman*, for instance – and also his apparent ignorance of, or disregard for, major Continental theories on editing. The suggestion of selective intellectual myopia is picked up by his grandson:

> what I find much more surprising [than his indifference to 'the great theological controversies of the nineteenthth century', the 'conventional piety' of his sermons, and his old-fashioned habit of wearing Geneva bands rather than a dog-collar], and especially to someone in Cambridge, is his apparent indifference to the great advances being made in the textual study of the New Testament, since these involved going back to the testimony of the earliest surviving MSS., a course which he had so often championed in English studies. And the publication of the Revised English translation of the New Testament in the opening days of 1881 was an event of intense national interest, but I have never seen any reference to it in his publications.[32]

The *Oxford Magazine* described him as 'a shy man, who made little impression in mixed society, and his gentle, placid, almost tired manner gave little indication of the consuming energy that possessed him'. *The Times* obituary reported that 'apart from his lectures, he was not the ideal professor; he was too inaccessible, being too busily occupied with his books and his book-making'. Moreover, 'in the fullest and highest meaning of the word "friend", he was a friendless man – his friends were his books'; although, of course, he 'knew many distinguished men both at home and abroad'. But the obituary written by his long-time associate, the co-editor of the *Oxford English Dictionary* Henry Bradley, insists that he was 'one of the most faithful and warm-hearted of friends'.

Skeat himself makes occasional reference to the 'scientific' nature of the new philology: for example, in his *Questions for Examination in English Literature*, first published in 1873, he wrote of the need to institute the discipline of English studies: 'It is high time that a true critical school should be established, and a true scientific method of instruction and enquiry should be adopted.'[33] And in 1881, urging undergraduates to attend his lectures (in an echo of Sweet's words quoted above), he described how

[32] Letter to the author. It should be noted that T. C. Skeat is himself an eminent New Testament Greek scholar.

[33] *Questions for Examination in English Literature*, xii. Quoted by Sherbo, 'Walter William Skeat', 116.

the study [of philology] has made extraordinary advances during the last ten or twelve years, and the treatment of it has become much more scientific. Guesswork that twenty years ago was reverenced would to-day be not much regarded ... in order to keep up the work and to gain more ground, we require specialists regularly trained, not amateur workers, as heretofore. Such specialists are being trained in Germany; it seems hard we can train none here.[34]

Contemporaries were fully appreciative of his remarkable achievement in establishing English studies as a proper academic subject in both schools and universities. 'There is still much to do', says Wyatt, 'but to gain some faint idea of what Skeat achieved we need only compare the position of English studies in Cambridge or indeed in England today with their abysmal neglect when he entered upon his professorship thirty-four years ago. And what he did, it is only fair to add, no one else could have done.' That judgement would apply equally well to much of his editorial work. As Sisam observed, 'it is Skeat's great merit that he resisted counsels of perfection. If he had waited until everything was cleared up to his satisfaction, we should have been without a major Chaucer and *Piers Plowman*, all of which he produced to a very creditable standard for the time ... I pardon all his imperfections.'[35]

Presumably it was as a result of an invitation by Furnivall that Skeat took on the project of editing *Piers Plowman*, although, as no records survive of the early days of the Early English Text Society, it is impossible to know for certain. A few of the surviving letters between the two men indicate that Furnivall had been interested in the poem for some time, and that he and Skeat at first undertook the task of editing it jointly. On 20 May 1865, Furnivall wrote in a postscript to a letter to Bradshaw,

> Thos Warton's note says there are 3 versions of P. Plowman [sc. in Price's 1824 edition of Warton's *History*]. Why can't you lay hold of a young Kingsman [Bradshaw's college was King's], and make him take up P.P. He could collate all the Cambridge texts at least. If any unoccupied man comes [illegible] me here, I shall try to set him on the London MSS.[36]

---

[34] *Ibid.*, 117.   [35] Letter to R. W. Chambers; see p. 298 below.
[36] CUL Add. 2591: 250; cf. CUL Add. 2591: 252: 'A good account or clarification of the MSS of Piers Ploughman would be more valuable to us, though, than those of any Romance [the topic under discussion]. If you'll do the Cambridge ones, I'll do, or get done, the London ones.'

And an exasperated letter from Skeat to Furnivall of 23 January 1866 indicates that the collaboration was not harmonious:

> You've made a most fearful blunder somehow with the P.Pl. bits. It beats me. The piece you give me from MS 10,574 (Whitaker's) is *not* in Whitaker!! – and your account of the types is consequently all wrong. Whitaker never mentions either *mayors* or macero. I enclose what he *does* say that you may see for yourself.[37]

As already indicated, Skeat's approach towards *Piers Plowman* differed fundamentally from that of previous editors. The most obvious indication of this is that he – or perhaps Furnivall – considered that the first task was to trace as many manuscripts as possible. This in itself is an interesting and highly significant development in editorial method. Presumably Skeat, whose only previous experience of editing (astonishing as this now seems to us) had been *Lancelot of the Laik*, extant in one manuscript only, was struck by the contrast in editing a work which survived in a large number of known manuscripts, and for all he knew perhaps as many again unknown manuscripts. As we have seen, the attitude of previous editors towards assembling and comparing as many different manuscripts as possible of the poem had been decidedly dilettanteist. Crowley used several manuscripts, but gave his readers no clear or full information about them; Whitaker used one manuscript belonging to his friend Richard Heber as his base-text, and sporadically consulted another of Heber's manuscripts, the B-Text in Oriel College Oxford, and Crowley's text; while Wright claimed, with some pride, to have consulted various manuscripts, but in practice confined himself to the Trinity A-Text and to Whitaker, and even then did not do the consulting in any sort of reliable or consistent way. In Skeat's view, knowledge of the manuscripts was to be linked closely with duty towards and respect for their contents. Presumably his experience with *Lancelot* had also taught him to distrust previous editors' printed versions; and this cautious attitude was fully justified.

The information Skeat gives us on the inception of his edition relates principally to manuscript identification and clarification. He describes years later (in *A Student's Pastime*) how

---

[37]   Quoted by Benzie, *Dr. F. J. Furnivall*, 153, from the Furnivall Papers at King's College Library. The mistake was Skeat's: as we have seen, the BL MS 10574 was not the copy-text used by Whitaker. Skeat may have been misled by Wright, who made the same mistake (see p. 59 n. 30 above). The implied discrimination between 'types' of manuscripts indicates that Skeat and Furnivall were preparing the 1866 'Tract'; see further below.

a particular passage of the poem was selected by Dr. Furnivall, and transcripts of this passage came to hand from many helpers; from Dr. Furnivall himself [who reported on British Library manuscripts], from the Rev. H. O. Coxe, Bodley's librarian, and from Mr. W. Aldis Wright [then librarian of Trinity College Cambridge]; whilst other aid was forthcoming from many quarters. Mr. (now Dr.) E. A. Bond gave his opinion as to the age of some of the MSS., and, at a later date, MSS. were either lent or shown me by the Earl of Ilchester, the Duke of Westminster, Mr Henry Yates Thompson, and Lord Ashburnham. Not the least pleasant of my experiences were some valuable hints sent me by Mr. Thomas Wright, who had made a very useful edition of this great poem on his own account. (p. xxvi)

What seems to have happened is that Furnivall and Skeat between them realised that many more manuscripts of the poem existed than had been used for the previous editions. The problem was, how to identify them. Furnivall hit on the expedient of transcribing a typical passage from the poem (from Passus III), which would surely exist in all copies of it that were not prohibitively defective, and circulating the passage to various librarians with the request that they would report back on any manuscripts in their care which they discovered contained this passage. The scheme of printing parallel texts was typically Furnivallian, according well with the practice of his Chaucer Society; and it seems that Furnivall led the project to begin with. This is indicated by a letter to Bradshaw of 1 January 1866:

> My dear B.,
>
> When a slip with an extract of 20 lines from Passus 3 of the London and Bodl. MSS of Piers Plowman reaches you, do please go off to the library, copy out the corresponding passages from all your MSS, & send them up to me, with the dates you put on them [i.e., presumably, Bradshaw's dating of them], or at least the order of time they seem in.
>
> I want to get a sample from every MS of P. Pl.
>
> The Vernon is the best, I expect.
>
> Yours ever
>
> F.J.F.
>
> Skeat is away just now, & has other work

Written on the reverse of the page is the following query: 'Where ought one to send for extracts besides Corpus, Dublin, & the Oxf^d

Colleges that Coxe notes'.[38] But it is difficult to imagine Furnivall holding his nose to the same grindstone without intermission for very long, something which this particular project would certainly require; and it is not surprising that the results of their preliminary inquiry were published (in 1866) under Skeat's name alone.[39]

They took the form of a pamphlet (or as Skeat called it, a tract), no. 17 in the EETS series, entitled *Parallel Extracts from Twenty-nine Manuscripts of Piers Plowman, with Comments, and a Proposal for the Society's Three-text Edition of this Poem.* The intention was to elicit information on the whereabouts of further manuscripts of the poem from EETS members and readers, so as to produce an edition of *Piers Plowman* (described as 'the most valuable work in Early English Literature before Chaucer wrote') which took into account as much of the extant evidence as possible. Skeat emphasised in his opening words the nature of his project, a vast and scholarly under-taking atypical of the EETS editions published so far, but serving the same ends, 'the bringing to light the whole of the hidden springs of the noble Literature that England calls its own':[40]

> With a view of obtaining information as to the language, age, and type of every known MS. of the Poem, the [EETS] Committee have, on Mr Furnivall's suggestion, resolved to print one and the same passage from every MS. which the goodwill of Librarians and owners of collections may place at their disposal, so that, by a collation of these extracts, the relative dialectal peculiarities, ages, and types of the MSS. themselves may be determined, and attention afterwards concentrated on those most likely to yield the most valuable results. The Committee, then, appeal to every one who has a copy of this noble poem under his control, to render them assistance in carrying out the great work they have in hand. (p. 1)

Skeat buttressed his entreaty with an appeal to the patriotic spirit of his readers, emphasising the importance of *Piers Plowman* to the nation: 'the Committee are sure that their appeal will not be left without response by any one who remembers how the old poem had called up before him the picture of his forefathers' life, and shown him the earnestness with which they strove for Truth amidst the many corruptions of their time' (pp. 1–2). The response, as we shall see, was

---

[38] CUL Add. 2591: 281.
[39] A further letter from Furnivall to Bradshaw of 27 June 1867 says, '... I hope you are, & will be, pleased with Skeat's Piers Plowman. He *is* doing it well.' (CUL Add. 2591: 377.)
[40] As Furnivall had put it; see p. 72 above.

very satisfactory. 'And so it came about', Skeat says, 'that I began editing this poem in 1866, and only finished the last page of the General Introduction in 1885.'[41]

Given Skeat's almost amateur status as an editor, the initial speed with which he produced his substantial editions was phenomenal. His EETS edition of A appeared almost straightaway, in 1867, followed by B in 1869 and C in 1873.[42] A fourth volume containing a glossary and a wealth of notes and other matter was finally completed after a more leisurely interval, in 1885.[43] Then in 1886 the Clarendon Press published Skeat's three texts all in one, in a two-volume parallel-text edition. The first volume contained the texts of the poem, arranging the three versions side by side across each double-page spread, thus making it much easier for the reader to compare and contrast the three versions. The second volume reprinted with some abridgement the notes and glossary from the fourth EETS volume. It was this edition of the poem that became the best-used scholarly one – for obvious reasons: the utility of the parallel lay-out and the comparatively uncumbersome format of two volumes rather than four. The consequences of this scholarly preference were not insignificant. For example, the two volume edition has much less information on the characteristics of the manuscripts than the previous editions, and it does not spell out clearly and fully Skeat's editorial principles and practice. Hence the provisional nature of his A-Text, and the sporadic character of Skeat's collation of many of the manuscripts, are not clearly evident from a reading of the Parallel-Text edition alone.[44]

Skeat's task was an overwhelming one. As we have seen, none of

---

[41] *A Student's Pastime*, 26.

[42] Describing in 1878 his work on *Piers Plowman*, Skeat writes that 'no other editor would attempt' the edition, and comments, 'The labour was certainly enormous, but I succeeded in examining, describing and arranging the 44 MSS., and in collating all that were worth collating. It is easily proved that, in the course of the work, I read 150,000 lines of Early English *in the original MSS.*, and that too *twice over*, carefully watching the spelling of every word, and recording all the variations, whether in the text or the spelling, that seemed to be of any value' (*Testimonials in Favour of the Rev. Walter W. Skeat*, 4). This may have been something of an exaggeration; see further below.

[43] For more detail, see pp. 174–6 below.

[44] The Parallel-Text edition pared down the recorded collations still further, making the choice between editorial variants seem even less taxing than did the critical apparatuses of the three separate editions. The scholarly popularity of the Parallel-Text edition makes it easier to understand how both Knott and Fowler and Kane came to overlook the existence of Bodley 851 when editing A (cf. p. 421 below). J. M. Manly, as we shall see later (p. 186), came to feel that this edition was responsible for an unthinking acceptance of the hypothesis that the poem's three versions were written by one and the same author.

the previous editors had worked out with any degree of thoroughness or accuracy what the relationships between any of the manuscripts were, or how these related to the work that the author (or authors) had (presumably) written in the first place. Reading through the leisurely, occasionally chatty introductions to Skeat's successive editions, one receives an engaging impression of how his perceptions, insights, and assumptions about the poem and its various stages gradually developed and accumulated. In the 1866 tract, Skeat explains that, hitherto, two versions of the poem have been identified (principally by Whitaker and Wright); but that

> a further separation of the MSS. can easily be made, so as to distribute them not only into *two* distinct classes, but into *three*. A close and careful scrutiny of several MSS. shows that those which most resemble the one printed by Mr Wright can be separated into two kinds, which may very conveniently be named the *Vernon* and *Crowley* types. The first of these is best exemplified by the text of the Vernon MS. at Oxford, and it is remarkable as presenting the earliest or original version of the poem. It is easily recognized by observing that it omits many long passages, and, in particular, the one containing the story of the rats in the Introductory Passus. It also contains *very few* Latin quotations, and does not extend much beyond ten *Passus*, though it is sometimes [i.e., in some manuscripts] supplemented by a later text. Its readings are, in general, peculiarly good, and the sense more simple and distinct than in later versions. (p. 3)

This statement looks as if it is made in ignorance of Price's earlier discovery, in his 1824 edition of Warton's *History of English Poetry*, that there were three distinct versions of the poem, two represented by the texts of Crowley and Whitaker respectively and a third to be found in two of the Harley manuscripts (pp. 46–7 above). It also suggests that Skeat did not work so closely in conjunction with Furnivall as we might have expected, since, as we have seen, Furnivall had referred to Price's discovery in his mention of 'Thos. Warton's note' in a letter to Bradshaw written in 1865. Skeat lists the six manuscript versions of the Vernon type that he has so far come across – Vernon itself, the two BL Harley manuscripts (875 and 6041) which Price had consulted, one manuscript in Trinity College, Cambridge (T), one manuscript in the Bodleian (Digby 145), and one in University College Oxford (No 45). He goes on to say,

> The *Crowley* type is adopted as a convenient name for the MSS.
> which resemble the text printed by Crowley in 1550, to which class
> the one printed by Mr Wright also belongs. The *three* texts, then are
> (1) those of the *Vernon* type; (2) those of the *Crowley* type; and (3)
> those of the *Whitaker* type. It is proposed to publish one of each
> kind in the above order, so as to show the gradual development of
> the poem from its briefest into its most elaborate form. (pp. 3–4)

Here one can already see taking shape the unargued assumption that
the shortest version must precede the longest, and that the poet would
have expanded, rather than contracted, as he wrote. (Skeat subsequently did produce some reasons for this assumption.)[45] He goes on
to observe that the 'variations' between the printed texts, Whitaker's
C and Wright's B, 'are far more numerous and important than has
been supposed' (he lists some of the major examples), and also stresses
that 'it is obviously very desirable to ascertain whether all of the MSS.
of each supposed type follow the same difference of arrangement,
&c.; and whether any new MS. of value can be anywhere discovered.
The present tract is put forth in the hope of obtaining further
information on these points' (p. 5).

EETS 17 nicely records Skeat's attempts at analysing and making
sense of this 'vast mass of unsifted material'.[46] He categorised the
various manuscripts according to the way in which they represented
two key passages of the poem (in Passus III and VI). As he describes,
he found that there were, in the manuscripts that he had seen, three
reasonably separate versions of these.[47] But Skeat's choice of these
passages was necessarily made without a full and extensive knowledge
of the various manuscript versions of the poem: it represented a
preliminary organisational foray into uncharted territory. The choice
turned out to be highly significant in the respect that it excluded the
possibility of the version of *Piers Plowman* found in Bodley 851, now
commonly known as the Z-Text, being identified as a copy of the
poem: for the simple reason that Z does not contain one of the
relevant passages, that in Passus III.[48] Hence Skeat formed his
hypotheses on the nature, organisation and development of the poem

---

[45] See below, pp. 115, 159–60. The assumption that A was composed before B and B
composed before C has until recently never been challenged, and rarely discussed; see
below, pp. 429–30.

[46] As it was later to be described by R. W. Chambers; see p. 248 below.

[47] Skeat prints the lines of the poem as half lines, following Wright; he drops this practice in
his *A-Text* (see his explanation in *A-Text*, xxvii–xxviii).

[48] For the details, see below, pp. 170 and 420ff.

without taking Z's unique characteristics into account. When he did come across the manuscript, as we shall see in chapter 9 below, he rejected its early part as incompatible with the ideas on the poem he had now irrevocably established, and which were to survive unchallenged for many years to come.

7

Skeat's *A-Text*

By the time his A-Text was published the following year, in 1867, Skeat had made considerable advances in his understanding of the manuscript relations and his hypotheses about the original versions they might be supposed to represent. But he begins with a more popular introductory section attempting to answer the question, 'What *is* Piers Plowman?' 'A poet of the reign of Edward the Third', comes the reply, 'of whom scarcely anything is known but the name (and even that is uncertain), wrote a poem in alliterative verse which he threw into the form of several successive visions; in *one* of these he describes his favourite ideal character – Piers – and in course of time the name was used as a common title for the whole series of them.'[1] Langland's 'vivid descriptions and earnest language', Skeat continues, 'caused the poem to be very popular, and the fertile imagination of the author induced him to rewrite the poem twice over, so that what may fairly be called three versions of it exist in manuscript'. Skeat notes that 'the vivid truthfulness of its delineations of the life and manners of our forefathers has often been praised, and it is difficult to praise it too highly', and he stresses its historical value: 'As indicating the true temper and feelings of the English mind in the fourteenth century, it is worth volumes of history.' Langland supplements the writings of Chaucer, since 'Chaucer describes the rich much more fully than the poor, and shews the holiday-making, cheerful, genial phase of English life; but Langland pictures the homely poor in their ill-fed, hard-working condition, battling against hunger, famine, injustice, oppression, and all the stern realities and hardships that tried

---

[1] *A-Text*, iii–iv. Possibly this description suggests that Skeat was not as yet fully familiar with the other versions of the poem, since it is only in the A-Text that Piers appears in 'one' alone of the visions; although in a footnote (iii n. 1) Skeat does acknowledge that Piers is, at least, referred to elsewhere in the poem: 'The character of Piers, in its highest form of development, is identified by Langland with that of Christ the Saviour – "Petrus est Christus".' This is a misquotation from the B-Text, Passus XV 212.

them as gold is tried in fire ... Each, in his own way, is equally admirable, and worthy to be honoured by all who praise highly the English character and our own dear native land.'

These terms of praise and description clearly recall those in the Early English Text Society reports by Furnivall, with their constant appeal to the subscribers' interest in and curiosity about the lives, customs, and mentality of their forefathers. Skeat allows that the poem could be found difficult: 'there is a danger that some who take up "Piers Plowman" may at first be somewhat repelled by the allegorical form of it, or by an apparent archaism of language, and some passages are sufficiently abstruse to require a little thought and care to be taken before one can seize their full meaning'. But once initial difficulty is got over, great rewards will be reaped: 'The reader who does not throw it aside *at first* will hardly do so afterwards'. Where the language is concerned, Skeat has little sympathy for any flagging readers. '*Some familiarity*' with 'old English' [i.e. the English of Chaucer, Langland and Gower], he says sternly in a footnote, and certainly

> enough to enable one to understand a large portion of our early literature, may be picked up in a few weeks – almost in a few days. It is amazing to find what a bugbear "old English" is to many Englishmen; they look upon it as harder to learn than Chinese. Yet any one who will take the trouble to master one or two of the Canterbury Tales has the key to much of the wealth of our early English literature; and the man who will *not* take the trouble to do this deserves to be guided by guesswork rather than by evidence in his notions of English grammar; as he probably will. (*A-Text*, p. v n. 1)

Once again, Skeat – very sensibly, in this context – sees understanding of the language as central to the discovery of our past culture. He goes on to recommend Langland's peculiarly *'practical* turn of mind', how he 'loves best to exercise his shrewd English common sense upon topics of every-day interest', and he finishes the Introduction with several pages of long quotation from the poem illustrating Langland's strength in depicting details of social realism (Glutton in the alehouse and the typical peasant diet), his skill in satire (Liar escaping to the pardoners), and his admonitions against social and religious irresponsibility (the end of A Passus VIII).

The Introduction was intended as a taster for non-specialists. Once into the Preface, Skeat gets straight down to what Furnivall would call the 'facts' of the matter, i.e. the manuscripts. He reports on the results elicited by his 1866 tract: a second manuscript at Dublin (D. 4. 12) has now come to his notice,[2] two belonging to Lord Ashburnham (now BL Add. 35287 and Hm 128), one in Lincoln's Inn library (where it remains), three more in the Bodleian (Douce 104 and 323, together with Ashmole 1468), and one other in private possession (belonging to H. Yates Thompson, Esq., of Liverpool; now at Newnham College, Cambridge). This brought the total up to thirty-seven, but 'I feel sure that there are yet more in various parts of the country, many probably in private hands, and I should be much obliged for any information concerning them' (p. xii). He has now discovered that 'the poem takes no less than *five* different shapes, but *two* of them are merely owing to differences of arrangement made by the scribes; and there are really no more than *three* forms of it'.[3] He has also discovered Price's note to Warton's *History of English Poetry*, which as we have seen had suggested as early as 1824 the existence of a text separate from and previous to the two versions printed by Whitaker and Wright.[4]

The additional manuscripts had strengthened Skeat's view that A came before B and B before C: 'we have abundant evidence of its being really the first and original draught of the poem ... Type B is obviously derived from it almost wholly by amplification and addition, and preserves nearly the same order in the narrative, even when C wanders away from both.' Also, '(which greatly helps the argument) the Latin quotations occurring in A are much fewer than those found in the corresponding parts of B and C, even when all allowance is made for the amplification of the story'. The new A-MSS had not, in Skeat's opinion, displaced the primacy of the Vernon manuscript as the best representative of text A, and the early date of the manuscript (late fourteenth century)[5] reinforced the view that the A-Text was the first of Langland's three versions, since it was the earliest known of all *Piers Plowman* manuscripts.[6] 'This MS.', Skeat says, 'is indeed a noble and admirable one. Its immense size, and the beauty of the vellum, of the writing, and of the illuminated letters have long since attracted notice, and it has already been made considerable use of by editors

---

2 Skeat heard of this manuscript, a version of A, too late to be able to incorporate information on it into his edition of A, and instead describes it in his *B-Text*, vi–vii n. 1 (see pp. 137–8 below).

3 *A-Text*, xlii. Skeat later settled on *ten* different forms; see pp. 174–5 below.

4 *A-Text*, xiv; cf. p. 110 above.   5 See Kane, 17.

6 *A-Text*, xiv: 'It is also to be noted that the oldest and best MS. yet found, the Vernon MS., belongs to the earliest type [A].'

and several extracts from it are in print.'[7] The terms of this description immediately arouse the suspicion that it was the appearance of the manuscript as much as its content which recommended it to Skeat, but he specifically rebuts this possible inference: 'This MS. was taken for the *text*, not solely because it is the oldest and best written, but also because a careful collation of it with the rest has shewn that its readings are, on the whole, better than those of any other. It seems to me the best known MS. of "Piers Plowman" *in every respect*' (p. xvi).

Skeat is perfectly straightforward and open about his selective use of the manuscripts, which is interesting in the light of reviews of his work. As time went on, and one edition after another appeared, the combined *œuvre* took on a cumulative weight and authority. Critics must have been perfectly well able to consult component parts of the editions and see that Skeat was building hypotheses on sometimes only partly consulted manuscripts, but no acknowledgement of this appears in their reviews, which are almost without exception overwhelming in their praise, particularly of the comprehensiveness of Skeat's editorial enterprise.

In fact, Skeat collated very few of the manuscripts in any detail, and only collated three other manuscripts in full against the text of Vernon (which he possessed in the form of a transcript made by a Bodleian library assistant, George Parker).[8] The first of these was Harley 875 (H), which Skeat judged to be 'valuable':

> This MS. is, in general, very close to the "Vernon", and pairs off with it better than any other does, as will soon be seen by studying the foot-note [he means the critical apparatus]. It contains additional lines occasionally, and seems to be the *fullest* of the series. It is therefore very useful for completing the sense, in passages that seem incomplete. It may be, however, that a few of these extra lines are spurious. (p. xviii)

Later scholars have found *all* of H's unique lines spurious, and regarded Skeat's inclusion of them as a disfigurement of his text. The

[7]   *A-Text*, xv. Skeat goes on to say that 'it has received the name of "Sowlehele", as containing things useful for the *soul's health*; and the name is a good one: the poems and treatises in it, which are very numerous, being chiefly of a religious cast.' Part of the Vernon version of the poem was published by Skeat's friend Richard Morris in the same year, 1867, in his *Specimens of Early English*, 249–90; but Morris did not apparently notice that the manuscript presented a different version of the poem from that found in Crowley, Whitaker and Wright.

[8]   See xvi n. 1; 142*. Parker was a Middle English scholar who also transcribed the manuscript of Sir Ferumbras (Ashmole 33) for S. J. Herrtage's edition of *Sir Ferumbras* (see EETS ES 34, xxvii–viii).

second manuscript Skeat collated in full was the A-Text in Trinity College, Cambridge, R. 3. 14 (T), the one sporadically consulted by Wright, which Skeat found 'very remarkable and valuable'; and the third was University College, Oxford 45 (U), 'an important and valuable MS., especially from its evident independence of the rest, agreeing sometimes with one and sometimes with another, sometimes even with none, yet corroborating them in the main' (p. xx). U had a curious misarrangement of material, part of Passus VII occurring in Passus I, suggesting that the leaves of its exemplar must have been disturbed. All three of these manuscripts were, like Vernon itself, checked repeatedly against the proof-notes.

In addition to the four main manuscripts, V, H, T, and U (whose variants he recorded in his footnotes),[9] Skeat drew sporadically upon the readings of three others, thus producing an edition based on seven manuscripts in all. First, Harley 6041 (H^2), which was a poor manuscript, Skeat judged, in comparison with the previous four: 'It is remarkably close to MS.T; and hence, after collating it closely with the text from the beginning down to l. 146 of Passus II., I ceased to do so; finding that it is, practically, little else than an inferior duplicate of T, and may be neglected without much loss. Yet it has occasionally been consulted in difficult passages, and readings from it will be found here and there throughout the book.' The second occasionally consulted manuscript, Douce 323 (D), Skeat came across after publishing his 1866 tract. D 'follows T rather closely, but is full of gross blunders. On this account, after collating with Passus I.–IV., I desisted, finding that it only tended to choke the foot-notes with inferior readings' (p. xxi). Finally, there was Ashmole 1468, also new to Skeat, about which he is similarly dismissive. He realised that it was quite a late manuscript,[10] and thought that it had 'many corrupt readings'. Hence 'very little use has been made of this, as it seems an inferior MS.; yet it furnished a few good readings at the end of Passus XI.' (pp. xxi–ii).[11]

One problem with the Vernon text is that it stops before the end of the A-Text found in other manuscripts, breaking off at Passus XI 183. So Skeat used the version in T to complete the text down to the end

---

[9] According to the spot-checks I have made, Skeat records the variants of these four manuscripts fully and accurately, although not as fully as Kane later. Thus, unlike Kane, he does not notice spelling variants or alternatives such as *ac* and *but*.

[10] Kane (2) dates the hand to the third quarter of the fifteenth century, while noting that the paper may be a hundred years younger.

[11] Cf. Skeat's summary description of his collation of these three manuscripts, *A-Text*, xxviii.

of Passus XI, a further 120 lines, collating it, as he says, against H^2, U, and D, and also taking the odd variant from Ashmole, which 'furnished a good few readings'.

Of these seven manuscripts, the only ones that Skeat used to form his A-Text, five – V, T, U, and H^2 – were already known to him when he put out his preliminary tract. In the intervening year before he published the A-Text, he did, evidently, consult the two manuscripts new to him, Douce 323 and Ashmole 1468, which indicates that he was open to new ideas on the text. Nevertheless, it is highly likely, given the fame and comparatively wide exposure to medievalists that Vernon had so far enjoyed, that Vernon's was the first A version of the poem that Skeat had read: and that inevitably, its text would tend to seem paradigmatic to him, with other versions to be compared against it as a base, and rated as good or bad depending on their extent of agreement with Vernon.

This is borne out by the summary way in which Skeat describes the text of the three A-MSS he made no use of for establishing his version of A. The first of these was the imperfect copy in Lincoln's Inn, which was another manuscript that stopped short before the end of Passus VIII, which Skeat appears to have found rather irritating: 'On comparing a transcript of a considerable number of lines kindly made for me by Mr. Furnivall, I found that the text has been much corrupted by the scribe, and that to collate it would only fill the footnotes with false readings, except in places where the text is sufficiently ascertained without it' (p. xxii). The scribe tended to amplify the alliteration, replacing the last, normally non-alliterating stave in the line with a word that alliterated with the three previous staves. Skeat concludes that 'careful examination of the MS. shews, in fact, that it is best dismissed'. The second manuscript, Harley 3954 (H^3) was even worse: 'At the beginning, it follows Type B, giving a long prologue which contains 'the story of the rats,' but it omits many passages which occur in such MSS., and, towards the end, approaches Type A. I do not consider it of much value, and believe it to be frequently corrupted' (p. xxiii). This description is interesting, since it reveals that Skeat did not read the manuscript with great thoroughness: in fact, as George Kane many years later described, it provides a fairly standard B version up to around Passus V 105, where the scribe appears to have switched to an A-Text exemplar.[12] The third manu-

---

[12] Kane, 7–8.

script, Digby 145 (K), was similarly dismissed. It is another of the AC combinations, transferring, rather inelegantly, from an A-Text exemplar to a C-Text one at the end of A Passus XI. Skeat calls it 'but a poor copy, and is a mixture of texts. The early part of it is, like the last one [H³], an amplification of Text A; the later part follows Text C ... I have made no use of this MS., and do not think it worth much attention' (p. xxiv). He does not comment on the quite striking number of C lines in its A-Text, one of which occurs in the first five lines; but this is presumably what he refers to by 'amplification' of A.

All of this suggests that Skeat was pretty content with Vernon's text, and reluctant to rethink it substantially in the light of new evidence. The speed with which he produced his edition altogether precluded the sort of thorough reading and digestion of the different manuscript versions which was essential for making a balanced and disinterested judgement on their relative characteristics. Subsequent textual critics, who have had the benefit of Skeat's edition, and have been able to consult, on perhaps less prejudiced grounds, the manuscripts which he was crucially instrumental in bringing to light, have disagreed with him. Skeat himself came to accept many years later that he had been wrong to adopt Vernon as his base text. On 18 June 1909 he wrote to R. W. Chambers, his immediate successor in editing A, to say,

> My A-text was one of my earliest attempts: & I had no guide. The trouble was that no A-text had ever been printed. The B-text had been printed twice (Crowley & T. Wright): & the C-text by Whitaker. – I do not know whether you have ever tried editing a text from many MSS. for the first time. And then I did not know (no one knew) what MSS. existed! – Certainly, no one would now start with V as a basis. That was wrong.[13]

Skeat was also, evidently, inclined to judge the worth of a manuscript on grounds which would not be wholly acceptable today: if there was a scribal overlay of corruption, as in the Lincoln's Inn manuscript, where the scribe seemed to have rewritten a number of lines in order to make them more alliterative, Skeat did not consider the possibility that it would be worthwhile collating the manuscript in full anyway, just in case the exemplar from which the Lincoln scribe (or whichever scribe in the history of transmission of the Lincoln manuscript) made his copy was actually a good and reliable version of

---

[13] Chambers Papers Item 5:11.

the A-Text. This principle of course applies to *all* manuscripts, however corrupt they may seem – or as Skeat would put it, with however many 'gross blunders' their text is defiled. Axiomatically, *all* versions of a text must descend from an authorial original, however far removed, which means that *some* original readings will have survived even in the most corrupt of texts. That this is so is shown by the fact that, by and large, manuscripts of the A-Text do present versions of the poem that are recognisably similar, or as George Kane put it in 1960, 'the majority of scribes did, after all, copy a very large number of words in a great many lines faithfully, often to the point of keeping spelling and dialect forms of the exemplar'.[14] At some stage in its history, the Lincoln version may well have been a relatively good copy of the original text; hence one or two original readings might, in theory, have survived in places where all the other extant manuscripts have varying degrees of error (see pp. 204–5 below).

But Skeat shows no sense of this. It is striking, in fact, that he provides his readers with no discussion of the proper way to edit a poem which exists in so many manuscripts, or explains how he himself made decisions between the extraordinarily large number of manuscript variants. There is no reference to any theory of editing. Instead, he presents a tailored account of the evidence, and throughout relies upon his own intuition, intelligence, and shrewd judgement (all major virtues in editing, of course). The reader, meanwhile, receives a reassuring feeling that the editor is tackling the problems with common sense and coming to wise but obvious decisions.

Another important judgement Skeat had to make was on the *extent* of the A-Text. This presented something of a puzzle, for the different manuscripts had varying lengths. None of them went beyond Passus XI, which made it seem likely that 'the early draught of the poem' stopped at this point. The addition by three manuscripts, T, H², and K, of a C-Text unskilfully grafted on to the end of Passus XI seemed likely to be a scribal form of the poem, and this is something with which later editors have concurred: it is now supposed that, when scribes came to the end of their A-Text exemplar, they searched around for a copy of the long continuation that they knew existed (in B and C), and simply joined it on to what they had already written.[15]

---

[14] Kane, 126.

[15] Four other subsequently discovered A-MSS also have C-Text continuations: the Chaderton MS (Ch), the *Piers Plowman* in the National Library of Wales (N), the Duke of

Two other of the manuscripts, however, H and L, stop before the end of Passus VIII, a 'significant circumstance'. Skeat believed that the manuscript rubrics furnished a further clue to the history of the composition of the A-Text, explaining why 'probably neither [H nor L] ever went further than the end of this Passus, i.e. than the end of the Vision of Piers Plowman, *properly so called*'.[16] Many of the A-MSS (TUDH²VAK known at this stage to Skeat, RJM discovered subsequently) have rubrics in between Passus VIII and IX reading as follows: 'Explicit hic visio willhelmi de Petro Plouʒman: Eciam incipit vita de do-wel do-bet et do-best, secundum wyt et resoun.'[17] Skeat thus thought that there were in origin two *separate* poems comprising the A-Text: the *Visio*, consisting of the Prologue up to Passus VIII, and then the *Vita*, consisting of Passus IX–XI.

This theory is an interesting and forceful one, which was later adopted by Knott-Fowler. See p. 330 n. 3 below. As Skeat puts it,

> Each poem is complete in itself, and the concluding passages of each are wrought with peculiar care with a view to giving them such completeness, by stating, at the end of each, the result which in each case the author wishes to bring out strongly. The only connection between them is that the second is a sort of continuation of the first, and supposes that the dreamer, not being wholly satisfied with the first result of his inquiries, sets out once more to renew and extend them. It is a mark of the later forms of the poem that the distinction between them is less heeded, as though the author had accepted the necessity of their being written and considered as *one*.[18]

It may well be thought that editors, too, have been inclined to regard the A-Text as representing *one* poem, rather than two. But how can we evaluate the force of Skeat's hypothesis? First, it is interesting to note that three manuscripts (unknown to Skeat) in addition to H and L also stop at or before the end of Passus VIII: N (in the National Library of Wales), Z (Bodley 851), and E (MS D. 4.

Westminster's MS (W), and Bodley 851 (Z). The puzzle is why scribes should have used a C-Text to supplement their A exemplar, rather than a B-Text. See pp. 356–7 below.

[16]   *A-Text*, xxvi.

[17]   DVAK omit the *explicit*. A and K are not mentioned by Skeat, either because he did not consider their witness to be reliable, or because he did not consult them. See the manuscript descriptions in Kane and Kane–Donaldson for the wording of A- and B-MS rubrics respectively, and for those of the C-MSS, see Robert Adams, 'Langland's Rubrics: The *Visio* and *Vita* Once More'. In both this and an earlier article, 'The Reliability of the Rubrics in the B-Text of *Piers Plowman*', Adams provides the most authoritative discussion of the rubrics in the poem, coming to the conclusion that they are at least as likely to be scribal as authorial in origin.

[18]   *A-Text*, xxv.

12 in Trinity College, Dublin).[19] But three of these manuscripts (H, L and E) are physically imperfect at the end of their A-Text, so that it is impossible to tell whether they originally continued up to the end of Passus VIII and beyond or not. Also, if they are copies of an archetype representing an earlier stage of composition of the A-Text than that of the other A-MSS, would we not expect to find some genetic link between them, i.e. agreements in readings shared by these two (or five) manuscripts which are not found in the other A-MSS? Skeat does not think of this question, and he would not have had the information to answer it: this is in fact a good illustration of the weak aspects of his editorial method identified by Henry Nicol. The full collation carried out by George Kane, however, shows that there is no particular genetic link between H and L or between H, L, N, E, and Z. At first glance, this would seem to scotch the theory that the shape Prologue–Passus VIII could be authorial, rather than scribal.

Neverthless, it is worth noting Skeat's point that 'the concluding passages of each [i.e. both *Visio* and *Vita*] are wrought with peculiar care with a view to giving them such completeness, by stating, at the end of each, the result which in each case the author wishes to bring out strongly'. The passages in question are as follows. Passus VIII:

> At þe dredful day of dom · þer ded schullen a-rysen,
> And comen alle bi-fore crist · and a-Countes ȝelden,
> How þou laddest þi lyf · and his lawe keptest,
> What þou dudest day bi day · þe Doom þe wol rehersen;
> ¶A powhe ful of pardoun þer · with Prouincials lettres,
> þþauh þou be founden in Fraternite · a-mong þe foure Ordres,
> And habbe Indulgence I-doubled · bote Dowel þe helpe,
> I nolde ȝeue for þi pardoun · one pye hele!
>
> FOrþi I counseile alle cristene · to crie crist merci,
> And Marie his Moder · to beo mene bi-twene,
> þþat God ȝiue vs grace · er we gon hennes,
> Such werkes to worche · while þat we ben here,
> þþat aftur vr deþ day · Dowel reherce,
> þþat atte day of dom · we duden as he us hiȝte.[20]

Passus XI:

---

[19] Skeat knew of the existence of the Dublin manuscript by the time he published his edition of A (1867); see pp. 137–8 below.
[20] Quoted from Skeat's *A-Text*, Passus VIII 174–87; I have not in this or subsequent quotations represented expansion of abbreviations in italics as Skeat's own text does.

Arn none raþere yrauisshid · fro þe riȝte beleue
þþanne arn þþise grete clerkis · þat conne many bokis;
Ne none sonnere ysauid · ne saddere of consience,
þþanne pore peple as plouȝmen · and pastours of bestis.'
Souteris & seweris · suche lewide iottis
Percen wiþ a pater noster · þe paleis of heuene,
Wiþoute penaunce, at here partynge · in-to heiȝe blisse!
   Breuis oracio penetrat celum.[21]

There is no doubt that the end of A Passus VIII is a perfectly good place to stop, and represents an obvious break in the poem.

In fact it seems likely that Langland (if we may for the sake of convenience imagine a single author)[22] had several different shots at ending the *Visio*. Three manuscripts, to varying degrees, preserve an extra *twelfth* passus. Skeat first came across this in one of the manuscripts he used to establish his A-Text, U, which has an additional eighteen lines at the end of the poem under the rubric heading 'Passus tercius de dowel, &c.'.[23] Skeat prints the eighteen lines at the end of his Critical Notes, adding 'If there exists any other copy of these lines, I should be glad to have it pointed out to me' (p. 154 n. 1). He suggests two possible explanations:

> either that they were added by some person not the author of the poem (though they are very much in his manner), who attempted a continuation of it; or else that the author himself began a continuation which he afterwards abandoned, betaking himself to an expansion of the part already written, and afterwards adding thereto a continuation different to the one he at first contemplated. The latter supposition seems to me very probable; especially as there must have been a little more of this Passus, and yet not much more – (pp. xxvi–vii)

and he points out that the two folios (four sides, or pages) missing from the end of U indicate that 'the utmost that is lost is probably not more than 112 lines, as there are 28 lines to the page'. Adding these

---

[21] Quoted from Skeat's *A-Text*, Passus XI 297–303. As Skeat observes in his critical notes (*A-Text*, 154), the quotation *Breuis oracio penetrat celum* 'does *not* strictly belong to the A-class of MSS., but to the C-class [i.e., as found in MSS TH², which are completed with a continuation from the C-Text]. But I have introduced it for two reasons: (1) because it is very appropriate and makes an excellent concluding line, and is closely connected with the sense of the lines before it, and (2) because it is *useful* as indicating the point of junction of the A and C texts, as the reader will find when he consults Text C.'

[22] The question of multiple authorship was to be raised in 1906, see further below, pp. 184ff.

[23] U stops after A Passus XII 19a (Kane's numbering), having omitted Passus XII 6.

112 postulated lines to the 19 (including the Latin) that survive gives us 131 lines, which is, Skeat says, 'a fair average length for a Passus'.[24]

As Skeat later reports in a supplement to his A-Text, issued together with the B-Text in 1869, there is in fact another witness to the *Passus tercius de Dowel* among the Rawlinson manuscripts in Bodley. This 'most important and satisfactory discovery' was made by George Parker, the Bodleian Library assistant who had written out the transcript of Vernon for Skeat, and who came across the version during the process of cataloguing the Rawlinson manuscripts. MS. Rawlinson Poet. 137 (R) went beyond U's 18 lines to a total of 112, killing the author off and ending with 12 lines allegedly by one 'Johan But'.[25] Skeat was much excited by the discovery and convinced of Rawlinson's authenticity: 'I have not the slightest doubt of the entire *genuineness* of the new portion. It is Langland's beyond a doubt, every word of it, from line 1 down to the end of line 100. All these lines are not only in his manner, but contain his favourite words, phrases, and turns of expression, and have the same changes of rhythm as we find elsewhere ...'[26] Another copy of this mysterious twelfth passus came to light some years later, in a manuscript belonging to Sir Henry Ingilby, of Ripley Castle in Yorkshire, and Skeat reports on it in his volume of notes published in 1885.[27] He had hoped, obviously, that it would shed some light on the last few lines, perhaps offering an alternative, more clearly authorial version. But he was disappointed. The Ingilby manuscript (J) has eighty-eight lines only of Passus XII, corresponding very closely to the version of R and (so far as it goes) U, and even including five new lines, but not providing any easy solution to the riddle. J's last line is written at the top of a blank sheet (fol. 54*b*), which may suggest that the scribe knew that there was more to come, but the evidence is tantalisingly incomplete.

Subsequent editors have preserved an open mind on Passus XII.

[24] In fact it is on the short side, but not prohibitively so; Passus IX, for example, contains 109 lines.

[25] *A-Text*, 143*. Skeat printed R's lines and his commentary on them on pages numbered 137*-144* issued with his *B-Text*, but designed to be extracted and rebound into the A-Text edition.

[26] Skeat carefully distinguishes between the bulk of the new passus in R and the last 'superfluous' twelve lines: 'The commonplaceness of these lines, and the smallness of their number, is of some importance. It shews us how men fared who attempted to add to the master-poet's words, and it affords some proof of the genuineness of the numerous additions which Langland made in his later versions, and which are not in the 'Johan But' style by any means' (144*).

[27] *The Vision of William concerning Piers Plowman ... General Preface, Notes, and Indexes*, 856–9. The manuscript is now in the Pierpont Morgan Library of New York (M 818).

'Some of this "Passus"', Kane says, '... (106–17) is evidently spurious; more (99–105) ... should probably also be rejected out of hand.
What remains after these subtractions (1–98) ... although its general
character makes this seem unlikely, may be wholly or partly
authentic, representing wholly or partly an imperfect or abortive
continuation of the poem by the author.'[28] Consequently he prints it
in an appendix to his edition, as did Knott and Fowler before him.
Kane goes on to agree with Knott and Fowler that Passus XII,
although possibly authorial, 'was probably not in the archetype of the
extant manuscripts'.[29] This is an interesting admission, for it allows
that there may have been another version of A, distinct both from 'the
archetype of the extant manuscripts' and from B and C, which
circulated independently of the A-Text proper.[30] In particular, of
course, it lends implicit support to Skeat's theory that Langland
originally finished the poem at A Passus VIII, since if a poet is
capable of tinkering with his ending once he is capable of doing it
more than once.

Further support for Skeat's idea comes from a controversial source.
The highly eccentric version of the A-Text found in Bodley 851 also
ends at Passus VIII, though in a unique form which omits the famous
tearing-of-the-pardon scene. There is a close resemblance in sense
between its last few lines and the end of Passus XI, as may be seen by
comparing Z's version:

> Blynde men and bedereden ant broken in here membris,
> That tacut this mischef meklyche han as myche pardoun
> As Perkyn the plowman ant yut a poynt more:
> [For] loue of here lownesse oure lord hem hath grauntet
> Here penaunce ant here purgatorye vpon thys puyr erthe.[31]

Here the old, weak, and sick who take their suffering meekly –
experience their penance and their purgatory in this world rather than

---

28   Kane, 51. For discussion of the nature and authorship of Passus XII, see R. W. Chambers,
      'The Original Form of the A Text of "Piers Plowman"'; Edith Rickert, 'John But,
      Messenger and Maker'; Oscar Cargill, 'The Langland Myth'; Anne Middleton, 'Making a
      Good End'.
29   See Knott–Fowler, 150–3, and their discussion on 148–50. Knott–Fowler, of course,
      believed that several different authors wrote the poem.
30   We shall return to this point later (p. 358). Kane, a fierce believer in single authorship of the
      A, B, and C versions of *Piers Plowman*, normally resists interpretations of evidence which
      lend any credibility to the multiple authorship theory. The postulation of two separate
      archetypes for A does exactly that.
31   Quoted from Rigg–Brewer, 109–10; I have not reproduced the italics indicating expansion
      of abbreviations in the manuscript. These lines correspond to A Passus VIII 84–8 (Kane's
      text), A Passus VIII 85–9 (Skeat's text).

the next – inherit the earth; at the end of Passus XI the poor people 'pierce with a Pater-noster the palace of heaven, / Without penance at their departure into the High Bliss'.

Rigg–Brewer argue that Z represents the poet's first version of A, written before he wrote A, B, and C. If this is accepted (and many scholars do not accept it), then it would be possible to argue that Langland first 'ended' his poem with the explication of Truth's pardon (as in Z), which leaves the dreamer still asleep and does not really tackle the complexities his poem had addressed. So he went back and rewrote the whole thing, this time adding the pardon-tearing scene at the end of Passus VIII, waking his dreamer up, and having him briefly reflect on his dream (conventional enough for the dream-poem genre). But evidently this did not satisfy him either, since the end of Passus VIII raises as many problems as it resolves. So he returned to the ending again, setting the dreamer off on his search for Dowel in a new passus (IX), continuing for another three passus (to the end of XI) but leaving the dreamer still in his dream. No proper ending there, either, so Langland wrote a further stretch which continued the argument at the end of Passus XI but petered out, to be continued by a scribe calling himself John But. And next time he returned to the poem, he revised it from the beginning, to produce the version now surviving as B.[32]

As we have seen, then, Skeat fixes on Vernon as a paradigm text, using it as a bench-mark against which to rate other manuscripts. This process makes it virtually impossible for him not to attribute to Vernon some sort of authoritative status, if only by default. New manuscripts, like Ashmole, or Digby 145, were read only in part, to get a representative idea of how they compared with Vernon. If a manuscript looked obviously scribally corrupt, then it was dismissed, without regard for the fact that it might record stages previous to the one in which it was badly corrupted, and hence bear some sort of witness to authorial readings. And Skeat does not explain how he identifies scribal corruption, or in what he believes it to exist. What were these 'gross blunders'? Sheer nonsense? Or simply readings which made sense in context but which he regarded as inferior? The only manuscript on which he gives us such evidence is L, where he describes the over-alliteration.

---

[32] Though cf. Donaldson's 1955 interpretation of B-MSS R and F, p. 264 n. 15 below.

No doubt an unavoidable element in his decisions about which manuscripts to collate, and to what degree, was their relative accessibility. He possessed a transcript of Vernon, and had an assistant (Edmund Brock)[33] who helped him collate this with the three Harleian manuscripts in the British Museum (*A-Text*, p. xvi n. 1). He would have had easy access to the Trinity manuscript used by Wright in Cambridge. All the others were further afield: the Lincolns Inn manuscript was in London, and the four remaining manuscripts in Oxford (one, University, in a college library, and three – MSS Douce, Digby, and Ashmole – in the Bodleian Library). The fact that Skeat collated Vernon with University throughout may suggest either that he borrowed the manuscript from the college, or that he again used a transcript.[34]

Skeat's A-Text wore the trappings of a critical edition, that is, one constructed from the readings of the different available manuscript witnesses; but in fact, Skeat collated only *four* manuscripts in full, and consulted only *three* others (although he describes a total of ten). So while his method might have appeared inductive, with his call for manuscripts and his comparison of different versions in the 1866 tract, once embarked on editing A, Skeat proceeded by prior hypothesis – the hypothesis that Vernon was more likely than not to represent the original version of what (again by hypothesis) he regarded as the first discrete version of the poem. To some extent, this was inevitable: it is impossible to be entirely free from preconceptions.[35] But we would now recognise that a better approach would have been to wait, read through all the manuscripts thoroughly, and then come to some sort of conclusion as to the relation between manuscripts and versions: in other words, to have tested the hypothesis in a more open-minded way against much more evidence. Had Skeat done this, however – had he had the temperament *not* to rush into print – would he ever have published? In this respect it is irresistible to compare the pragmatist Skeat with the perfectionist Bradshaw, who could not 'bear the thought of any publication *coming forth with authority*, when it is merely the result of a few hasty and crude speculations, which a little fair preliminary discussion

---

[33] Brock also helped Skeat with transcribing C-MSS; see p. 161 below. He re-edited *Morte Arthure* for EETS (OS 8, 1871).

[34] University College manuscripts were not deposited in the Bodleian Library until 1882; see E. Craster, *History of the Bodleian Library*, 189.

[35] On the inevitable circularity of editing, cf. p. 349 below.

would get rid of'.[36] To call Skeat's speculations crude and hasty is harsh, but in some respects just.

Skeat's A-Text Preface included a number of other sections: an explanation of the method of printing the critical apparatus (indicating the unfamiliarity of this sort of edition, drawing on more than one manuscript source, to the EETS readership); a 'few words on alliterative verse', briefly explaining the principle that each line contained three alliterating staves; discussion of the poem's date and the relation between the three versions; an account of the author's life; and finally a summary of the A version passus by passus.

He dismisses the possibility that different writers were responsible for the later versions ('There were not two Langlands, surely'), and reviews the known evidence on Langland's name, quoting Bale on Robert, but preferring the evidence of the Dublin manuscript ascription discovered by Madden that the author's first name was William. He adduces further internal support for this theory, referring to Tyrwhitt's quotation of the C-Text reading, 'And sayde, *Wille*, slepest thou' at Passus I 5, and adding the reference to 'Wille' (in Vernon 'oure Wille') at Passus A IX 118. He has far more to say about the likely biographical profile of the poet than anyone before him, for the simple reason that he is the first person to have read the various versions sufficiently thoroughly to build up some idea of the picture which the poet paints of the narrator. (He rejects any notion that it is helpful to distinguish between the author and the dreamer in *Piers Plowman*: 'I can see no reason why we should think that the author is always trying to deceive us about himself; and certainly, Langland is the last man one would suspect of not speaking everything straight out'.)[37]

So what sort of edition of A did Skeat actually produce? As his Introduction indicates, he signalled with square brackets in the text all his departures from the testimony of Vernon. His footnotes record the readings of the three other collated manuscripts, and, as he says, periodically the readings of the three further manuscripts which he also consulted. He retained the thorns and yoghs of his manuscript, reverting to the practice of Whitaker (Crowley and Wright had replaced thorns and yoghs with modern spelling equivalents). At the end of the text he included a section of 'Critical Notes', which 'explain a few things more at length with respect to the various

---

[36] G. W. Prothero, *A Memoir of Henry Bradshaw*, 216–17.
[37] *A-Text* xxxvi; cf. George Kane, *The Autobiographical Fallacy in Chaucer and Langland Studies*; Anne Middleton, 'William Langland's "Kynde Name"'.

readings of the MSS.; to have inserted them in the footnotes [i.e., critical apparatus] would have been inconvenient' (p. 138). To some extent, these notes appear to be afterthoughts; they make illuminating reading since they spell out more clearly some of Skeat's assumptions about the text of *Piers Plowman*. The issues that repeatedly arise are (1) the accuracy and reliability of Vernon, (2) the relationship between the A- and B-Texts, and (3) Langland's alliterative practices.

Often all three of these issues combine as in Skeat's discussion of one of the first lines in the poem, Pro 14. Here Vernon reads

I sauh a Tour on A Toft *wonderliche* I-maket.

Three other manuscripts known to Skeat, TUH³, read *triȝely* instead of *wonderliche*, and in this they agree with the B-Text.[38] H, as often V's close partner, reads *wondurly*, while the other manuscript Skeat consulted, D, reads *trewlich*. (Unusually, he has looked up the reading in all seven of the manuscripts he used.) By three separate criteria *triȝely* is the superior reading: first, that it makes as good (or better) sense in the context as *wonderliche*, but seems to have been a rarer and harder word (cf. *OED* s.v. *try*, *a.*, which cites two occurrences of the adverb, one of them this one. This dictionary would not, of course, have been available to Skeat). Secondly, it causes the line to alliterate regularly, as it does not with *wonderliche*. And finally, *triȝely* is the variant that, if assumed original, *explains* the existence of the other two readings. Since it is a hard word, it would have been liable to misunderstanding by scribes: and it is both feasible and plausible that the ancestor of V and H simply substituted a simpler word, approximating very fairly to the guessed-at meaning of the original; while D's reading resulted from a misreading: the word *trewlich* has roughly the same palaeographical shape, it alliterates, and its sense is not intolerable in context.

Skeat does not mention the first or third of these criteria for discussion. (Where the first is concerned, it is remarkable how little he comments on the content of the poem in these Critical Notes, and how little he invokes nuances of sense as a reason for making a choice between variants.[39] As for the third criterion: the principle that the

---

[38] The line occurs in fifteen of the seventeen A-MSS. They vary as follows: *triȝely* TRUH²EKW; *trewlich* DChJLM; *wonderliche* VH. Z (the version in Bodley 851) reads *tryeliche*. B has the same line as A, while Skeat's C-Text reads, 'And sawe a toure, as ich trowede · truthe was þer-ynne' (Passus I 14).

[39] Though he elsewhere invokes the 'canon of criticism that a *rum* reading is very likely to be *right*'; see below, p. 136.

probable original of a number of different variants is the one that will, among other things, explain how the rival variants came into existence, seems not to have penetrated Middle English textual criticism for some forty years.)[40] Instead, Skeat is merely concerned with the alliteration. His remark is so interesting that I shall quote it in full.

> I have altered *wonderliche* to *triȝely* to preserve the alliteration, although MS. H supports the reading of V. The fuller alliterations found in the later copies were no doubt due, partly to corrections by the author himself, and partly to emendations (often ignorantly made) by copyists. Thus in l. 20,[41] *Erynge* [the reading of MSS VH in the line *In Eringe and in Sowynge swonken ful harde*] was soon changed (no doubt by the author) into *settyng*, but it does not follow that the alteration should be made in this early text. Nevertheless, I have ventured to write *triȝely* here, for the reason given by Mr Wright in making a similar change. 'Though we find instances of irregularity in the sub-letters (or alliterative letters in the first [part of the] line) in Pierce Plowman, the chief-letter is not so often neglected.' [Wright and Skeat understand the 'chief-letter' to refer to the third stave in the line – that occupied by *triȝely* in the first example and *swonken* in the second.][42] In other places, I have not always given my reason for making alterations in the text, but the footnotes will generally supply one; and besides, I have always had regard to Text B. (p. 138)

This raises a number of different issues. First, it is not quite clear what Skeat (or Wright) means by stating that the third stave in a line is the one least likely to be irregular, since there are very frequent instances of this in the manuscripts (as indicated by the fact that a large number of the emendations made to the B-Text by Kane and Donaldson, for example, *correct* non-alliterating third staves).[43] Since Skeat had already, even so early in his editing career, almost certainly read more

---

[40] See p. 230 below.   [41] *Sic*; actually line 21 in Skeat's text.

[42] The term 'chief-letter' corresponds to 'head-stave'; cf. Old Icelandic *höfuf[*eth]-stafr*. See Richard Cleasby and Gubrandur Vigfusson, eds., *An Icelandic-English Dictionary* (Oxford, 1874), 308; also R. K. Rask, *Angelsaksisk Sproglære* (Stockholm, 1817), 108, translated (with revisions by Rask) by Benjamin Thorpe, *A Grammar of the Anglo-Saxon Tongue* (Copenhagen, 1830), 135; James Bosworth, *The Elements of Anglo-Saxon Grammar* (London, 1823), 216 n. 7; E. Guest, *A History of English Rhythms* (London, 1838), vol. II, 14 (note), and the re-edition of Guest by Skeat (London 1882), 313 n. 1. I am grateful to E. G. Stanley for these references. Skeat's quotation is from Wright's justification for his emendation of *synnelees* to *giltles* at B Pro 34 (*The Vision and the Creed of Piers Ploughman*, vol. II, 505–6); for discussion of this crux see pp. 332–3 below.

[43] Possibly Wright and Skeat mean that the *author* did not tolerate non-alliterating third staves, but Wright's phrasing ('we *find* ... ') suggests they mean that scribes did not *write* non-alliterating third staves.

Piers Plowman manuscripts than Wright ever did, he need not have deferred to the senior editor in this respect. A more important point is raised by Skeat's speculation that 'The fuller alliterations found in the later copies were no doubt due, partly to corrections by the author himself, and partly to emendations (often ignorantly made) by copyists.' By 'the later copies' Skeat seems to mean copies of B and C, which do indeed, in the line he instances, read *settyng* rather than *erynge*. But so also do the A-MSS TH²D (as Skeat records in his critical apparatus), together with all extant manuscripts except VH *eringe*, J *sowing*, and RUE *seedtyme* (the latter two variants are evidently alliterating alternatives). Later editors (Knott–Fowler and Kane) have decided that *erynge* is a scribal error and that the original A-Text reading was the same as that of B and C, *settyng*. Skeat offers no explanation for the existence of *settyng* in TH²D, and the agreement between these manuscripts and the two later texts. But what might he have suggested? Did he mentally classify it as an example of scribal emendation? If so, why not consider the simpler alternative that VH's reading was in error here? It is difficult to answer these questions.[44] But the phrasing of Skeat's remark, which links together the author with 'ignorant copyists', raises a problem that perhaps should have bedevilled *Piers Plowman* textual criticism far more than it has: the question how much of the differences between texts should be attributed to the author, and how much to scribes. How do we know whether a scribe was responsible for emending apparently defective alliteration in a text that the author himself made revisions to? By the standards of later editing, Skeat acts very boldly by deciding that an apparently inferior reading is to stand, even though it is corrected – by author or scribe – in subsequent versions.

Classical editing by recension, according to the method popularly attributed to Lachmann, or according to older eclectic methods,[45] proceeds on a number of important premises: for example, that authors wrote uniformly well (in contrast with scribes); that where a number of textual variants exist, the best reading is the original; that the criteria for distinguishing 'good' writing' and the 'best' reading are unambiguous and not subject to question. But these premises do not consort well with what are generally agreed to be the facts of the

---

[44] He might also have considered that the agreement was due to contamination of these three manuscripts from B and/or C.

[45] For discussion and references, see Kenney, *The Classical Text*, 21–74.

composition of *Piers Plowman*: that the author changed his mind about the desirability of readings, and substituted one for another as he rewrote the poem. This suggests that, in his eyes at least, some of his readings, authorial though they might be, were inferior to others.

Where the third stave is concerned, however, as with *triȝely*, Skeat regularly emends V's defective reading to the reading found in T and related A-MSS together with B (and often C). Examples occur at Passus IV 11, 69, V 199; VI 30, 98, 99; IX 3, 11, 32. Skeat's remark on the first of these, IV 11, gives a good idea of how unreliable his collation can be. The line reads 'And A-Counte with Concience · (so me [Crist] helpe!)'; and his critical apparatus gives VHUD as reading *god* for *Crist*. Skeat comments that he has inserted '*Crist* for *god* on the sole authority of T, because it is the reading of Text B, and supplies the chief letter'. But H², a manuscript Skeat says he consulted 'in difficult passages', also reads 'Crist' – and would, had he cited it, have given his emendation additional authority. And he emends to the reading of the other A-MSS and B on other occasions too – when V has defective alliteration in another part of the line, as at Passus IX 24, or when it omits an apparently necessary word, as at Passus IX 24, or when other A-MSS have whole lines that are found in the later versions – as at Passus VI 57, IX 4–5, IX 12, and notably V 202–7. In the last instance, Skeat comments, 'Though these lines are in U only, they appear in all the later versions of the poem, and are certainly genuine.' His successor George Kane disagreed with him, regarding the agreements between B/C and a few A-MSS in small numbers of lines scattered throughout Passus V as due to some form of contamination.[46]

Skeat emends V far more frequently in the later than in the earlier part of the poem, indicating that he gained confidence in dismissing the readings of his base manuscript as his editing experience increased. His final remark quoted above, 'I have always had regard to Text B', is borne out by a number of emendations towards the end of the poem where he adduces B's reading as confirmatory support (e.g. Passus VIII 73, 106, 109, 114, 128; X 204–5, 213; XI 79, 85, 96).[47] Skeat's notes often look like second thoughts, written after he had decided on the text – perhaps, given the speed with which the edition

---

[46] See Kane, 30–1, and pp. 358 and 391ff. below.
[47] Contrast his retention of V's readings earlier, and his respective discussions in the Critical Notes, at Pro 14, 75; Passus I 39, 79, 87, 135; II 9, 118, 129, 206; III 32, 174, 266–9; V 125 (where he states, 'My object is to avoid alteration as much as possible').

was produced, after the text had reached the proof stage. So they sometimes seem to record what he would do were he now to re-edit the text: so at V 195, he reproduces Passus V's reading *I-wipet* in the line 'And weschte þat hit weore I-wipet · with a wesp of Firsen'; but he comments in the Notes, 'I suppose the true text to be *wexed*, as in Text B, and in T, H, and U.' (For similar examples of second thoughts, see the notes on Passus II 9 and II 64.)

Skeat shows some considerable interest and skill in tracing the process of scribal error, an area of expertise almost completely unexplored by his predecessors. Passus III 99–100 reads in his text

> Corteisliche þe kyng · Cumseþ to telle,
> To Meede þe Mayden [meleþ þeose] Wordes.

As Skeat comments, 'there is no doubt that such should be the reading; but in V the scribe has mis-written it *melodyes*, which is nonsense; in T and H² we find *melis þise*; in U it is *moueþ þese*; D corruptly has *mekely þese*'. His note to line 100 describes how V's reading arose: 'the *y* and þ are, throughout, only distinguishable by careful inspection; and thus *melodyes* is put for *melod þes*, i.e. spake these. Nevertheless, it seems better to use the *present* tense *meleþ* (as in the other MSS.), and to adopt the usual spelling *þeose*.' It is also interesting to see how his natural reluctance to alter manuscript testimony leads him to retain word order which he regards as inelegant, but which would now be seen as characteristic of Langland's abrupt and knotty *usus scribendi*: on Passus III 105 he comments 'It would greatly improve the alliteration to read *late com* instead of *com late*; but the chief-letter is not unfrequently thus badly placed; *see* ll. 93, 124.' The three lines in question, whose placing of the third stave is shared by all Skeat's A-MSS, are

þþe suffraunce þat ȝe suffre · such wrongus to be wrouȝt (93)
Ichaue a kniht hette Concience · com late from bi-ȝonde (105)
þþer nis no beter Baude · (bi him þat me made!) (124).[48]

As the above examples will make clear, Skeat's text looks reasonably different from the one with which we are now familiar, that of George Kane. The frequent occasions on which Vernon's reading diverges from that found in most of the other manuscripts (Kane records 230 readings which it shares with Harley 875 alone, many of

---

[48] Other examples of careful discussion of variants occur at Passus XI 285, X 191–3.

which are reproduced in Skeat's text),[49] result in a significant number of lexical differences between the two editions. And Skeat's respect for Harley 875 (H), and his consequent retention of the occasional single or two or three lines found in that manuscript alone, immediately strike anyone comparing the two texts. These lines are not found in any other manuscript, and they often fail to alliterate, and restate in an obvious way matters already clearly communicated in the poem. The result is sometimes flabby or diffuse; but occasionally they rise to a higher standard, leading one to question whether they might not be worth retaining (see e.g. the lines after Passus II 129, listed with the other unique material in H, about sixty lines in total, at Kane pp. 45–7).[50]

Skeat maintains that all important manuscript variants were recorded in his critical apparatus. He states that he has not always noticed minor variants such as *ac* for *but*, and that 'The object, throughout, has been to crowd into the foot-notes as much information as possible, so that the amount of *additional* information which might be gained from a perusal of the MSS themselves should be the smallest possible, and that they may be found to be well represented in print as far as need be' (xxix–xxx). This statement – in essence false – caused a great deal of trouble, as we shall see. It gives the clear impression that Skeat's text of A was a *critical* text: viz. that it was a version of the A-Text constructed from a careful comparison of all the variants in the cited manuscripts.

It also gives the clear impression that Skeat's critical apparatus reliably indicates the range of manuscript support for any particular reading. Both these impressions would be strengthened by a light reading of Skeat's notes, which illustrate analytic, thoughtful, and sensible consideration of the various textual cruces.

However – and the speed with which Skeat completed his work is a sufficient explanation for this – his text frequently retained Vernon's readings in instances where it agreed with no or few other manuscripts, and Skeat sometimes failed to indicate in his critical apparatus or his notes that this was the case. A particularly interesting example is at Passus V 218, a line which in Vernon has the deadly sin Glutton declaring

---

[49] See Kane, 73–4.
[50] Skeat's text also looks different from Kane's because he paragraphs it, as he does his text of B and C. In this he followed Wright, and was himself to be followed by Knott–Fowler, Schmidt (see his note on punctuation and paragraphing, ix) and Pearsall. Crowley and Whitaker printed unparagraphed text, as do the Athlone editors.

For hungur oþer for Furst I make myn A-vou.

This is what Skeat prints in his text, although he notes in his critical apparatus that two other A-MSS, T and U, have the line in narrative form:

And auowide to faste for (any) hungir or þrist;

and that the A-MS H differs from either of these versions.[51] But he does not discuss the line in his notes. Had he consulted the other A-MSS known to him, he would have found that they agreed with TU rather than with Vernon (or H). Had he consulted the B-MSS (at Passus V 382), he would have found that they also agreed with T and U. In other words, the Vernon reading which Skeat prints in his text is entirely eccentric, and all but one of the remaining A-MSS, together with the B-MSS, agree on an alternative reading. If Skeat had been aware of this, he might have reconsidered his decision, judging instead that Vernon's version of the line was a corruption – not least because it makes rather less sense in context than the line almost unanimously found elsewhere.

Skeat later used this line to identify the *Piers Plowman* version in Bodley 851 (Z) as a B-Text rather than an A-Text, since it agreed with B not Vernon. Evidently his own collations let him down badly here, since most A-MSS agree with the B-Text and hence it is not possible to use the line as a distinguishing characteristic of one text rather than the other.

As we have seen, however, Skeat had on the whole mastered the B-Text pretty thoroughly during the process of editing A; and he passes on some of the fruits of his comparisons in a short but useful section, following his notes, which compared texts A and B line by line.[52] One consequence of reprinting the A-Text later in a completely different form, as part of a parallel-text edition which set A beside B and C across a double-page spread, was that the room for critical apparatus was drastically cut down, and Skeat – or his editors – pruned the recorded variants still further.[53]

Some flavour of the enthusiasm and attack with which Skeat went at his editing of A is conveyed by his remarks on a tiny crux, which I

---

[51] See Kane V 209 for A-MS variants.
[52] The extent to which it is proper or advisable to consult one text when editing another was later to become a significant issue; see p. 256 below.
[53] Skeat at this stage may still have believed that a parallel-text edition of the poem would be too difficult to produce: see *Parallel Extracts from Twenty-nine Manuscripts of Piers Plowman*, iv.

have identified as A Passus VIII 56 (corresponding to Kane VIII 55), written at the end of a letter to Furnivall which is largely on other matters. The letter is dated 28 February 1868, after the A-Text had been published, and presumably Skeat is replying to a criticism of Furnivall's. In a discussion of the rightful merits of lawyers, the poem reads (Skeat's text):

> Ac to bugge water, ne wynt [ne] wit, (is þe þridde),
> Nolde neuer holy writ God wot þe soþe!

As he records in his apparatus, Skeat follows the reading of manuscript T; *ne* is omitted by Vernon and H and U differ. Skeat does not record any other reading, and it is apparently this for which he has been taken to task by Furnivall, who is likely (given what we know of him) to have accused him of not sticking to the reading of his main source Vernon. Skeat writes,

> I am full of fight about my reading in Piers Plowman "ne witte" etc. for MS T *has* it. And the *three* Oxford MSS *have it* !!![54] I'll undertake to get 6 MSS for it easily – of *A* type – and I'll bet you'll find *no* MS that omits it altogether, except the *Vernon* only. Is it not a canon of criticism that a *rum* reading is very likely to be *right* – especially when 5 or 6 MSS agree about it? It is for *you* to *prove* it wrong. *I* stick by the *MSS*. And can count on your backing me if I do.[55]

Skeat was *almost* right: most A-MSS other than Vernon read *ne witte*. The two MSS UH, however, both frequently consulted by Skeat, read *or witte*, although Skeat in his eagerness to win his argument seems not to have noticed this.[56] Clearly, he should have checked all the manuscripts known to him before going into print rather than after, but his almost correct judgement is an illuminatingly typical instance of his ability to make sound guesses based on minimal evidence.

[54] Skeat presumably refers to the University College manuscript, and to the Ashmole and Douce manuscripts. This is puzzling, however, as while A and D read *ne*, U reads *or*, a reading it shares with H.

[55] I am grateful to Professor William Schipper for providing me with a transcript of this letter.

[56] Both the Rawlinson Poet. MS 137 (R), probably unknown to Skeat at this stage, and the National Library of Wales MS no. 733B (N), which was discovered in the next century, read *and witte*.

8

Skeat's *B-Text*

New manuscripts continued to turn up. By the time Skeat published his B-Text in 1869 he had discovered two more copies of *Piers Plowman* in Oxford, an A-MS and a B-MS, both identified during the process of re-cataloguing the Rawlinson collection in Bodley, and had been supplied with further information about the A-MS in Trinity College Dublin, of whose existence he learned just before the publication of his edition of A.

The interesting thing, of course, is to see how Skeat absorbs new information. He welcomed the discovery of the Rawlinson A-MS (p. 124 above) because it bore further witness to the extra twelfth passus hitherto found only in the University College A-MS (U), and he read the rest of the manuscript carefully enough to realise that it had a close textual relationship with U. This was signalled by the fact that both manuscripts have the same misordering of material (part of Passus VII occurring in Passus I). When Skeat went on to compare details of their readings, he found they often agreed in variants found in no other manuscripts; and for this reason he assumed that they shared a common exemplar.[1] Skeat did not, however, comb through the Rawlinson A-MS's text in order to search out possible original readings – not surprisingly, since he had not done this with any of the other manuscripts.

The other manuscript of the A-Text which Skeat had come across, the manuscript in Dublin to which he assigned the sigil E, seems to

---

[1]   Kane (81–2) records 210 variational agreements between these manuscripts, way ahead of the closest rival behind, WN's 130 agreements, and second only to VH's 230 agreements. It should be noted that these numbers are the result of a calculation that assumes that Kane's A-Text is exactly the same as Langland's original text – or perhaps the A-Text archetype. If Kane had made different identifications of original readings, then the figures would be correspondingly different. (If, for example, he had decided that many of the agreements between R and U were in right readings, which accurately represented Langland's original text, then the number of variational agreements between these two manuscripts would have been far fewer, indicating that they were not so closely genetically linked.)

have been first identified by Sir Frederick Madden.[2] Skeat gained
sufficient information from a detailed description of the manuscript
sent him by a Professor Dowden to work out that, in the Prologue at
least, it had links with U and R but also, confusingly, the B-Text and/
or C-Text.[3]

What is notable in Skeat's accounts of both R and E, brief as they
are, is his identification of their relationships with each other and with
U. Not only did he match the end of R with the end of U – an
obvious thing to do, given the fact that they both finished with an
extra passus – but he went back to the rest of their text and identified
other similarities. He found this an enlightening procedure, and so
applied it to the next manuscript he came across, E. Skeat makes no
reference to the Lachmannian procedure of establishing a stemma of
manuscript relationships by this sort of reading-by-reading comparison, and it may be that he almost stumbled into it, as a way of
making sense of the existence of so many different versions of the
same text. Certainly his edition of B builds on his apparently new
awareness that such a procedure of comparison may be very useful
for establishing a trustworthy picture of the character of the manuscripts and their variants. His description of the B-MSS follows the
same pattern as his edition of A; in each case he gives a full account of
the manuscript's appearance and contents, an indication of its probable date, and some characterization of its text. But with the B-MSS
he adds a new ingredient, viz. a classification into sub-groups,
although he provides us with no discussion or illustration of the
principles by which this sorting process has been conducted. Skeat
simply adds to the end of his description of the manuscripts the
following passage:

> *Comparison of the MSS., and their sub-classes.* I would here add, by
> way of recapitulation and a more complete exhibition of the relation
> of the MSS. to each other, that they are divisible into *sub-classes,*

---

[2]   See *B-Text*, vi–vii n.1. Madden presumably came across the manuscript at the same time
that he discovered the Stacy de Rokayle ascription in the Dublin C-Text manuscript (see
p. 52 above). On the two Dublin manuscripts, see further E. St John Brooks, 'The *Piers
Plowman* Manuscripts in Trinity College, Dublin'.

[3]   *B-Text*, vi n.1. It inserts material apparently derived from the later two versions at two
points in the Prologue; see Kane, 30. A letter written by Skeat dated 29 September 1869 (in
the possession of Karen Thomson), addressed to 'Dear Sir' (probably Dowden), makes clear
Skeat's excitement at the discovery that MS Dublin D.4.12 'is clearly the A-type'. He directs
his correspondent to compare it with his *A-Text*, now published, and is particularly anxious
to learn whether this manuscript too contains a copy of the twelfth passus.

each of which possesses certain characteristics. The agreement of those in the same sub-class is very strong.

And he produces a list dividing eleven of the manuscripts into four sub-classes (a, b, c and d). At the end of this he says, 'To the remaining MSS. I cannot certainly assign the right class.'[4]

Exactly what procedure of classification did he engage in? Since Skeat offers no explanation for the rationale of these so-called 'sub-groups', other than the implication that they are ranked according to their reliability, it is difficult to be quite sure. But he has presumably found that certain manuscripts group together in sharing variational readings, so much so that it seems a reasonable inference that the manuscripts thus linked share a common ancestor, i.e. are in some way genetically related. Two questions immediately arise. First, on what basis did Skeat decide what constituted a sub-class? Did he collate readings systematically from the manuscripts, or did he do spot-checks, of say, one passus? What did he count as significant agreement between the manuscripts? Obvious errors, dialect or spelling similarities, striking and unusual readings whether original or spurious? And secondly, what use did Skeat make of his classification? The standard (Lachmannian) procedure would be to classify all the manuscripts on the basis of shared error, and then use the resulting genealogical information to reckon up the strength of support for any one individual reading. So, for example, a reading found in the five manuscripts constituting Skeat's sub-class (b) (viz. YCBmBoCot) would not count for more than one original manuscript – the common ancestor of those five manuscripts – and an editor could justify the choice of a rival reading found in one manuscript in each of the other three groups (a), (c), and (d) on the grounds that they represented three separate original manuscripts. (It would be important that the other manuscripts in the various groups did not offer alternative possible readings, and it would help if the chosen reading was clearly superior, by whatever criteria, to that of the group (b) manuscripts.)

But it does not seem that Skeat formed or used his sub-texts with anything approaching even this rather basic degree of sophistication:[5] I have been able to find no indication in his critical apparatus or his

---

4 *B-Text*, xxxi. Sub-class (a) contained LR, (b) YCBoBmCot, (c) OC^2, (d) WCr. Skeat retrospectively classified the A-MSS in a similar way; see p. 175 below.

5 Skeat's parenthetic reference to the classification of L and W is hard to read; see p. 153 n. 42 below and cf. pp. 163–4.

notes that he *applied* his information on the way in which the B-MSS were related: not least because the alterations he made to the text of Laud were minimal.[6] As we have seen (p. 82 above), Skeat was later (1873) criticised by Henry Nicol for his failure to 'give a genealogical table' of the manuscripts of *Piers Plowman*, and thus 'test the truth of the proposition he apparently assumes, that if two or three of the best MSS. give a reading good in itself, we may, without consulting the others, infer it to be the author's'. It may be that Nicol, apparently alone of Skeat's contemporary readers, had analysed Skeat's text to discover that the classifications he provided were unsatisfactory.

Skeat took as the base for his B-Text the Laud manuscript in the Bodleian Library, again transcribed for him by George Parker.[7] 'I look upon this MS.', Skeat declared,

> as of the very highest importance. My original reason for printing it was that it seemed to me, after a short examination, much upon a par with the MS. printed by Mr. Wright, and I considered that, supposing the MSS. to be of nearly equal value, it would be a great gain to print the unprinted one, in order to have two complete copies of the poem in type.

This remark indicates a Furnivallian enthusiasm for reproducing manuscripts rather than editing them, but it is evident from Skeat's further remarks that he applied critical evaluation to the manuscript's readings from the start. 'I began my collation', he continues,

> with no very great respect for the MS., and was ready to amend it whenever it seemed to have inferior readings. But when, in several instances, after making some such alterations, larger knowledge compelled me to alter them back again, the case was altered. The conviction was gradually *forced* upon me that the MS. is of the highest order of excellence, and the chief authority on all difficult points. When, in certain doubtful places, after consulting the other MSS. of the B-class, the A-text, Whitaker's text, Crowley's text, the Cotton MS. of the C-text, &c., I found this Laud MS. helping me

---

[6] Thus Skeat makes nine emendations, almost all minor, to the text of Laud in the Prologue (a total of 230 lines), at lines 20, 39, 41, 67, 99, 151, 179, 224, 226 (I refer to his numbering, not that of Schmidt). Five of these (at 20, 67, 99, 151, and 226) are to improve grammar or spelling, two are slightly less insignificant (41 and 179), and two are substantive: 39, where Skeat adds a half-line, *is luciferes hyne*, omitted in Laud; and 224, where he substitutes *longe* for Laud's *dere* in the line 'And dryuen forth þe [longe] day with "*Dieu vous saue, Dame Emme!*"'. In both these cases, as Skeat notes, he follows the text of A (see further below, p 156).

[7] Parker also helped him with his collations of Bodley manuscripts (xlvi).

out of the difficulty for about the twentieth time, I felt compelled to
pay to it all due respect. (p. viii)

This account of the way in which Skeat's initial resistance to the
manuscript was overcome by increased acquaintance with it is proof
of his open-mindedness. It is also a clear indication that Skeat was
now reading the three texts side by side as he attempted to establish
the text of B. He was particularly convinced of the importance of
Laud by numerous crosses, both large and small, that appear in the
margin. The small crosses generally indicated an error in the text,
while the large ones occurred at points in the B-Text where, Skeat
says, changes were later made by the C reviser. This, coupled with the
fact that the hand looked possibly late fourteenth century,[8] tempted
Skeat to think, 'Indeed, it may be an autograph copy, as Langland was
very probably himself a poor professional scribe, and speaks with
scorn of those who could not write things out properly (B. xi. 299);
and this MS. is a good specimen of calligraphy.'

These may well seem slender grounds on which to base the
supposition that Langland himself should have been responsible for
the text of Laud. Such a theory virtually ruled out the possibility of
accepting readings from other manuscripts into the texts except under
extreme circumstances, when the reading of Laud was intolerable or
clearly in error. And Skeat's interpretation of the significance of the
crosses, both large and small, is highly questionable. There are many
differences between B and C which are not marked with a large cross
in Laud, and it is very possible that the marks were made by a scribe
or reader who simply made occasional comparisons of Laud's text
with a C-Text. The small crosses are susceptible of the same interpretation: several other of the manuscripts, notably the B-MSS M (BL
Add. 35287) and Hm (Huntington Library Hm 128), are marked by
correctors, and there is no reason why a corrector should not have
been responsible for the marks in Laud also. It is decidedly illogical of
Skeat to plump for this interpretation and argue for it on such
uncertain evidence, and it is difficult not to believe that he was moved
to present the evidence as he did simply to bolster up his independent
fondness for the quality of Laud's readings. Such partiality does not
indicate logical and rigorous scholarship.[9]

---

[8]   Kane–Donaldson date it to the beginning of the fifteenth century (10).
[9]   He later changed his mind: Jusserand reported in 1910 that Skeat no longer believed that
     Laud 581 was the poet's autograph copy of B; see '*Piers Plowman* ... A Reply', 24.

Skeat tries to anticipate criticism of his theory that the manuscript is Langland's own autograph:

> It has been objected, that the spelling is faulty; but is there any reason for supposing that Langland could or would have spelt better? It may also be objected that there are a few mistakes not marked for correction; but let any one try the experiment of writing out 7000 lines of poetry, and reading it once over afterwards. It is quite as correct as any autograph MS. can fairly be expected to be, and in any case it is (as far as the *sense* and *metre* are concerned) by far the best MS. of the B-text extant.[10]

Skeat returns to his defence of Laud in his discussion of dialect, as we shall see below (p. 152).

Skeat collated five B-MSS in full against Laud's text. One of these was the newly discovered manuscript in the Bodleian, Rawlinson Poet. 38 (R). Skeat triumphantly describes how he came across some folios removed from this manuscript in a process of 'shameful' maltreatment – during a bout of successful detective work he found them bound up in a manuscript in the British Museum. He reckoned that this manuscript was closely related to Laud: 'It agrees with the text, for instance, in giving the right date of Chichester's mayoralty,[11] and generally corroborates the reading of the text in difficult passages. It is therefore to be classed with the Laud MS as regards its general character.' But the manuscript raised difficult problems in another respect: when Skeat collated it closely against Laud's text, he found that 'it abounds in *omissions* and *additions* of no insignificant kind, although the mere *variations* are few. It is necessary to account for them ...' Comparing the manuscript with the A- and C-texts supplied the correct answer to the problem, Skeat believed. He found that 'the omissions (amounting to more than 150 lines) are mostly due to mere carelessness; a few coincide with the briefer narrative of the A-text; and some of them occur at points where the B- and C-texts vary'. The additions, on the other hand, which amounted to about 160 lines,

> almost invariably occur at points where the C-text is fuller than the B-text, and it is easily seen that the Rawlinson MS. really exhibits

[10] *B-Text*, x. Skeat adds a cautious footnote: 'That is, as far as I know at present. I am not at all sure that my list of MSS. is complete'; in fact, he knew of all extant B-MSS, although he did not (for some reason) take notice of the B-Text portion of Harley 3954 (H³ of A, H of B), already mentioned in his *A-Text* (xxiii), when describing B-MSS.

[11] Skeat had now discovered that 1370 is the correct date and changed his dating of B accordingly; see *B-Text*, iv.

the poem in its transition stage between these two forms, and the best idea of it is formed by calling it a copy of the B-text *with later improvements and after-thoughts*. (p. xii)

Skeat goes on to list both additions and omissions, but does not press his case any further.

This startling theory is not signalled with any prominence, and is not taken up by any scholars and critics for three-quarters of a century.[12] But it is remarkable nonetheless. Unlike Skeat's opinion that Laud was the author's own autograph copy of B, it has a good deal to recommend it. Skeat's method of presenting his argument is the same with both Laud and Rawlinson: he states his interpretation of the evidence, and then gives a list of line-references so that the reader may make some sort of assessment of his hypothesis by looking up instances referred to in the text (although to do so would have been a long and laborious task).[13] But where an alternative hypothesis instantly springs to mind to explain the presence of the various crosses in Laud – that they were made by a corrector comparing his manuscript with other versions of the poem, a practice not infrequent with *Piers Plowman* manuscripts – the alternative where R is concerned is less easily arrived at. That an author who spent his life writing and rewriting a poem, and who seems to have produced at least three distinct versions, may have left traces of intermediate versions recording partial revision of one text to another might seem an obvious theory to anyone untrammelled by the 'search for editorial certainty'.[14] But it is a theory that, as we shall see, causes immense problems for editors trying to produce full critical editions (as Skeat's, in fact, were not) of any one of the three texts. (In this way it is very similar to another obvious supposition, put forward by Whitaker, that Langland, as he wrote and rewrote, may sometimes have 'debased' his original version.)

The second manuscript Skeat collated in full against Laud was the Trinity B-Text printed by Wright, to which Skeat would have had easy access in Cambridge. He found it 'somewhat inferior to the Laud MS.', and to exhibit a 'slightly varied form of the poem; but the difference between them only comes out after verbal collation of the whole poem'. He judged it to be closely related to the manuscript

---

12 See E. T. Donaldson, 'MSS R and F', and p. 264 n. 15 below.
13 Skeat's list is not exhaustive. Compare Kane–Donaldson, 66–9.
14 Pearsall's phrase; see below, p. 350.

used by Crowley (a view confirmed by later collation),[15] and groups the putative Crowley manuscript with Trinity in his sub-class (d).

Also collated in full was the Oriel College manuscript used by Whitaker: 'the first thing I discovered in it was a piece of paper marking the passage which he [Whitaker] printed at p. xxxv. of his Preface. His quotation is printed with such great carelessness, that the only way of giving the reader a fair idea of what the MS. is like is to print it again', which Skeat does. He describes the manuscript as 'much the neatest, and probably altogether the best, of the MSS. which are written *continuously*, i.e. without a break at the end of each paragraph'[16] – suggesting that he assumes a correlation between neatness of handwriting and accuracy of text. Here, for the first time in his description of either A- or B-MSS, Skeat mentions the *dialect* in which the version is written – 'Midland'.[17] He notes that it agrees in places with two other B-MSS, C and B (see below), 'but it is clearly superior to both of these MSS., and, as it frequently offers *peculiar* readings, and is, as it were, an independent witness, it was very necessary to collate it throughout.'[18] Oriel was accordingly put in a separate sub-group, (c), where it was joined by the Cambridge University Library MS Ll. 4. 14 (C²), which Skeat thought was probably a copy of Oriel. He collated it, therefore, throughout the two passages where Oriel lacked text (owing to lost leaves at Passus XVII 97–344 and XIX 283–355), and 'occasionally consulted [it] in other passages'.[19]

The vast folio MS CUL Dd. 1. 17 (C) was also collated throughout. Despite its many 'defects, corruptions, and peculiarities', Skeat felt it was an important witness which 'follows the text very closely', and he

---

[15] Cf. Kane–Donaldson, 38ff., 42ff., 49ff.

[16] Skeat notes that Laud, Rawlinson, Trinity, Yates-Thompson, and the Ashburnham MS now BL Add. 35287, are all paragraphed, while the remaining manuscripts are written continuously. He reproduces Laud's paragraphs in his text. See p. 134 n. 50 above.

[17] M. L. Samuels identifies the Oriel manuscript's dialect as N. Herts. See 'Dialect and Grammar', 206–7.

[18] *B-Text*, xvii. Evidently Skeat borrowed the manuscript for some length of time; cf. Furnivall's account of how, when visiting Skeat in Cambridge, 'before tea, Mr. Skeat showed me the copy of *The Vision of Piers Plowman* which the Provost and Fellows of Oriel had been good enough to lend him for his edition of "Text B"' (*Caxton's Book of Curtesye*, v). Blackman later observed that 'the collations of O in the accepted B-text are often erroneous', and provides a short list of those necessary for her paper ('Notes on the B-Text MSS of *Piers Plowman*', 507 n.47).

[19] The two manuscripts are closely related; Kane–Donaldson (21) identify 330 agreements, the largest number to be found between any pair of B-MSS other than the 504 agreements between R and F. As noted above, C² contains a short glossary to its text of *Piers Plowman*, which Skeat reproduces, with comment, as an appendix to his *B-Text* (421–6).

even incorporated into the text a handful of its unique (or nearly unique) lines.[20] He classed it as (c), a group into which fell the last manuscript to be collated in full, Bodley 814 (Bo). This manuscript was unusually closely related to two in the British Library, Add. 10574 (Bm) (the manuscript originally belonging to Heber which Wright, and initially Skeat, wrongly thought had been used by Whitaker as his copy-text), and Cotton Caligula A XI. (Cot). Skeat regards these manuscripts as a disappointment, especially Bo, since its neatly written appearance and early date seemed to promise well. But the text of the three is eccentric in shape: it starts off as a C-Text, switches to A around the end of Passus II, and finally turns to B from III onwards.[21] Skeat seems to have approached this bizarre combination without prejudice: 'Whence this form of the poem arose it is not easy to tell. As MS. R represents the B-text, with amendments in the *latter* part of the poem, it may be that MS. B [i.e. Bm] represents the same, with amendments near the *beginning*. But this is not very likely.' The adoption of an A-Text in between the C and B portions led him to 'feel tolerably sure that it is, in fact, a corrupt version, the misarrangements of which are due to the scribe only, who pieced together the Prologue and three first Passus as well as he could, and then followed a B-text copy throughout the rest of the poem'. This opinion was corroborated by the fact that many of its readings in its B-text section were corrupt. Nevertheless, he collated its text throughout on account of its closeness to Bo and Cot ('to collate one of these is precisely the same as collating all three; and to collate *three* MSS. at a time is a thing worth doing' – a very Skeatsian view, one feels).[22] And there was another reason for collation as well, one which Skeat has not previously mentioned but which indicates an increase in editorial experience: 'the collation … shews how corruptions arise, and where to expect them, and even helps to establish the correctness of the text by mere force of contrast'. This suggests Skeat is beginning to get a 'feel' for typical scribal errors, and to derive benefit from examining even faulty manuscripts, because this increases his knowledge of typical scribal behaviour. And indeed, as in his edition of A,

---

[20] Though he later decided this had been a mistake; see xii n.1.

[21] Skeat evidently did not realise that these three manuscripts contained any A lines when he edited A, and Kane, too, seems to have been ignorant of this when he published his edition of A many years later; see his second edition, 459. Skeat did use the three manuscripts for his edition of C; see *C-Text*, x.

[22] Skeat makes various further remarks on Bo in his Critical Notes, *B-Text*, 391–3. But he later felt that he had given the manuscript undue attention; cf. *C-Text*, x.

Skeat shows clear signs of a developing interest in tracing the processes of scribal error.[23]

Skeat did not, however, make the results of his collation of these five manuscripts against Laud fully available to his readers. On the first page of his text, he lists the sigils for Laud, Trinity, Oriel, Rawlinson, Dd. 1. 17 and Ll. 4. 14, and states, unclearly, that 'readings from the last of these are given only occasionally'.

The remaining manuscripts were collated either not at all or in part. BL Add. 35287, one of the former Ashburnham manuscripts (Appendix 129; M) was read but not collated, despite being judged 'a very fair copy of the B-text'. (As pointed out by Kane–Donaldson, this manuscript presents a problem insofar as it appears written in a varying hand – possibly several hands, and extensive alterations have been made by correctors at various different stages. So it has all the signs of a seriously contaminated manuscript: its genealogical character irretrievably adulterated by correctors comparing other manuscripts and introducing alien readings into it.)[24] The second Ashburnham manuscript (130), now Huntington Library MS 128 (Hm, Hm[2]), Skeat regarded as 'altogether inferior' to M. He was interested in it chiefly on account of the fifteenth-century note inside the front cover which reads 'Robert or william langland made pers ploughma*n*.' John Bale's note on the author of *Piers Plowman* is 'squeezed in between this older note and the lower margin of the cover', and the fact that the hand of the first note is older made Skeat judge it to be more reliable than Bale's testimony, and valuable, of course, since it offered the alternative *William* for the author's first name.[25] Otherwise, the second Ashburnham manuscript was notable chiefly for the peculiar way in which it was bound up. Skeat says of this version that it 'has been much spoilt by attempted corrections. These are written over erasures and are almost always alterations for the worse,' and Kane and Donaldson agree with this judgement nearly one hundred years later.[26] The most obvious example is in the

---

[23] See e.g. the remarks in his notes on Passus V 627, VII 137, XII 192–3, XV 564–7, XVIII 41.

[24] See Kane–Donaldson, 11, 44, and 50.

[25] The second note is in Bale's own hand. See Kane, *The Evidence for Authorship*, 37–42, for discussion of both this and the ascription to 'Robert or william'.

[26] The manuscript contains one complete version of the B-Text (fos. 113a–205a), together with two portions from (apparently) a different version of B – Passus III 50–72a, written out on the recto side of fol. 95, and Passus II 209–III 49, written out on both recto and verso sides of fol. 96. (The line references are Kane–Donaldson's.) Both *Piers Plowman* versions are written in several hands, not clearly detectable by the naked eye; after the manuscript reached the Huntington Library it was carefully examined with ultraviolet light and

first line, 'In a somer sesoun whanne softe was the sonne', where *softe* has been altered to *set*, as in Crowley's text.[27]

Another Cambridge manuscript was CUL Gg. 4. 31 (G) – 'an unpromising MS. to look at, but ... considerably better than it appears to be, having been transcribed from a very fair and tolerably complete older copy. It follows our text pretty closely, its chief variations seeming generally to agree with the readings of MSS. Y and O.' This must have troubled Skeat, since such affiliation cut across his sub-classes (b) and (c), and he does not classify the manuscript. Apparently he did not collate it in any detail or with any consistency, and he does not cite its readings in his critical apparatus or notes.[28]

One of the most interesting of the B-Text manuscripts is Corpus (Oxford) 201 (F). Curiously enough, Skeat did not expend much effort on it, although this would certainly, in the eyes of subsequent editors, have repaid his pains. 'The MS. is of the B-type, but frequently, it appears to me, corrupt. It contains several lines not in other copies, but their genuineness is doubtful ... It is evidently an inferior MS.; yet it may be worth consulting in a case of difficulty. Thus in xiv. 188 it reads – "& if þe *powke* plede," &c. – which is unquestionably right' (F's reading *powke*, 'devil', is shared – as Skeat might have discovered – with R; the remaining manuscripts read *pope*, which as he indicates will not work in context). Skeat was chiefly impressed by Corpus' novel arrangement of the passus divisions: 'it would seem as if the scribe had endeavoured to divide it into Passus how he could, without any guide, and had added a few lines by way of conclusion and introduction to each, for it is just at the points of division that the readings seem to be the wildest'.[29] In fact, the divisions are not as wilfully eccentric as Skeat suggests; they tend to

---

microscopes, and the hands of three text-writers and two correctors in the main version were identified. See Kane–Donaldson, 9–10; also R. B. Haselden, 'The Fragment of *Piers Plowman* in Ashburnham No. CXXX', and R. W. Chambers, 'The Manuscripts of *Piers Plowman* in the Huntington Library'. A. I. Doyle comments, 'the number and nature of the conspicuous alterations ... suggest that they were from pedantic rather than commercial motives, and occasioned by difficulties in the exemplar' ('The Manuscripts', 94).

27 Skeat comments that this 'seems to prove that the alteration was made after Crowley's edition [which also reads *set* for *softe*] was published. It is incredible that any MS. should have had *set*, when the time referred to is the early morning; nor have I seen *set* in any other MS. whatever. Nor do I believe that Crowley's MS. had *set*; it must have been his mistake' (*B-Text*, xxii n.1; cf. xxxiii n.1, and discussion of this crux by Warton, Percy and Ritson mentioned above, p. 28).

28 G contains a novel feature, a table or index to the poem, entitled 'here ynsuethe yᵉ table off pyers plowman' (on fos. 101b–3a). As Skeat says, it is 'merely a sort of abstract, made to serve the purpose of a brief index, and is of no value [for editing the poem]' (*B-Text*, xxiii).

29 *Ibid.*, xxvii.

coincide with the divisions between *dreams*.[30] It is difficult to be sure how closely Skeat looked at the manuscript; he actually reproduces in his edition the first and last lines of F's passus divisions, which means it is barely credible that the reasonably strong correlation with the beginning and endings of dreams did not strike him. Much more significant is his failure to realise that F agrees time after time – both in individual readings and in its omission and addition of lines – with the Rawlinson B-MS, which as we have seen Skeat took very seriously. Both Kane–Donaldson and Schmidt have identified these two manuscripts as a separate branch of the B-Text tradition, descending from an exemplar in many respects superior to the common exemplar of the remaining manuscripts, and adopted many of the readings peculiar to RF (or just F) into their texts.[31]

The Yates-Thompson manuscript (Y) seems to have been the last of the B-MSS turned up by Skeat.[32] He collated only three passages from the later part of the poem, totalling some 800 lines.[33] Skeat thanks Mr. Thompson 'for his kindness in lending me this MS., and so enabling me to become thoroughly acquainted with its contents at my leisure' (p. xv); so his partial collation must have been due, not to pressure from Thompson to return the manuscript, but to the fact that his text was already established, and he thought it of little interest to include Y's variants from other parts of the poem. This supposition seems to be confirmed by his letter of thanks to Thompson, preserved in Newnham College Library, which is dated 9 December 1869 – i.e., very shortly before his edition appeared. He writes,

> I am so much obliged to you for your loan of the MS. of Piers Plowman. I hope the E. E. T. S. will duly send you a copy of my book. Meanwhile, I send you a description of your MS. on a separate slip – thinking you may like to have it in that form. On p. xxxi of my preface, you will find a scheme, shewing the *exact* place of your MS. as compared with others. I call it copy 1 of sub-class *b* of class B. [A footnote here adds 'B. b. *alpha* will be my final notation'.] This defines it to a nicety.

This letter may have impressed Mr Yates-Thompson but can scarcely have enlightened him.

---

[30] For a recent discussion of the scribe's organisation of his material, see James Weldon, '*Ordinatio* and Genre in MS CCC 201'.

[31] See pp. 386–8 below.

[32] He later came across another B-MS, the second Heber manuscript used by Whitaker, now Hm 114, bringing the total known to him to fifteen. See p. 162 n. 9 below.

[33] Viz. 'XVI. 56–91, XVII. 96–340, XVIII. 411–XX. 27' (*B-Text*, xiv).

So much for the B-MSS and Skeat's description of them. As with the A-MSS, it appears that he collated in their entirety few manuscripts in comparison with those available – six out of fourteen, a point again completely missed by his enthusiastic reviewers (other than Nicol).[34] Nevertheless, he evidently looked at each with some thoroughness – more, possibly, than was the case with the A-MSS,[35] and hence was able to make some general observations about the character of the B-Text that still hold true today.

Compared with the A-MSS, the B-MSS were remarkably homogeneous. Skeat says of the A-Text that it 'shewed the poem as originally sketched, and the MSS. were found to be in most cases imperfect either at the beginning or the end, and there were a considerable number of various readings'. The unspoken implication here is that the copies of A were made before the poet had finished his poem properly; and indeed, as we have seen, there are various indications that this was the case. In great contrast,

> the B-text, though nearly three times the length, is frequently found in a perfect state, and the numerous MSS. of it agree together in a way which is sometimes astonishing. It is not uncommon to find five consecutive lines alike in all the MSS. as far as arrangement of the words is concerned, and this likeness sometimes prevails even to minute correspondences of inflections and spelling. (p. xxxix)

This is certainly true, and may be observed by any reader who opens the two *Piers Plowman* editions of Kane and Kane–Donaldson, lays them side by side, and measures the difference in length of the space taken on the average page of text by the critical apparatus of A and B respectively.[36] The inference Skeat draws from the consistency of agreement between B-MSS may seem at first sight an obvious and fair one:

---

[34] Collated in full against the Laud MS were the Rawlinson, Trinity, and Oriel B-MSS together with MSS Dd. 1. 17 in the Cambridge University Library and Bodley 814. For characteristic reception of Skeat's editions, cf. *North British Review*, OS 52 (NS 13) (April 1870), 241–5. As already mentioned, Skeat did not refer to the conjoint B/A-MS Harley 3954 (H³) in his account of B-MSS or in his critical apparatus and notes. He does, however, include mention of a transcript of Rogers' printed edition of 1561 in the library of Caius College, Cambridge (*B-Text*, xxx), and in his edition of C (l) the extracts from a B-Text copy of *Piers Plowman* in MS James 2, Bodleian Library (on which see p. 20 above and Chambers and Grattan, 'The Text of "Piers Plowman"' (1931), 50 n.3; the writers seem to be correct in dismissing this as 'almost negligible').

[35] For example, Skeat has changed his principles for recording variants in footnotes. In the *A-Text*, he explicitly stated that he did not bother to note 'and' for 'ac' (xxix); in the *B-Text* it is clear that in many instances he did note this particular variation (xxv).

[36] Skeat makes the same point for his two editions (*B-Text*, xxxix).

> Hence there is a certainty, a firmness, and a conclusiveness about the text which is very satisfactory. There are probably more doubtful points in a single Canterbury Tale or in a single Act in some of Shakespeare's plays than in the whole of the B-text of Piers the Plowman.... I wish especially to draw the reader's attention to this, that he may remember, once for all, that any 'conjectural emendations' are, in general, entirely out of the question. (p. xxxix)

But this remark will seem astonishing to twentieth-century *Piers Plowman* scholars, who are familiar with the notion that the poem raises textual problems of unparalleled, indeed appalling difficulty, most of which centre on the B-Text, the very version which Skeat regarded as the most straightforward of the three, and which is now thought to require extensive editorial correction in the form of the conjectural emendation that Skeat here rules out. This assessment of B's textual character by the father of *Piers Plowman* editing sets the present view of B in its proper twentieth-century context.

Skeat also tells us that, when in doubt, he consulted 'either the A-text, or the C-text, or else more MSS. of the B-type, so that the resulting text has almost always plenty to support it'. This reduced the need for conjectural emendation still further: since so much of the A-text is found in B, and so much of B found in C, problems in one text can sometimes be resolved by appeal to the equivalent section in the other. As I have described, Skeat had to a certain extent done the same in editing A: 'I have always had regard to Text B' when editing A, he remarks parenthetically when discussing a problem of alliteration in his Critical Notes to the *A-Text* (p. 138); and when alliteration, particularly, could be improved by printing B's reading – often, as it happened, the reading found in the other A-MSS too – he frequently overrode Vernon's text and replaced it with the superior B reading.[37]

As we have seen, however, this procedure raises an important question of editing principle. If the B-MSS disagree or produce an unacceptable reading for a word in the poem, and A and/or C have satisfactory readings, unanimously attested, at the equivalent points in their texts, is it justifiable to import their readings into the B-Text? Or put more generally, are minor differences between A and B (or B and C) due to the poet *changing his mind* between writing one version and another, or to scribal error? Skeat's emendations of Vernon's text were usually justified by the fact that more than one of

---

[37] See pp. 130–2 above.

the other A-MSS agreed with the superior reading found in B. But what if all the B-MSS agree on a reading which seems inferior to the equivalent readings of A and C – what, indeed, if A and C agree on a reading different from the one unanimously attested by the B-MSS? All depends, of course, on editorial judgement in deciding when differences between texts are likely to be due to scribal error and when to authorial revision.

These points were to assume major importance in the twentieth-century editing of the poem. Skeat's successors, Chambers and Grattan, were unable to complete their edition of the A-Text owing to their belief that it was impossible to edit A without full knowledge of the witness, and probable original sources, of the B- and C-MSS; while the editor of the Athlone edition of A, George Kane, shut his eyes to the B- and C-Texts. He did complete his edition; but his failure to consult the evidence of the two other traditions of the poem has resulted in serious methodological flaws in the Athlone editorial project.[38]

Skeat's edition of B is in general a fuller and more mature work than his edition of A. He includes more sections in the Introduction, and thus manages to set the various aspects of the poem in a larger context. The *B-Text* contains an expanded discussion of the poem's date, and entirely new sections on the previous printed editions (not possible with A, of course), the 'character' of the B-Text (containing the remarks on B's textual straightforwardness quoted above), 'allusions' in the B-text (i.e. to places – many of these, as Skeat notes, in London – historical events, and what Skeat took to be the author's own circumstances), and dialect. He also provides, as before, an argument of the poem, and explains his method of annotating the text, which this time includes a system for marking in the margin the places where A diverges from or agrees with B, thus facilitating the comparison of one text with the other.

Skeat's remarks on previous printed editions are thorough and perceptive. He has worked out that Crowley printed three separate editions and used at least four manuscripts, an A-MS, a C-MS, and two B-MSS (p. xxxiv n.4; p. xxxv n.2), and also that Crowley's base-manuscript was a good witness to the poem, better in places, he thinks, than the Trinity manuscript used by Wright. Consequently Skeat frequently gives the variant readings of Crowley's three editions

---

[38]   See further below, pp. 374–8.

in his notes.[39] Skeat also knew of Rogers' edition and was able to dismiss it as 'a careless reprint of Crowley's *third* impression ... almost worthless' (p. xxxvi). By contrast he soft-pedalled on the shortcomings of Wright's edition, which he described as 'well-known and excellent', acknowledging 'my *very great* obligations to it. Without its help my work would, at the least, have been doubled.' He helpfully listed a few misprints and errors in Wright's text, and also a table aiding collation and comparison of Wright's edition with his own.[40]

Skeat's views on the 'Dialect of the B-Text' (pp. xli–xlv) demand to be quoted at some length, both for the illumination they shed on his attitude towards editing, and for the criticisms – as far as I have been able to discover, unpublished – that he says he is responding to. His defensiveness over Laud's inconsistencies of spelling and the mixed dialect suggests that he has argued over the manuscript's merits with someone like Bradshaw, who firmly believed that it was appropriate to emend manuscript spelling or dialect if it deviated from a posited norm. It is quite possible Skeat had Bradshaw at his elbow, criticising his choice of base-text on the grounds of its forms rather than its substance.[41] Skeat writes,

> From a careful comparison of the various MSS. of the poem, I arrive at the conclusion that the text here printed represents the probable dialect of the author with great fidelity, as, indeed, might be expected when we remember that it is a probable autograph copy.

And this is all he presents in the way of argument. Presumably Skeat chose to see Laud's dialect as original to Langland, because he believed – on shaky grounds, as we have seen – that the manuscript was Langland's own work. Skeat continues,

> I have been told that the spelling and grammar of my text are faulty, and that the Vernon MS. (or A-text), printed in vol. 1., is far better.

---

[39] He provides all the variant Crowley readings up to Passus X, recording them more selectively thereafter (see his comment on p. 408).

[40] *B-Text*, xiv, xxxvii–ix. Wright, who was only fifty-nine at the date of the *B-Text*'s publication in 1869, was still active as a scholar, and well known to Skeat. Nearly twenty years after his death in 1877, Skeat wrote, 'I remember him as a quiet but cheery old gentleman, who more than once stayed with me when he came to Cambridge to consult MSS. He had sharp quick eye-sight, and wrote a very legible hand at a quite unusual pace; he used to say of himself that he was "pretty quick", and perhaps he trusted to his quickness a little too much in later years, as some of his errors of reading are somewhat surprising... We were excellent friends, with a common interest in Middle-English and in things relating to Shropshire' (*A Student's Pastime*, lxi–xii).

[41] For Bradshaw's views, see pp. 86–9 above.

To this I can only reply that, as a matter of fact, the Vernon MS. seems to be, as far as the spelling and grammar are concerned, an 'improved' text [Skeat apparently means by this, 'improved' by a scribe], and very unlike the majority of the rest. Indeed I know of none that agree with it. It is a very great mistake to suppose that the MS. which exhibits the best grammatical forms, is therefore the best MS. It is obvious that, if the author had small regard for grammar, then the MS. which is very correct in that respect, does in effect, in the same respect, represent him least.

This looks like a suspicion of 'improved texts' born of Skeat's initial trust in Vernon, and his eventual realisation, as indicated by his Critical Notes and occasional emendations, that Vernon was not as reliable as he first thought. As we have seen, Skeat readily acknowledged in 1909 that Vernon was the wrong A-MS to choose as base-text. All we know of Skeat's personality (his interest in swift and regular output, efficiency in the use of time, and preparedness to sacrifice a possibly elusive search for the best solution in favour of the pragmatically satisfactory hunch) suggests that he would not have been the person to re-edit A even though he realised at the end of the exercise that he had probably made something of a mistake.

In this light, his immediately following remarks about Vernon seem like an attempt to shore up a self-evidently weak position: 'The Vernon MS. was chosen for the A-text because it seemed, upon the whole, to give the best sense, and satisfactory MSS. of the A-text are somewhat scarce.' This observation is, of course, silently belied by the frequent importation of the readings of the Trinity A-MS (T) into his text. Skeat then continues:

The Laud MS. has been chosen for the B-text because it is, also as regards the sense, by far the best. It has been suggested to me that the MS. printed by Mr. Wright is more correct from a grammatical point of view. I have examined this point, and hardly find it to be true. The truth that results from the comparison is a very curious and significant one. It is, namely, that the coincidences between the Laud MS. and the Trinity MS. are frequently startling. They agree in many instances with a most singular minuteness. And when it is remembered that the two MSS. are quite independent of each other (except in so far as they are due to the same author), and belong to different sub-classes,[42] I think their frequent resemblances corrobo-

42 This observation is baffling. If the coincidence between W and L is striking, why did not Skeat assign them to the same sub-class? What were the criteria by which he originally assigned them to different sub-classes? See p. 139 above. Kane–Donaldson do not list WL

rate and confirm the general genuineness of both in a very remarkable way. It is none of our business how Langland *ought* to have written; we have merely to ascertain how he probably *did* write; and for this reason I think it a great gain to have the Laud MS. in print, exactly as it stands, without any improvements or alterations except such as can be fairly justified by other MSS. and by other passages in the MS. itself.

Skeat is discussing grammatical forms here. But it is also true that the B-MSS frequently unanimously agree on words, phrases, and lines which later editors and textual critics have judged to be not what 'Langland *ought* to have written'. The current explanation for this is that the archetype of the B-MSS, to which all the manuscripts adhere far more closely than do the A-MSS to their archetype, was a significantly corrupt copy of the B-Text. So the forms and readings it presents are not only not what Langland *ought* to have written, but not in fact what he *did* write. I shall discuss this theory in detail later; for the time being, however, it is interesting to observe the distinction Skeat makes between our editorial wish to reconstruct a text that conforms to (what we judge to be) the highest possible standard, and what he clearly recognises as the possible historical truth of the matter, *viz.*, that such a standard was not always, necessarily, adhered to by the poet.

Of Laud's dialect itself, Skeat says little. He gives several examples of alternative verb-forms, and comments, 'beyond a doubt, Langland used a mixed dialect ...' He will 'not offer an opinion' on 'the part of England which the dialect of the text represents' (in fact Laud does, as he says, exhibit mixed dialectal forms – although there is no need to suppose that this was true of the author rather than his scribes).[43] Skeat finishes by saying that 'we may, however, feel confident that his conversation is more of the lower and less educated classes than of the upper classes. I think it very likely that grammar was a thing about which he troubles himself but very little, and he certainly makes some singular mistakes' (pp. xliii, xlv); Skeat evidently assumes that lin-

---

among the B-MS variational pairs of 'a dozen or more agreements'; this indicates that the agreements detected by Skeat were in what Kane–Donaldson would identify as 'right readings'. Cf the caveat on Kane's classification of A-MSS given in p. 137 n. 1 above.

43 Samuels identifies the language of Laud's 'main and oldest layer' as 'unmistakably the same south-west Worcestershire dialect as is found in MSS X, U and I of the C-Text', although of 'a fainter and more diluted form' than that found in the B-MS R. See 'Langland's Dialect', 241.

guistic self-consistency characterises only the 'educated classes', which he calls the 'upper classes'.

These are important remarks, because they represent a view of Langland – as a rough, unsophisticated, chaotic, practically-minded poet (cf. Skeat's Introduction to the *A-Text*) interested in content rather than form – that predominated in the criticism of the poem for many years. Such a view fitted well with the theory which took off in 1906, that the poem was not in fact the work of one man, but of several different authors. Apparent inconsistencies, changes of view, and what can come across as a confusing, or confused, rambling quality in certain parts of the poem, could thus be readily explained as due to the fact that more than one author was responsible for the various forms and stages of the text. Those who resisted this theory were keen to argue that, on the contrary, there was discernible in the putative originals of the manuscripts a single-minded and coherent artistic purpose: hence editors with this view tended to be those unable to accept a pluralistic attitude towards their texts. To put it more straightforwardly, one of the characteristics of the main proponent of the single-author view, George Kane (whose book on the subject published in 1965 effectively scotched the opposition), is an impressive certainty in his decisions as to which variants are scribal, which authorial. The sceptic may well see this certainty as attributable to the fact that Kane's editing technique produces the text that (in Kane's view) Langland *ought* to have written, rather than, necessarily, what he did write.

As we have seen, Skeat's critical apparatus to B offers partial records of the readings of his six collated manuscripts in much the same way as did that of his edition of A; while the Critical Notes are chiefly taken up with comparison of the readings printed in Crowley's text. His transcription of Laud was in general accurate;[44] and true to his word, he rarely emends, other than in very minor details, the reading of the Laud manuscript, although he occasionally suggests that it is at fault (see e.g. Passus XV 464–7; V 357; VIII 64), and he frequently supplements it with the lines found in R (often also found in F, but Skeat was evidently unaware of this).

One interesting example of these various policies occurs at Pro 122. Here, the king, Kind Wit and the Commons 'Shope lawe & lewte

---

[44] See J. A. W. Bennett, 'A New Collation of a *Piers Plowman* Manuscript', 22 n.2, who notes that Skeat's Parallel-Text edition of the poem contained more errors in its representation of Laud than did Skeat's EETS edition.

eche man to knowe his owne'. Skeat comments of this line, found only in the B-Text, 'The chief-letter [i.e., third stave] is wanting. Without doubt we should read *lif*, not *man*; for Langland often uses *lif* in place of *man*' (p. 388); he does not, however, incorporate this emendation into his text. In fact, his suggestion is supported, perhaps confirmed, by a source known to him but presumably unconsulted. The Corpus manuscript F, which as we have seen Skeat did not rate very highly, also reads *lyf*; and this reading is accordingly adopted into the B-Text by subsequent editors (Schmidt and Kane–Donaldson).[45] Another interesting point is that Skeat now – very occasionally – appeals to the testimony of the A-Text as supporting a reading in the B-Text (as he stated in the portion of his Preface already quoted, p. xxxix). Thus at Passus IX 47 (Schmidt IX 48), where MSS W and R read *his* (which Skeat prints in his text), Crowley *our*, and Laud and the rest omit the word entirely, he comments 'But *his* is right, as proved by the A-text' (which also has *his*). He also emends Laud's reading to one found in the A-Text, together with a few of the other B-MSS, at Pro 39, 224 (Schmidt 225), and Passus I 37–8. And – slightly differently – he prints Laud's reading at Passus V 357 (Schmidt V 351) but suggests that the A-Text's reading is in fact the correct reading. In other words, Skeat on occasion uses A's text as an arbiter in determining B's text.

This takes us back to the question of authorial revision and scribal error. How is an editor to know to which of these two causes to ascribe differences between A and B? Is it really satisfactory to affirm that, if there is a difference in quality between an A reading and a B reading, the superior reading must have been the original to *both* texts? Supposing that Langland wrote one reading in A, and then improved it when he came to write B? Or – alternatively – supposing that Langland wrote one reading in A, and then 'debased' it when he came to write B?

Where *Eringe/settyng* were concerned at A Pro 14, Skeat preserved the non-alliterative reading of Vernon. As we have seen (p. 130 above), he argued that although the author may have later changed his mind and written *settyng* in the B-Text, it was not the duty of an editor to import that reading retrospectively back into A, and he considered that the presence of *settyng* in other A-MSS should not displace the primacy of Vernon. As already mentioned, subsequent editors –

---

[45] The remaining B-MSS agree in reading *man*.

156

Knott–Fowler and Kane – have disagreed with this decision, printing the reading *settyng* in their editions of A on the grounds that it is present as a variant in the A tradition as well as in the B, and therefore is very likely to be the original of A as well as of B. The problem here seems to be that Skeat chose the wrong manuscript of A for his base-text, and then decided to stick to it too closely. And it is certainly the case that many of the differences between Skeat's A and B texts simply disappear if you take the reading of A to be something other than that of the Vernon manuscript.[46]

Other instances, however, are more troublesome. At Passus III 213 (Schmidt III 214), Skeat's B-Text reads 'For ʒiftes han ʒonge men to renne and to ride'. Crowley's and Wright's texts, together with all the B-MSS save R and F, read *renne* here, producing an irregularly alliterating line, and *renne* is also found in all the A-MSS save one (see A Passus III 201; the two texts run in parallel at this point), and had been printed by Skeat in his A-Text. The B-MSS R and F, by contrast, read the lexically more difficult ʒerne, which restores the alliteration. Skeat records in his critical apparatus that R reads ʒerne for *renne* (he does not record R's agreement with F here, probably because he did not know of it; as we have seen he took little notice of this manuscript). But there is no reference to this variant in his notes; Skeat instead comments that Crowley's substitution of *giftes* for *ʒiftes* and *go* for *renne* makes it look as if 'the alliteration depended on the initials of *giftes*, *ʒonge*, and *go*. But we know from Text A that *renne* is correct. The alliteration follows a rule, according to which each half-line is alliterative within itself' (p. 395) (*abab* rather than *aaax*; many Middle English scholars would allow that *abab* was an acceptable Langlandian line).[47] As he tells us, Skeat always had reference to B when editing A, especially in matters of alliteration. But he did not know of the Rawlinson B-MS until he had completed A (see p. 142 above), so the B-Text information he relied upon when editing A – probably drawn from the printed editions, Crowley and Wright – would have given him no particular reason not to stick to Vernon in reading *renne* (especially since this reading is also found in all but one of the other A-MSS, M, which rewrites this part of the line; see A Passus III 201). However, Crowley occasionally replaces obsolete words with sixteenth-century equivalents that preserve the allitera-

---

[46] As Chambers and Grattan were later to point out in their criticisms of Manly and others; see pp. 198–9 below.
[47] Cf. Schmidt, 507.

tion, so it is not an unreasonable inference that Crowley's manuscript also read ȝerne, in common with the B-MS R. This would make it a possibility that ȝerne was the original of the B-Text. It is revealing that Skeat does not notice this possibility: having established his A-Text, he is reluctant to allow a different text in B, especially if this means emending Laud, although a preferable reading is to be found in one of the other B-MSS, R (and also, had he consulted it, in Corpus 201 (F), R's regular partner, with which it represents an independent branch of the B tradition), and although it might well have been the case that, having written *renne* in the A-Text, the author 'corrected' it to the alliterating *yerne* when he wrote B.

Editors of *Piers Plowman* seem to find it very hard, when editing B, to allow one-word differences between the two texts, A and B, in an otherwise unchanged line. There seems to be some sort of compulsion to deny the possibility that the author revised on so small a scale, and instead to attribute such differences to scribal corruption. There is also a reluctance to rethink the editing of A when editing B. We shall see below how this is true of the editing of Kane–Donaldson.[48]

Where this textual crux is concerned, we can see Skeat quite as enmeshed as later editors in the intolerable problems of editing an authorially revised work surviving in many manuscripts, whether or not he recognised the logical and methodological traps into which he fell. We can also see his reluctance to budge from the testimony of Laud.[49]

[48] Kane (III 201) emends the reading *renne* found in all but one of the A-MSS to *yerne*, which is a preferable alternative on both metrical and semantic grounds (it is the harder reading). His justification is that the single differing manuscript, M, reads *þey desiryt*, for the phrase *han ȝonge men to renne and*, which he takes to be 'a mistaken scribal attempt to gloss a harder reading' (161). He makes no reference to the existence in the B (and as it happens, C) tradition of ȝerne (some C-MSS read *renne*, some ȝerne; Skeat (IV 271) prints the former and Pearsall (III 269) the latter), despite the fact that this would have bolstered his defence for introducing into the A-Text a reading found in none of the A-MSS. On Kane's views on the appropriateness of consulting the B- and C-Texts when editing the A-Text, see below, pp. 374ff. For another example of Skeat's reluctance to admit small differences between the texts of A and B, see his text and note on Passus V 189.

[49] In the same year as his *B-Text* (1869), Skeat published an edition of B Prologue and Passus I-VII, derived from the EETS volume, designed for students. Many times revised and reprinted, it contained an introduction, notes, and glossary, all of which took material from the EETS series of editions as they progressed, together with additional matter for the student audience. As Pearsall comments, 'It is a work of great importance in the history of *Piers Plowman* studies, since it shaped the perception of the poem for generations of readers (until superseded by Bennett ...), particularly in fostering the view of the poem primarily as social commentary' (*An Annotated Critical Bibliography of Langland*, 32). For Bennett's edition, see p. 410 below.

9

Skeat's *C-Text*

Skeat's edition of C is altogether more circumspect.[1] He begins with a recapitulation and expansion of some of the material first presented in the previous two editions, noting that 'the C-Text MSS. require peculiar care'.[2] This includes an analysis of the five different forms in which *Piers Plowman* manuscripts are found,[3] and a discussion of the poem's date and order of composition. Here he appeals straightforwardly to common-sense intuition:

> it is ... as well to shew, first of all, that the C-text is really later than the B-text; in other words, that no mistake has been made in the order of the recensions of the poem. On this point the internal evidence is most conclusive; given the B-text, it is not difficult to see how the C-text was formed from it, by various omissions, additions, transpositions, and corrections. But it is hardly possible to turn the C-text into the B-form, without the most improbable and contradictory suppositions. The transition in the one direction is simple and natural, but in the other direction is difficult and unlikely. This will appear so clearly upon a careful perusal of the two texts that it is hardly worth while to go into particulars. (*C-Text*, p. xi)[4]

And he explains that the only reason for raising the question at all is that Whitaker had suggested the reverse, that B came after C. 'This may', Skeat comments, 'in some measure account for the difficulty which he had in seeing his way clearly, and for the extraordinary

---

[1]   Some of the following material originally appeared as part of the Introduction to *Piers Plowman. A Facsimile of the Z-Text in Bodleian Library, Oxford, MS Bodley 851.*

[2]   *C-Text*, ix.

[3]   These five different forms comprise three 'real' forms, due to the author, viz. A, B, and C, and two scribal forms: (1) the AC conjoint texts exhibited in Trinity R 3 14, Harley 6041, and Digby 145, and (2) the BC (*sic*; properly CAB) conjoint texts found in Bodley 814, Add. 10574, and Cotton Caligula A XI. Later, Skeat distinguishes ten different forms; cf. p. 174 below.

[4]   Cf. p. 159 above.

159

views, founded upon no premises whatsoever, which he formed respecting the respective merits of the two versions.'[5]

Skeat also strengthens his argument for the compositional order BC rather than CB by adducing the existence of an A version, unnoticed by Whitaker and Wright:

> Now, when we proceed to place the *three* texts side by side, it is at once apparent that the B-text is *intermediate* in form between the other two; so that the order of texts must either be A, B, C or C, B, A; but the A-text so evidently comes *first*, that the C-text can only come *last*, and this settles the question.

To clinch this point, Skeat quotes the first ten–odd lines of each of the three texts, commenting that this 'will suffice to shew' that he is right.

But of course it does nothing of the sort. A and B are virtually identical over this very short stretch of the poem, while C makes a few changes. It is not in the least clear that any one of the versions should precede the other two; although it makes some sense that A and B should be either the poet's first two or last two attempts, given their extreme similarity. Skeat could have made a stronger case by quoting passages from the quarrel between Conscience and Meed in Passus III or the confessions of the Deadly Sins, where there is a progressive expansion from A to B to C, so that what appears in germ form in A is successively developed in the two supposedly later versions.[6] But what is missing altogether from his account is a discussion of what it is reasonable to assume about how a poet would compose. Why should we think that a poet might not reduce an earlier, longer version, with the intention of producing a text more suitable for instructional purposes? If this is unlikely, then what are the reasons that make it so?[7]

Skeat's closing remark in this section is an important one: 'Now that all three texts are in the reader's hands, he can prosecute the comparison of them as far as he pleases, in a way that could never

---

[5] Skeat then demolishes Whitaker's only stated argument for B's anteriority, that it contains an allusion to burning heretics and therefore must be later than the second year of Henry IV's reign, by citing similar allusions before 1401 (*C-Text*, xi–xiv). He believes C is to be dated to 1393, largely on the basis of interpreting the political allegory in Passus III (Passus IV according to Skeat's numbering) as applying directly to contemporary events. C may, in fact, have been written as early as 1388; cf. Anna Baldwin, *The Theme of Government in Piers Plowman*, 59, 101 n. 9.

[6] See Charlotte Brewer, 'Z and the A- B- and C-Texts of *Piers Plowman*'.

[7] See p. 429 below.

have been done before' (p. xv). This is Skeat's greatest achievement: he subjected the *Piers Plowman* manuscripts to their first real process of digestion, and made the result available in an intelligible form to the scholarly public.

Skeat took much longer to edit C than he did the two previous texts. I suspect that this was because the manuscript tradition of C, like that of A, is complex. He was able to dispatch A very swiftly, probably because he did not fully grasp the problems it raised, while B was also dealt with expeditiously, being self-evidently straightforward on account of the extraordinarily frequent unanimity of the manuscripts.

Skeat's description of the ups and downs he experienced in editing C gives us some insight into the ways in which his editorial techniques had developed. He eventually took as his base-text the same manuscript as that used by Whitaker, Hm 137 (by this time in the Phillipps collection). One would expect Skeat to have chosen a different manuscript, in order to increase the number of manuscripts in print and thus satisfy the good Furnivallian principle that was achieved by printing the Laud B-MS rather than Wright's Trinity B-MS. This was in fact his original view with the C-Text: 'I thought it would be well to avoid printing the same one as had been printed already, because I considered that it would be a distinct gain to have two MSS. printed in full instead of one, and I rather disliked the look of Dr. Whitaker's text, as seeming to indicate a faulty source.' He chose instead the Cotton MS. Vespasian B. 16 (M);[8] 'but this plan soon broke down, as I found that it was constantly requiring emendation, or else that the readings were frequently inferior to those of Whitaker's edition'. He next tried the Earl of Ilchester's *Piers Plowman* (now London University Library MS S.L.V.88), another good C version, 'but this MS. would not do to print from, on account of its incompleteness'. Finally he turned to the beautifully written Cambridge MS, Ff. 5. 35 (F), setting up the whole of its Passus II in type and collating the text with every other C-MS he knew of. 'Then the whole truth came out at last': that Whitaker's MS was in fact the best, but had been grossly disfigured in the printing. This Skeat settled when his assistant Edmund Brock was allowed by Sir Thomas Phillipps to collate Skeat's own copy of Whitaker with the manuscript itself, a collation that Skeat completed personally on a visit to

[8] Transcribed for him by three helpers and checked by another (Lucy Toulmin Smith); see xxi, xxxix–xl.

Cheltenham, Phillipps' seat.[9] 'From this *corrected* copy of Whitaker', Skeat proudly announces, 'the present text has been printed, and the text is sufficiently satisfactory. Most of the absurd readings', he informs us,

> turned out to be Dr. Whitaker's mistakes; some others were due to marked peculiarities in the scribe's spelling, easily removeable; and the rest have been amended by collation with six or seven other MSS. The resulting text is a peculiarly good one, and is, at any rate, ascertained on sufficient grounds to be the best that can be procured from the existing materials.[10]

This is an interesting account of his search for the right text. Skeat's methods of editing have become vastly more sophisticated than they were in 1866, when he plumped for Vernon as a base-text of A in a fashion that was not clearly argued or worked out. A sample collation of a significant stretch of the poem is an obvious way to begin in the struggle to rationalise and make sense of a large number of different manuscripts. Presumably, also, Skeat had built up considerable expertise in recognising typical patterns of scribal error, although he never discusses this point. Skeat continues,

> For a long time, the state of the text was a great puzzle to me, and it has been a great satisfaction to be able to find so full and clear a solution to that puzzle. I think it must have been nearly two years before I saw my way quite clearly; and I have no doubt that that chief part of the difficulty arose from my assuming that Dr. Whitaker's print, so obviously *intended* to be correct, really *was* so. Certainly experience has taught me, as an editor, to put no trust in editors, but always to verify their work by a reference, where possible, to the originals which they profess to represent.[11]

---

[9] It was probably at this time (before Phillipps' death in 1872) that he came across another Phillipps manuscript, formerly Heber 1088, now Hm 114. This manuscript was discussed briefly by Whitaker, and obviously, as Skeat observes (p. xix n. 1), a source of confusion to him. Skeat himself regards it as 'one of those MSS. which are best avoided'. It preserves a mixed text, a highly eccentric blend of A, B, and C; see George Russell and Venetia Nathan, 'A *Piers Plowman* Manuscript in the Huntington Library'; also Wendy Scase, 'Two *Piers Plowman* C-Text Interpolations'.

[10] *C-Text*, xxii. When the manuscript came up for sale as part of Sir Thomas Phillipps' library, Skeat wrote to the librarian of CUL (Jenkinson) on 11 March 1890 to persuade him to buy it, describing it as '*the*' manuscript of the poem, 'worth much more than the other 2 [Phillipps, formerly Heber, *Piers Plowman* manuscripts] put together'. See CUL 8635:11:5; and cf. p. 44 n. 11 above.

[11] Skeat had learned this lesson at the beginning of his editing career, with *Lancelot of the Laik*; see pp. 97–8 above.

Subsequent editors, who have been able to learn both from Skeat's triumphs and his mistakes, have also heeded – in some cases – his advice to mistrust other editors, primarily, of course, Skeat himself. As he says, experience has taught him to be slower and more careful, and to test initial impressions against a sufficiently large swathe of other evidence. His treatment of the C-MSS differs significantly from that of the A-MSS: he collated most of the manuscripts against Passus II, so as to get some idea of their general characteristics, and collated 'six or seven' additional manuscripts throughout the text (in contrast to the three and five additional manuscripts he collated for A and B respectively).

As he did with the B-MSS, Skeat assigns most of the C-MSS to a sub-class, identifying five in all (a–e).[12] But he still does not reveal the procedure he used to establish his classification, although one would have expected that his collations against Passus II must have made this a more systematic operation than the equivalent B-MS analysis. The collation information Skeat slips into his individual descriptions of the manuscripts is nevertheless decidedly confusing. Thus of M, the Cotton Vespasian manuscript, Skeat says, 'this MS. should not be put in the same sub-class with P, E, and Z, nor with I, T, and B, but in a third class, along with F and S' (p. xl). This clearly implies that S (Corpus 293) is in a different sub-class from P, E, and Z. Yet Skeat groups S *with* these manuscripts in his list of sub-classes on page li. Elsewhere he states that 'when [S] differs from [Skeat's edited] text, it commonly agrees with G, M or F' – which manuscripts are all in *different* sub-classes (a, d, and e respectively). It is possible that the explanation for these apparent discrepancies is either that S is wrongly included in sub-class (a), perhaps as a result of a misprint (yet Skeat later repeats the classification),[13] or that there is a large number of 'cross-cutting' agreements in C-MSS linking manuscripts in one sub-class with manuscripts in another. But we cannot tell whether either of these explanations is correct: Skeat simply furnishes insufficient information; and the fact that later editors have identified conflicting groupings among the manuscripts does not help matters (see n. 12 above). It seems that, where the classification of the manuscripts was concerned, Skeat regarded himself as writing and editing for

---

[12] Sub-class (a) contains PEZSGVR, (b) IYDTH^{2}D^{2}BOL, (c) K, (d) M, and (e) F. This categorisation should be compared with that of Allen (p. 267 below); as she notes, there is little correspondence between the two.

[13] See *The Vision of William Concerning Piers Plowman ... General Preface, Notes, and Indexes*, 848.

those interested in the poem, not for those interested in his editing of the poem.

Insufficient information is also given to readers anxious to interpret the casual remarks thrown in at the foot of the list of sub-classes: 'It must be observed that the MSS. of sub-class (b) represent a slightly *earlier* cast of the poem than those of sub-class (a); as has been already explained. But the texts of MSS. M and F are *later*.' What has been explained is that *one* of the manuscripts in sub-class (b), Ilchester, has passages which Skeat believes mark it out as 'an *earlier* draught of the C-text' (p. xxxvii). But none of its fellow members of sub-class (b) share those lines: and so there can be little justification for supposing that they also represent this posited '*earlier* draught'. As for the statement that M and F are later than the C-Text proper: I have been able to find no reference to this theory anywhere else in Skeat's writings on *Piers Plowman*. But it is evidence that Skeat, at least at one point, may have held the view that the C-MSS between them represented *three* different versions (if that is not too definite a word) of the poem.[14]

Skeat believed that MS P, whose scribe records his own name as Thomas Dankastre,[15] was very close to the author's original:

> its mistakes are commonly of a very transparent nature; we can easily see through them, especially with the aid of collation with other MSS., and hence perceive clearly that Dankastre *made his copy from a very good original*, probably from an early copy of the poet's own *autograph* copy, and that we are thus brought as near to that original as is *now* possible (p. xxiv; Skeat's italics)

But this remark is curiously belied by a following one, viz. 'Dankastre's copy of the true text is not the *only* one, since there are two others.' These were Laud 656 (E), and the C portion of Bodley 851. Remarkably enough, Skeat believed that Bodley 851 was even closer to the authorial original version than P, and '*may*' have been a copy of Langland's autograph (p. xxiv n. 1) – a notable theory. If this was so, one immediately asks, why did he not take it as his copy-text in preference to P? The answer to this question is given in

---

[14] This impression may be contradicted by the statement on p. lxviii that 'there is no trace whatever of any later revision'. See p. 174 below for Skeat's final views on the number of authorial versions of the poem, and p. 268 below for later comment on his identification of different versions of C.

[15] His identity is unknown; cf. Russell, '"As They Read It"', 179 n. 8, for the suggestion that his name is 'Lancastre'.

his account of Bodley 851: as we shall see, Skeat came across this manuscript well after he had established his text. Clearly he was loath to scrap the work he had so far done and go back to the beginning again.[16]

The manuscripts Skeat chiefly relied on for establishing his text were E, which as we might expect from the above information was very closely related to Skeat's copy-text P, Ilchester (I), M, F, and S: a total of six including P. He tells us that 'the number of MSS. on which the text is based varies from five to nine, the most usual number being six or seven' (p. lxxv). As before, all the manuscripts were described in some detail, with accounts of their misarrangements or omissions of text (characteristic of C-MSS), and occasional information about the other items occurring in the manuscript.

Skeat believed that E 'must have been a close copy from the same original' as P. Hence it had been 'very useful to me, and enabled me to see my way more clearly in many places'; he collated it throughout and assigned it along with P to sub-class (a). He also reproduced a photographic plate of a portion of the text – Covetousness's confession – and provided a transcript, noting pedagogically that this would help those unfamiliar with the manuscript characters (pp. xxiv–xxx).[17] Another important manuscript was the one belonging to the Earl of Ilchester. This initially gave Skeat a good deal of trouble:

> Perhaps no MS. could be better devised for completely puzzling a critic unfamiliar with the poem. The text has been made up from two imperfect texts, an A-text and a C-text; some of the matter comes twice over; several leaves have been lost; the remaining ones have been numbered wrongly, and then bound up in the wrong order ... The MS. has been somewhat spoilt, particularly at the end, by damp, and much injured by the rats, which have eaten away, in some places, nearly half the leaf, so that sometimes the last half, sometimes the first half of a line is entirely gone, and many lines are more or less imperfect. (p. xxxiii)

---

[16] A section of the type-set text of C Passus XVIII 1–20, scribbled over with corrections and addenda, survives in the Skeat–Furnivall collection at Kings' College, London (F3a); 'Keep this: & note readings of Z' is written roughly across the top of the first page. Presumably this set of proofs was produced before Skeat had come across Z, but after he had established his text. On p. li of his Preface Skeat describes Z (in its C-Text portion) as 'even more correct in its readings than P'. For Skeat's views on Bodley 851, especially its early portion, see further below.

[17] He later tells us that 'the expense of supplying this autotype was mainly borne by myself' (*The Vision of William Concerning Piers Plowman ... Notes to Texts A, B, and C*, xv).

Nevertheless, Ilchester was in many ways a remarkable manuscript. Its prologue, particularly, was notable for an insertion of lines that seemed to belong much later in the poem, to Passus IX. Skeat's receptiveness to new information is illustrated by the fact that he does not dismiss these unconventional passages, but instead quotes from them with approval, commenting, 'These lines do not read to me as spurious; it is just possible that they represent the poet's first cast of this curious passage, peculiar as it is to the C-Text' (p. xxxv). Skeat's conclusion on Ilchester is that it represents a separate branch of the C-text tradition. This has been confirmed by later scholarship.[18] But his inference is a bold one:

> Just as MS. R [of the B-Text] differs from the true B-text in being of a somewhat later date and thus embodying a few after-thoughts, so MS. I differs from the true C-text, but in the other direction; for it is clearly an *earlier* draught of the C-text, and does not contain quite so many alterations of the text as do most of the other MSS. Its readings, in consequence, sometimes *point back* to the B-text. (p. xxxvii)

M was another important manuscript, which Skeat reckoned the best and earliest of the *Piers Plowman* versions in the British Museum. He collated it throughout: 'Every reading of M that is of any consequence is recorded in the footnotes.' But as we have seen, he found that it was 'not so good, as regards the character of its readings, as might have been expected'; and 'my attempt to make it the basis of the text entirely broke down' (pp. xxxix–xl).

F was also collated in full. This was the manuscript whose Passus II he had set up in type in order to use it as a collation base for sorting out the relationships between the other manuscripts. Skeat's description of how this procedure failed gives a good indication of his increasingly sophisticated techniques of editing the text:

> Then [i.e. after comparing the typeset Passus II with the other manuscripts] it came out that the readings of F are frequently peculiar to itself, and that its apparent smoothness of metre and diction must be due to the text having been touched up. This is a point which cannot very well be exemplified by special instances, as it is necessary to collate or observe the readings of a long passage, at least 400 or 500 lines, before the exact characteristics of the MS. can

---

[18] See the important article by Wendy Scase already referred to, 'Two *Piers Plowman* C-Text Interpolations'.

be clearly apprehended; the reader will be content, perhaps, to accept the fact as the result of my experience, since I have collated it with the text throughout, and give every variation in the footnotes that is worth giving. (p. xli)

The recognition that a manuscript needs to be thoroughly studied over a significant portion of its text before its character can be ascertained is a new one for Skeat, and conveys how the experience he refers to has improved his judgement and understanding of the processes of text reception. It is yet another indication of how he towers above other EETS editors, none of whom approach his degree of sophistication. But at the same time he is reluctant to explain precisely how his judgement and understanding work, asking the reader to accept their results on trust. Partly, perhaps, this is because Skeat worked in an intuitive way; probably he was also averse to devoting considerable time to discussion of detail, in the belief that his methods of tackling that detail were unassailably commonsensical, obvious, and right. The tone is similar to his discussion of the text of the *Astrolabe* quoted earlier (p. 90): why bother the reader with unnecessary information? He is, of course, editing not for editors but for readers. Skeat goes on to apologise even for the detail he has given: 'Indeed, I believe that [F] has received more than its fair share of attention, since, on account of its peculiarities, the letter F appears oftener in the footnotes than any other ... Except when supported by other MSS, its readings are, in general, to be regarded with suspicion' (p. xli).

The last two manuscripts which Skeat collated in full were S, another imperfect version of the C-Text about whose relationships with the other C-MSS, as we have seen, Skeat gives us conflicting information, and the C-Text portion of T, which began at Passus XII 297, and was collated from that line to the end of the poem. It was very close to Ilchester, Skeat found, and therefore useful where this manuscript was deficient (p. xxxviii); he cites its readings in the critical apparatus.

The remaining fourteen manuscripts were consulted only in part or not at all. The other two conjoint AC manuscripts, Harley 6041 (H^2) and Digby 145 (D^2 of C, K of A), whose A-Texts Skeat had already looked at for his first edition of the poem, were briefly dealt with, Skeat appearing to assume that the quality of their A-Texts would be reproduced in their C-Texts. This meant that, because their A-Text portions were close to the A-Text portion of T, he assigned them to the same sub-class as T and I (p. xxxviii). The C-Text portion (i.e. Pro–III 128) of Bodley 814 (Bo) was found to be close to Ilchester again, but 'as this MS. cannot be much depended on, very few readings have been cited from it'; its close partners Bm and Cot do not seem to have been even consulted (pp. xxxviii–xxxix).

CUL Dd. 3. 13 (G) was another imperfect copy of the text, which also missed many lines. 'Yet the text, as far as it goes, is a good one, and differs from [that of Skeat's printed version of C] but slightly'; it 'bears a likeness to S', so was occasionally collated where S failed. However, Skeat warns against over-interpretation of his critical apparatus: 'the collation of the text must not be taken to be *complete*, even where S fails; as I have frequently omitted to record readings from it that seemed of no particular value' (p. xliii). This caveat suggests Skeat was now aware of the confusing nature of the information he provided in his critical apparatus.[19]

Digby 171 (K) was again 'Imperfect and only partly collated', from Passus XII 1 to its ending at XVI 65 (p. lxxv).[20] The scribe actually leaves a blank page after the last line that he writes, as if his exemplar ran out at this point and he was unable to find an alternative continuation. Perhaps for this reason Skeat did not 'at first perceive the full value of it, or I would have collated it sooner'. It seems that he only gave it serious attention once his text had been set in type, and so its variants are not recorded in the footnotes. To compensate for this oversight, Skeat notes down 'the few readings that are most worthy of record' in his Introductory section on the manuscript, and adds, somewhat defensively,

> It will be seen that these readings confirm or help out my results in almost every instance. Indeed, I may say that further collation with this MS. will, I believe, be found merely to confirm my results, and not to give new information. It possesses, on this account, more interest for myself than for the reader. (p. xlv)

The remaining manuscripts are summarily dismissed. Douce 104 (D)

---

[19] He attempts to explain further his rationale for including material in his critical apparatus on lxvi–lxvii, making it clear that what he prints is only a *selection* of the variants of the manuscripts he consulted.

[20] Skeat records the approving but admonitory inscription on this manuscript of Stephen Batman, one of its previous owners, the chaplain to Matthew Parker: 'This Booke is clepped: Sayewell, Doowell. Doo better. & Doo Best / Souche a booke az diserueth the Reeding. Bookes of Antiquiti are wel be-stowed one those whose sober staied mindes can abyde the reding; but commonly ffrantike braines suche az are more readye to be pratlers than parformers, seing this book to be olde, Rather take it for papisticall than else. & so many bookes come to confusion. S. B. Minister.' See further *C-Text*, xliv.

was notable for its 'very rudely drawn coloured pictures'; but 'As I have not collated this MS., I cannot give its peculiarities with certainty; but it is obviously an inferior MS. of the same sub-class with I and T' (p. xlvi). Its fellow Bodleian MS Digby 102 (Y) is unique among *Piers Plowman* manuscripts in being written as prose. Skeat seems to have done sufficient spot-collation to class it with I and T (pp. xlvi–xlvii). The Harley MS 2376 (N), despite being clearly written and relatively early (1440 or earlier, Skeat judges), was 'a most disappointing MS., as it looks so promising, and is yet so unsatisfactory. I had intended to collate it ... but so many readings seemed to be corrupt that it proved to be no sure guide, and is, indeed, best neglected' (pp. xlvii–viii). Furnivall collated Passus II of this manuscript against the printed copy of F, and Skeat prints some of the variant readings which resulted from this – many of them seem to have been prompted by the scribe's desire to gloss the original, although this has several times been done inaccurately.

Skeat was again dependent upon the good offices of Professor Dowden for information about the C-MS in Trinity College, Dublin (V). Dowden also used the printed copy of F's Passus II as a basis for comparison, and Skeat worked out from his results that it was probably a poor member of the P sub-class (p. xlviii). The British Library MS Royal Library 18 B XVII (R) was collated by Lucy Toulmin Smith against the printed copy of F Passus II. This manuscript was very close to P, with spellings of a later form, and Skeat did not take it into account when forming his text. Similarly with Phillipps 9056 (now BL Add. 34779, P^2): 'It is clearly wholly of the C-type, but not much can be made of it, and I have therefore set it aside. The last page is scarcely legible, and a note states (correctly) that the last 42 lines are wanting. I doubt if it was ever a very good copy' (p. xlix). Skeat finally mentions a manuscript in the possession of the Duke of Westminster (W). He reports an article published in the *Academy* which stated that the manuscript was unlike those so far printed by EETS, allowing Skeat to infer that it was a C-MS. Unfortunately, he was unable to consult it for his edition of C; later he discovered it to be a conjoint AC text.

Skeat thus struggled far more with the text of C than he had with his other editing enterprises. Nevertheless, the extent of his knowledge of several of the manuscripts ran only to a comparison of their version of Passus II with the printed copy he had made up of F's text; and he seems not even to have done that with the third Phillipps manuscript (9056). His open-mindedness on Ilchester is remarkable, but perhaps explicable, like his treatment of the Rawlinson B-MS, as the attitude of someone still searching for a solution to an editorial problem, and not yet confident that he had found the answer.

Such, at least, is my explanation for why Skeat took such a different attitude towards the first of the two *Piers Plowman* versions preserved in Bodley 851 (which he suggested should be denoted by the letter Z, presumably because this was the last manuscript he came across). It is easy to reconstruct the manner in which Skeat finally discovered this manuscript, for he reports it himself with engaging candour:

> The copy of Piers the Plowman ... was entirely unknown to me until quite recently. This oversight arose in the most natural way possible. When making my collection of "Parallel Extracts" [described above, pp. 107–8], Mr Coxe, Bodley's Librarian, whose kindness to me from first to last has been of the greatest service to me, himself sent me copies of the passage I had selected [near the start of Passus III] from the various MSS. of Piers the Plowman under his charge. But he sent me no copy from this MS. Z, for the sufficient reason that the passage is not to be found in it; whilst at the same time it never occurred to me to make further inquiry, because no other MS. omits this passage, and I did not suppose that any MS. *could* omit it. When however I at last lighted upon the MS. and examined it, this mystery was soon cleared up.[21]

It turned out that Bodley 851 contained another example of a text made up of two separate components, in this case written out in very different hands:

> The first part exhibits an extremely corrupt text, mere rubbish, as it seems to me, and written out from imperfect recollection; but the latter part exhibits, though in a late hand, a copy of the C-text which is remarkable for the extreme general *correctness* of its readings, and may have been copied from an autograph or from an early copy of it.

Skeat observes, wrongly as it turns out, that 'the former part of the MS. approaches rather to the B-text than the A-text ... But the text is greatly corrupted, abridged, transposed, and in every way altered for the worse; so that it is worthy of no attention except as a curiosity.' To illustrate this, Skeat quotes from part of its description of the Deadly Sins, a passage abridged, he says, by cutting down B's 216

---

[21] This and the following quotations on Z are taken from *C-Text*, xxx–xxxiii.

lines to 19, 'a considerable liberty'. The passage has several Norfolk allusions: Covetousness' 'Norfolk' nose, his oath, 'so thee ik', i.e. 'as I may thrive', which is in Norfolk dialect, and the mention of the worsted that Covetous will give up making now that he is reformed.[22] (This local name for wool is derived from the name of the town Worsted in Norfolk.) Curiously, instead of identifying the anti-Norfolk joke as a virtual commonplace in contemporary literature – found, among other places, in Chaucer's Reeve's Tale, and nearer still to home in Covetousness' B-Text protestation that he knows no French except that spoken in Norfolk[23] – Skeat rather jokily takes exception to the Z poet's insults, and rises to Norfolk's defence. 'This description of Covetousness having "a Norfolk nose" contains some covert satire that is lost upon me. Having resided two years in Norfolk, I may be allowed perhaps to observe that I never remarked any peculiarity in the noses of the people there. But as they are, in these days at least, remarkably hospitable, this may account for my difficulty!!'[24] And a propos of the apparent insinuation 'that the makers of the worsted fabrics at Worsted did not put in good work and workmanship', he comments, 'it is too bad to suppose that the convenient proximity of the shrine at Walsingham caused them to be careless of their commercial integrity'.

It is interesting, to say the least, that Skeat is content to write off, without further discussion, the rather distinctive characteristics of these lines as 'mere rubbish', while he was very open to the possibilities presented by the unique lines, and unusual versions of orthodox lines, in Ilchester's and Rawlinson's texts. Z contains many other unique lines and readings, and several other unique passages, all of which, with one exception,[25] make satisfactory sense in context. When read through and considered on its own terms, it produces a coherent and shaped narrative. But it seems unlikely that Skeat did read it through and consider it on its own terms. His remarks on the C portion of Bodley 851 indicate why this should have been:

... on comparing my printed C-text with the latter portion of [Z], I

---

22 The dialect form of Covetousness' oath, found also in the B-Text (Passus V 224) may well have been the original reading of the A-Text as well; see the manuscript variants recorded by Kane at Passus V 142 of his edition of A. Kane does not consider this possibility in his discussion of the crux (164) and does not later review his decision (see Kane, *Piers Plowman: The A Version*, second edition, 459–63).

23 B Passus V 235; see Rigg–Brewer, 16–17, 81.

24 Skeat had been a curate at East Dereham; cf. p. 95 above.

25 The repetition of material between Passus IV and V; see Rigg–Brewer, 14.

made the very satisfactory discovery that this MS., representing as it does a very pure text in spite of its rather late spellings, tended greatly to confirm the various emendations which I had made in the text after collation with other MSS. It was, as it were, an unexpected and satisfactory testimony to the correctness of my text, confirming many results of careful thought, and shewing me that I had been working upon right principles.

Skeat makes it clear that he came across Z right at the end of his editing process, after he had sorted out the puzzles and difficulties involved in teasing out from the manuscripts some sense of the probable authorial and transmission history of the poem.[26] The C portion of Z confirmed his theories, and was therefore highly acceptable to him, while what he identified as the B portion of Z presented evidence that was simply indigestible in terms of his existing hypotheses, unless it was regarded as a scribal, not an authorial product.

But those hypotheses had been formed on a preliminary view of the evidence. At the outset of the editing project, Skeat and Furnivall between them had set up a criterion for identifying a *Piers Plowman* manuscript, namely that it should contain certain lines from Passus III. Since Z did not satisfy this criterion, it was unidentified by the Bodley librarian, and slipped through their net. Skeat went on to establish and fix his ideas about the authorial process of composition of the poem, and its scribal transmission, without taking Z's eccentric version into account. When it surfaced seven years later, he scanned the first section for recognisable passages, probably going first of all to the Deadly Sin section because that was a swift and efficient way of working out which of the three versions Z most nearly corresponded to. What he found, as we saw, repelled him. His identification of the first part of Z as approaching 'rather to the B-text than the A-text' is illustrated by one line, also in Passus V, where Z does indeed agree with Skeat's edition of B rather than of A. But that is because Vernon reads uniquely at this point; most other A-MSS read the same as B – and as Z.[27] Skeat's A-Text reading for this line is an unfortunate consequence of his following the text of Vernon far too closely, without taking sufficient account of the other A-MSS (his critical apparatus records no variation among the other A-MSS). This oversight on Skeat's part seems to suggest that he spot-read the first part

[26] See n. 16 above.   [27] See p. 135 above.

of Z, and rejected it almost immediately. His account of Bodley 851 effectively put it out of the running for serious consideration by later editors.[28]

Later work on the C-Text has not confirmed Skeat's view that P was the best witness to the C tradition. The manuscript now reckoned to be the most reliable was discovered in 1924 and sold by Sothebys to the Huntington Library, where it is now Hm 143; an edition of it, by Derek Pearsall, appeared in 1978 and it is the base-text for the forthcoming Athlone edition of C.[29]

Skeat followed his account of the manuscripts with a full treatment of Whitaker's edition, noting its various limitations and defects and 'observing that it is, in its way, a great work ... However deficient Whitaker's edition may seem to others, I can truly say that *to me* it has been invaluable; and but for the help it has afforded me, the difficulty of my task would have been at least doubled.' Given the large number of errors and misjudgements in this edition, Skeat's gratitude may seem hard to understand. But we should remember that he would have been thankful for any preliminary sorting of the three editions, and that the only printed witness to the C-Text, allowing him to form his views of what the various versions of the poem consisted in, was to be found in Whitaker. And this is what Skeat himself says: 'From the first moment of undertaking the comparison of the three texts, I have always had it at hand to refer to, and have referred to it hundreds of times; and many are the difficulties which a mere reference to it has solved' (p. lxii).[30]

Sections on the 'Character of the C-Text', 'Allusions in the C-Text', and 'Dialect' follow (pp. lxvi–lxxiv). Skeat believes that 'The C-text is generally inferior to the B-text in general vigour and compactness', but that 'we must never forget that the C-text is the best possible commentary' upon B. He also believes that the C revision involved rewriting B in its entirety, including the last two passus (most scholars now believe they were transferred to the C-Text virtually unrevised) (p. lxviii). Skeat is fascinated by the biographical information provided about the dreamer in the C-Text, which he takes without discussion to be autobiographical of the poet.[31] He is also now convinced that, as he suggested in his *B-Text*, the poet used

---

[28] See pp. 420–1 below.
[29] See further pp. 284–5 and 337 below.
[30] His gratitude led him to include a brief biographical sketch, lxiii–lxvi.
[31] He dismissed the danger of the authorial fallacy earlier; see p. 128 above.

a 'mixed' dialect; and he notes that the prevalence of southern forms in some of the C-MSS would support the notion that the poet wrote this version after his return home from London to Worcestershire in old age (p. lxxiv).[32]

As we would expect, Skeat has made a very thorough comparison of C with the two previous versions. He lists the additional passages in C and provides a table showing the parallel progression of the three texts, as well as adding marginal annotations to his text indicating the equivalent passages in A and B. He finishes with a passus-by-passus summary of C.

The text is followed, as in the other two editions, by a section of Critical Notes; here Skeat provides a full comparison of his text with Whitaker's, exhaustively pointing out Whitaker's mistranscriptions and other errors. J. A. W. Bennett compared Skeat's own text against the manuscript in 1948 and discovered something under 350 errors of transcription, almost all minor ones of spelling, which over so long a text may well be as accurate as we should expect of an editor as extraordinarily swift as Skeat.[33]

A fourth volume of Notes and Glossary was published in 1877 and 1885, a total of 910 pages. 70–odd pages of prefatory matter recapitulate some of the introductory matter of the preceding editions. Skeat offers summary sections on dialect, the poet's name, the author's life, and nineteenth-century criticism of the poem (based on Whitaker's and Wright's editions), etc., adding new information where appropriate (for example, he believes he has now discovered the 'bourn' mentioned in the first few lines of the poem).[34] He also summarises his views on the author's processes of composition and revision, identifying ten forms of the poem of which eight represent different stages of authorial writing.

As we have seen, he believed that the poem first stopped at Passus VIII (as in the A-MSS H and L), but that the poet subsequently added first Passus IX–XI, and then Passus XII (found in R, U, and J), making three different versions in all of A. The peculiar form of the poem found in H[3], an A-Text to part-way through Passus V followed by a B-Text, suggested 'that the revision of the A-Text may not have been accomplished all at once'; in other words that this manuscript

---

[32] Cf. Samuels, 'Dialect and Grammar', 207–8.
[33] See Bennett, 'A New Collation of a *Piers Plowman* Manuscript (Hm 137)'.
[34] xix n1. Skeat first describes this in a letter of 25 September 1884, now in the possession of his grandson T. C. Skeat.

represented a fourth stage in writing the poem.[35] The B-Text proper was the fifth form of the poem, with Rawlinson Poet. 38 and Ilchester representing intermediate versions between B and C and thus forming the sixth and seventh forms of the poem respectively. And the eighth authorial form was found in the C-Text proper. The two other forms were scribal: the AC combinations found in T, H[2], Digby 145, and the Duke of Westminster's manuscript (which Skeat has now ascertained falls into this category; see 853); and the BC combinations (properly CAB) found in Bm, Bo, and Cot.

The great mass of the volume is taken up with copious notes on the three texts, supplying quantities of historical, lexical, and interpretative information and frequently comparing other contemporaneous works. These notes are an unparalleled store of explanatory and critical elucidation and have been mined again and again by subsequent editors and critics; they are still well worth consulting on cruces in the poem. Skeat then provides a series of indices – to the explanations in the notes, to the books referred to in the notes, to the quotations made by the author, to the books Skeat guessed – with an appropriate degree of shrewdness and common sense – might have been in the poet's library. There follows an index to proper names and then a full glossary, which continues to be an important source for Langland scholars as it is the only one available, and can also be used as a sort of minimal concordance to the poem.

Skeat also attaches a summary account of the manuscripts, including the version found in each one of the 'parallel extract' from Passus III which he had originally used as a way of identifying *Piers Plowman* manuscripts and discriminating between them. (There is, of course, no example of this from Z.) Most interesting here is Skeat's retrospective allottment of the A-MSS to sub-classes in the same way as he had done with B- and C-MSS. He distinguishes four of these, but they correspond only in the roughest way with the classification later established by Kane, and it is impossible, as with the sub-classes of the two later versions, to infer the basis on which Skeat decided to group the manuscripts.[36] Skeat describes the two manuscripts which had come to light since his publication of Texts A and C: the Ingilby manuscript (now Pierpont Morgan M 818), an A-Text which con-

---

[35] Skeat nowhere pursues this notable theory, which if it were correct would suggest that the peculiar variants in this manuscript would be of special interest.

[36] The sub-classes are as follows: (a): VH; (b) REU, ?J; (c): TH[2]WDAL; (d): H[3]K. See 835–40, and on Kane's classification see p. 362 below.

tained an imperfect version of Passus XII, and the Duke of Westminster's manuscript, one of the AC conjoint texts (pp. 835–9). He gave a great deal of attention to the Westminster manuscript (W), comparing its A section thoroughly with that of his own text and noting with obvious interest the large number of B and C lines which this version introduces. Skeat judged W to be related to the other A-MSS T and D, and reckoned its many peculiar readings were 'of considerable interest, at any rate to myself ... In some instances the scribe has inferior readings which impair the alliteration; in others he supports many of the emendations which I have already made in the text.' The C section of the manuscript he found less interesting but nevertheless scrutinised it sufficiently to ascertain that it did not agree exclusively with any of the sub-classes he had already established. He thus treats W far more thoroughly than he had earlier treated Digby 145 (A-MS K), the other 'contaminated' A-MS known to him.[37]

It is tempting to assume that Skeat's fuller treatment of W is a mark of his increased editorial experience and knowledge, hence sophistication and understanding: he now has a clear idea of the material peculiar to each of the three versions, and he is consequently better able to detect and analyse deviations from the three-text model. But this theory is belied by his treatment of J, which he examined with much less thoroughness. Skeat was interested in its preservation of all but the last few lines of the Passus XII found in R and U, which he quotes in full, but seems to have made little investigation of its readings throughout the rest of the poem.[38]

Following this account is an entertaining and instructive selection of critical comments on *Piers Plowman* by various authors from 1381 to 1883. Finally there is a tightly packed list of Additions and Corrections covering all four volumes, and a General Index to the entire work.

This vast work of scholarship appeared in a differently organised form the following year, 1886. The Clarendon Press printed two volumes, the first containing the three texts printed in parallel form, and the second a reduced version of the introductory matter, notes and glossary.[39] This is the edition which has been used most

[37] Cf. Kane, 31–3.
[38] See his remarks at 836–7, 856–9; he linked J with R and U (in fact the three manuscripts have, according to Kane's collation, ten agreements in common).
[39] It seems likely that Skeat would have got the idea for the parallel presentation of his texts from the Chaucer Society's grand six-text parallel edition of the *Canterbury Tales*. But

extensively during the course of this century. One point of interest is that Skeat adopted a different classification of the manuscripts, that published in 1885 by Richard Kron, who claimed to have examined the less important manuscripts with greater care than Skeat himself. This classification was authoritatively demolished by Chambers and Grattan in 1909, who observed that 'Dr. Kron appears to have seen most of the MSS., but he has not recorded a single reading of a single A-MS. which he has not derived from Skeat ... his work ... is not only useless but misleading with reference to the relationship of the A-MSS.'[40] But as illustrated above, Skeat's classification of the manuscripts seems to have had little or no relationship with his method of establishing the text of the poem, and consequently his espousal of Kron's scheme had no practical consequences.

The Parallel-Text edition was received with overwhelming praise. An anonymous review in *Notes and Queries* gives a good sense of the respect Skeat now commanded among the scholarly public:

> In these two handsome volumes we have at last a standard and definitive edition of a great English classic, which has scarcely yet received its due recognition. Probably there is not another man in England besides Prof. Skeat who could have produced an edition so satisfactory. There is certainly none other we know of who has given himself to the work with such long and consistent devotion, and there is hardly another who could bring to the task in the same high degree the necessary qualifications here manifested – wide knowledge of the language in its historical development, the most painstaking and conscientious accuracy in minute details, textual and critical, such as we seldom meet with except in some of the great commentators, continued at the same time with a *légèreté* and lucidity of treatment more suggestive of French than German scholarship.[41]

Skeat's edition of *Piers Plowman* was accurately identified by his colleagues as the 'crown' of his 'long and arduous labours in Middle

---

there is an important difference between the two enterprises. Furnivall wanted to print transcriptions of the major manuscripts of Chaucer so as to correct the false impressions given of the poem by unduly creative past editors; Skeat, on the other hand, offered what was taken by many of his readers to be critical texts of the three versions of *Piers Plowman*. A small amount of correspondence between Skeat and the Clarendon Press on the 1866 edition survives in the OUP archives (April 1883–November 1886).

[40] 'The Text of "Piers Plowman" ', 373–4 n2.

[41] *Notes & Queries*, 7th series, vol. III, no. 57, 99–100 (99). For other reviews see DiMarco, *Piers Plowman*, 69–70. One of the few criticisms voiced was that of James M. Garnett, who asked for more information on the poet's dialect.

English' (Henry Sweet), 'probably the very best specimen of critical English scholarship ever produced' (James Murray), and 'one of the finest feats of modern editorship, – nothing less than the first adequate resuscitation for English students and the English public of that extraordinary contemporary of Chaucer who most deserves to be remembered in connexion with him and in contrast to him' (David Masson).[42]

---

[42] Quoted from the collection of *Testimonials in Favour of the Rev. Walter W. Skeat*, assembled by Skeat for his application for the Elrington-Bosworth chair in Anglo-Saxon at Cambridge in 1878 (pp. 58, 22 and 40). David Masson was Professor of Rhetoric and Engish Literature at the University of Edinburgh.

PART III
The Skeat aftermath

Manly versus Chambers and Grattan

Far more than previous editors, Skeat grappled with the problem of texts and manuscripts, coming up with various hypotheses that really did seem to supply reasonable explanation for the characteristics of the different manuscripts.[1] He was the first person to show convincingly that there were three main separate versions of the poem, all authorial, which he called A, B, and C. The assumed author, William or Robert Langland, first wrote a short version, A, and then revised and extensively rewrote A to produce B, which was three times A's length. Several years later, so the theory goes, the poet began revising and rewriting B to produce C. Skeat's editions were received with great enthusiasm, and with clear understanding of the outstanding contribution he had made to the establishment and interpretation of the text. What, one might ask, was there left to do?

The answer is, a considerable amount. Several important manuscripts came to light after Skeat published, but even before that, scholars began to debate his position fiercely. And here it is possible to trace some of the characteristics of the way in which theories about texts, and editions themselves, develop.

So far, from Crowley to Whitaker to Wright to Skeat, there seems to be, largely speaking, some progression in textual criticism and editing. Wright is more scholarly and more accurate than Whitaker, and Skeat is superior to both in understanding the importance of consulting as many manuscripts as possible, making informed and shrewd, if not infallible judgements on their relative significance, coming up with the very respectable hypothesis of three original authorial versions as an explanation for the variety

---

[1]   This chapter in part recapitulates material first published in 'Editors of *Piers Plowman*'.

and diversity of extant manuscripts, and providing a superb set of notes. How much progress we have made since then is arguable, although perhaps we should take this as a mark of Skeat's outstanding achievement rather than a criticism of modern editors and scholars. Nevertheless, even with the editions that I have described, I think that the relationship between them is not one of straightforward progress.

Characteristically, textual scholars approach a problem by looking at what has already been achieved or settled in the past, and deciding to kick away some aspect of this in order to argue that their own views are valid, interesting, and new. So Whitaker, for example, deliberately picks a different manuscript from Crowley, and argues that this text is superior; Wright reverts to Crowley's version but edits a better manuscript of it, pouring scorn on Whitaker for his various scholarly ineptitudes; Skeat levels the work of his predecessors (with great courtesy and much regard for their contributions, it has to be said) to such an extent that he produces an entirely new landscape. What can his followers do to make their own contribution to the field?

To answer that question, we can look at what Skeat set up as major assumptions about the poem, assumptions with which followers in the field could therefore take issue.

In effect, Skeat established three principles:

(1) that there were three and only three original versions of the poem: A, B, and C;
(2) that his own editions of A, B, and C presented a reasonably faithful picture of what Langland actually wrote;
(3) that one author was responsible for the three original versions of the poem.

As it happens, every one of these three principles can be contested. To take the first, the hypothesis of A, B, and C. Not all the manuscripts fit as comfortably into the three-text grid as one might hope, and as Skeat himself recognised: there are various 'rogue' manuscripts such as Corpus 201, Hm 114, and Bodley 851 which by no means conform to the pattern that Skeat set down. Moreover, as any editor of the poem has found, comparing the line-by-line readings of even relatively orthodox manuscripts of any one version, and placing the three versions side by side, raises delicate and at times almost insoluble difficulties. The extraordinary variety of readings begins to strain credulity: is it really plausible, or feasible, that only one authorial original gave rise to this sort of diversity? Perhaps Langland wrote more than three versions of the poem? or perhaps he changed his mind back and forth between versions in a way now impossible to retrace, but making the whole enterprise of producing critical texts of the three supposed versions at best problematic? Skeat nowhere in his printed work (so far as I know) suggests such a thing, although he comes close to it in a letter written some years later (see p. 234 below); and although, as I have just described, he thought that there were as many as eight separate stages in the authorial composition of *Piers Plowman*.

The second principle, that Skeat's versions of A, B, and C were reasonably faithful to the putative originals, is similarly problematic. Skeat's editions can give the reader a somewhat false impression of textual completeness: he describes every known manuscript in his Introductions, and every page of his text has a learned array of footnotes. But in fact, as his Prefaces makes clear, his texts of the three versions are not critical editions. In essence, he reproduces the readings of one manuscript each for his editions of A, B, and C (Vernon for A, Laud for B, and what is now Hm 137 for C), and he regularly collates only a handful of manuscripts for each edition, making judgements of the others which are often sweeping, and not wholly reliable, on the basis of selective reading and occasional collation. Equally as important, he had to take pragmatic decisions about editing A before he was fully conversant with the manuscripts of the other two versions. It subsequently became clear that, as his successor R. W. Chambers put it, 'we cannot be sure of our critical A-text till we have at least a provisional B-text, nor of our B-text till we have a provisional C'.[2] Skeat's copy-text of A, the Vernon manuscript, looks much less convincing in the light of his B and C editions, as he himself came to accept.

The third principle, single authorship of *Piers Plowman*, was also somewhat insecure. Crowley had suggested that some material in the poem was 'lyke to be a thinge added of some other man than the fyrste autour', and Hearne had thought the same. Thomas Wright, noting the differences between his text and that of Whitaker's text (i.e. between B and C), had also stated his belief that his own text, B, 'was the one published by the author, and that the variations were made by

---

[2] P. 32 of Chambers' draft Introduction to his projected edition of A (Chambers Papers Item 20).

some other person, who was perhaps induced by his own political sentiments to modify passages and was gradually led on to publish a revision of the whole'; and the idea had been repeated by George Marsh in 1860.[3]

MANLY

We can expect that at least one of these three principles (ABC model, reliability of Skeat's texts, or authorship of the poem) will be seen by subsequent scholars as something to get their teeth into. Perhaps not surprisingly, it is the last, the simplest and in a way the biggest issue, that is most immediately taken up for dispute, by Professor J. M. Manly of Chicago (later to become co-editor of the famous Manly-Rickert edition of *The Canterbury Tales*).[4] What is particularly interesting for a historian of the editing process, however, is that Manly, together with all subsequent major *Piers Plowman* scholars up to 1955, did not begin to question an equally important mainstay of Skeat's position, his assumption that Langland wrote three, and three only, original texts.[5] In fact, Manly *emphasises* the supposed security of the assumption that there were only three original texts, elevating it to the status of fact, in order to make his attack on Skeat's hypothesis of single authorship the more devastating.

Manly's work first appeared in an article published in 1906.[6] He describes how,

> Summer before last, in the enforced leisure of a long convalescence, I reread *Piers the Plowman*, or perhaps I had better say, read it for

---

[3] 'The manuscripts of Piers Ploughman vary so widely, that Whitaker can explain the discrepancies only by the supposition of a *rifacimento* by the author himself, at a considerably later period, when his opinions had undergone important changes; but a comparison of Whitaker's and Wright's texts reveals so wide differences in grammar, vocabulary, and orthography, that it is quite unreasonable to refer the two recensions to one writer, and it is by no means improbable that both are very unlike the author's original' (*Lectures on the English Language (First Series)*, 422n.).

[4] Manly and Rickert began work on this edition in 1924, well after Manly's involvement in *Piers Plowman* studies. As an editorial undertaking comparable in size and complexity to the edition of *Piers Plowman* projected, but never completed, by Chambers and Grattan, it took the same sort of overwhelming toll on its editors. See J. M. Manly and Edith Rickert, eds., *The Text of the Canterbury Tales*, vol. I, vii–viii, 1.

[5] See p. 264 n. 15 below. Cf. the school edition of the poem published in 1879 by J. F. Davis, *Langland: Piers Plowman Prologue and Passus I–VII. Text B*, vii–viii, where the matter is regarded as still open.

[6] 'The Lost Leaf of "Piers the Plowman"'. Page references hereafter are to the EETS reprint. Manly gave a paper on the subject to the Philological Society at about the same time; see p. 221 below.

the first time, for although I had more than once read the first seven passus of the B-Text[7] and various other parts of the poem, I had never before read the whole of the three texts in such a way as to get any real sense of the relations of the versions to one another.

'Fortunately', he goes on to say, he 'did not at that time possess a copy of Professor Skeat's two-volume edition', which printed the three texts in parallel fashion on the page, and he was consequently obliged to read the individual editions of A, B, and C that Skeat had published earlier, with the EETS. This was a salutary experience, he found, for 'I read each version separately and obtained a definite sense of its style and characteristics' (p. viii). The impression Manly thereby gained of the differences between the three texts led him to formulate the hypothesis that these differences were better explained as the consequence of different authors than as one author's changing style over many years of writing and rewriting. He describes how his 'suspicions' of multiple authorship have now been changed into 'certainties': 'I am now prepared, I think, to prove that the three versions are not the work of one and the same man, but each is the work of a separate and distinct author.'

In brief, his view was that the A-Text was far superior to the two later versions. Consequently, any perceived defects in the A-Text could not be attributed to the A-Text author. The particular defects Manly had in mind were to be found in Passus V, and were the attribution of several lines to Sloth on receiving stolen goods which in Manly's view belonged to Robert the Robber, and the omission of Wrath from the catalogue of Deadly Sins. (In fact, as his opponents severally pointed out, the characteristics of the Deadly Sins tend to run into each other in most medieval accounts, so that a contemporary audience would have had no difficulty with the proposal that Sloth would have been a receiver of stolen goods.)[8] To explain both these flaws, which are found in all extant manuscripts of A, Manly posited the loss of a leaf in the A-Text archetype. According to Manly, the B author also noted these deficiencies in A, and wrote extra lines to compensate for them, lines however which were 'confused, vague, and entirely lacking in the finer qualities of the imagination, organization, and diction shown in all A's work' (p. xiii). Hence A and B were by different authors. This conclusion, together

---

7   Presumably in Skeat's student edition (1869) of the Prologue and Passus I–VII of the B-Text.
8   See e.g. R. W. Chambers, 'The Authorship of "Piers Plowman"', 9.

with the hypothesis of the 'lost leaf', were the 'certainties' Manly sought to establish.[9]

Manly's candid admission that he had never read the three texts through separately somewhat vitiated his claim to familiarity with the poem.[10] Yet it is worth giving some weight to his point: that the physical characteristics of the edition in which a work is read – characteristics which need have nothing to do with the form of the original work, but which are entirely the product of the modern editing and publishing process – will inevitably influence the way in which the work is perceived by the modern reader and critic. Manly identified the Parallel-Text edition as a medium which tipped the reader towards assuming that all three versions were by the same man. But it is also true that Skeat's individual editions encouraged readers to think of the texts of Vernon, Laud, and Phillipps as the final and authoritative versions produced by the author, rather than what they really were: landmarks among the manuscripts somewhat arbitrarily selected, in relation to which the rest of the manuscript tradition might be mapped out. Manly could see how Skeat's editions influenced readers in one way, but not in the other.

His article caused a great stir, not least on account of the somewhat ill-judged sanction it received two years later in 1908, when he rewrote it in an enlarged form as a chapter in the *Cambridge History of English Literature*. This gave Manly's speculations highly authoritative status, and enraged his opponents. Scholars swiftly took up positions on either side of the debate. Furnivall seized on the quarrel as a suitable subject with which to regale EETS subscribers, and in between 1908 and 1910 reprinted several of the major articles for their

---

[9]   It should be noted that the Z-Text of *Piers Plowman*, believed by some scholars to be an authorial version of the poem anterior to A, does not omit Wrath from its list of Deadly Sins. Instead, the poet lists the sin in the same line as he lists Envy ('Enuye ant Yre ayther wep faste', Passus V 91). If the poet composed the A-Text from a copy of Z, his omission of 'Yre' may be explained as a form of eyeskip, his glance moving from the double treatment of 'Enuye ant Yre' in Passus V 91–4 to the next sin mentioned, 'Couetyse', in Passus V 97. See Rigg–Brewer, 18–19.

[10] Manly later refers to his 'lucky chance of reading [the poems] in the right order' ('*Piers the Plowman* and its Sequence', 41). Manly was not always reliable on matters of fact; for example, he claims in 'The Authorship of *Piers Plowman*', 43 n.1, that he is well aware of the A-MS variants which Chambers and Grattan suggest may vitiate his case for the discrepancies between A and B, but defends himself at 39 n.1 by saying that he did not have access to his pupil Knott's collations. These two remarks appear flatly contradictory. Manly – and more especially, his pupil Knott – do not come well out of the authorship debate; this may be why George Kane, the pupil of R. W. Chambers, attacks Manly so very strongly on his scholarship in another field, the major critical edition of the *Canterbury Tales*. See 'John M. Manly and Edith Rickert'.

consumption. He heartily endorsed Manly's theory, in a way that suggests that he may always have had doubts about Skeat's editing – not surprisingly, given their different editorial orientation (see pp. 83–90 above).[11]

It would take a book to rehearse the various arguments that went to make up the '*Piers Plowman* controversy'; and one has indeed been written, by George Kane, editor-in-chief of the Athlone Press edition of the poem.[12] Kane no doubt felt it necessary to clear the ground for his own edition, which axiomatically assumed that one single author was responsible for all three versions of *Piers Plowman* (though the book may be felt to be retrospectively self-justifying, appearing as it did five years after the first volume of Kane's edition).

As I have described, Manly takes over some of the received ideas on the poem, but completely overturns others. Presenting his argument to the reader, Manly first reports the 'undisputed facts' established by Skeat's 'monumental editions'. Skeat had 'conclusively shown ... [that] there are three principal versions or texts, which he designates the A-text, the B-text and the C-text ... respectively ... The B-text and the C-text are successive modifications and expansions of the A-text' ('*Piers the Plowman* and its Sequence', pp. 1–2). Manly then moves to the question of authorship, introducing this topic with the words 'Let us turn now from fact to theory.' Yet the first hypothesis, that the manuscripts all relate back to three separate (and separable) authorial versions, and no more than three, is just as much a theory as (and no more fact than) that of single (or multiple) authorship. Such an observation rarely, if ever, surfaces in the fast and furious debate on authorship that Manly's article initiated.[13] But as I

---

11 Furnivall's racy account of Manly's theory is to be found in one of the Forewords to the EETS reprint of Manly's *Cambridge History of English Literature* chapter (EETS o.s. 135B: iii–v). As Derek Pearsall has suggested to me, 'Furnivall's zest for Manly was typical of his usual boyish love of upsetting stately apple-carts. He had no established views or thought on the matter' (despite his protestations quoted below, pp. 190–1).

12 *Piers Plowman. The Evidence for Authorship.* Kane was presumably dependent on the excellent account of the controversy found in S. S. Hussey, 'Eighty Years of *Piers Plowman* Scholarship: A Study of Critical Methods', an unpublished MA thesis of 1952 (whose subject was suggested and supervised by Kane). The controversy is succinctly and perceptively discussed by Anne Middleton, in Albert E. Hartung, ed., *A Manual of the Writings in Middle English*, vol. VII, 2224–7, and also, with wit and judicious clarity, by E. T. Donaldson, in 'Piers Plowman: Textual Comparison and the Question of Authorship'. The most useful bibliography is to be found in Derek Pearsall, *An Annotated Critical Bibliography of Langland*, 45–64; cf. 6–31.

13 Twenty-seven years later, Manly's opponent R. W. Chambers speaks in much the same terms: 'The controversy as to the authorship of *Piers Plowman* fortunately does not apply to the fundamental facts of the texts, which have been accepted equally by Skeat and by Manly, and are indeed beyond dispute. *Piers Plowman* is extant in three versions ...' ('The

have already pointed out, in order to make his attack on Skeat's views of authorship as convincing as possible, Manly actually shores up Skeat's hypothesis of the ABC model: as if the first element in Skeat's position was somehow more securely based than the third.

Manly argues at some length, in three successive articles, that a total of five authors had been responsible for the various forms and stages of the poem: the first wrote the A-Text up to Passus 8 (A1), the second wrote Passus VIII–XII (A2), and John But was responsible for the last few lines of Passus XII (A3). B and C respectively were written by two separate and additional authors. He thought this a necessary thesis for a number of reasons. A, he felt, was vastly superior to the other two versions: it was 'distinguished by remarkable unity of structure, directness of movement and freedom from digression of any sort. The author marshals his dream-figures with marvellous swiftness, but with unerring hand; he never himself forgets for a moment the relation of any incident to his whole plan, nor allows his reader to forget it, or to feel at a loss as to its meaning or its place.' These remarks have the twin faults of being vague on the one hand, and – despite their vagueness – eminently refutable on the other. It is true that A has fewer digressions than B and C, but this is easily explained by the fact that it is less than a third of the length of the two longer versions. As for the integrity of the A author's plan and his skill in organising his material, that argument turned out to depend on Manly's posited lost leaf. The A-Text's catalogue of the confessions of the Seven Deadly Sins omits any mention of Wrath, and allows Sloth to confess to receiving wicked winnings. Such carelessness was unthinkable in Manly's A author, so Manly argued that a leaf had fallen out of the author's original manuscript before the latter had been copied into the archetype of all extant A-MSS. As Donaldson astutely perceived sixty years later, Manly's strategy – one that was also adopted by his opponents – was to argue not about the *texts* (or, as one might say, the evidence), but about a hypothetical construct, the *author*(s). Manly could not tolerate the idea of an author of such a poem as A1 being written by anyone who could combine apparently contradictory characteristics: fine organisation and sharp imaginative power on the one hand, and on the other, an

Manuscripts of *Piers Plowman* in the Huntington Library', 2). This view has persisted for many years. Cf. the statement by S. S. Hussey: 'The existence of the A, B and C versions is one of the few facts in *Piers Plowman* scholarship, and unless and until new manuscripts are discovered we had better hold on to it' (*Piers Plowman: Critical Approaches*, Introduction, 8), and also by Russell, 'Some Aspects of the Process of Revision in *Piers Plowman*', 27.

inability to get right one of the simplest imaginable lists – the Seven Deadly Sins. His solution, a postulated lost leaf for which there is absolutely no manuscript evidence, saved his author's face, but led to the strange consequence that the B author, who *did* produce a complete list of the Deadly Sins in his equivalent passage (B Passus V), was berated for supplying a confession for Wrath which Manly judged to be below par. The C author, similarly, is castigated for only partly repairing B's botched attempts.[14]

J. J. Jusserand – and others – responded to these and other arguments in a variety of ways, which can all be very briefly summarised as the point that we should not expect authors to be consistent in their writing or their revisions, especially since, as seemed to be the case with Langland, he devoted his entire life to his poem and wrote it over a long number of years.[15] But Manly felt that the single-authorship camp was labouring under a historical fallacy, which recently increased knowledge should be able to correct. Towards the end of his *Cambridge History of English Literature* article, he gives potted accounts of other satirical alliterative poems which appear to be in something of the *Piers Plowman* mould: *The Parlement of the Thre Ages, Wynnere and Wastoure, Pierce the Ploughman's Crede, Death and Liffe,* and others, nearly all of which were published or republished during the nineteenth century. He uses this evidence to suggest that we now know (or should know) that there were more than just two significant poets writing in the late fourteenth century. Expatiating on this, Manly's style shifts into an embarrassingly grandiose key, worth quoting at some length since it reveals his conception of how his revolutionary views on the poem are part of a forward thrust in the march of knowledge:

---

14 E. T. Donaldson, 'Piers Plowman: Textual Comparison and the Question of Authorship'.
15 Skeat's letters to Chambers on Manly are a good illustration of this type of argument; see further pp. 234ff. below. Jusserand himself puts the main point forcefully in a letter to Chambers dated 7 February 1910 (Chambers Papers Item 29, unnumbered), in which he welcomes Chambers (whom he addresses as 'My dear fellow-Plougher') into the fray: 'I felt till now somewhat lonely in my fortress ...' '... It seems incredible that Manly could say: here are differences, therefore there must have been several men at work, for everybody knows that men never change, they never contradict themselves, and all their words are on a level. No thought of comparing, of verifying if men were really so, if poets answered his beliefs seems to have crossed his mind ...' J. J. Jusserand was the first person to resist Manly's theories in print; see 'Piers Plowman, the Work of One or of Five', answered with some irritation by Manly in 'The Authorship of Piers Plowman', which article was in its turn replied to, with increased irritation, by Jusserand, 'Piers Plowman, the Work of One or of Five: A Reply'.

We are accustomed to regard the fourteenth century as, on the whole, a dark epoch in the history of England [which epoch Manly sketches out for us in dramatic terms] ... Against this dark background we seemed to see only two bright figures, that of Chaucer, strangely kindled to radiance by momentary contact with the renascence, and that of Wyclif, no less strange and solitary, striving to light the torch of reformation ... With them, but further in the background, scarcely distinguishable, indeed, from the dark figures among which he moved, was dimly discerned a gaunt dreamer, clothed in the dull grey russet of a poor shepherd, now watching with lustreless but seeing eye the follies and corruptions and oppressions of the great city, now driven into the wilderness by the passionate protests of his aching heart [Manly continues further in this vein] ... Our study of the *Piers the Plowman* cluster of poems has shown us that [the dreamer's] confused voice and ... mighty vision were the voice and vision, not of one lonely, despised wanderer, but of many men, who, though of diverse tempers and gifts, cherished the same enthusiasm for righteousness and hate for evil. (p. 42)

Manly's work would have reached a number of readers in the pamphlet printed for EETS by Furnivall referred to earlier (p. 187 n. 11). Furnivall was overwhelmed by Manly's claims, and opened his Foreword to the pamphlet with a strongly felt claim for their revolutionary qualities:

> Prof. Manly's discovery of the multiple authorship of *Piers Plowman* is, to me, the best thing done in my time at Early English. Henry Bradshaw's lift up to the Man of Law of the Tales forming the rest of Group B of the Canterbury Tales,[16] Nicholson's proof of the humbug of the genuineness and reputed authorship of Mandeville's *Travels*,[17] Henry Bradley's setting right the run of the *Testament of Love*, and his demonstration that Thomas Usk was the author of it,[18] are the most memorable events in our section of study since I began work in 1861. But I set Manly's achievements above them, because of the greater importance of the Plowman's vision for the student of Literature and Social England, and because the Chicago Professor for the first time clears away from the poet of the A version the tangential strayings and confusions of the author

[16] See Donald C. Baker, 'The Evolution of Henry Bradshaw's Idea of the Order of *The Canterbury Tales*'.

[17] See E. B. Nicholson, letters to *The Academy*, vol. 10, 11 November 1876, 477, and vol. 19, 12 February 1881, 119–20.

[18] See Henry Bradley, 'Thomas Usk: The "Testament of Love"'.

of the B revision, and the rewritings, changes, differences of opinion, and spurious biographical details introduced by the writer of the C version, and leaves us a poet more worthy of being Chaucer's contemporary and ally than we had thought possible.[19]

These remarks are significant in that they indicate the light in which Manly's 'discovery' was seen – as a literary pushing back of the barriers of knowledge, stripping away obfuscation from a true work of art and restoring it to its pristine newness. 'Discovery' may seem a curious term for Manly's speculations, which is why I put the word in quotation marks. But Manly's theory of the lost leaf took on a remarkably concrete quality, both in his eyes and in those of others, on account of his postulating a lost *object* – the leaf itself: there actually was – or might be – something there to be 'discovered'. In fact, what Manly was proposing was a conjectural emendation of enormous proportions – the sixty to eighty-odd lines written on the recto and verso sides of the lost leaf.[20] Without the physical, or material dimension afforded to his ingenious argument by such things as the calculations of the number of lines per page on the average A-MS, or the reference to the typical structure of the manuscript quire, Manly's ideas would not have appeared nearly so objective and logical. But the stress on the physical aspects of his argument diverted attention from the purely subjective impression from which the argument sprang: that there was something wrong with the A, B, and C rendering of the Deadly Sins. Generations of scholars and readers before Manly, and many more since, have read these passages in ignorance of Manly's hypothesis and found them perfectly satisfactory. This is not a proof that he was wrong, but it is a notable fact nevertheless, and indicates how purely personal, even idiosyncratic,

---

19 Foreword, iii, in EETS OS 135B. As we have seen (p. 84 above), Furnivall felt Middle English literature was important not because it was an art form but because it provided evidence for the state of the depressed classes.

20 A point made by Donaldson, 'Piers Plowman: Textual Comparison and the Question of Authorship', 243–4. Such emendations were not unusual in codicological studies; cf. the *Beowulf* criticism of Müllenhoff, set in context and described (with some scorn) by John Earle, *The Deeds of Beowulf*, Introduction, esp. xlff. This codicological form of literary criticism was to continue; Manly's later opponent, R. W. Chambers dismissed one of the less convincing examples (by F. A. Blackburn) in his article entitled 'The "Shifted Leaf" in "Beowulf"' (1915). Skeat had already, we have seen, discovered missing leaves from Rawlinson Poet. MS 38 in the British Library, and he was also, just before his death in 1911, to come across what he believed to be fragments of *Havelok* in the Cambridge University Library. See 'A New "Havelok" MS' (ironically published in the same volume of *MLR* as one of R. W. Chambers' rebuttals of Manly, 'The Original Form of the A-Text of *Piers Plowman*'); also Skeat's second edition of *The Lay of Havelok the Dane*, revised by K. Sisam (1915), Introduction, ix–xi.

was the response to the poem which formed the mainstay of Manly's elaborate theory.

Manly himself saw his role as one who upsets received conventions of the day, or – to adopt Thomas Kuhn's later terminology – one who initiates a paradigm shift. Replying to Jusserand, one of his most forceful and persuasive opponents, he says:

> Mr Jusserand warns us that if my methods are adopted, the whole history of literature will have to be rewritten. This warning is not unfamiliar; we have heard its like from the housetops on almost every occasion when a new truth in literary history, in science, or in social, political, or economic science, has been announced ... I am merely a humble follower in paths of science long known and well charted. The history of literature has been rewritten very largely, and rewritten to no small degree by precisely the same methods that I have employed. And unless human energy flags and men become content to accept the records of the past at their face value and in their superficial meaning, many another ancient error will take its place in the long list of those which could not bear the light of historical and critical research.[21]

It is clear that Manly adopts his epoch-making role with relish.

He was certainly right in thinking that such a violent shake-up could do only good to *Piers Plowman* studies. As Anne Middleton has pointed out,

> Manly's critical axioms were ... characteristic of the period. In fragmenting authorship to explain an additive or reiterative literary structure, his interpretive strategy followed a late-nineteenth century pattern in accounting for the form of long poems of early societies. *Beowulf* and the *chansons de geste*, for example, were analysed as layered assemblages of the work of several hands.[22] His perception of flaws of sense and structure was based on a firm conviction that the A *Visio* defined the genre and merits of the entire work: it was a satire, its author a man of 'unerring hand', and thus B and C represent a decline from the original inspiration and form of the first two visions, not the expansion of a poetic plan. Since disputing Manly's views required scholars to define more carefully both the generic conventions of the poem and its distinctive usages, his challenge had the ironic and unintended effect of hastening the advent of modern comparative literary study.[23]

[21] 'The Authorship of *Piers Plowman*,' 52–3. [22] See n. 20 above.
[23] 'The Critical Heritage', 8.

This observation is precisely confirmed by the letter which R. W. Chambers, the principal scholar involved, wrote many years after the controversy to Kenneth Sisam:

> It is rather a tragedy that Manly discovered two things about *Piers Plowman* which, if he had at that time had access to the MSS. and been willing to work them out, would have led I think to great results. He realised that so far as his A1 was concerned at any rate, there was very much more structure in *Piers Plowman* than had generally been supposed. If he had followed this up carefully he would have found the same to be true of A2 and the B additions and I think probably of the C additions, though this is much less certain.

Manly's second discovery was that 'Skeat's A, B and C, if regarded as critical texts, could not be by the same author, but in 1907 he did not realise how entirely elementary had been the state of our knowledge when Skeat began work in 1864.'[24] This was an important point. If one reads carefully through Manly's three articles, it is difficult not to come to the conclusion that he was almost wholly dependent on Skeat's editions for his knowledge of the various readings and characteristics of the *Piers Plowman* A-MSS, and Chambers had earlier pressed this home in his attacks on Manly.[25] There are a few indications that Manly looked at some of the British Museum manuscripts on one of his trips to England, but he seems never to have put his hand to any serious attempts at collation, of the sort that would have revealed to him the weaknesses of Skeat's editions as anything very much more than reprints of single manuscripts.[26] Manly mentions only one other source of authoritative information on the A-MSS, the work of one of his graduate students at the University of Chicago, Thomas A. Knott, who was to become an important figure

---

[24] 4 February 1942, EETS Papers. Morton Bloomfield made a similar point: one of Manly's contributions to *Piers Plowman* studies was that he 'made us more conscious of the merits of A1 [i.e. the first part of the A-Text] which had been rather neglected since Skeat chose the *Visio* of the B-text for his abridged edition' ('The Present State of *Piers Plowman* Studies', 217).

[25] See Manly's calculations on the average number of lines per page of the manuscripts, which quotes Skeat ('The Lost Leaf of "Piers the Plowman"', xii); his dismissal of the Lincoln's Inn manuscript (e.g. 'The Authorship of *Piers Plowman*', 93), which clearly follows Skeat and Skeat alone; his discussion of A Passus V 49, which relies entirely on Skeat's collations (*ibid.*, 114 n.2). Chambers observes that Manly's arguments are 'avowedly unsupported by a shred of MS. authority' in 'The Original Form of the A-Text of "Piers Plowman"', 304, and accuses him of having 'arrived at his conclusions before examining the evidence' ('The Authorship of "Piers Plowman"', 25).

[26] His remarks in 'The Authorship of *Piers Plowman*', 96 nn.1 and 2 indicate that he looked at the MSS Add. 35157 and 35287 in the British Museum.

in *Piers Plowman* textual studies. Knott had, 'at my [i.e. Manly's] suggestion, been working for the past two years upon a critical text of the A version, the materials for which he collected in England and Ireland in the summer of 1907'.[27] But Knott's collations had not been made when Manly wrote his first (and probably second) article, and he did not have access to them when writing his third.[28] Manly's promised book on his multiple-authorship theory[29] never appeared; probably, as he later wrote to Chambers, because he came to realise that his arguments had in the end to depend on textual evidence, and that the only available textual evidence, that of Skeat's editions, was unreliable and incomplete:

> Meanwhile I hope you will go on with the text of Piers Plowman. I certainly agree with you that the points at issue between us depend in many instances on the readings of the texts. Naturally, I understood this from the first, but I did not realise how purely casual were Skeat's records of the readings & there is no doubt that I took his silences to mean more than they did.
>
> Until we have a critical text of the three visions argument is futile. I dropped the discussion because there was obviously no profit in merely repeating what we had already said … So – as we say in America – it is 'up to you'. When your text appears, you will admit that I am right, or I will admit that you are right, or we shall have a good discussion to determine the question.[30]

We shall return to Knott later. Meanwhile, Manly's observation that decision on authorship must be deferred until the texts had been properly edited is a significant one. It was fundamentally mistaken,

---

[27] 'The Authorship of *Piers Plowman*', 125 n.1. Manly first refers to Knott in 1908 in 'The Lost Leaf of "Piers the Plowman"', xii–xiii. A letter from Manly to Chambers dated 13 July 1909 repeats this infomation and states that 'Mr Knott has taken the Trinity MS as the basis of his work' (Chambers Papers Item 5).

[28] As reported in his letter to Chambers of 13 July 1909, a response to the offprint Chambers had sent him of his 1909 article (described below): 'I might have made full use of the full collations of my friend and pupil, Mr T. A. Knott, but unfortunately they were not available when I was writing, as my article was written partly in Germany and partly on the boat which brought me home.'

[29] See e.g. 'The Lost Leaf of "Piers the Plowman"', ix.

[30] Letter dated 26 June, no year given (probably 1926), Chambers Papers Item 6 (unnumbered). It would appear that Manly had at the time of writing given up hope of Knott's projected text ever being published (see further below), and his softened attitude to the authorship question is confirmed by the report of A. H. Smith that 'according to statements made by Chambers to Professor A. G. Mitchell and myself in 1938, Manly … had finally abandoned the theory of multiple authorship'. '*Piers Plowman* and the Pursuit of Poetry', 35. Cf. T. A. Stroud, 'Manly's Marginal Notes on the *Piers Plowman* Controversy', for evidence that he still believed in his theory in 1928.

but is a key note sounded again and again in the aftermath of the authorship controversy.[31]

Manly's chief opponent in the *Piers Plowman* controversy was R. W. Chambers (1874–1942), librarian of University College, London, where he eventually (1922) became Quain Professor in succession to W. P. Ker. Together with his collaborator, J. H. G. Grattan (1878–1951), a University College colleague who subsequently became Professor of English at Liverpool University, he published three major articles refuting in substantial detail the claims for multiple authorship made by Manly and his pupil, T. A. Knott. Chambers and Grattan embarked on an edition of the A-Text, which gradually expanded into a major research project intended to produce authoritative texts of all three versions. These never came to the light of day, but the project was inherited by several of Chambers' graduate students, one of whom, George Kane, eventually published major editions of A and B many years after Chambers' death, in 1960 and 1975 respectively.

Chambers had been an undergraduate at University College under W. P. Ker and A. E. Housman, and both these men wrote testimonials for him when he applied for a job as assistant librarian at Gray's Inn Library. They speak of diligence, accuracy, good character, considerable ability, and 'methodical industry' – no mention of charm, imagination, or originality; though it is probable that such attributes were not thought useful in an assistant librarian.[32] Chambers was very much a college man with strong feelings of filial piety (see e.g. his lecture on 'Philologists at University College', reprinted in the collection of essays published as *Man's Unconquerable Mind*). He was a traditionalist; for example he supported the preservation of classics and of philology in the English syllabus at University College.[33] He was regarded by his contemporaries and colleagues as a 'stout, true-hearted Englishman' (so H. C. Wyld calls him in a generous letter of congratulation on his appointment to the Quain chair); and his patriotic spirit was an important element in his devotion to *Piers Plowman*, which had by now come to be seen as a

---

[31] It was not to be finally routed until 1965; see p. 321 below.
[32] The testimonials survive in Chambers Papers Item 1.
[33] See materials preserved in Chambers Papers 2 and 4,.

national document of some significance. Chambers called it 'the most thoroughly English of all our religious poems', and commented, 'any Englishman who will take the trouble to understand it can sympathise with it'.[34] Scant matter of truly personal interest survives among Chambers' many letters and papers, though some endearing quirks emerge, for example his love of bears. He seems to have put much of his emotional and professional energy into his librarianship at University College. One of the college porters tells how, during the Second World War, he came back from fire-watching one dawn to check anxiously on the building. He found the library in ruins, with Chambers sitting on the steps weeping at the loss and destruction of treasures he had spent much of his life accumulating for the honour of the college.[35] Chambers' principal works were an edition of *Widsith* (1912), *Beowulf: An Introduction to the Study of the Poem* (1921), which for sixty years remained the authoritative study of the poem's background, *On the Continuity of English Prose from Alfred to More* (1932), which traced a chronological line between his two main interests, and a biography of More (1935). He also produced a great and original edition of *Beowulf* (1914), although characteristically he preserved the name of A. J. Wyatt on the title page since he had taken the latter's unfinished work as his starting point.[36]

Grattan is a more shadowy figure. He moved to Liverpool after the First World War, published an inadequate edition of the *Owl and Nightingale* (originally embarked upon by G. F. H. Sykes, an *OED* lexicographer) in 1935, and struggled on with the *Piers Plowman* editing after Chambers' death in 1942 until his own death in 1951. But it seems clear that Chambers was the moving spirit in the partnership, and although they jointly signed the three major articles which turned out to be their only published contribution to textual investigation of the poem, Grattan himself insists in a letter to Chambers of 1930 (see below, p. 272 n. 4) that he had contributed little other than collation of the various manuscripts.

The work of both Chambers and his successor, George Kane, can be seen to fit into the previously established pattern of relationships

---

[34] *Man's Unconquerable Mind*, 90. Cf. p. 73 above, and p. 296 below. Chambers' 'sense of England's greatness and consequence', and the relation of this to his critical writings, is illuminatingly discussed by J. A. Burrow, 'The Sinking Island and the Dying Author'.

[35] I have this story from Lord Quirk.

[36] See further Chambers' obituary, by C. J. Sisson, in *PBA* 30 (1944): 427–39, followed by a bibliography of his writings compiled by Winifred Husbands, 440–45; also John Wilks, 'The Influence of R. W. Chambers on the Development of University Libraries', and C. J. Sisson, 'R. W. Chambers. A Portrait of a Professor'.

between editions of the poem, a pattern which is not entirely accurately described as one of straightforward, chronological improvement. I shall try to show that Chambers came to the poem with certain ends in view, and under the influence of certain current, and powerful, textual theories derived from classical textual criticism, but that, as he began to see the inappropriateness of these theories to *Piers Plowman*, his work on the text of the poem lost impetus. His pupil, Kane, inherited the theories (and brought many fresh insights of his own), but did not take full notice of some of the implications of Chambers' collations militating against those theories. So the edition of the A-Text he eventually produced, eighteen years after Chambers' death, is in many respects a magnificent achievement, but in other respects flawed.

It seems probable that Chambers' principle interest in the text (as opposed to the contents) of *Piers Plowman* derived at least in part from his passionate devotion to rigorous and logical argument, an interest evident in his initial contribution to the *Piers Plowman* controversy, and also in the very syntax and vocabulary he uses.[37]

Chambers' and Grattan's first article, 'The Text of *Piers Plowman*', was published in the *Modern Language Review* of 1909.[38] Here Chambers makes it clear that he is concerned with one particular aspect of Manly's argument. Manly had tried to pin part of his claim that B was written by a different (worse) poet from the person who wrote A by basing a complicated argument on Skeat's critical apparatus. Manly had discovered that many B readings credited to the B poet were in fact also to be found in A variants (as printed at the bottom of the page in Skeat's edition of the A-Text). So he concluded that the B reviser used a 'vicious transcript' of A from which to make his own version, and that this person was not himself responsible for

[37] It is an interest attested to by those who knew him – Lord Quirk, for example, a protégé of his, has told me that he always felt Chambers should have been an advocate. And cf. the remarks of A. G. Mitchell: 'Whatever was forgotten of his writings, the brilliance and sureness of the arguments were remembered. His gift for interpreting fragmentary and uncertain evidence, for revealing the fault in an apparently satisfactory theory, was paramount. The remote student often found an unkind delight in following his destruction of an elaborate theory' (from unpublished notes for a biographical memoir in EETS Papers).

[38] Although this article, like the two others on the text of the poem (written in 1916 and 1931) is signed by both men, it is clear that, as stated above, Chambers was the leading force in the partnership, writing the articles and relying on Grattan for collation evidence rather than conceptual input into the argument. Grattan himself acknowledged this, and it seems to have been perceived by many of their contemporaries, who wrote to Chambers as if he alone were the author (see chapters 12 and 13). In what follows, I likewise refer to Chambers as sole author.

the changes from A. Manly's motive, of course, was to devalue B in comparison with A.[39] As Chambers rightly points out, the suggestion that the B reviser had 'used as the basis of his B-text a vicious transcript which had travelled, by successive corruptions ... far from his original work', would certainly 'seem to clinch finally the argument in favour of multiple authorship', since it was 'hardly conceivable' that the A-author would not have used an accurate copy of his first version when rewriting to produce B.[40]

Manly thus, as I have described, attacks the third of Skeat's three principles, that one author was responsible for all three texts of *Piers Plowman*. Chambers questions this attack by demonstrating the unstable nature of the second of these principles, that Skeat's editions of A, B, and C represent with reasonable fidelity what the author originally wrote. Manly's argument for multiple authorship, Chambers points out, and as we have seen above, depends on the assumption that Skeat's texts were authoritative. But this is not, in fact, the case. Chambers puts it as follows:

> It has not been recognized that the received A-text is not an attempt to reconstuct the original text, as written by the poet. It is a reprint with some corrections of a single MS. – the Vernon (V) – which Prof. Skeat selected, believing that its readings were, 'on the whole, better than those of any other.' Having selected this MS., the editor's object was to print it *with as few corrections as might be*. With this object, readings admittedly inferior were retained in the text,[41] and have been reproduced alike in the Early English Text and Oxford editions.[42]

Chambers begins his article with convincing documentation of his case. He lists a number of instances where Vernon's text is clearly inferior to that of B, but where B's reading is to be discovered in several – often many, or most – of the A-MS variants, both those printed by Skeat in his critical apparatus and those from manuscripts not collated, or only partially collated, by Skeat. The obvious conclusion, Chambers felt, was that Vernon's text in these places is the result

---

[39] '*Piers the Plowman* and its Sequence', 23.
[40] Though cf. the letter written by Craigie to Chambers in 1919 (p. 253 below), and Chambers' own theory, first expressed in 1910 (pp. 228ff. below) and subsequently developed by Blackman and then Kane and Donaldson, that the poet used corrupt manuscripts of his poem when writing his revisions.
[41] This observation had been previously made by Eduard Teichmann, 'Zum Texte von William Langland's Vision'.
[42] 'The Text of "Piers Plowman"', 358.

of scribal error, and that the original reading of A is the one found in the other A-MSS and also in B.[43]

Chambers, who had had the advantage of being taught by A. E. Housman, substantiates these observations with something quite new in *Piers Plowman* textual criticism, an appeal to the principles of Greek and Latin editing.[44] It has been long recognised in classical editing, he says, that 'a text, which adheres to one MS. in every case except where the reading of that one MS. is untenable, cannot arrive at a reconstruction of the original'. Any single manuscript, however close it is in the copying chain to the author's original, will inevitably be marred to a greater or lesser extent by scribal error; and this means that, in the case of many Old and Middle English works, whose text survives in one manuscript only, we must give up hope of recovering the words in the form in which they originally left the author's pen. But where many manuscripts of a work survive the situation is entirely different. It may well happen that where one scribe has miscopied, another has copied accurately, so that minute comparison of the different manuscripts can give the editor material with which to supplement the deficiencies of one by the strengths of another. This, as Chambers sees, is the case with *Piers Plowman* and its 'peculiarly rich supply of MSS.'.

It seems that Chambers was making genuinely important strides forward in textual criticism as practised by English scholars, by bringing to bear on Middle English texts the techniques of analysis by now familiar to classicists, whether drawn from the German genealogical studies of the previous century or the eclectic tradition stretching back to the Renaissance. German editors of Middle English had been aware of the 'genealogical' method in editing for some time, as instanced in the editions of Lydgate by the German scholars Schick and Glauning (in 1891 and 1900 respectively) already mentioned. But while it is clear that German (and French) techniques of recensionist analysis were known to English editors, they seem not to have been discussed or investigated in any detail.[45] The Chaucerian editor Mark

---

[43] For Skeat's treatment of these instances, see pp. 130ff. above. Chambers writes, 'Many passages, vigorous, energetic, and metrically correct in B, are feeble and tentative in A' ('The Text of "Piers Plowman"', 359). Manly, of course, had regarded Skeat's A as *superior* to B. The fact that the two critical judgements could so differ illustrates the variability of textual criticism of this sort.

[44] For an entertaining account of Chambers' relationship with Housman, see *Man's Unconquerable Mind*, 365–86.

[45] See, e.g., S. J. Herrtage's edition of *Sir Ferumbras* (published in 1881), xix, and George McKnight's edition of *King Horn, Floris and Blauncheflur, The Assumption of our Lady*

Liddell (a Texan Professor of English who believed that language and literature presented 'a field for scientific study much like that of Economics or Ethics ... provided one took the trouble to investigate the phenomena in a scientific spirit')[46] wrote a letter to the *Athenæum* in 1901 making it quite clear that *he* understood the notion of a 'critical text' as established in German textual scholarship, but also indicating that neither the term nor the method of editing it described were familiar to educated circles in England.[47] Liddell claimed to have just produced the first 'critical' edition of some of the *Canterbury Tales*, based on the genealogical analysis of the manuscripts carried out by Zupitza, the German critic of the EETS publications quoted by Sweet in 1877.[48] (The first complete critical edition of the *Canterbury Tales* was not to be produced until 1940, edited by the multiple-authorship proponent Manly, whose pupil Knott – as we shall see below – shows himself aggressively familiar with some of the terminology and techniques of the genealogical method.) Editions of Gower's *Confessio Amantis*, the other major (i.e. literary) Middle English work to survive in a significantly large number of manuscripts, show no signs of textual sophistication until the edition of Macaulay published in 1900–1, an edition which still stands today.[49] Macaulay identified three different classes among the forty-odd manuscripts of the poem, corresponding to three different stages of authorial composition. His discussion of scribal error and authorial

(published in 1901), xxviii–xxix, xlii–xliv, liv–lvi. Cf. also the letter written in 1868 by Paul Meyer to Furnivall quoted above, p. 88, which makes mention of a 'critical text' with the obvious expectation that Furnivall will recognize the term, and Skeat's rather meaningless adoption of Kron's analysis of the *Piers Plowman* manuscripts (p. 177 above).

[46] *An Introduction to the Scientific Study of English Poetry*, vii.

[47] 'When I used the term "critical" ... I was thinking of the German *kritisch*, as used by scholars: as so used the word designates a text constructed in the light of all the "critical" evidence obtainable, regardless of the editor's personal opinion as to the inherent desirability, so to speak, of one reading over another. In such a use of the term no "critical text" is possible until the mutual relations of the MSS. have been ascertained, for until that is done there is no way of discerning critical, essential, and significant evidence from evidence that is not significant, not essential, and therefore not critical' (*The Athenæum* 3862 (2 November 1901), 597–8).

[48] See p. 75 above, and Liddell, ed., *Chaucer: the Prologue to the Canterbury Tales; the Knightes Tale, the Nonnes Prestes Tale*.

[49] The edition of Henry Morley in 1889, *Tales of the Seven Deadly Sins: Being the Confessio Amantis of John Gower*, makes no mention whatsoever of the origin of the text he prints, although he gives a very brief account of previous editions (x), including that of Reinhold Pauli (1857). Pauli had based his text on that of Berthelette (*Jo. Gower de Confessione Amantis*, 1532), collating it with two manuscripts throughout and two others sporadically, and commenting 'The text of a work like the Confessio Amantis does not require the same scrupulous attention to every existing MS. as that of an ancient classical author' (see Pauli, *Confessio Amantis of John Gower*, xliii–xliv).

revision is extremely brief, however, and there is no indication that he applied principles derived from classical textual criticism to the manuscripts to distinguish between scribal and authorial readings, nor that he had carried out an analysis of the manuscripts of the sort referred to by Liddell and to be later recommended by Chambers.[50]

Elsewhere in the 1909 article, Chambers draws on precisely these textual principles, indicating that he had indeed made himself properly familiar with the canons of classical editing. For example, he comments that the significance of *majority* manuscript support for a reading has to be shrewdly assessed: 'MSS. must be weighed, not counted' (p. 363).[51] So that if (as frequently happens), Vernon and its partner, Harley 875, preserve one reading, while the remaining ten A-MSS plus B preserve another, this does not *of itself* prove that the latter reading is the right one. Until the genealogy of the manuscripts is sorted out, it is impossible to tell how likely (or unlikely) it may be that any given manuscript should have reproduced the original reading while all the others have a corrupt substitute. But, he says, it *is* possible to argue that 'the reading of the ten is vigorous, picturesque, and metrically accurate, that of the two commonplace and metrically defective'. And he goes on to comment 'anyone, therefore, who believes that the received text of A reproduces in these passages the original author's words, will have to admit that the text received material improvements at the hand of a scribe, whose phrasing was more effective, and whose ideas of metre were more strict, than those of the original author'.

This is a reference to a standard and, traditionally speaking, quite unexceptionable maxim in classical textual criticism: that it is reasonable under almost any circumstances to attribute the superior reading of two or more alternatives to the author, and the inferior to a scribe or scribes. Yet, as we shall see later, it can become a dangerous maxim if exercised to its logical extremity. There are some texts where, on occasion, *none* of the manuscript readings seems satisfactory or acceptable. In these cases, conjectural emendation, the substitution of a reading thought up by the editor in place of the evidence of the manuscripts, becomes necessary. But in the case of *Piers Plowman*, where the author himself revised his work, such decisions become far

---

50 See G. C. Macaulay, *John Gower's English Works*, esp. vol. I, cxxxi–ii.
51 Kenney traces the lineage of this remark back to 1574 (*The Classical Text*, 44). It was to assume great importance in later *Piers Plowman* textual criticism with Kane–Donaldson's decisive rejection of majority attestation as a significant factor in determining originality of readings. Cf. Brewer, 'The Textual Principles of Kane's A-Text', 76–7, and p. 392 below.

more difficult. Is a weak reading in A necessarily a scribal one? Or might it simply be the weakness of an early draft?

Another principle alluded to by Chambers is that of the sophisticating scribe. As he concedes, notwithstanding its various blemishes, 'the merits of the Vernon text are undeniable'. But even where its text seems admirable, we have to be on our guard. There are various indications that the Vernon scribe went out of his way to improve his exemplar. As Chambers puts it, 'it is natural that a scribe, engaged in copying and turning into his own speech poems often written in widely differing dialects, should become something of an editor. Sometimes he makes a slip, and we can detect him at work.' One example is Vernon's version of a passage where the lady Meed, a personification of bribery, is accused by Conscience at Passus III 116 of having felled 'Your fadir' (most manuscripts) or 'Vr Fader Adam' (Vernon).[52] The person being addressed is the king of Passus III, who stands for Edward III, as several references to the French wars of the time make clear. So the 'your father' found in the majority of manuscripts should probably be taken as referring to Edward II. The Vernon scribe, we may suppose, failed to understand this, and so substituted the reference to Adam, a somewhat ingenious if inappropriate emendation of a reading that evidently puzzled him. As Chambers remarks, 'whatever sins may have contributed to Adam's fall, Bribery can hardly be said to have played a part' (p. 365).

This is one of several 'slips' which Chambers detects in the Vernon scribe's text. He comments, in some irritation, that 'it is the very cleverness of these plausible corruptions which makes their danger. A scribe who is intelligent enough to do this kind of thing, is likely to mislead us more than a bungler who copies, more or less incorrectly, the text before him.' And he refers to the remarks of Edward Moore on the early manuscripts of Dante's *Divine Comedy*: 'their writers are not exact copyists, but editors, although working without an editor's sense of responsibility'.[53] This observation, Chambers says, applies to some extent to all the *Piers Plowman* manuscripts.

Chambers has now invoked two principles of traditional textual criticism that might well seem contradictory; although he himself evinces no recognition of this. On the one hand, he has stated that an

[52] Chambers cites Skeat's line reference, A Passus III 122, and states that nine manuscripts read 'Your fadir'. In fact, the number is fourteen, taking into account the manuscripts discovered since 1909.
[53] See Moore, *Contributions to the Textual Criticism of the Divina Commedia*, viii.

editor should choose the 'better' (by whatever criteria) of two textual variants, since to do otherwise is to act on the assumption that a scribe might write better than the poet (or might be able to produce corrections or alterations of original work which improve on what was there before). On the other hand, he has identified the phenomenon of the sophisticating scribe. Such a scribe acts with the motive of improving his copy. He can be identified in some instances because he makes slips. But why, in other cases, should his behaviour be distinguishable from that of the author? That is to say, if you have two variants, both acceptable, but one less sophisticated than the other – or worse, one acceptable and one unacceptable – how are you to tell whether it is the scribe or the poet who is responsible for the 'better' of the two? In the latter case, the acceptable reading could be the sophisticating scribe's attempt to make sense of the corrupt variant surviving in the other manuscripts. Despite Chambers' failure to notice the problem, editorial dilemmas of this nature bedevil the editing of *Piers Plowman*.

So what is the editor to do, given Vernon's untrustworthy nature? Chamber's solution, clearly, is that the editor should prepare a critical text: compare the manuscripts one with another so as to map out their family tree and get some sense of the relative reliability of the various texts they bear witness to. The procedure he suggests is evidently Lachmannian in origin, but it is immediately derived from that set down in Hort's Introduction to the edition of the Greek New Testament by Westcott and Hort (as Chambers explicitly acknowledges in his later articles).[54]

As Henry Nicol, the genealogically minded critic of Skeat's editions, no doubt realised (see p. 82 above), it is precisely the sort of thing that Skeat would have found useful in dealing with the 'vast mass of unsifted material' that he confronted in 1866. When you wish to make some sense of a large number of different manuscripts of the same work, how can you begin to classify them so as to try to work out which of them are nearer, which further, from what the author originally wrote? There are two types of evidence, Westcott and Hort decided: internal and external.[55] The internal evidence is the quality of the individual readings, taken one by one, while the external is the quality of the manuscript as a whole: its general reliability as a witness. Pretty clearly, the latter is dependent on the former. But it is

[54] See e.g. 'The Text of "Piers Plowman:" Critical Methods', 263, and also p. 212 below.
[55] See Westcott and Hort, *The New Testament*, vol. II, 33.

useful to make the distinction between internal and external: for a manuscript which is generally reliable may yet slip up in the odd reading; and *vice versa*. The way to start is to examine individual readings of a number of different manuscripts on their own merits, and build up a sort of league table to show how the manuscripts compare against each other. There are three stages to this process. Chambers began by taking the four manuscripts on which Skeat placed most reliance, V, H, T, and U, and comparing their texts one against the other over the entire extent of Vernon's text (i.e. up to Passus XI 183). He found, as expected, that VH often agreed with each other, and he found that frequently TU shared an alternative variant on these occasions.[56] Making what were obviously subjective judgements on the quality of the variants, he decided that TU's text was more often right than VH's,[57] although *occasionally* TU's text was inferior to VH's. This was the second stage, which led him to conclude: 'On the evidence, then, of the four MSS., of which full collations have been published [sc. in Skeat's edition of the A-Text], we are led to suspect that, whilst neither the TU tradition nor the VH tradition is to be despised in our search after the original A-text, the greater weight is to be placed upon the TU tradition' (p. 373).

This conclusion enabled the third stage of analysis, in which Chambers reassessed individual VH/TU conflicts in the light of his overall result. It might well be the case that, with the knowledge that TU were on the whole more reliable than VH, he could make a choice between two variants neither of which was clearly superior to the other. Statistically speaking, the TU variant was more likely to be correct than the VH one, and this knowledge gave the editor a useful crutch.

One of the most important principles of a critical text is that *all* manuscript witnesses should be consulted. Chambers went on to show how, given that neither TU nor VH were wholly reliable, additional help in fixing the text might be derived from judicious use of other manuscripts, however unpromising they might initially seem.[58] The Lincoln's Inn manuscript (L), for example, did indeed, as

---

56   As Chambers says, 'there is no necessity to argue, what has been recognized by all students of the subject, that V and H form one group and T and U another. If anyone wishes to satisfy himself of this afresh, five minutes' study of Skeat's footnotes, taken at random anywhere, would prove it' (373). Cf. also Kane, 73–4, 82, 85.

57   H's text ceases at Passus VIII 144.

58   The position (as witness of an author's text) of outlying manuscripts is always difficult to establish in Middle English stemmatology, for scribes knew the language well and the poetic art is not so unique that the scribe's will will not (on occasion) match it. This is a crucial

Skeat thought, have an overlay of scribal corruption, but it was independent of both the TU and the VH families, and hence useful as an independent witness when those two families disagreed or were both in error.[59] Many of these – for example H²KWRE – were, he thought, descendants of the same family as TU. For this reason, they could be used as an additional check on the text of TU. In some cases, their texts had not been fully collated either because Skeat had dismissed them as too faulty or because he had not come across them early enough to make use of them for his edition of A.

Chambers offers us some preliminary findings on them. H², for example, was collated only up to Passus II by Skeat, since he believed that it was so close to T's text as to be useless as an independent witness. Chambers disagrees fundamentally with this reasoning, on two separate accounts: first, that there are occasions where T blunders but where H² preserves the correct reading; and second, because 'even where H² blunders together with T, it is sometimes with a difference which helps us see what the reading of T's original was, and why T went wrong' (p. 374). The same applies to other of T's close relatives.

A different issue arose with W and K. Both these manuscripts have a number of lines normally found only in B- and C-MSS; and the same is true, although to a far lesser extent, of E. Chambers concludes that these lines are present as a result of scribal conflation: scribes somewhere in the history of copying W, K, and E must have had access to manuscripts of the two later versions, and occasionally incorporated their lines or passages into roughly equivalent places in the A-Text.

But as Chambers clear-headedly points out, these diagnoses of supposed conflation need further support: was it a possibility that, as the author wrote and rewrote, he 'issue[d] from time to time additions to his work, so as to give rise to a series of transitional texts?' As we have seen, Skeat thought that this was the correct explanation of the textual characteristics of the Rawlinson B-MS and of the Ilchester C-MS. It was also the assumption of Jusserand, who up to the arrival of Chambers and Grattan on the scene had been the only prominent

difference between Middle English and Classical stemmatology; although not, as it happens, one mentioned by Chambers.

59   See 'The Text of "Piers Plowman"' (1909), 380–2. The Ingilby MS (J), about which Chambers says very little, was a similarly independent manuscript, although the fact that it seemed to have received some correction from a scribe familiar with the C version meant that an editor had to use it with caution. (This manuscript was not collated by Skeat, since he came across it too late to make use of it for his edition of A.) See 'The Text of "Piers Plowman"' (1909), 382–3. On J and L, see further pp. 220–1, 237–8 below.

Manly opponent.[60] Manly had explained the occasional incoherence to be found within and between the three versions by positing separate authors. Jusserand, by contrast, attributed the incoherence to Langland's style of working:

> Tentative additions, written by the author on the margin or on scraps, to be later definitively admitted or not into the text, were inserted haphazardly anywhere by some copyists and let alone by others. In his next revision the poet never failed to remove a few errors left in the previous text, always, however, forgetting a few.
>
> As shown by the condition of the MSS, the poet let copyists transcribe his work at various moments, when it was in the making (it was indeed ever in the making), and was in a far from complete and perfect state; sometimes when part or the whole of an episode was lacking, or when it ended with a canto or passus merely sketched and left unfinished.[61]

Jusserand provided chapter and verse for these assertions, which he drew from the evidence and editorial analyses in Skeat's editions. But like Manly, he seems not to have examined the manuscripts personally or in further detail than Skeat.

With his superior knowledge, Chambers is able to dispense with much of Jusserand's argument. He presents his arguments with his customary courtesy, shrewdness, and rhetorical skill. He concedes at the outset that there may in theory be something in Jusserand's point of view – 'It may be that, when the evidence of the MSS. has been finally sifted, there will be left over certain passages supporting this theory' – but ably demonstrates that 'the bulk of the phenomena which might seem at first sight to support it, on further examination do not so'. Thus Harley 875 and the Lincoln Inn manuscript are not evidence of an early version of the poem stopping at Passus VIII, because both manuscripts are defective at the end of their *Piers Plowman* text, giving no clue whether their respective exemplars also stopped at this point or not. Similarly, the argument that the lines unique to Harley 875 are original to the poem is a difficult one to win, given that the lines are not also present in Harley's twin manuscript Vernon. Chambers thinks they are spurious, a judgement with which subsequent editors have concurred.

And close line-by-line examination of K (and, as Kane later showed, of W also) points unequivocally to the conclusion that a

---

[60] See above, p. 189.   [61] '*Piers Plowman*, the Work of One or of Five', 4–5.

scribe, not the poet, was responsible for the importation of B/C material into an A exemplar: it is done too unskilfully to be attributable to the author.[62]

There is no doubt that Chambers' dismissal of the 'rolling revision' proposition put forward by Jusserand is, as he says, justified on the evidence he discusses. But an interesting and knotty theoretical problem is presented by his method and conclusions. While it is unexceptionable to argue that awkwardly placed lines in W and K are due to scribal conflation, the occasional lines in E – and what Chambers does not mention, the many 'BC' readings in E and A and H^3 – are not self-evidently due to the same scribal interference. They read perfectly well in their context; the only peculiar thing about them is that they are not found in the other A-MSS. When Chambers found B readings in TU, as against a different reading in VH, he claimed that the TU reading was the original of A as well as of B. Why should one not claim the same of the 'BC' readings in E, A, and H^3 (and, as it happens, in several other manuscripts)? We will return to this problem in more detail below (pp. 374ff.).

The 1909 article was a turning point in textual analysis of the poem, marking a departure from the unsystematic consideration of manuscripts and manuscript relations that had previously characterised discussions. In a way, Chambers' advances on Skeat were almost as great as Skeat's on his predecessors, with the signal and vital difference that Skeat produced texts. But Chambers' work was by no means flawless. For example, he dismisses manuscripts A and H^3 as valueless for editing purposes, which is inconsistent with his championship of H^2 as a useful, though weak, witness. And more importantly, his stated intention 'later in the year, to print either MS. T or R, with collations of all the other MSS.' (p. 384), is strangely at odds with the preceding analysis. The logical thrust of the argument against the reliability of Skeat's text, couched as it has been in terms drawn from classical textual criticism, points relentlessly towards a critical edition – that is, a text constructed from the evidence of the A-MSS as a whole, not a staightforward reprint of one or another manuscript.[63]

---

[62] See Kane, 31–5.

[63] The statement puzzled its readers too, as can be seen in the following remarks made by W. W. Greg, librarian of Trinity College, Cambridge, in a letter to Chambers dated 22 June 1909, congratulating him on the *MLR* article. He asked, 'if you give us a reprint of T or R, who is going to give us a critical edition? However, until the relation of the versions is finally settled, I suppose your plan's the safest' (Chambers Papers 5, unnumbered item).

But in 1909, Chambers' and Grattan's work was at a very pre-liminary stage, as they themselves acknowledge. They had made some collations of the A-MSS, but these were only partly digested, since they had 'not had time to sift thoroughly our transcripts and collations'.[64] It also emerges, from other evidence, that the collations were made only of selected passages from the A-Text.[65] It is perhaps too much to expect that the two authors should have fully perceived the revolutionary effect their application of a new form of textual analysis would have on the poem. In this regard, another of their statements is significant: 'only when we know what is the "diction, metre, and sentence structure"[66] of the original A-text, can we argue with certainty whether these are, or are not, materially different from those of the B-additions, or decide whether B's treatment of the A-text is really inconsistent with unity of authorship' (p. 384). This is the first sounding of the keynote identified earlier, one which was to be echoed constantly over the next half-century: without properly established texts, no sensible view on authorship could be taken. In fact, it would be truer to say that establishing the texts was itself impossible without adopting a prior position on authorship, but it was some years before the more sophisticated among *Piers Plowman* scholars could bring themselves to acknowledge this paradox.[67]

Greg was later to play an important, though indirect, role in the editing of *Piers Plowman*, through the influence his work exerted on first Chambers then Kane. See pp. 279 and 355 n. 28 below.

64 'The Text of "Piers Plowman"' (1909), 383.

65 In fact the job was never completed. See further below, pp. 303ff. Chambers and Grattan printed sixty-odd lines from Passus V at the end of their article, a transcript of T with collations from twelve other manuscripts (RUEH²DKWLJAVH).

66 The quotation is from Manly.

67 See p. 321 below.

Excursus: Westcott and Hort

At this point, it will be helpful to step back and consider some more general issues on the editing of *Piers Plowman*. The authorship debate was partly fuelled by the perception of differences between A and B. For a number of reasons, there is strong psychological resistance to the possibility of variation in a canonical text. In the years following Manly's bombshell, advocates of single authorship felt the need to argue that the differences Manly perceived between A and B did not exist (as in the cases of dialectal or alliterative distinctions), or that they were not significant, or that they were due to faulty scribal copying preserved in Skeat's edition. Manly and his followers explained the differences by positing more than one author, and suggesting scribal disruption of A, thus assigning to other hands all the major flaws which were perceived to exist in the canonical text.

There also exists an accompanying resistance to the notion that the author may have changed his mind. He would presumably have done so for some reason, the most obvious being that he regarded his first version as unsatisfactory. But to admit this necessitates admitting also that not all of the author's writings were of the same high quality – an admission which many critics seem to find intolerable, when an alternative explanation is at hand, viz. attributing the variation to scribal corruption.

That these views should have played much part in the textual criticism and editorial construction of the texts of *Piers Plowman* may seem absurd, since the certainty that the author, or someone else, revised and rewrote the poem was almost universally recognised from Skeat onwards,[1] and had been suggested as early as 1550.[2] But a

---

[1] The sole exception seems to be G. Görnemann in 1916, *Zur Verfasserschaft und Entstehungsgeschichte von 'Piers the Plowman'*. Her argument that the differences between the versions are best explained as scribal variations from a single common original was authoritatively demolished by Chambers and Grattan; see below p. 281.

[2] By Crowley; see p. 14 above.

curious phenomenon is discernible: the more sophisticated the textual criticism exercised upon the poem, the greater the reluctance to concede that the source of the textual critic's search, the original manuscript of the poem, is anything other than single and perfect. This must have something to do with a notion of the poet as speaking a language divinely inspired, a magic text whose conception takes place within the soul and which is, in the first instance, sublimely figured forth in words whose luminous and transcendent quality unmistakably stamps them as literature of the highest possible quality.[3] All subsequent processes of transmission – commitment by the author to paper, editing, publishing – are, axiomatically, processes by which change, and therefore error, may creep in. The task of the critic is to purge the error, and recover the original text in all its pristine purity, rather as one might set out to restore a painting, recovering its original state by removing the accretions of age, and inexpert retouchers, on the one hand, and by judicious reconstruction (i.e. conjectural emendation) on the other.[4] The fact that the poet may have willingly complied with changes, recognising them as a necessary part of the process of bringing his or her work before a public, is inconvenient, and until recently, largely ignored. In the case of modern works, irrefutable evidence of such compliance survives – in letters written by the poet and the poet's publishers, different versions of the work during its various stages from first manuscript through proofs to print, different editions, and so on; but in the case of medieval poets, there is almost nothing to give us any hint of what publication consisted in, or how authors oversaw the process. Hence it is easier to preserve the notion that a mass of different readings does not, as in the well-documented cases of Shelley and Byron, reflect different views the author took of his work at different times, but must instead result solely from scribal misprision and miscopying.[5]

---

[3] This notion is an ancient one, going back at least as far as Homer. It is commonly associated with the thought of the Romantic poets; see Shelley, 'A Defence of Poetry', 294, col. 1. E.g., 'the mind in creation is as a fading coal ... this power arises from within like the colour of a flower which fades and changes as it is developed ... the most glorious poetry that has ever been communicated to the world is probably a feeble shadow of the original conceptions of the poet. I appeal to the great poets of the present day, whether it be not an error to assert that the finest passages of poetry are produced by labour and study.'

[4] The current debate on the propriety and efficacy of the restoration of paintings is directly analogous to the debate on how to edit texts.

[5] These ideas are now commonplace. The seminal account of the way in which the social circumstances of a writer mesh with the text he or she produces is to be found in Jerome J. McGann, *A Critique of Modern Textual Criticism*, a work briefly discussed in its historical context by D. G. Greetham, *Textual Scholarship*, 337–8. Greetham provides a very useful

Differences between the texts of *Piers Plowman*, even the reconstructed archetypes of the three texts, are time and again attributed to scribal miscopying rather than to authorial revision. None of the editors of A, B and C will allow that the poet may have changed his mind back and forth between versions, for example writing a line in one way in A, changing his mind in B, and returning to his first choice in C. Instead, there is an apparently irresistible impulse to fix on one line or reading as the original of all three versions, with manuscript variation being written off as scribal error. Consequently, as we shall see, editors expend enormous intellectual energy on establishing methods of detecting scribal error, but very little on what one might have thought would be a logically required corollary, considering how and in what respects the author would have revised his poem.

Some of the resistance to the possibility of authorial variation in Langland's text is undoubtedly attributable to the major influence on the poem's editors of the Introduction to Westcott and Hort's edition of the *New Testament*. As we have seen, the Westcott and Hort method was implicit in Chambers' and Grattan's 1909 article, and it became a mainstay of Chambers's textual analysis in later years.[6] It was published in Cambridge in 1881 and 1882, but appeared to have exerted little influence on Skeat.[7] By contrast, Westcott and Hort were invoked by Manly's successor, T. A. Knott, and also influenced Chambers' successor, George Kane (as he acknowledged at an early stage in his editing career).[8] Consequently, a reading of their Introduction, which gives a full account of their method, is crucial to understanding the textual history of *Piers Plowman* this century.

The Introduction synthesised and restated some of the major principles of classical editing established during the previous years of the century. Westcott and Hort espoused a good deal of the principles of Lachmannian genealogy, yet they fully understood its limitations. They stressed the importance of evaluating the individual quality of

---

summary history of textual criticism and editing at 295–346. The articles in the 1990 edition of *Speculum*, edited by Stephen G. Nichols, devoted to 'The New Philology' reflect and reflect on some of the ways in which recent changes in critical and textual theory impinge on the editing of medieval texts. See also Derek Pearsall, 'Theory and Practice in Middle English Editing', 'Authorial Revision in Some Late-Medieval Texts'.

6 A piece of paper in Chambers' handwriting listing 'important passages in Westcott & Hort *introduct*' survives among his papers at University College (Item 24).

7 See above, p. 104, on Skeat's equal lack of interest in the 1881 publication of the Revised Version translation of the New Testament.

8 See p. 315 below.

manuscript readings, thus encouraging a flexible application of the recensionist method. This can be seen in the three-stage method they advocate for analysing manuscripts (adopted by Chambers for his study of the A-MSS): the method utilises genealogical information, but tries to avoid the sort of mindless application of genealogical theory indulged in by Knott (described below, p. 241). This three-stage method is concisely summarised by Chambers:

> Faced by a large number of MSS., how are we to start estimating their value and relationship? ... We select the passages where one reading seems, on various grounds of *intrinsic* probability, superior to another or others. We then notice in which MSS. the inferior readings occur, and so obtain data to judge the worth and relationship of MSS. Having done this we can, for the first time, begin to speak of MS. authority, and of one MS. being better than another. But, as we decide where the weight of MS. authority lies, we must look back, and be prepared to alter our original judgement as to readings if ... 'very strong *a posteriori* evidence from the best MSS. should seem to overbalance the admittedly inconclusive *a priori* evidence'.
>
> The three stages are repeatedly emphasized by Westcott and Hort: first, *provisional* judgement of readings on intrinsic evidence: then, estimate of MS. authority by these readings: then, final decision.[9]

For our purposes, certain additional salient features of Westcott and Hort's method stand out. The opening sentence of the Introduction sets the scene: 'This edition is an attempt to present exactly the original words of the New Testament, so far as they can now be determined from surviving documents'. This statement is amplified by the following:

> ... textual criticism is always negative, because its final aim is virtually nothing more than the detection and rejection of error. Its progress consists not in the growing perfection of an ideal in the future, but in approximation towards complete ascertainment of *definite facts of the past, that is, towards recovering an exact copy of what was actually written* on parchment or papyrus by the author of the book or his amanuensis. *Where there is variation, there must be error in at least all variants but one; and the primary work of*

---

[9] Chambers and Grattan, 'The Text of "Piers Plowman": Critical Methods', 263. The quotation at the end of the first paragraph is from Edward Moore's *Contributions to the Textual Criticism of the Divina Commedia*.

textual criticism is merely to discriminate the erroneous variants from the true'. (vol. II, p. 3; my italics)

The assumption that there was one single authorial original is virtually indispensable in the case of the Bible: the word (or voice) of God must be singular not plural.[10] We speak of the 'word', singular, fixed, unchangeable, unsubstitutable. This view adapts very easily to the conception of the author as divinely inspired sketched out above. But it is not a happy principle to apply to an authorially revised poem like *Piers Plowman*: it is not necessarily a 'fact' that there was one original and one original only. We shall see later the difficulties that assumption of a single original caused in the Athlone edition of *Piers Plowman*, where the editors time and again showed themselves unable to tolerate small differences between the A and B texts, correcting the evidence of the B-Text on the assumption that only one authorial reading could have given rise to the variants to be found in both A and B, and resisting all implications to the contrary.

Another interesting feature of Westcott and Hort's analysis is their constant appeal to 'facts'. Thus they write

> Every method of textual criticism corresponds to some one class of textual *facts*: the best criticism is that which takes account of every class of textual *facts*, and assigns to each method its proper use and rank. The leading principles of textual criticism are identical for all writings whatever. Differences in application arise only from differences in the amount, variety, and quality of evidence. The more obvious *facts* naturally attract attention first; and it is only at a further stage of study that any one is likely spontaneously to grasp those more fundamental *facts* from which textual criticism must start if it is to reach comparative certainty. We propose to follow here this natural order, according to which the higher methods will come last into view. (vol. II, p. 19; my italics)

This language is reminiscent of that to be employed years later by Kane, as amply evidenced in the quotations in Part V below. It gives a good idea of the style of the Introduction, with its forthright appeal to logic and its appearance of relentless rigour. The language is that of empirical scientific investigation, a discipline with which Kane has explicitly associated textual criticism.[11] This coexists rather curiously with what is too often lacking in the writing of *Piers Plowman* textual

---

10   Cf. *Piers Plowman*, B Passus IX 35.
11   See p. 405 below.

scholarship, a recognition of the essential subjectivity of the editing process:

> There is much literature, ancient no less than modern, in which it is needful to remember that authors are not always grammatical, or clear, or consistent, or felicitous; so that not seldom an ordinary reader finds it easy to replace a feeble or half-appropriate word or phrase by an effective substitute; and thus the best words to express an author's meaning need not in all cases be those he actually employed. But ... it concerns our own purpose more to urge that in the highest literature ... all readers are peculiarly liable to the fallacy that they understand the author's meaning and purpose because they understand some part or some aspect of it, which they take for the whole; and hence, in judging variations of text, they are led unawares to disparage any word or phrase which owes its selection by the author to those elements of the thought present to his mind which they have failed to perceive or to feel. (vol. II, pp. 21–2)

These two quotations are a good example of Westcott and Hort's remarkable seesawing between recognition of the subjectivity of the whole exercise, and insistence upon logic and rigour, even though the former would seem to obviate some crucial applications of the latter. As we shall see later, a comparable see-sawing can also be perceived in the Kane–Donaldson edition of *Piers Plowman*.

The second of the quotations is part of Westcott and Hort's discussion of the difficulty of choosing between alternative variants on what they call 'internal' or 'intrinsic' grounds – i.e., considering them on their own merits without reference to the overall quality of the manuscript they appear in. 'In dealing with this kind of evidence', Westcott and Hort say, 'equally competent critics often arrive at contradictory conclusions as to the same variations' (p. 21). The reason for this is clear. If the job of the editor is to 'perceive or feel' what was in the mind of an author who wrote centuries ago, it is inconceivable that editors will not disagree with each other. This is because we have moved beyond the realm of 'facts' into that of mere surmise. Westcott and Hort stress that 'The value of the evidence obtained from Transcriptional Probability [postulating what appears the most likely sequence of scribal error] is incontestable. Without its aid textual criticism could rarely attain any high degree of security' (p. 24). But it is of limited use only:

> If we look behind the canons laid down by critics to the observed *facts* [my italics] from which their authority proceeds, we find, first, that scribes were moved by a much greater variety of impulse than is usually supposed; next, that different scribes were to a certain limited extent moved by different impulses; and thirdly, that *in many variations each of two conflicting readings might be reasonably accounted for by some impulse known to have operated elsewhere.* (vol. II, p. 25; my italics)

For obvious reasons, this last point presents particular difficulties. If we allow that a scribe would have written more emphatically than an author, and that a scribe would also have written less precisely than an author, we can find ourselves unable to decide whether to attribute a variant to a scribe or to an author (consider, for example, the difference between 'blaze' and 'fire'. Is 'blaze' more emphatic or more precise?). The problem is, that many of the criteria for distinguishing between scribal and authorial writing (or, 'what are not very happily called "canons of criticism"', p. 23) are reversible. Westcott and Hort recognise this; as we shall see below, their successor George Kane did not (pp. 372ff.). The two editors continue, stressing the extreme precariousness of their processes of inference and deduction:

> In these last cases decision is evidently precarious, even though the decision may seem to be stronger on the one side than on the other. Not only are mental impulses unsatisfactory subjects for estimates of comparative force; but a plurality of impulses recognised by ourselves as possible in any given case by no means implies a plurality of impulses as having been actually in operation. (vol. II, p. 25)

And besides, the operation of 'accidental circumstances beyond our knowledge' make it impossible to know how our judgement of the relative force of the impulses would have been perceived and acted on by the scribe in question at any particular moment. These and other observations (such as the rather desperate attempt to distinguish between scribal sophistication and authorial original, p. 27)[12] give a strong impression of the fragility of the reasoning process that otherwise so strongly characterises Westcott and Hort's writing. But the prevailing appearance of their work is one of ruthless and unimpeachable logic, which subjects a chaotic plethora of manuscript detail to rigorous analysis and brings to light the original words of the

---

[12] Cf. Chambers' struggles with the sophisticating scribe of Vernon, described above, p. 203.

author through a process of objective and scientific examination. As such it had (and has) enormous appeal.

Chambers may have come across Westcott and Hort through Housman, although it is possible that (as a medievalist) he first read of their work in the study by Edward Moore he also cites, the *Contributions to the Textual Criticism of the Divina Commedia* (Cambridge 1889). Both Westcott and Hort and Edward Moore were cited as models for analysing the manuscripts of *The Canterbury Tales* in Eleanor Hammond's *Chaucer. A Bibliographical Manual*, which was published by the University of Chicago in 1908, and it is possibly through this route that their work came to the attention of T. A. Knott, who as the pupil of Manly, Professor of English at Chicago, would presumably be aware of the latest textual work on Chaucer.[13] (On the other hand, Knott's discussion of textual principles is so crude as to suggest his familiarity with Westcott and Hort and Moore was minimal, despite his invocation of their examples.)

Whatever its route, the filtering of their work into Middle English textual criticism was an event of great significance. It answered the criticisms of Sweet thirty years earlier, and fulfilled the requirements of Henry Nicol that the manuscripts of *Piers Plowman* should be genetically studied. It marked a new stage in Middle English editing, indicating that the era of Furnivallian printing, as opposed to editing, was beginning to come to an end.[14]

[13]   Though work on the Manly–Rickert edition of *The Canterbury* Tales did not begin in earnest until 1924; see p. 184 n. 4 above.

[14]   Though it is probably true to say that in some areas of Middle English editing, such as the Romances, it has now been accepted that the sort of editing advocated by Westcott and Hort, which received wide currency through the favourable reception given to Kane's edition of the A-Text of *Piers Plowman*, is simply impracticable. For a summary discussion, with references, see Pearsall, 'Theory and Practice', 111–12 and 112 n.10, who comments 'The practical solution here is to edit the different witnesses in parallel texts' – i.e. return to the Furnivallian mode of printing.

Chambers 1909–1910

A considerable stash of letters and papers belonging to R. W. Chambers now survives in the library of University College, London.[1] Chambers made very few copies of his outgoing letters, but–fortunately for us–kept a number of the interesting and important communications that he received from scholars such as Henry Bradley, Skeat, and Furnivall. These give a valuable insight into the contemporary reception of Chambers' work on the poem, particularly his first article. Chambers also kept some of his notes on *Piers Plowman* manuscripts, along with copies of his correspondence with Grattan and with various librarians. Piecing these all together is a difficult, one-sided, and ultimately speculative task, but it does give us some idea, albeit sketchy, of the manner in which his textual work on the poem progressed.

The surprising indication of some of the material is that Chambers' and Grattan's consultation of the manuscripts themselves, as opposed to their reading and digestion of Skeat's editions and Manly's articles, may have begun as late as January 1909. A letter dated 7 January 1909 from W. W. Greg, librarian of Trinity College Cambridge, grants Grattan permission to see a Trinity manuscript, apparently for the first time.[2] This was presumably the Trinity A-MS (R. 3. 14), which Chambers and Grattan's 1909 article, discussed in chapter 10 above, pinpoints as one of the most important of the A-MSS, and a major, indeed superior, rival to Skeat's Vernon. The letter indicates that much of the first-hand work for the article must have occurred after this date, and possibly in as little as three months.[3] This may seem

---

[1]   A. H. Smith made some use of the papers on pages 34–6 of his article on '*Piers Plowman* and the Pursuit of Poetry' (1969). Otherwise they have not, so far as I know, been quoted in print. See Janet Percival, *The Papers of Raymond Wilson Chambers*.

[2]   Chambers Papers Item 5, unnumbered.

[3]   At the same period, the two men were working intensively on T's close genetic partner, U (University College 45), as indicated in a letter Grattan wrote to the librarian of University

barely credible, but it would explain why the two scholars' initial estimate of the time required to complete an edition of the A-Text (one year) was so sanguine, for their initial work on the poem had proceeded with remarkable speed.

Chambers' considerable familiarity with *Piers Plowman* must have begun some time before this, however, studying Skeat's editions and critical apparatuses carefully to check the truth of Manly's observation that many B readings were to be found in faulty manuscripts of A—meaning manuscripts of A which read differently from Vernon.[4] The Trinity A-MS figures most largely among these, and was the obvious choice for Chambers and Grattan as the first manuscript to collate in detail.

Even at this comparatively early time, Chambers and Grattan had heard that someone else was working on the A-MSS of *Piers Plowman*. Writing to Sir Henry D. Ingilby, Bart., on 16 February 1909, to make inquiries about the A-MS in his possession, Grattan refers to 'the American', and his fear that he and Chambers 'may be working on another man's ground'. Ingilby seems to have written back to reassure them, for a copy of a letter Chambers subsequently wrote to him on 9 March 1909, making arangements for the manuscript to be sent to the British Museum for him to consult there, says gratefully: 'the information you kindly gave me that Professor Skeat was the last person to make critical use of your MS., shows that the American who we feared might forestall us, is pursuing some plan different from ours'.[5] The manuscript cannot have arrived in time for Chambers to have made much use of it, since his article gives it fairly brief and unspecific attention, merely stating that it is a valuable witness, independent of the two major families, but must be used with

College on 25 February 1909, asking whether he might look at the manuscript again to check a few extra collations. He finishes 'we are most anxious to consult the U. C. MS at as early a date as possible, since the results of our investigations (practically complete, but for the verifying of Skeat's work) must be in the printer's hands by the middle of March'. University College manuscripts had by this stage been deposited in Bodley (see p. 127 n. 34 above). An undated scrap of paper in Chambers' hand (Chambers Papers Item 5, unnumbered), apparently also from this early period, records the lines so far collated from each manuscript. H² and U have been collated up to the end of Passus II, H for most of Passus III, K, D, A up to varying points in Passus V; W and V up to Passus VI 46, and only R, J, E and L throughout. This suggests that Chambers and Grattan's work was not systematically carried out, confirming many other indications to this effect.

4   A. G. Mitchell suggests that Chambers set to work immediately after hearing Manly's paper delivered to the Philological Society in 1906 (see n. 8 below); it is possible, however, that Chambers (his informant) had in retrospect collapsed the time schedule.

5   Both letters survive (unnumbered) in Chambers Papers Item 5, as does all other correspondence cited hereafter in this chapter unless otherwise indicated.

care.[6] And he and Grattan must have been dashed by the letter they received a month later (10 April) from Ingilby, telling them that, alas, he had just come across three letters among his past correspondence showing that he must have lent the manuscript to a Mr Knott of Chicago in 1907. Skeat had written to Ingilby in Knott's favour, which is why Ingilby had recollected Skeat as being the last person to whom he had lent the manuscript. 'If you have spent labour in vain in consequence of my mistake', the baronet writes apologetically, 'I can only repeat my great regret.' He enclosed with his letter the three letters from Knott, asking for their return at Grattan's convenience. Grattan complied with this request, but made transcripts of certain portions of the letters, including the following remark from a letter of 30 August 1907: 'Trusting to have the privilege of presenting you with a copy of my edition of the poem–to be published in two years.'[7] It seems that Chambers and Grattan were not alone in underestimating, by a very considerable margin, the time it would take to produce a critical edition of A (Knott's edition was finally to achieve posthumous publication in 1952). The two English editors' optimism, at this stage in the proceedings, is revealed in the letter Grattan wrote to Ingilby in May 1909:

> We hope this time next year to do ourselves the honour of asking you to accept a copy of a complete variorium edition of the A-Text of Piers Plowman. For we have been fortunate in receiving an offer from Dr Furnivall to bring out an edition in the Early English Text Society's publications. Professor Skeat has previously encouraged this; and Mr Knott, we find, will not hurt, or be hurt by, our work.

The information that Chambers and Grattan were to bring out an edition for the EETS is delightfully fleshed out by several of the other letters in the Chambers Papers, along with related matter in the EETS archives. It is reported by A. G. Mitchell that 'Chambers was present as (in his own words) "a young and unknown librarian" at the meeting of the Philological Society at which J. M. Manly propounded his theory of the multiple authorship of *Piers Plowman*. At that meeting were present such giants of scholarship as W. P. Ker, Henry Bradley and Dr. Furnivall.'[8] It seems possible that Furnivall subse-

---

[6] See p. 205 n. 59 above.
[7] Chambers Papers Item 6 (unnumbered).
[8] The account survives in the EETS archives as part of an unprinted biographical memoir of Chambers. Its chronology and other details are probably not reliable, as indicated by the description of Furnivall as a 'giant of scholarship'. It continues, 'Bradley and Furnivall

quently talked to Chambers about his work on the A-Text, decided that it would be a good project for the EETS, and gave him a letter of introduction to Skeat, whose assent to a new edition it would be only courteous to procure. Chambers had by this time written, but not published, the 1909 article; and he was worried by the possibility of Knott's pre-emptive work on the A-Text. Skeat replies to his inquiry as follows (the letter is dated 24 April 1909):

> Dear Sir –
> I do not know Mr Knott's address. He called here, & I did what I could for him. I seemed to gather that he wished to collate *all* the MSS. of the A-text of P. Plowman. –
> I shall be glad to do what I can for you likewise – of course. – If you can kindly come here tomorrow at half-past four, or there-abouts, to afternoon tea, we could easily talk things over. On Monday I am out in the morning – to lecture – & have a College Meeting all Monday afternoon. –
> Yrs
> W. W. Skeat.[9]

Chambers evidently accepted Skeat's invitation and went up on the train to see him. Over tea on the Sunday afternoon he asked Skeat to read a copy of the proofs of his forthcoming article on the A-Text. Back came a letter from Skeat written on the following day (Monday 26 April):

> Dear Sir -
> I have just had time to glance at the proofs: & I can see that the whole essay is of great importance.
> It all comes to this – that we cannot profitably discuss a question till we know *precisely* what we are talking about. And – for reasons such as you adduce – we cannot discuss Text A till we know *precisely* what Text A really is.
> That is quite correct.
> Further, owing to difficulties which could not be adequately understood or got over at the time when the "Vernon" Text was printed, but which *can* be adequately considered *now*, it has now become much easier to construct a correct A-text than it was in

accepted Manley's [*sic*] theory and later wrote in vigorous support of it. W. P. Ker was won over. Chambers alone stood out in uncompromising opposition. He believed in the single authorship of the three recensions of the poem, and felt sure that the name of the author was William Langland. He went quietly away to get his ideas together and write an article....'

9   Chambers Papers Item 5:2.

earlier days. This is all in the natural order of progress. -

Two things follow. (1) That your Essay ought to be at once printed and circulated. (2), That I am quite aware that it *may* become necessary for my A-text to be superseded. -

I comfort myself with the reflection that my work is *by no means* set aside; because it is really a reasonable basis for fresh work, and will lead to right results in the end & hereafter.

Yrs

W. W. Skeat[10]

This is a remarkable letter, illustrating as it does Skeat's magnanimity and generosity to the younger man as well as his ready grasp of Chambers' argument. Chambers' article, as we have seen, consisted almost entirely of a demonstration of the notable but unobvious imperfections of Skeat's A-Text; not only his choice of an undesirable copy-text, the Vernon manuscript, but also his failure to record in the footnotes significant variants found in the other A-MSS, even those he claimed to have collated rigorously against the text.

The next letter in the sequence (so it seems; it is headed only '10 am. 1909') is one from Furnivall to Grattan explaining Furnivall's views on the EETS producing a second edition of a text already in print:

Dear Mr Grattan, I've read the PPl. article by Chambers & you, & I think it's a capital bit of work, & am willing to say so in the way of a Testimonial. I am also willing to take an edition off [*sic*] the A text by you two, using TU – or such MS. as you choose as the best – as the basis, but editing it by necessary improvements, such as supplying the 2 half-lines it leaves out in v. 91–2, & – adding full collations – making the best text you can of it, & your having the right to use the text for a 6/- or other school or Coll. book. I will not take a simple print of 1 MS with collations. I wrote to Skeat about it.

Dr. Thos. A. Knott, 6 [?] St. Cambridge, Mass., U.S.A, is the address you want. Write on the envelope – if gone, forward to the University of Chicago.[11] With the many unprinted MSS [?]needing

---

10 Chambers Papers Item 5:3.

11 That Chambers did write to Knott (presumably in his continued anxiety over what 'the American' might be doing) is confirmed by a rather bullying letter from Manly to Chambers dated 13 July 1909, 'thanking' him for an offprint of the 1909 article: 'I am very glad that you and Mr Grattan intend to publish a text of the A-version with a complete collation of the manuscripts. Mr Knott tells me that he has just received a letter from you in regard to the possible interference of his plans and yours. I entirely agree with you that there need be no interference especially if you carry out your plan of making MS. Rawl Poet. 137 the basis of your publication. Mr Knott has taken the Trinity MS as the basis of

type, I don't want to have many of [?] EETS Texts re-edited; but I
hold this A case to be an exceptional one, & therefore am willing to
take your edition. Before we can deal satisfactorily with the relation
of B & C to A, we must, as you say, know what A is.

Truly yrs,

F. J. Furnivall.

If you can spare your proof for 3 days, post it to Dr. Hy. Bradley,
North House, Clarendon Press, Oxford.[12]

Here is an important statement indicating that Chambers and Grattan's original plans would have to be revised. Furnivall had plainly
taken on board the logic of Chambers' textual arguments rather more
successfully than Chambers himself, and perceived the necessity of a
proper critical edition, not one based, as Skeat's had been, on a single,
occasionally corrected manuscript. Furnivall evidently did write to
Skeat, for he posts the latter's reply, dated 11 May 1909, on to
Chambers:

> My dear Furnivall –
>
> I am very much obliged by your note. I don't know that I could
> have done better *at the time*: as the whole problem was in a different
> stage then to what it is now. I presume that, *but* for the E.E.T.S.
> edition, the present advancements of the Problem would hardly
> have been made. –
>
> But we move on: & I can see *now*, what no one knew *then*, that it
> is better to take another MS. – and not the Vernon MS. – as the basis
> of the A. text. I shd. strongly support the issue of a new & improved
> edition – it would become the E.E.T.S. to do it, as soon as is
> convenient.
>
> It is, as you say, not an ordinary case: & so the E.E.T.S. money
> wd. be well spent in remodelling the text. I can only hope that the
> editors will find that I have made the way a good deal clearer than it
> would have been otherwise. If they find it so, & will be so kind as to
> say so, I shall be quite satisfied.
>
> Yrs. W. W. Skeat.[13]

---

his work, and it will be of the highest interest and value to have the two publications.' As
we have seen, Chambers and Grattan had not stated a final decision to make the Rawlinson
manuscript their base-text, merely that they hoped 'to print either MS. T or R, with
collations of all the other MSS.' ('The Text of "Piers Plowman" ' (1909), 384), and they had
reproduced at the end of their article a sample of text using T as a base.

[12] Henry Bradley, the co-editor with J. A. H. Murray of the *OED*, had come down with
Furnivall on Manly's side in the *Piers Plowman* controversy. He wrote several articles on
the debate, including 'The Misplaced Leaf of "Piers the Plowman" ', 'The Authorship of
"Piers the Plowman" ', 'Who was John But?'.

[13] Chambers Papers Item 5:5.

This passing about of letters from one correspondent to another is typical of Furnivall, who operated more as a facilitator of relationships and a communicator of information between different parties, than as a participating scholar in the controversy. The full analyses of Chambers' work are to be found in letters to him from Bradley and Skeat, not from Furnivall, who merely scrawled hasty comments, encouragement and sometimes ideas on the edges of other people's letters or on the back of brightly painted postcards.

After Chambers' article had been published, Furnivall discussed it with Henry Bradley and subsequently forwarded to Chambers a section from Bradley's reply.[14] Bradley's contributions to the debate on authorship are found in a number of letters preserved in the Chambers Papers, and are marked by three characteristics: the tenacity with which he continued to hold his views (despite his appreciation of the force of Chamber's position), the disinterestedness with which he expressed them (*parti pris* acrimony–or as another of Chamber's correspondents put it, the *odium philologicum*[15] – never enters into his remarks), and finally his continual emphasis, shared with all his contemporaries, on the need for proper texts: for until these were established, so they believed, no satisfactory conclusion on authorship could be reached. All these characteristics can be found in the following letter, written to Chambers on 1 June 1909:

> My dear Sir,
> When I returned your paper I inadvertently left out of the envelope a note that I had written. I now write to express my admiration for the article, and the satisfaction which I feel in learning that you and your colleague are engaged in a critical edition of the A-text. You have given every reason for confidence in the soundness of the method you are following in its preparation. I have all through felt strongly that until we have before us a trustworthy reconstruction of each of the three texts, any detailed argumentation on the question of authorship must necessarily contain much that is fallacious. Probably every serious student of Piers Plowman has seen that the Vernon MS. is no fit basis for the constitution of the A-text. At the same time, it has been equally obvious that haphazard dipping into Skeat's collations will not help

---

14 The snippet is undated, but the envelope in which it is enclosed, addressed in Furnivall's hand to Chambers, is postmarked 1 June 1909.

15 A letter from the librarian of Corpus Christi College, Cambridge, thanking Chambers for an offprint (probably of the 'Authorship' article), remarks that although he hasn't read Manly, 'one can estimate your conservative arguments against him fairly well; and they are as convincing (to me) as they are free from the *odium philologicum*.' (25 February 1910).

us greatly. Whether individual differences of the other MSS. from the Vernon ones are traces of the original reading or due to acquaintance with some form of B & C can only be determined by systematic work. The task before you – even assuming that the great labour of collation has already been accomplished by you – is terribly difficult, but your paper leads me to believe that you have the industry, patience, and freedom from bias which are essential to its successful accomplishment.

    Believe me,
        Yours sincerely
        Henry Bradley[16]

These salutary words of caution were repeated by Skeat (possibly with the slightest hint of malicious pleasure): 'I am rather interested in the question as to what can now be done. It seems to me that, *even now*, the man who edits the A-text has not precisely a "soft" task! ... Your admirable text of T shows that it requires emendment, as you (in fact) say. There are plenty of problems left.'[17]

His judgement was corroborated by Furnivall, who told Chambers 'You're in for a big and long job, but the work is so important that effort is well worth while at it.'[18]

Chambers' next published paper, on 'The Authorship of "Piers Plowman"' (1910) gives some indication of how Grattan and he were tackling those problems. It appeared, like the previous paper, in the *Modern Language Review*, but was circulated for consultation beforehand to Furnivall and Bradley. It is a masterly attack on Manly's position. Chambers writes with greater cogency and elegance than either Manly or Jusserand, and it is this paper more than any other which sets forth clearly the various issues under discussion.

Chambers devotes the first part of his paper to dealing with Manly's assertions that three passages in A were miscopied by scribes, and subsequently wrongly adopted–i.e. in their flawed form–by B.

[16]   Chambers Papers Item 5:9. Cf. also Bradley's letter of 30 June 1909 to Furnivall (Item 5:14), which includes the following passage: 'What both you and I desire is truth, and not the confirmation of our own theories. Mr Chambers' paper at any rate contains much that is valuable, and has distinctly raised my hopes that eventually the whole question may receive a decisive solution. But exhaustive work on the texts is needed before that result can be attained.'

[17]   Chambers Papers 5:11, dated 18 June 1909. The letter concludes: 'But it is quite certain that you & Mr. Grattan (I don't know him, but hope we may meet some day) have *very materially advanced* our knowledge of the A-text: & that you are doing work which will be *permanent*'.

[18]   19 August 1909, Chambers Papers Item 5:18. Furnivall also offers financial support from EETS funds in photographing manuscripts.

The three passages in question were the supposed misplacements of Robert the Robber's confession, the concluding lines of Sloth's confession, and the lines on Piers' wife and children.[19] In all three cases, Chambers shows that Manly's argument and assumptions will not hold: the passages are perfectly satisfactory as they stand, and any identification of incoherence, awkwardness, or inconsistency must, if it is made to stick, apply also to many other passages in A which Manly has not questioned. Chambers then summarises, very sensibly, the basis on which decision between Manly's theory and the A-Text evidence must be made:

> It must be remembered that the question is not whether, on the whole, the text would make better sense if rearranged. Where MS. evidence is equally divided we can, of course, only choose the most plausible arangement. But here there is no particle of MS. evidence in favour of a rearrangement of the received text. The proposed arrangements are pure conjecture. Unless the advantage to be gained by a rearrangement is very great indeed a cautious editor would not, under these circumstances, accept it; still less found a theory on it [by which Chambers means, the theory of multiple authorship].
>
> Only (1) if the MS. reading absolutely refuses to make sense, and (2) if the proposed rearrangement of the text is so convincing that it has only to be stated to be at once recognized as right, do we get that certainty which is necessary, before we can build argument as to authorship upon conjectural emendation. (pp. 15–16)

But neither of these conditions applied.

After demonstrating that B's supposed (by Manly, that is) misunderstandings of A are not that at all, Chambers moves on to demolish his next argument, that 'a careful study of the MSS. will show that between A, B and C there exist dialectal differences incompatible with the supposition of a single author'. Chambers is able to prove from the parallel passages printed by Skeat in his volume of Notes to Piers Plowman (EETS OS 81) that the manuscript forms differed very considerably, making it impossible to infer the author's (or authors') dialect from the evidence of manuscripts.

Here an important point emerges. Manly had, of course, relied on Skeat's texts for his information about dialect. But Skeat had chosen his copy-manuscript in all three cases for the sake of the quality of its readings, not of its dialect. As we have seen, Skeat collated only those manuscripts which he thought helpful in fixing the text, and he

---

[19] See above, p. 185.

frequently did not trouble to record minor variants such as *but* for *ac*, or *sche* for *heo*.[20] So it was futile–and utterly misguided–for Manly to have based his argument on such a precarious foundation. Chambers rightly concludes 'that work upon the dialect of Piers Plowman should be based upon a new and minute examination of the MSS.' (p. 25).[21]

Chambers now rehearses some of the conclusions to which he had come, even as early as 1910, on the problems of editing *Piers Plowman*. Clearly he had spent many rewarding hours with the B-MSS, for he comes up with the theory that is usually attributed to his ultimate successors, George Kane and E. T. Donaldson, that the archetype of the surviving B-MSS was corrupt. Skeat had observed that the B tradition was far less complex than the A, so that there were 'probably more doubtful points in a single Canterbury Tale or in a single Act in some of Shakespeare's plays than in the whole of the B-text of Piers the Plowman' (see p. 150 above). But Chambers plumbed the matter further. Very likely he was prompted to do this by Manly's provocative assertion that B, being a different person from A, and a poorer poet, had adopted an inferior reading, found among the variants of the A-Text, in place of the better one in the A-Text proper. Chambers had shown in his previous article that 'the more the MSS. are examined the more probable does it seem that these variants from the received text of A, adopted by B, are, in fact, the true readings. That this is so in the majority of cases seems hardly to admit of dispute.'

But what if there were other cases where Manly was right, and where B did present a text which was unmistakably at fault? Here, Chambers advised, the 'utmost caution' was necessary, 'lest we should make the writers of the B and C versions responsible for what are, after all, but the errors of their scribes.' And he gives an example of the 'famous and excellent Laud 581' slipping up, along with ten other manuscripts, in its rendering of B Passus XVIII 383–4:

> in the scene of the Harrowing of Hell, Christ claims that He, the King of Kings, may save the wicked from death, since, if an earthly king comes

---

[20] Skeat, *A-Text*, xxix.
[21] He susbsequently set a graduate student of his, Elsie Chick (later Blackman) to work on the manuscript relations of the B-Text as a prelude to a study (which never came to the light of day) of their dialect. See further below, pp. 256ff.

There þe feloun thole sholde deth or otherwyse,
Lawe wolde, he ʒeue hym lyf, if he loked on hym.

> *deth or otherwyse*, the reading of Laud and the received text, can
> hardly be right; for the point is that even the extreme penalty may
> be remitted for a king. The right reading is obviously that of the C-
> text *deth oþer Iuwise* (justice, execution). This is the reading of only
> three B-MSS, whilst Laud's corrupt reading has the support of ten.
> (pp. 26–7)

So majority support for a B reading, even when the majority includes
manuscripts of high general quality, does not necessarily indicate that
the reading is correct. That is a perfectly sound doctrine, and one that
illustrates the strength of Chambers' argument that Skeat's reprints of
'best' manuscripts must be replaced with critical editions which make
use of the evidence provided by all the manuscripts.[22]

But occasionally a further development occurs: when *all* the extant
B-MSS agree in a reading which seems inferior to the equivalent one
in A or C. Chambers does not fully thrash out the issues in a case
such as this, although many of the arguments (and assumptions) later
to be found in the work of Kane–Donaldson are already implicitly
present in his analysis. As an instance of unanimous B support for a
poor reading, he cites the reading at A Pro 41, where

> some A-MSS. speak of beggars with bags *bretful* or *bredful*
> *ycrammed*, another of beggars whose bags *with bred full be cromed*.
> The old rule, that the harder reading is to be preferred, would lead
> us to suppose *bretful* (*bredful*) right; for this would easily be
> corrupted into *of bread full*, whilst the reverse process is hardly
> credible. A, then, almost certainly wrote *bretful* (*bredful*). The B-
> MSS. are unanimously in favour of *of bread full*. It might be argued
> that 'the B-reviser' had before him a MS. of A with this reading, and
> took it over into his revised text. But when we come to the C-text
> we find the original reading *bretful* reappearing there. The advocates
> of separate authorship will have to admit that there *was* a B-MS.
> (viz. that used by C as a basis) which had the reading *bretful*; for the
> same line of argument which led us in the first place to decide that
> *bretful* in A could not be corrupted from *of bread full* again applies
> here. *Of bread full* is not, then, a genuine B-reading at all, but a very
> early B corruption, inherited by all the extant B-MSS., but not

---

[22] Chambers had already indicated the editorial caution necessary for assessing the force of
majority support for a reading in his 1909 article; see p. 201 above.

belonging to the original B. Hence no argument can be drawn from it. (p. 27)

Here are a number of assumptions. First, that the principle of *difficilior lectio* is applicable: the harder of two variants is the one most likely to be original. In the case of the A variants, this seems reasonable: not only might *bretful ycrammed* be thought to be harder than *with bred full be cromed* (though *MED* evidence does not suggest that *bredful* was a particularly unusual word at this period), it also explains how the other variant came into existence: as an attempt to unpack and clarify the harder reading, in effect provide a gloss of it, while preserving the alliteration of the line and the general shape of the original.

The moment we turn to the B-Text, however, several problems appear. Chambers does not overtly raise the question who wrote the B-Text–the A author or another person–but, as Kane, Donaldson and Russell were to acknowledge many years later, assumptions about the identity of the author are inextricably bound up with the process of analysing the textual variants of the two later versions of the poem.[23] If we assume that the author of B is *the same as* the author of A, we will find it strange that he should incorporate a scribal reading into his text of B. This is clearly Chambers' assumption, and he consequently looks for an alternative explanation for B's reading. One comes readily to hand: that if the A variant *with bred full be cromed* could be–and apparently was–a corruption of an original *bretful ycrammed*, then there was no reason why the same should not have been true of the B reading *with bred full be cromed*. The fact that no existing B-MS accurately reproduces this assumed original reading is (pretty much) neither here nor there: Chambers has already demonstrated that majority support of a reading is not always reliable, and he is merely taking his principle to its logical extent by arguing that unanimous support is not necessarily reliable either. And he can claim confirmation from C, for, as he in effect asks, where could C possibly have got its reading *bretful ycrammed* from if not from a copy of B– i.e., the manuscript of B on which the C reviser based his revision?

It is an easy inference from this sequence of argument that one and the same person wrote all three versions. But the sequence is not a necessary one. There are two major alternative lines of argument that Chambers does not explore. Firstly, the one that Manly would

---

[23] See pp. 321–2 below.

espouse; this would no doubt go as follows. The A author wrote the superior *bretful ycrammed*; the B author–a different person, not up to the standard of his predecessor–rewrote A using a scribal manuscript, and reproduced the scribal corruption *with bred full be cromed*; finally the C author, who had access to both B and a better version of A than the one used by the B reviser, was able to substitute A's superior reading. (It is possible to find many instances where A and C agree against the unanimous testimony of B.) There is nothing logically amiss with this hypothesis, although it seems never to have been advanced by Manly, who was quite properly silenced by Chambers' crushing revelation of his undue reliance on Skeat's unreliable collations.[24] The only way to anticipate it is to argue (or assume), as Chambers does, that the inferiority of the B-Text is due to its faulty transmission by scribes rather than to the person who wrote it. No doubt one of the reasons for Kane–Donaldson's vehement espousal of the latter theory was in part prompted, whether consciously or not, by a desire to argue that the author of B was a poet of the highest possible quality, and thus on a par with the author of A– namely, the same person.

The second possible line of argument assumes that a single author was responsible for all three versions, but manages to be subversive nevertheless. As before, it would start with accepting that the A author wrote the superior *bretful ycrammed*. What comes next is optional. *Either* (1) the B author–the same person, but on an off-day – rewrote A using a scribal manuscript, and allowed the scribal corruption *with bred full be cromed* to slip past him. This may seem a preposterous suggestion on two counts–first that the author would have used a corrupt scribal transcription, rather than his own correct version, of the earlier text; and second that he would have let the error pass by unnoticed. Both assertions, however, have been generally accepted by the admirers of Kane and Donaldson's major edition of B, in which the two editors argue that precisely the same happened in the case of the C reviser's rewriting of B: he used a corrupt B manuscript,[25] and let some of its errors slip past him. The other option (2) for what happened in B is as follows: the B writer knew of the scribal corruption *with bred full be cromed*, and actually chose to

---

[24] So far as public utterance went, at any rate; see further above, p. 194 n. 30, and cf. T. A. Stroud, 'Manly's Marginal Notes on the *Piers Plowman* Controversy'.

[25] Though not so corrupt as the manuscript of the extant B-MSS; see Kane–Donaldson, 98–127. They also suggest that the B-reviser used a corrupt A-MS; see e.g. 211 n.172 and pp. 401ff. below.

reproduce it in his new version of the poem, on the grounds that it was easier to understand and would therefore communicate his desired meaning more effectively to the audience.

Neither of these two alternative lines of argument is investigated by Chambers. The reason for ignoring the first is obvious, since it would support the hypothesis that the author of A was different from the author of B. As for the second line of argument, it may simply not have occurred to him. Both branches of it, (1) and (2), offend against traditional canons of textual criticism, since they assume that the author may, for two different reasons, have written into his text a reading manifestly inferior–by the criteria normally employed to differentiate between the quality of readings–to one that he *could* have chosen. (1) assumes that the author allowed a poorer reading to pass him by unnoticed; (2) assumes that he *chose* to incorporate a reading whose origin was scribal.

Common sense tells us that both these things are possible. Many authors have failed to notice printers' errors in their proofs, and have subsequently reproduced them in revised versions of their work. And many authors (the most notable and notorious example being Joyce) have been struck by the greater appropriateness of the printer's error than the original, and hence have adopted the error into their text.[26] Incontrovertible examples of this sort of authorial behaviour only survive from the comparatively recent past, partly because it is more likely that less of the crucial evidence will have disappeared, and partly because the printing process allows us to draw more hard and fast lines between author's manuscript and edited and published product than is possible in the medieval period. Therefore it is in the case of texts written in more recent periods that such possibilities have been contemplated, and discussions have taken place of the consequent difficulties involved in applying canonical textual principles to their analysis. Medievalists have largely fought shy of such damaging assumptions as that an author may have written less well than a scribe, or may have deliberately chosen to write in a way that falls below what present-day critics would wish to think of a proper authorial standard. The reason for this is relatively clear: that to accept such possibilities renders the act of editing, i.e. distinguishing between authorial and scribal writing, so difficult as to become almost impossible.[27]

[26] J. A. W. Bennett suggested in 1977 that this might also have happened in Langland's case (Review of Kane–Donaldson, 326).

[27] Cf. Westcott and Hort's rather tortured account of such difficulties, quoted above, p. 214.

Despite these limitations to his examination of the textual problems of *Piers Plowman*, it is nevertheless remarkable that Chambers was able so early, and on what must have been a merely preliminary scanning of the various manuscripts, to sketch out the theory both of the corrupt B archetype, and of the less corrupt C reviser's B-MS, both of which theories were taken up and substantiated in detail by Kane and Donaldson sixty-five years later. Chambers' associated assumption that agreement between A and C against B indicated error in B rather than an authorial change of mind back and forth between readings is also significant, and fits in with the syndrome referred to above, the reluctance to concede the possibility of variation in a canonical text.

Chambers completes his article with two short sections, one on the supposed change of views between A, B and C, and one on the apparently autobiographical references in all three versions to an author 'Will'. He argues that any differences in outlook between the poems may be easily tolerated, adding that 'If the discrepancies pointed out by Prof. Manly under this head are sufficient to prove anything, then no English author from before Chaucer to after William Morris can escape being divided into four or five' (p. 28). This is a mere assertion of difference of opinion. His material on 'Long Will' is more analytic, adducing several medieval parallels (Chaucer, Dante, Gower, Lydgate) of authors referring to themselves in their own works, and pointing out that 'before the invention of the title-page, the surest way in which an author could mark his work was by introducing his name into the body of it' (p. 30).

The Chambers Papers again shed light on how this major contribution to the *Piers Plowman* authorship debate was received. Furnivall's response may serve as representative:

> Many thanks for your very able and temperate article. It is a regular twister for us, & convicts us of too hasty judgement, as we certainly didn't wait for your arguments and facts. I don't yet give up the belief in the differences of authors, but you have made me see that the question is far more difficult that I at first supposed, & that till we get new ed^{ns} of the 3 Texts, no real conclusion can be arrived at. I congratulate you on the power & cogency of your article. (21 December 1909)[28]

In a later letter (23 December 1909), Furnivall reiterates the comment

---

[28] Chambers Papers Item 5:22.

that is constantly echoed throughout this correspondence: 'till Knott's or your new A text is out, no certainty on many points can be attained'.[29]

Skeat must have been a more whole-hearted admirer of Chambers' incisive work, not least on account of its many graceful references to his pioneering work, even though these do not shrink from pointing out what Skeat had by now accepted as its inevitable limitations. Skeat's response to Chambers' second article indicates that he was delighted with it, and glad at the opportunity to let off steam at Manly. He returned the draft of Chambers' authorship essay to him with a letter (dated 7 July 1909) that sets out in the fullest detail that I have come across Skeat's own views on the author's process of composition, and the way in which the poem was transmitted in its earliest stages. For this reason I quote it almost in its entirety.

> The writers of A, B, C (being all different people, if not five people) seem to have been all alike tarred with one brush, viz. inconsistency! That is rather an argument in favour of their being *one* man. Surely it is obvious that the author never meant to be consistent – he only meant to say cutting things about dishonesty – and in *this* he is consistent enough. One wonders what he would say *now*, about such a Trades-Union rule as that which forbids a workman to lay more than a fixed number of bricks an hour. I shd. like to have his opinion very much –
>
> There is a presumption that Wille was *himself* a scrivener: & one reason why he took so readily to rewriting things was precisely because he had no need to be beholden to any one for making his rough drafts. He could alter his work easily enough, because he *could do it himself*!
>
> Then his friends would borrow his rough-drafts which were not on loose sheets,[30] but in regular quires, and probably loosely (or well) bound. And his friends would copy them out (& a nice mess they sometimes made): & if any of them liked to add lines on his own account, there was nothing to prevent him. I believe we are utterly misled by modern notions, & clean forget how *casual* our ancestors were. How did *they* know that they were anything more

---

[29] Chambers Papers Item 5:24. Other responses are preserved in Chambers Papers Item 5:12, 14, and 15. Chambers sent Manly an offprint, and received a sharp but superficially suave letter in reply (25 February 1910). Chambers' argument on Sloth and Robert the Robber, Manly says, 'really strengthens my position in regard to the lost leaf, for it suggested the necessity of a transitional passage'; though why Manly thought this to be the case is not clear. 'As to the rest of your arguments', Manly finishes, 'I think I shall be able to meet them successfully.'

[30] This is a dig at Manly's 'lost leaf' theory.

than ephemeral productions? They looked upon them much more as we should regard a modern 'leading article'. They copied them because they wanted to *read them over again*! *not* because they wished to perpetuate them. They never regarded posterity one bit. What – as the famous remark runs – had posterity done for *them*? The utter feebleness of some of Prof. Manly's remarks, is amazing...

– I think Manly's remark about *Calote* my [*sic*; an interesting slip] daughter is disgraceful[31] ... Surely no author yet accused himself of living with his own daughter while she was no better than she should be. It is so terrible an insinuation that it not [*sic*] to be believed: & I do *not* believe it. There is absolutely no reason why he should not have lived with his wife and daughter, & whether kitte & kalote were their real names or not we don't know. If they were not, their names are only playfully disguised, much as if we were to say Molly & Meggy, & had no such lewd connotation. – Faugh! –

"C (says Manly, p. 35) is a *better scholar* than either *A* or *B*." Could anything be feebler! As if a man could not *possibly* get to know better in a year or two than he did at first!! – I *know* this argument to be utter rubbish. For I *myself* know that I made, not one, but *hundreds* of blunders, 20 years ago that I *could* not make now. And can't you say the same? What clutches at cleverness these "critical" remarks are! –

– I fully believe that the *five* authors, or the *one*, whichever it is, all contradict each other at times. And why not? –[32]

– As to your notes upon the dialect, & upon *ben* and *aren*, they are all right. But they are not so utterly *smashing* as an argument I can offer you. What do you think of *this*?[33] ...

Clearly, it's a *far* more complex problem than your statement indicates. So why not pile up the agony?

Yrs,

W. W. Skeat

---

[31] Manly had suggested that the names Kit and Calot, given to the wife and daughter mentioned by the narrator at B Passus XVIII 428 (cf. C Passus V 2) were names commonly used by (or given to) prostitutes. See 'Piers the Plowman and its Sequence', 34, 'The Authorship of *Piers Plowman*', 137–8, and Jusserand's and Chamber's responses to this point in, respectively, 'Piers Plowman, the Work of One or of Five', 325, and 'Robert or William Longland?', 447.

[32] In a card written to Chambers on 2 February 1910, thanking him for what was presumably the offprint of his and Grattan's paper, he says 'The idea that no author is ever inconsistent is surely a mere craze. – I am afraid I have corrected myself more than once, but that does not prove that I am 2 different people.'

[33] Here Skeat gives a list of *-eth/-en* endings (as *worcheth*, *buggen*) occurring constantly as alternatives in the poem–i.e., inconsistently throughout.

– However, it is perhaps sufficient to say that there is plenty of confusion, and that it all proves *nothing*.[34]

Skeat continued to encourage Chambers in his work, and to approve of his borrowing from Skeat's own editions: on 16 February 1910 he wrote to Chambers 'By all means annex the "side-notes", or any other similar comments. I am glad to think that they may come in useful.'[35]

[34]   Chambers Papers Item 5:16.
[35]   Chambers Papers Item 5:30.

Chambers versus Knott

It is tantalisingly difficult to trace the course of Chambers' and Grattan's work, but it seems clear that they felt some considerable pressure on them to complete their text of A as soon as possible. A copy of a hastily written letter from Chambers to Grattan seems to belong to this early period, and was presumably written in February 1910:

> I chucked the whole of Trinity [the A-MS of Trinity College Cambridge, thought by most scholars to be the best MS of A, and the one that Chambers and Grattan were planning to use as their base-text. Presumably Chambers refers to the rotograph of the MS, not the MS itself] into my things which were going off to Clacton [where Chambers spent his summer holidays during this period] I would therefore suggest your getting on with Univ. [i.e. with transcribing the A-MS of University College, Oxford]. I think, if you are in London with more or less free time it might be well if you could collate say Lincoln's Inn upon it, this being more useful even than Univ, wh. if necessary can be done, so to speak, in bed. We have now all the evidence we really want *Rawlinson, Univ, Ingilby, Lincoln's Inn, Vernon* in Skeat's Reprint, *Trinity.* The other MSS so far as I can make out are purely ornamental Westminster and Digby almost worthless, Douce and Ashmole, Harl 129 [there is no such A-MS; perhaps Chambers means Harley 3954] little better. I should be very sorry to do it, but should things become desperate we might go to press without *West, Dig* Ash. I doubt much whether in a single instance these will help
>
> If we can get Trinity transcribed, and L. Inn upon it we really could make up a text which we should not want to alter in half a dozen places, and might get that to Clays [the EETS printer] forthwith, to Furnivall's great delight probably.
>
> The text would, in the first place be set up separately, the notes being arranged under later. But what I am really anxious to prove is

the non-contamination of Lincoln's Inn, upon which, after all, most of our theories depend.

This suggests some development of their theory on Lincoln's Inn, which had in the 1909 article been argued to be a manuscript independent of both the other two families.[1] If the 'independence' turned out to be due to contamination from B or C (as Chambers and Grattan thought was the explanation for some of the readings of Ingilby, for example), they would be in trouble. More importantly, the hastily scribbled letter gives some indication of the pell-mell speed with which they were tackling their edition, with manuscripts being flung into suitcases, and views on them formed long before any systematic collation had taken place. And the preparedness to go to press, at a pinch, without several of the manuscripts, reveals that whatever text Chambers and Grattan were putting together, it was scarcely a satisfactory one by the criteria they themselves had established in 1909. Furnivall may have got some sense of their headlong and precipitate attack on the edition, for he writes on 4 March 1910: 'Don't hurry the A text. It needs lots of care and time.'[2]

This advice seems to have been heeded, for proofs of the first four passus were not produced until January 1912. A copy is preserved in the Chambers archive at University College, printed from the Trinity College A-MS, with a small quantity of unattributed variants at the foot of each page. Evidently these proofs were circulated to various medievalists and textual scholars for comments, for letters referring to them survive from Bradley and Greg, both men querying the precise status of the variants (Greg described them as 'a bit cryptic').[3] Recording them in this way was unsatisfactory, for it gave no indication why Chambers and Grattan's text had any claim to be superior to Skeat's, and it was incompatible with the editorial standards set down in their 1909 article.

Chambers had meanwhile (1911) published another article on the poem, on 'The Original Form of the A-Text of "Piers Plowman"', a reply to an article by Bradley which had appeared the previous year.[4]

[1] See pp. 204–5 above. Chambers and Grattan subsequently dropped this theory, perhaps, as David Fowler suggests (in Knott–Fowler 22, and in his unpublished dissertation, 'A Critical Text of Piers Plowman A-2', 4 n. 7) because they were persuaded by Knott's classification of these manuscripts with his group *y*.

[2] Chambers Papers Item 5:32.

[3] Bradley's letter is dated 6 April 1912 (Chambers Papers Item 5:38), Greg's 3 April 1912 (Chambers Papers Item 5, unnumbered).

[4] 'The Authorship of "Piers the Plowman"'.

Chambers concludes that *all* the A-MSS represent an original that went beyond Passus VIII, to the end of XI; the absence of IX–XI in the Harley and other manuscripts being more likely explained by accidental loss of the end of their texts than by A Pro–VIII representing the poet's first version of the work. He believes that Passus XII was probably the result of a separate piece of writing by Langland: the three manuscripts which contain it (RUJ) are genetically linked, whereas those which omit it are less closely linked: 'this was the conclusion arrived at thirty-six years ago by Professor Skeat, and I do not see that any other is possible'.[5]

The article is notable for its moderate tone and the complete absence of vitriol in dealing with the arguments advanced by the proponents of multiple authorship. Chambers thanks Bradley for 'having read through this paper in an earlier draft, and for having suggested modifications which add greatly to any force the arguments may carry'. This is a clear indication of the usefulness of cooperation with those of different views, for the sake of clarifying the issues concerned. As we have seen, Bradley repeatedly reiterates his desire for disinterested uncovering of the truth, regardless of whether it favours his side of the argument or that of his opponents, and this is certainly an attitude of mind subscribed to by Chambers. Such an approach is markedly absent from the next important contribution to the authorship debate, which came from the explosively choleric pen of Thomas Knott, the pupil of Manly and the 'American' whose 1907 visit to England to look at the manuscripts had so scared Chambers and Grattan earlier.[6]

Knott describes how

> I was so fortunate as to be a student under Professor Manly in 1905, when his belief in the diversity of authorship was daily receiving fresh confirmation from his investigations, and we recognized the need for an adequate critical text in order that the differences

---

[5] See pp. 120ff. above.

[6] 'An Essay Toward the Critical Text of the A-Version of "Piers the Plowman"'. The article was originally submitted as Knott's Ph.D. dissertation to the University of Chicago in 1912. Knott wrote one further article on *Piers Plowman*, 'Observations on the Authorship of *Piers the Plowman*', a long and immoderate attack on the theory of single authorship. He also edited the text of A up to Passus VIII 126 (the edition was posthumously completed by David Fowler; see pp. 329ff. below). Otherwise, he turned his interests to lexicographical matters, becoming the general editor of the second edition of Webster's *New International Dictionary*, and the second editor of the *Middle English Dictionary* from 1935 to 1945, when he was replaced by Hans Kurath. His tenure of the latter post was an unhappy one; see Hans Kurath et al., *The Middle English Dictionary. Plan and Bibliography*, ix–x.

between the three versions might be determined satisfactorily. Accordingly, in my first subsequent vacation, in the summer of 1907, I began the necessary work by collating the fourteen MSS of the A-version. (p. 129)

Knott had gone from one library to another, and from one great house (e.g. Ingilby's, the Duke of Westminster's) to another, and simply transcribed the manuscripts. On his return home he must have sat down and produced lists and tables of agreements and disagreements, for his article provides an impressively full account of manuscript relations. The job would have been a long and arduous one, and it is not altogether surprising that publication of his result should have taken eight years, especially since it appears that he worked on the material only 'as time and opportunity offered'.[7] Knott tells us that he has used the Trinity College, Cambridge A-MS as the 'basis' of his text, carefully explaining that

> by 'basis' I mean, of course, not that I shall print that MS as it stands, nor with such occasional readings from other MSS as may seem better to me. On the contrary, the readings adopted into the CT [critical text] must always be the critical readings, as attested in every case by the weight of the evidence, genealogical and other. No matter how plausible the reading of T may seem, it must not be retained if not supported. By 'basis' I mean, therefore, little more than the basis for spelling and dialect. (p. 131)

He now launches into the account of his editorial principles which aroused great wrath from a number of different critics. Throughout (as in the above quotation) he refers to his text somewhat portentously as the 'CT', and speaks of it as an independent, almost autonomous entity, that has been constructed by purely 'scientific', objective means unaffected by editorial whim or even judgement. He begins with an account of the method he seeks to overturn:

> The older method of printing a text was to select an old, well-spelled, well-written MS, the readings of which seemed to the editor to give 'the best sense'. In case of dissatisfaction with a reading, support for it was looked for in other MSS, and, if support failed, a reading was adopted from some other MS or MSS which the editor thought gave the 'best sense'. (p. 132)

---

[7] Knott had in the interim published a defence of Manly in the 1909 edition of the American periodical *Nation* ('The "Lost Leaf" of "Piers the Plowman"'), defending Manly's thesis against the modifications suggested by Bradley and Carleton Brown earlier.

Skeat's name is never mentioned, but clearly it is Skeat who is the chief exponent of this 'older method of printing' – not, be it noted, of 'editing'. Like Chambers and Grattan before him, Knott points out that the trouble with such an 'eclectic' practice is that non-original readings will survive into the edited text. Knott describes the method as 'unscientific and unreliable': 'The editor left in his text a large number of readings which gave "smooth good sense," but some of which were sophisticated, that is, introduced by copyists who were practising conjectural emendation; and others of which (introduced carelessly) were intelligible, but which could not be supported by scientific proof.' The 'eclectic' method was also unsatisfactory for a second reason, Knott claims: it 'laid too much responsibility on the unchecked discretion of the editor, who often adopted a reading merely because it was in the greater number of MSS, and who, on the other hand, often adopted readings merely according to his whim or his personal taste'.

Certain terms stand out in this account, for example, 'scientific proof', versus an editor's 'whim or personal taste'. What was the miraculous scientific method discovered by Knott, which would make the editor's decisions for him, i.e. render them objective? None other, it turns out, than the Lachmannian principles of recension. 'Adequate expositions of these processes have long been accessible', he says, 'especially' in Westcott and Hort and Edward Moore's *Contributions* ... and the principles 'have been admirably stated recently by Dr Eleanor Prescott Hammond in her *Chaucer: A Bibliographical Manual*';[8] this means, he says that 'it is hardly necessary to recount here in great detail the processes that must go toward the determination of a critical text'. Knott comments: 'The dangers arising from the exercise of personal taste or whim ... are avoided by the critical text.' And this is to be constructed through establishing the genealogy of manuscripts: examining the relationships between the manuscripts so as to discover which was copied from which, and how their ancestors may be traced back to the hypothetical archetype, a copy of the author's original:

> Two or more MSS, or two or more groups of MSS, are assigned to an identical, hypothetically reconstructed ancestor, or archetype, if they possess in common a number of clear errors, omissions, and additions. Common errors, deviations, and omissions in two or

[8] At pp. 106–13. See above, p. 216.

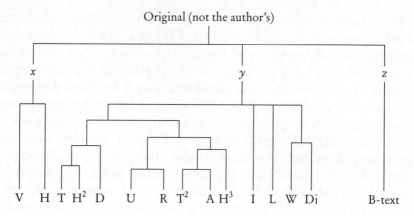

Figure 13.1. Knott's genealogical tree

> more MSS must be due to coincidence, or to contamination, or to
> their existence in the MS from which copies were made. If there are
> more than a very few significant errors, the laws of probability
> forbid attributing them to coincidence. (p. 133)

Applying this method, and various more sophisticated variations on
it, Knott has been able to slot each of the A-MSS into place on a
genealogical tree showing the family relation that they bear to each
other. Then,

> after the genealogical tree of the extant MSS has been plotted, the
> determination of the reading of the Original in a given passage is
> usually comparatively simple, especially if more than two indepen-
> dent lines of descent from the Original copy have been established.
> (p. 134)

The idea is that the editor judges the relative qualities of readings by
applying knowledge of the relative qualities of the manuscripts in
which they are found: and it is the genealogical tree which supplies
the information about the latter. All the editor has to do is to see
where in the tree the manuscripts occur. Knott also warns us that the
text reconstructed by such genealogical means is not necessarily the
same as the one the writer originally wrote: all the genealogical
method can do is reconstruct the original (or archetype) of the extant
manuscripts, which may simply have been a copy – necessarily
flawed, therefore – of the author's original.

Knott moves on to give us some specific results of his genealogical investigations. He draws a tree (see figure 13.1) and gives details and examples of the various major groups: VH, WK, EAH³, TH²R, RU (Knott uses different sigils for three MSS: T^2, rather than E, for MS Trinity College, Dublin D 4.12; Di, rather than K, for MS Digby 145; and I, rather than J, for MS Pierpont Morgan M 818). Altogether his analysis is far more thorough than that of Chambers and Grattan earlier, and this is mainly because he provides full evidence: the lists of agreements that support his groupings of the manuscripts.

His analysis does not entirely accord with that of Chambers and Grattan: for example he identifies various patterns of agreement between manuscripts that they have overlooked (as between A and H³ – see p. 149).[9] Knott takes the English pair severely to task for this. 'Such different results', he says, 'cannot be due to mere difference in opinion. How then are they to be accounted for?' And his judgement is harsh:

> First, the method employed by these students has been at fault; secondly, they have stated their opinions before they have had the necessary material in hand to formulate sound opinions; and, thirdly, they have not collected the evidence afforded by MS readings which were perfectly accessible. (p. 150).

Further, 'the most serious fault in their presentation is that they cite almost no specific evidence whatever for their classification of the MSS' – which means that 'other students who would like to know what Chambers and Grattan regard as errors, significant or insignificant, are left absolutely in the dark'. This is a little unfair, especially as Knott himself has not presented his evidence with outstanding clarity: many of his lists of A-MS agreements in error are by line number only, but these refer to manuscript variants and to a text (Knott's 'CT') that are as yet unpublished (see p. 131).

Nevertheless there is some truth in Knott's accusations. Chambers and Grattan did present preliminary results on the basis of partial collations only, and there was, as we have seen, some fundamental inconsistency in the thinking behind their proposed editorial method. On the one hand they fully perceived that Skeat's method was an

---

9   On Ashmole, alluding to Chambers' unsatisfactory and unjustified dismissal (383), Knott says (155), 'as I have shown above, H³, A and T² [E] are bound together in a minor sub-group by a very large number of common errors and variations; and most of the contaminations from the B-text in MS A are in the source of all three MSS'. Cf. Chambers' 1911 article on the A-Text (312), where he makes it clear that he has still not yet noted H³'s affinities with any particular manuscript or manuscripts.

imperfect tool to exploit the rich stores of evidence to be found in the numerous manuscript variants; on the other they persisted in the curious plan to reprint one manuscript, and only make use of the variants found in the other manuscripts by recording them in the footnotes. And they used the rigorous methods of Westcott and Hort in analysing internal and external evidence of readings, only to apply them to some manuscripts and not others. Why make use of H^2, perceiving it, despite evident corruption, to be nevertheless a useful check on its near relation T, but altogether dismiss manuscripts like Ashmole without bothering to find out whether they were closely allied to other manuscripts which might also benefit from such a check?

In one other respect, also, Knott goes far beyond Chambers and Grattan: his understanding of the importance of B to editing A. At the start of his article he warns readers of the provisional nature of his results so far: 'The critical text, with the collations, must wait until similar work on the B- and C-versions has been finished (when all will be printed together), but the text I hope to publish in a short time in the form of a reading edition' (pp. 129–30). The apparent distinction between 'critical text' and 'text' is not transparent: but it seems that Knott means that his first 'text' of A (which is to be published very soon) is provisional, and that the full, 'critical text' of A will be his final version, revised to take account of the full evidence of B and C. As we have seen, Knott is well aware of the 'insecurity' of the text of B (and, presumably, C), as represented by Skeat's edition, which was based on incomplete collations, and consequently the possibility that readings in A will have to be revised once the 'critical text' of B is available (see p. 150 n. 1). This recognition is one from which George Kane would have done well to profit in his successive editing of the A- and B-Texts (see further pp. 376, 391ff. below.)

He is thus well aware of the interdependence of the three versions, especially from an editorial point of view. ABC share roughly 1,900 lines in common, and AB 400 lines in common: so in places where reconstructing the original A-Text from the extant A-MSS is not straightforward, it can be helpful to look both at B and at C.[10] Knott reckons (see p. 149) that B was copied from an archetype independent of the archetype from which the extant A-MSS were copied, since B does not share any of the characteristic errors of A-MSS. (VH

[10] Cf. Skeat, 'I have always had regard to Text B [when editing A]' (p. 130 above), and p. 333 n. 8 below.

descend from hypothetical archetype x, the remaining A-MSS from hypothetical archetype y, and B from hypothetical archetype z). 'Consequently, whenever x and y differ, but when neither is clearly in error, we have the independent evidence of B to help us in determining the reading of the Original': that is, if B agrees with x against y, then that makes it likely that B's reading was also the original A reading, and that y's is the result of scribal error. This is a sensible and straightforward inference. Knott recognises the problem that arises when all three, x y, *and* B, differ. Here 'we are without reliable genealogical evidence of the reading of the Original of A. In cases like this, we are logically obliged to follow the reading of that group which is less often in error when error can be determined' – namely y (TRUD etc.)

The clear implication of these observations is that the B-reviser based his text on an A-MS in some respects superior to any of the A-MSS which now survive. But Knott adds as a warning, 'The CT, of course, can never safely adopt the reading of B alone, however tempting that reading may appear' (p. 150); in other words, one must never completely disregard the evidence of the A-MSS and substitute a superior B reading. Knott does not say why not, and it may be simply that he felt that this was too interventionist. But if one believes in single authorship (as Knott of course did not), one would have to allow for the possibility that the poet, on revision of A to B, *improved* on A, so that both readings, the inferior A reading and the superior B reading, must be regarded as original. Hence it will not do to substitute one for another.

As can be imagined, Chambers was incensed by this article. In a draft letter to Grattan dated 22 March [1915 or 1916], written in haste and crammed on to three small cards, he writes,

> Dear Grattan,
> I'm making good headway with Knott. Whether any one will take the trouble to read it all is a question, but there is no doubt as to our being able to guy him most efficiently. Honestly, with our work before him, he ought to have been able to do better! Anyway, if he had read Moore's Prolegomena.
> One difficulty is that attacks on us on the score that we did not give sufficient data – which is true. If one gives data as one goes along, bulk becomes immense Our last essay filled 32 pages, & had we given all our collections [*sc.* collations] would have filled 80 or 100

The proper way to explain the A text and rout Knott will be in an essay of some 30 pages, say, on text relationship: but to meet his criticism about not quoting facts that needs to be followed by 50 or 60 pages of *Appendix*, quoting variants

I am inclined to think Robertson [the editor of *MLR*] will not give us the space we want – indeed cannot: and we owe it to Gollancz [the director of EETS] to give *him* what he wants Probably the best thing will be to print Text and Collations of Prol. & Pass I–IV = 70 or so pp + 80 pp or so of Introduction + Appendices, explaining our system. & refuting Knott. Altogether with some critical notes, title page etc a vol. of approaching 200 pp. which would be quite respectable.

... as we know, MS relationship varies often from passus to passus. Our introduction will deal with the *MS relationship of the portion we print* (I–IV) When we print V–XII we must note any changes which come over our relationships We must check every reading with ultra-scrupulous accuracy: because we have to deal with a very venomous oponent. Any score Knott has made is on the latter passus which we had not collated so carefully when we wrote. On I–IV we are on our strongest ground.

Can you get ahead every available moment on the rest of the collation of III. Let me have all of II that you can spare, as I am wanting the collations daily.

Another point. The silly fool Knott tries to demonstrate

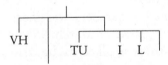

on the strength of 7 asserted variants common to TU & IL. If we deal with I–IV separately his case is peculiarly bad since *only two* of his seven come there, and those peculiarly feeble. The only decent ones come in Passus V. There are some striking variants common to I & TUI & one common to IL & TU in Pass I–IV. In fact our chief difficulty is the extraordinary feebleness of Knott's case, lest we seem to the ignorant to prove that I.L, belong to the VH family Knott bases the whole of his scheme on their belonging to TU.

> I think we had better abandon our idea of an article in MLR –
> people would not read it and bring out an article in EETS.[11]

This is helpful for indicating the present state of Chambers' plans: and
also the stage which his labours with Grattan at the *Piers Plowman*
laboratory (as Grattan later referred to it) had so far reached.[12] It
seems that they were still a long way from completion, and confirms
that the collations (assembled, it seems, primarily by Grattan) which
had formed the staple of evidence for the previous article – written six
years previously – must have been sparing indeed.

But their hope of completing an edition instead of an article was
unfulfilled, not least, presumably, because both were engaged in war
work. Despite this, Chambers was able to move quickly: in July 1916
he published (again under Grattan's name as well as his own) a
rebuttal of Knott entitled 'The Text of "Piers Plowman": Critical
Methods' (completed in Rouen). This was a skilfully controlled
response, which carefully praised Knott's essay as 'packed full of
diligent research', and stressed what was indeed the case, the degree to
which the two sets of research on either side of the Atlantic agreed
with each other. Chambers pounds Knott mercilessly, if always
courteously, for the flaws in his argument and accusations. He points
out, rightly, that some of the differences between the results thrown
up by the two editing projects were trivial or inaccurately described
by Knott, and much of the material was mutually confirmatory rather
than, as Knott had suggested, mutually contradictory. Far more
importantly, however, Chambers expends considerable energy – to
notably successful effect – in deconstructing Knott's ideal, supposedly
realised in his own practice, of 'scientific' editing.

He demonstrates that the procedures of editing which Knott had
mocked them for following were in fact precisely those specified by
Westcott and Hort. This devastating body-blow left little room for
doubt that Knott had failed to consult one of the most important
discussions of the method of textual recension he was avowedly
following (pp. 261–4). And Chambers makes it clear that it is Skeat
whom Knott is covertly criticising in his unflattering allusions to the
'older method of printing a text', characterised as 'unscientific and

---

11 Chambers Papers Item 6: unnumbered. Gollancz refused to publish Chambers' projected
article, on the grounds that EETS should retreat from Furnivall's example in printing the
Piers Plowman controversy and restrict itself to publishing texts, not monographs. He
offered to publish Chambers' work as an Introduction to the text when the text was ready,
as stated in a letter from Chambers to Mabel Day of 20 January 1938, EETS Papers.

12 See p. 311 n. 5 below.

unreliable', pointing out that 'Dr Knott's attitude to Skeat's work may be gathered from the fact that, when he has to compare Skeat's edition with the edition which he himself is preparing, he speaks, not of Skeat's edition as compared with "my forthcoming edition", but of Skeat's edition as compared with "the Critical Text"' (p. 265). Chambers defends Skeat stoutly: he was faced with a great mass of 'quite unsifted material', and his work on it represents the only possible first stage in dealing with such a wealth of evidence: he chose the best available manuscript and printed it, with a selection of collations, as a first attempt to clear a path through the maze of manuscript variants. The difference between him and his followers

> is simply that which must be found between the results of the first pioneer who, like Skeat, breaks fresh ground, and those of subsequent investigators like Dr Knott or ourselves who, having the spade work already done for them, are able to spend their time on a more minute and precise working over of the old ground. If Dr Knott's results – and ours – are more accurate than those of Skeat (and we hope they are) it is not because our methods are 'critical', whilst Skeat's were 'unscientific and unreliable', but because we start with the benefit of the material which Skeat collected, whilst Skeat had, in the case of the A-text, to begin at the beginning. (p. 267)

Chambers then exposes what his successors, Kane and Donaldson, were later to term 'the ultimate absurdity' of recension, the 'scientific' method Knott so confidently espoused.[13] If an editor must, in order to construct his family tree, determine which are the errors to be found in each manuscript, so as to match error with error and trace the family resemblances between the manuscripts, then this is an exercise of editorial judgement quite as whimsical, subjective, and unscientific as any displayed by editors using the 'older method'. The subsequent process of editing – ascertaining the worth of the reading by checking its relative position in the family tree – may indeed be objective, but it is based on an inherently subjective framework. And if the editor is prepared to use his subjective judgement to establish the family tree, why not go straight ahead and use subjective judgement to establish the text itself? To do the first, in fact, necessarily implies the second.

Talbot Donaldson many years later described the situation thus:

---

[13] Cf. p. 383 below.

It is always carefully pointed out that MSS may be grouped together only on the basis of shared error, but it is seldom pointed out that if an editor has to be able to distinguish right readings from wrong in order to evolve a stemma which will in turn distinguish right from wrong *for* him, then he might as well go on using this God-given editorial power to distinguish right from wrong throughout the whole editorial process, and eliminate the stemma. The only reason for not doing so is to eliminate the appearance – not the fact – of subjectivity: the fact remains that the whole classification depends on purely subjective choices made before the work of editing begins. It is as if the editor believed he had created a very complex machine, into which a god had made his way who could dictate to him the true text, and the editor must reverence the god; while in fact the voice is merely the echo of the editor's ancient preconceptions, the choices made so long ago that he has forgotten it was he who made them; the voice is his own, made to sound divine only through time and forgetfulness: *vox Dei, vox ed.*[14]

Chambers puts it more prosaically: 'A sturdy common sense was Skeat's great characteristic, and he would have been the first to see that he was no more capable of "classifying all extant MSS. according to their family relationships" and "constructing a family tree" "before anything is done toward determining what readings should be adopted in the text" than he was of walking a mile with his right foot before moving his left foot from the ground' (p. 268).

Chambers is able to call on his superior knowledge of textual criticism to demonstrate that Knott's recensionist method, vaunted as new and scientific, was in fact established in the nineteenth century. (Chambers makes somewhat disingenuous play with this, considering that this method was, as we have seen, virtually unknown to Middle English scholars.) He claims that it was used by Skeat to the extent that he did try to put his manuscripts into families. 'That he did not attempt to tabulate these relationships in the form of an actual family tree does not mean that his methods were the less critical' (p. 271): but as we have seen, Chambers' own arguments depended on demonstrating the degree to which Skeat had erred in judgement by adopting Vernon as his copy-text and taking insufficient notice of other of the manuscripts which he had not collated in full; and Skeat's allotment of manuscripts to families was in any case unsatisfactory.[15] Chambers

---

[14] 'The Psychology of Editors', 107; Donaldson is attacking the method expounded in Eleanor Hammond's *Chaucer: A Bibliographical Manual*, referred to by Knott.

[15] See above, pp. 138–40, 163–4 and 175.

goes on to say that, though trees had been, during the third quarter of the nineteenth century, 'a favourite recreation of the learned' as a means of illustrating the way in which Indo-European languages developed (branched out) from one single original, they were helpful up to a certain point only: 'no two were ever the same'. And for scholars to criticise each other because of differences between their trees was 'ludicrous'. Knott had done just this in his article attacking Chambers and Grattan, but even more ludicrously, for Chambers and Grattan never made a tree: for the very good reason that 'the phenomena are, in fact, so complicated that no genealogical tree can properly express them'. The manuscripts 'undergo the most kaleidoscopic transmutations' – switching allegiances from one exemplar to another, and being subject to variable but significant amounts of contamination – 'and this often makes the construction of an actual family tree impossible'.

Chambers distinguishes carefully between the 'genealogical method' on the one hand, which 'seeks to get at the traditions which lie behind different MSS. or groups of MSS., and to estimate the value of these traditions', and one of the *applications* of the 'genealogical method' on the other hand, that which results in the construction of a stemma. In such a case as *Piers Plowman*, where cross-copying and contamination prevailed, a stemma was a chimera, a 'pious hope' (Moore, *Contributions*, p. xxxi). And Chambers shows up Knott mercilessly in his counter-citation of the three authorities that, as we have seen, Knott fleetingly adduced before launching into his self-assured and simplistic account of the 'scientific method'. Eleanor Hammond outlines the method of the 'family-tree' in her *Chaucer Manual*, but adds the important proviso that her description altogether omits to take account of the difficulties raised by 'the possibilities of contamination'.[16] Westcott and Hort, 'amongst the greatest expositors of the "critical" or "genealogical method" … brought out their critical text of the New Testament without any family tree of the extant MSS. at all'. And 'Dr Moore, in his book on Dante, several times reflects on the undoubted contamination that has muddied the clear waters of transmission', and fears that it may be impossible to construct 'anything like an *albero genealogico* of MSS.' (pp. 273–4).

---

[16] A point made more famously in the last sentence of Paul Maas's *Textual Criticism*, 'Gegen die Kontamination ist noch kein Kraut gewachsen.' See E. J. Kenney, *The Classical Text*, 140–2.

Chambers roars to a resounding finish with a quotation from the letter written to him by Skeat in 1909:

> Owing to difficulties which could not be adequately understood or got over at the time when the "Vernon" Text was printed, but which *can* be adequately considered *now*, it has now become much easier to construct a correct A-text than it was in earlier days. This is all in the natural order of progress ...
>
> I am quite aware that it *may* become necessary for my A-text to be superseded. I comfort myself with the reflection that my work is by no means set aside; because it is really a reasonable basis for fresh work, and will lead to right results in the end & hereafter.[17]

Chambers received a number of warm and congratulatory responses to this article, one of which was from A. W. Pollard: 'I have read it with keen pleasure; firstly for the quality of the swordsmanship, secondly for the justice it does to old Skeat, and thirdly for the intrinsic interest of your remarks on critical method.' W. A. Craigie commented that 'some men never understand how much their predecessors have done for them'. Another letter, from Henry Burnett Hinckley, describes Knott as 'a little whippersnapper', adding 'I believe Dr Knott is a very young man, else I hope he would not have been so cavalier.'[18] A long letter from R. A. Williams (13 December 1916), previously of Trinity College, Dublin (from where he had sent Chambers details of the Dublin A-MS) and now Professor of English at Belfast,[19] comments

> I think you show very clearly that Knott is an ass – it seems a pity it should be so since he's apparently very industrious, but it's just as well people should know. Personally I think you are entirely right in what you say both about yourselves and Skeat. Of course 'scientific' editing is an imposture, as Knott conceives it. Editing is not a science but an art, and as such science may be applied – but the applications of science are very different from science itself.

Williams continues with a discussion of editorial principles, to the effect that an editor should emend his manuscripts if the readings are plainly unworthy of the author (in an interesting adumbration of the editorial policies of Kane and Donaldson in editing B many years later), returning to Knott at the end of his letter:

---

[17] See above, pp. 222–3.
[18] All three letters, with others, are preserved in Chambers Papers Item 6, unnumbered.
[19] He later wrote a book on *Beowulf*.

My main point is that Knott seems to be one of these pestilential 'objective' rascals, who evade their own stupidity by appealing to facts they do not understand. I am glad you laid into him about his precious genealogical tree. I hope for the sake of readers that if you & Grattan bring out your edition of Piers you will take the best MS. readings as the basis of your critical text & emend these where it can be done. If you could print a parallel text from the best MS. with the chief variants of the others in the notes, so much the better. But Heaven preserve us from Knott's 'scientific' text with the readings mechanically based on a 'scientific' tree. I think it quite possible that the best text which could be constructed from the Mss. is worse than the original of them all, and it's the bounden duty of the editor towards the reader to improve on it if that can be done.[20]

Other papers, preserved, it appears, almost at random, indicate that progress at the *Piers Plowman* laboratory continued, perhaps by fits and starts. Between 1915 and 1918 Chambers made arrangements to see and then purchase photostats of the newly discovered *Piers Plowman* A-MS (N) held by the National Library of Wales, Aberystwyth (1915–18);[21] in 1917 he was corresponding with the Clarendon Press on the possibility of producing an edition of the B-Text which re-used the plates of the original edition – Chambers dismissed this scheme out of hand, but by March of the following year, he was in correspondence with the Delegates of the Press again, offering to re-edit Skeat's school edition of the poem, Prologue and Passus I–VII of the B-Text. The Delegates decided that it would be best to wait until 'your big critical edition has appeared', so that it would be possible for the school edition to glean from this and from other scholars' criticisms.[22]

The edition was greatly set back by the war. Chambers worked for four months in Rouen in 1916 (during which time he completed his reply to Knott) and again in Belgium in 1917. Grattan was similarly distracted. Two rather miserable letters from this period (January 1919) survive, written from Shrewsbury, where Grattan had been in

---

[20] Chambers Papers Item 6, unnumbered. Relations between Chambers and Knott eventually became cordial: a letter from Knott dated 11 March 1935 discusses his plans as editor for *The Middle English Dictionary*. No mention is made of *Piers Plowman* (Chambers Papers Item 100, unnumbered).

[21] He published a very brief description of the manuscript in 1941, noting its affiliations with the Duke of Westminster's manuscript and giving some examples. He states that the line references he gives 'are to the forthcoming Early English Text Society edition' (see 'A Piers Plowman Manuscript').

[22] Letter dated 26 March 26 1918 (Chambers Papers Item 6, unnumbered).

government employment for the last four years and was now involved in a demobilisation exercise.[23] He offers some cogent criticism of Chambers' latest article, on 'The Three Texts of "Piers Plowman" and Their Grammatical Forms' (1919). The second letter was evidently a response to Chambers' defence of himself, which does not survive. Grattan says, mollifyingly, 'Of course I was not such an idiot as to wish to dis-regard the *B-Text* in editing A' – though perhaps he had been tempted by this plan as a way of expediting their edition of A; for, as we shall see, it was the determination to edit A *in relation to B and C* which fatally delayed their joint editorial project. Grattan's first letter talks of his depressing surroundings, the 'Philistine atmosphere', and his 'slavery'. 'I am isolated here from everything, so am possibly writing nonsense.' He goes on to say

> Circumstances have delayed our original scheme, and my own circumstances are still such that no one can tell when I shall be able to carry out my share of whatever development of the original plan we now have to decide on. It is therefore clear that you will have to go on with the scheme in whatever way you think right.

A letter from W. A. Craigie to Chambers, written on 12 June 1919, illustrates how topical the subject of *Piers Plowman* and its various versions and authors was felt to be: everyone seemed to have a pet theory on it. Chambers' recent article ('The Three Texts of "Piers Plowman" and Their Grammatical Forms') reminded him, Craigie wrote, of an idea 'which occurred to me some time ago as possibly accounting for the differences between AB on the one hand and C on the other.' Langland produced, or at any rate, published, A and B in London, A being an 'advance copy' of B:

> The finished copies of A and B were taken up as fast as they were produced (whether by Langland himself or by professional scribes), and in the end the author remained with only his scroll copy. In this he had written out some portions in a fairly finished state, while of others he had merely set down the general drift, not even worked out into alliterative form.

Langland then returned 'to his native dialect', and prepared a new edition of the now well-known work.

> The fact that he had with him no finished copy of B is the

---

23 The letters are dated 20 and 24 January 1919 respectively (Chambers Papers Item 6, unnumbered).

explanation for the apparently pointless departures from it, while the more serious differences are due to further reflection on various parts of the subject. If he was hard up, as is usually supposed, there is good reason for his keeping no reliable copy of the finished text … the possibility of an author [of a medieval work] being left without a finished copy of his compositions is one that should be taken into account.[24]

This is a striking anticipation of the theory to be notoriously advanced by Kane and Donaldson many years later, that the poet used corrupt copies of his poem to make his revisions.

In 1921, Chambers published his most famous work, *Beowulf. An Introduction to the Study of the Poem*, which was widely recognised as a major contribution to scholarship.[25] But he continued to pursue his interest in the manuscripts of *Piers Plowman*. He followed the fortunes of the Ashburnham manuscript (No. 130, now Huntington Library MS 128) sold to Quaritch, the London bookseller, in 1899, corresponding both with Quaritch and with American friends over a number of years. In 1922 a new manuscript of the poem was discovered. The owner, Allen Bright, got in touch with Chambers through Mabel Day of the EETS, and Chambers and Grattan called on Bright to look at the manuscript, which turned out to be an A-Text.[26] They collated it and made some attempt to establish its relationships with the other A-MSS and map its readings on to the portion of A-Text which they had already established.[27] Bright carried out extensive research on the poet's supposed connections with the Malvern area, and published a book on the subject in 1928 to which Chambers wrote the preface.[28] In June 1924 Chambers bought rotographs of MS Rawlinson Poet. 137; in July 1924 he was collating a 'wretched' Piers Plowman C-MS due to be sold at Sothebys (the manuscript was subsequently bought by the Huntington Library and

[24] Chambers Papers Item 6:41.

[25] Allen Mawer wrote, 'The Introduction finally and definitely places its author in the front rank of the great English scholars who have handled the problems of Ango-Saxon literature and at the same time removes the last vestige of reproach that might be brought against English scholars of letting themselves be outrivalled by scholars of German and Scandinavian nationality.' Mawer signs this review from Liverpool; he had not yet become Provost of University College and therefore closely associated with Chambers.

[26] Now Society of Antiquaries 687 (M).

[27] A scrap of paper survives among the Chambers Papers (item 20) listing a number of M's readings with the other A-MSS E, A, and the B-Text, etc., apparently in Grattan's hand. For the significance of this group of A-MSS, see e.g. pp. 400ff. below.

[28] A. H. Bright, *New Light on Piers Plowman*. The book set out to demonstrate that the poet was indeed William Langland, native to the Malverns, and was one man not five. A large number of letters from or about Bright survive in the Chambers archive.

became Hm 143, now regarded as the best extant C-MS; Chambers visited the Huntington Library in 1935 to study it further);[29] four years later he was buying photostats of one of the Dublin manuscripts.[30] The continued non-appearance of the edition indicates that Knott's 1915 article had delivered a serious blow, despite Chambers' triumphant retort. Knott's clear demonstration that it was unacceptable to reprint a single manuscript with collations was only a reiteration of the points Chambers and Grattan had themselves made in 1909. But it may have pushed them into a far more ambitious project than they would have otherwise envisaged.

[29] The evidence is a draft letter dated July 1924, addressed to a Mr Gibson, apparently at the British Museum (Chambers Papers Item 6, unnumbered): 'I have been collating the wretched Piers MS still further. It certainly belongs to that family which I mentioned. The other MSS are the Earl of Ilchester's which is fragmentary & contaminated, Digby 102 which is imperfect, your Add 35157, & Douce 104. According to our judgement (which is painfully fallible) it is upon that family that a text should be based. Add 35157 is disqualified because of its very erratic spellings from being made the basis of an edition. It looks rather as if the best documents were either Douce or this Sotheby MS.' Cf. also 'The Text of "Piers Plowman"' (1931), 51 n. 2.

[30] He had begun investigation of these manuscripts nearly twenty years earlier. A letter dated 19 June 1909 from the librarian of Trinity College Dublin thanks Chambers for his 'by-print' of 'The Text of "Piers Plowman"', and agrees that the two *Piers Plowman* manuscripts in his charge should be sent to University College, London for Chambers to work on 'when the time comes' (Chambers Papers Item 5, unnumbered).

14

Chambers' graduate students

One of the important observations that Knott had made in his 1915 article was that establishing a text of A was contingent upon establishing a text of B. Chambers and Grattan had explicitly recognised the truth of this remark: 'So inter-related are the texts, that before you can have a final A-text, you must have an adequate B- and C-text.'[1] This crucial point is one that has seriously bedevilled *Piers Plowman* textual investigation, for reasons that become distressingly evident as familiarity with the manuscripts increases: if editing A requires prior editing of B (and C), then by the same token editing B (and C) requires prior editing of A and C (or A and B). The circularity of these requirements is daunting, and at the very least means that the editorial project is destined to eat up a good deal of time. Almost certainly one of the reasons why Chambers' editing of A stretched out over so many years, and seemed ultimately to lose impetus, is that he realised the strength of Knott's observation that, given the insecurity of Skeat's text of B (and by implication C), decisions on editing A made with the help of these two editions could only be provisional: once the three texts had been edited in the first place, it would be necessary to start all over again (see p. 244 above).

Chambers addressed the problem of B at an early stage, setting to work a remarkably able graduate student, Elsie Blackman, on a study of the poem.[2] Blackman was the first person to produce thorough and

---

[1] 'The Text of "Piers Plowman": Critical Methods', 271. Chambers and Grattan note that this principle had been acknowledged by Thomas A. Knott, in 'An Essay Toward the Critical Text of the A-Version of "Piers the Plowman"', 129. But they had probably taken it on board at least as early as 1910; see n.2 below.

[2] Chambers had examined B- and C-MSS from an early date; a letter survives from the Librarian of Newnham College dated 21 October 1909 granting him permission to see the Yates Thompson B-MS (Chambers Papers Item 5:21), and in 'The Authorship of "Piers Plowman"' (1910), 28 n.1, he had declared his and Grattan's 'hope, next year, to print some notes on the relationship of B and C MSS., especially in passages bearing upon problems of the A-text'.

systematic work on the classification of the B-MSS, and for that reason deserves a place of special honour in the *Piers Plowman* editing canon. She completed her MA thesis for the University of London in 1914 (under her maiden name, Chick), restating and summarising its main conclusions in an article published four years later, over-modestly entitled 'Notes on the B-Text MSS of *Piers Plowman*'. Blackman had begun work intending to study the dialect of the B-Text, presumably at the suggestion of Chambers, who was anxious to amass material to prove Manly wrong.[3] When Blackman realised how doubtful were some of the readings of Skeat's B-Text, she decided to undertake an investigation of all the extant B-MSS instead. She thanks both Chambers and Grattan 'for the help and advice they have given me throughout this work'.

Blackman set out to classify the manuscripts into genetic groups, ascertain which of the manuscripts were most valuable, and set down the lines on which reconstruction of the B-Text would have to be based. She worked on sample passages only, taken from different points in the poem and amounting to about two thousand lines in total, something under a third of the B-Text's total of seven thousand-odd lines. She identified three main sub-groups of B-MSS:

(1) λ, containing LMRF;
(2) τ, containing WCr;
(3) ω, containing CB, YO, C^2, and G^2.[4]

G^1, she found, was independent of any of these groups. This compares with Skeat's classification of the manuscripts into four sub-groups:

(a) LR;
(b) YCB;
(c) OC^2;
(d) WCr.

(The remaining manuscripts he was unable to assign to sub-groups.) The difference between Skeat and Blackman is no doubt due partly to the decline of Laud from editorial popularity, partly to the fact that Blackman analysed sample passages only, and partly to the unsatisfactoriness of Skeat's categorisation.[5] Skeat's views on manuscript relations had been fixed while under the impression that Laud's was

---

[3] See p. 228 above.   [4] G^1 stands for Pro–Passus VII of G, and G^2 for the remainder.
[5] See pp. 138–40 above.

the most faithful text; hence his conclusions as to which manuscripts were related – which manuscripts agreed in error, or in other words agreed in deviating from Laud – were (presumably) dependent on the assumption that Laud's text was indeed the right one.[6] Blackman came to believe that Laud was far less accurate than Skeat had originally supposed, although still the most serviceable basic manuscript; hence her detection of agreement in error, and consequently her classification of the manuscripts, were necessarily different.

She decides that 'L and W are, in each case, the only trustworthy representatives of their groups' (p. 505), and that Y is the best representative of the third group. In general, the readings she instances as the errors on which she has based her classification into different groups are uncontroversial.

She goes on to investigate the relative value of the manuscripts. First, she finds that there are many instances (161 in 499 lines of text common to A B, and C) where the agreement of AC against B indicated that B was faulty. She does not consider that Langland may have reverted to an A reading when writing C, having in the interim chosen a different reading for B, and she puts this point very clearly:

> If it is certain
> (a) that the C-text was written from a B-text
> (b) that the B-text was written from an A-text
> (c) that the C-text is not contaminated from the A-text
> then it follows that all cases where the A- and C-texts agree against the B-text must be cases where the accepted B-text is faulty, and where it must be emended to agree with the readings of the other versions. (p. 518)

This baldly stated syllogism is not justified or explored. It is presumably advanced on the unacknowledged assumption underlying her entire article, that all three texts were written by the same person. Otherwise, there would be no reason not to suppose that A might have chosen one reading, B another, and C have reverted to the choice of A: consistency, or what one might term a linear development in choice of reading, is not necessarily to be expected from three different authors. But even given a single author, it is not *demonstrably* the case that a writer should not have changed his or

[6] Skeat had, as we have seen, changed his mind on Laud by 1910. Blackman refers to Jusserand's report of this in '*Piers Plowman* – The Work of One or of Five: A Reply' (312), and comments, 'I am unable to trace Professor Skeat's change of opinion in his published works'. Presumably Skeat was strongly influenced by Chambers' 1909 paper.

her mind back and forth during the course of rewriting a work. It is hard to be too critical of Blackman for failing to recognise this, however, since her successors make the same assumption with almost as little acknowledgement and justification.[7]

Blackman's notion that – given single authorship – A and C can be used as a 'control' on the faulty archetype of B was to become a powerful tool in B-Text editing, and indeed a necessary one if many of the changes editors later made to the B archetype were to be justified. Donaldson pointed out in 1968 that it was *only* the assumption of single authorship which validated the use of the AC control: without it, the editor was left perpetually shrugging his shoulders. The B reading might appear inferior to the AC one, but who was to say it was not in fact the choice of the B-author? On the other hand, if a single author had demonstrably chosen the AC reading on two different occasions – so the argument went – it stood to reason that he probably chose it for B as well, and that the B reading which survives is a scribal corruption of the ABC original.[8]

Blackman uses her AC versus B rule to attempt to distinguish between B-MSS: the B-MSS closer to A and C are, she thinks, more reliable than the others – provided, of course, that the correspondence is not attributable to contamination. On this test, G^1 and W – and to some extent O and C^2 – emerge superior. Her second investigation is of the other portions of her sample material; and here she finds that G^2 and Y are also relatively reliable, while L, definitely, is not. Finally, in an independent investigation, she assesses the relative number and quality of errors found in the B-MSS over all her material, and comes to the conclusion that L is, by this criterion, 'the first authority', and that ω and W come next; while R is to be treated with suspicion (given its possible contamination, with F, from the A- and C-Texts) and G^1 with respect.

Putting all this material together allowed her to advance some theories on her third objective, the way in which the B-Text should be edited. She draws a 'table' (see figure 14.1), on which the B-MSS figure in relation both to each other and to A and C. By weighing the genetic groups one against another, and making judicious use of outlying manuscripts such as M, G^1, and R, it was possible to construct the probable original reading of Bx, the B-MS archetype.

---

[7] See e.g. Kane–Donaldson, 149ff, and p. 349 below. As we have seen, Chambers had adumbrated the principle in 'The Authorship of "Piers Plowman"', 26 ff.

[8] 'Piers Plowman: Textual Comparison and the Question of Authorship'.

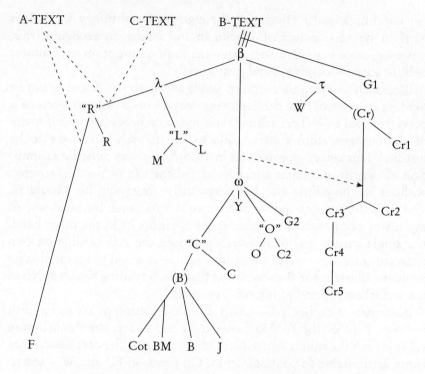

Figure 14.1. Blackman's table of the B-MSS

But this was of limited use, given her belief that the archetype was faulty. Comparing it with A and C would, according to her assumptions about the relationship between the three texts, determine the correct reading in *some* instances – so that where AC agreed against B, the true B reading would be the same as that of AC – but in numerous other instances the other two texts would not be available as controls. So 'at present', she says, 'this seems to be as near as one can get to the original B-text, though a nearer approximation can be made when further collations of the B- and C-MSS are available' – particularly of the last few passus, where B and C agree very closely. (Presumably acting on this hint, it was to the last three passus of B that George Kane first turned his attention when he came to work on the poem, editing them for his Ph.D. thesis in 1946.) Blackman is also clear that 'there is one significant fact that cannot be overlooked by students of *Piers Plowman* – the extant evidence suggests that the writer of the C-text worked from a B-text MS. which, in certain

respects, was better than the ancestor of the extant B-text MSS.'
(p. 530), an important corollary of the perception that agreements
between AC versus B indicated a faulty B archetype.[9]

Blackman tells us that she hopes to print at a later stage 'some
Passus at least of the reconstructed B-text, when it will be seen that
many apparent roughnesses of the B-text are innovations', and that 'it
is even possible that some of the passages in the B-text from which
the argument in favour of multiple authorship is drawn owe their
present form to scribal errors' (p. 530) – this despite the fact that her
own textual investigations were premised upon single authorship.
Her hope was not fulfilled. Unfortunately for *Piers Plowman* studies,
she had married by the time the article appeared, and moved to
Cambridge and had her first child in December of that year. Thereafter, although she returned to London and taught regularly for
University College, she never produced further published work on
the poem (other than a book review). Nevertheless she was apparently
still working on the B-Text in 1923,[10] and communicated with
Chambers on textual matters on various occasions over the next
nineteen years (see pp. 286–302 below).

Despite the clarity and intelligence of Blackman's exposition, her
account of her investigations occasionally gives the reader pause for
thought. First of all, there is the question of method, a question she
does not raise. As already described, she must have established a
rough and ready view of the original B-Text *before* she embarked
upon her classification of manuscripts. On what grounds does she
decide that readings are authorial or scribal? No discussion of the
principles for such discrimination is provided; it seems clear that
Blackman must regard them as, in the main, too obvious to need
stating. Her technique for reconstructing Langland's text is adopted
from Westcott and Hort, presumably under the instruction of
Chambers; she follows the three-stage method outlined above, first
collating the manuscripts to establish some sense of genetic relations,
and then using the tool thus provided to inform her reassessment of
variant readings. She handles this method with considerable facility,

[9] In this respect, as she acknowledges, she develops the suggestion of Chambers in his 1910
article (see above, pp. 288ff.).
[10] As reported by B. F. Allen, in her unpublished MA thesis, 'The Genealogy of the C Text
Manuscripts of *Piers Plowman*', 1; cf. also Chambers and Grattan, 'The Text of *Piers
Plowman*' (1931), 2. A note written some time after 1935 by Chambers on English tutors at
University College, perhaps for purposes of assessing relative salary or promotion deserts,
records against Blackman's name 'no research after 1918'; presumably he referred to
published research (Chambers Papers Item 96, unnumbered).

demonstrating an ability unprecedented in the *Piers Plowman* editorial tradition for understanding how manuscripts may be used as checks on each other's reliability, if they can be demonstrated to descend from the same source (see e.g. her discussion of her four manuscript families, pp. 498–516). Presumably this method seemed to her unimpeachable, but as we have seen it is peculiarly unfitted to an analysis of a manuscript tradition such as *Piers Plowman*. The Westcott and Hort method, both for constructing a stemma and for establishing a text, is predicated on the assumption that only *one* of the conflicting variants witnessed by manuscripts can be original. But where an author revises his own text, some of the variants available in the manuscript tradition may be both authorial *and* less satisfactory, by the usual criteria, than other variants which the editor judges to be original.

Blackman's views on scribes and their motives are sometimes troubling, indicating that she was not fully alert to the difficulties of distinguishing between scribal and authorial readings. She is not above the occasional witty put-down, clearly enjoying the sense of her own editorial superiority. Thus she says of the scribe of the notorious Corpus 201 manuscript of B (F), that the scribe was 'often puzzled by his copy, but he made sure that no one else should suffer in the same way ... [his] text is, for the most part, so bad that it is useless' (p. 502). This is a reference to the F-scribe's remarkable powers of composition, which have (no doubt) given the modern editors of the B-Text cause for much heart searching, in the hope of distinguishing between an excellent scribal guess and original authorial text. Kane and Donaldson on the one hand, and Schmidt on the other, have adopted many of F's readings into their texts,[11] and this difference of opinion alerts us to the subjectivity of editorial judgement, despite Blackman's certainty (shared, as we have seen, with Skeat) that F's readings were usually inferior to the ones she judged authorial.

Elsewhere Blackman writes of the scribe of W 'faking' his copy (p. 526), and of the scribe of C as 'careless and dishonest':

> he was also so indifferent that he had no objection to writing a meaningless line. The student does not grumble at him for his want of invention, for a faithful rendering of an original is obviously of more value than an unfaithful one, however interesting the latter

---

[11] See further below, p. 387 and note 17.

may be; but his carelessness in copying has very greatly negatived the advantage that should have resulted from his lack of initiative. (p. 506)

This easy and impatient contempt is a familiar editorial attitude towards scribes: the modern editor likes a scribe to be as diligent but unthinking as possible, so as to provide the optimal circumstances for reconstruction of the author's original – or, a less charitable explanation, the best possible foil to the editor's own acuity, perception, and wit. If a scribe is 'careless and dishonest' – note the moral disapproval – it is tiresome for the editor who has to correct his mistakes; if he is intelligent, it is equally or even more tiresome since editorial ingenuity must then compete with scribal ingenuity.

Blackman's remarks illustrate her lack of interest in the original circumstances of transmission; as she says, 'Very little is known of the method of publication in the 14th and 15th centuries' (p. 530). This is less true now than in 1918, and modern editors question the proposition that scribes were necessarily stupid, recognising that differences between standards of accuracy in the fifteenth century and today may reflect not only improved methods of transmission, but also different aims on the part of those involved in the transmission process.

Lack of knowledge of the circumstances of transmission hampers Blackman's discussion of contamination between manuscripts of the various versions, although it cannot be said that we have much more information to aid us today. Blackman scratches her head over the peculiar characteristics of G. Were its frequent agreements with A the result of contamination from an A-MS or were these readings really B readings all along, misrepresented by the other B-MSS? Many of them are trivial, so it seems unlikely a scribe would have picked them out in preference to more distinctive A readings – which rarely turn up in G.

Contamination is a difficult concept under any circumstances, but particularly so in the case of *Piers Plowman*, and Blackman deserves credit as the first scholar to consider the problem in any detail. It does seem possible that a reading from one version of the poem might leak into another, especially if scribes were in the habit of making copies from more than just one of the versions. As they copied out their exemplar of one of the versions, they might accidentally or intentionally introduce from memory a reading which belonged to the equivalent passage in one of the two other versions (memorial

263

contamination). Some manuscripts show clear signs of extensive correction – the B-MS M, or the A-MS H^2, for example. But the triviality of many of the corrected readings makes the phenomenon impenetrable to modern editorial reconstruction of scribal motive. It is also possible that agreements between manuscripts of different versions is to be attributed to coincident scribal error.[12] Blackman was particularly disadvantaged by the fact that neither of the other texts had been fully edited, and no satisfactory record of their collations existed.[13] So what appeared from Skeat's editions to be a distinctive 'A' or 'C' reading, which had somehow found its way into a B-MS, might turn out, once all the evidence had come to light and been analysed, to be (on the balance of probability) a scribal reading – or even a reading present in a non-B-MS because it had been borrowed from B.

Finally, Blackman's confident drawing of a stemma, and her assumption that its logic might be mechanically applied, is puzzling in the light of Chambers' destruction of Knott's similar assumptions. Chambers had been able to show that A-MS relations were more complex than Knott's scheme allowed for, and the same is unfortunately true of the B-MSS. Blackman had based her conclusions on sample evidence only (a technique specifically warned against by Westcott and Hort, although practised by Moore).[14] Her results were initially confirmed by George Kane, her successor, in his doctoral thesis of 1946, which analysed the manuscript relations in Passus XVIII–XX of the B-Text, but were overturned by his subsequent work, which took into account the B-Text in its entirety.[15] Kane and Donaldson found that the inconsistent patterns of agreement between B-MSS made it impossible to construct a credible stemma, in the same way that it had proved impossible to construct a stemma for the A-MSS.

Blackman nevertheless made a substantial contribution to the initial

---

[12] For a recent discussion of the apparent contamination in both G and other *Piers Plowman* manuscripts, see Robert Adams, 'Editing *Piers Plowman B*', 54–9.

[13] Other than Prologue and Passus I–IV of the A-Text, for which she had Chambers and Grattan's proofs. But their collations were neither complete nor wholly accurate.

[14] See Moore, *Contributions*, xxxiiff.

[15] See p. 384 below. An interim stage of this study was reported by Kane's collaborator, Talbot Donaldson, in 'MSS R and F in the B-Tradition of *Piers Plowman*', by which time the two editors had completed their B-Text collations. Here Donaldson demonstrated that RF represented a branch of the B-Text tradition separate from LM, and that the B-MSS fell into two families only, RF and the rest; he concluded that RF represent an authorial stage of the poem intermediate between A and B. For the two editors' final position, which rejects this conclusion, see Kane–Donaldson, 57–69 (and pp. 381, 386–8 below).

classification of the B-MSS, and this was duly recognised by her successor on the B-Text, George Kane (see p. 315 below). Yet in one way her results must have seemed depressing to Chambers. Her analysis of B was, as she asserted, provisional, since she collated only a portion of the poem. She believed that it would be necessary to collate and analyse the readings throughout the entire poem to be sure of her conclusions, or in some cases even to come to a conclusion; and in this she was absolutely right. Chambers must have regarded her conclusions with some dismay. If it was impossible to edit B properly without comprehensive collation of all the B-MSS, then there could be no question but that comprehensive collation of the A-MSS would also be required for the much more complex manuscript tradition of A. And such collation, as we shall see later, was still far from complete.

The C-Text was worked on by several different pupils. The first was Bessie Allen (later Tapping), who wrote an MA thesis under Chambers on the relationship of the C-MSS in 1923. She did not consult the C-MS in Trinity College, Dublin, D. 4.1, or the Duke of Westminster's manuscript, an AC conjoint manuscript, and she did not know of the manuscript now Hm 143, which was discovered the following year. But she examined all the other manuscripts save Ilchester and Skeat's base-manuscript P (then Phillipps 8231, now Hm 137), for whose readings she relied on Skeat's text and critical apparatus.

Allen writes with a clarity and decision which give a rather false impression that the problems she discusses are easily susceptible of resolution. Thus she alludes in the space of a sentence to the authorship controversy, and comments 'The last word seems to have been said on the subject.' She was wrong, of course. The matter was not settled to general agreement until 1965, with the publication of Kane's book on the subject; and in the eyes of a small number of scholars it is still open to question.[16] The establishment of the original texts of the three versions she regards as a perfectly distinct matter, necessarily separate from, and prior to, deciding on authorship. She thus makes explicit the mistaken assumption implicit in Blackman's work, viz. that it is possible to decide between many of the variants in the textual tradition of *Piers Plowman without* already having assumed single or multiple authorship of the various versions.

[16] Allen, 'The Genealogy of the C Text Manuscripts of *Piers Plowman*', 1. Cf. Pearsall, *An Annotated Critical Bibliography of Langland*, 45–64 (and also 6–31), and p. 322 below.

Here is how she states the relationship between the two issues:

> To establish the genealogical tree of the MS. is the first step towards
> reconstructing the original C ... when once the genealogical tree has
> been found the way should be clear towards determining the
> original readings. And when the original A., B., and C. texts have
> been reclaimed, purged of the errors of their many scribes, then it
> will be possible to argue with some degree of certainty about their
> authorship, and about their metre, and dialect, and style. Then we
> shall know what *Piers Plowman* was, and perhaps may be able to
> determine whether William Langland made it, – or Robert – or
> whether it is indeed the work of five. (p. 2)

This view, that recension is the key to the original text, evidences a
quite remarkable belief in the objective security of the genealogical –
or as Knott would call it, the scientific – method, one which it is
curious to read in the light of Chambers' scathing dismissal of Knott
in 1916.

Allen continues with a comparison between Skeat's work and her
own. She arrives at a different classification of the C-MSS partly, she
says, because she has collated eleven manuscripts which he did not,
but also owing to 'the advance in the principles of textual criticism
which I have been able to apply to the study, but which had not been
generally accepted in Skeat's day' (p. 5). These are (1) that persistent
identity of error in two or more manuscripts implies identity of
origin, (2) that agreement between manuscripts in a *correct* reading
does not imply identity of origin, and (3) that in order to establish
their genetic connections and characteristics, manuscripts must be
examined in their entirety – affiliations might change from passus to
passus, and so confining the examination to one stretch of the poem
only will not do. This last point gives the misleading impression that
Allen, unlike Skeat, fully collated all her manuscripts in their entirety.
Such a task would have been a very substantial undertaking, and she
did not attempt it. Instead, she seems to have selected, pretty much at
random, examples of interesting variations and agreements between
the C-MSS throughout the poem; although she nowhere describes the
policy governing her selection.

Her analysis of the C-MS relations is represented by the stemma
shown in figure 14.2. She detects three separate groups of manuscripts: the P group (PERMNQSZFGK), the I group (UYIP^2-
OLBD), and the T group, TH^2. The P and I groups derive from the

The autograph

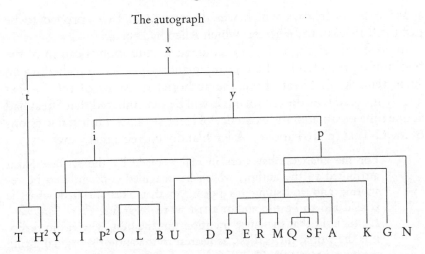

Figure 14.2. Allen's analysis of C-MS relations

same sub-archetypal source, 'y', and therefore the stemma is essentially bifid. Clearly, this classification does not correspond to that of Skeat (see p. 163 above; Skeat did not class N and P², and U and Q were unknown to him when he published the C-Text). Group T, Allen thinks, is the oldest, for TH² 'retain certain archaic or rare words not understood by the scribe of 'y' (the parent of the I. and P. groups) and moreover their readings often explain those of the other two' (10). So although T and in particular H_2 have many errors, they are 'of extraordinary value'. Since T is incomplete (being another of the conjoint AC manuscripts), however, it cannot be taken as a copy-text. Neither can any of the P group manuscripts, as this tradition 'is sophisticated and given to expansion', and on comparison with the other groups proves to be lower down the chain of transmission and therefore furthest from the author's original. Allen concludes, therefore, that 'the C. text is best given by a MS. akin to Ilchester; that when established the C. text will be much nearer to the B. text than the printed edition shows; but the general character of C. will not be altered; the additions made by the author will remain much as they now stand' (p. 11). The manuscript she suggests is U (Add. 35157). These conclusions are apparently considered by the Athlone editors to be still essentially valid:[17] Hm 143, the C-MS now regarded as

---

[17]   As reported to the author by Professor Kane in a conversation of 1 September 1993. See also Kane, *The Evidence for Authorship*, 36 n.1.

superior to its fellows which was discovered in 1924, proved to be just the 'MS. akin to Ilchester' which Allen had specified.

Interestingly enough, in her comments on the sophistication of the tradition represented by the P group manuscripts, Allen picked up on some remarks of Skeat about the authorial revisions of the C-Text largely ignored by other scholars. It will be remembered that Skeat had at one time postulated the existence of *three* separate authorial versions of the C-Text (p. 164 above). Allen blandly corrects this view:

> For the changes that were in reality made by the scribes, Skeat attributed to the author, whom he imagined constantly to be re-writing and re-issuing his poem. So that Skeat printed what he considered to be the author's last word regarding *Piers Plowman*. He thought that the latest tradition was the best; whereas in reality it is the worst; the earliest, as nearest to the author's original, being the best C.text. (pp. 11–12)

This judgement was later confirmed by A. G. Mitchell, who reports it with the approving comment that it further undermined Manly's argument on multiple authorship: the fewer the number of distinct versions of the poem, the less likely that more than one author was involved.[18] Yet the question of the number of authorial versions of C was later to be reopened (see p. 355 below). This would seem to have been inevitable. The hypothesis that the revising poet (even assuming that only one person was involved) limited his rewriting of C to one attempt alone is intrinsically improbable, given the substantial variation between the C-MSS.

At the end of her Introduction, Allen corrects what may have been thought to be a fault of Blackman's dissertation, and provides a very brief account of the principles of textual criticism by which she distinguished between authorial and scribal error (pp. 6–7). She alludes in her last paragraph to 'well known maxims' for detecting scribal error: *lectio difficilior principatum tenet*, from Bengel, *brevior lectio praeferenda est verbosiori*, from Griesbach, and 'the rule emphasized by Tischendorf, that the reading that explains the origin of other readings is preferable'. These remarks, perfunctory though they are, suggest she had done a little more reading in the history of textual criticism than Blackman.[19] However, her analysis has none of

---

[18] Mitchell, 'A Critical Edition of Piers Plowman, Context, Prologue, and Passus I–IV' (unpublished Ph.D. thesis), 43–4.

[19] A University College library slip dated 30 August 1923 records that Chambers had borrowed, among other books, Westcott & Hort, the *New Testament* editions of

the intellectual power and control, and indeed none of the polish, of Blackman's, and gives little indication that she had come to grips with the peculiar editorial problems of the poem.[20]

In the same year, another pupil of Chambers, F. A. R. Carnegy, submitted an MA thesis on the C-Text. He devoted the first part of his Introduction to the refutation of Görnemann's theory that the various manuscripts of the poem represented a single authorial original,[21] and the remainder to illustrations of and notes on Allen's discussions of the relations and characteristics of the C-MSS. He agrees with Allen entirely, and nothing in his Introduction gives any hint of the problems confronting the editor of the poem. Carnegy edits Passus II, III, and IV (equivalent to AB II, III, and IV) of the C-Text, taking U as his base-text, and provides a critical apparatus listing the variants of the thirteen other manuscripts he collated. No indication is given of the principles on which he emended the readings of his base-text. The thesis was later reproduced as a book in 1934.[22]

Carnegy and Allen were obviously unlucky to complete their work in 1923, the year before Hm 143 (X) was discovered. This was sold by Sothebys in 1924, and Chambers was able to make 'as full an examination of it as time permitted' while the manuscript was in their care.[23] He subsequently (1935) visited the Huntington Library to work on the manuscript further, using Allen's analysis of C-MS relations as the basis for classification of its affiliations.[24] He found that it belonged to her I group, that XU and D alone of this group were qualified to form the basis of a text, and that X was unequi-

---

Tischendorf and Griesbach, and Bentley's *Proposals for a New Edition of the Greek New Testament* (Chambers Papers Item 20, unnumbered). An accompanying scrap of paper in Chambers' handwriting, perhaps dating from the same period, reads

Lectio difficilior principatum tenet
Bengel
Brevior lectio praeferenda est verbosiori
Griesbach
Tischendorf reading which explains the other readings preferable

Evidently he was continuing to investigate the degree to which classical principles of textual criticism could be applied to Middle English, and it is possible that he was checking these references on Allen's behalf.

[20] Later in her thesis, Allen devotes a short chapter (180–9) to the discussion of the possibility of contamination in the C-MSS from the B-Text, suggesting that memorial contamination would have been likely. This suggestion was to be later picked up by Mitchell.

[21] A theory finally dispatched by Chambers and Grattan in 1931; see pp. 281–2 below.

[22] Cuttingly reviewed by Blackman (1934), who had received a free copy from Carnegy; see his letter to Chambers dated 28 February 1934 (Chambers Papers Item 99, unnumbered).

[23] 'The Text of "Piers Plowman" ' (1931), 51 n.2; cf. pp. 254–5 above.

[24] Chambers had written to Bessie Tapping (as she now was) before his departure, requesting a copy of her thesis to take with him to California (Chambers Papers Item 100, unnumbered).

vocally the most superior of these three manuscripts, with U second in importance. This was a finding of major importance for the editing of the C-Text. X was the manuscript printed by Pearsall as his copy-text of C in 1978, and is to form the basis of the forthcoming Athlone edition of C.

It is appropriate at this point to run ahead of ourselves chronologically, and look at the work of one of the two remaining *Piers Plowman* graduates whom Chambers enlisted in the editing project, A. G. Mitchell. (The other is George Kane; in chapter 16 below I describe how these two men came to take over the editorial burden of Chambers and Grattan.) Mitchell's Ph.D. thesis, again supervised by Chambers, was an edition with Introduction of C Prologue and Passus I–IV, completed in 1939. He pays extensive tribute to the work of Allen, reporting Chambers' elevation of X to the position of first among the C-MSS as a confirmation of Allen's prior analysis of the C-MS relations, which remained valid in every other respect. He was able to supplement Allen's work by identifying the Trinity College, Dublin C-MS (D. 4. 1), which she had not been able to examine, as a separate member of the sub-group PERMQSF (although he does not mention, and therefore does not classify, the other manuscript unconsulted by her, that belonging to the Duke of Westminster).

Mitchell nowhere gives any detailed information on the principles on which he had established his text, apparently assuming, like Blackman and Allen before him, that these would be unproblematic. Instead he makes merely general comments, as 'In emendation we have sought to be as conservative as possible, without carrying conservation to an unreasonable extreme.' In this respect his dissertation is vastly inferior to that of George Kane, submitted seven years later, who discusses in some detail the criteria for distinguishing between authorial and scribal readings. But in another respect his work is superior to Kane's, namely in his discussion of the phenomenon of scribal contamination between the various manuscripts and versions of the poem.[25] In including such a study, Mitchell was following in the footsteps of Blackman and Allen; and his account is more sophisticated than Kane's, both in the latter's Ph.D. thesis of 1946, and also in his published editions of A and B (1960 and 1975 respectively).

---

[25] 'A Critical Edition of Piers Plowman, Context, Prologue, and Passus I–IV', 90–110.

He looks at the problem of contamination not only by *lines* (as Kane was later to do in the case of A-MSS WN and K),[26] but also by *readings*. The phenomenon of contamination by readings poses a much more sticky problem for the editor of *Piers Plowman*, as it can render the process of decision between the variants for any one version of the poem almost intolerable. (For example, if two variant readings, roughly equivalent in value, are found in two or more versions of the poem, then it can be literally impossible to guess whether their presence is due to authorial revision or to scribal contamination. Some individual instances of this problem are discussed in chapters 20 and 21 below.)

Like Blackman and Allen before him, Mitchell considers the possibility of memorial contamination – scribes having previously copied A- and/or B-MSS, and incorporating a reading from that manuscript into their C-Text – 'inherently probable'. And he seems fully to understand the problematic nature of the concept of contamination as applied to the editing of the poem: 'Both by being too ready to assume contamination, and too reluctant to assume contamination, we run the risk of misrepresenting the manuscript evidence, on the one hand by over-riding it, on the other by failing to take into account important modifications of it' (p. 97). Mitchell's understanding of the difficulty presented by contamination is the result of his comparing the readings of A-, B-, and C-MSS over a portion of the poem which evidences both a good deal of authorial revision and a large number of roughly equivalent lines between the three versions. Kane, who cut his teeth editing a very different section of the poem (B Passus XVIII–XX), did not acquire so keen a sense of the phenomenon, especially since in editing the A-Text he did not examine the manuscripts of the B- and C-Texts. As we shall see, his editing was to suffer as a result.

[26] See Kane, 31–8.

271

15

Chambers 1931

There is no doubt that Chambers' editorial work on *Piers Plowman* was beginning to lose its impetus by the mid-1920s. He had published an article on 'Long Will, Dante, and the Righteous Heathen' in 1924, but this did not deal with textual matters. His colleague A. H. Smith later described how 'a growing distaste for work of an analytical character turned Chambers to other fields and the work [on *Piers Plowman*] lagged, especially after Grattan's departure to Liverpool, except for fitful pricks of conscience'.[1] E. G. Stanley remembers that C. J. Sisson (one of the other English professors at University College, London) used to tell how he would lock up Chambers and Grattan (on his visits to London) in a room together in order to get them to work on their edition of the poem. Later, Chambers complained that his work on the text had been needlessly delayed by the printed opinions of Mabel Day, who published articles in 1922 and 1928 arguing on the basis of evidence in Skeat's editions that as many as five authors (not counting But) had written the poem. The fact that Day 'had never consulted a MS.' made him particularly angry.[2]

In 1930 Chambers wrote to Grattan, 'we must do our duty to old William Langland (and to Skeat) before the night comes when no man can work',[3] his melodramatic turn of phrase revealing his sense of responsibility to a text of such national importance; the result was the publication in 1931 of an article entitled 'The Text of *Piers Plowman*'. The work is signed by both Chambers and Grattan, but Chambers as always played the leading role.[4]

[1] 'Piers Plowman and the Pursuit of Poetry', 36.
[2] Letter dated 16 May 1939 to R. B. McKerrow, the distinguished textual scholar and editor of *RES*; Chambers Papers Item 102, unnumbered. See Mabel Day, 'The Alliteration of the Versions of "Piers Plowman" in Its Bearing on Their Authorship', and 'The Revisions of "Piers Plowman"'.
[3] Quoted by Smith, 'Pursuit of Poetry', 36.
[4] As is made clear by a letter from Grattan (now promoted to the chair in Liverpool) to Chambers of 21 October 1930: 'Your article is a masterly summary. I know of course that

This third article partly recapitulates, and partly develops, the ideas and principles the two editors had established earlier. They fully acknowledge the enormous gap that has intervened between the 1909 article (which had been given the same title) and its continuation, and explain that 'these intervening twenty-two years have more and more shown us how closely related are the problems of the three texts, A, B, and C, and how impossible it is to reach final results upon any one of them without the fullest consideration of the others' (a supremely important principle in the editing of *Piers Plowman*, and one first identified, as they acknowledged in 1916, by Knott).[5] But Chambers and Grattan do not give much hope that their labours are about to be brought to a conclusion. 'Even now', they say, 'although the exploratory work is done, and the system on which the A-, B- and C-texts must be edited seems, to us at any rate, fairly clear, it must be years before the mere labour of collation can be finished; and "the blind fury with the abhorred shears" spares text-editors no more than poets' (p. 18).[6] Nevertheless, their discussion demonstrates how increased familiarity with B and C has enhanced their understanding of the problems of editing A.

This can be seen in their account of the archetypal manuscripts of

some of your facts are based on toil that I have had a share in. I know that I have even had an exceedingly small share in thrashing out some of the problems. But your logical and comprehensive grasp of the whole issue is a thing far beyond my powers... I have done my best to work at 'PP' all these years; and I am prepared unashamedly to say that I can see the right reading through the welter of variants in MS MSS. [*sic*] quite as well as Housman can spot the right Latin reading. So much I *have* learnt. But the comprehensive view, the syntactic powers which you possess, will never be mine. And I have always felt – perhaps I have not always let my feelings be seen? – that, in my association with you on this great piece of work, I am getting a bigger share of the credit than my own, rather mechanical, skill has entitled me to... I myself have never omitted to make clear to any friend who spoke to me of our joint articles, that my share has been only a share in the spadework, and that you with your keen and logical mind have been, throughout, the architect' (Chambers Papers Item 6, unnumbered). This well illustrates the formidable intellectual difficulty which the textual problems of the poem presented even to someone who had been working on them for a considerable number of years. It should be noted that, despite Grattan's remarks here, Smith refers to one of the most important elements in the 1931 article, the theory of 'Substitution of Similars', as Grattan's in origin ('Pursuit of Poetry', 35).

5   'The Text of "Piers Plowman"' (1931), 1; cf. 'The Text of "Piers Plowman"' (1916), 271, and T. A. Knott, 'An Essay Toward the Critical Text' (1915), 129.

6   The Chambers Papers, Item 116, contain an offprint of the 1931 article annotated by Chambers. A list of *Piers Plowman* manuscripts appears at the end of the article (50–1), and Chambers has marked with handwritten annotation the manuscripts of which he possesses either rotographs or transcriptions. These do not include the A-MSS Ashmole 1468 (A), Digby 145 (K), Harley 3954 (H[3]), or National Library of Wales (N). He has only a 'very bad transcript' of the Trinity College Dublin A-MS D. 4. 12 (E), and a photograph of Passus V–XI 225 of the Duke of Westminster's manuscript (W). This information bears out his gloomy prognosis of the likely time it would take to complete the collations.

the three versions. The archetype of A was – in a very few instances (which, regrettably, they do not list) – faulty, so that all the A-MSS agree in error. At these points, B 'seems to have had the correct reading before him': i.e., the B-MSS offer a superior equivalent; and Chambers and Grattan infer from this that the A-MS used by the B-author for his revision of A was in some respects better than the archetype of the existing A-MSS. This is not an implausible inference, given that 'every extant A-MS. is later (and all but one are much later) than the date when B was working on the A-text' (p. 1).[7] But in many other cases it was difficult to use B-MSS as straightforward evidence about the reading of the original text of B.

It was for this reason, of course, that they had cause to be grateful to Blackman. It was she who had developed and substantiated Chambers' theory of the corrupt B-archetype, first enunciated in 1910, and also – for to edit B in its turn necessitated some preliminary classification of C-MSS – confirmed his suspicion that 'the writer of the C-text worked from a B-text MS. which, in certain respects, was better than the ancestor of the extant B-text MSS.' The evidence for this was that, in a significant number of instances (some presented by Blackman and some independently discussed by Chambers), B and C had roughly equivalent text, but C preserved a slightly better version of the text than B. In many of these cases, B's version looked more like a scribal corruption than an authorial revision – although, unfortunately, the relative probability of these two explanations is not explored by either Chambers or his pupil Blackman.

Some of Chambers' discussed examples are cogent. For instance, B XIX 184–6 describes how 'Christ, before His ascension, entrusts to Peter power of remitting sins':

> And ʒaf Pieres power · and pardoun he graunted
> To alle manere men · mercy and forʒyfnes
> Hym myʒte to assoile · of alle manere synnes (p. 5)[8]

Various of the B-MSS have different readings, apparently trying to

---

[7] They qualify this remark as follows: 'The fact that B's MS. was earlier than any A-MS. now extant does not necessarily mean that it was better; but age establishes a presumption of superiority in MSS., and the presumption is in this case justified.' They refer the reader to Westcott and Hort, 33, for confirmation of the general principle. See further below, pp. 357 and 429, on the curious circumstance that the extant A-MSS of the poem are later than the extant B-MSS; and on the B-reviser's A-MS, see pp. 401ff. below.

[8] Chambers quotes Skeat's text; the line is equivalent to Schmidt XIX 184–6 and Kane-Donaldson XIX 183–5.

make sense of this difficult passage. But if one turns to the C-Text, 'everything' (so Chambers says) 'is clear':

> And ȝaf Peers power · and pardon he grauntede
> To alle manere of men · mercy and forȝyuenesse,
> And ȝaf hym myghte to asoyle men · of alle manere synnes (p. 6)[9]

Chambers believes that C's addition of a single word (*ȝaf* in the last line) transforms an opaque passage into a transparently clear one, and it might seem convincing indeed that C's reading is, in truth, the original of B also. The case is not unarguable, however. Kane–Donaldson later took the view that 'the B and C archetypes agree in unmistakable and complex scribal error' at this point, and introduce an elaborate large-scale emendation, while Schmidt, more moderately, does not adopt C's reading but instead emends the B archetype by inserting 'To' at the beginning of the third line.[10]

In fact, none of Chambers' examples are unarguable – not surprisingly, since judgement between textual variants of this nature must always be uncertain. So it is disquieting that Chambers himself regards such instances as

> typical of important cases where we can *prove* [my italics] that a reading, although found in *all* the extant B-MSS., cannot really have been the reading of the original B-text, *but is a blunder which had crept into the archetype of all extant B-MSS.*, yet from which the B-MS. used in the preparation of the C-text was free. (pp. 7–8; remaining italics are Chambers' own)

More importantly, what is disturbing about Chambers' analysis of his examples is that, once he has fastened on the notion that B's archetype was corrupt, he takes that as a licence for preferring C on numerous occasions where it is different from B, but where it is not inconceivable that the difference is to be attributed to authorial revision in C rather than to scribal error in B. Chambers never considers this as a possibility. Instead, taking it for granted that his arguments can be considered 'proof' that the B archetype was corrupt, he uses this 'proof' to argue that even where B error is not obvious, it almost certainly existed:

> Now it must always be remembered that for one case in which we

---

[9] C Passus XXII 183–5 (Skeat's text); equivalent to Passus XXI 183–5 (almost identical) in Pearsall's edition.

[10] See Kane–Donaldson's (unconvincing) justification for their emendation, 120–1, and Schmidt's textual note (first edition, 299–300; second edition, 405).

> can *prove* a reading erroneous, there will be many instances of erroneous readings which we cannot prove to be so; because it is only a small percentage of blunders which are so obviously blunders as to be incapable of defence. To assume otherwise is as if we should assume that a pick-pocket has picked no pockets except those for picking which he has done time. (p. 8)

This bluff, apparently common-sense image is seriously misleading. The key question is, to what extent, and under what circumstances, do the errors (or picked pockets) we have 'proved' to exist, licence our sniffing out other possible ones? The term 'pickpocket', like the designation 'corrupt archetype', tends to tip the balance against the veracity of the witness not only in doubtful cases, but also where the witness looks unimpeachable.[11]

Chambers feels that now, after his accumulated experience of the manuscripts, he has built up a picture of the way in which the poems were written and disseminated. This goes as follows. The A-Text was probably never formally published. At the end of Passus XI (i.e. the end of the A-Text found in most of the manuscripts) the narrator denounces Clergy and asserts that ignorance is better than learning. This seemed to have produced something of an intellectual impasse for the poet, and A breaks off, unfinished, with the narrator still asleep, in what is effectively the middle of an account of Dowel. The poet made some attempt to complete the A-Text at a subsequent stage, since three of the A-MSS, as we have seen, preserve a continuation of sorts; but this attempt too is unfinished. The B-Text begins with a roughly parallel version of A, but at around the point where A breaks off, it introduces a 'short episodical vision' (in Passus XI), where the narrator describes how he went astray during his earlier years and abandoned the search for Truth. Chambers takes this account as literal and autobiographical, for it helpfully explains the gap between A and B, and elucidates the way in which B solves some of the problems presented in A, which had (presumably) stood in the way of A's completion; principally, B has the narrator reproved for the angry words in which the earlier poem had broken off.

Chambers thinks that it was unlikely that the A-Text, this unfinished poem, was ever formally published. During the years before his completion of B, the poet's friends and admirers made copies of his

[11] Chambers' pupil Kane indulges in the same sort of fallacious argument in order to justify the same end, viz. extensive emendation of the B archetype. Cf. p. 390 n. 21 below and Adams, 'Editing *Piers Plowman B*', 41–2.

first version. One might imagine that such copying would have been by non-professional scribes for personal use, and would have taken place sporadically, perhaps without authorisation. This process would explain the textual characteristics of the A-MSS – far more various and at odds with each other than the B-MSS, and rarely agreeing unanimously on an erroneous reading. And it also would fit in with the A-MSS' physical characteristics: they tend to be smaller, scruffier, and less professionally produced than the B-MSS, which (as Chambers says) 'are for the most part much more elaborate than the A-MSS. – more spacious, with broader margins, and written with more care' (p. 9). By contrast the A-MSS

> have very much the appearance of having been derived from originals which go back, if not to the author's actual autograph, at any rate to something very near it. There are passages where all the extant A-MSS. are confused or imperfect. This may be due to confusion in the author's autograph. But the A-MSS. have not the air of being all derived from one original into which a large number of scribal errors have intruded themselves. (p. 10)

The assumption implicit in these suggestions is radical, though there is no indication that Chambers recognised it as being so. While he is evidently happy to assume that the B-MSS all descended from one single archetype, 'into which a large number of scribal errors have intruded themselves', he thinks that the A-MSS are the result of a different process of transmission. In what way different, exactly? I think there are two main possibilities, assuming single authorship of A and B. Either (1) copies of the A-Text were made by different people at different times from the author's single original manuscript of the poem, and these were then variously disseminated; or (2) such copies were made from *more than one* authorial version of A. Given that the author did return to his A-Text in order to write the three extra passus, it seems likely that he may also, at different periods, have gone back over the text he had written, and changed a few words, perhaps making both his original text and his corrections or revisions difficult to read; so that it is difficult to assume (1) without also allowing for the extreme probability of (2). But to assume that extant manuscripts derive from more than one authorial original is to undermine, quite fundamentally, much of the received practice of textual criticism, and in particular textual criticism of *Piers Plowman* (see pp. 212–13 above and p. 385 below). Perhaps Chambers retreated from this possibility as 'almost too complicated to bear thinking about'.[12]

The B writer – evidently the same person, Chambers thinks, as A – used a manuscript of B 'which had none of the characteristic mistakes of the different extant A-MSS. or groups of A-MSS.' Yet all the *extant* B-MSS derive from a copy at some considerable distance from this original B-Text, 'into which a large number of errors had crept'. The C writer, in turn, used a copy of B which was free from these errors: 'nevertheless, whether he was the original poet or an editor, we can say that no poet – or, alternatively, no editor – ever dealt more recklessly with the work he was revising'. And Chambers quotes lines from the B-Text Prologue which are flabbily rewritten in the C-Text, to indicate the regrettable nature of this recklessness, commenting 'we should ourselves hesitate to say how far it is inconceivable for an author, in revision, to spoil his own work' (p. 11).

Behind this careful delineation of the process of composition and transmission of A, B, and C lies a curious, but unstated logic. Chambers did not need to argue, for it was then generally agreed, that the C-Text was in some ways a sorry rewriting of B.[13] In specific cases, however, Chambers argues – with varying degrees of force – that C's readings are superior to B's. He takes it that this superiority of C to B is to be explained, not as the result of authorial revision (C improving upon B as he rewrote), but as the result of C correctly preserving an authorial original which was also the original of B, but which has been (unanimously) corrupted in the extant B-MSS. Chambers does not set out the rationale for this assumption, and refers, as we have seen, to his arguments for the B-archetype's alleged corruptions in these instances as 'proof', rather than, as would be more reasonable, 'probability', or even 'possibility'.

Why should Chambers have so signally failed to consider the possibility of the C reviser making at least some local improvements as he rewrote the B-Text? This is difficult to explain, but may have something to do with a feeling that it would have been inconsistent of the poet to revise for the better in this way, given his removal of much that is poetically remarkable in B, and his interpolation of markedly leaden passages not found in B. Local differences between B and C, where C seemed better than B, must, Chambers presumably instinc-

---

[12] See p. 351 below.
[13] It was partly to rescue the C-Text from such critical neglect and misprision that E. T. Donaldson wrote *Piers Plowman: The C-Text and Its Poet*. See below, p. 312.

tively felt, be due not to the imaginative fertility of the C poet but to his simply copying out what was in front of him, and what must therefore have been originally present in B. The plausibility of this unstated assumption is less apparent, however, when one reflects on the fact that the C-poet was undeniably inconsistent in other respects. He may have written the gruelling passage on grammatical consonance in Passus III, but he also wrote some striking lines which have met with universal praise, both then and now, such as the so-called autobiographical passage which describes the poet living in Cornhill with his wife and daughter (anthologised by Sisam in his influential collection *Fourteenth Century Verse and Prose*), or the lines on beggars and poverty in C Passus IX. Chambers' striking reluctance to allow that differences of wording between B and C might be attributable to authorial revision in C, and hence his readiness to emend the archetypal reading of B, were to be inherited by Kane and Donaldson, who make an enormous number of changes to the B archetype.[14]

Chambers goes on to a discussion of the textual principles which underlie his proposed edition. These are far more crisply and assuredly put than in previous articles. He appeals directly to the method laid down by Westcott and Hort, the threefold process by which manuscripts can be sorted and a text provisionally arrived at, and he emphasises strongly the circular and provisional nature of this process, which necessitated a constant reference forward and back to decisions on textual characteristics of manuscripts, leading gradually – it was hoped – to greater and greater sureness in settling the text.

But now an interesting new element has appeared. W. W. Greg's *Calculus of Variants* was published in 1927, and Chambers has evidently pondered its contents carefully (see e.g. p. 17). One of Greg's dicta was 'the easier it is to explain how an error arose, the less valid the assumption that it only arose once' – i.e., if an easily explained error is present in different manuscripts, it is likely to have occurred independently, rather than as the result of genetic connection.[15] This was not quoted, but clearly taken to heart by Chambers, who emphasises very strongly that, while it is possible to identify manuscript families, the many cross-cutting agreements undermining

---

[14] See p. 390 below and cf. pp. 210–11 above.
[15] *Calculus*, 20, n.1. Greg also exerted a fundamentally important influence on George Kane, Chambers' succcessor in editing A, whose eclectic edition was an example of the editing procedure recommended by Greg. See Kane, 57ff.

the integrity of these families *must* be the result of massive coincidental error.

The genealogical method assumes, on the contrary, that agreement in error indicates a genetic relationship between the manuscripts sharing the error: at some point in their history, they derive from the same source. This information is in turn used to help construct the stemma. But of course, there are other reasons why manuscripts should agree in error: first, contamination, which Westcott and Hort briefly acknowledge introduces all sorts of problems into the construction of the stemma,[16] and second, as Chambers now perceives, coincidence. Knott had momentarily referred to this third possibility when presenting his classification of the A-MSS in 1915, and had assumed that coincidence was not a significant factor ('An Essay Toward the Critical Text of the A-Version', p. 133). Chambers has now worked on the *Piers Plowman* manuscripts for many more years, and has come to feel that many of the agreements in very minor readings between manuscripts which cut across established families (such as VH, or TH²) *must* be due to coincident error. It is inconceivable that they are due to contamination, for why should a scribe have laboriously chosen to incorporate such minor readings into his text, while ignoring far more substantial ones? On the other hand, the sort of error which would be very easily introduced into a text while copying – the substitution of *ac* for *but* and *vice versa*, omission or addition of *and* between clauses, and so on – might well have been introduced by *more* than one scribe.[17]

This is an enormously significant step forward in sorting out the relations between A-MSS. Westcott and Hort had taken quite a different view on the matter: 'except where an alteration is very plausible and tempting, the chance that two transcribers have made the same alteration independently is relatively small', so that 'while a certain number of identities of reading have to be neglected ... the great bulk may at once be taken as evidence of a common origin'.[18] But Chambers believes this simply does not hold for fifteenth- and sixteenth-century English manuscripts: 'Many scribes did not look back to their originals as often as verbal accuracy demands, and, whilst retaining the general sense, they carried in their heads more

---

[16] Vol. II, 46; cf. the discussions of Blackman and Mitchell, pp. 263–4 and pp. 270–1 above.

[17] On the other hand, Greg regards 'the herd of dull commonplace readings' (such as these) as likely to reveal the genetic source of the text. Kane corrects this view; cf. his Introduction, 59.

[18] Vol. II, 46.

than they could remember quite perfectly. By accidental coincidence, two such scribes must have occasionally used the same synonym in substitution' (p. 16). And he suggests that textual scholarship of the past has taken insufficient note of this important syndrome.

If Chambers was right, then the high probability of coincident error dangerously undermines the principle by which stemmata are constructed: that shared error indicates shared ancestry. The problem was recognised by Greg in his *Calculus of Variants*: 'we do habitually make' the assumption that common error has not risen independently, 'and although it is not necessarily correct in any individual case, without it no inference as to the relations of manuscripts would be possible'. This is a typical human reaction to the recognition of a seriously undermining element in some system of belief that has come to seem irreplaceable. Since the recognition is so perilously threatening, it is only momentarily acknowledged, and then set to one side. Chambers has the courage to look it more closely in the face, and to come up with some sort of solution. If coincident error really is a significant feature in the manuscript relations of *Piers Plowman*, then, 'it is vital that we should attempt to discriminate between the type of variant which we can reasonably assume not to have arisen independently, and the type where such assumption would be unjustifiable' (p. 17). This sounds promising, but Chambers does not expatiate beyond asserting that, while 'there are a large number of variants upon which we can safely argue', those variants consisting simply of '*substitution of similars*' (i.e., as in the examples above) 'can prove relationship only where they occur constantly and repeatedly. It is not the occurrence of such variants, but their occurrence *in overwhelming proportion*, that provides the argument for common origin' (pp. 12–13). The phenomenon of coincident variation was later returned to by Grattan in 1947, and its implications developed to the full by Kane and Donaldson in 1975.

The remaining thirty-odd pages of the 1931 article are taken up with a defence of Chambers and Grattan's position against rival suggestions on the relationships between the manuscripts and versions, principally by Mabel Day and Gertrud Görnemann. Görnemann had taken the view, in a book published in 1916, that the three versions were all scribal variations of a single authorial original.[19] Chambers and

---

[19]   *Zur Verfasserschaft und Entstehungsgeschichte von 'Piers the Plowman'.*

Grattan deal with her briefly and damningly, pointing out that her reliance on Skeat's text, and her failure to consult any of the manuscripts – inevitable, as it happened, since she worked on the poem in Germany during the First World War – completely vitiate her various assumptions and arguments (p. 22). Day took longer to demolish, and must have aroused much greater irritation and distress in the two men, not least because one of her articles was most approvingly summarised (by Dorothy Everett) in the 1928 volume of *Year's Work in English Studies*. Day claimed on several grounds that the three texts of the poem were by at least five different authors, and she based her arguments, some closely textual, on Skeat's editions. It would be tedious to rehearse the detail of her assertions or of Chambers' and Grattan's rebuttals; their strategy is to illustrate how, time after time, she relies on the manuscript variants reported in Skeat's critical apparatuses, but that independent consultation of the manuscripts, which Chambers and Grattan have carried out but which Day has not, shows her assumptions, arguments, and conclusions to be wrong. Skeat did not record all interesting or significant variations from – or agreements with – the three texts which he printed, and it is impossible to deduce anything from his silences. All this should have been evident from a careful reading of Chambers' 1909 article (or Knott's of 1915, or indeed the Introductions to Skeat's own editions), and one can sympathise with Chambers' and Grattan's weariness in being virtually forced to reply to influential articles which were wrongly based on insufficient information. 'We should have preferred to get on with our editorial work', they say, 'rather than spend time on controversy' (p. 24).

Their dismissal of Day is hampered by Chambers' close relations with her as Assistant Director and Secretary of the Early English Text Society, in which capacity her work was 'known to everyone', and they fall over themselves to explain the reasons why she should have innocently committed the delinquency of which they find themselves forced to accuse her.[20]

Such tortuous efforts to preserve courtesy and cordiality at all costs, while at the same time demolishing a view on the textual relations of *Piers Plowman* which is quite at odds with the authors' own, is entertaining to read. It is also a notable demonstration of the general (certainly the outward) good nature with which Chambers

---

[20] She briefly replied to some of their criticisms in an article published in the same year, ' "Din" and "Doom" in "Piers Plowman" '.

and Grattan conducted the *Piers Plowman* controversy – a temper not shared by Manly, and decidedly absent in his pupil Knott. Curiously enough, it is Chambers' successors who – with one exception – take up the mantle of Knott when it comes to the tone in which textual debate is conducted. Kane, Mitchell, and Russell all tend towards dogmatic assertion, and occasionally searing denunciation of views different from their own. Knott's pupil David Fowler, on the other hand, despite the merciless mauling he received in Kane's discussion of his A-Text, gave the book in which that discussion occurs a fair, open-minded, and generous review. Kane's collaborator, Talbot Donaldson, is in some ways the most remarkable of all contributors to the textual debate, combining keen intellectual penetration into the most tangled and resistant of textual issues with an almost distressing (to his readers, that is) acknowledgement of the force of positions alternative to the one he has chosen to adopt himself.[21]

But despite the diverting spectacle of Chambers and Grattan wriggling in their efforts to damn Day without insulting her, it is a great pity that so much of their final published contribution to textual discussion of the poem was spent on clearing the good name of arguments previously well established. Of course, they had only themselves to blame. Had they made faster headway with their edition of A, the difference between their text and Skeat's would have opened critics' eyes far more effectively than could tedious exegesis to the limited nature of Skeat's editions, and other scholars would have been less tempted to place their trust in these.

[21] See e.g. p. 381 below.

16

Chambers 1935–1942

In 1935 Chambers published a biography of Thomas More, indicating that his productivity in some respects continued apace. But still he doggedly returned to *Piers Plowman*.[1] In the same year the Huntington Library funded a trip to San Marino, California to examine its manuscripts, where Chambers worked closely with the librarian, R. B. Haselden, and produced an important article on the library's *Piers Plowman* manuscripts, identifying Hm 143, the manuscript he had looked at when it came on to the market in 1924 (see p. 254 above), as the most valuable of the C-Text manuscripts.[2] This was swift, efficient, and productive work; presumably he was highly stimulated by the change in scene. Max Ferrand, a Director of the Huntington Library, wrote affectionately to him some years later: 'Your visit to San Marino was one of the most satisfactory of all our visiting scholars – *because you cleared up your job.*' And he goes on to say, somewhat over-optimistically as poor Chambers must have felt, 'It is to be hoped that when the war is over, the several texts of Piers Plowman will be published and that work of scholarship cleared off for a generation or two.'[3] But the important finding of Chambers' study, that Hm 143 was the most significant extant C-MS, merely underlined the depressing unpredictability of *Piers Plowman* textual work. The two graduate students, Allen and Carnegy, who had been set to work on the C-Text in order to clear the ground for the A-Text, had analysed the manuscripts in ignorance of Hm 143. Chambers' 1935 work thus simultaneously advanced and retarded textual

---

[1] A letter from C. T. Onions of 4 August that year thanks Chambers for a copy of the More biography, adding 'And now, I suppose, you will be back again at Piers Plowman,' marvelling 'how you do it all, and with such freshness' (Chambers Papers Item 100, unnumbered).

[2] 'The Manuscripts of *Piers Plowman* in the Huntington Library'.

[3] Letter dated 27 January 1942 (three months before Chambers' death), Chambers Papers Item 103, unnumbered.

progress: it demonstrated the incomplete nature of the work so far done. A facsimile edition of Hm 143 appeared the following year, 1936, with an introduction by Chambers in which he declared that the manuscript was the best extant C-Text of *Piers Plowman* and the one to be used in a future edition.

In 1937 Chambers had a major operation, and in his sixty-fourth year must have had to confront the question whether he would live to complete his work on the poem. It was time to secure his succession. Surviving correspondence between Chambers and Grattan indicates that by November 1937 EETS had appointed the two main editors together with Elsie Blackman to a Committee to 'see after the editing of "P.P"'; and that the names of A. H. Smith, Edmund Colledge, and A. C. Cawley, three younger scholars, were being floated as possible co-editors. Colledge's and Cawley's names do not reappear, but Smith was to figure in reports of the editing enterprise for several years to come.[4] On 26 April 1938 Grattan wrote to Chambers to thank him for a letter written nearly six months previously, in which Chambers had put his scheme to him. He explains at length that he has been very ill with problems such as bronchitis resulting from chronic catarrh; and his diffuse and troubled remarks on the editing project give some idea of his state of mind:

> I wish I could have a *talk* with you about 'Piers Plowman'; but I cannot undertake a journey to London yet.
>
> Since I left UCL. a variety of circumstances has prevented you & me from getting together to finish Part I of the A-Text.
>
> I wish very much that we could devise a plan for finishing it before we introduce any new co-editors officially. Compared with the enormous labours which we have already put into it, the work should not be very heavy.
>
> Except for consulting you further about B- & C-readings, I could probably carry out a good deal of this task here with the help of my assistant, Mr. E. Colledge, if you were willing for him to be associated in the work. He would regard it as an honour to be associated with us, 'even in an humble capacity'. He is young,

---

[4] Smith's support was warmly acknowledged by George Kane in the Preface to his edition of A, although a recent observation by Kane in a letter to the author suggests that his help was political rather than textual; he is remembered by former colleagues as a tower of strength on university committees, and evidently played an important part in securing the Athlone Press' agreement to publish the edition. Smith published one article on *Piers Plowman* but was chiefly known for his work on place names; Colledge went on to produce distinguished work on Middle English mystics; Cawley subsequently established himself as an expert on Middle English drama.

strong, & full of energy, and he has already considerable experience of MSS. (Richd. Rolle &c).

I myself have real hope that, when once I have got rid of my catarrh, I shall have renewed energy and enough leisure to do such work.

I was very glad to learn from you that the EETS has made you, Mrs. Blackman, & myself into a joint committee to see after the editing of 'P.P'.

I agree with you that it is most desirable to coopt some younger men; although I think that you (if not I) have still several years of vigour & of good work before you.

But – unless you feel very strongly about it – I myself would much rather postpone adding to the SubCee. until Pt I is in the press.

Such a course ought not to prevent us ensuring that there are trained younger men ready & willing to finish our work.

How would it be for you to guide Smith & Cawley in preparing Pt II of the A-Text, while Colledge & I get Pt I ready for the final touches which you & I must give to it?

There would then be *three* young men to carry on: Smith, Colledge, & Cawley (I place them thus in order of knowledge & experience).

I have met Smith, and I have the highest opinion of him as a man & as a scholar. If *you* do not live to edit the C-Text, he will doubtless become in time the chief editor of the EETS 'P.P.'

You will, of course, train Cawley; and I shall like to think that, when I drop out (through disability or death), a man whom I have trained will have a hand in the work.

My suggestion, then, amounts to this: that we *coopt helpers* as soon as possible but that we postpone a little longer the question of new *co-editors*.

Probably I shall have to drop out altogether, through failing sight, long before you leave the helm; but I would rather not decide on this until Part I has appeared.

Will you please let me have your views, fully & frankly, about the above suggestions?

There are two other matters which we ought to have settled long ago:–

1. As the bulk of the A-Text material is in your possession, I ought to have some evidence in your handwriting that this material is owned jointly by us.

2. We ought to have some written guarantee from the EETS. that Gollancz's verbal promise will be carried out, *viz* that the Society will pay (in EETS. vols.) the cost of our rotographs as soon as Pt I is in the press.[5]

But it was to another person altogether that Chambers turned for help. Presumably he realised that Grattan had insufficent drive and energy to be relied upon. A. G. Mitchell, a graduate from the University of Sydney, had recently arrived at University College and under Chambers' supervision embarked on a doctoral thesis, a critical edition of C Passus I–IV (see p. 270 above). A quantity of correspondence from Mitchell survives in the Chambers Papers, providing ample evidence of the degree to which the older man was venerated by the younger. The letter quoted below confirms that Chambers had now fully grasped that work on the three texts had to proceed side by side and had to be distributed to younger and more able collaborators than Grattan. Mitchell writes on 2 January 1939 from an address in Oxford (where he was collating manuscripts) to thank Chambers for

> your note of 30/12/38. It was no ordinary experience to receive it.
>
> I can hardly believe still in the great good fortune which allows me to hope that I may continue to work on Piers and perhaps complete the C-Text, having, as it were, a commission to do so from you. I have been very excited about such a prospect ever since in conversation with you at your home, you led me to hope that something of that kind might yet fall to my lot. At that time I purposely refrained from saying more than that I was most willing to continue the work, and very much honoured by the thought that you might like me to. I did not mean to say anything then that might lead you to think you had committed yourself to even the vaguest of promises ...
>
> I hope you have not thought that this attitude on my part has suggested lack of enthusiasm for the work ahead, or lack of appreciation of the extraordinary opportunity you have given me. One who simply inherits the fruit of the labours of such men as Skeat, the accumulated results of your work over so many years, and of such recent workers of the quality of Miss Allen, feels humble and grateful indeed. The responsibility of bringing such work to future fruition, and of trying to interpret such a magnificent thing as Piers, is sometimes rather crushing. I am too well aware of my deficiencies to imagine that I can bring much more to the work than industry and a certain very average competence. But all that I can do you may be sure that I will ... You have spoken yourself of Skeat's magnanimity in handing the work over to you; I think you

---

[5]   EETS Papers.

have been more magnanimous to me and with infinitely less cause than Skeat had: for he must have had some idea of the great things with which you were to enrich the world's store of knowledge.

And Mitchell, who seems to have been a loyal and impressionable person, continues at some length in this vein, affirming that he, Mitchell, would be content to produce, as his life's work, one paragraph of the quality of Chambers' work. Such extravagant and uncritical praise may raise doubts about the reliability of the young man's judgement, given that Chambers' record of productivity on *Piers Plowman* had so far been less than wholly satisfactory. Mitchell has more to say about Chambers' plans towards the end of his long letter:

> It is good to think of a 'British Empire' team as you describe it . We from the Dominions are keenly aware of our membership of the Empire and of our common loyalty ... To you who have made it possible for anyone at all to be editing the C-Text now, I can only give my thanks and my promise that in working on it I shall do my best. I see no reason why your work should not be completed. That you will is both an earnest hope personally, and also the hope of all who know that this work needs your guidance if it is to be done as well as it can be done; as well as those other things which only you can give the world.[6]

The mention of the Dominions is evidence that the most significant actor in *Piers Plowman* textual studies this century had now appeared upon the scene. George Kane was a Canadian (born 1916) who had completed his first degree, in classics, at Vancouver. He came to University College in 1938 to do post-graduate work on the Renaissance epic, but was assigned to Chambers since there was no one else available to supervise him.[7] He was immediately sucked into the *Piers Plowman* project and set to work collating B-MSS. By the time war broke out, he had completed about 2,000 lines.[8] As Mitchell reports, he enlisted in 1939, defended Calais, was shot through the lung, and taken prisoner on 27 May 1940.[9] Correspondence between Chambers and Mitchell, now returned to Sydney, witnesses to his friends' constant anxiety about Kane's whereabouts and treatment. In August

---

[6] Chambers Papers Item 101, unnumbered.
[7] For a brief résumé of Kane's career, see *Medieval Studies Presented to George Kane*, ed. E. D. Kennedy et al, xi–xiii.
[8] As he has told the author in conversation.
[9] EETS Papers.

1940 his survival was confirmed,[10] and Mitchell wrote to Chambers to rejoice: 'he is as near to me as a brother. A fine fellow now with a glorious record of duty done.'[11] Eventually letters were exchanged, and in September 1941, feeling that Kane wanted 'some stiff reading',[12] Chambers sent Kane a copy of his *Beowulf*, his *Introduction to Beowulf*, Skeat's two volume edition of *Piers Plowman*, and the one-volume *Cambridge History of English Literature* to work on in captivity.[13] Later that year, another correspondent wrote of her joy that Kane was still alive: 'What a knack he must have for insinuating himself into all our hearts'.[14] As we shall see, Kane himself reported that he had been 'spared for Piers'.

Meanwhile Chambers had revived Elsie Blackman as an active worker on the B-Text. As we have seen, she had been put on the EETS sub-committee along with Chambers and Grattan, and surviving correspondence indicates that she and Chambers between them were carefully considering the relative worth of B-MSS, as well as busily pursuing manuscripts and manuscript rotographs at various libraries in order to supplement the work she had earlier done.[15] Chambers' sense of urgency is communicated in the frustration he expresses over the difficulty of getting photographs in wartime: 'If this war is going to last years, all photographers will be absorbed for war work and rotographs will become unprocurable, so at my age it is a question of now or never; and I very much want to leave the Piers Plowman work is [sic] as satisfactory a position as possible ...' Elsewhere he indicates the level of hope and trust he had already, on so brief an acquaintance, lodged in George Kane: he ends a discussion of B-MSS with the words 'Hereafter, in a better world than this, we will, with the help of the boy Kane, get on with the B-text.'[16]

Further evidence that Grattan was a weak reed is supplied by a letter from him dated 30 December 1940. In this he explains that his chronic catarrh has – despite an operation in 1938 – 'made a semi-invalid of me. I can get through my teaching and academic work; but

---

10 A handwritten note by Chambers among the EETS Papers records that 'News of Kane's safety arrived 12 Aug 1940' and that he wired Mitchell the same day.
11 2 October 1940 (EETS Papers).
12 Chambers to Mitchell, 11 September 1941 (EETS Papers).
13 Mitchell's response to this news was 'It is good to know that he has now a number of books of a scholarly kind on which to spend his energy. He is a lad of such strong vitality that time must hang heavy on his hands' (31 March 1942; EETS Papers).
14 Patricia Lusher, 2 December 1941 (EETS Papers).
15 EETS Papers; surviving letters are dated between 14 May and 29 August 1940.
16 16 May 1940; EETS Papers.

I have little time or energy for either research or lighter entertainment – including correspondence'. The letter (like many of Grattan's) is somewhat self-pitying, and self-absorbed; at the end of it he abruptly turns to *Piers Plowman* matters: 'I suppose the P.P. material is at the Welsh Nat Liby?' and goes on to ask, 'If you are killed by a car in the black-out, what happens to my share of the material? Would not EETS seize all, and repudiate any claim I might make without documentary support?'[17]

Chambers evidently attended scrupulously and instantly to this implicit request, for Grattan writes again on 3 March 1941 to thank him for two letters, one written on 2 January enclosing a 'copy of your appointment of Dr Hitchcock as your post-mortem-"P.P."-representative', and a second – sent in the absence of any reply from Grattan – written on 22 February. After some excuses as to why he has not written earlier, Grattan launches into another diffuse discussion of the state of the Piers Plowman project, which makes it clear that Chambers was carefully setting up a team of researchers to take over after his (and Grattan's) death, consisting of Blackman and Kane (B-Text), Mitchell (C-Text), and Smith (role unspecified). There is no further mention of Cawley, and Chambers seems not to have responded to Grattan's offer of Colledge. In July 1939 Chambers had apparently proposed a parallel-text edition of all three versions, on the model of Skeat's, but his more recent mention to Grattan of Kane and Mitchell 'getting the BC-Texts out' after his and Grattan's death, leads Grattan to ask whether he has gone back to the original scheme of three separate editions. Grattan also asks, presumably ironically, 'is the title-page to bear the names: Chambers – Grattan – Blackman – Smith – Kane – & Mitchell?' In general, the letter is as disorganised and troubled as his previous ones, and expresses in plaintive tones Grattan's wish to participate in the project, at the same time making it clear that he is unable to do so effectively on grounds of both health and safety.

His next letter follows unusually early (18 March), reporting the devastating effect of an air-raid on Merseyside which smashed his house's roof to fragments and killed forty of his near-neighbours. His study came off better than other rooms, owing to some stout shutters, and all his books had now been transferred to the new University (Henry Cohen) Library for keeping – although, as Grattan fears, not

---

[17]   EETS Papers.

necessarily safe keeping. Consequently, he says to Chambers, 'do not on any account send me my "Piers Plowman" material yet'. He has received a 'splendid report' (of which, unfortunately, no trace survives) on the editing project, for which he thanks Chambers, saying also that 'I feel ashamed that I am now giving no help with the heavy task of getting something ready for printing as soon as printing shall become possible.' Further letters reiterate the request that Chambers not send him any editing material for fear of destruction in more bomb attacks.

There are a couple of more public statements on the progress of Chambers' work which must have given hope to those waiting for the text to appear. An important article on *Piers Plowman* came out in 1939 in the United States, written by Chambers' old pupil Morton Bloomfield. Entitled 'Present State of *Piers Plowman* Studies', it surveyed *Piers Plowman* scholarship since Skeat, and gave a full account of the authorship controversy which had been sparked off by Manly's article of 1906. Bloomfield takes the view that prior establishment of the text is necessary in order to determine the number of authors (failing to see, like so many, that the two issues were pretty well indistinguishably bound up together), and in connection with this reports confidently that 'The A-text will soon appear, but Professor Chambers has informed me that it will still be many years before the textual work on the three recensions is finished' (p. 217 n.2). Given Bloomfield's previous connection with Chambers, it seems likely that the optimism about the forthcoming appearance of A was Chambers' own.[18]

In March 1939 A. W. Pollard resigned from the EETS Directorship and Chambers took over the office, which he regarded as 'something of a sacred trust'.[19] Presumably this encouraged him to keep one of the most important of the old EETS projects, the edition of *Piers*, at

---

[18] Morton Bloomfield spent a year (1935–6) at University College London, and was encouraged by Chambers to embark on a research project on the seven Deadly Sins, a subject with particular interest for Chambers since he believed that ignorance on the nature of medieval representation of the Sins had been partly responsible for Manly's misinterpretation of the B-Text account of Wrath, and his consequent attribution of B to a different author from that of A (see Chambers Papers Item 6, unnumbered items, letters dated 7 December 1936 and 9 December 1937). Bloomfield worked on the subject as a doctoral dissertation on his return to the States (at the University of Wisconsin, Madison), and it eventually appeared as a book (*The Seven Deadly Sins*). Along with the first of his letters to Chambers is the abstract of his dissertation, one of whose paragraphs reads 'The variations in the list of the sins in the three versions of Piers Plowman give no support to the theory of multiple authorship.'

[19] EETS Papers, undated letter to J. R. R. Tolkien (probably May 1938).

the top of his list of priorities; and the indications are that he now made a substantial effort to draw together his energies for a final assault. In May 1940, Chambers was awarded a grant of £200 from the Leverhulme Trust, for a one-year project entitled 'An investigation of the 51 known manuscripts of *Piers Plowman*, with the object of producing a definitive text (with apparatus) of the three versions of the poem'; obviously Chambers' return to concentrated work on *Piers* had started to take definite shape.[20] In particular the decision to edit all three texts simultaneously now seemed established. The EETS annual report of 1941 – perhaps written by Chambers himself – reminded its members of the existence of an 'obligation' of very long standing:

> the re-editing of *Piers Plowman*, mainly from manuscripts which were unknown when Skeat produced his edition. This task was handed over by Skeat in 1910 to R. W. Chambers and J. H. G. Grattan.[21] The Leverhulme Trust, in September 1940, made a grant of £200 to Professor Chambers for the expenses of his work, and some statement as to its position and progress seems therefore called for. [A description of Chambers' investigation of Hm 143 in the Huntington Library follows.] Hm 143 ... proved to be the best MS. of the C-text, and its discovery, following the somewhat earlier discovery of a cognate MS. which was acquired by the British Museum (Additional 35157) revolutionizes our conception of the C-text. Dr Mitchell, at the University of Sydney, is now working on the C-text, with Hm 143 as his basis. Mr George Kane, who was engaged upon the B-text, is now a prisoner of war in Germany. His work, so far as finished, is in the keeping of Professor Chambers, but recent events have impeded the work of Professor Chambers and Professor Grattan on the A-text. Printing in any case will be held up till after the war, but the Leverhulme grant makes it possible to duplicate material in such a way as to minimize the danger of destruction. Much of the most essential matter, including a facsimile of Hm 143, is now in both Great Britain and in Australia.

In a letter accompanying a copy of the report, which he sent to Godfrey Davies of the Huntington Library, Chambers is already sounding plangent tones: 'I do not know whether I shall live to gather

---

[20] The letter informing Chambers of the grant award is dated 6 May 1940, and survives in the EETS Papers. A draft of Chambers' application also survives.

[21] A pleasing mythology, that Skeat initiated the proposal of re-editing and chose his followers in a form of apostolic succession, has intervened here.

up the fruits of all this, but I hope I have arranged that none of the work shall be wasted.'[22]

Chambers made two reports to the Leverhulme trustees of his progress during the course of the year.[23] The first is an interim account from September 1940 to March 1941, describing how the University of London had been evacuated and the English Department of University College moved to Aberystwyth. Many of the British Museum manuscripts of *Piers Plowman* had been deposited in the National Library of Wales at Aberystwyth, and Chambers had had photostat negatives made of six of them. He had taken other precautions too:

> I have caused to be copied, in triplicate, a critical text, with complete collations, of the A-text of *Piers Plowman: Prologue, Passus* I, II and III to line 23.[24] This is a part of the work upon which Prof. Grattan and I have been engaged for many years. A copy of this will be placed with Prof. Grattan, who is, with me, jointly responsible for the text. A copy has also been sent to Dr. A. G. Mitchell of the University of Sydney, NSW, and has been placed by him in the University strong room there for safe keeping. I propose to continue this work for the rest of *Passus* III, *Passus* IV, and perhaps *Passus* V and VI of the A-text.[25] It forms the beginning of what Prof. Grattan and I hope will be the definitive edition of *Piers Plowman*, to be published by the Early English Text Society. Probably it will not be possible to print anything until after the war
>
> ...
>
> A certain amount of my material was lost in the partial destruction of my library and of the library of University College, London, by enemy action on September 25 last. That material, however, was only of secondary importance, and in so far as its loss compels me to concentrate upon the portion of the material which I had already placed in safety (a task quite sufficient to occupy the rest of my life) it may even prove advantageous ...
>
> It is clear that at the age of sixty-six a man cannot look forward with any certainty to the fruits of his work through the press. But by communicating my work step by step to Prof. Grattan [he evidently did not do this] and Dr. A. G. Mitchell I am doing all I can to ensure that it will not be wasted. A third collaborator,

22 Chambers Papers Item 103, unnumbered, letter dated 22 November 1941.
23 EETS Papers.
24 A typed copy of the collations (not the text) of the remainder of Passus III survives in the same EETS folder; it is marked in Chambers' hand as being 'for Dr. Mitchell', and he notes that the preceding material has already been sent to Mitchell.
25 See pp. 303ff. below.

George Kane of the Universities of Vancouver and London is now a wounded prisoner of war. He writes from Oflag VII c/H. 'I am quite fit now, having been spared for *Piers*. I hope you will let me go on seriously with the work after the war.' Other former collaborators are Mrs. F. F. Blackman of Cambridge, and Mrs. T. W. Tapping ... Dr. A. H. Smith, Treasurer of the Early English Text Society, is at present in the Air Force, but his help and cooperation after the war will, I hope, be available.

The completed edition will, I think, demonstrate the unity of the poem, and the authorship of William Langland [and he refers to his forthcoming article on authorship in *London Medieval Studies*.][26]

The present standard edition of *Piers* is the result of the work done single handed by W. W. Skeat between 1867 and 1884. To improve on Skeat's work is no light task, but I trust that before 60 years have elapsed from its publication the new, revised edition begun by Prof. Grattan and myself will be well on its way, and that it will be on record that even in the midst of war, the Leverhulme Trustees could support the editing of a great poem produced under conditions of world crisis by no means dissimilar to those which prevail now.

This last remark indicates the patriotic significance attributed by Chambers to the poem, echoing the views of Furnivall and Jusserand before him that *Piers Plowman* represented an account of a peculiarly English struggle against the forces of evil and oppression.

Chambers' final Leverhulme report begins with the sorry statement that 'up to date I have been able to spend upon expenses for my work on *Piers Plowman* only £61.13.11 out of the grant of £200'. He explains that owing to the destruction of Grattan's house in the blitz on Liverpool, he cannot at present look to him for help, and reports that he is sending books to Kane in his prisoner of war camp. 'Though detailed collaboration is impossible', Chambers writes, 'he ought to be able to put in a good deal of work which will be useful when we can bring out an edition.' This remarkable statement, with its untroubled assumption of civilised conditions in Kane's prisoner-of-war camp, let alone heroic powers of concentration and tenacity in the unfortunate inmate, once more reveals Chambers' accurate perception of Kane's outstanding qualities. He further reports that Mitchell is steadily progressing in Sydney, and unlikely to be dispatched to military duties; he quotes from a letter stating that 'the

---

[26] 'Robert or William Longland?', an article Kane judged 'Chambers's greatest contribution to the [authorship] discussion' (*The Evidence for Authorship*, 53 n.2).

provisional critical text [of C] is well on the way now'. Chambers explains, though, that his own time is greatly taken up with an increased teaching load (standing in for younger men who are engaged on war service), and trying to ensure the solvency of the EETS – upon which the *Piers Plowman* project was of course crucially dependent for its eventual publication.

Mitchell had returned to Australia with his wife in July 1939. He corresponded regularly with Chambers after his arrival home, where he took up a lectureship at the University of Sydney, and he continued steadily with his work on the C-Text, displaying an impressively gung-ho and confident spirit when reporting to his former supervisor. This is distressing to read in the light of the retrospective knowledge that almost nothing of the material into which he was pouring his energies was published then or since.[27] His letter dated 2 October 1940 made it clear that he was basing his critical text on a limited number of manuscripts: Hm 143, Dublin D. 4. 1, the Oxford manuscripts, 'Cambridge MSS in part', and Skeat's transcript of P. 'As you will see these are quite sufficient for working out the critical text. The rest will not make much difference'; and when the rotographs of the other manuscripts arrived it would be 'only a clerical job of completing the list of variants'. This was how Chambers and Grattan had started out at first, with a cheerful assumption that they could edit by instinct, making initial judgements on manuscripts and then slotting in any other useful evidence as it came to hand. Mitchell was also sure that he could settle the question of authorship: 'I have proved single authorship of B- [*sic*] and C to my own satisfaction but am keeping the article by for further confirmation from the critical text' (it never appeared), and he was working on various critical and interpretative problems in C: 'There will be quite a heap ready when we can think of publication' (a small number of these, 'Notes on the C-Text of *Piers Plowman*', were published in 1949). On 1 January 1941 he wrote, 'I find work on the text increasingly easy and swift. I believe I shall be sorry when the job is finished'; in April that year he published a two-page account of 'A

---

27 Mitchell's only substantial contributions to discussion of the poem were a response written jointly with George Russell to an article on multiple authorship by David Fowler (see below, p. 335), and an essay on allegory ('Lady Meed and the Art of *Piers Plowman*', delivered as the third Chambers Memorial lecture at University College in 1956. Other than this he published 'A Newly-Discovered Manuscript of the C-Text of Piers Plowman', and three short notes on individual readings: 'The Text of *Piers Plowman* C Prologue l. 215', 'Notes on the C-text of *Piers Plowman*', and 'Worth Both His Ears'.

Newly-Discovered Manuscript of the C-Text of "Piers Plowman"', in Sir Louis Sterling's library;[28] on 15 September 1941 he reports

> good progress on *Piers Plowman*. With the manuscripts that I have
> and Skeat's notes, I am able to arrive at a critical text which I am
> sure will not require modification when the other Manuscripts are
> available. By next week I expect to be able to send you copies of the
> critical text of C passus V and VI ... I am very hopeful that by the
> end of the year the editing of C will be half done.

By 31 March 1942 he had, on the basis of the manuscripts available to him (X, Y, P, E, V, K, and the manuscripts fully collated by Skeat) 'worked out a critical text to the end of Passus 10'. Yet he was constructing his text in ignorance of the readings of 'the most important Cambridge MS, and all the BM MSS', together with Q, S, F and G. He was imminently expecting rotographs of the last four, and asks Chambers whether he could send him rotographs of the others. He adds, 'My article on the single authorship of B and C is coming along quite nicely, but I am taking my time and do not want to run the risk of presenting anything but a fully convincing argument.'[29]

For much of this difficult time Chambers' morale seems to have kept relatively high, although the consciousness of war and destruction, and the consequent threat of danger and loss both near and far, hang like a cloud over him and his correspondents. In this context, as we have seen, the pursuit of the text of *Piers Plowman*, a repository of English cultural values, took on the character of patriotic war work. To one colleague, Professor E. Norman, who was engaged in a different sort of war work at the Foreign Office, but also trying to get off the ground a new periodical, an in-house journal for the University of London (*London Mediaeval Studies*) due to publish Chambers' authorship article, he wrote (on 14 August 1940),

> I hope you will not think that I am fiddling while Rome is burning,
> but I am still trying to keep Piers' plough going. One of my
> colleagues in the work is in Sydney, New South Wales, and the
> other, George Cane [*sic*], a prisoner of war in Germany, lucky to be
> alive: he was at Calais. Could you tell me if London Mediæval

---

28 The manuscript (A) is mentioned in a catalogue of Sterling's library in *TLS* 4 February
    1939. Mitchell found it to be closely related to V (D. 4. 1 in Trinity College, Dublin); the
    handwritings are contemporary, probably dating from around the first quarter of the
    fifteenth century.

29 All these letters survive among the EETS Papers.

Studies is going to be published and about my offprints? ... We are frightfully busy although our work is less vital than yours.[30]

But all this changed when the library at University College, over which Chambers had presided for many years, was virtually destroyed in the bombing raid already referred to, which took place in the following month, on 25 September. His buoyancy and resolve were dealt a devastating blow. He told Mitchell in a letter of 6 November 1940 that about one third of his private library had been destroyed, although 'the most valuable things have been saved, including almost all the Piers Plowman material'.[31]

A year later he was still in need of consolation, and Kenneth Sisam, the Secretary to the Delegates of the Clarendon Press who was also a distinguished medievalist, wrote to administer comfort, offer advice, and encourage him to bring to light some of the *Piers Plowman* material that had been stored away unpublished for so many years. 'You must soothe your loss by writing something', he suggested. 'And if you can't tackle anything big, couldn't you amuse yourself by doing what must be all in your head – the short Selection from Piers Plowman that is much needed, to replace Skeat's selection with its old-fashioned notes?'[32] Chambers' response seemed reasonably positive: 'I am grateful to you for reminding me about the short selection from *Piers Plowman*. I will try to get ahead with it. I suppose you are thinking of something which in bulk would be about equal to Skeat's small edition of Passus I–VII of the B-text, filling some 200 pages, more or less.'[33] Sisam replied to confirm this and discuss the project in more detail, ending with more words of comfort: 'You must feel, after wrestling with *Piers Plowman* for many years, that a very small and unambitious work is a relaxation. I am sure it would be a great help for the next generation of students, who ought to start off where we finish'.[34] A month later Sisam had rethought the project, deciding

---

[30] EETS Papers; a copy is preserved in Chambers Papers Item 27, unnumbered.

[31] EETS Papers. It seems that Chambers feared that Tapping's thesis might have been destroyed along with much else of the library's contents, for Tapping wrote on 30 December to reassure him that she still had her own copy. She offered her services freely to Chambers, expressing longing for the 'privilege' of becoming involved in the recapitulation of the editing project: 'if at any time there is any work on Piers to be done, I should be very happy if you thought me able to do it' (Chambers Papers Item 103, unnumbered).

[32] 17 September 1941; Chambers Papers Item 103, unnumbered. Chambers had first proposed a replacement of Skeat's student edition to the Clarendon Press in 1918; see p. 252 above. The replacement was eventually edited by J. A. W. Bennett; see p. 410 below.

[33] Item 103, unnumbered, letter dated 20 September 1941.

[34] Item 103, unnumbered, letter dated 22 September 1941.

that what was wanted was an independent selection to complement Skeat, since this latter volume still sold well and the Press had decided to keep it in print as long as was justified by demand. There was also 'a real difficulty about revising any of Skeat's work: the family are interested and are inclined to treat it as monumental, so that an editor could not be given a free hand, and there are difficulties, too, of terms'.

> I agree with you that a new edition of Skeat's two-volume *Piers Plowman* is needed, but there it is a case of doing afresh, with better knowledge, exactly what he attempted. The Notes are good, and it is Skeat's great merit that he resisted counsels of perfection. If he had waited until everything was cleared up to his satisfaction, we should then have been without a major Chaucer and *Piers Plowman*, all of which he produced to a very creditable standard for the time. When he relied on his own knowledge and good sense, and was not overawed by the latest edition or article, he was always worth reading, and I pardon all his imperfections. But I think anyone coming after him is entitled to use his notes, as he used Tyrwhitt's [in his edition of Chaucer].[35]

The discussion evidently continued, so as to whet Sisam's appetite for more information: on 11 February of the following year he wrote

> what you tell me about *Piers Plowman* gives me a great desire to see the problem of the text set out at not too great length, so that I can digest it, and with selected evidence only. I hope you are going to get time to do that without waiting for a complete statement.[36]

But Sisam's delicately tactful hints, including the no doubt carefully chosen and certainly apposite account of the expedience in Skeat's case of sacrificing perfection to production, did not do their work: neither the selected edition of *Piers Plowman*, nor the suggested outline account of the *Piers Plowman* textual problem, nor the 'complete statement', ever appeared; although in the same year (1941) Chambers published a very short account of the *Piers Plowman* manuscript in the National Library of Wales which referred to his 'forthcoming Early English Text Society edition'.[37]

---

[35] Item 103, unnumbered, letter dated 27 October 1941.
[36] Item 103, unnumbered. Sisam's curiosity about the text of *Piers Plowman* must have been greatly stimulated – and partly assuaged – by his reading of Kane's draft Introduction to the A-Text ten or so years later for the Athlone Press; see pp. 344ff. below.
[37] See p. 252 above.

Meanwhile there was concern beyond Europe about the fate of the *Piers Plowman* project undertaken so many years ago. An anxious letter came from George R. Coffmann, chairman of the Advisory Committee on Research of the Medieval Academy of America (the publishers of the medievalist journal *Speculum*). He had heard 'the rumour that the notes which you had been assembling for a critical edition of *Piers Plowman* through many years were destroyed in the London raids of a year ago. I can only hope that this is not true.' Literally, of course, it was not true, but it is difficult to believe that Chambers' energy was not greatly sapped by this personal, professional, and institutional disaster. Coffmann asks for information on the progress of the edition.[38] But by this time Chambers, already debilitated by an attack of 'flu a month earlier, had suffered a heart attack in Swansea where he had gone to deliver a lecture. Elsie Hitchcock, the friend, collaborator, and former pupil who had shared a house with Chambers and his sister since 1917,[39] and took care of Chambers in his illness, scribbled across the top of the letter that she would 'refer to RWC when *sufficiently* recovered'. He died a few weeks later, on 23 April 1942.

It was Hitchcock to whom the task fell of sorting through his papers. They were in a fairly chaotic state, and the *Piers Plowman* material presented particular problems, since it was unclear who owned the project and who should be responsible for its continuance. Leverhulme had invested money in it; EETS appeared to have publication rights; Grattan – whose letters Hitchcock would have been able to discover among Chambers' collections of correspondence – regarded himself as joint owner; while Mitchell's involvement must have seemed essential if the material was ever to be published.

Some of the confusion is suggested by the letter written by C. J. Sisson, one of Chambers' University College colleagues, to Hitchcock on 26 May 1942, urging her to confirm with the Leverhulme Trust that work on *Piers Plowman* would be continued, and opining 'the choice of the successor will probably rest with the Council of the EETS.' He adds, 'I think it quite probable that Professor Grattan does not in fact know where the work stands. I imagine that Dr Smith has been more in Q. P.'s [the Quain Professor's] confidence upon this

---

[38] Chambers Papers Item 103, unnumbered.
[39] She had been a lecturer at University College for many years and had published EETS editions of three lives of Sir Thomas More (notably N. Harpsfield, *The Life and Death of Sir Thomas Moore*, EETS 186, as an Introduction to which Chambers had written his famous article, 'The Continuity of English Prose') and also of Pecock's *Donet*.

than anyone for some considerable time'. Hitchcock replied the same day: 'it is certainly Grattan who should know best the stage reached – it was their joint job, and he would have been kept informed'. As we have seen, this is unlikely. The Treasurer of EETS, Mabel Day, Chambers and Grattan's old opponent over multiple authorship, was trying to clear up Chambers' EETS business, and wrote to Hitchcock on 6 June 1942:

> W. r. to Piers Plowman, I don't see that much can be done until peace comes. I suppose that Prof. Grattan will take the responsibility for the A text; & I will try to keep him at it ... Was Mrs Blackman supposed to be working on B?

Hitchcock replied that 'Mr. [*sic*] Blackman was working on the B-Text, so also Kane.' Hitchcock herself found the burden of responsibility in dealing with the *Piers Plowman* material a source of trouble and distress, wishing to do her best by her friend's unfinished life work, and trying to throw off the threat of co-editorship, a post for which (as her letters reveal) she felt herself unfitted and disinclined.

She sent a good deal of information to Blackman for identification, and tidied the surviving nine folders of 'Text and Collations, Passus i–vi', typing up the missing pages and dispatching the completed material to its intended owners (who included Grattan, Kane, and Blackman; Mitchell had his already). A biography of Chambers was planned by Robin Flower, who had taken over the Directorship of EETS, and she collected together a mass of material to be passed on to him.[40] No news came from Mitchell, and Hitchcock wrote despairingly to Blackman on 17 June 1942, 'I keep on saying that I will do all I can, but for a totally ignorant person to assume any *Piers* responsibility is absurd, and I do not believe Q. P. intended it.' Later (17 July 1942), in reply to various queries from Blackman, she commented 'I do not know Q. P.'s ideas as to the A-Text. I quite see how you feel about it [Blackman was also reluctant to take charge of the project], and I myself cannot really do anything of value. I feel crushed by the responsibilities I have already – complications seem to increase ...'

Grattan's first decisive action was to claim his half-share of Chambers' *Piers Plowman* material. Hitchcock seems to have resisted

---

[40] Chambers Papers Item 117. Flower, when working at the British Museum, had given Chambers palaeographical advice on the *Piers Plowman* manuscripts, as the latter gratefully acknowledged in his interim report to the Leverhulme trustees.

his request for papers, storing all the material in the National Library of Wales in Aberystwyth.[41] By 14 June 1942 Grattan was negotiating with Leverhulme to take over the A-Text money, and arranging to visit Flower in London;[42] another letter of 21 June 1942 made it clear that he was determined to move forward with the A-Text work. He had decided in view of previous letters from Chambers himself 'that the right man to collaborate with me in finishing the A-Text wd be Lieut. Kane – *when* he is available'.[43] Hitchcock replied on 23 June to confirm that Robin Flower had agreed that the balance of the Leverhulme money should be handed back to the Trust as soon as possible after probate, but would be available for the EETS and Grattan when necessary. She added 'With regard to Kane, the Q.P. thought a lot of him. How he will be after a long period of Prison or War life, one cannot tell, and he may be anxious to return quickly to Canada.'[44]

But Grattan continually put off his projected visit to review the *Piers Plowman* material, pleading illness, while on 12 July 1942 Blackman wrote formally to Hitchcock, in response to a request for information on the state of the B-Text, 'Piers has been out of my thoughts for three years, and my mind won't go back to it easily, but as soon as I can I will try to give Dr Flower some idea of the B-text position. It cannot be more than an "idea" because practically all my papers are packed away. Some of them, I remember, are serving as sandbags!' She fears that she can do nothing towards *Piers* during the war, and cannot give any commitment afterwards. She finishes, 'I did

---

[41] A typed account of the material thus stored survives among the EETS Papers. The following were stated as having permission of access: Chambers' sister Gertrude, Hitchcock herself, Grattan, Mrs Francis Blackman, Mitchell, the Director of EETS (then Dr Robin Flower, of the National Library of Wales), The Provost of UCL, Prof. C. J. Sisson. The material comprised (1) rotographs of A-MSS (TRUDHJW), B-MSS (MCotYOGHm), and C-MSS (TUXLRMV); (2) copies of theses by Mitchell, Tapping, Carnegy, Kane, together with a loose-leaved notebook with notes on the A-, B-, and C-Texts; (3) material previously deposited by Chambers: 'A. Text. Introduction and collations, Prol., Passus i–vi. 9 folders. Letters on Piers Plowman [presumably those he treasured from such correspondents as Skeat]. Rules for collating Piers Plowman' (see further below p. 309); (4) a parcel described as containing 'P.P Authorship. 2 uncorrected copies of provisional Text. Rough collations, Vita de dowel. Carbon of essay on *Piers Plowman* as far as finished.'; (5) two further boxes containing 'A. Text, Trinity, with collations', and 'A. Text, Rawlinson 137, with collations' respectively.

[42] EETS Papers.

[43] EETS Papers. Grattan quotes from two letters (not now surviving) from Chambers which suggest that Chambers, as well as Grattan, felt lonely and isolated in his professional and private life. No other indications of Chambers' loneliness survive among his papers or writings, but it could be that depression contributed to his failure to complete his work on *Piers Plowman*.

[44] EETS Papers.

not know that the Q.P. thought of me as collaborating with J.H.G.G. over the A-text. He certainly never spoke to me about it. He did once talk of a team of workers and "Smith with his enormous energy", as a means of carrying on the work, but did not elaborate ...'

At this point a cable arrived from Mitchell:[45] 'THANKS TETTER IF GRATTAN UNABLE PREPARED COMPLETE CHAMBERS A TEXT AS REVISER WITHOUT MENTION MY NAME WRITING = MITCHELL', interpreted by Hitchcock as 'Thanks letter. If Grattan unable prepared complete Chambers' A-Text as reviser without mention my name. Writing. Mitchell.' Hitchcock gladly seized on this (24 July 1942), passing it on to Flower and also informing Grattan: 'it does seem a splendid solution to the A-text problem'. Grattan confirmed on 6 August that he 'should greatly value [Mitchell's] collaboration'. But he continued to defer his trip to Aberystwyth, pleading one excuse after another, despite Hitchcock's urging that it was in his own 'essential interest' to come as soon as possible.

On 23 September 1942 Mitchell wrote to report he was 'making fairly good progress on my C-Text', at the same time assuring Hitchcock,

> I am prepared at all times to undertake anything you or the other editors may desire in seeing to the completion of Chambers' A-text. That I regard as an obligation almost sacred to the man to whom I owe more probably than I shall ever know ... I am anxious above all things that *Piers.* should be completed as nearly as may be in the form Chambers would have wished and with no greater delay than is forced upon us by the troubled times in which we live.[46]

Unfortunately, this wish was never realised. Mitchell did not complete his work on the C-Text. He was appointed to a chair at Sydney in 1947 (for which, as recorded in the EETS Papers, Chambers had recommended him), and fourteen years later gave up his research to become Deputy Vice-Chancellor, having 'finally elected to devote himself to administration'.[47] He passed on his work on the C-Text to George Russell, and its publication is still (in 1995) pending.

---

45 Still surviving in the EETS Papers.
46 EETS papers.
47 Russell's phrase, in 'The Evolution of a Poem' (34); although Russell also records (33) that (in 1962) Mitchell had still 'a distinguished contribution to make' towards the textual study of the poem. See below, p. 337.

17

The Chambers and Grattan collations

As we have seen, Hitchcock tidied up the *Piers Plowman* material left by Chambers and dispatched it to the National University of Wales for safekeeping in June 1942. After the war, it was transferred to the library of University College, where access was restricted to Grattan and Kane.[1] It seems likely that much of the material she records as having lodged at the University of Wales was either lost, or dispersed by Grattan in the process of re-examining the embryo edition and sorting out the papers and rotographs.

The surviving material, which is piecemeal, makes it difficult to work out precisely how Chambers and Grattan conducted their work after 1912, when proofs were printed of the Trinity A-MS Pro–IV.[2] The most interesting element is a set of master collations.[3] Reading through these gives the impression that the process of collating, checking and revising was unsystematic and at times chaotic. A note in Chambers' hand on the 'Present Condition of Collations' in October 1919 (Item 8), states that all the A-MSS save W, N, and K had been collated as far as Passus VIII. Of W, Chambers notes that occasional passages only have been collated beyond Passus VI 46 'for special purpose' – i.e., at points of particular textual difficulty. Continuous collation of K had stopped at around the same place, at Passus VI 38. Chambers notes in an underlined jotting that *'neither of*

---

[1] See Chambers Papers Item 8, letter dated 27 September 1947.
[2] Two sets of proofs of this material survive (Chambers Papers Items 7 and 8). Those in Item 8 are probably subsequent to those in Item 7. 'Grattan' rather than 'Chambers' is printed at the head of the first page, and while some of Chambers' handwritten corrections in Item 7 have been incorporated into the text (for example, '[Hic incipit liber qui vocatur pers plowman - prologus]' now appears between 'TRINITY TEXT OF A' and the first line of the Prologue), others, including manifest errors corrected by Chambers in Item 7, remain, e.g. the beginning of Passus I 160 is printed 'Iames be ientil' in all three copies; Chambers' handwritten correction in Item 7 indicates that *be* should be changed to *ſe*, but the error remains in the two copies of Grattan's proofs.
[3] Chambers Papers Items 11–17.

these are of any value for fixing the text, and can if necessary be put in subsequently', which strongly indicates that, as yet, his ideal of a critical edition was not being logically implemented, and that he was constructing his text in ignorance of some of the manuscript witnesses. On Passus IX–XI he notes '*All* MSS collated except W and H^2 need doing throughout: H^2 important. Ashmole and K need doing for XI: of these Ashmole is important'; whereas for Passus XII it was 'only necessary to check Skeat's collation of Ingilby upon Rawlinson'.[4] This seems to mean that, by 1919, the two editors had collated all of the manuscripts for the later passus except W, H^2, A, and K.

The collations themselves are like a set of geological specimens, with different layers – dated and undated notes, insertions, etc. – marking the different stages of the process of evolution. Chambers and Grattan used foolscap sheets of quarter-inch squared paper, at the top of each of which they wrote out one line as it appeared in T. Underneath were recorded the variants of the other A-MSS, with a different colour ink accorded to each manuscript and (to start with, at any rate), a different line on the page for each manuscript as well. For some portions of the poem more than one set of collations exist, recording what are probably earlier stages in the process of collation.[5] Each of the passus is stored away in a folder, presumably for easy transportation, with a note inside stating that the material was the property of Chambers and Grattan of University College London, and that 'if lost, a reward will be repaid on its return with contents'. At the head of each passus Chambers and Grattan inserted an extra sheet of paper, which recorded – again, in varying hands written at different dates – the manuscripts which had been collated, checked, and rechecked for that passus.

The Prologue was treated relatively systematically. Twelve manuscripts (RVUJTDHLKH^{2}EKW) are recorded as collated throughout, with proofs and variants revised on 4 April 1921 by both editors. A second check was carried out, again by both editors, on 20 July 1921. By May 1922 the collations had been checked against Carnegy's C-Text, and against the B-Text information found in Blackman, Wright, and Crowley. A 'third revision, settling *finally* the B & C

---

[4] Chambers' revised opinion of the importance of Ashmole indicates that he had taken to heart the views of Knott published three years earlier in 1915 (see p. 243 n. 9 above).

[5] As for example the collations of A-MSS RVEJ, in Grattan's hand (Chambers Papers Item 9:3).

insertions and the obeli', was made, by both editors, on 7 April 1923. On 12 November 1928 the variants of the recently discovered manuscript belonging to Allen Bright (M; see p. 254 above) were incorporated by Grattan, and on 21 February in the following year they were checked by Chambers. On 11 August 1930 Grattan records that the readings of six of the manuscripts, H^2, V, E, K, W, and N, are to be 'looked through in order to list omitted checkings', and subsequent crossings-out indicate that in the case of all but V and E, this was done.[6] One of the interesting things revealed by the information preserved on these sheets is that regular checking of the A-MSS against B and C took place from a comparatively early stage, 1922, confirming the indications we have already seen that the two editors regarded it as essential to edit A with a constant eye to the evidence of the two other textual traditions.[7]

Passus I was dealt with in a similar way, with checkings and re-checkings noted and (mostly) dated. As before, B and C were recorded as being checked against the readings. There is also an undated pencil note: 'Remember to collate with Knott.' The last dated note is at the bottom of the sheet: 'looked through in order to list some omitted checkings JG 11/8/30'.[8] Passus II and III seem both to have been last looked over in 1928–9, when Chambers and Grattan inserted the readings of M. Passus IV,[9] however, received subsequent attention in 1948, when someone – presumably Grattan – inserted on 25 September the variants of the Chaderton MS, which had been discovered in 1943.[10] Grattan also noted that 'longhand variants & galley proofs' had been revised on 19 September of the same year.

The material for Passus V–VI takes a different form; presumably the collation of these later sections was undertaken at a different stage.[11] There is now a typed text, with corrections, as well as handwritten collations. The initial sheet of paper is set out differently, and records many more overlays of subsequent accretions. There is an instruction dated 24 April 1928 to 'check D first', and another lower down the page, dated 24 June 1948, recording that this manuscript's readings are 'not yet checked after 20 years (!)'. Lincoln's readings were checked in August 1930, the Dublin manuscript's in July 1948,

---

6 Chambers Papers Item 11:2.
7 Chambers Papers Item 20 contains a list of 'possible B contamination in Pro-IV' – i.e., B readings in A-MSS. This is by no means comprehensive. See p. 253 and p. 256 n. 2 above.
8 Chambers Papers Item 12.   9 Chambers Papers Item 15.
10 See p. 311 n. 5 below.   11 Chambers Papers Items 16–17.

at which time also Grattan notes that data on Ashmole is 'not very satisfactory'. M's readings were inserted and checked at an undated period; a subsequent note reads, despairingly, 'but they are not full enough'. The (undated) 'settling of B & C insertions' was carried out for lines 43–105 only, and an apparently later annotation comments that 'these all need revision'. Among the July 1930 remarks is the note, written diagonally across the bottom of the page, that 'several readings in Text are yet to be re-weighed 15/7/30 JG viz. 176 203 204'; the list of line numbers is continued eighteen years later, almost to the day (on '1/7/48') with no indication that the problems noted earlier have been sorted out.

The records of accretions to the collation of Passus VI are also increasingly haphazard. Apparently only T had been fully checked by 1948, while U and D were partially so. The readings of RH^{2}VHJE had been inserted but not checked, while AKWNM had received inconsistent treatment: Grattan notes on 5 July 1948 'Chambers has inserted *some* readings, I find', but 'no checking done'. Two days later he records that he has added all barring the last seven lines of the Chaderton manuscript, but he has not rectified the absence of the other collations. An earlier note (7 April 1930), in Chambers' hand, oberves that 'Our text is not well fixed to l. 64. Better after that'; in reply Grattan writes despondently on 6 July 1948, 'not much better'. Another note, in the hand of one or other of the editors, heavily emphasised and underlined, reads 'BC only provisional!!!'

Turning to the text and collations themselves, one is struck by the unmethodical jotting down, in sometimes scrawled handwriting, of various comments, queries, indications of absent information, and so on, to produce a collection of material which must have struck George Kane, who inherited these records, as a nightmarish mess. One of the main problems was that the two editors were seriously inconsistent in the way they chose to record variants, only later coming to realise that the fullest possible record was necessary in order to establish a text with all relevant information: often it was only at a late stage that the editors were able to perceive what was relevant information and what was not.

The dates attached to the various annotations suggest that one wave of corrections was carried out in 1930, and the material then left untouched until 1948, when Grattan finally returned to the editing project with the help of Kane, who had been occupied on the B-Text before that date.[12] At the head of the initial sheet of Passus V a note in Grattan's hand reads that 'typed text and (written) variants checked & emended by G. Kane & J. Grattan Sept '48'. Kane was involved in working over Passus VI as well as V, for in both sets of collations there is the odd note in his handwriting. It is immediately identifiable by its neat appearance and its clarity and syntactic coherence, compared with the wildly written short-hand comments of the other two editors. These are sometimes illegible and often elliptic to the point of incomprehensibility: for example, on Passus VI 71, 'BC alternate half line', or on Passus VI 69, 'Has any MS *hald*?' By contrast, Kane's comments were designed to serve as full drafts for the textual notes, and they are of a standard well beyond that of his two seniors: they appeal to such criteria as standard alliteration and scribal behaviour, and even leave careful blanks for references to be later filled in. The overwhelming impression is of an infinitely more thorough, controlled and meticulous mind at work. One example, duly supplied with *NED* reference, is the comment on *friþed* at Passus VI 68, a line which (in Kane's subsequent edition) reads:

> He is fre[þ]id in wiþ Floreynes & oþere [fees] manye,

and where many manuscripts read *fretted* for *freþid* and some *floures* for *fees*. Kane writes,

> friþed in *v. fretted in*. The expression *fretted in* would have exactly the same meaning, 'adorned within', as the A-reading. (v. *NED* s.v. *in* adv. 5.) Such a meaning here, however, is scarcely consistent with the line that follows. It seems clear that the other, minority A-reading (which is also found in B and C) is the original: the brook of truthful witnessing is hedged in or bordered with a thicket of bribes against the truth, from which the pilgrim is admonished to 'pluck no plant'. 23/9/48.[13]

Overleaf, he adds

> 68 ctd.
> The substitution of *frettid* 'adorned' for *frithed* 'hedged', may ~~also~~ well have brought about the substitution of 'flowers' for 'fees' in some A-MSS.

Grattan ticked and initialled this note, dating his approbation the

---

[12]   In 1948, as we learn from Grattan's second *Speculum* bulletin (p. 311 below), Kane broke off his work on B to help Grattan with A. For a hint as to the photographs and transcripts of the A-MSS available to Chambers and Grattan in 1931, see p. 273 n. 6 above.

[13]   Kane improves on this note in his edition; see 444.

same day. Kane's comment on an important crux at A Passus VI 2 ('blustrid forþ as bestis ouer [baches] & hilles', where most manuscripts read *valeis* for *baches*, which is found in MS W only) also gives the flavour of his measured and logical deliberations:

> on .l. 2 The absence of alliteration in the second half line of our text suggests that *valeis* is the product of an early A-substitution and that the original reading was the extant synonym *baches* found in our MS. W. This W reading however can hardly ~~have been~~ be a genuine survival, but must have been restored from the C-text.

This is particularly interesting in view of the fact that W is a manuscript which Chambers and Grattan regarded with little respect: Kane has nevertheless identified in it a reading that – so he argued – preserves the original A-Text accurately where all other extant A-MSS – and all other extant B-MSS too, for that matter – have failed.[14] It may well have been such a discovery that convinced him of the absolute necessity of collating *all* available extant manuscripts with the same loving care, whether superficially reliable witnesses or not.

He was later to revise his opinion that W came by this reading as a result of contamination from C,[15] but the problem – did a good reading in one or only a few A-MSS come through uninterrupted A-Text transmission, or was it the result of clever or gifted scribal 'correction', perhaps from a more faithful text of one of the two later versions? – clearly exercised the A-Text editors very considerably. Another comment, partly scrawled diagonally across the page, and therefore presumably by one of the two senior editors rather than the methodical Kane, asks of the agreement between EMH[3] and BC at Passus VI 71 (where the A archetype reads '[And] loke þat þou leiȝe nouȝt for no manis biddyng', and BC (Passus V 584/VII 231) together with A-MSS EMH[3] – and Z – read, instead of the first half of the line, 'In no manere ellis noght'),

> Has the A-tradition
> gone wrong [?illegible]

---

[14] At Passus VI 42 below Chambers writes 'Collation of W groggy from this point', and Grattan comments underneath 'very'.

[15] Or so it would appear from the note to his edition (444). Both the crux and Kane's treatment of it are discussed with characteristic penetration and erudition by Robert Adams, who believes that Kane was wrong to identify *baches* as the original reading ('Editing and the Limitations of the *Durior Lectio*'). See further discussion below, pp. 415ff.

or has B (&C)
   improved on the original?[16]

It would have been difficult for the two editors to clear up this matter even if they had had the evidence of full collations of the A-, B-, and C-MSS before them. And other of the BC readings found in A-MSS were simply not noted by them – for example, EAM share three lines after Passus VI 81 which are not found in the other A-MSS. Two of these closely resemble two lines in B and C, found in both Skeat's editions and in all extant B-MSS (and also in Z).[17] Chambers and Grattan make no reference to this agreement with B and C in their collations.

Also extant are several pages of foolscap describing editorial policy on the text and collations, presumably destined for the printed edition of A, together with a long handwritten draft introduction which sets out the theories of editing the text which Chambers had previously established in his published work.[18] Other material includes a copy of lines from the C-Text with some Blackman collations recorded against them;[19] various notes on C-MSS, including collations;[20] and assorted scraps of paper with incomplete lists of manuscript readings and agreements. All in all the material is a sufficient explanation for the continued non-appearance of published work.

[16] See further Charlotte Brewer, 'George Kane's Processes of Revision', 81, and also below, p. 400.
[17] See Charlotte Brewer, 'Z and the A- B- and C-Texts of *Piers Plowman*', 213.
[18] Chambers Papers Items 11 (another copy in 18) and 24 respectively.
[19] Item 23.   [20] Item 9.

18

Grattan and Kane

Information on the fate of the edition is now (post-1942) much harder to come by. Elsie Hitchcock died at the end of the year, and there is no evidence that Chambers' sister ever played a part, as amanuensis or otherwise, in her brother's academic affairs. The next clue comes in a short article which appeared in *Speculum* in 1945 under the name of George R. Coffmann, who had written to Chambers just before his death in April 1942.[1] The article reproduced a formal report (last revised 27 June 1944) prepared by Grattan on the state of the *Piers Plowman* edition.

At this stage, the edition was still intended for the Early English Text Society. Grattan writes, 'Dr Chambers and I had worked out our principles of editing, and the first volume [presumably Pro IV] of our Critical A-text was practically ready ten years ago and more.' He continues,

> Almost at the last moment, however, it was found advisable to modify the original plan of printing the A-, B-, & C-texts separately (as in Skeat's E. E. T. S. edition) in favour of exhibiting the three texts of [*sic*; *sc.* 'on'] one page or opening (as in Skeat's Oxford edn.). This change of plan, by which no portion of the Critical A-text could be published until the corresponding B- & C-texts should be ready, necessarily involved a somewhat indefinite post-ponement of the publication of the first volume of the projected E. E. T. S. edition.[2]

Grattan also gives the whereabouts of his current collaborators. He explains that help had been called in 'at an early stage in our work', 'for the collation of B- and C-MSS' – although it is fair to say, as

---

[1] See p. 299 above.

[2] It seems likely that this new information is to some extent a *post hoc* explanation for delay. The first mention of the parallel-text edition that I have come across is that of 1939 in Grattan's letter to Chambers of 3 March 1941; see p. 290 above.

Grattan does not, that the work of Blackman and Tapping had far exceeded mere collation. The first helpers had dropped out, and the others – unnamed, but identifiable as Mitchell, Kane, and Smith, had had their work curtailed by the war. Grattan warns that although he hopes to make faster progress on his work 'here in Liverpool' after his retirement begins in October, 'I do not forget that I am nearly through my sixty-seventh year.' And he has gloomy news of Robin Flower, the much younger man whom he counted on as a link between him and the other collaborators, and to whose energy he had trusted to see through the project. Ill-health had forced him 'to retire completely from such work', and Grattan now looked to his successor as E. E. T. S. director, C. T. Onions, to fulfil his role. Flower died soon afterwards, in 1946, and no further mention is made of Onions' association with the project. By 1950, the prospective editors were negotiating with the Athlone Press of the University of London, since 'changes in the [EET] Society's policy' had made the previous arrangement, standing since 1909, 'impracticable'.[3]

Kane returned to England immediately after the end of the war, and finished his doctoral thesis with astonishing swiftness in 1946.[4] The thesis was an edition of the last three passus of the B-Text of the poem, together with critical notes, full critical apparatus, a description of the B-MSS and discussion of the principles by which Kane's critical text of B had been arrived at (with particular reference to the C-Text). In a second *Speculum* report, dated 1951, Grattan announced that Mitchell had meanwhile continued to work on C, while his own work on A had been restricted until 1947.[5] By 1947 Grattan was in his seventieth year, and age as much as anything else must have slowed

---

[3] See Grattan's second *Speculum* bulletin on progress on the edition, 'The Critical Edition of *Piers Plowman*'. George Kane has told me that Onions would only consider the edition for EETS if Kane worked under a supervisor, which condition he refused.

[4] Hitchcock records his thesis as being one of those stored away in the underground library of the National Library of Wales, which suggests that it already had a substantial existence by 1939; as we have seen, he had collated 2,000 lines by the time he enlisted. In ' "Piers Plowman": Problems and Methods of Editing the B-Text', 5, Kane states that he began collating the B-MSS in 1938.

[5] In an article published in 1947, Grattan corroborates this statement, referring to his and Chambers' '*Piers Plowman* laboratory' at University College, London, assembled 'nearly a generation ago', and stating, 'to my regret, I have not been able to consult this material' (8). The article was an account of the Chaderton manuscript (Ch), an A-MS recently acquired by the Library of Liverpool University and closely affiliated to the Trinity College A-MS (T). Like T, it is another example of a copy of an A-Text completed by a C-Text. See 'The Text of "Piers Plowman": A Newly Discovered Manuscript', and cf. Quaritch Catalogue no. 613 (1943), 9–11 (the manuscript's first public notice).

down his progress. Thus in 1948 Kane broke off his work on B to collaborate with Grattan on A, presumably in the hope that this text could be more speedily brought to completion. This explains how, after Grattan's death in 1951, Kane took on the editing of A as his first task in dispatching the *Piers Plowman* inheritance left him by Chambers and Grattan.

Grattan was able to set up a fairly elaborate plan of succession. His 1951 report describes what is now a grander and more ambitious project: 'a comprehensive critical edition … under the editorship of Grattan, Kane, Mitchell and Smith'. The four editors had met for the first time after the war in September 1949, and decided to revert to the original scheme of printing the three texts of the poem in separate volumes. They had also decided to add three extra volumes, making a total of six. Volumes I–III were to be editions of A, B, and C respectively, A edited by Grattan and Kane, B by Kane, and C by Mitchell. Volume IV was to contain *'The linguistic apparatus and glossary'*, provided by Grattan, Smith, and (a newcomer on the scene) C. R. Quirk; volume V was to contain *'Annotations* under the general direction of Kane, with the collaboration of Professor Morton W. Bloomfield of Ohio State University, and E. T. Donaldson of Yale University'; while the same team were to collaborate on a 'discussion of the background, interpretation, authorship, etc. of *Piers Plowman'* for volume VI.

Randolph Quirk, a pupil of Chambers, published a couple of articles on *Piers Plowman* in 1953 and 1954 but subsequently directed his energies into the field of Modern English Language studies. Bloomfield, another pupil, continued his interest in the poem but dropped out of the editing project. Donaldson was to become one of the most significant *Piers Plowman* textual and interpretative scholars. In 1943 he had completed a thesis on the C-Text of the poem, and in 1949 he published a major book on *Piers Plowman: The C-Text and Its Poet*. Here he argued strongly that the alleged inferiority of the C-Text had fuelled the multiple authorship theory, since it made joint authorship of both B and C by the same poet appear far less likely. By contrast, Donaldson put up an implicit counter-argument with his attempt to demonstrate that the C-Text was 'a magnificent poem, intellectually profound, artistically effective' – i.e. certainly not a poem which could be judged unworthy or uncharacteristic of the B poet. Kane read his book, and in 1951 sent him a copy of his own book, *Medieval*

Literature, together with an invitation to join the project. Donaldson accepted.[6]

Grattan finished his account of the state of the edition in 1951 with the confident statement that 'The work on the A-text now approaches completion; it is expected that Volume I of the edition will be ready for the printer in the winter of 1951. Volume III [C] is almost ready; II [B] will, it is hoped, be ready by 1953, and the remaining volumes will follow at short intervals thereafter.' This prognosis now appears as one of a long and sorry string of grossly over-optimistic forecasts on the speed with which the textual work would be concluded.[7]

The Ph.D. thesis which Kane completed with such remarkable expedition is an interesting document, for it records Kane's 1946 views on certain textual issues about which he was later to change his mind significantly, as well as illustrating the genesis of theories crucial to his later editions.

He affects the same somewhat scathing tone when discussing scribes and their products as that of Blackman earlier; for example he says of the most eccentric, and in some ways most controversial, B-MS, Corpus 201 (F):

> The division into passus corresponds to nothing on earth ... Capitals are illuminated with elaborate bad taste. This is not a cheap manuscript, but the money spent on it did not go into the text. The scribe was an individualist as to spelling: he used ʒ promiscuously with no apparent intention of affecting the sound of words. He generally tries to remember too much text, and if he cannot recall the exact words of his copy, he does not look back, but puts his own words to the sense as he remembers it. (pp. 4–5)

These remarks illustrate the confidence with which he identifies the cause of the textual variants found in this peculiar version of the B-Text. Kane makes the almost unthinking assumption that the manuscript's unusual readings are to be attributed to delinquency on the part of the scribe (which he describes with some perception), rather than any other cause – such as contamination, or even, in however convoluted a way, descent from the author's original. He

[6] I have this information from Professor Kane.
[7] Another had appeared in the 1946 article by Kane discussed below: 'Professor Grattan hopes now to take up the A-text again where he left off before the war; Professor A. G. Mitchell of Sydney University has almost completed the collation of the C-text manuscripts; and we may hope that critical texts of at least these two versions of *Piers Plowman* will be in print within the next three years' ('"Piers Plowman": Problems and Methods', 4).

offers no evidence for this hypothesis, and he was later to revise it markedly. By 1975, he and his co-editor of B, Talbot Donaldson, had become convinced of the quality and value of F's idiosyncratic readings, and put forward an elaborate and tendentious argument in their edition of B that many of these readings were original to the poem.

Most interesting from our point of view are the remarks Kane makes on textual criticism and on his indebtedness to Chambers, his supervisor. Tacitly, but unmistakably, he marks out his position in the Chambers and Grattan/Manly and Knott debate of the previous forty-odd years by the simple expedient of failing to recognise the existence of the other side:

> No one who so much as glances at the *Piers Plowman* [critical] material can fail to be impressed by the extent to which each new student in this field is under obligation to his predecessors. Skeat was the pioneer: he discovered most of the manuscripts, worked hugely at their classification, and made a beginning by publishing three of the best of them. Professor Chambers, following him, first applied the principles of scientific editing to these manuscripts, and subsequently inspired and directed the work of students like Mrs Blackman, Mrs Tapping, and Dr Mitchell to the greatest effect. (p. 14)[8]

No mention of the importance and influence of Manly and Knott here, although the *Piers Plowman* controversy had done much to bring the poem into the limelight, and had stimulated productive discussion of its literary qualities.[9]

In discussing editorial method, Kane explicitly states his debt to and regard for Chambers. He attributes to him a unique place in Middle English editing, one which Kane is now widely regarded as occupying himself:

---

[8] Kane rarely mentions Grattan, and often refers (as I have done) to the articles signed by the pair of them as if Chambers alone were the author.

[9] See Anne Middleton's remarks quoted above, p. 192. In the words of Bloomfield, writing in 1939, 'If his contention has not been proved, Manly has, at least, focused attention on a great poem which had been neglected unjustly, and stimulated an interest that has produced notable results, so that we are able to appreciate much that was lost to our predecessors.' Despite Kane's failure to mention the issue, Bloomfield evidently felt that the dispute over authorship remained current ('The Present State of *Piers Plowman* Studies', 215–22, esp. 217 n.8), as did S. S. Hussey, writing six years later than Kane, in 1952: 'The authorship controversy now looms so large in *Piers Plowman* scholarship that some critics have felt compelled to state categorically on which side of the fence they stand or whether they sit balanced on top', 'Eighty Years of *Piers Plowman* Scholarship', 108. On the other hand, E. G. Stanley has told me that 'by 1948–51 (when I was an undergraduate) the "multiple author" theory was quite dead in Oxford (as well as London, I presume)'.

Except among those who knew him, it is not generally realised how far Professor Chambers carried the work of adapting the principles of editing applied to classical texts to the conditions of Middle English poetry. His formulations of method must henceforward fix the manner in which Middle English texts will be edited. (p. 31)

and he points out that Chambers' published output on such matters consisted of 'articles which were poor in bulk if rich in substance', offering this as an explanation for the neglect of his work. Kane was trespassing on Blackman's ground in his work on the B-Text, and he also makes grateful acknowledgement of her formative influence on and preparation of his way:

The work and the results set down in these two productions [her MA thesis of 1914 and her article of 1918] have put me under an obligation to her which I am at a loss to express. I have constantly used her conclusions ... I have made use of her conclusions freely and gratefully throughout my work. I should like to state most emphatically that I am greatly in her debt. (pp. 14–15)[10]

These 'conclusions' – largely concerning manuscript relations and the importance of individual manuscripts and manuscript readings – were, Kane makes clear, reached by her application of the principles of editing taught by Chambers:

He was one of the first to apply these principles to the inspection of Middle English texts: they were earlier formulated by Westcott and Hort during their work on the New Testament, and by Dr Moore in his attempt to classify the manuscripts of the *Divine Comedy*. (pp. 16–17)

Kane emphasises that he merely follows these principles in his analysis of the variant readings of the B-MSS and his attempt to produce a critical text (see p. 30ff.), and during the course of his discussion of individual manuscripts and editing methodology he comes up with remarks that look significant in the light of his later editing practice.

---

10   This generosity and explicitness is repeated by Kane two years later in his reference to Blackman's 'brilliant and painstaking researches' and his statement that her work 'is of such value that no future student of the B-text will be able to avoid an enormous obligation to her' ('"Piers Plowman": Problems and Methods', 7 n.2 and 8). Acknowledgement of Kane's indebtedness to Blackman, and of the seminal influence of her work, is absent from his joint edition of B (1975); see Kane–Donaldson, 18 n.11 and scattered footnote references thereafter. It is very likely that years of independent study erased the memory of her guiding steps from his mind. Blackman's 'excellent study' is acknowledged by Donaldson in 'MSS R and F in the B Tradition of *Piers Plowman*' (181).

For example, his recognition that any one of a number of 'inferior' B-MSS (MRFC²GCotBoBmHmCr) 'may upon occasion provide a surprise in the shape of a correct reading where the best manuscripts appear to have gone astray' picks up on Westcott and Hort's warning that the pedigree of manuscripts may not always be the best clue to the quality of individual readings, and adumbrates his own later rejection of recension as no more than an ancillary editing tool in the production of a critical text.[11] On the other hand, his discussion of the Rawlinson B-MS shows an open-mindedness on the question of authorial revision that was later to disappear. He refers to a private letter from Chambers of 1939, in which Chambers went back on his 1935 views about R (stated in 'The Manuscripts of *Piers Plowman* in the Huntington Library', where he had classified R as a manuscript contaminated with C readings), and discussed the possibility that R might show signs of authorial revision to C, or alternatively that R's additions were those of an interpolator, and were incorporated by the C reviser, who did not know they were interpolations (pp. 21–2).[12]

Many pages (pp. 31–50) are taken up with a painstaking discussion of the interrelatedness of editing B and C: decisions on the one text *cannot* be made without reference to decisions on the other. His fullest statement of this principle is as follows:

> Where the two texts run together, B- cannot be edited finally without C-: but the editing of C- will often in its turn be influenced by the reading of the B-manuscripts. My work here has borne out the point which Professor Chambers constantly made, that the editing of the several texts of *Piers Plowman* must go forward side by side and step by step, each editor making use of all the information provided by his colleagues, and in his turn helping them. (p. 49)[13]

This remark is immensely significant in the light of Kane's subsequent editing of A. For there, Kane turned his back on the principle that, to

---

[11]   See p. 361 below.

[12]   Kane repeatedly points out that until R and F have been fully collated, it will be impossible to make up one's mind: 'It is a tantalizing thought that R and F may be giving us a fleeting glimpse of a B-tradition now preserved nowhere else but in their lines. The sad fact is that they would be of more use to the editor of B- if he knew for certain that they are contaminated, than they are at present, when they offer the possibility of something much better. If it eventually appears that R and F, or either singly, represent a stage in the revision of B- into C-, then their role in the editing of the B-text will have to be reconsidered. For the present they are not of much use' (25–6).

[13]   Kane refers to Chambers, 'The Text of "Piers Plowman"' (1916), 271, and 'The Text of "Piers Plowman"' (1931) 1–2, 11, 30. The same principle is very clearly stated in the MA thesis of Kane's pupil, S. S. Hussey, e.g. at p. 44.

edit any one text of *Piers Plowman*, it is essential to consult the other two at every possible stage. Instead, as we shall see, when editing A, Kane explicitly did *not* take B and C variants into consideration, except in very unusual circumstances. This limitation was almost certainly an influential factor in the comparative speed with which Kane completed his edition of A. By contrast, when he came to edit B with Donaldson, he constantly had recourse to the text of A he had previously established – a major, if unsignalled, change of policy, which reverted to the original principle established by Knott and then Chambers – but he consulted only that established text, and did not compare B variants with A variants. (Had he done so, he might have been moved to alter not only his B-Text but also his A-Text.) Knott had long ago understood that, once the preliminary texts of A, B, and C had been established, the process of editing would have to start all over again, with the editor returning to edit A in the light of the newly established critical text of B and C. This editorial logic has never been acknowledged by the Athlone editors.[14]

Several other arguments point to Kane's marked conservatism at this stage in his editing career. He explicitly states that, in accordance with the principles for editing A inherited from Chambers, and followed also in editing C by Mitchell, 'we [i.e. he and Mitchell] have attempted to refrain from admitting the element of personal preference into our choice of readings, and to maintain the greatest possible conservatism consistent with the reconstruction of our several texts' (p. 51). So he is cautious of conjectural emendation, for example: 'an ill-founded emendation is worse than no emendation at all, for it merely adds another error to the text, and one made with less excuse than the medieval scribe had' (p. 34), and he condemns in particular emendation *causa metri*:

> To have emended for reasons of metre or alliteration would have been to presume, first, that we had the right to expect a rigidly consistent practice of the author, and secondly, that we were sure of being able to discern, on the entirely personal basis of taste and individual preference, what he wrote. The function of an editor is to approach as nearly as possible within the bounds of certainty to the author's autograph, *but not to set down opinions as to what it should have been*. (p. 52)

Kane was to change his mind notoriously on the propriety of

14   See further below, pp. 374ff., 391ff.; and for Knott's view see p. 244 above.

emending on metrical grounds, and on conjectural emendation generally, in his triumphant discovery that the B-Text of *Piers Plowman* presented classically appropriate conditions, as described by Maas, for the exercise of conjectural emendation.[15]

For negligible differences between the B- and C-Texts over equivalent stretches in the last two passus, Kane coins the term 'scribal differences', by which he means, differences it is impossible to decide between, as either variant might be authorial, and where the choice between variants 'does not in any way affect the quality of the text' (p. 45). He comments,

> If Middle English alliterative verse were bound by rules as uncompromising as those which governed Greek and Latin prosody, or if these readings affected the sense, it would be important to secure conformity in cases [such as these]. But as matters stand, we have nothing but our own preference to guide us, and this is not a ground for emendation. (p. 47)

Here we have a marked contrast to the clarity and decision with which Kane distinguishes between scribal and authorial readings later in his career – and in fact, one of the three readings Kane adduces as examples of differences between B and C where 'no great case can be made for the poetry or alliteration of one or the other' (p. 46) he later changes his mind about, emending the B reading to that of C in his B-Text edition of 1975, partly to secure an *aaax* alliterative pattern in B, but also because, contrary to his view here, the B reading 'could have been derived from the [C reading] by one of the known processes of scribal variation'.[16]

In Chambers' and Blackman's cases, unshakeable certainty about the distinction between scribal and authorial readings went with a belief that differences between versions are to be attributed to scribal error rather than authorial revision. So we might expect that Kane's early acknowledgement that some variants are difficult to choose between would be accompanied by an acknowledgement that the author might, as he revised, make minor changes between his texts.

But this is not the case. Kane does not fully discuss the issues

---

[15] See 'Conjectural Emendation', 168–9, and ch. 21 below. In 1948 Kane repeats the view (echoing Skeat; see p. 154 above) that an editor should not improve the author ('"Piers Plowman": Problems and Methods', 7).

[16] The archetypal B reading (Passus XX 19) is 'That he dronke at ech dych er he *for thurst deide*', the b-half of which Kane–Donaldson emend to that of C (Passus XXII 19), 'er he *deye for purst*'. See Kane–Donaldson, 92 and 95.

involved in editing two texts, one of which is assumed to be a revision of the other. Consequently he does not acknowledge the difficulty in determining whether differences between the texts which suggest a higher quality in the second version are to be attributed to faulty scribal copying of the first text, or improved authorial revision in the second. Kane cites B Passus XX 126, which, he says, 'is a dangerous line because at first glance it appears to be adequate: "Symonie hym sent to assaile conscience". The C-text', he continues, 'upon inspection, proves to have what may be a much superior reading: "Symonie hym sewede to assaile conscience"'; and he comments, 'Without C- we might easily have accepted the B-reading for this line' (p. 48). What is missing from Kane's consideration of the variants is any recognition of the possibility that the archetypal B line, admittedly inferior, might conceivably have been Langland's own first shot, and that he improved it when revising from B to C.

Kane is presumably tipped towards regarding the B reading as purely scribal by his belief that authorial revision between B and C in the last two passus of the poem was very unlikely (p. 35ff.). He concludes, with Chambers earlier ('The Three Texts of "Piers Plowman" and Their Grammatical Forms', p. 129), that 'There is no C-text for the last two passus, such trifling variations as exist being apparently due to the scribes.'[17] This means that 'The manuscripts of C-, for the final two passus of *Piers Plowman*, produce a B-text' (p. 38) – although the C-MSS bear witness to a better archetypal text than the B-MSS. 'There are occasions', Kane continues, 'when it would be convenient to believe that differences between B- and C- are the result of revision, but there seems to be no means of proving this. We must therefore conclude that the C-poet had in his possession and used for his revision a very good manuscript of the B-text, often better than we can reconstruct from B-evidence.'

This is a strange but important conclusion. Why should revision between the last two passus of B and C be ruled out simply because, if it did occur, it occurred on so small a scale that we cannot be absolutely certain that the differences between the two texts might not be scribal? There may be 'no means of proving' that the differences are authorial; but on the other hand, there is equally 'no means of proving' that they are not. The problem deserves deeper consideration than Kane is prepared to give it.

---

[17] This view is generally held, although contrast Skeat, *C-Text*, lxviii.

Kane cut his teeth editing a comparatively small portion of the B-Text, 1,300-odd lines out of a total of about 7,000. The last two of his three chosen passus, XIX and XX (together amounting to well over half of this portion, some 800 lines) are unique in the significant respect that they differ less than other parts of B from the C-Text, making it reasonable to assume that there was indeed very little revision between B and C at this stage. Many of the weaknesses in Kane's later editing practice can be attributed to a reluctance to notice the pitfalls lying in wait for the editor of authorially revised texts, in particular the difficulties of distinguishing between authorial revision and scribal error. It seems likely that Kane's choice of which portion of the poem to edit first had a formative effect on his editorial views; consequently (and unfortunately), the reasons for and characteristics of authorial revision, both on a large and (especially) on a small scale, were not matters to which, at this stage, he devoted very much of his remarkable intellectual energy.

For what marks out Kane's thesis, in contrast to those of his University College predecessors, is his willingness to make clear the theoretical grounds for his editorial practice. He has read and assimilated Chambers and Grattan's writings on editorial theory, along with those of Westcott and Hort, and he foregrounds these as the basis for making decisions between variants.[18] Blackman, Tapping, and even Mitchell, talk about decisions between variants as if they are unproblematic; they simply state their conclusions about the originality of readings, without attempting to describe the ratiocinative processes they presumably exercised as a means of coming to their decisions. It is Kane's far superior theoretical knowledge, and in particular his readiness to see practical issues of choice between variants in terms of the theoretical issues such choice imply, which was later to make him so distinctive an editor.[19]

Many of the ideas expressed in Kane's thesis reappear in the article he published two years later, entitled ' "Piers Plowman": Problems and Methods of Editing the B-Text', which updated the scholarly public on the state of the joint editorial project. Much more than

---

[18] He recapitulates Chambers' recapitulation of Westcott and Hort's three stages of editing (32); and his later discussion of the intricacies of editing B in relation to C make it clear he is fully aware of many of the practical and theoretical ramifications of editorial decisions.

[19] He describes this intellectual awareness as a legacy from Chambers and Mitchell, e.g.: 'We have tried to bear in mind the various principles by means of which errors in a text are to be detected, while remembering that each separate case must be decided on its individual merits' (52).

Kane's thesis, the article is marked by what was to become Kane's characteristic tone of stern rigour.

This time he begins (as he hardly could not) with a brief account of the authorship controversy, taking to task the 'learned editors' of the *Cambridge History of English Literature* for their 'freakish error of judgement' in printing Manly's essay as a standard and authoritative account of *Piers Plowman*. And he reiterates the mistaken point we have seen made time and again, that 'in the case of *Piers Plowman* the question of authorship has been allowed to take precedence for a long time over the problem of the text, when in actual fact no point regarding this poem, and certainly not that of its authorship, can be settled upon internal evidence until the text itself has been fixed' (p. 2).

This point was not to be finally laid to rest for another twenty years. Commenting on the multiple authorship debate, and the belief that hostilities would have to cease until truly authoritative texts were published, E. T. Donaldson later wrote, in a typically exploratory and provocative article published in 1968,

> it is ironical that Professor George Kane and I, who are among the editors presumably producing these better texts, found ourselves virtually unable to perform our work until we had committed ourselves to a position on authorship: I think part of the long delay in the production of the B-text was, indeed, due to our slowness – or at any rate my slowness – in realizing that it is impossible to work at all from a neutral position and, in fact, that the only way one can work profitably is from overt assumption (which, to be candid, was congenial to us) of single authorship ... And so it is clear that a text edited upon an assumption concerning authorship is not going to provide any sort of firm foundation for a solution to that problem.[20]

Donaldson goes on to explain how, especially where B is concerned, it is vital, for editing purposes, to assume that A and B are written by the same author – otherwise, how can the editor presume to correct B from either of the other two texts? Similarly, it is impossible to use the evidence of the other traditions *at all* if single authorship is not

---

[20] '"Piers Plowman" Textual Comparison and the Question of Authorship', 241–2. In the same article, Donaldson apologises to Kane (who had by now changed his mind) for having 'clung long – too long – to the hope that some sort of proof of authorship could be made to emerge from textual comparison of the three versions: I went on trying to square the circle long after I should have known better' (242 n.1).

assumed: ' "Show me," one says to the text, and the text remains inert' (p. 247).[21]

Kane's book *Piers Plowman: The Evidence for Authorship*, published in 1965, is generally regarded as the definitive statement on the topic. It is an exhaustive and scrupulous review of all the evidence, both internal and external, relating to authorship and to possible theories on authorship. Its conclusion is that there is no basis for the assumption that more than one poet was responsible for the work. It is true that many inconsistencies between the versions exist, but as Skeat commented in 1910, 'The idea that no author ever is inconsistent is surely a mere craze. – I am afraid I have corrected myself more than once: but that does not prove that I am two different people.'[22] However, despite the severe claims of Kane's book, where he rejects with freezing contempt the arguments against his own, the question of authorship is not finally susceptible of proof one way or another. It is simply an easier proposition that there was one author of *Piers Plowman*, not five; and there now prevails what David Fowler, the last of the original advocates of multiple authorship, has disappointedly called 'a gentleman's agreement to the effect that the problem no longer exists'.[23]

Certainly, assumption of single authorship is the unspoken premise underlying Kane's 1948 article. After due recognition of the role in editing played by Chambers and Grattan, he moves to a close discussion of the importance of C for editing B. Here he utters an important caveat on his analysis of the B- and C-Texts. Knowledge of C was, at present, derived from insufficient evidence, since Mitchell had not yet made available all the C-MS collations. But when possible, Kane would take into consideration *all the manuscript variants* of both B and C when editing B. 'This consideration of the full evidence

---

[21] Kane himself had made the same point three years earlier in *Piers Plowman: The Evidence for Authorship*, 3: 'It used often to be said that the question of authorship would never be finally settled until "critical" texts of the three versions were available … That this prospect was illusory must be stated without delay … What the editor of *Piers Plowman* does when he edits is to create, out of textual detail, a hypothesis of original readings based ultimately on an assumption (however well or ill founded) about authorship.' The words of his two colleagues were taken to heart by the third Athlone editor, now George Russell, who wrote a couple of years later, 'editors … must accept either the theory of single authorship or one or other of the theories of multiple authorship. The decision taken will, of course, profoundly influence the nature of the editorial process and, as a consequence, the nature of the text which is its product' ('Some Aspects of the Process of Revision', 34).

[22] Card dated 2 February, from Skeat to Chambers (Chambers Papers Item 5, unnumbered).

[23] 'Editorial "Jamming"', 215. See also the essay by Eric Dahl, '*Diverse Copies Have It Diverselye*', which argues that the theory of single authorship evolved by default and has been unthinkingly accepted, to deleterious effect, by modern scholars.

will prevent readings from being "submerged" in the process of editing the separate archetypes' (p. 14). And Kane explains that a decision made on B variants *in ignorance* of C variants might lead the editor to assume that a B variant, strongly supported by B-MSS, was the original one. Had the editor consulted C-MSS, however, and found that they bore witness to a rival reading also found in B-MSS, but hitherto disregarded as insignificant, then that might well affect judgement on what was the original reading of B. Here is strongly expressed Kane's clear-thinking apprehension of how the relationship between B and C must affect the editor's actions and decisions every step of the way. As we have seen, however, he did not later recognise that, by the same logic, A-MS variants (rather than just the edited A-Text) *as well as* C-MS variants must be consulted to establish the readings of B, over those passages where there is roughly equivalent text; nor, similarly, did he recognise that both B- and C-MS variants must be consulted when establishing the text of A.

Kane's point (inherited from Chambers and Blackman) was that, given that the C reviser seems to have used a manuscript of B better than the archetype of the existing B-MSS, C-MS evidence can constantly be used as a corrective of the B archetype. But, as in his thesis, Kane gives almost no consideration to the question of what sort of changes the poet might have introduced between B and C.[24] In other words, he does not consider the criteria an editor might use to distinguish between two theoretically possible situations: (1) where the poet starts off with a (possibly inferior) reading in B and then changes it to an improved reading in C, and (2) where the original B reading has been *corrupted* by the B-MSS, and C's improved reading is also the original reading of B. It is reasonable to suppose, as Kane points out, that 'when the reading of the B-archetype for any passage is so bad as to be either impossible or meaningless, while C's reading for the corresponding passage is good, then there is a strong likelihood that B- requires emendation from C-' (p. 12). But it is worrying that Kane seems to think the case for scribal error in B proved if he can show how a variant *might* have arisen as a scribal misreading of the text of C. It does not seem

---

[24] Except at 9 n.2, where he does consider the possibility that, where A and C agree against B, B may 'represent a departure from the text of A-, and C- a return to the original reading'. Kane comments that such a possibility 'seems remote but cannot entirely be ignored', and refers to Chambers, 'The Authorship of "Piers Plowman"', 27 and Blackman, 'Notes on the B-Text MSS of *Piers Plowman*', 518–21 (discussed above, p. 258). Cf. the observation of James Thorpe referred to below.

to occur to him that '*revising authors and erring scribes can some-times change texts in ways that are either attributable to the same causes or, at the least, indistinguishable in their results*'; or, as his colleague Donaldson crisply noted in an article published (indepen-dently) four years later, that there is no reason to assume that 'a poetic revision will never produce the same mechanical pattern as a scribal error'.[25]

Throughout his discussion of the degree to which it is justifiable to use C evidence to correct that of B, Kane considers only the relative likelihood that B- and/or C-MSS are corrupted, not – except very briefly indeed – the likelihood of authorial revision between B and C. An example of such brief consideration is his statement that the 'lost original' of B from which C made his revision – i.e. a highly superior B-MS – will be preserved 'only in the unrevised lines of the C-archetype', implying that it is no good using C to emend B where differences between the two versions are due to authorial revision. But Kane does not discuss how one would distinguish between scribal error and authorial revision – he seems to take such distinction for granted, as unproblematic. It is likely, as suggested above, that the importance of authorial revision between the versions of *Piers Plowman* was obscured for Kane, since his first editorial acquaintance with the poem was over B Passus XVIII–XX, where authorial revision is comparatively slight.

Although he states that 'To force a reading produced by C-manuscripts upon the B-text is a serious undertaking, and not even the very strongest presumption that C-'s original was superior to the B-archetype can excuse the editor from considering every possible relationship between B- and C- at such a point' (p. 11), Kane reveals time and again his disposition to emend the archetypal reading of B to that of C (thus denying the possibility of authorial revision) whenever he can. Thus he says, 'All differences between the B- and C-archetypes other than the trivial sort must be taken to indicate a possible wrong reading in the B-archetype' (p. 12). Half a page later, he writes,

> There will be occasions when the B- and C-readings for a passage differ, but appear on *prima facie* grounds to be equally good. In such cases, before a decision can be made, it will be necessary to show either that one of the two readings is required by the sense of

---

[25] See Robert Adams, 'Editing *Piers Plowman B*', 50; Donaldson, 'The Texts of *Piers Plowman*', 271.

the passage in both texts, or that one of them can easily have developed out of the other by a scribal error or succession of errors. (p. 13)

This comes across as somewhat perverse. It seems the editor already *knows* that one of the two readings has to be scribal, even though he acknowledges that each is acceptable. But why should this be so, when the alternative explanation of authorial revision – in principle, at least as likely – is readily available, which would allow *both* readings, 'equally good', as Kane himself ackowledges, to be authorial? Kane writes with the appearance of relentless and almost scientific logic (note the phrase *prima facie*, and the use of the impersonal construction 'it will be necessary to show', which implies an impartial demonstration of impeccable logic). Yet he simultaneously exemplifies striking illogicality in his failure to consider the possibility that the difference between two readings in two versions of a poem revised by the author could be due to the author's revision; in other words, that both are original. His position was to be aptly delineated some years later by James Thorpe, in his observation that authors will always, if given the chance, revise, but that editors will usually avoid recognition of this possibility – for obvious reasons, given the disabling editorial complexities opened up by authorial revision – 'unless the evidence to demonstrate the fact of revision has been overwhelming'.[26]

Kane summarises his position thus:

> When the present writer began his work on Passus XVIII–XX of [the B-Text], he intended to produce a critical text of this portion of the poem by reconstructing the archetype of the B-manuscripts and correcting this, where it was obviously defective, from the C-text. During the course of this undertaking it became increasingly evident to him that the simple and arbitrary correction of the B-archetype from C-readings is not to be tolerated as a part of the process of editing, but that in every single instance the value of the evidence of the C-manuscripts must be carefully weighed before it can be applied to the correction of the B-archetype. As his work went forward he saw more and more clearly the inadequacy of the archetype, and came to realize the extent to which the editor of B is dependent upon the C-manuscripts. The reconstruction of the B-archetype consequently became simply a step toward determining the relation between the B- and C-texts where the latter does not

---

[26] *Principles of Textual Criticism*, 36. Cf. also John G. Griffith, 'Author-Variants in Juvenal'.

represent a revision of B-. At the same time that the extent of the editor's dependence upon the C-text became apparent, it was, however, also made evident that the certain superiority of the C-poet's original B-manuscript could not be invoked as a simple and arbitrary principle of editing, but that the decay of the unrevised portions of the original in the course of the transmission of the C-text must be taken into account. (p. 25)

Kane finishes by saying that 'the present writer' could 'now proceed with confidence that his methods have been carefully defined, and that the critical text of B- will be nearer to the autograph of the poet than the simple archetype of the B-text manuscripts' (p. 25).

Kane's choice of language is again significant. He refers to himself in the third person, which has a distancing effect and also makes the various processes of judgement he describes sound both dispassionate and rational – whereas in fact they all involve quite considerable issues of taste and personal preference, in the exercise of which rationality plays only a small part. He uses the language of scientific discourse: once his 'methods' have been 'defined', it is simply a matter of proceeding along established processes of reasoning to arrive at a correct result. But textual criticism is often a long way away from such logically determined paths, and it is of course impossible to test textual hypotheses in the way that one can test scientific hypotheses, given the continued absence, in the case of *Piers Plowman*, of a manuscript known to be written by the author. Kane refers not to 'my' critical text of B but 'the' critical text: as if the text has an independent autonomous status, and is not in fact the product of what must inevitably be a number of idiosyncratic and problematic decisions. It seems hard to compare Kane with the egregious Knott, writing thirty years previously, but there is a disquieting and unmistakable echo of the latter's similar reference to an objectively constructed 'CT'.[27]

Meanwhile, Kane's elderly colleague Grattan had published one of the most important contributions to the textual discussion of the poem, an article somewhat portentously entitled 'The Text of *Piers Plowman*: Critical Lucubrations with Special Reference to the Independent Substitution of Similars' (1947). This developed some of the material in his and Chambers' article of 1931.[28] It undermined the

---

[27] See further below, p. 405, on the parallels drawn by Kane between scientific methodology and textual criticism.
[28] See above, pp. 279–81.

recensionist method still further, anticipating Kane's later work in two significant ways: first, in subjecting variants to a minute analysis, organised under various different categories, in the attempt to detect the direction of corruption – regardless of genetic considerations; and second, in emphasising the significance of coincident variation as a factor in interfering with what one would otherwise take to be genetic links between manuscripts. He writes,

> When we find a MS deserting its own and running with an alien family, *our first step*, before labelling this phenomenon 'contamination' or 'mixture', must be to test every such suspicious reading for the possibility of fortuitous and independent change. Agreement in a sufficiently large number of instances will, of course, render the assumption of mere chance unjustifiable; but our opinion as to what constitutes a large number will to some extent depend upon the type of substitution found and upon our estimate of the probable immediate cause of scribal error. (pp. 603–4)

Grattan is more cautious than Kane was later to be about the possibility of detecting the direction of change; thus he points out that in the case of minor changes of word-order, 'it is not always possible to decide which was the original' (p. 596). Another of his remarks is also interesting in view of Kane's reluctance to consider the existence of small-scale authorial revision. Grattan (p. 598) quotes Skeat, 'our great pioneer', on the reading þroly (A Passus IX 107), preserved only by Vernon among the A-MSS: 'I suspect this was the original word, afterwards altered because our author found that many did not know what it meant.' To accept such a motive for change devastates the long established principle for distinguishing between scribal and authorial readings, *difficilior lectio*, since it acknowledges that an author may have simplified his work in order to make it better understood. Grattan might have gone on to quote the rest of Skeat's remarks:

> I draw attention to it [the variant þroly] because I think it will be found that the A-Text contains several provincial words which were after eliminated in order to make the poem more widely understood. William's residence in London enabled him to realize that some of the words of his native country were not known there.[29]

---

[29] *The Vision of William Concerning Piers Plowman ... General Preface, Notes, and Indexes*, 215. Kane discusses the variant on page 156 of his edition of A, commenting that 'it is not manifestly an inferior or easier reading', but that 'the overwhelming manuscript support for [the rival reading] þre dayes, the greater emphasis in þroly, and the sophisticated character of V fully authorize the reader to reject þroly as unoriginal'.

It is fair to say that such awkward, but entirely reasonable, considerations as these are wholly absent from the thinking behind the texts of A and B that Kane later produced. It is easy to see why: if it is allowed that an author might revise his text to produce a reading with characteristics which the 'canons of editing' require us to attribute to a scribe, then the sort of editing which Kane practises becomes hard indeed, if not impossible, to justify.

Grattan does not appear to be aware of the complex issues raised by his quotation of Skeat, and merely comments, 'To [Skeat's] "our author" it would be right to add "or some scribe".' He thus further highlights the difficulty of distinguishing between scribal and authorial variants in the poem.

19

Knott and Fowler, Donaldson, Mitchell, and Russell

In 1952 an important new development took place. The first scholarly edition of *Piers Plowman* since the appearance of Skeat's Parallel-Text in 1886 was published under the joint names of Thomas A. Knott and David C. Fowler, the eventual outcome of the project undertaken in 1907 by the multiple-authorship adherent Knott, pupil of Manly. Knott had completed a critical text of A up to Passus VIII 126, but subsequently turned his interests towards other aspects of Middle English research.[1] His work was continued by David C. Fowler, in a posthumous collaboration, who reproduced his text of A 'virtually as he left it',[2] and added the text he himself had prepared for his Chicago Ph.D. dissertation (completed in 1949), which picked up from where Knott had finished and continued until the end of the poem. The edition is now little used, having been superseded by Kane's Athlone edition of the A-Text in 1960, in which Kane set out the justification for his own textual method by means of demolishing that of Knott–Fowler (see pp. 358ff. below).

Knott–Fowler is the first edition designed for a mainly academic audience. Undergraduates were provided for with a set of explanatory notes, a glossary, and an Introduction with sections on the authorship, metre and alliteration of the poem together with a substantial account (nearly thirty pages) of its historical background, and a bibliography. Fowler's summary of the authorship question tries to steer an equal path between single- and multiple-authorship adherents, but, not surprisingly, presents the case for the latter more persuasively. His long historical section (which deals with matters such as 'The Parish', 'The Three Kinds of Monastic Rule', 'The Pestilence') reaffirms the editorial tradition established by Crowley, and continued by

---

[1] See Knott–Fowler, vii, and p. 239 n. 6 above.
[2] 'except that I have restored four lines (7. 70–73) which [Knott] considered, I think rightly, to be a scribal insertion' (Knott–Fowler, vii).

Whitaker, Wright and Skeat, of viewing the poem primarily as a social and historical document rather than a literary text.

For the '*Piers Plowman* scholar', Fowler wrote a more technical, but short (pp. 20–8), section of the Introduction, on the critical text of the edition. This provided stemmata (slightly different) for both A^1 (see figure 19.1) and A^2 (see figure 19.2), and referred the reader to Knott's 1916 article and Fowler's own doctoral dissertation for evidence of readings (see p. 243 above for Knott–Fowler's use of different sigils).[3]

Fowler acknowledged that

> Of course no single diagram can account for all of the complexities that we inevitably find in a study of this kind, where the text exists in seventeen MSS, copied over a period of more than a hundred years ... No attempt is made to indicate ... aberrations. (p. 26)

He also emphasised that, although the Trinity A-MS had been taken as the copy-text for their edition, its readings had been adhered to only when they could be justified 'by the weight of the evidence, genealogical and other. No matter how plausible the reading of T may seem, it must not be retained if not supported.' T's dialect and spelling had been used as the basis for the text, but 'It should be said that the critical text would have been exactly what it is, save for dialect and spelling, no matter what particular manuscript had been chosen for a basis' (p. 28). The putative scholar is also provided with a further section of 'textual notes', in fact a line-by-line list of (select) collations. Fowler's discussion is disappointingly concise, and does not address the textual problems of the poem raised by Knott earlier; for example, there is no recognition that the editing of A is contingent on that of B and C.

A brief comparison of Knott–Fowler's text with that of Kane's (which appeared several years later in 1960) is illuminating. Visually, the two editions appear very different, owing to the absence in Knott–Fowler of an on-the-page critical apparatus. Kane's critical apparatus often occupies more room on the page than the text, and the text itself is further cluttered with square brackets (indicating depature from the readings of the base manuscript T) and italics (indicating editorial expansion of scribal abbreviations). Both these

---

[3] Knott and Fowler believe that the A-Text comprises two textually separate poems: A^1, i.e. Pro–Passus VIII, edited almost in its entirety by Knott, and A^2, i.e. Passus IX–XI, edited by Fowler alone. See Knott–Fowler, 3, 5–7.

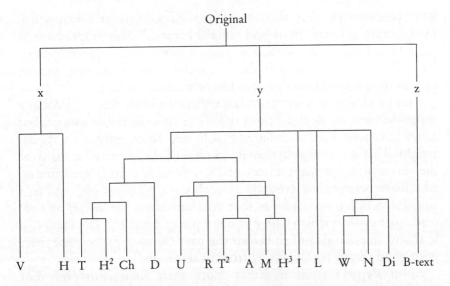

Figure 19.1.   Knott–Fowler's genealogical tree of A¹. (Knott–Fowler's tree is the same as that of Knott in 1916 (Figure 13.1) except that it includes A-MSS Ch, M, and N, all of which had been discovered since that date.)

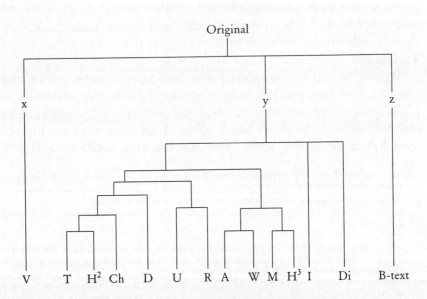

Figure 19.2   Knott–Fowler's genealogical tree of A²

latter characteristics are also absent from Knott–Fowler's text, which by contrast appears clean and unproblematic.[4] This impression is reinforced by the end-section of textual notes, which gives a much less full set of collations than those found in Kane, excluding spelling variations and sometimes more substantial lexical variants.

Knott's choice of text varies unpredictably from Kane's, Fowler's somewhat less so. Both editions took T as their base manuscript, but as we have seen Fowler declared that he and Knott gave it no special weight. This is a strange statement in view of the fact that so many of the variants in the manuscripts of *Piers Plowman* are impossible to adjudicate between on grounds of quality – a plural as opposed to a singular, a difference in tense that does not affect the sense, or rival readings between which 'there is not a pin to choose'.[5] In practice, it is almost impossible not to favour the base manuscript, because there is no good reason for departing from its testimony.

Knott departs from it rather more than Kane, however. For example, he chooses to substitute the reading 'synneles' for 'giltles' in the line (Pro 34)

> And gete gold wiþ here gle giltles, I trowe

which as it stands produces *aaa/ax* alliteration (Schmidt's Type Ic).[6] Here *giltles* is found in TCh alone. Three other manuscripts have readings that look palaeographically similar: *gylelas* L, *gylously* W, and *gylefully* K.[7] The remaining read *synneles* or something very close, producing alliteration equally Langlandian, *aaa/xx* (Schmidt's Type IIa).

Arguments can be mustered for and against both *giltles* and *synneles*. For example, an original *giltles* explains the existence of LWK's respective readings, which are all close enough to *giltles* to be misreadings. On the other hand, *giltles* could have been substituted by a hyper-alliterating scribe. But *synneles*, too, could be a typical

---

[4] They replace thorns and yoghs with equivalent modern spelling, following the customary practice with editions of Chaucer, presumably in order to render the text more palatable to student readers. Salter – Pearsall and Schmidt do the same (see p. 40 n. 8).

[5] Chambers, 'The Manuscripts of *Piers Plowman* in the Huntington Library', 10, quoting Housman.

[6] See Schmidt, 507.

[7] This reading highlights the varying treatment by the poem of minstrels. In A and B at this point, minstrels are sinless/guiltless; in Z (if that version be admitted as authorial) and in C, they are condemned. See Z Pro 34–6, A Pro 33–4, B Pro 33–4, C Pro 35–40 (which runs together two categories, minstrels and 'japers and janglers', kept distinct in A and B). K's reading may be the result of C contamination, by sense if not by specific reading, since it was evidently subject to contamination from elsewhere in C; cf. Kane, 36–7.

scribal substitution of a more emphatic, less precise, more usual original. This was presumably the reasoning which led Kane to retain T's reading in his text, along with the consideration that, given that it is hard to make any sensible decision between these various alternatives, one might as well stick to the reading of the base text.

Since Knott and Fowler offer us no discussion of individual readings, it is impossible to tell why Knott rejected T's *giltles*. We know that Knott, however, believed that it was important to consult the B- and C-Texts when coming to a decision between A variants (Kane, as we have also seen above, did not share this view despite its championship by Chambers and Grattan earlier). Thus it is likely that Knott consulted Skeat's B-Text, to find that B too reads *synneles* at this point, and decided that B's support clinched the decision against *giltles*.[8]

The tortuous (and torturous) nature of constructing editions of *Piers Plowman* is well illustrated by this example. Who can say whether either Kane or Knott was right? It is, moreover, interesting to note that Kane–Donaldson and Schmidt (in his first Everyman edition), presumably without reopening the question of decision between the A variants, emend the reading of B to that of Kane's edited text of A.[9]

This is a specific case. But it is also impossible to tell the general grounds on which Knott and Fowler made their judgements between variants. Analysing a small sample (Pro I) of Knott's text reveals that the manuscripts whose readings he rejects from his text do not consistently fall into any genealogical family. Hence, although he has constructed a manuscript stemma, he does not seem to have made any use of it for establishing his text. He must then have used the eclectic method of establishing the text later espoused by Kane: with the crucial difference that he does not explain his methods to his readers.

---

[8] To be precise, WHmCrGYCLMFH read *synnelees* (F has omitted the first half of the line and run it together with the preceding one), while OC² read *not synles*. The line is B Pro 34. It is worth adding that, although I have not systematically collated Knott–Fowler's text against the A- and B-MS variants (as given in Kane and Kane–Donaldson respectively), I have come across a number of other instances where (*pace* Knott's stated policy, described p. 245 above) their text does *not* follow B's at points of difficulty. Thus at Passus VI 2, VI 71, and VII 5 (all in Knott's portion), Knott–Fowler retain MS T's reading despite the fact that the alternative B-Text reading at this point is found in some of the other A-MSS present (at Passus VI 71 Knott–Fowler fail to record the A-MS variation in their textual notes). I discuss all these readings elsewhere; see pp. 417, 400 and 376 respectively.

[9] In his new editions of the poem (the Longman Parallel-Text, and the Everyman B-Text, both published in 1995), Schmidt reads *synneles* in both A and B. His Everyman textual note (363) observes that the emendation *giltles* (as he points out, originally Wright's) is unnecessary on alliterative grounds.

As might be expected, Knott's taste does not correspond with Kane's. Kane prefers his Langland elliptic, terse, understated, and punning, while Knott will choose variants which fill out the syntax and offer transparent meaning. Thus Knott retains conjunctions such as 'and' between clauses where Kane rejects them; Knott keeps 'but' and 'full' where Kane will choose 'ac' and 'well'; Knott chooses *fayneden*, *poundis*, and *bond men* where Kane has *flitte thanne*, *poundide*, and *bondage*.[10] Fowler's text, by contrast, is extremely close to that of Kane.[11]

In the same year, 1952, Fowler published an article designed to support the thesis that A and B were by different authors.[12] His strategy was (1) to establish (with A-MS evidence) what scribes do to texts, and (2) to seek to show that the differences between B(C) and A are of exactly the same order as scribal changes of original A-Text material. Thus it would look as if the differences between A and B(C) must be attributable to scribes, not to an author. Fowler's analysis of these scribal errors in A-MSS is simply concerned to show how one version might have arisen (by means of eyeskip, dittography, etc.) from another. He does not consider the relative quality of lines and readings, and nor does he consider that he could in some instances reverse his arguments, and by applying the same rules derive the supposedly authorial version from the supposedly scribal. It is as if he makes up his mind in advance, and then finds *post hoc* reasons for justifying his decision.

Another problem with his argument is that he supposes the B and C versions as witnessed by the extant manuscripts to be accurate copies of the B and C originals (whether produced by the same person as A or a different one). But that is unlikely to be the case. When he shows that the B and C versions read texts which, in the light of A, look scribal rather than authorial, he by no means proves that the B and C versions are hence by a writer different from A. The B- and C-MSS could be corrupt scribal copies of B and C originals which were *exactly the same as A*. In other words, even if we accept that scribal error took place in the production of B and C manuscripts, there is no need to locate it in the process of composition of B and C – instead, it could take place *after* the composition of B and C.

---

[10] Pro 42, 86, and 96 respectively. For discussion see Kane, 160 and 434.

[11] For example, there are fewer than ten differences, all very minor, between Kane's and Fowler's texts over the first 100 lines of Passus IX.

[12] 'The Relationship of the Three Texts of *Piers the Plowman*'.

Fowler states (p. 16 n. 11) that 'Throughout this analysis I am trying to avoid making literary judgements about the quality of the B- and C-revisions. One reason for this, which I hope seems obvious by now, is that many of these are not revisions at all, in the literary sense, but rather adjustments of error in transmission.' The objection to this is that identification of 'error' as opposed to 'revision' must be inevitably reliant upon a literary judgement. Fowler is making the same mistake as before: just because the difference between one version and another *may* be explained in terms of known scribal processes of transmission, that is not to say that the difference *should* be thus explained. Fowler goes on to give a second reason for his avoidance of literary judgements: 'my thesis does not depend on literary evaluation of any passage, although it is to be expected that scribal tampering with a poem as excellent as the A-version will produce debasement of the text'. But how does he then explain those passages in B (but not in A) which show undoubted literary talent?

Fowler's article was immediately attacked on two sides at once. Donaldson replied from Yale in the following issue of the same journal, while five months later A. G. Mitchell published an article in a different journal, writing jointly with a colleague, G. H. Russell, from the University of Sydney.[13] Donaldson wrote with characteristic urbanity, acuity, and wit, making criticisms of Fowler's argument such as those given above. Mitchell's and Russell's work is less elegant and more tendentious. They dispute Fowler's hypothetical reconstruction of the B reviser's misreading of A on grounds which are sometimes not acceptable;[14] although other of their main points, made also by Donaldson, must stand, for example that, given 'the chances of error coming in between the author's original and the archetype of the known manuscripts ... the relationship of the archetypes is [not necessarily] the relationships of the autographs' (p. 445).

Both of the retorts to Fowler, amusingly enough, make judgements on the quality of specific B lines and passages which later prove to be hostages to fortune. As we have seen, Fowler argued that differences between A and B were due not to authorial revision but to the misreading of A by a corrupting B reviser. The three single authorship advocates claim that the B lines in question are not due to error but

---

[13] E. T. Donaldson, 'The Texts of *Piers Plowman*'; A. G. Mitchell and G. H. Russell, 'The Three Texts of "Piers the Plowman"'.

[14] See for example the first paragraph of 451, or the argument on 455–6, where Mitchell and Russell make absurdly unverifiable claims about how and why a scribe's eye would skip from one piece of text to another.

are, on the contrary, the original words of the revising poet. Yet in several instances, notably A Passus I 96–102/B Passus I 98–104, the B editors Kane and Donaldson subsequently agree with Fowler that the B reading is scribal, and in 1975 emend B to read as (Kane's) A.[15] This illustrates how precariously subjective can be the judgements of the relative qualities of readings, especially when the driving force behind the editorial analysis is a wish to demonstrate the virtue of a hypothesis subscribed to on prior grounds.

Fowler's first article on *Piers Plowman* was ill-judged. And the textual claims of his edition probably deserved the excoriating reception they met at Kane's hands in 1960. But it is striking that Fowler's later work on the text of the poem has been unfailingly perceptive, judicious, and highly intelligent, although his continued advocacy of multiple (or dual) authorship has consigned him to an eccentric fringe of *Piers Plowman* studies. His powers of analysis are well illustrated in his devastating review of Kane and Donaldson's B-Text, which Fowler was in many ways uniquely equipped to write as one of the very few scholars of the poem whose textual knowledge rivalled Kane and Donaldson's own. In this review, as in that of Kane's edition of A, Schmidt's (first) edition of B, and Pearsall's edition of C, Fowler has shown that he is prepared to carry out the back-breaking examination of text and variants, line by line and word by word, essential for a comprehensive picture of how textual principles have been applied. Yet at the same time he is able to retain the larger view of textual issues implied by an editor's individual decisions,[16] while maintaining throughout a moderate and generous tone of collaborative discussion, far removed from the occasionally Housemanesque savagery of George Kane.

George Russell, Mitchell's co-author, joined the Athlone team

---

[15] See Mitchell and Russell, 'The Three Texts of "Piers the Plowman"', 447–8, Donaldson, 'The Texts of *Piers Plowman*: Scribes and Poets', 269–70. Other examples occur at A Passus V 95–7/ B Passus V 113–16 (Kane–Donaldson: V 115–18), discussed Mitchell and Russell, 'The Three Texts of "Piers the Plowman"', 447–8, Donaldson, 'The Texts of *Piers Plowman*: Scribes and Poets', 271; A Passus IX 53–4/B Passus VIII 62–3, discussed Mitchell and Russell, 'The Three Texts of "Piers the Plowman"', 449.

[16] Thus at the start of his review of Kane–Donaldson, he points out that, in the first half of the B-Text, which contains 2,200 lines found also in A and 1,100 lines new to B, the editors make emendations *causa metri* to 35 of the 2,200 lines carried over from A, but by contrast make emendations *causa metri* to 125 of the 1,100 lines new to B. The statement of so striking a disparity stops one in one's tracks. If we accept Kane and Donaldson's editorial decisions, we must also accept that material new to the B version was copied *eight times less accurately* by scribes than material previously present in A – a literally incredible hypothesis. The only tolerable alternative is to accept that Kane and Donaldson were far too zealous in their emendation of the B archetype.

some time between 1956 (when the minutes for 4 May of the Athlone Press Board of Management record Mitchell as still the editor of C) and 1962, by which time he had replaced Mitchell. The previous year Mitchell had become Deputy Vice-Chancellor of the University of Sydney, and seems to have given up research, moving in 1965 to become Vice-Chancellor of Macquarie University. Russell was appointed to his Sydney chair, and delivered an inaugural lecture entitled 'The Evolution of a Poem: Some Reflections on the Textual Tradition of *Piers Plowman*' (1962).

Russell was to make a far more significant contribution to the textual history of the poem than his senior colleague. He has written a number of thoughtful and illuminating articles on the genesis of the poem and on the C-Text scribes and commentators.[17] More importantly, by 1973 he had completed a provisional text of C up to the point where its line numbers could be cited (see Kane–Donaldson, p. vi). But the edition has been subject to very extensive delay and has not yet appeared; it is now said to be due in spring 1997, edited by both Russell and Kane.[18]

Russell's essays on the poem are characterised by a sort of reverent ruminativeness, which both treats its subject with immense respect and licenses violent editorial action upon it. A number of different assumptions and perceptions coexist in his work, often in awkward tension. Thus he writes of Langland's greatness of a poet, 'To generalise and, more, to rationalise the working of a creative mind as large, as subtle, and as obliquely allusive as that of Langland is clearly so hazardous as to constitute an impertinence. No kind of summation or discussion can confidently or adequately identify the strategy of the poem or expose the dynamic of its realisation.'[19] On the other

---

[17] His work on the C-Text scribes has been particularly valuable; see 'Some Early Responses to the C-Version of *Piers Plowman*' and ' "As They Read It" '.

[18] This information comes from the Athlone Press, who have periodically advertised the book as forthcoming since 1990. A biographical account of Russell may be found in his Festschrift, written by Vincent Buckley, 'George Russell as a Topic in his Own Right'; see also the note in the same volume by Clive James, a former pupil, 'George Russell: A Reminiscence'. Buckley makes it clear that Russell, who has had a peripatetic professional life, selflessly devoted much of his career to administration and teaching in the interests of his various colleagues, pupils, and institutions, and comments that, as he moved from one appointment to another, Russell's 'opportunities for research shrank slightly year by year' (5). He also writes 'He hated to choose *finally*; his spirit rejected finality' (12), which may shed some light on the continued non-appearance of his edition of C, as may the quoted reminiscence of a former pupil that Russell would mention places in the poem where he was not certain whether or not to emend, and 'say how he was putting off making a final decision about it' (5).

[19] 'The Imperative of Revision in the C Version of *Piers Plowman*', 234.

hand, he on several occasions concedes – as his fellow editors never do – that 'no mediæval author in the alliterative tradition would have felt sufficiently strongly about the minutiæ of his line structure to attempt a word-by-word check of his manuscript' – in the way, for example, of a modern-day editor of the stamp of George Kane, or indeed Russell himself. He continues,

> Perhaps I am wrong, but I feel that a poem whose metrical structure is relatively free and whose verbal organization only occasionally gains its force from the close interrelation of elements within the line might easily fail to proclaim to its reviser, even if he were the author, that at that or this point a scribal corruption had been allowed to enter.[20]

Elsewhere, in an article written for George Kane's Festschrift, he refers to the C-reviser 'often' rephrasing 'the poet's own infelicities and inadequacies' (sc. in the B-Text) (p. 241), with no apparent recognition of the problem for C-Text editing caused by Kane and Donaldson's refusal to allow that any such 'infelicities and inadequacies' might exist in the B-Text in the first place, the two editors as it were anticipating the action of the C-reviser, in their extensive emendation of B, in a way that places severe logical strain on the editorial enterprise. Again in this article, Russell declares, 'it would seem also to be the case that the revising poet did not – for whatever reason – always concern himself with what we may venture to call the detail of the line. What may appear to a modern hypercritical eye as more explicit, more emphatic, easier, or accidental seems not always to have concerned the revising poet.'[21]

These remarks, which seem unexceptionably reasonable, would appear to undermine fatally the 'deep' editing engaged in by his two fellow editors, since they remove any justification for the sort of meticulous and pervasive alterations Kane and Donaldson make to the B archetype, on precisely the grounds that readings which appear to us 'as more explicit, more emphatic, easier, or accidental' cannot be attributed to the author, but must be the work of scribes. It is difficult to imagine how one of the Athlone editors can have made such comments, given the extraordinarily interventionist nature of the editorial behaviour evidenced in the edition of B.[22] Yet there is no

---

[20] 'The Evolution of a Poem', 43–4.   [21] 'The Imperative of Revision', 242.
[22] Though Donaldson comes close to Russell's position when he writes of the difficulty of distinguishing between scribal and authorial writing in *Piers Plowman*, 'particularly when

suggestion that either Russell or Kane and Donaldson recognise the havoc that Russell's views wreak upon their editorial enterprise.

Russell frequently stresses what he believes to be the sporadic and unfinished nature of the revision from B to C, and postulates the existence of an 'editor' of C, 'a reader of special authority' who read the poem 'reverently', and 'made no heavy-handed attack upon a text which was only occasionally patently defective'.[23] He accepts that editorially perceived errors in B have been let stand by the author in C (and considered, at any rate in 1969, that they should continue to be let stand by the editor in C).[24] These and others are extremely complicated hypotheses, which can be neither proved or disproved. If acted upon, they authorise an alarmingly wide range of editorial activity, despite the fact that the remarks already quoted might seem to advise editorial caution and restraint in emending the evidence of the manuscripts. But Russell writes strongly against the sort of pusillanimous editing which allows the scribes priority over the editors, urging that we demand of our editors 'that they supply us with texts edited in such a way that the true lineaments of the original are revealed. This can only be done', he says, 'by courageously and unremittingly eliminating that mass of scribal corruption which is endemic in almost all Middle English texts.'[25] In keeping with this, he strongly supports the line taken by Kenneth Sisam, and quoted above (p. 79 n. 38), on the editing of Old English texts, that conjectural emendation should be vigorously pursued for purposes of 'probing as well as healing' (although his advocacy of editorial conjecture is somewhat less extreme than that of his colleague George Kane).[26] Thus he declares, 'Certainly in their work on the *Piers Plowman* manuscripts,

---

we cannot be sure that he [the author] was operating under our own aesthetic doctrine that trifles make perfection' ('The Texts of *Piers Plowman*', 272).

23   '"As They Read It"', 175–6.   24   See p. 391 n. 23 below.

25   'Editorial Theory and Practice in Middle English Texts', 168.

26   *Ibid.*, 168–71. This article is evidently a meditation on Kane's 'Conjectural Emendation', published three years previously in 1969. There Kane had argued (following Chambers) that the editorial principles evolved from the study of classical texts and of the New Testament should be applied to Middle English editing and in particular *Piers Plowman*, and had quoted Sisam's advocacy of more active editing without noting, as Russell does, the qualification that Sisam wrote 'of Old English manuscripts, and in particular of Old English verse which survives in a single late manuscript' (170). As I observe below (p. 373), it is questionable whether emendation practices designed to correct manuscripts written by scribes who copied their texts many years, often centuries, after they were originally written, should be applied to manuscripts written by scribes in their mother tongue (though perhaps of a different dialect) within a few decades of original composition. See K. Sisam, *Studies in the History of Old English Literature*, 30, 38–44, and cf. E. G. Stanley, 'Unideal Editing of Old English Verse', esp. 256–7, 263.

the Athlone editors have come to the view that Sisam's general position is sound and that really adequate editorial work on Middle English texts presupposes a most exacting scrutiny of the witnesses offered by the manuscripts and a generally sceptical attitude towards their testimony.' This means that 'The resulting texts will consequently contain a good deal of conjectural emendation where we have felt obliged to depart from the archetypal testimony'.[27]

At the same time, however, Russell claims that the Athlone editors' 'guiding principle' has been 'that the testimony of the manuscripts is not to be abandoned unless it can be shown beyond reasonable doubt that the present state of the text is indefensible'.[28] The next two chapters will make it clear, I hope, that while this is a reasonably fair description of Kane's practice, it could not be further from a satisfactory account of that of Kane and Donaldson.

[27] 'Editorial Theory and Practice' 170, 172–3.   [28] *Ibid.*, 173.

PART V

The Athlone Press edition

20

The Athlone A-Text

KANE AND THE ATHLONE PRESS

We have seen from the announcements made in *Speculum* in 1951 by Grattan that there had been some considerable changes of plan over the form and editorship of Chambers and Grattan's original edition of *Piers Plowman*. Changes in EETS's 'policy' had made their publication of the edition 'impracticable', and hence the editors were negotiating with the in-house press of the University of London, Athlone.[1]

The Athlone Press was sold into private hands in 1979, and then or earlier most of its records were destroyed. Fortunately, the minutes of the Board meetings, together with a few other items, were preserved and are now accessible to readers of the University of London's library. Item 26 of the meeting of Friday 13 October 1950 records the Athlone Press Board of Management's resolution 'That the offer by Professor A. H. Smith on behalf of himself and other scholars of a definitive edition of *Piers Plowman* in 6 volumes be accepted in principle, subject to the proviso that pending further discussions with the promoters the Board shall not be regarded as committed to a specific number of volumes.'[2] A later minute (12 October 1951) records autumn 1953 as the projected date for the submission of volume I (the A-Text), but Kane did not actually deliver his manuscript until October 1955, when he became Professor of English Language and Medieval Literature at Royal Holloway College, London (having in the interim become Reader at University College). Since Grattan's death in 1951, Kane had recast the edition of A in its entirety.

---

[1] See p. 311 above.
[2] The minutes of 8 December 1950 record that two members of the Athlone Board had been satisfied after a discussion with Smith that 'all six volumes were integral to the plan of the edition'.

The Athlone Press recognised the work as exceptional. At the suggestion of A. H. Smith, the Secretary (W. D. Hogarth) sent the manuscript to a friend of his, Kenneth Sisam, for assessment. As we have seen, Sisam had corresponded with Chambers fourteen years previously about an edition of *Piers Plowman* for OUP, expressing 'great desire' to learn more about the poem's textual problems. Hogarth explained to him that Smith, under whose auspices the Press had originally accepted the edition, was now no longer active as general editor, and asked Sisam for confirmation that the work produced by Kane, 'quite a young man [Kane was by now thirty-nine] who has not yet made his name by other textual work', was 'not merely the promising effort of a young scholar but what, in the circumstances, it really ought to be' – a 'solid monument'. In particular, he asked for answers to two questions: first, whether Kane had been accurate in his handling of the manuscripts; and second, whether he had adopted a sound method. As regards the latter, he commented,

> he has started from the point, and very much with Smith's blessing, that the methods of textual criticism used by previous editors of *Piers Plowman* are faulty and out-of-date, and that it is necessary to tackle the problem by using canons of criticism that have been much more fully worked out in the Classical Field than in English studies. He is principally concerned to demolish the edition of Knott–Fowler. This accounts for the enormous length of the Introduction. To our own lay eyes he seems to have built up a pretty formidable and carefully argued case, but perhaps to have done it still a little too much in the spirit of the able young man out to upset his elders and, if he can, to make their flesh creep.[3]

The minutes of the Athlone meeting dealing with the submitted edition (10 February 1956) record an unparalleled amount of attention devoted to it. The Board were concerned to establish that Kane's work was utterly sound, given the importance of the work for Middle English studies and also the expense of producing so large and typographically complex a volume.[4] The minutes reproduce the Secretary's account of Sisam's report (which apparently amounted to 2,000 words).[5] The report seems to have been extremely favourable, and probably displayed the pragmatism and good sense typical both

---

[3] Letter dated 15 October 1955, now in the possession of Miss Celia Sisam.
[4] See Item 390, 10 February 1956.
[5] The sole surviving copy of this report is in the possession of Professor Kane.

of Sisam himself and of the qualities in books and scholarship that he most admired.[6] He warned the Board that he wrote 'from the point of view of an ex-publisher and a probable user of the book ... not competent to give an opinion on fine points in *Piers Plowman* on which students of the text disagree'. He approved the Board's commitment to publishing B and C, but expressed some doubt as to the value of a glossary. He suggested there was need for

> more caution over a commitment to volumes of commentary, partly because 'almost anything medieval might be said to have some bearing on something in *Piers Plowman*', and therefore a commentary might be 'sprawling' or 'partial', and partly because an Oxford scholar, Mr. J. A. W. Bennett, is known to be at work at a replacement of the OUP. Skeat edition in which the commentary would be the special new feature.[7]

In fact, Bennett never completed this undertaking, which Sisam admitted was 'far distant'. Instead, OUP issued a reprint of Skeat's Parallel-Text edition in 1954, with an updated bibliography provided by Bennett, who later went on to produce a new version of Skeat's student edition of the Prologue and Passus I–VII of the B-Text (something Sisam had first discussed with Chambers).[8]

In Sisam's view, the 'special feature' of Kane's edition was his lengthy Introduction, in which he 'sets forth the history of the MS tradition, describes the problems whch arise and gives a reasoned statement of the principles upon which he has founded his edition and which involve certain important departures from the canons of textual criticism followed by the previous editors of *Piers Plowman*'. But his opus was

> 'a comprehensive, not a definitive edition: it contains more facts or material than any in existence or in contemplation'; it should not be called *definitive* because it may well be impossible ever to produce

---

[6] See p. 298 above. Hogarth wrote back to thank Sisam for his '*magnificent*' report. In a letter Sisam later (17 March 1963) wrote to his daughter, Miss Celia Sisam, three years after the publication of Kane's edition, he commented, 'Kane's *Piers Plowman* has merits: he has worked hard and is sane. But I see no signs of brilliance. I think Knott–Fowler was right to use the B-text in many places where they are virtually coincident, because it must be based on a copy of A *in the author's hands* if all the work of one man.' This is an important point (Kane–Donaldson get round it by postulating that the B-reviser used a corrupt manuscript of A; see pp. 401ff. below). As noted above, however, it does not appear that Knott–Fowler *did* use B in this way; see p. 333 n. 8.

[7] Quoted from the Secretary's report.

[8] See p. 252 above and p. 410 below.

an unchallengeable text, 'since in the end, all the MS. variants must be considered and the choice made by personal judgement.'[9]

In certain sections of the Introduction, apparently, the argument was 'not fully established', while others contained 'more detail than is needed to support the conclusions reached'. Summing up, Sisam felt that 'the faults of this edition are mainly in its superfluities and would be removed with these'. Kane was informed who the reader was, and wrote a letter of reply to the Board. He stood up for the importance of a glossary, 'pointing out that the glossaries of previous editions are notoriously inadequate but constantly cited, e.g. in OED, and that the need for an authoritative glossary is frequently reiterated in current articles on *Piers Plowman*'. And on the commentary, he suggested there was no need for an early decision: 'Let us wait and see what the position is when the texts are out.' Kane further stated the current position on editorial collaboration: 'the closest collaboration is desired by all three editors (himself, Professor Mitchell of Sydney, and Professor Donaldson of Yale) ... all available information is shared ... the only restriction has been that imposed by distance'.

One important criticism made by Sisam explains what many have felt to be a defect of the edition when it eventually appeared.[10] As it now stands, Kane's edition includes only brief descriptions of the manuscripts. Apparently, his early version contained full ones, but Sisam felt that these might well be pruned. Kane promised that 'he would be prepared to shorten this section if required to do so by the Board "which should also then assume responsibility"'. He would himself regard the omission of such palaeographical material as 'a pity'.

The Board resolved to ask Kane to act as general editor in replacement of Smith. Quirk is mentioned as a co-compiler of the projected glossary, 'on which Professor Smith may also be able to give some help'. But 'no other scholar is effectively connected with the enterprise'. Both Mitchell and Donaldson expected to be in London during the summer of that year (1956), so it was 'particularly desirable that arrangements for editorial control should be decided now so that the three text editors can work out its implications while

---

[9] Hogarth reports Sisam's words to the Athlone Board, placing exact quotations within (single) quotation marks.

[10] For example by A. I. Doyle; see his review. The only comparable edition in Middle English, Manly-Rickert's *Canterbury Tales* (1940), had included very full descriptions of the manuscripts.

they are together'. Evidently the Board were highly impressed by Kane's scholarship and by his reply to Sisam, for they decided to accept Kane's A-Text 'on the understanding that Professor Kane shall be free to make such use as he may judge proper of the comments furnished by the Board's adviser'. On 19 February 1956 Kane wrote to accept 'with pleasure' the Board's invitation to become general editor, 'provided that Professors Mitchell and Donaldson agree to that arrangement'. Further minutes record that they did, and that discussion as to possible differences in editorial opinion between the three editors had been satisfactorily resolved. The Athlone Press Annual Report of 1955–6 stated that Kane's A-Text 'is now in production' (its delayed appearance, in 1960, might possibly have been due to a dispute in the printing industry reported in the draft annual report of 1958–9 as having held up the publication of thirteen of the Athlone Press books). On 6 December 1957 the edition was in proof, and the Board agreed that the three editors should receive 10 per cent royalties from the sales of their respective volumes after the costs incurred on production and publication had been recouped by the Press. It was decided to print 2,000 copies of A, at a cost later estimated as £7,450; the volume eventually produced was a massive 457 pages long, priced at £3. 10s. a copy. Athlone's draft annual report for 1959–60 mentions the publication of the A version as being 'of special interest', noting that 'this impressive contribution to Middle English scholarship stems from a project launched over half a century ago by the late R. W. Chambers and J. H. G. Grattan', and records the Board's 'natural pleasure in being able to report the completion of the first stage of an important and costly undertaking which has been so long and closely associated with the University'. By 19 June 1964 Kane's edition had sold 982 copies; by 31 July 1972 the initial print run of 2,000 copies was nearly exhausted and the book's credit balance stood at £621. The Press considered the possibility of a reprint, but its finances were on the point of collapse and the reprint was deferred until 1988, when Athlone had been transferred to private hands.

THE ATHLONE EDITIONS: GENERAL CONSIDERATIONS

Before discussing in detail the characteristics of Kane's edition of the A-Text, and Kane–Donaldson's edition of the B-Text, it will be helpful to step back and look at the two Athlone editions from a more distant perspective.[11] Both editions inherited the hypothetical model of three original texts: it is supposed that Langland wrote first A, and then two revisions, B and C. As we have seen, this model was first established by Skeat, who nevertheless believed that the B-MSS RF and the Ilchester C-MS represented intermediate versions. When Skeat's views were first challenged, by Manly in 1906, it was his hypothesis of single authorship rather than his hypothesis of three original texts that came under attack. Both Manly's opposition to Skeat, and Chambers' subsequent defence of Skeat, took over almost without question the three-text model. The ferocity of the authorship controversy effectively blinded critics to the fact that the exclusive existence of A, B, and C had never been proved, and was perhaps not susceptible to proof.[12]

As stated above, the three-text model has much to recommend it, since most of the fifty-odd surviving manuscripts do fall roughly into one of three distinct narrative shapes, that of A, or B, or C. But it also has significant limitations. If one compares the manuscripts by lines and readings rather than by broad narrative shape, the multiplicity and diversity of variational readings become overwhelming, forcing the question whether the three-text model is a sufficient explanation for the chaos of divergent and convergent readings.

As we shall see, Kane was most unwilling to entertain the possibility of authorial revision other than from A to B and B to C; and the editing of B did not change his mind. The question of the validity, integrity and authenticity of A, B, and C is raised in both editions, but only briefly, and in highly theoretical terms. The conclusion is that there were three original versions, and three only, and consequently that everything pointing away from this is scribal (Kane, pp. 19–20; Kane–Donaldson, pp. 70–72). Closely linked to this conclusion are a number of significant and pervasive assumptions about Langland as author, sometimes clearly set down in black and white and sometimes not. For example (and both editions make this perfectly clear), Kane and Donaldson assume that Langland's writing

---

[11] Some of the following material in both this chapter and the next originally appeared in the form of articles: 'The Textual Principles of Kane's A Text', 'George Kane's Processes of Revision', and 'Authorial vs. Scribal Writing in *Piers Plowman*' (Copyright, Center for Medieval and Early Renaissance Studies, SUNY Binghamton). The important article by Robert Adams, 'Editing *Piers Plowman B*', is essential reading for an understanding of the editing of Kane and Kane–Donaldson; many of Adams' observations, explications and insights run in parallel to the points I make here, and he discusses a number of significant additional matters.

[12] See above, pp. 182ff., esp. p. 187 n. 13.

was of a totally consistent and invariably high quality, and of a completely different order from anything a scribe was capable of, so that, once editors have worked out his (supposed) *usus scribendi* from the corrupt manuscript evidence, they can turn round and apply this standard back to the manuscripts, and usually distinguish infallibly between what Langland would have written and what is the result of scribal tinkering or misprision.[13] This applies down to the smallest textual detail. (There is a troubling element of circularity here, although it is true that all editing involves some degree of comparable circularity.)[14] The notorious example of this is Kane and Donaldson's metrical theory: they assume that Langland wrote according to one and one only alliterative pattern, so that lines not conforming to this pattern are, *prima facie*, scribal.[15] More generally, the assumption that Langland wrote to a consistently high standard is in some ways a peculiar one given the evidence we have about the poet. Langland's obsessive rewriting of the poem, involving deletion of lines and readings as well as additions, suggests that, in his own opinion at least, the quality of his output could vary.[16]

Another example of Kane and Donaldson's beliefs about Langland (and one which they never convincingly or even explicitly argue for) is their assumption that he revised his poem from A to B to C in a logical and consecutive way, never, for instance, going back to an A

---

13 Examples of this belief abound in both Introductions. Consider for instance Kane–Donaldson, 82ff., where the two editors repeatedly consider, and reject, the possibility that readings in B which they judge defective in comparison with equivalent ones in AC could be attributable to a failure of judgement in the poet: 'in this situation it seems to us right to reject the possibility of the erratic poet for the established certainty of the inaccurate copyist'. Kane and Donaldson never, so far as I can see, consider the possibility that their identification of the respective quality of some of these readings might be fallible, although this has been suggested by various of their critics. See for example Robert Adams, Editing and the Limitations of the *'Durior Lectio'*, esp. 14 n.3.

14 See Kane–Donaldson, 212, and cf. A. E. Housman, *Selected Prose*, 29, and p. 279 above on Westcott and Hort's three-stage method of textual analysis.

15 Their method of argument is revealing here. They judge that 'almost a third of the B version's two-stave lines are scribal from considerations other than of versification' (136), and take this as an overwhelmingly strong indication that *all* two-stave lines are scribal. But the propositions (1) that scribes frequently corrupt by dropping a stave, and (2) that Langland sometimes wrote two-stave lines and considered them acceptable, are not mutually exclusive. As Donaldson had pointed out over twenty-five years previously, there is no good reason for 'the assumption that a poetic revision will never produce the same mechanical pattern as a scribal error' ('The Texts of *Piers Plowman*', 271; cf. the independent rephrasing by Adams quoted above, p. 324). Two-stave lines are accepted as Langlandian by Schmidt (507); his account of Type III alliteration includes the forms *axax* and *abab* rejected by Kane–Donaldson. Duggan, however, does not accept two-stave lines; see e.g. 'Notes Toward a Theory of Langland's Meter', 43.

16 The third Athlone author, G. H. Russell, takes a different view of the uniform quality of the poet's writing; see above, p. 338.

reading for his C version, having written something different for B.[17] In this they follow in the footsteps of Elsie Blackman (see p. 258 above). Agreement between A and C against B is thus regarded as *prima facie* evidence that the B archetype is corrupt, and in almost all cases where this occurs Kane and Donaldson emend B to read as AC.[18] Kane and Donaldson also assume that each time Langland rewrote, he rewrote for the better, so that a reading in B which is (by their lights) inferior to the equivalent one in A, is necessarily a scribal reading. Both Wordsworth and Auden have been held up as counter-examples to this theory of progressively improved authorial revision.[19]

It is clear why Kane and Donaldson should have made these assumptions. Believing in three texts as they did, and having to get these out in a reasonable form to the printer, they were under what Derek Pearsall has called 'the pressure of the search for editorial certainty'.[20] To acknowledge the possibility of more than three original versions, of inconsistent revision, of authorial and scribal interdependence, is to do away altogether with the possibility of constructing a three-text critical edition of the poem; for such possibilities fatally undermine the grounds on which such an edition can be produced. There is another explanation also for the Athlone editors' striking reluctance to allow for the possibility that the author may have changed his mind back and forth between versions or written more than just three. When Kane inherited the *Piers Plowman* project, there may still have been a need to argue against the theory of multiple authorship – a view pretty much laid to rest by his own edition.[21] In order to beat down the threat posed by the multiple authorship party, there was an incentive to minimise the differences between texts so as to argue that all three were written by a single author. The end result was the same: a tendency to attribute differences between texts to scribes, not author(s).[22]

---

[17] The assumption is similarly unquestioned by Russell; cf. e.g. 'The Imperative of Revision in the C Version of *Piers Plowman*', 235.

[18] See, e.g., Kane–Donaldson, 149 ff.

[19] E.g. by Thorlac Turville-Petre, in his review of Kane–Donaldson. Cf. Whitaker above, p. 39. The large and indeterminate number of the various revisions Wordsworth made to his poems form an interesting comparison with what may have been Langland's textual practice also: see Jonathan Wordsworth, 'Revision as Making', and Stephen Gill, 'Words-worth's Poems'. Gill comments 'Criticism must recognize that Wordsworth's poems exist in varying states and that it is neither responsible nor sensible to vest authority in a single version' (59).

[20] 'The Ilchester Manuscript of *Piers Plowman*,' 192.   [21] See p. 314 n. 9 above.

[22] Cf. Allen's rejection of Skeat's notion that the manuscripts of C represented three separate authorial stages of composition, p. 268 above.

But the three-text model, and the assumption that editors can meditate on the tangle of manuscripts and variants to construct, or reconstruct, something satisfactorily close to three original texts, has never been finally established. Some editors of selections from the poem at the turn of the century seem to regard the question as not finally settled;[23] while Kane and Donaldson themselves make it clear that they believe that the C reviser, at any rate, produced his version with some substantial inattention to detail.[24] If this is true, then it significantly undercuts the notion that editors can painstakingly restore scribal copy to original pristine masterpiece simply on the grounds of superior poetic quality. As we shall see, Donaldson took a more exploratory view of R and F in 1955 – a view later repudiated; and in 1981 Derek Pearsall discussed the possibility that the Ilchester manuscript might represent a fourth, a D-Text of the poem – written by Langland himself – but turned away from reopening the question of 'the exclusive integrity of the three texts' as 'almost too complicated to bear thinking about'.[25] Some of the suggestions of his work were subsequently built upon by Wendy Scase, who discovered that Ilchester had lines and readings in common with the extremely eccentric manuscript HM 114, and proposed that the two manuscripts represented an authentic second tradition of the C-Text.[26] Some years earlier Anne Hudson had anticipated such lines of inquiry in her discussion of the editorial principles of Kane–Donaldson:

> one is tempted to wonder whether adequate consideration has been given to the likely way in which the revisions were made – almost certainly haphazard, spread over a period of time, often re-revising or restoring the first reading, quite probably using more than one copy. [27]

If this was so, then the chaotic state of the manuscripts may be as much a reflection of the way in which the author composed the poem, as it is of the way in which the poem was transmitted.

---

[23] See e.g. J. F. Davis, ed., *Langland: Piers Plowman Prologue and Passus I–VII. Text B*, vii–viii.

[24] See e.g. 125; their view is shared by Russell (see p. 338 above). Kane–Donaldson provide no comparable discussion of the characteristics of AB revision, except very briefly at 75. Curiously enough, Russell has slightly more to say about AB revision than they do; see 'Some Aspects of the Process of Revision', 36–7.

[25] 'The Ilchester Manuscript of *Piers Plowman*,' 193.

[26] 'Two *Piers Plowman* C-Text Interpolations'.

[27] Anne Hudson, 'Middle English', 44. Cf. Hudson's more recent, and equally subversive, remarks about the likely order of composition of the various texts of the poem (p. 430 below).

As my discussion so far will have made clear, the central problem confronting the editor of *Piers Plowman* is the decision between the two alternative textual camps: one explaining the textual variation in the manuscripts as due to a more or less indeterminate combination of authorial rewriting and corrupt scribal transmission, the other attributing it to corrupt scribal transmission alone. Essentially, this decision boils down to determining the degree to which one can distinguish between authorial rewriting and scribal variation. The editor must be prepared to account for the manifold differences between manuscripts and versions of the poem – differences that must be referable either to the poet or to the scribes – in terms of a number of assumptions: about Langland's methods of and motives in revising, about his judgement of his own work, about the relations between authorial and scribal *usus scribendi*. These assumptions are often articulated, and certainly acted upon, in the introductions to the two Athlone editions. But they are rarely acknowledged as assumptions. Consequently the hypothetical and provisional nature of the conclusions they produce is not acknowledged either.

KANE'S EDITION OF A

Kane's edition of the A-Text is remarkable in several ways. It stands out as the only edition of a major Middle English work to set down in full detail the criteria for analysing variants so as to work out which is authorial in origin, and which scribal. As we have seen, Kane felt that one of Chambers' chief – though undervalued, and indeed insufficiently recognised – contributions to Middle English editing was his application of classical principles to Middle English texts. Kane follows through and realises that contribution.

With that in mind, it is worth scrutinising closely the statements Kane makes at the start of his edition. A foreword, presumably written, or sanctioned, by Kane, briefly recapitulates the history of the edition, noting that it 'owes its conception to the late Professors R. W. Chambers and J. H. G. Grattan who, in 1909, embarked upon an edition of the A version, and later encouraged others to examine the textual problems of the B and C versions'. Work on the project was 'suspended and eventually abandoned' – one suspects this is a more truthful report than any other so far recorded – as a result of the two editors' 'prolonged ill-health', and also the outbreak of the Second World War. Mitchell and Kane, however, 'continued to gather materials', and in 1950 the project was taken on by the Athlone Press. No mention here of EETS, which seems sad given Furnivall's boundless energy and enthusiasm, and the support provided by the Society up until the deaths of Chambers and Flower. In his Preface, Kane sets out his position more fully, choosing his words with care:

> Although I am in some degree the successor of the great initiators of this edition, and although I have enjoyed unrestricted access to their materials, I cannot claim the honour of collaboration with them. I was privileged, at various times, to learn from both Professor Chambers and Professor Grattan, and it is hardly possible for me today to distinguish my own findings from what they taught me, by writing and by word of mouth. But because opinions about textual criticism are much changed since their time, with an inevitable effect upon me, I cannot claim that they would have much approved of the direction which my conclusions have taken.
>
> Independence has, indeed, been forced upon me. When I undertook to edit this version of *Piers Plowman*, Professor Grattan was still alive; the plan then was that my uninformed energy would be guided by his greater experience. But with his death all responsibilities fell upon me; at the same time I was deprived of any source of interpretation of the materials collected by my predecessors. If I was to continue with the work, no course seemed possible except to treat it as my own. For, in a situation of this kind, although credit can be shared, responsibility is indivisible. Therefore I recollated in full that part of the poem already examined by them, instead of simply completing their collations as originally planned; I reviewed all editorial decisions taken by Chambers and Grattan or Grattan and myself; and I replanned this volume as the present state of the subject seemed to require. I did not let considerations of piety affect my decisions; that is, I know, the last thing they would have wished. True piety seemed to me to lie rather in following to the utmost of my ability the high tradition of scholarship which they represented. They would at all costs have wished me to obey the direction of the evidence. Still, it remains a fact that their interpretation of the evidence might not have been the same as mine. Therefore, while my relation to them is one of obligation in almost every respect, and they must share in any credit attached to my performance, the responsibility for this volume is mine alone.

This is a very graceful way of indicating that all the significant work had been Kane's alone. As none of the rotographs referred to by Chambers and Grattan survives in the Chambers archive, it seems likely that Kane took these over as vital evidence in his newly established task of recollation. We know from the Athlone Press minutes that he completed his text and much of his Introduction by 1955, so he evidently continued to work with formidable speed. His Preface tells us that 'the Leverhulme Research Fellowships Advisory Committee awarded [him] a grant towards the expenses of preparing the edition' in 1948, and that the University of London gave him further financial aid to go to Ann Arbor to consult the files of the recently established Middle English Dictionary. Both these pieces of information suggest that Kane, once he had decided to devote himself to the A-Text, did so with an authority and dispatch that impressed others as worth backing. Kane further details many of the libraries housing *Piers Plowman* manuscripts as having given him much help and support, which indicates that he checked any rotograph material he inherited from Chambers and Grattan against the manuscript originals (and this is confirmed by the formidable accuracy of his edition).

Why was it that Kane took so much less time, and was so much more successful, than his two predecessors, Chambers and Grattan? The answer must lie mainly in his superior determination and abilities, but can be fleshed out in other ways. To start off with, he would have been able to benefit from lengthy discussions of the textual problems of the poem by Chambers, Grattan, Manly and Knott, together with later researchers such as Blackman, Tapping, Carnegy, Mitchell and Day. Just as Chambers was able to enter the *Piers Plowman* field with a much better grasp of the conceptual issues involved than Skeat, so Kane was at the tail end of a lengthy debate which had clarified some of the main points of discussion, if not solved them. The advantages of hindsight in enabling an observer to identify and detect significant issues in the long debate are splendidly illustrated in the MA thesis written by S. S. Hussey, who was directed by his superviser, Kane, to search out, summarise, and analyse the scholarship on *Piers Plowman* written over the last eighty years.

Another reason, no doubt, was that Kane could consult the preliminary analysis made of the various readings by Chambers and Grattan, available to him in their collations, which covered Prologue and Passus I–VI. As he says, he then reconsidered their decisions, but at least he was provided with some sort of bench-mark in relation to which he could then proceed.

A third reason would be that he was the beneficiary of the

innovation made by Chambers which he so generously recognises in his Ph.D. thesis and 1948 article: Chambers' application of classical principles of editing to Middle English. Any reader of Kane will immediately recognise the logical character of his turn of mind, and understand how receptive such a temperament would be to the apparent rigour and relentlessness with which discourses such as those of Griesbach, Hort, Housman, or Greg, are written.[28] Kane greatly expanded his reading in textual criticism while working on the edition of A.[29]

A fourth reason for Kane's remarkable expedition in completing his edition was that he confined himself to A variants when editing A. This might seem an obvious limitation; but as we have seen, it was not one accepted by his predecessors Chambers and Grattan, who (at the prompting of T. A. Knott) had recognised since 1916 that the three texts of the poem were 'so inter-related ... that before you can have a final A-text, you must have an adequate B- and C-text'. The consequent attempt to master the tradition of B and C as well as that of A had probably been the single most important factor in their failure to produce an edition before they died. Certainly it had been the reason for their enlistment of Blackman, Tapping, Carnegy, Mitchell, and eventually Kane himself. In 1946 Kane had quoted their views on the matter with approval (see p. 316 above). One can only assume that he subsequently steered clear of their policy in his determination not to become bogged down in the same morass of manuscripts and versions which had finally overwhelmed his two seniors.[30]

Kane's chosen method of editing is described in detail in the four long and densely written chapters of his Introduction, totalling 172 pages. His prose is calculated and rigorous, proceeding at a measured yet relentless pace, behind which it is possible to detect a certain heady intellectual excitement as the logic of the narrative unfolds. Unfortunately there is no index to the Introduction, and no subdivision of the chapters into smaller sections, so the reader must work

---

[28] Greg's *Calculus of Variants* exerted a strong influence on Kane, who thanks Greg in his Acknowledgements for reading his Introduction before publication.

[29] See his bibliography, 53 n.3.

[30] In 1950, Kane's friend and colleague A. H. Smith, who was to be largely responsible for securing the Athlone Press' support of the edition, again refers to the principle of the inter-relatedness of editing the ABC versions, with no sense that it is questionable or problematic. See 'Pursuit of Poetry', 35, on the enlistment of co-editors of the other versions: 'It also became clear after a time that to edit the A-text the B-text would also be needed, and so Mrs. Blackman began work on the B-text.'

through the material consecutively. The text is furnished with a full critical apparatus giving the variant readings of almost all the manuscripts, and it is this feature as much as any other which makes the Athlone edition worth its weight in gold, since for the first time a large proportion of essential textual evidence is made available to scholars. At the end of the volume is a rather sparse body of textual notes, which provide cross-references to discussions in the Introduction when appropriate. A major defect arising from the absence of indexing has since been independently corrected by the invaluable publication in 1993 of a line-number index (by Peter Barney), which now makes it possible to trace a discussion in Kane's Introduction of a textual decision unmentioned in his textual notes.

There is no treatment in Kane's Introduction, nor in that of Kane–Donaldson, of the social and historical background to the poem, such as has characterised each of the editions of the poem published so far (even Crowley's, although there the discussion is exiguous); and nor is there any overt discussion of the poem's literary qualities such as is to be later found in the Everyman edition of Schmidt. The two volumes are directed at the textual scholar. On the other hand, both the Athlone editions take as read the assumption that Langland is a poet of great literary power, and the absence of historical contextualising material in the Introductions fits in with what Lee Patterson has identified as the New Critical literary tradition in which the Athlone editions are conceived.[31]

MANUSCRIPTS AND VERSIONS

Kane starts with a brief palaeographical account and description of each of the A-MSS,[32] and then moves to a discussion of manuscripts and versions. Here he thrashes out with far greater rigour than Skeat the argument that there actually is a distinct A version. He discusses the fact that the different A-MSS have different shapes – some end as soon as Passus VIII or before, some have the extra Passus XII which Skeat found so interesting, and some have a C continuation tacked – at various different points – on to the end of their A-Text. And he shows that the fact that the *genetic* links between manuscripts do not correspond to their shape suggests that the variation in shape is

---

[31] See 'The Logic of Textual Criticism', 73–6, 85–7.

[32] Except for Bodley 851; and the largely B-Text manuscripts BmBoCot, all three of which begin with an A-Text. See further below, p. 421.

unlikely to be authorial – unlikely to reflect different authorial versions of A which ended at different points. Some manuscripts may preserve a shorter version of A because an earlier manuscript in the transmission process lost its final pages for reasons now irrecoverable; or perhaps, given that A-MSS are in general younger than B- and C-MSS, and hence the two longer versions already in existence at the time when the extant copies of A were being made, scribes may have stopped copying their A exemplar (at various different stages) in order to transfer to a longer text.[33] The advantage of this hypothesis is that it explains why, say, R and T should be (to some extent) genetically linked, but have very different quantities of A-Text. If the varying lengths of A material in A-MSS were due to varying lengths of *authorial* text (i.e. more than one version of A), then one would expect the manuscripts to have genetic links *in accordance* with their varying lengths – the shorter versions would be more closely linked than the longer ones. But this is not the case.

Kane goes on to provide a useful list of the lines characteristic of the A version, and this amounts, more or less, to a definition of the A-Text. But it is not of course the whole story. Some of the manuscripts (W, N, and K most notably, but also, sporadically, U, V, H, J, E, A, W, and H³) have additional material, one or sometimes three or four or more lines together, which Kane believes properly belong to the B and C versions. How could this come about? Kane looks in detail at the chief offenders, W, N and K, and shows pretty conclusively that at some stage in the copying ancestry of these manuscripts, scribes had compared the A versions in their exemplars with one of the two longer versions, and added lines from the latter. The evidence for this is that the additional lines partially repeat or interfere with the local sense in the A passage, so that it seems unlikely that the author himself would have been responsible for such a misunderstanding of his own work.

Kane does not go into much detail as to the motives for scribal conflation of versions, and indeed they are often hard for us to conjecture. Nor does he discuss, or even mention, the fact that many

---

[33] Why the scribes should have chosen C-MSS rather than B-MSS to tack on to their A-MSS is another matter. Kane later (1988) suggested the choice 'may be an accident of local availability, but could just possibly reflect the compilers' awareness that in some senses C was more "complete" than B' ('The Text', 181). On the relative ages of surviving A- and B-/C-MSS, see A. I. Doyle, 'Remarks on Surviving Manuscripts of *Piers Plowman*', 36–7.

of the A-MSS which are minor offenders in the business of conflation of BC *lines* are, as it happens, far worse at conflating BC *readings*.[34]

On Passus XII Kane retains an open mind. He agrees with Knott–Fowler that it was probably not in the archetype of the extant manuscript, and repeats their caution 'that the imperfect ending of the manuscript V and the concealment of the original form of the ending of TChH^{2}KWN by the various C additions obscure the evidence and stand in the way of a firm conclusion' (p. 51). It seems likely that some of this passus – though we cannot know how much – was authentic: or, as Kane puts it with exemplary caution: 'It seems as if textual evidence by itself is insufficient to close this question, or to exclude, for the present, the possibility that some at least of Passus XII is authentic' (pp. 51–2). Now this is an interesting and significant admission. As we shall see in due course, it is important for the credibility of Kane's general view of the A-MSS that they all derive from one single archetype, which was not subsequently corrected or altered in any way by the author. Yet here he concedes that there may well have been *more* than one archetype from which A-MSS are descended: that of Pro–Passus XI, and a second, of indeterminate length, which contained *some* of Passus XII.

DISMISSAL OF KNOTT – FOWLER'S GENEALOGICAL METHOD;
ESTABLISHMENT OF KANE'S ECLECTIC METHOD

Kane's third chapter, entitled 'Classification of the Manuscripts', moves on to the meat of his Introduction. This is the best source for tracing the evolution of Kane's theory of editing. Interestingly enough, it at first sight appears that Kane's method only crystallised on his reading of the Knott–Fowler edition, which was published in 1952. We might thus surmise that in the four years intervening since 1948, when Kane gave up his work on B to help Grattan, he had been checking Chambers and Grattan's recording of A-MS variants, and perhaps sorting out some sort of preliminary approach to the editing of A. The appearance of Knott–Fowler would have presented him with a distinct challenge, perhaps even a crisis. If this new edition was adequate and satisfactory, then the Athlone project would be seriously shaken: clearly it would be undesirable to launch a flagship volume that turned out to be fairly indistinguishable from an existing and recently published edition of A.

[34] Cf. Kane, 38, and pp. 391ff. below.

There is an alternative explanation for the way in which Kane describes the evolution of his theory of editing as a response to the edition of Knott and Fowler, namely that it provides a narrative structure for the explication of his method. This imparts a sense of logical progression, even suspense, into the telling – will Knott and Fowler's method turn out to be workable, or will it not? The narrative is thus a rhetorical device for making the method more easily apprehensible by the reader. It is improbable, after all, that Kane left the construction of his method so late, especially when the way to it had been cleared so effectively by Chambers and Grattan in their articulation and discussion of the theory of the 'Substitution of Similars'.[35]

Knott–Fowler was based, as we have seen, on the genealogical method established by Knott in the 1915 article which so seriously provoked Chambers and other supporters of Skeat. Kane undermines this method in masterly fashion.

First, he places it in the context of the various possibilities of textual analysis, observing that 'Classification of manuscripts has been attempted in various ways, but always upon one of two broad principles: either analysis of all agreements in substantive readings, or the scrutiny of agreements in selected "common errors, deviations, and omissions"' (p. 56). And he quotes from Knott's account of his own adoption of the second method ('An Essay Toward the Critical Text of the A-Version', pp. 393–4). With some irony, in view of Knott's insistence on the 'scientific' (i.e. objective) nature of his method, Kane immediately points out that it is one in which 'the editor's judgement operates at all stages, first to identify erroneous readings, then to determine what are "significant errors", and then to distinguish between "legitimately descended errors" and "contaminations"' (p. 57). The rebuttal is reminiscent of that directed at the same article by Chambers many years ago.[36]

Having dealt a bruising blow to one of Knott's most fundamental claims, he moves on to examine the reliability of the genealogy that he actually comes up with. In order to test Knott's genealogy, Kane independently replicated the process of analysis that Knott described. Once he had completed his collations of the entire body of manuscripts, he made his first attempt to classify them into genetic groups, according to their sharing of obviously erroneous readings. Many of

[35] Pp. 279ff. and 326ff. above.   [36] See p. 248 above but cf. also p. 326 above.

the results, he says, appeared to confirm those of Knott's. But several problems turned up which Knott had failed to tell his readers about. First, although Kane in many regards identified the same basic groups as did Knott, he found that there was a large number of cross-cutting agreements between the groups – or as he puts it, 'the evidence for classifying these manuscripts was grievously obscured by the existence of many random groups which must signify coincidence or conflation of error'. And many of the cross-cutting agreements were just as significant in quality as those binding the main groups together; they differed only 'in relative persistence from those on which the classification would be founded'. Thirdly, Kane felt that several of the main groups were suspect because they were the products of traditions that were evidently corrupt. Finally, supposing that he did, like Knott, treat the best attested groups as the genetic ones, and then go on to use that classification in distinguishing between rival variants at any given point in the A-Text, he found that he would be in the unhappy situation of choosing an easier reading for his text, or 'a reading repugnant to the context', or 'a reading from which the variants rejected by recension could not conceivably have originated'. In Kane's view, these various limitations – concealed from us by Knott – made his genealogy 'a most dangerous instrument to use for recension'. 'Tested by the method employed to form it', he censoriously concludes, 'Knott's genealogy was found inadequate' (p. 61).[37]

So what would be a better alternative? Kane tells us that, since his first attempt to classify the manuscripts had suggested that 'no method of analysis would produce usable results', he next proceeded to 'scrutinize the variants themselves'. And, 'as it turned out', he found that this scrutiny 'had far-reaching results that determined my subsequent approach to the editing of A manuscripts' (pp. 61–2). Thus Kane's eclectic method of editing was born.[38] He took as his watchword one of Greg's principles for establishing the originality of a variant outside the framework of recension: 'To show that a reading

---

[37] Cf. my analysis above (p. 333), which suggests that Knott did not in fact make significant use of his genealogy.

[38] Much of the rhetoric of Kane's account of his investigations represents his conclusions as empirically driven, in a way that is perhaps dictated by the narrative drive in the Introduction identified above. But it is of course the case that many of those conclusions – his rejection of recension, or his identification of typical scribal motives for alteration of copy-text (see further below) – conform to the editorial practice of his predecessors, whether Chambers and Grattan or the eclectic editors of classical texts and the New Testament of the past. On the latter, see E. J. Kenney, *The Classical Text*, 21–74.

is original two main lines of argument are available: that the reading is itself satisfactory, and that it explains the origin of the erroneous alternative.'[39] Kane found that his 'scrutiny' brought to light several regular distinctions between what he identified as authorial and non-authorial readings. Most importantly, he felt that he could explain many of the non-authorial readings as having arisen from 'well-defined tendencies of [scribal] variation', where scribes, confronted with an original reading, would coincidentally produce the *same* error as a consequence of misreading the original. Thus he was able to establish a long list of typical scribal tendencies to variation, which could distinguish between scribal and authorial readings far more reliably and effectively than could a dubiously established genealogical tree. So Kane decided that he 'would fix [his] text without using recension, and would treat recension as only one of a number of available indications of originality' (p. 63).

Once his text was fixed, he 'made a second analysis of the variant groups of the A manuscripts, in relation to this text'. And he found that

> *i.* certain very persistent groups took shape;
>
> *ii.* a large number of relatively less persistent groups, frequently in conflict among themselves or with the groups in *i,* could not be ignored;
>
> *iii.* more than a thousand random groups testified to the existence of either abundant conflation, or excessive coincidence of variation, or both;
>
> *iv.* no stemma of these manuscripts could be reconstructed.[40]

These findings convinced Kane that recension was useless as a means of establishing the text of A.

He made this additionally clear by printing lists of variational groups of two, three, four and up to six manuscripts – i.e., agreements in error between manuscripts, where the 'correct' text (i.e., the text deemed by Kane to be correct) read something different. He then showed that Knott's and Fowler's evidence for variational groups simply did not stand up: they based their evidence for a genealogical stemma on poorly attested groups, and groups where there was so much cross-cutting agreement with other manuscripts that the groups they were pleading for ceased to have any convincing identity.

---

[39] Greg, *Calculus* 20 n.1, quoted Kane, 62.   [40] Quoted from Kane 63–4.

Knott and Fowler emerge devastated from this analysis, and they probably deserve to do so. It is however appropriate to make one reservation. Identification of variational groups depends crucially on one's choice of original text. If, for example, at A Pro 21, you decide that *settyng* is Langland's original reading, then manuscripts RUE, which agree in reading *seedtyme*, constitute a variational group. If on the other hand you determine that *seedtyme* is the original reading, then the agreement between RUE cannot be taken as evidence of genetic relationship, since their agreement is in a right reading: each of these manuscripts may have inherited the reading independently. Kane does not mention this problem, and makes no allowance for the fact that it may have made a distinct difference between his analysis of the groups and that of Knott and Fowler's, possibly to the extent of invalidating his invalidation of their classification of the manuscripts. Nevertheless, Kane's strictures against Knott seem justified. In many respects, he merely repeats the points made against the same target by Chambers and Grattan in 1916, although his evidence is vastly superior to theirs, deriving as it does from a complete collation of the A-MSS. As his two predecessors emphasised then, it has been well recognised for some decades, that, whatever the advantages of recension as a method of editing, it falls down completely when the manuscript witnesses have been to any significant extent interfered with by scribal contamination, against which, to quote again Maas's phrase, 'no specific has yet been discovered'.[41]

Kane does, however, concur to some considerable extent with the genetic analysis that Knott–Fowler finally come up with, although – as must by now be clear – he is extremely chary about using it as a tool for editing. He finally determines upon a statement of genetic relations that looks like this: $\{<[(TH^2)Ch]D>RU\}$, $(E)A(W)MH^3$, VH, WN, with J, L, and K separate.[42] The enormous incidence of convergent variation makes it impossible to define the relationship of the groups to each other.

So Kane concludes that 'the comfort and the appearance of authority afforded by recension are denied to the editor of the manuscripts of the A version of *Piers Plowman*. He can neither evade the responsibility for decisions about originality by referring them to

[41] See above, p. 250. For the context of Maas' remark, and its place in the history of textual criticism – particularly the work of Pasquali which was partly generated in response to Maas – see Kenney, *The Classical Text*, 140–2. See also Kane 114 n.1.

[42] 112–14. Cf. Knott–Fowler, 13–14; Fowler's account is far more confident and definite than Kane's, as is indicated by his bold drawing of stemmata (p. 331 above).

a genealogy, nor put his text beyond criticism [as the unfortunate Knott had tried to do] by calling it "critical".[43] So, he declares, 'Evidently then it is necessary to seek some other means of determining originality of readings. The history of transmission of the poem was not one of mechanical copying; it was, indeed, very much the contrary. Thus the method of editing cannot be mechanical' (p. 114).

EDITORIAL RESOURCES AND METHODS: DISTINGUISHING SCRIBAL FROM AUTHORIAL WRITING

This launches him into the description of his 'Editorial Resources and Methods' (chapter IV). The logic is impeccable and relentless. Recension, as Kane has now so clearly established, 'is not a practicable method for the editor of the A manuscripts. Nor', he goes on to say, 'is the creation of a hierarchy [of manuscripts], with some one copy elevated to a rôle of authority', for the very good reason that, 'while some of these manuscripts are certainly more corrupt than others, all are corrupt to an indeterminate but evidently considerable extent'. This means that 'the sole source of authority is the variants themselves, and among them, authority, that is originality, will probably be determined most often by identification of the variant likeliest to have given rise to the others' (p. 115).

In other words, Kane is returning to the dictum established by Greg, and quoted earlier. Where recension is not usable as an editorial method, two main lines of argument are available to show that a reading is original: 'that the reading is itself satisfactory, and that it explains the origin of the erroneous alternative'. Kane now moves to a very brief consideration of the historical circumstances under which the poem was copied, providing us with a useful account of the processes by which he thinks that manuscripts would have been copied (and corrupted). (He does not, however – and this is a significant omission – consider the circumstances under which the poem may have been composed: once again, he explores the nature of scribal transmission while taking that of authorial composition for granted.)

> *Piers Plowman* was especially subject to variation as a living text with a content of direct concern to its scribes. Its relevance to

---

43   Though cf. Kane's own use of this term earlier.

contemporary circumstances would not merely distract them from the passive state of mind ideal for exact copying, but actually induce them, whether consciously or subconsciously, to make substitutions. Professional copyists 'just able to take an unintelligent interest in what they were doing' as well as educated amateurs taking copies for their own use might be so affected. In this *Piers Plowman* resembles the *Divine Comedy*.[44] In one respect the Middle English poem was even more susceptible to correction than the Italian. Because it was written in non-stanzaic, unrhymed lines with an indeterminate number of syllables, little skill or ingenuity would seem to be required of those who set out to alter their copy. Indeed, scribes ignorant of the practice of alliterative poetry, or with an imperfect grasp of it, might receive an altogether false notion of freedom from formal control. The copyist's sense of obligation to follow his exemplar might be further relaxed by awareness that the poem was current in several shapes, or from knowledge of discrepancies between copies, whether of the same or different forms of the poem. If the exemplar before a scribe was evidently corrupt in parts he might cease to respect it as a whole. These conditions: the liveliest personal interest in the theme and content, the apparent absence of technical discipline, and the suggestion that form and expression were to some extent fluid, combined to make the scribes of *Piers Plowman*, in many cases if not all, 'amateur, uncritical and anonymous editors, unchecked by the editor's sense of responsibility'. (pp. 115–16)[45]

This is an important passage, for it articulates some assumptions about the nature of the authorial output, of its qualities relative to those of a scribe, and about the duties and responsibilities of an editor. Standing behind it is a notion of authorial writing as in some essential way different in quality from anything a scribe would be capable of producing, so that scribal interference with authorial original will inevitably produce identifiable and significant corruption of that original. At the same time there is a paradoxical acknowledgement of the fact that, to contemporary readers (scribes), both authorial and scribal writing might be viewed as a sort of continuum, with no necessary distinction being made between the two sorts of material.

These reflections put the exercise Kane carried out in his second

[44] Here Kane refers to Moore's *Contributions*, as had Chambers and Grattan before him.
[45] The quotation is from Moore, *Contributions*, viii; Chambers had earlier alluded to it in 1909 (see p. 202 above). The idea of the scribe as critic has become very popular in recent years, but it is not one approved of by Kane. See ' "Good" and "Bad" Manuscripts', 139.

and third chapters into a slightly different context. The identification of the A version now appears to have, in a certain respect, something of a rhetorical function. From the start, Kane assumed that there had been one single text of A, one single original, and that all variants other than one must by definition be scribal. This was an important manoeuvre for clearing his editorial path. What he doesn't consider are such difficult possibilities as authorial revision of that hypothetical single original version, and how this would be manifested in the surviving manuscript evidence, or – in chapter 3, his classification of the manuscripts – that some of the numerous cross-cutting agreements which upset any attempt to form a genealogical tree may result from the fact that there was more than one original version of the A-Text.

Having established his model of how scribes copied, and (implicitly) his assumption of how authors wrote, Kane sets out his principles for detecting scribal as opposed to authorial writing. He concedes that, in the circumstances of copying he has just described, 'it might seem that substitution [of scribal for authorial readings] would be not merely frequent but also wild and wayward'. But this is not the case. In fact it is possible to divide scribal error into two broad categories: those originating in mechanical error, 'which hardly seem problematic', and those deriving from more conscious, deliberate and discriminating scribal substitution. By mechanical error Kane means such things as eyeskip – the scribe's eye passing from say the end of one line to the identical end of another several lines away, and hence failing to copy out the intervening material; or dittography – writing the same word or phrase twice. He gives approximately eight and a half pages of examples of mechanical errors, categorised under such headings as 'confusion of e and o' (in the handwriting of the exemplar), 'confusion over division of words', 'anticipation of copy'. All these have been found useful categorisations by subsequent Middle English editors in sorting out their texts, and all had been previously enunciated by classical scholars.

Some mechanical error shades into the ill-defined border between conscious and unconscious error, the distinction between which depends, as Kane says, 'on the possibility of discovering motives for any variation'. Kane recognises several instances where 'the editor is powerless' to distinguish between variants, on account of the impossibility of discovering either an occasion for mechanical inaccuracy or a possible motive for substitution. Examples of this are where the readings differ over minor omissions or additions (say of 'And' at the beginning of a line, or an article), or where there are 'variants of dialect, construction, tense, mood or number, word order or vocabulary equivalents, which do not materially alter the substance of the communication in any way now determinable'. This is a significant recognition of the limitations of an editor's power to distinguish between scribal and authorial readings; for, as we shall see, later on in his editing career Kane became far more confident of his ability to ascribe such tiny variants to scribe rather than author, or *vice versa*.

So far, Kane's description of his editorial procedures is uncontroversial. It is manifestly the case that all sorts of minor errors of the sort he designates 'mechanical' did occur, and do occur, in any attempt to copy out a text by hand. Far more interesting is his account of the second sort of scribal error, conscious substitution of a reading for the one found in the scribe's exemplar. As Kane says, 'there is a *prima facie* improbability that all variants, whether substitutions, additions or omissions, were merely careless or erratic. The majority of scribes did, after all, copy a very large number of words in a great many lines faithfully, often to the extent of keeping spelling and dialect forms of the exemplar' (p. 126). Scribes did run into problems, of one sort or another, with their exemplars, finding what was written in front of them unreadable, unintelligible, or in other ways unsatisfactory. And in these cases, occasionally, they seem to have made a deliberate decision to change their copy, substituting an alternative word or phrase for the one giving them trouble.

As with mechanical errors, all of these possible motives for scribal substitution had long been established in classical textual criticism, for example the principle that scribes tend to substitute an easier for a harder reading (*difficilior lectio*).[46] Kane's strong representation of the relevance of such an analysis for Middle English texts is one of the features which has made his edition so significant and so influential; in this respect he was, as he acknowledged in the 1940s, following in Chambers' footsteps.

Here it is important to note that, according to his own description, Kane proceeded on a specifically inductive basis in identifying the typical scribal motives for substitution, as if his independent investi-

---

[46] See Kane, 130 n.2, and cf. Kenney, *The Classical Text*, 43 and 43 n.2. Cf. also Allen's allusion to 'well known maxims' described on p. 268 above. An important discussion of the limitations of this principle for the editing of *Piers Plowman*, particularly as evidenced in Kane's editorial practice, is to be found in Adams, 'Editing and the Limitations of the *Durior Lectio*' (see p. 417 below).

gations of *Piers Plowman*, which are reported rather as one might report the various stages of a scientific experiment, confirmed the inherent rightness of the 'canons of editing' which had evolved from the study of classical texts. On the other hand, as already suggested, it may be that Kane's narrative mode in the Introduction is a retrospective imposition of a dramatic sequence on the various elements of his textual practice. In this case, the congruity between Kane's 'findings' as to typical scribal behaviour and the 'canons of editing' of the classical editors might be due to Kane's prior expectations of the sorts of error he would be likely to come across, expectations which then influenced his interpretation of the evidence (without his necessarily being aware of the fact). It is worth making this point, and sounding a warning alarm at this stage in the account of Kane's relation of the evolution of his method, for it is, of course, highly questionable whether it is appropriate to apply theories such as *difficilior lectio*, derived from the study of the transmission by scribes centuries after their composition of classical texts and the Greek New Testament, to texts written by Middle English scribes in their own language.

Kane does not give us a full account of his procedure, but so far as I can make it out it was as follows. He examined a number of instances (he does not specify how many) where there were two main variants among the manuscripts, where one variant was attested by a minority and the other by a majority of manuscripts, but where neither was obviously the result of mechanical error, or was manifestly inferior to the other. In each case, he made the significant, but unstated, assumption that the two variants could not *both* be original (i.e. that Langland did not at any stage revise, touch up, or otherwise rewrite his text of A in such a way as to give rise to alternative authorial A variants still surviving in the A-MS tradition), and that one of the variants, therefore, had to be the result of scribal error. As a general rule, it seemed much more likely that the majority variant was original, and the minority variant scribal. This is because the erroneous reading has to be explained as the result of independent coincident substitution on the part of the scribes concerned. Evidently, it is easier to assume small-scale rather than large-scale coincident substitution of the same variant; so it is easier to assume that the majority reading, not the minority reading, is the correct one.[47]

---

[47] Kane must here have assumed that genetic relationships were not, in general, responsible for the agreement between the majority manuscripts; see further below, p. 373.

He summarises his procedure as follows:

> The frequent recurrence of *presumably unoriginal variants* with similar effects on the substance of the poem, and therefore presumably made from similar motives, allows the editor to deduce the existence of several general tendencies of scribal substitution ... Such circumstances both account for the large number of material variants and afford a means of interpreting these in crucial passages. (pp. 143–44; my italics)

This method corresponds precisely to that described in the major work of textual criticism in the tradition which Kane inherited from Chambers and Grattan, Westcott and Hort.[48]

Time after time, Kane found that the minority variant was (say) more explicit than the majority variant. In view of his *prima facie* assumption that the more manuscript support a variant had, the more likely it was that that variant was original, he was able to conclude that one characteristic scribal motive for substitution was to alter copy in such a way as to make it more explicit. This is how he describes his process of induction:

> Motives of substitution were inferred from comparison of the variant readings where the distribution of support gave a *prima facie* suggestion of the direction of variation. For instance, it was observed that of two available readings one was sometimes more and one less explicit. *Until direction of variation was fixed the situation was ambiguous, and the motive of substitution might have been either to increase or diminish the explicitness of statement. Acceptance of the majority variant as probably original* pointed, in many instances, to a wish for more explicit statement as the motive for substitution. (p. 127; my italics)

According to his own narrative, then, Kane did not, at the outset of editing the poem, regard more explicit readings as self-evidently scribal; instead, it was the circumstance that the balance of manuscript support often went against them that led him to associate greater explicitness with a scribal, not an authorial style.

Kane was able to repeat this process of comparison between majority and minority variant many times, so as to establish a wide range of 'possible motives for scribal substitution'. In general, he felt, 'scribes set out to produce what seemed to them a more correct, or a more easily intelligible, or a more emphatic, or a more elegant text.

[48] Vol. II, 23–4.

Their substitutions seem designed to make the meaning clearer, or to express it more forcibly, or to embellish the form of its expression' (p. 128). Scribal variants 'may show [the copyist's] concern for the convenience of readers, but may also record an active interest in the subject matter ... or, by contrast, record a probably unconscious protest against the necessity for unremitting, intelligent attention to meaning. They tend to more complete grammatical representation of meaning, more explicit reference, and more precise designation' (p. 131). Frequently, when faced with a difficult word, a scribe would substitute a word with roughly the same palaeographical shape but with little applicability to the context; Kane calls such substitutions *homeographs*. Scribes were also concerned to remove from their text

> terms of esoteric vocabulary of alliterative poetry; words of regionally restricted use which may not necessarily belong to this vocabulary; words falling into disuse; new words, presumably not yet in general currency; punning words; words used allegorically or otherwise figuratively; ambiguous expressions; or expressions otherwise difficult in the context. The change is in the direction of flat statement, simplifying not only language but connotation, and sometimes losing or altering denotation. It favours the obvious and the colourless, and rejects language pregnant, or mannered, or fanciful. [Footnote: 'The effect of some substitutions to increase emphasis is a separate matter. See pp. 138–9 below.'] The results of this tendency are a prosy utterance and loss of force in the communication of meaning, weakening of poetic tension, dilution of the archaic flavour of the style, and general loss of efficiency. *It should be remarked that many of the variants are adequate readings in the sense that they would pass muster if not exposed to comparison.* Some are near or exact glosses of the supplanted readings. (pp. 133–4; my italics)[49]

Implicit in this account are further editorial assumptions that need to be extracted and examined. First of all, Kane is assuming that, of any number of manuscript variants, only one – if that – will be original. The remaining will have come about through one or other of the operations of scribal miscopying; and it is possible that *all* the variants may be the product of such miscopying. Is this a reasonable assumption? It supposes that the author composed his poem in a particular

---

[49] Cf. 143, where Kane repeats that 'exercise of scribal preference ... [may have] produced variants of more or less equivalent value'; and 152, where 'balance of evidence' is said to be 'probably the editor's worst problem'.

way, and that it was transmitted in a particular way: that circumstances were such that the author left no trace of variants in any of the ancestors of the surviving manuscripts. It is thus a peculiar assumption to make about the author of *Piers Plowman*.

It was certainly assumed by Kane that one and the same author was responsible for all three versions of the poem, and hence that the author was one unusually prone to revision. He is unique among English poets in being responsible for one work only; so far as we know, he dedicated his whole life to the single poem. Why limit his processes of composition and revision to three stages only? As Donaldson indicated in 1955, every writer need only observe his or her own writing processes to become aware of how unusual it is to produce one version only of a piece of writing, and never subsequently change, polish, revise, cut, or add to it.[50] It is probably true that in every single documented case of a literary writer preparing his or her own work for publication (in whatever form), evidence survives of authorial variants, which often present editors with considerable problems.[51] So why should we exclude this possibility in Langland's case?

One of the notable characteristics of the *Piers Plowman* textual tradition is its plethora of variants. Perhaps we might again pick up a point made in Donaldson's 1955 musings, and consider ascribing some of these not only to the way that the poem was copied – to which Kane gives so much attention – but also to the way that the poem was composed. A particularly worrying phrase used by Kane in his description of scribal variants is that 'many of the variants are adequate readings in the sense that they would pass muster if not exposed to comparison'. This is exactly what we would expect of the difference between one authorial version and another. To consider the question on a larger scale: if we had to choose absolutely between the A version and the B version, most of us would choose B, while accepting that A would certainly pass muster if not exposed to comparison. Langland himself evidently felt that there was room for improvement of A; that was why he wrote B. Why should we not at least consider the possibility that the same may have been true on the scale of alternative readings within a version? Langland may have

---

[50] His remarks are quoted below, p. 381.

[51] James Thorpe, in *Principles of Textual Criticism*, 36, lists some fifty writers (of the late sixteenth to twentieth centuries), investigation of whose works has revealed that they were subject to extensive authorial revision. Authors may readily be added from the medieval period, e.g. Chaucer, Petrarch, Deguilevile.

come back to his first version of A and improved some of its readings. We know that he rewrote his poem at least twice (or three times); it is often assumed by critics that he spent his entire life on the project. It seems to fit in perfectly well with this view that he should have tinkered and rewritten at all stages of the work; indeed, it seems on the contrary surprising that he should not have done this.

Kane's observation that some scribal variants 'are adequate readings in the sense that they would pass muster if not exposed to comparison' is worrying in two further respects. Here is his characterisation of these readings:

> The change is in the direction of flat statement, simplifying not only language but connotation, and sometimes losing or altering denotation. It favours the obvious and the colourless, and rejects language pregnant, or mannered, or fanciful. The results of this tendency are a prosy utterance and loss of force in the communication of meaning, weakness of poetic tension, dilution of the archaic flavour of the style, and general loss of efficiency.

To the extent that this is an account of the *relative* characteristics of the 'scribal' variants, the characterisation is perhaps acceptable; though it would be possible to question further the critical criteria it implies. The terms 'pregnant', 'mannered', 'fanciful', and 'archaic' are not unproblematic labels, and it is certainly not clear that the author may not have sought to reduce such characteristics of his poem in the rewriting, in order to reach a wider audience.[52] It would also be difficult to define 'efficiency' in verse in a way that would satisfy more than a few Langland (and other) scholars at a time. However, the remarks just quoted tend towards an account of the *absolute* characteristics of these scribal variants, as in 'prosy utterance', etc. If Langland is capable of such poor writing – for such is implied by the statement that these readings would 'pass muster if not exposed to comparison' – then a substantial difficulty arises for the editors of B and C, and also for anyone recognising (as I have argued we should) the probability that Langland will have revised his text *within* a version. The possibility has to be faced that Langland may occasionally have revised his poem for (what we would now regard as) the worse.

Recognition of this possibility places a heavy burden on the shoulders of the editor. Criteria for distinguishing between variants

---

[52] It will come as no surprise that Skeat suggested this long ago; cf. p. 327 above.

almost invariably assume that the authorial reading will be 'better' than the scribal. But in the case of a poem like *Piers Plowman*, which was revised several times over a period of many years, such criteria may be valid to a limited extent only. There is no mention of this serious problem by Kane.[53]

A second issue is obliquely acknowledged, but not tackled (or resolved) in Kane's footnote to his remarks on scribes favouring 'the obvious and the colourless, and reject[ing] language pregnant, or mannered, or fanciful'. The footnote reads: 'The effect of some substitutions to increase emphasis is a separate matter. See pp. 138–9 below.' The relevant passage on these pages is the following:

> the most striking of the variations originating from the scribe's association of himself with what he copied are those designed to increase the emphasis of statements.... . Such variation took place because scribes were enthusiastic for the poem, and consciously or unconsciously, if sometimes without intelligence or taste, strained to participate in the experience that it recorded, as well as to contribute to its purpose.

But Kane does not indicate how we are to distinguish between the effects of these two opposite scribal tendencies: those that increase emphasis, and those that reduce it. This is one of several 'reversible criteria' for distinguishing scribal readings that Kane uses: another is his characterisation of scribes' 'indolent (perhaps even habitual) pruning of unessential words' (p. 122), versus their tendency to 'more complete grammatical representation of meaning, more explicit reference, and more precise designation' (p. 131). The reader may well grow uncomfortably suspicious that Kane chooses his original reading on grounds of intuitive preference, and is then able to justify this by appealing to the appropriate criterion of the relevant opposite pair – the reading is original because it is more emphatic or because it is less emphatic, because it is more explicit or because it is less explicit.[54] Westcott and Hort, whose writings exerted so great an

[53] The problem raises substantial questions about the aim of an editor: for example, is this to establish what the author originally wrote, or to construct the best possible text? Kane and Donaldson implicitly touch on such questions when they assume that Langland incorporated readings which they judge to be scribal in his revision of A to B and of B to C (see Kane–Donaldson, 205 n.154, 211 n.172; Kane, 2nd edition, 463). In some of these detected instances, the editors emend the readings concerned. But if Langland wrote them into his text, by what criterion can they be scribal? and with what justification may an editor remove them? See further below, p. 391 n. 23 and cf. Skeat's views, e.g. pp. 131, 154 above.
[54] Cf. John A. Alford's comments on Kane and Donaldson's criteria for distinguishing scribal variants, which they inherit almost wholesale from Kane: 'the great danger of [Kane and

influence on Kane's predecessor Chambers, were well aware of the reversibility of 'what are not very happily called "canons of criticism"'; but it seems to have gone unnoticed by Kane himself.[55]

A further problem arises in relation to the way in which Kane decided how to designate the characteristics of competing variants. As is clear from the above discussion, he felt that, in most cases, the fact that the majority of manuscripts supported readings of one characteristic (say 'less explicit') than another ('more explicit') meant that it was reasonable to assign the majority characteristic to the author, not to a scribe. But later in his career – specifically, when editing B – he comes to feel that in many cases majority readings are not to be trusted. If this is true, then one of the important bases on which he establishes his identification of scribal characteristics of substitution begins to look logically shaky.[56]

But it is also possible, as I have suggested, that Kane's representation of the inductive process by which he arrived at his identification of the typical characteristics of scribal substitution is rhetorical, the result of a retrospective imposition of a consequential narrative on the various elements of his analysis. In this case, a logical flaw is not particularly significant. What is significant, however, is that Kane's identification of typical scribal behaviour conforms to the characteristics established many years previously in classical editing.[57] We may then ask how appropriate it is to apply such an analysis to *Piers Plowman*. Scribes of Ancient Latin and Greek manuscripts (including the Greek New Testament) are far removed in their own language from the language of the texts they copy, and divided from their texts not only by language but by several centuries. They are very considerably less learned in them than the best editors from the

---

Donaldson's] method ... is the possibility that scribal tendencies of the fourteenth and fifteenth centuries may be used to answer uniquely twentieth-century questions. By means of an infinite variety of scribal "errors", we can make the text say almost anything our ignorance requires'; *Speculum* 52, 1002–5 (1003). Adams' article 'Editing and the Limitations of the *Durior Lectio*' illustrates this point in detail.

[55] See p. 215 above.

[56] The force of this criticism may be mitigated by the difference in nature of the textual traditions of A and B. The B tradition is much simpler, and most or all of the manuscripts frequently agree in a reading which represents that of beta (i.e. one of the two main B-MS families, to which all the B-MSS other than RF (alpha) belong), or of the archetype (Bx) itself. Therefore dismissing the reading of Bx involves dismissing the reading of two main families only. The A tradition is more complex, and so majority agreement more compelling, firstly, because it probably represents more than one (or two) post-archetypal ancestors, and secondly, because the A archetype is generally regarded as less corrupt than Bx.

[57] Cf. p. 360 n. 38 above.

Renaissance onwards, who established the 'canons of editing' which Kane applies to *Piers Plowman* in order to identify and diagnose the sorts of errors made by copyists truly unfamiliar with the linguistic and lexical characteristics of their exemplars. The scribes of *Piers Plowman*, on the other hand, copied texts written in the same language they themselves spoke (though perhaps of a different dialect), and usually only decades after the date of the poem's original composition.[58] It is questionable, therefore, whether the tools for distinguishing between scribal and authorial writing developed for a quite different set of textual problems may prove adequate or satisfactory here, especially given the likelihood that some of the alternative variants surviving in the *Piers Plowman* textual tradition are authorial.

EDITING A WITHOUT EDITING B: THE 'B/C' READINGS IN EAMH[3], Z, AND OTHER A-MSS

One of the most significant features of Kane's editorial method is that, as stated above, he limited himself to A-MS variants when determining the text of A. I have suggested that the reason for this may have been, quite simply, the entirely commendable intention to get the edition out at all costs, and not fall into the same editorial bog as Chambers and Grattan, whose struggle with B and C at the same time as A had fatally undermined their textual labours. Chambers and Grattan had recognised as early as 1916 that editing one text implied editing the other two, and as we have seen, Kane in 1946 accepted this proposition without question: 'the editing of the several texts of *Piers Plowman* must go forward side by side and step by step' (see p. 316 above). But by 1960 he had come to a different view on the matter, pronouncing strongly in his edition of A (albeit in a footnote) as follows:

> The limitation to A variants [in establishing the text of A] is unavoidable, since this is an edition of the A version. In theory all variations of corresponding lines in the three versions might afford indications of a common, presumably unrevised original form of such lines. In practice the intrinsic likelihood that the authorial revision responsible for the major differences between versions will also have introduced smaller differences, makes it impossible to say

[58] Cf. Eric Stanley, 'Unideal Editing of Old English Verse', 257.

of many lines whether their various forms in the three versions originated with scribe or author. The editor of any version is thus restricted to the evidence of the variants in manuscripts inferentially descended from the archetypal copy of that version. He will employ the evidence of variants from other versions only in special circumstances .... . This restriction is to be regretted, since it cannot fail to have some effect on the quality of the text of each version. But it is inherent in the nature of the editorial problem. (p. 147 n. 1)

One type of 'special circumstance' is 'when most or all of the A variants for a passage are unsatisfactory in a way which casts doubt on their originality, and when, at the same time, the reading of another version could easily and naturally have given rise to the A variants if it had been the original of A as well' (p. 157).

It was identification of such instances on a massive scale in the B-MSS which led Kane and Donaldson to believe that the B archetype was seriously corrupt. Between editing A and editing B Kane changed his views radically on the acceptability of using the evidence from one tradition to determine originality in another, returning to the position held by Chambers and Grattan. In the Athlone *B Version*, he states that 'the editor of A now considers that he allowed insufficient weight to readings from other versions in his editing, and that his earlier view of the situation (Vol I, 147 n1 and 157) was mistaken'. His 1975 view is that 'determination of originality in any version must include consideration in the first instance of all differences between the versions' (p. 75).[59]

Kane and Donaldson set down logically and clearly the reasons for this:

> Given single authorship and a sequence of composition where B is the middle version [of the three versions of the poem] its editors are placed in an unusual logical position. For about a third of the poem, that is to the end of B X, there are many single words, as well as passages of various length, where the three versions recognizably correspond and can be minutely compared at the textual level with respect to local expression and to technical form, without distraction by larger considerations of meaning and structure. Because inaccurate copying axiomatically occurs at all stages in the transmission of manuscript texts all differences of reading revealed by such comparison are possible indications of unoriginality. Not all can be

---

[59] Cf. 164: 'It is comparison with readings outside the tradition of the B manuscripts which enables accurate assessment of the quality of their archetype and its frequent correction.'

authorial; some must necessarily have been created by scribal variation in one or more of the archetypal traditions. Therefore determination of originality in any version must include consideration in the first instance of all differences between versions and in the second particularly of those differences not evidently or probably resulting from authorial revision. In the editing of B this principle has special force because the archetypal text of B can be compared over so much of its length not only with the text of A or the text of C but also, where all the versions correspond, with both, that is with two texts of itself preserved in distinct manuscript traditions. There are thus exceptional resources for assessing the quality of the B archetype. (pp. 74–5)[60]

In this crucial respect, therefore, Kane's text was constructed on a radically different principle from that of Kane and Donaldson. They refer to this difference between the two editions only in three footnotes to the B-Text Introduction (on pages 75, 159, and 205), despite the fact that the textual principles involved are of sufficient importance to merit full treatment in the main body of the introduction.[61] For the shift in editorial methodology between A and B produces a substantial problem for the Athlone project. When, time after time, Kane and Donaldson dismiss the reading of archetypal B and revert to that of Kane's A, they do so without rethinking the editing of A. But Kane arrived at his A reading by a process of textual analysis that Kane and Donaldson reject as inadequate; that is, Kane took into account the readings *only of the A-MSS* in establishing his text, and not those of B- and of C-MSS. Thus Kane and Donaldson's final text is based on mutually inconsistent premises: in implementing their B-Text methodology, they treat as relevant evidence textual decisions arrived at by an irreconcilably different methodology, that of Kane's A.

A single example will serve to illustrate both the force of this point and the dangers inherent in Kane's method of determining originality among manuscript variants. In the first few lines of A Passus VII, Piers offers to guide the pilgrims to Truth after ploughing his half acre. As printed in Kane's edition, these lines read

---

[60] Kane had first set out this position in 1969, in the intellectually exciting essay 'Conjectural Emendation', where he pointed out that the peculiar textual conditions of the B-Text of *Piers Plowman* represented those laid down by Maas as ideal for the employment by an editor of conjectural emendation (168–9; cf. Kane–Donaldson, 75 n.16).

[61] It is conceivable that Kane and Donaldson recognised the shift as posing significant problems for their editorial enterprise only at a late stage in their composition of the B-Text Introduction, and hence were unable to take full notice of these in the body of their text.

'þis were a wikkide weye, but whoso hadde a gide
þat miȝte folewe vs iche fote [forto] we were þere.'
Quaþ perkyn þe plouȝman, 'be seint poule þe apostel,
I haue an half akir to er[e]n be þe heiȝe weiȝe;
Hadde y [erid] þat half akir
I wolde wende wiþ ȝow til ȝe were þere (A Passus VII 1–6)

For line 5, B and C both read 'Hadde I eryed þis half acre and sowen
it after' (B Passus VI 5/C VIII 2; no significant manuscript variation).
As Kane points out in his textual note (p. 446), the line that he himself
prints is 'unusually short'. In fact – although Kane does not explicitly
acknowledge this – none of the manuscripts reads a line of such
unusual brevity, as becomes clear on scrutiny of his critical apparatus.
Of the seventeen A-MSS, two omit the line, one rewrites it completely, and seven run it together with all or part of the following line,
thus increasing its length to something more normal. The remaining
seven add an extra phrase, again bringing the line to a normal length:
TChH² add 'so me god helpe', and EAMH³ add '& sowen it after'.
EAMH³'s reading is thus exactly the same as that of B and C.

Kane does not tell us of the agreement between EAMH³ and BC,
but instead comments, 'whether the form adopted [i.e. in his text] is
original can hardly be established, but it does seem that the variant
readings of TChH² and EAMH³ filling out the line are unoriginal'.
This remarkable statement has at least two significant implications.
First, it confirms that, when editing A, Kane did not systematically
compare the readings of B and C. Otherwise, he would surely have
told us that EAMH³'s reading was to be found in BC, and he would
presumably have hazarded an explanation for this. There are two
obvious explanations for the agreement between EAMH³ and BC:
either that the reading '& sowen it after' is the original A reading; or
that it is not, and that EAMH³ read it as a result of contamination
from the later traditions (it could hardly be the result of coincident
error).[62] The second implication of Kane's remark is that his editorial
judgement on unoriginal readings is not entirely secure. He puts
TChH²'s (presumably scribal) 'filler', 'so me god helpe', in the same
category as the (undeniably authorial) 'filler' of EAMH³, '& sowen it
after': both, he says, 'seem ... unoriginal'. Kane offers no explanation

---

[62] As observed above (p. 270), Kane's consideration of contamination is much less satisfactory
than that of A. G. Mitchell. This would seem to be partly because he did not compare the
versions of the poem with each other to any great extent when editing A, and so was not
made aware of contamination *by readings* as a possibly significant phenomenon.

for his judgement, although we can supply appropriate ones from his Introduction. TChH^2's reading might be designated 'obvious, colourless', tending towards 'prosy utterance and loss of force in the communication of meaning, weakening of poetic tension, dilution of the archaic flavour of the style' (p. 134), or as 'more complete grammatical representation of meaning, more explicit reference, and more precise designation' (p. 131), or as a substitution 'designed to make the meaning clearer, or to express it more forcibly, or to embellish the form of its expression' (p. 128); all these descriptions are provided by Kane as characterisations of typically scribal utterance. Unfortunately, as indeed implied by the way that Kane brackets TChH^2's reading together with that of EAMH^3, some of these remarks (as on pp. 131 and 128) would apply equally well to '& sowen it after'. Yet this is, by the witness of B and C, an indisputably authorial reading (and reproduced as such in Kane–Donaldson), despite Kane's surprising failure to identify it as such in his edition of A. As it happens, '& sowen it after' is also the reading of the Z-Text (Passus VII 5). If one believes that Z is a copy of a draft of a pre-A version of the poem by Langland himself, then the line-up of agreements in favour of '& sowen it after' as the original of all four versions will look compelling, since Z, EAMH^3, B, and C all agree in a reading over which the remaining A-MSS manifestly had a great deal of difficulty. Even if one believes, with Kane, that Z is a late scribal version of the poem, the evidence in favour of '& sowen it after' looks strong.

If the criteria Kane uses to distinguish scribal readings from authorial are as unreliable as this, could it be that other of the readings he rejects in his A-Text, which are found in A-MSS, Z, B, and often C, are also authorial?[63] I pursue this question at greater length in the next chapter.

Kane's edition was received with universal acclaim, and criticisms such as those made here were almost entirely absent from the reviews (indeed, it would be impossible to make many of them without the information provided in his later edition of B). It immediately became the standard edition of the A-Text, and has come to serve as a monument to editorial theory and practice. J. A. W. Bennett's remarks give a good indication of the regard in which the work is

---

[63] For a demonstration of the fallibility of standard editorial methods for distinguishing between scribal and authorial variants, see John Bowers, 'Hoccleve's Two Copies of *Lerne to Dye*'.

generally held: 'The briefest acquaintance with this book will bring some notion of the years of thought, planning, collation, and painful rearrangement that have gone into it ... for Mr Kane there is a secure place in the history of medieval scholarship.'[64]

[64] Review of Kane, 71. See also reviews by Morton Bloomfield, Gervase Mathew, David C. Fowler, A. I. Doyle.

21

The Athlone B-Text

GEORGE KANE AND E. T. DONALDSON

As we have seen, E. Talbot Donaldson became involved in the *Piers Plowman* project in 1951, at the invitation of George Kane. He was to be partly responsible (with Bloomfield) for volume V, the *'Annotations'*, and for volume VI, the 'discussion of the background, interpretation, authorship, etc. of *Piers Plowman'*. By 1955 he was established as co-editor of B, had together with Kane made complete collations of all the B-MSS, and was working in detail on B-MS relationships.[1] As early as 9 March 1960, the text and apparatus of the Athlone B-Text were in typescript;[2] but the final version was not delivered to the Athlone Press until March 1973. The resulting volume – a substantial 681 pages, to process which the Press engaged the services of an extra proofreader – was published in 1975. 2,500 copies were printed, at an estimated cost of £8,500, and the book was priced at £20 a copy.[3]

As mentioned above, Donaldson's cast of mind was essentially different from Kane's. Kane's writing is magisterial, its constant appeal to the dictates of logic sometimes bullying, certainly wearying

---

[1]   The Athlone Press minutes record Donaldson as one of the three co-editors at this date, when Kane submitted his completed edition of the A-Text, and Donaldson's 1955 article on B-MSS R and F 'was based on the complete collations of the B-MSS which Prof. Kane and I have made'; see 'MSS R and F in the B Tradition of *Piers Plowman*', 182 n.15.

[2]   According to a letter of that date written by Kane to Kenneth Sisam, now in the possession of Miss Celia Sisam. The letter also states that Kane is working on an analysis of B variants which he hopes will bring out 'the nature of the treatment suffered by the text at the archetypal stage'. In an earlier letter, dated 4 February 1960, Kane commented that he was now hard at work on the second volume. It was 'a relief to work on something untouched by controversy' (presumably he refers to the complications of the A-Text inheritance from Chambers and Grattan), but apart from that the editorial problems of B were, if anything worse than those of A. However, he now had the help of E. T. Donaldson from Yale University, 'an acute and strenuous scholar'.

[3]   These details are recorded in the Athlone Press minutes.

the reader. Donaldson by contrast writes more lightly, with an intellectual flexibility which comes across as dispassionate, exploratory, and often suavely ironic. These characteristics become increasingly ' evident as Donaldson grew older, but can still be seen comparatively early, as in the following reflections in 1955 on the manuscript tradition represented by B-MSS R and F (which he originally believed to represent an authorial version of B written before the B-Text proper):[4]

> I wonder whether, in the present instance, the peculiarities of the B-MSS are not more easily attributable to the revisions of a poet than the machinations of a contaminator. Everything we know about the B- and C-poet suggests a constant and loving reviser of his poem. Indeed, I sometimes wonder whether the C-text, the B-text, and even the A-text are not merely historical accidents, haphazard milestones in the history of a poem that was begun but never finished, photographs that caught a static image of a living organism at a given but not necessarily significant moment of time.[5] It may be that the very act of surrendering his autograph to be transcribed ... gave him the impulse towards further revision. This is something that happens quite regularly to twentieth-century scholars. And having added a few passages ... he began to think again of what he had written, and to feel the old discontent with it, and hence to revise and rewrite. Such a return to what one had hoped to be completed is not peculiar to presumably disorderly poets. I imagine that some of my readers, released from the awful deadline of eventual publication, would go on revising their work from typescript to typescript, from galley to galley, from pageproof to pageproof, until Kingdom Come.

This disinterested appraisal of different possibilities, whose implication fatally undermines the enterprise undertaken in his joint editing project with Kane, is reminiscent of Skeat's remarks in his letter to Chambers forty-odd years previously:

---

[4] 'MSS R and F', 211–12. As we have seen (pp. 142–3 above), Skeat had supposed these manuscripts to represent a version intermediate between B and C. Donaldson acknowledges Skeat's related hypothesis, commenting 'Skeat's instincts seem often to have anticipated our most laboriously reached conclusions' (211). He thanks Kane for his help but notes that 'he is in no way responsible for the perhaps eccentric ideas set forth here, nor is he committed to their acceptance' (182 n.15). Kane had earlier considered the possibility that R and F might represent a separate authorial revision of the poem, and postponed decision until the manuscripts had been fully collated (see p. 316 n. 12 above). Donaldson later repudiated the views expressed in this article; see Kane–Donaldson, 64 n.101.

[5] Cf. Adams' comment on this remark in 'Editing *Piers Plowman B*', 33 n.3.

I believe we are utterly misled by modern notions, & clean forget how *casual* our ancestors were. How did *they* know that they were anything more than ephemeral productions? They looked upon them much more as we should regard a modern 'leading article'. They copied them because they wanted to *read them over again!* *not* because they wished to perpetuate them. They never regarded posterity one bit. What – as the famous remark runs – had posterity done for *them*?[6]

The same detachment is found in the typically engaging article published by Donaldson in 1968, where he reviewed the published material on the authorship question (see above, p. 321), and in his 1965 paper on 'The Psychology of Editors'.[7]

EDITORIAL ASSUMPTIONS

The Introduction to the joint edition of B, written by Kane but the product of a 'perfect collaboration, if ever there was one',[8] between the two scholars, entirely lacks this exploratory and self-undermining dimension. The edition is organised on lines similar to Kane's earlier edition of A, with five long chapters (compared with Kane's four), no subheadings, and no index. It is thus almost impossible to use for casual reference.[9] The first chapter lists and briefly describes the methods the two editors used to classify the manuscripts, while the remaining chapters outline editorial resources and methods. Unlike the A Introduction, the B Introduction does not devote an entire chapter to 'Manuscripts and Versions', regarding this matter as sufficiently fixed by the preceding edition.[10]

It is chapter 2, on the 'Classification of the Manuscripts', which begins to make clear the editors' assumptions about and general attitude towards their editing task. After a brisk account of the material peculiar to the B-tradition, for example, they state

> Common possession of these broad features, together with innu-
> merable less striking resemblances, creates a presumption that these
> copies represent a single manuscript tradition: they are descendants
> of an exclusive common ancestor, differentiated from this and from

---

[6] See pp. 234–5 above.   [7] Printed in 1970; see p. 406 below.
[8] Kane's phrase (in conversation).
[9] See 'Authorial vs. Scribal Writing', 61–2; Peter Barney's line-number index has now made it possible to trace the discussion or mention in the Introduction of individual lines and passages.
[10] Kane–Donaldson, 16–17.

one another entirely by the effects of scribal transmission. The correctness of this presumption will now begin to appear from our account of their classification. (p. 17)

But the editors do not consider the possibility that the 'presumption' they begin by making has determined the findings they come up with. They take a rigid and traditional approach to the business of analysing a manuscript tradition, assuming almost without question that the peculiarities of the B-MSS are more easily attributable to scribal error than to 'the revisions of a poet'. This approach, entirely in keeping with that of Kane's edition of A, is notably different from the attitude Donaldson took in the article quoted above. I shall return to this point shortly.

Kane–Donaldson now describe how they established their text, and consequently arrived at their classification of the manuscripts. As they say, in presenting the account of their classification immediately after the description of the manuscripts they follow traditional editorial practice. But in fact, their classification was only carried out *after* establishing the text. In this, they again follow the lead set by Kane's edition. Kane, as we have seen, found that relations between A-MSS were so complex that full-blown editing by recension was to all intents and purposes impracticable. Kane and Donaldson reinforce this point with a more theoretical objection to the illogical circularity of recension: because it is only agreements in *unoriginal* readings which can be taken as evidence of genetic relationship between manuscripts, 'classification of MSS cannot be safely undertaken until the whole text they contain is for practical purposes fixed'. And they comment in a footnote, 'In this situation lodges the ultimate absurdity of recension as an editorial method: to employ it the editor must have a stemma; to draw the stemma he must first edit his text by other methods. If he has not done this efficiently his stemma will be inaccurate or obscure, and his results correspondingly deficient; if he has been a successful editor he does not need a stemma, or recension, for his editing' (p. 17 n.10).[11]

Having established their text, however, Kane–Donaldson did go to the trouble of constructing a genealogy (or an attempt at one): not,

---

11   Cf. Donaldson's earlier remarks on recension, quoted above p. 249. This is an extreme view; as we have seen, Westcott and Hort recommend a gradual process of analysis, oscillating between genetic and internal assessment of readings. Kane–Donaldson's own method, as they fully acknowledge, is not exempt from the charge of circularity; see p. 212. For further discussion, see Adams, 'Editing *Piers Plowman B*'.

however, 'as a formality'. 'For one thing', they say, 'we were obliged to test the accuracy of a published genealogy of the B manuscripts', that of Elsie Blackman. And

> For another we believed (with justice, as it has turned out) that examination of the variational groups assumed by the manuscripts of our poem could not fail to be rewarding, notwithstanding our total scepticism about recension, and all genetic considerations apart. Whether or not the results of the process of classification supported earlier genetic conclusions, or even brought a new stemma to light, the operation would establish whether the B manuscripts were in fact descended from an exclusive common ancestor. (p. 18)

This is an unsubstantiated claim: the editors give no precise indication of *how* investigation of the manuscript relationships (as indicated by their determination of the original text) would 'establish whether the B manuscripts were in fact descended from an exclusive common ancestor'.

They then describe their method of classification, which was dependent, as they have explained, on their prior determination of the original B-Text:

> Our method of classification was that employed in editing A. We first established a text at all possible points by comparison of variant readings, identifying or restoring the original reading from knowledge of typical scribal substitutions and on considerations of sense, alliteration and the poet's *usus scribendi*. All agreements in substantive variation from this text, that is all agreements in certainly or presumably unoriginal readings affecting its sense, we treated as potential evidence of genetic relation. The variant groups formed by such agreements, whether in simple variation or in complex variation (if this could be traced), we collected, analyzed and attempted to interpret. (p. 18)[12]

The results of their classification demonstrated that Blackman had been right to qualify her findings with the caveat that examining the B-Text in full, rather than by sample passages, might bring to light additional information conflicting with her conclusions. Kane and Donaldson establish that the archetype of the extant B-MSS (Bx) was copied by two main families, one consisting of MSS R and F, and the

---

[12] A footnote explains certain 'deliberate exclusions' they made from the evidence.

other of the remaining MSS (WHmCrGYOC²CBmBoCotLM(H)S), thus correcting her earlier categorisation.[13]

The editors recognise, in a remarkably frank statement, the essentially subjective nature of the identification of originality on which this proceeding was based:

> We do not know of any method of classification which would answer as well as this one to the circumstances of manuscript tradition; nevertheless we must, before presenting our results, insist on its limitations. The first is human: because the method requires exercise of judgement at every stage, in the determinations of originality which afford its data, in the tracing of complex variation, and in the discrimination of variational and genetic groups, it implies successive possibilities of error. The second limitation is set by the almost always conflicting, often obscure quality of the evidence and the problem of interpretation by assessing relative probabilities that this poses. (p. 19)

The wonder is that this acknowledgement of the precarious and fragile nature of their undertaking goes hand in hand with the editorial confidence, indeed boldness, to be found in their edition.[14] It is worth picking out one particular flaw in their reasoning, since this relates to the question of *versions*. We have seen that Kane set out to establish his A-Text on the assumption that only *one*, if that, of the extant A variants could be original, and that consequently he diagnosed all the remaining variants as scribal. In doing this, he did not allow for the possibility that the author might have composed or rewritten A in such a way as to leave traces of more than one authorial reading at any point in the text. Subsequently, he regarded his findings as *proving* what he had originally assumed as premise, that the A-MSS derive from one authorial version and one version only. Kane and Donaldson exactly replicate that method, and hence that fallacious argument, in the procedure briefly outlined in the quotations above. They analysed the B variants with the assumption that one and one only (if that) was to be attributed to the author, and that hence all others were to be attributed to scribes. But they also assume that their method will subsequently 'establish whether the B manuscripts were in fact descended from a common ancestor'. They do not recognise that their method of determining originality among B-MSS

---

[13] See Kane–Donaldson, 63–9.
[14] Cf. also 212–13, where the editors discuss the hypothetical nature of their work.

will *inevitably* establish that the B-MSS were descended from an exclusive common ancestor.

Kane and Donaldson's three-text premise requires that they distinguish absolutely between the texts of A, B, and C. This is not as easy or straightforward as it sounds, since over substantial stretches of the poem either all three, or two, of the versions read essentially equivalent text. Considerable manuscript variation characterises these passages as much as it does the rest of the poem: the question then arises whether the variation is due to authorial revision or to scribal corruption. The variation comprises two different categories: first, where the manuscripts of any one version disagree among themselves over any particular reading, and second, where similar disagreement is found in the equivalent reading of the other version(s) too.

Kane and Donaldson consider the possibility of authorial revision within the B tradition towards the end of their discussion of B-MS textual relationships. They write as follows:

> The text of RF contains about 175 lines not found in WHmCrGYOC²CBmBoCotLMS [viz., the remaining B-MSS, other than H]; and these latter manuscripts (with H where it is a B text) contain about 170 lines not found in RF. These differences have suggested some form of authorial differentiation: specifically, that RF might preserve an authorial form of the poem intermediate between B and C; or conversely that the text of WHmCrGYOC²CBmBoCotLMS might incorporate changes made by the poet. (pp. 63–4)

They explain that both these explanations rest on inaccurate assumptions: first, that the B-MS tradition was otherwise relatively uncomplicated (sc. in comparison with that of A), and second, that RF were genetically linked with LM, which 'made it difficult to account for differences between these pairs of MSS, or agreements of LM with WHmCrGYOC²CBmBoCot against RF, except by assuming some form of authorial intervention, or contamination' (p. 64). 'But it is now clear', they say, 'that the difficulty was unreal': 'Full collation of the B manuscripts has done away with any impression of their uniformity of attestation; they are frequently and strikingly corrupt'; and full collation has also brought to light the extensive cross-cutting agreements between all the manuscripts, which places the apparently inconsistent relationships of LM in a context of a far more general inconsistency. (Kane and Donaldson attribute this inconsistency to convergent scribal variation.) The problem of attestation of different lines remains, however, and Kane and Donaldson explain this as the result of mechanical error on the part of the two scribes responsible for the two respective common ancestors (see pp. 64–9). They conclude that the apparent distinctiveness of the two manuscript families in B is referable to scribal omission of lines, not to authorial addition of them; and they thus preserve intact their theory that textual complexity in *Piers Plowman* is due to corrupt scribal transmission, not to authorial rewriting.

There are two objections to Kane and Donaldson's analysis here. First, they make no comment on the distinct oddness of their theory: why is it that the two scribes concerned omitted copy in this way? No other *Piers Plowman* scribes (of either A or B, that is) omitted comparable quantities of lines. One hundred and seventy-odd lines is a very large number to account for; and it is also peculiar that the (supposedly accidental) omissions of the longer passages do not result in narrative disruption.[15]

The second objection is that Kane and Donaldson discuss the matter principally in terms of *lines*, not of readings. Yet later in their Introduction they argue that MS F contains more than 100 original readings not found in the other manuscripts (p. 165 ff.).[16] It seems that this peculiarity might also be referable to the question of different authorial rewritings of B; but Kane and Donaldson never reopen it. Their prior conclusion that Langland wrote only one version of B, a conclusion they based on an analysis of F's lines, not its readings, does not seem to have allowed them to respond to the evidence presented by the readings in an unbiased way. There is a striking contrast between the apparent rigour with which they discuss various explanations for F's authentic readings, and their failure to investigate the most obvious one, that F may represent a separate, authorial strand of the B tradition.[17]

---

[15] A point made by Derek Pearsall in his review of *The B Version*. See also David Fowler's review, 'A New Edition of the B Text of *Piers Plowman*', 34ff. The two sets of omitted lines are listed in Kane and Donaldson, 66–9.

[16] In thirty of these instances, R is defective, so that 'F's reading is explicable as probably or possibly that of the main genetic group (RF)' (165).

[17] On Kane–Donaldson's use of F, see further Adams, 'Editing *Piers Plowman B*', 51. Their treatment of F here is an example of their failure to reconsider existing hypotheses in the light of new evidence; see p. 406 below. Schmidt, who also dismisses the notion that RF

Even if Kane–Donaldson are right in their belief that the differences between RF and the remaining B-MSS (except H) do not in any way reflect the original existence of different authorial *versions* of B, that is still no reason for discounting the possibility that they may reflect original authorial *rewritings*. Langland may have revised or retouched his poem sporadically, word by word rather than line by line (or passage by passage.) We have no reason to think this unlikely, especially since something similar has been suggested in the case of other medieval authors. [18]

The second category of *Piers Plowman* textual variation, that between one tradition and the next, is considered somewhat more explicitly in both A and B editions. Kane states that, 'in practice the intrinsic likelihood that the authorial revision responsible for the major differences between versions will also have introduced smaller differences, makes it impossible to say of many lines whether their various forms in the three versions originated with scribe or author' (p. 147 n.1). This contrasts significantly with the self-confidence of Kane and Donaldson's pronouncement, where they state as axiomatic the principle that 'not all [variations between the three versions over text common to all] can be authorial; some must necessarily have been created by scribal variation in one or more of the archetypal traditions' (p. 75). While this may seem reasonable, Kane's earlier diffidence on the possibility of being certain which of the variations can be confidently determined as scribal, which authorial, is conspicuous by its absence. Later, Kane and Donaldson describe how they determined 'whether differences between the archetypal readings in the B tradition and those of AC or A or C were created by authorial revision or scribal variation', and comment

> This minute delimitation of versions, which, we appreciate, is the most crucial operation in the whole editing of *Piers Plowman*, we have endeavoured to conduct with restraint, permitting ourselves to

might represent an authorial rewriting of the poem, appears to be even more reliant on this family than Kane–Donaldson, adopting 'some 500' of their readings into his text of his first edition (xxxvi; cf. his second edition, lx–lxv).

[18] See Derek Pearsall, 'Authorial Revision in Some Late-Medieval Texts', for an account of recent editorial attitudes towards authorial revision in Middle English writings. An example from Old English can be found in Malcolm Godden's positing of sporadic authorial revision as an explanation for textual relationships in the manuscripts of Ælfric's Catholic Homilies: 'One suspects that much of the revision of detail originated when Ælfric was checking newly copied manuscripts for errors, rather than as a deliberate process of revision, and that revisions were often copied sporadically from one pattern-manuscript to another within Ælfric's scriptorium' (*Ælfric's Catholic Homilies*, lxxxvi).

reach conclusions only in cases which seemed beyond serious doubt. (pp. 149–50)[19]

Various critics have argued that several of their textual decisions can scarcely be admitted under this description; meanwhile, the language Kane and Donaldson use in their development of this statement reveals their underlying resistance to the possibility that authorial variants rather than scribal corruption are responsible for differences between the archetypal versions of the three texts:

> we *accepted* as authorial not only all large differences of structure or meaning, but also every small difference which did not seem explicable in terms of scribal imperception or evident stupidity, and every stylistic difference which might conceivably reflect an author's taste rather than a scribal tendency of variation. Where we could see so much as a possibility that the difference between B and another version might reflect some authorial intention we *allowed* this full force. Further we *allowed* the greater likelihood of finical and relatively insignificant revision in certain positions ... [e.g., where Langland was unarguably responsible for substantive differences between A and B or B and C; my italics]. (p. 150)

This suggests that their expectation is of scribal error, and that they are prepared to admit the possibility of scribal accuracy only under certain specified conditions.[20] The last sentence also suggests that the same phenomena were interpreted as symptomatic of scribal corruption or of authorial revision depending on their position in the text rather than on any inherent characteristics, a criterion which does not seem to square with the scrupulousness of those listed immediately above.

Kane and Donaldson's Introduction furnishes many further instances of the editors' certainty about their discrimination of scribal from authorial readings, even though the criteria they bring to bear on their decisions are never fully discussed or justified. They say of instances where they do detect authorial revision between versions that

the determination of the likelihood is inevitably subjective; *a poster-*

---

19 Cf. the similar statement by Russell, written before the publication of Kane–Donaldson, that the 'guiding principle' of the Athlone editors has been 'that the testimony of the manuscripts is not to be abandoned unless it can be shown beyond reasonable doubt that the present state of the text is indefensible' ('Editorial Theory and Practice in Middle English Texts', 173).

20 Kane and Donaldson together appear to have a significantly higher expectation of scribal error than Kane alone did earlier. Compare, for example, Kane's remark that 'the majority of scribes did, after all, copy a very large number of words in a great many lines faithfully, often to the extent of keeping spelling and dialect forms of the exemplar' (Kane, 126).

iori because a purpose imputable to the author, as the whole poem reveals him, seems discernible behind the change; or aesthetic because the change seems of a kind which a poet rather than a scribe would make. In other words such differences suggest enlargements of imaginative conception, insights into new modes of development, altered senses of the poetic or doctrinal value of topics, or intensified homiletic purpose. (p. 75; cf. pp. 83–4)

These remarks make it clear that Kane and Donaldson do not seriously consider the possibility of whimsical, inconsistent revision, or revision from a good to a less good reading, whose purpose may not now be recoverable by an editor. Kane and Donaldson also reject the possibility that Langland may have decided against an A reading for his B text, but subsequently have reinstated it in C.[21] It is clear why these possibilities should have been unpalatable: they remove the rationale by which one may distinguish with confidence between authorial and some scribal readings.

An examination of the textual apparatus to even a short specimen passage of their text reveals that Kane and Donaldson emend the archetype of B to read as A very considerably indeed.[22] Comparison of their text with that of Kane shows that many of the differences between the readings of Kane's text and of the B-MSS are construed by Kane and Donaldson as indicating corruption in the B archetype rather than authorial revision between A and B. Such differences vary from the very minor (e.g., singular as opposed to plural nouns where the meaning of the context is unaffected, or omission or inclusion of *And* at the beginning of a line) to major lexical changes between the versions. The B archetype or majority B-MS reading is emended to read as Kane's A-Text even when the C-MSS are in agreement with the B-MSS. Kane and Donaldson justify such emendation by their hypothesis that in his revision of B to C Langland used a scribal copy of his original B-Text (although one less flawed than the archetype of all existing B-MSS), so that many agreements between B-MSS and

---

[21] See Kane–Donaldson, 75ff., esp. 82: 'it seems to us right to reject the possibility of the erratic poet for the established certainty of the inaccurate copyist, and to recognize the agreements of AC against B as evidence of the corruption of the archetypal text of B'. The process of reasoning recalls Chambers and his argument on pickpockets, p. 276 above. Cf. also p. 258 above.

[22] Kane later (1986) stated, 'Donaldson and I professed to identify, in [the archetypal text of B], some 760 unoriginal readings, that is to say, corruption in 11 percent of its 7,200 lines' ('"Good" and "Bad" Manuscripts', 143). But it should be noted that their reconstruction of the B archetype was itself an editorial process in which emendation of manuscript evidence played an important part: thus Fowler estimated Kane and Donaldson's total number of emendations to amount to 'more than 1,600'; see 'Editorial "Jamming"', 213–14.

C-MSS are due to the same post-archetypal corruption.[23] This means that in practice their text of B very closely resembles that of Kane's A (much more so than does Schmidt's B-Text, although Schmidt adopts many of Kane and Donaldson's editorial principles).

Such consistent emendation of B to read as (Kane's) A argues distinct views on Langland's methods and motives in revising A. Unfortunately, Kane and Donaldson nowhere provide us with a detailed account of what they believed these were. The reader is not left completely helpless; one can infer, for example, that Kane and Donaldson assume Langland did not revise his poem to make B readings more explicit and more emphatic than the corresponding ones in A, since B readings with these characteristics are invariably struck out as scribal. But the editors do not justify or defend their implicit assumptions on Langland's mode of revision, and it is inappropriate that the reader should be reduced to such inferences. It would have been very useful if Kane and Donaldson had spelt out clearly the ways in which, in their view, B differs from A, so as to justify their decisions on textual cruces where, despite the over-whelming or unanimous testimonial of B-MSS, they make B read the same as A.[24] It would also have been useful if they had explored more explicitly the implications of their pervasive use of Kane's A-Text during the early part of the poem, for this raises some substantial methodological problems for their two editions. I shall now turn to look at these in more detail.

IMPLICATIONS OF THE ATHLONE B-TEXT FOR THE ATHLONE A-TEXT: THE 'B/C' READINGS IN A-MSS REVISITED

As we have seen, Kane established his A-Text without reference to the variants of the other *Piers Plowman* manuscripts, despite the fact

---

23 A theory first put forward by Chambers (p. 228 above). See Kane–Donaldson, ch. 4, 'The C Reviser's B Manuscript', 98–127. Such emendation raises a difficult problem for the editor of C: if Langland incorporated a B reading identified by Kane and Donaldson as scribal into his C-revision, does that not amount to authorial sanction? Or is the editor of C to revise his text to read as (Kane's) A? Further: if Langland found the reading acceptable, might that not indicate that Kane and Donaldson's identification of error is fallible? I have been able to find only one notice of this problem in the writings of the Athlone editors, by George Russell in 1969: 'A reading originally scribal in origin is transformed by the fact of its admission by the C-reviser into a genuine reading of the C-version. It is, in my opinion, hazardous to edit these readings out of the C-version since we have no way of judging the motives which led to the retention. It may have been inadvertence: it may also have been a deliberate decision' ('Some Aspects of the Process of Revision', 40 n.21).

24 Cf. p. 351 n. 24 above.

that such a policy flew in the face of the dictum established by Chambers and Grattan, and earlier accepted by Kane himself: 'so inter-related are the texts, that before you can have a final A-text, you must have an adequate B- and C-text'. When he came to edit B, he had changed his mind, presumably because he believed that the B archetype – unlike the A archetype – was so corrupt that it was intolerable to retain its readings. Substitutes had to be found, and the first recourse was to the manuscripts of the other versions. In other words, Kane and Donaldson assumed that the pervasive differences between A and B, AC and B, and C and B were, in many cases, due not to authorial revision – Langland changing his mind in between one version and the next – but instead to scribal corruption in the B archetype. As we have seen, their belief that the B archetype was substantially corrupt sanctioned their emendation of its readings on a very considerable scale.[25]

To assume that the hypothetical archetype of all existing manuscripts of a poem is corrupt brings with it certain weighty textual consequences. Notably, this assumption taught Kane–Donaldson to attach very little (if any) significance to majority attestation of a reading within a version, if this conflicted with their editorial judgement. The B-MSS evidence a quite remarkable degree of uniformity (*pace* the remarks of Kane and Donaldson quoted above) and many B readings are attested unanimously by all the B-MSS. (As we have seen, this uniformity made a strong impression on Skeat, who believed that there were 'probably more doubtful points in a single Canterbury Tale or in a single Act in some of Shakespeare's plays than in the whole of the B-text of Piers the Plowman'.)[26] But many of these B readings, despite their unanimous testimony, were – in the view of Kane–Donaldson – corrupt.[27] It followed, presumably, that

[25] David Fowler's review of Kane–Donaldson provides a useful analysis of Kane–Donaldson's emendations in the Appendix; he lists 1,600-odd instances where he believes the emendations to be unacceptable ('A New Edition of The B Text of *Piers Plowman*', 39–42). He also, as already noted, provides a devastating analysis of their *rate* of emendation of the archetypal B-Text over B Pro-Passus X, indicating that they emend B nearly eight times more often over stretches of the poem when A is not available as a control than when it is available (25). So striking a variation in the perceived rate of originality in B is remarkable, to say the least, and more likely to be attributable to Kane–Donaldson's varying editorial policy than to genuine fluctuations in the B archetype's accuracy. A comparable analysis is made by Patterson, who works out that, if we are to trust Kane–Donaldson's judgement, the B archetype is ten times more corrupt by itself than over stretches of the poem where it has text in common with C. This is simply not credible. See 'The Logic of Textual Criticism and the Way of Genius', 217 n.52.

[26] See p. 150 above.

[27] They stress 'the relative unimportance of strength of attestation as evidence of originality',

unanimous or majority attestation in A and C needed also to be treated with extreme caution.

Retrospectively applying his new insights to his old A-Text, Kane must have realised that he had to rethink some of the principles by which he had edited the first version of the poem. There, he had applied more conservative principles: he had placed considerably more faith in the probability that, other things being equal, the reading of the majority of manuscripts at the point of variation was likely to be original; and where evidence was divided between two or more variants which were, for whatever reason, indistinguishable in poetic quality, he had printed the reading of the base manuscript T.[28] As we have seen, he did not think it proper to bring in the testimony of B or C, except in very unusual circumstances. In a footnote to the B version (p. 159 n.78), Kane describes his embarrassment at having stuck to these principles so doggedly. 'Various differences', he now says, 'between [the A-Text] as printed in Vol. I and that of B are in fact scribal and will disappear on more rigorously logical editing of A. Its editor is now embarrassed to recall his conservatism with respect to some of these.' In similar vein, he records towards the end of the B version Introduction that he was 'deluded by the "ideal" of conservative editing', and hence failed to correct several instances of 'post-archetypal or archetypal corruption in the A tradition'. For this was the crucial point. Kane's edition of A was in fact an attempt to reconstruct the hypothetical archetype of the extant A-MSS, and not, except very exceptionally, to get past that archetype to the author's original. No doubt this was, at least in part, because Kane judged that the A archetype was pretty accurate: that is, that there was little difference between the text he could reconstruct from existing A-MS evidence and Langland's original text of A. (He later revised this opinion, as we shall see below.)

and caution against undue credibility in the face of majority attestation: 'The old maxim "manuscripts should be weighed, not counted" should be revised to run "readings should be weighed, not manuscripts counted". But to the inexperienced in textual criticism an array of sigils after a variant is bound to seem impressive' (63, 63 n.100).

[28] He makes this practice clear throughout ch. IV of his Introduction, 'Editorial Resources and Methods'; see for example 150: 'A very large number of readings in various manuscripts were excluded because they were in the first instance minority readings; many such were not intrinsically inferior to those adopted, but were simply less well attested. The employment of this standard was inevitable when rival readings were of equal intrinsic value, and neither contained an argument for originality over the other. The frequency of such situations can be illustrated by the following examples from the first hundred lines of Passus V ...'

What would have happened if Kane *had* systematically consulted the testimony of B- and C-MSS when analysing A variants? This is of course a difficult question to answer. But we have a resource available to us that Kane himself, at the time of editing A, did not: namely a full record of the evidence of the B-MSS, clearly and accurately listed for us in the textual apparatus of Kane–Donaldson.

If we compare the texts and critical apparatuses of the Athlone A and B Versions over the Prologue and first eight passus of A, we find many occasions where a reading witnessed by some of the A-MSS, but rejected by Kane as scribal, is also the reading of the B archetype – and often of C as well.[29] The number depends on criteria for collation, but is something over 250 – or in other words, once every seven or so lines in A Pro-VIII. In these instances, the following line-up of agreements, somewhat disquieting, appears as a result:

> Some A-MSS & Bx (& C) versus Ka (& other A-MSS) & (usually) KD.[30]

(Bx designates the reading of all or most B-MSS.) Kane–Donaldson emended the Bx reading to that of Kane's text in about 70 per cent of these cases – despite the absence of B-MS support for such emendation – since the two editors were predisposed to regard the B archetype as faulty, and regularly inferior to A. It could be that there is acceptable justification for Kane's and Kane and Donaldson's choice in these instances. Kane offers no justification, since he does not acknowledge that such a pattern of agreement exists. But Kane and Donaldson, who did consult the readings of the other *Piers Plowman* versions, evidently knew of the existence of agreements between the B-Text and A variants rejected by Kane. They signal their presence, however, only where B *and* C are in agreement with the A reading rejected by Kane, and where they themselves reject the B reading – in other words, only in what one might take to be the most damaging of these instances. Surprisingly, they do not regard these agreements as in any way challenging or undermining Kane's

---

[29] I list the B readings in A-MSS over A Pro-Pass VIII in my unpublished D. Phil. thesis, 'Some Implications of the Z-Text for the Textual Tradition of *Piers Plowman*'.

[30] In about half of these 250-plus instances, C agrees with the A-MS reading *not* adopted by Kane; in about a fifth, it agrees with Kane's text, and in the remainder its text deviates from that of AB. Schmidt chooses the B-MS reading for the text of his first edition in nearly 80 per cent of the instances, and rejects it to read as Kane's and Kane–Donaldson's texts for the remaining 20 per cent (as contrasted with Kane–Donaldson's 30 per cent and 70 per cent respectively). In just under half these cases, the A-MS and B reading rejected by Kane and Kane–Donaldson is also found in Z.

(and their own) textual decisions. Instead, they take agreements between rejected A variants, B, and C against their two texts as confirmation of their decisions, in the following way:

> the observable generation in one textual tradition of certain specific kinds of readings by the identifiable operation of known scribal tendencies establishes something like a certainty that the same or similar readings in another tradition will have a similar origin. We therefore reject the possibility of authorial revision. (p. 102)

The logic seems to be that the more often a variant occurs, the less likely it is to be original.[31] This passage makes it very clear that Kane and Donaldson were determined to attribute much textual variation within and (especially) between versions to scribal miscopying, and reluctant to admit the possibility of authorial rewriting.

This again prompts one to ask the following question: if Kane had been aware of the relative weighting of the textual variants across all three versions, would he have made the same decision between variants when editing A in the first place? One test-example, chosen because it presents a genuine difficulty of interpretation, is a reading at A Passus II 144, which Kane prints as

As fo[bb]is & faitours þat on here feet iotten

Here, all A-MSS except four, together with C and all B-MSS except one, read *rennys* for the fourth stave of the line; Kane however prints *iotten*, which is the reading of two of the other A-MSS (TH²). Kane–Donaldson also print *iotten*, despite the fact that this reading is found in no B-MS.[32] Kane explains that his reason for choosing *iotten* was that it is a harder reading than *rennen*, and that it is not easy to see how the latter reading would have been misunderstood by scribes to produce *iotten*. *iotten*, on the other hand, which 'is probably a past tense of the verb "to go"; see *NED* s.v. *Yode, Yede* v. γ²', might have

---

[31] This assumption is in direct opposition to Kane's original views on the significance of majority manuscript support for a variant, on which he based his criteria for detecting the direction of scribal variation: 'In practice unanimity of support must be accepted as establishing the strongest presumption of originality, unless the reading attested by all the manuscripts is patently unsatisfactory,' 148. Cf. Kane–Donaldson, 129 n.1, and the previous chapter, where I have tried to show that Kane's identification of the 'known scribal tendencies' referred to here is in fact predicated on the assumption that variation in A-MSS is never due to authorial revision.

[32] See B Passus II 183 and C Passus II 193. Z also reads *rennes* (Passus II 153). The single B-MS, H, reads ȝede. Schmidt prints *rennen*. There is also considerable variation in the first half of this line; see the critical apparatuses in Kane and Kane–Donaldson.

been misunderstood, and have given rise to scribal *trotten* (A-MS Ch's reading) on the one hand and *rennen* on the other (p. 436).[33]

The particular problem raised by this example is that Kane's argument seems absolutely right where the A-MS variants are concerned. It is only when we look at the overwhelming evidence of B and C – which Kane himself, presumably, did not consult – that we may start to question his decision – not only in B, but also, retrospectively, in A. Could it be, for example, that *iotten* and *rennen* are authorial variants, both present in the A tradition as a result, perhaps, of the poet's marginal annotation, and that Langland subsequently rejected *iotten* in favour of the clearer and more communicative variant *rennen*? Such a hypothesis does not square with traditional criteria for distinguishing between scribal and authorial readings; but that is no reason to reject it.[34]

Another example, less controversial perhaps, is chosen more at random. Kane's Passus A III 138 reads *She* – i.e., Meed – *blissiþ þise bisshopis ʒif þei be lewid.* The reading *ʒif* is supported by five A-MSS; three other A-MSS, all B-MSS, and C read *þeigh* instead. Kane–Donaldson dismiss the unanimous testimony of the B-MSS and emend to read as Kane's A. In this example, the decision between the two A variants is a fine one, with *ʒif* perhaps having the satiric cutting edge over *þeigh* – and also being a less obvious, and therefore harder, reading than *þeigh*. On the other hand, it is not *that* hard, and one of the other A variants which Kane rejects, *þey þat* (RD), is arguably more satiric and less obvious.[35] Whatever the decision on A variants – and it seems certainly justifiable for Kane to have followed his base-manuscript, T, at this point – most editors would have qualms about emending B-MSS on the basis of so slight a justification, especially when none is found among the B-MSS themselves. We may revert to our question: would Kane have emended T's reading had he known of that of B and C? And would Kane–Donaldson then have preserved the B-MS reading?

Disputing individual examples is always tendentious, and can distract attention from the general issues underlying choice between rival variants. If we turn instead to a general consideration of this category of variants (agreements between A-MSS, B, and C, against

---

[33] The remaining A-MS, E, reads *ganges*.

[34] Cf. Skeat's speculations on *throly*, quoted above p. 327.

[35] The remaining A variants are *þif* W, *þeigh þat* UV, *þere þat* M, *of all* E – most of which have more in common with *þeigh* than with *ʒif*.

the texts of Kane and Kane–Donaldson) we can ask a second question which may shed light on our first. What are the theoretically possible explanations for their peculiar pattern, namely that, on average, more than once every ten A lines, a reading found in some A-MSS, in all or most B-MSS, and in C as well, is rejected by Kane and Kane–Donaldson, who instead print an alternative reading in A (often well attested by other A-MSS), and the same reading in B (often in the teeth of the testimony of *all* B-MSS)? There are, I think, four main possibilities:

(1) Kane made the wrong decision when editing A. The agreement between A-MSS and Bx (and C) versus Kane and KD is the one *original* to AB(C), despite Kane's choice against it (which was made, presumably, without considering the readings of B and C). Kane's text therefore prints a scribal error, and where Kane–Donaldson carry over his reading into their edition of B they are simply reproducing this error.

(2) The reading chosen by Kane is an authorial variant in the A tradition, which survives (for whatever reason) in some A-MSS; Langland carried over the *other* variant into his writing of B (and C).

(3) Kane's reading is the one original to A (but not to B). The scribes of the A-MSS rejected by Kane coincidentally corrupted their manuscripts to read the same as the authorial B Text – or, perhaps, introduced this reading into their manuscripts as a result of contamination from a post-archetypal B-MS (which they knew from having read or copied B-MSS). In this case, Kane–Donaldson would be wrong to emend the reading of the B archetype to that of A, for the difference between A and B at this point is due to authorial revision.

(4) Kane's reading is the one original to A *and* B. The A variants rejected by Kane agree with Bx (and C) *in error*: Bx is, as often, corrupt (if applicable, the error survives, for whatever reason, in C too), and A scribes *either* contaminated their texts with this reading, *or*, alternatively, miscopied their exemplars to produce exactly the same error coincidentally produced by the scribe of Bx. This is the 'hardest' explanation, i.e., the one which requires the greatest number of assumptions, but it is the only one that 'saves' Kane's and Kane–Donaldson's texts.[36]

---

[36] Chiefly, it requires the assumption of a good deal of coincidence. On coincidence, Kane–Donaldson themselves remark that 'to explain textual phenomena as random is (we believe) permissible only when other explanations in terms of established processes of cause and effect are not acceptable' (103, though cf. 103 n.8). 'Established processes of cause and effect' would, in the cases under discussion, be the retention of A readings in B, and AB

It would seem reasonable to assume that, during the process of editing B, Kane retrospectively compared his 1960 A-Text with that of the various B- and C-MSS, to determine whether, in the light of evidence which he had not systematically brought to bear on A-MS variants, his original decision had been the best one. Implicit in such rethinking of his text would be views on Langland's processes of revision. Would the author be likely to change his mind back and forth between versions, returning to a reading in C that he had discarded (for whatever reason) in B? How likely is it that the explanation for a reading in A which looks weak beside that of B and C is that Langland improved his wording between B and C? Or might A's reading – or the one that Kane himself printed – instead be due to archetypal or post-archetypal corruption? What *were* Langland's motives for rewriting A? Might the famous 'corruption' of the B archetype be to any extent attributable to Langland's desire to make his text more straightforward and communicative to his readers, e.g. 'flatter', 'prosier', 'more explicit', 'more emphatic' – namely, precisely those characteristics that Kane–Donaldson attribute to scribes? What is the likelihood that, as he revised, the poet 'debased' his original choice?[37] Unfortunately, none of these issues receive any serious overt attention in the Athlone A- and B-Text Introductions.

As the two editors recognise, the principle that *all* manuscripts of *Piers Plowman* are to be taken into consideration when editing any one version means that two editing operations have to take place: first, reconstructing the hypothetical single archetype of the extant manuscripts of the version (supposing that there was indeed just one archetype), and second, comparing it with the correspondingly reconstructed hypothetical archetypes of the other versions.[38] These operations are distinct in theory but may often fall together in practice: decision on the first operation, determining the original reading of the archetype, may well be influenced by carrying out the second, seeing what the other two (three) versions have to say. This is not least the case because many of the variants present where all three (four) texts read equivalently are of the type 'which poses the editor's most serious problem' (Kane, p. 116), since they are roughly equivalent on the various grounds of style and sense. In other

readings in C, because Langland put them there – not because a number of different scribes all coincidentally (randomly) corrupted their exemplars to read the same.

[37] Whitaker's suggestion; see above, p. 39.

[38] Kane–Donaldson, 128. This understanding was in essence anticipated by Knott; see p. 244 above.

instances, it is possible to argue that one variant is superior to the other(s). In all cases, decisions between variants both within and between versions can only be made as a result of prior suppositions about Langland's motives for and methods of revision. Unfortunately, Kane–Donaldson do not make this clear, and they provide only scarce discussion of the problem.[39]

The difficulty of decision between the variants is illustrated by the example discussed in the previous chapter, where Kane assumed that the reading found in EAMH³, *& sowen it after* was scribal, and seemed unaware that it was the reading of both B and C. This brings us back to our original question: if Kane had known – as clearly he did not – that B and C agreed with some of the A-MS readings which he had at first sight rejected as scribal, would he have changed his mind, and recognised these readings as original to A?

This question can be partly answered by turning to Kane's second edition of the *A Version*, published in 1988 (referred to henceforth as A2, in contrast to Kane's first edition, A1). Here he reproduced his original text almost exactly, adding only a five-page section on 'The A Text in 1988'.[40] This brief essay listed fifty-three emendations to the 1960 text, Kane commenting that

> twenty five years of editing the B version of Piers, working with the editor of the C version, and studying the textual problems of *The Legend of Good Women* and *The Canterbury Tales* have confirmed or extended my cautious generalizations of the 1950s about what happened to the texts of great poems during manuscript transmission. I now see many more types of situation in which the actual language of the text itself induced variation, in particular unconscious substitution, through engagement with immediate or more extended context. (p. 459)

---

[39] As at 75–6, quoted above, pp. 389–90. Here they simply and briefly assert their views on Langland's motives for revision; for example, that only differences between versions suggesting 'enlargements of imaginative conception, insights into new modes of development, altered senses of the poetic or doctrinal value of topics, or intensified homiletic purpose' are to be accepted as due to the poet rather than to scribes. But many of the differences between A, B, and C are on a far less grand scale than this, as the editors implicitly accept by printing the texts they do.

[40] See 'George Kane's Processes of Revision', 84–96, for a detailed discussion of the changes Kane proposed in A2 to his original edition of A. A second edition of the *B Version* was published at the same time, virtually identical to the first, and containing only one, unacknowledged, change (at B Passus XIV 28). For notice of this and for a list of the typographical and other minor differences between A1 and A2, see Kathleen M. Hewitt-Smith, 'Revisions in the Athlone Editions of the A and B Versions of Piers Plowman'. The single alteration to the B Version was presumably made in response to the criticism of John Alford in his review of Kane–Donaldson, which discusses this specific reading.

These remarks arouse the expectation that many of the changes Kane now recommends will take the form of more radical emendations, and this indeed turns out to be the case. Kane lists his proposed changes to his original text under five categories (pp. 460-3), all of which comprise instances where he now feels that he adhered too rigidly to the readings of his base manuscript, or to his reconstruction of the archetype of the A-Text. It is particularly notable that thirty-six of his fifty-three proposed emendations are made as a result of subsequent comparison with the B- and C-Texts. We can expect, therefore, that readings such as '& sowen it after' may come up for re-evaluation.

As it happens, Kane does not include this particular reading as due for emendation in A2, which implies that he must think that EAMH^3 read as they do on account of contamination from B (i.e. he has chosen explanation 3 above) – although, as we saw in the last chapter (pp. 357-8), he originally dismissed contamination in these manuscripts as insignificant.

This is curious, since Kane does regard several other B readings in EAMH^3 as original to A. The supposition that some B readings in these manuscripts are attributable to contamination, but that others are the original of both A and B, needs acknowledgement, and indeed argument and defence. At Passus VI 71, Kane printed in A1 '[And]-loke-þat-þou-leiȝe-nouȝt-for-no-manis-biddyng', and commented (p. 71) 'this line seems to be deliberately unmetrical'. For 'loke ... nouȝt', EMH^3 read 'In none manere ellis', which is also the reading of ZBC.[41] As before, Kane seems not to have noticed the agreement between EMH^3 and BC, but he does list the line in his A2 note as due for emendation to the latter reading, commenting that '[And]-loke-þat-þou-leiȝe-nouȝt' is 'substitution of a more explicit and easier reading' (the issue of alliteration receives no mention, although the line remains unmetrical). At Passus VII 233, Kane originally printed 'Actif lif oþer contemplatyf; crist wolde it alse'. AMH^3 agree with Z and B in reversing the terms *contemplatyf* and *actif*; Kane lists this reading as due for adoption in A2.[42] In all three of these cases, and in many others, the same A-MS group, EAMH^3, turns out to agree with

---

[41] MS A's version is much the same as the text Kane prints.

[42] The textual situation here is complex. In fact, the full form of the line which Kane now advocates, and which Kane–Donaldson printed in 1975, is not found in any of the extant A-MSS or B-MSS. Remarkably, though, it is the reading of Z. This might be taken as arguing either that Kane–Donaldson did an excellent job of reconstructing Langland's original version, as found in Z, or that the Z scribe's editorial abilities rivalled even their own. See the texts and variants in Kane's A and Kane–Donaldson's B (Passus VI 235), and compare Z Passus VII 235.

Z, B, and often C, against the reading of Kane's first A-Text. Scanning Kane's A2 list turns up several further examples of his changing his mind in favour of the readings of this group,[43] but Kane makes no mention of this. In fact, the genetically linked group EAMH³, together with several other manuscripts, notably W(N), are those textually closest to Z, and between them these manuscripts account for the overwhelming proportion of B(C) readings to be found in A-MSS – as well as a handful of B/C lines Kane earlier decided were unoriginal to the A-Text.[44] It is obviously a possibility to be considered that these manuscripts, whose reading was in many instances rejected by Kane for his A-Text, in fact contain the authentic A-Text readings – i.e., that explanation 1 above is the correct one for their agreement with the two later texts (and, where applicable, with Z).[45]

THE CORRUPT MANUSCRIPTS OF THE B AND C REVISERS

Decision between the four explanations outlined above must have had great significance not only for Kane's rethinking the text of A, but also for Kane–Donaldson's determining the original reading of B. In many cases, the two editors came to the conclusion that Kane's text was the original of both A *and* B: that is, they chose the fourth explanation, and thus favoured Kane's text despite the agreement against it of some A-MSS, often all B-MSS, and frequently C as well.[46] But in other cases (at the time of editing B, 1975, over thirty separate instances), they decided that Kane's decision between A variants had been at fault. This, at any rate, is the process of reasoning which I believe lies behind the various qualifications to A1 offered by Kane in his footnotes to the Introduction of the B-Text, where these thirty-odd instances are listed (Kane apologising, as I have already mentioned, for having been earlier 'deluded by the "ideal" of conservative editing').[47] In most of these cases, Kane had, they

---

[43] Passus V 112, 113; V 254; VII 61 (MH³ only; this portion of text is absent in E); VIII 100; all listed in A2, 461–2.

[44] See Kane, 30-1. He believes that the BC lines in EAMH³ are 'unlikely to be the consequence of comparison of versions [sc. of BC with A]' (38).

[45] I discuss this matter in more detail in 'Some Implications of the Z-Text for the Textual Tradition of *Piers Plowman*'; it is an obvious topic of further research.

[46] For some examples, see 'The Textual Principles of Kane's A Text', 72 n.5, and cf. Kane–Donaldson, 101–2. Patterson, I think uniquely, notes the dangerous implications of such agreements, but (somewhat surprisingly) suggests they do not undermine Kane–Donaldson's editorial position ('The Logic of Textual Criticism and the Way of Genius', 65).

[47] See e.g. 205 and n.154, both discussed in more detail in 'George Kane's Processes of Revision', 84ff. Kane began to doubt the conservatism of his editing of A as early as 1960,

believed, wrongly reconstructed the A archetype, failing to detect the direction of error among the A variants; although in a few places, he had correctly reproduced the reading of the A archetype, but failed to identify it as corrupt. Unfortunately, the editors nowhere spell out in detail their process of reasoning, for they give no indication to the reader of the large number of agreements between rejected AB(C) variants, nor, consequently, offer us any explanation (along the lines of 1–4 above) why these should exist. Nor do they spell out in detail the implications of their own new policy of consulting the readings of other versions when establishing the original text of any one version.

If the reconstruction of Kane's and Kane–Donaldson's thinking which I have sketched out above is correct, then one of the hypotheses of the Athlone B-Text that has greatly vexed reviewers, the proposition that the C reviser used a corrupt version of B to make his revision, appears (I think) in a more intelligible light. As we have seen, the theory of the corrupt B archetype had been established by Kane's predecessors Chambers and particularly Blackman, although neither had anticipated the scale on which it was to be invoked by the Athlone editors. It seems likely that the proposition of the C reviser's corrupt B-MS, like the corresponding proposition of the B reviser's corrupt A-MS, was virtually forced upon Kane–Donaldson as the only way of 'saving' Kane's text. This is because their decision to opt for the fourth explanation, corroborating Kane's decision in A1 and treating this as the original reading of B also, meant that they had to find a way to explain why other A-MSS, B, and C all agreed in an alternative reading.[48]

This consideration seems to be behind the remarks made by Kane–Donaldson in the Athlone B-Text (and echoed by Kane in A2) on corrupt archetypal readings in all three texts. In another of their highly significant footnotes to the Introduction of the B-Text, the two editors state 'The agreements in unoriginality between A and B where C is revised and between all versions are to be explained as early archetypal errors of the A tradition which escaped notice in respectively one or both revisions. They are thus incidentally evidence that Langland used a scribal manuscript for revising to B', and they list or refer to nineteen AB or ABC lines which are marked by such

the date of publication, expressing his suspicions of the A archetype in a letter to Kenneth Sisam of 9 March 1960 (now in the possession of Miss Celia Sisam).

[48] My account here should be compared with that of Adams, 'Editing *Piers Plowman B*', e.g. 48–50.

archetypal corruption (p. 211 n.172). Kane says much the same thing at the end of his A2 note, listing ten 'evidently archetypal, unmetrical A lines which survive in B or in BC' as 'evidence that Langland used a scribal A manuscript for his B revision'.[49] He comments that, with one exception, 'it would not be hard to emend these lines conjecturally. But the consideration that Langland once or even twice missed or did nothing about them gives them a kind of sanction.'

The theory that Langland used a scribal manuscript of A when revising to B – and the better-known theory, propounded at length in the fourth chapter of Kane–Donaldson's Introduction, that Langland used a scribal manuscript of B when revising to C – may well, at first sight, strike readers as preposterous. Agreement between all or most of the manuscripts of two or more versions of the poem would appear, in the first instance, to be a strong indication that the readings in question are authorial. But many of these readings, Kane–Donaldson believed, were actually scribal: as I have described, this belief was the ineluctable consequence of their choosing explanation 4 above, which saves Kane's earlier text, but carries with it the corollary that the alternative readings witnessed by other A-MSS, and found also in B(C), had to be scribal. How then were they to explain the spread of agreement between manuscripts and versions in readings which they could not, without repudiating Kane's A-Text, allow to be authorial? The editors' solution was remarkable and ingenious: for both B and C, Kane–Donaldson posit the theory of the reviser's corrupt archetype, in order to explain how, respectively, A-MSS and B-MSS, and B-MSS and C-MSS, come to share readings which they believe are scribal, not authorial, in origin.[50] Such a theory raises several questions, not all of them answered by the two editors. For example, if Langland was – according to their own account – prepared to countenance readings which Kane–Donaldson judge to be scribal, does that not cast serious doubt on the reliability of the editors' identification in the first place? Further, the fact that

---

[49] The discrepancy between Kane–Donaldson's figure of nineteen lines and Kane's A2 figure of ten is a significant one, indicating Kane's failure in 1988 to acknowledge the full implications of his stated beliefs in 1975. See further 'George Kane's Processes of Revision', 89ff.

[50] They devote an entire chapter, thirty pages, to discussion of 'The C Reviser's B Manuscript'. Their references to the B reviser's use of a corrupt A-Text, on the other hand, is almost entirely limited to footnotes towards the end of their B-Text Introduction. As noted by Fowler ('A New Edition of the B Text of *Piers Plowman*', 26–7) this is a very striking disparity. It may indicate that the theory of the B reviser's corrupt copy of A was an afterthought.

the two editors are prepared to say that the same reading is in one version of the poem scribal, but in the corresponding place in one (or two) of the other versions authorial, would appear to make nonsense of (1) their characterisation throughout the A- and B-Text Introductions of scribal readings as unremittingly inept, and Langland's readings as consistently of the highest possible poetic quality,[51] and (2) their claim that distinctions between scribal and authorial readings can be made on the basis of their inherent quality. Even if we allow that Kane–Donaldson are correct in identifying the readings in question as scribal, the fact that Langland reproduced them when revising to B, rather than altering or correcting them, surely gives them effective authorial status – at any rate in B, if not in A. Kane's remark in A2 quoted above, that such errors are given 'a kind of sanction', would appear an understatement. Errors though they may be in Langland's scribal copy of A, by the time they enter the B-Text in Langland's own hand, they must be considered authoritative and original. The same applies to the reproduction of archetypal B 'errors' in C: by the time they appear, as a result of authorial action, in the latter text, these readings must be judged authorial, not scribal. Accordingly, such 'errors' should not be edited out of the second text, but retained.[52]

These three issues – consultation of other versions when editing any one, corrupt archetypes, and reviser's scribal copy of A and B – are, I think, the major areas in which Kane's thinking on editing shifted significantly between his edition of A1 and of B. How does the above discussion help us to answer our initial question, whether Kane would have edited A as he did if he had had readily accessible to him the manuscript variants of B and C? One can speculate that he would have applied the principles of his B-Text, and in many instances chosen the A-MS variant agreeing with B (and often C).[53] If that had been the case, Kane–Donaldson would presumably have stuck with the B-MS reading for their B edition. I have suggested that some of the most tortuous and difficult theories of Kane–Donaldson's radical B-Text were in fact imposed on the two editors by their need to protect Kane's earlier decisions when editing A. Had Kane made different decisions in the first place, that radicalism might have been

---

[51] See e.g. 83–4.   [52] Cf. p. 391 n. 23 above.
[53] As has A. V. C. Schmidt in the A-Text of his new (1995) Parallel-Text edition of the poem. Schmidt prepared his texts by editing the various versions of the poem simultaneously: see Brewer, 'Schmidt's Parallel-Text Edition of *Piers Plowman*', and p. 431 below.

substantially reduced – and the first two volumes of the Athlone Press edition of *Piers Plowman* would look substantially different from their present form.

THE SCIENTIFIC MODEL

One of the most striking characteristics of Kane's writing is its implicit appeal, in both style and vocabulary, to the methodology of the empirical sciences. His Ph.D. thesis of 1946 showed some signs of this, and it was further developed in his article of 1948 on the problems of editing the B-Text. By the 1960s this characteristic imbues his writing. In an article written in 1969 he openly adduced the parallel between the procedures of scientific experiments and those of textual criticism:

> An edition constitutes an attempt to account for available phenomena in terms of what is known about the circumstances which generated them. To that extent it has the character of a scientific activity. It operates by advancing hypotheses to explain data, and tests such hypotheses in terms of their efficiency as explanations. Those which pass the test it accepts as presumptively, not absolutely, true; they remain subject to revision or rejection if new evidence comes to light or more efficient hypotheses are devised. Its character implies an editorial obligation to expose its procedures and the precise extent to which their results are speculative to scrutiny.[54]

Most famously, the last two sentences of the Introduction to the edition of B announce that assessment of the work can be made only by repeating the experiment in order to test the validity of the result: that is, by re-editing the entire text.[55] This is clearly an impossibility for the overwhelming majority of readers and critics. It is also unimaginable that the result would be the same – as evidenced, for example, by the differences between the text of Kane and Donaldson's edition of the B-Text and that of the Everyman edition of Schmidt, which was established by using the same data (the manuscript variants

---

[54] 'Conjectural Emendation', 165–6. Cf. Kane–Donaldson, 212, and for Kane's positivist cast of mind, cf. *The Evidence for Authorship*, 1–2: 'There is some evidence; it must embody a necessary conclusion, and the truth should be attainable by right thinking.'

[55] 'How we have interpreted [the evidence of the B-MSS], and the evidence of the A and C versions bearing on it, has been laid wholly open to scrutiny in the preceding pages of this Introduction. Whether we have carried out our task efficiently must be assessed by reenacting it' (220).

as recorded in the Athlone B-Text critical apparatus). Repeating the experiment will not tell you whether it was right or wrong, for there can be no such thing as a control which will provide information that could not have been provided by other means, for example critical judgement. The only meaningful control would be the discovery of (one of) Langland's original manuscript(s), against which an editor could then test the accuracy of his or her guesses. This is an apt illustration of the difference between textual criticism and the empirical sciences, and hence the inapplicability of the scientific model.

Kane's thinking on the matters of evidence, truth, science, and textual criticism should be distinguished from that of Donaldson, despite the latter's co-editorship of the *B-Version*. Thus Donaldson writes, 'it seems true that almost all stages of the editorial process represent psychological achievements as much as they do scholarly ones: for the fact is that this branch of scholarly activity, which is often made to appear most austerely detached and objective, is almost wholly subjective'.[56] And indeed, Kane's (and Donaldson's) editorial procedures do not square with the scientific model. The physical layout of the two Athlone volumes so far published does not permit the exacting scrutiny he describes, given the absence of indexing and cross-referencing between text and Introduction (and between A-, B-, and C-Texts), which effectively prevents full examination of the relevant evidence and also access to such significant data as the rate and quantity of editorial emendation.[57] More importantly, as I hope I have shown, Kane and Donaldson do not go back over their hypotheses and reconsider them in the light of new evidence. We have seen this in the case of the B-MS F, and, far more strikingly, in the case of the A-Text as a whole, in effect a hypothesis, or a vast collection of hypotheses, which was not re-evaluated in the light of editing the B-Text but instead treated as a textual fact not subject to further question.[58]

In the discussion above of the Athlone A and B editions, I have

---

[56] 'The Psychology of Editors', 103.

[57] A point made by Patterson, despite his extravagant praise of Kane–Donaldson as 'not only the best *Piers Plowman*, but the true one' (69); see 64 n. 21, 85, and 85 n. 52. See also n. 25 above.

[58] Except in the tiny number of instances specified in the *B-Text* footnotes mentioned above. Cf. Robert Adams' identification of what he calls Kane's 'intellectual monism', in 'Editing *Piers Plowman B*'. E.g., '[Kane's] account of his procedures in editing *A* sometimes appears to imply that the mere act of explaining how a rejected reading may have arisen is tantamount to establishing that it did arise that way' (42).

concentrated particularly on the two editors' disinclination to entertain the prospect that Langland wrote more than three texts of the
poem, or the prospect that he wrote more than one version of each
text. I have also suggested that they were virtually forced into this
intellectual straitjacket by the constraints of the three-text publishing
project. In other words, it was impossible for them to take a
disinterested view of the situation, in the way that Whitaker, an
infinitely less talented and intellectually powerful editor, had done
nearly 150 years earlier. The Athlone B edition was less rapturously
received than the A edition, and a number of critics registered their
discontent with other aspects of the two editors' work. In particular,
there was widespread disapproval of Kane–Donaldson's readiness to
replace the perceived deficiencies of B with conjectural emendation.
This disapproval was registered in many of the reviews published in
scholarly journals,[59] and it no doubt facilitated the oral circulation of
the following limerick (although its original author, an unreserved
admirer of the edition, wrote it as a playful 'dig' against the editors
rather than as an expression of any criticism):[60]

> Say Donaldson and Kane as they edit,
> 'We don't give the scribes much credit;
> In a trice we divine
> The sense of each line,
> And when we say he said it, he said it.'

But just as there is no such thing as a disinterested editor, so is there
no such thing as a disinterested critic. It would be idle not to
acknowledge that the present writer's own concern with Kane and
Donaldson's insistence on the three-text model of *Piers Plowman*

---

59   See the articles by Traugott Lawler, John A. Alford, J. A. W. Bennett, Thorlac Turville-
      Petre, Derek Pearsall, David C. Fowler, E. G. Stanley, Manfred Görlach; and cf. the
      remarks by Anne Hudson in 'Middle English' (quoted in part above). The outstanding
      article by Lee Patterson ('The Logic of Textual Criticism and the Way of Genius') makes
      some searching and potentially damaging criticisms of the edition but appears to be written
      in a spirit of wholehearted approval. Patterson locates Kane–Donaldson in a 'Romantic'
      intellectual tradition inspired by notions of poetic genius, although at the same time
      evidencing an apparently contradictory commitment to positivist historicism (see esp. 85–
      6). The article contains much enlightening and penetrating commentary and many salient
      points, though cf. 'Authorial vs. Scribal Writing', 62–6.
60   I am most grateful to Professor Marie Borroff, who has kindly given me permission to
      reproduce her original version:
          Say Donaldson and Kane, 'When we edit,
          We don't give the scribes any credit;
          In a flash we divine
          The poet's each line,
          And if we say he said it, he said it.'

must stem from her espousal of a hypothesis at odds with this model, that the Z-Text of the poem, the first part of the peculiar version of the poem found in Bodley 851, represents a fourth authorial version of the poem. In the Epilogue we shall consider both the edition of the Z-Text and several of the other editions that have appeared in recent years.

PART VI

Epilogue: the Athlone aftermath: Schmidt, Pearsall, Rigg–Brewer, et al.

At the time of writing, no further volume has appeared in the Athlone *Piers Plowman* series since Kane and Donaldson's B-Text (volume II) of 1975. In their Preface to that edition, Kane and Donaldson state that Russell had completed a provisional C-Text (volume III) by 1973, but at the same time they comment, 'it will be understood that we cannot hold him to [the textual decisions he had made at that point]: it would be insufferable for our opinions to deprive him of his right to change his mind'. It is possibly Russell's acceptance of this implicit invitation that has delayed publication of his edition. As mentioned above, the volume is now due in spring 1997, edited by both George Russell and George Kane.[1]

In 1980, Kane reported that volume IV (the linguistic apparatus and glossary) was 'taking shape from indications of the evident needs of scholars in the field'.[2] By 1990, a group of five scholars had independently teamed up 'to annotate the magisterial Athlone Edition of *Piers Plowman*', in other words to produce volume V.[3] But no announcement has been made concerning volume VI, the 'discussion of the background, interpretation, authorship, etc. of *Piers Plowman*'.[4]

After the publication of the first Athlone volume, two important selections from the poem appeared. As long ago as 1918, Chambers

---

[1] See Kane–Donaldson vi, and cf. p. 337 n. 18 above.

[2] 'A Short Report on the Athlone Press Edition of *Piers Plowman*'. Kane goes on to say, 'Its main component will be a complete glossary of the three versions of the poem. It will also include studies of Langland's syntax and versification. Work on the glossary is underway. An absolute word index of the B version has been prepared. Lexicographical analyses of terms of particular interest have been carried out, and systematic glossing of B, to provide a frame for the references to and supplementations from A and C, will begin in the spring of 1980.'

[3] See Anne Middleton, in 'Life in the Margins', 167; she lists herself, John Alford, Stephen Barney, Ralph Hanna III, and Traugott Lawler as the scholars involved. John Alford has since withdrawn.

[4] See p. 312 above.

had corresponded with the Clarendon Press about a replacement for Skeat's student edition of Prologue and Passus I–VII of the B-Text of *Piers Plowman*, first published in 1869 and many times reprinted, and the discussion had been repeated (with Kenneth Sisam of the OUP) in 1941.[5] This replacement edition finally came into existence in 1972, edited by J. A. W. Bennett, who like Skeat took the Laud manuscript as his copy-text. He provided a short Preface (about 750 words), a select bibliography, a select table of variants (five pages), a glossary, and very extensive notes, which reproduced much of Skeat's information while adding more. The notes were the real justification for the edition; as Pearsall has commented, they 'are in the best tradition of Bennett's scholarship, alert to every allusion and backed by a comprehensive knowledge of every aspect of the poem's background'.[6] Textually the edition is not distinguished. Bennett in the main follows Skeat's decisions for emendation, and seems to have relied almost wholly on his collations, using Donaldson's article on 'MSS R and F' as his only other source.[7]

The other important selection was that by Elizabeth Salter and Derek Pearsall, in 1967. This excerpted a number of passages from the C-Text manuscript Hm 143, discovered in 1924, which Chambers had identified in 1935 as the best-known manuscript of the C-Text. The editors provided selected variants from the other important C-MS of the same family, Add. 35157 (U), and from Skeat's copy-text Hm 137 (P), occasionally incorporating readings from these manuscripts (or, much more rarely, other manuscripts collated by Skeat) into their text. They also supplied a linking commentary, full annotation, a bibliography, and a glossary. The Introduction, written by Salter, marked the edition out as a departure from its predecessors, since it provided a long and sophisticated, though very clear, literary analysis of the poem, particularly its allegorical procedures; Salter–Pearsall's annotation was similarly distinguished by its literary tone.[8]

---

5   See pp. 252 and 297 above.

6   *An Annotated Critical Bibliography*, 36. Bennett had originally (1956) planned a re-edition of Skeat's 1866 Parallel-Text edition (for a reprint of which he had provided a bibliography in 1954), with a commentary which was to be the edition's 'new special feature'; cf. p. 345 above. Instead he seems to have channelled his work on the commentary into the far less ambitious project of 1972.

7   Bennett notes that 'square brackets in the text represent editorial insertions ... bold brackets point to a suspect reading' (78); these do not appear in the edition.

8   In keeping with this aspect of their approach, they replace the thorns and yoghs of the manuscript with modern equivalent spellings, a practice found also in Knott–Fowler and Schmidt (and before them, in Crowley and Wright), presumably in an attempt to make the text look as linguistically familiar to the undergraduate reader as that of Chaucer.

Both these editions, in different ways, filled the slot previously occupied by Skeat's student edition, that of an introduction to the poem for the general reader, including the university undergraduate. Both were unequivocally ousted by the major new edition of the poem published in 1978, the Everyman edition of the B-Text by A. V. C. Schmidt, which now has no effective rival for the student market. Schmidt's edition was also a significant contribution to scholarly analysis of the poem, one that was initially made, it would appear, by using the collations invaluably recorded in the critical apparatus of the Athlone B-Text.[9] Schmidt thus picked up the gauntlet thrown down in the last two sentences of the Introduction to that edition: 'How we have interpreted [the evidence of the B-MSS], and the evidence of the A and C versions bearing on it, has been laid wholly open to scrutiny in the preceding pages of this Introduction. Whether we have carried out our task efficiently must be assessed by reenacting it.'[10]

Schmidt's first edition was prepared with utterly astonishing swiftness, coming out three years after the publication of Kane–Donaldson. It is, in Pearsall's words, 'a marvel of compression',[11] achieving the aim Schmidt himself identified of 'enabling the text to release its original power' (p. xvi). It contains a substantial introduction, a select bibliography, and a critical text of B based, like Kane–Donaldson's, on the Trinity College B-MS (B. 15. 17), with word glosses flanking the text at the side of the page and occasional translation of difficult lines at the foot of the page. Select textual notes also appear on the page, and there are two separate sections of commentary at the back of the book, under the headings 'Textual and Lexical' and 'Literary and Historical'. The volume also contains an index of proper names, and an appendix on metre.[12] The first edition was reprinted several times, adding small corrections together with a supplementary bibliography in 1984 and a select glossary in 1987. In 1995, a second edition has appeared, entirely reworked, incorporating the fruits of Schmidt's substantial reconsideration of the B-Text during the process of editing all four versions of the poem (i.e. Z, A, B, and C) for his major new parallel-text edition of the poem for Longman. I shall return below to

---

[9] Schmidt records that he checked against the originals all readings taken from sources other than his copy-text (Trinity College B. 15. 17), with the exception of the few taken from MS Hm 128, for which he relied on Kane–Donaldson (xl). Presumably he decided which readings to print after analysing all the variants (see n. 13 below) as printed in Kane–Donaldson.

[10] See p. 405 above.   [11] *An Annotated Critical Bibliography*, 23.

[12] Schmidt's views on Langland's metre have been extensively corrected by Duggan; see *YLS* 2 (1988), 167–74.

consideration of this new enterprise, whose publication has coincided with the completion of the present book.

The Introduction to Schmidt's first Everyman edition is divided into eight sections, on 'The versions of *Piers Plowman*', 'Authorship, Audience and Date', 'Literary Tradition', 'Structure', 'The Poem's Themes', 'Langland's Poetic Art', 'The Textual Problems of the B-Version', and 'Editorial Procedure'. In choosing to include a discussion of the authorship and date of the poem, Schmidt returned to the editorial tradition of Knott–Fowler, Skeat, Wright, and Whitaker (and also, to a lesser extent, Crowley), which had been bypassed by Kane and Kane–Donaldson: a recognition of the poem's historical and social context. This is also supplied in the copious 'Literary and Historical' commentary, which furnishes the reader with an abundance of information in the tradition of Skeat and also Bennett. But unlike his predecessors, with the exception of Salter–Pearsall, Schmidt explicitly presents the poem as a literary work of profound imaginative power, written by a poet whose command of language is superbly skilled. This is stated at the outset: '*Piers Plowman* has a serious claim to be the greatest poem of the Middle Ages' (p. xii), and developed and illustrated in the middle sections of the Introduction, in an essay which (like Salter's) matches the style and sophistication of scholarly explication of the poem in books and learned journals published over the last forty-odd years. It is clear that Kane and Kane–Donaldson would agree with this judgement of the poet (as evidenced in their references to 'the quality of Langland's art' (p. 212), 'the excellence of Langland's poem' (p. 213), etc.); indeed their decisions between rival textual readings were predicated on their assumption of Langland's literary merit. But they did not regard the demonstration or illustration of his literary merit as falling within their remit. Instead, as already stated, they addressed themselves to the textual scholar.

But Schmidt managed to cover textual issues as well as literary ones.[13] Both in his Acknowledgements and at the start of his Introduction, he paid tribute to the work of Kane and Donaldson, 'a guide, inspiration and challenge throughout... which must rank as one of the most important contributions to literary scholarship in our time'. He added, 'The basic arguments of Kane and Donaldson can only be accepted or refuted, they cannot be by-passed. There is no

---

[13] Schmidt's Acknowledgements tell us that his wife Judith analysed the variants, a massive task in the preparation of an edition such as this. She also compiled the Index and prepared the Bibliography.

way of going back to Skeat and no point in reproducing his texts as the original work of the poet or anything approaching it' (p. xii). In the remarkably brief section (four and a half pages) of his Introduction on 'Textual Problems of the B-Version', Schmidt 'put before the reader certain basic conclusions which have emerged from my editing of the B-text'. He stated that the section 'is not offered as a summary of all the problems faced by an editor nor as an outline of editorial method; these would require a whole book' (p. xxxv). Compression was presumably forced upon Schmidt by his publishers, and their need to keep the book to a size affordable by undergraduates and the Everyman book buyer, and also palatable to the same audience; as he says, his edition was 'intended for the widest possible use' (p. xii). So a lengthy account of the textual issues was out of the question. However, the briefness of the report gives the misleading impression that it is conclusive. There is no acknowledgement, as in Kane–Donaldson, of the tentative nature of the hypotheses which sanction the widespread emendation characteristic of both editions.

Schmidt accepts Kane–Donaldson's classification of the B-MSS into two families, that of RF (which he calls *alpha*) and WHmCrGYOC^{2}CBLMH (*beta*), and also believes, like them, that 'each family constitutes a (defective) representative of a homogeneous B-tradition, not an earlier or later stage in the evolution of the poem' (p. xxxv). He agrees with Kane and Donaldson that editing by recension is impossible, given the pervasive occurrence both of coincident variation and also, almost certainly, contamination among the manuscripts, which make it 'nearly impossible to eliminate from consideration the readings of any group or individual MS' (p. xxxv). 'Nevertheless', he went on to say, 'it is possible to acquire in the course of examining all the readings a certain understanding of the character and tendencies of particular MSS, even those like F which have a complex history' (p. xxxvi). And with arresting boldness he drew a stemma (see figure E.1), and explained the broad outline of his decision-making technique in uncompromisingly recensionist terms. Schmidt commented thus:

> The *Archetype* (Bx) is constructed from the sub-archetypes when they agree; from α or β when either appears superior on intrinsic grounds or in the light of secure readings in the A and C traditions; in a few cases from individual MSS where they are judged to preserve α or β either in isolation or against other witnesses; by reconstruction when neither α nor β can be securely established.

413

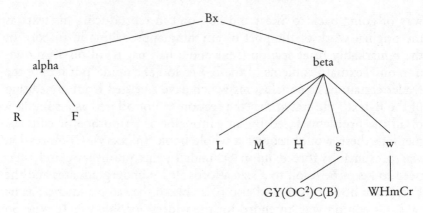

Figure E.1. Schmidt's diagram of the B-MSS

'Reconstruction' would appear to mean, emendation from A or C, or alternatively conjectural emendation. Schmidt favoured the divergent readings of the *alpha* group far more than the *beta* group (according to his own figures, 500 times as opposed to 260 times; the instances are not listed, presumably on the grounds of space). He does list, however, some of the other instances in his text where the reading is supported by one of the groups of manuscripts or by individual manuscripts.

In a sub-section entitled 'Emendation of the Archetype', Schmidt made it clear that he adopted wholesale the theory of the corrupt archetype of B, and the consequent necessity to emend this text from the evidence of A and C, or, in the absence of the two other texts, occasionally by editorial conjecture, although he had been more cautious than Kane and Donaldson in rejecting the reading of the B archetype. So despite the bold visual claim made upon the reader by the stemma, it turns out, on investigation, that the small print licenses exactly the same sort of widespread eclecticism and editorial conjecture practised by his immediate predecessors. Schmidt also followed Kane and Donaldson's (and Blackman's) example in refusing to countenance the possibility that agreement between A and C against B can indicate anything other than corruption in B; in other words he did not entertain the notion that the author might have changed his mind when writing B, and then reverted to his earlier choice when revising to C.[14]

---

[14] See xxxviii, and Schmidt's critical apparatus throughout. Thorlac Turville-Petre in a review of Schmidt comments: 'Mr Schmidt regularly rejects acceptable B readings in favour of AC

Schmidt states that he incorporated into his text fourteen emendations from Skeat, one each from Wright and Bennett, and 260 from
Kane–Donaldson, adding a further 163 of his own (p. xxxviii). This
came to a total of 439, 'fewer than K-D's total, partly because I
sometimes disagree with them that Bx [the B archetype] is corrupt
and partly because I occasionally refrain from emending for lack of
certainty either of corruption or of the worth of any available
correction ... I have been reluctant to diagnose corruption on
grounds of sense, metre, or style *alone.*' As we have seen, Kane–
Donaldson do not tell us how many emendations they have made to
their base manuscript, although it is possible to work through their
Introduction and text and come up with some calculation on the basis
of the lists of agreements with which they do provide us. Using this
evidence, David Fowler estimated the total as 'more than 1,600' that
is, nearly four times more than Schmidt's total (although, as we shall
see below, Schmidt provides us with rather different figures in 1995).
In this light, Schmidt's editing looks positively conservative, but as
Fowler comments, 'Before 1975 [i.e. the date of Kane–Donaldson's
publication], who would have dared make over 400 emendations?'[15]

Schmidt's textual apparatus to his first edition, although less
copious than Kane–Donaldson's in that it did not give the full
conspectus of B-MS variants, often provided more useful information.
This is because it indicated, as Kane's and Kane–Donaldson's did not,
agreement of the editor's chosen reading with A and C when it
occurs. This is an invaluable aid to understanding why the editor
made the choice he did, since (as we have seen) Schmidt, like Kane
and Donaldson, frequently jettisoned the reading of the B-MSS, even
if unanimously attested, in favour of that of A and/or C. Schmidt also
told us how Kane and Donaldson had previously judged. By comparing the critical apparatuses at one point in the text we may see the
advantages and disadvantages of each. At Passus V 514, Kane and
Donaldson's text reads

> But blustreden forþ as beestes ouer [baches] and hilles,

readings (e.g. VII 24, 48, 49, 104, 175) though he is certainly not unaware of the problems of
doing this. In a note on VII 166, discussing B's *loke* against A's *kepe* and C's *saue*, he
remarks acutely that "this type of small change provides strong presumptive evidence of
Langland's propensity for revision even in the case of seemingly indifferent particulars". To
grant this seems to me to be equivalent to admitting the practical impossibility of using AC
readings to correct those of B, where B is otherwise acceptable.'
15 Fowler, 'Editorial "Jamming"', 213. Fowler produces a useful numerical analysis of
Schmidt's emendations as compared with Kane–Donaldson's, together with further comments, on 213–14. See also above, p. 390 n. 22.

compared with Schmidt's slightly more economical, and more infor-
mative (in terms of the placing of square brackets)

> But blustreden forth as beestes over ba[ch]es and hilles

(it will be seen that Schmidt modernises spelling, replacing the thorn
with *th* and consonantal *u* with *v*).[16] The difference between the two
critical apparatuses is more striking. Kane–Donaldson read as follows:

> *line om* Hm. blustreden] blustred C²M; blusteren G; blustrenden C;
> blusterynge Cr. forþ] for C. baches] balkys F; bankes
> WCrGYOC²CBLMR

while Schmidt reads

> baches] **AC** (so K-D); balkys F; bankes W &*r*

For editorial purposes, the only important variant here is the one
Schmidt selects, *baches*. His editorial notation readily communicates
to us, as Kane–Donaldson's does not, that the preferred reading,
baches, is found in *no* B-MS, since all extant B-MSS other than F
agree in reading *bankes* (this is the significance of his invaluable
symbol &*r*)[17] To ascertain this important fact from Kane and
Donaldson's apparatus we must carefully note the cited B-MSS in the
entry, to work out that they between them comprise all the available
B-MSS, which in turn means that the reading *baches* must derive from
a source other than the B-MSS. But having done that, we are none the
wiser as to what that source might be. There is no way of knowing
whether or not the reading is discussed in the Introduction, or how to
find it if it is discussed. Instead we must turn to external sources.

Schmidt himself occasionally proves such a source, since he sometimes gives us the page reference for Kane–Donaldson's discussion of
or statement on individual textual decisions, though not in this
instance; as ascertainable from Barney's line index, the reading is
mentioned twice in Kane–Donaldson's Introduction as an example of
a B reading easier than the equivalent AC reading; it is tucked away in
lists on pages 79 and 151. (Schmidt did not appear to have a systematic
policy on his provision of page-references to Kane–Donaldson's
Introduction, presumably because the absence there of indexing and
cross-referencing made successful location of their mentions of individual readings largely a matter of luck, or heroic persistence beyond
the call of duty. Barney's line index has now removed this problem.)

---

[16] See p. 410 n. 8 above.   [17] Schmidt does not tell us that Hm omits the line.

Epilogue: the Athlone aftermath

The striking superiority of Schmidt's apparatus over Kane–Donaldson's is that he tells us the origin of *baches*, namely that it is the reading of A (Passus VI 2) and C (Passus VII 159). However, even this is inadequate information – though far more helpful than that found in Kane–Donaldson. For, as the reader will remember (see p. 308 above), the variant *baches* is found in only *one* A-MS, W, the remainder reading (variously) *valeis*, *dales*, and *bankes*. Kane decided that *baches* was the original reading of the A-Text, on the grounds that it was the most difficult of the variants. *baches* is also the reading of the Z-Text, a fact which may be taken as a vindication of Kane's judgement, on the assumption (with which Kane, of course, disagrees) that this version represents the poet's first draft. However, Robert Adams, in a probing discussion of the limitations of *durior lectio* as a criterion (much beloved by Kane, as we have seen) for distinguishing between scribal and authorial readings in a text such as Langland's, has suggested that Kane's decision may well have been wrong, given the biblical authority for the phrase *bankes and hilles*. (Why the C-Text – and the Z-Text – should also read *baches* is another question; Adams suggests that an intelligent scribe might easily have supplied the word, as 'an obsolescent term still readily available in the southwest Midlands', to remove the apparent redundancy of original *bankes* with *hilles* in the same line. Readers will divide as to the plausibility of this suggestion.)[18] But if we accept *bankes* as likely to be correct in A, then the justification for emending the same reading in B, in the absence of any manuscript support, looks much less secure.

Similar findings on comparing the two texts and apparatuses may be replicated time and time again. The great advantage of Schmidt's critical apparatus is that it gives to the reader eager to know more about the text an immediate steer in the right direction. Schmidt does not provide full textual information, but he nevertheless furnishes the reader with a helpful gloss on the decisions of Kane and Kane–Donaldson. And the absence of full information was not misleading in an edition such as this, an Everyman paperback, which by its very format makes no claims for full textual authority (although the editor sometimes writes as if views other than his own are untenable).

---

[18] 'Once this kind of change had been made, other C scribes, less esthetically inclined and perhaps less attentive to their job, could easily have introduced the non-alliterating synonyms of *baches* without even being aware of it (the evidence from A is more compatible with a process running in the opposite direction: that is, original error = *valeis*, altered by scribal conjecture or contamination to *baches* in one A manuscript).' See Robert Adams, 'Editing and the Limitations of the *Durior Lectio*', 8–12.

Many of Schmidt's textual decisions are discussed in his textual and lexical commentary, to which the apparatus refers the reader when appropriate. Here Schmidt almost always explained his own decisions to emend or not to emend in terms of Kane–Donaldson's previous example, defending the archetypal B reading which they have chosen to replace, or substituting a different editorial conjecture. In this respect again his first edition amounted to a commentary on theirs, and Schmidt makes it very clear that, like Kane–Donaldson, he often did not hesitate to reject the evidence of the B-MSS if he could think of a better reading in their stead.[19]

Such editorial practice brings home the force of Fowler's fear that Kane–Donaldson's extraordinary disregard for the manuscript evidence licenses similarly unlimited editorial activity by their successors.[20] And Schmidt's ready eclecticism in his choice between the various readings which *are* to be found in the manuscripts (again like that of Kane–Donaldson) reminds one of a comment made by Pearsall in 1985, that 'An intelligent contemporary editor, with an intimate knowledge of his poet's language and idiom, may hit upon readings that seem preferable, not only to him and his modern counterpart, but that might even have been preferred by the poet himself if he had thought of them.'[21] This is a just observation, and emphasises the link between textual and interpretative activities, in the case of both scribes and editors. Editors emend texts on the basis of their interpretation of those texts: it is impossible to discriminate between readings without invoking, whether consciously or unconsciously, literary critical criteria. At the end of his Introduction, Schmidt made a distinction between textual scholars of Langland and 'the many more experienced readers of Langland', by which he meant literary critics, offering his text and textual commentary to the scrutiny of the latter rather than the former. But as every page of his commentary reveals, there is no fundamental difference between the two.

Pearsall's edition of the C-Text was published in the same year, 1978, and dedicated to the memory of Skeat. Like that of Schmidt, the edition is aimed at both undergraduate and scholar. He provides a shorter Introduction, together with a select bibliography, and a wealth of on-the-page notes instead of glosses. A separate glossary

---

[19] Examples can be furnished from almost every page of the commentary; picking one at random, 281, see the entries for Passus X 244, 249, 272 (and contrast that for Passus X 246, where Schmidt retains a reading he believes to be unsatisfactory).

[20] 'Editorial "Jamming" ', 214. [21] Editing Medieval Texts', 95.

appears at the end of the book. The Introduction compresses an impressive amount of material into ten or so pages, yet is written with a clarity and vigour which defy the constraints of space. He presents a perceptive, judicious, and exciting account of the poem in its social, literary, and historical context. Many of the issues discussed – the relationship of the poem to Wycliffite and other contemporary sources, to the liturgy, to contemporary events, and its self-referential qualities and characteristics – are expounded further in the detailed and often extremely illuminating notes.

Textually, Pearsall's aim is far less ambitious than that of Schmidt, since he makes no claim to present a critical edition of C. Instead he takes the Huntington MS 143 (X) as his copy-text, in accordance with the judgement of Chambers, and corrects it conservatively from the witness of four other manuscripts: its close partner U (BL Add. 35157, the manuscript identified by Allen as providing the best basis for an edition of C before the discovery of Hm 143), the second half of the Trinity College MS R. 3. 14 (T, the conjoint AC manuscript), the manuscript taken by Skeat as his copy-text (P, now Hm 137), and the Ilchester manuscript (I). In a few instances towards the end of the poem (e.g. at Passus XXI 12, 75, 340, 408), he also has recourse to the text of B. Pearsall makes the limited nature of his edition very clear, pointing out that his text will 'inevitably contain inferior readings which have been introduced in the process of scribal transmission'.[22] And he throws the onus for excision of those readings fairly and squarely upon the shoulders of the Athlone C editor George Russell: 'It will be the business of Russell's critical edition to reconstruct, as far as possible, from the available evidence, what the author originally wrote.' Given Pearsall's clear-sighted apprehension, abundantly evidenced elsewhere, of the editorial difficulties of the Athlone project in particular, and of recovering from Middle English texts 'what the author originally wrote' in general,[23] it is difficult to read his following comments without attaching to them some element of irony:

> A particular complication is introduced by the fact that the text of B which the C-reviser used as the basis of his revision was already a

---

[22] It should be observed that Russell believes the scribe of X to have made one mistake every nine lines, which would imply a rate of emendation far in excess of Pearsall's. See ' "As They Read It" ', 178.

[23] See, for example, his review of Kane–Donaldson, and the articles 'Editing Medieval Texts', 'Textual Criticism and Fifteenth-Century Manuscript Production', 'Theory and Practice in Middle English Editing'.

> copy corrupted by scribal transmission ... though not in such an
> advanced state of corruption as the archetype of all extant B-MSS.
> Since the C-revision was neither systematic nor complete ... it is
> difficult to determine what degree of authorial endorsement has
> been given to inferior readings carried over from the reviser's B-MS
> [see p. 404 above] ... An examination of this problem, as of the
> textual status of those parts of C which are additions to B or where
> the revision is not close enough to make textual comparison
> possible, must await Russell's full critical edition. (p. 22)

But it is exactly these issues which make the production of a critical
edition of C so problematic.

Pearsall describes his text and notes as 'interim statements' (p. 1),
which gives the impression, as does the statement already quoted, that
he wishes his readers to understand that he defers to the forthcoming
edition of Russell. Indeed, one of the reviewers of his text and
Schmidt's went so far as to comment, 'Pearsall has not aspired to
enter the lists.'[24] But the question is well worth asking whether an
edition such as Pearsall's, which refuses the burden of a critical
analysis of all the textual variants, is not after all an infinitely more
sensible and practicable undertaking than that of Schmidt, which
presents a text less idiosyncratic than Kane–Donaldson's but still
bears little demonstrable relation to what a fourteenth-century reader
read or what the poet himself wrote.

A good deal of recent work in medieval studies has addressed itself
to the question of what contemporary readers read, and therefore to
the study of scribes and the dissemination of texts. It was in
pursuance of such work, a study of poetic anthologies, that A. G.
Rigg in 1978 came across the copy of *Piers Plowman* preserved in MS
Bodley 851, and suggested to the present writer, his graduate student,
that it would be worth studying the copy as an example of a scribal
rewriting of a major literary text.[25] As we have seen (chapter 9
above), Skeat discovered Bodley 851 well after he had fixed his views
on the text of the poem, and he therefore rejected the eccentric early
passus of its version as useless for editorial purposes. Chambers knew
of its existence, and referred to its rendering of the early lines of the
poem as 'corrupt and here practically a B-text'; presumably he was
influenced by Skeat's description of these lines as a B-Text, for in its
shape and the vast majority of its readings it must be classed as an

---

24 In other respects the review, by Stephen Barney, is exceptionally helpful and illuminating.
25 See Rigg's three articles on 'Medieval Latin Poetic Anthologies'.

A-Text.[26] Russell mentioned the manuscript in 1969, comparing it with the conflated version of the poem found in Hm 114. He concluded, 'It appears to be the characteristic product of the editor or editing scribe: and there seems to be little reason to dissent from Skeat's description "mere rubbish".'[27]

But the manuscript went unnoticed in Kane's 1960 edition of A. Almost certainly this is because no mention of it was made in the various discussions of A-MSS by Skeat, who listed Bodley 851 as a C-MS, and described it only in his edition of C. As we have seen, Kane had departed from the stated principle of his predecessors Chambers and Grattan, that when preparing an edition of any one of the versions of the poem, the other version(s) should be consulted at the same time. Hence Kane had no reason to check through the manuscripts of the B and C versions, and hence no opportunity to discover that Skeat's description of Bodley 851 had been faulty, and that the early part of the *Piers Plowman* version was in fact an eccentric A-Text, and due for discussion, therefore, in his edition of A.

Kane's policy of confining himself to the evidence of the A-MSS when editing A had, as we have seen, the great advantage that it limited the collation and editorial work to manageable dimensions, so that one person could take on and complete the edition within a reasonable space of time. On the other hand, the policy implies certain assumptions about the versions of the poem, the author's composition of them, and their corruption through scribal transmission, none of which was clearly articulated or argued by Kane, but all of which can, with hindsight, be seen to have led him subsequently to reject Z as an authentic part of the *Piers Plowman* canon.

The reader of the poem interested in making some sense of its textual and editorial history must ask the question whether these assumptions are valid. Many of them have been discussed in previous chapters, but it will be helpful to restate them here.

It is uncontroversial to claim that most of the fifty-odd manuscripts of the poem fall into three different shapes, corresponding to what Skeat called A, B, and C. But this implies a simpler set of

---

[26] 'The Authorship of "Piers Plowman"', 28 n. 1; the following year (1911), Chambers described Z as 'a confused MS. written under the influence of A-, B- and C-texts' ('The Original Form of the A-Text of "Piers Plowman"', 313 n. 1); in 1935 he noted that Z 'does not begin to be a reliable manuscript till Passus X' ('The Manuscripts of *Piers Plowman* in the Huntington Library', 21). The early part of Bodley 851 satisfies the requirements stated by Kane, 20–3, for an A-Text.
[27] 'Some Aspects of the Process of Revision', 28.

relations between the three versions than in fact exists. Over significant stretches of the poem, all three texts read roughly the same, although the fifty-odd manuscripts vary in their exact rendering of these stretches. The patterning of variation does not necessarily correspond with the different versions; for example, as illustrated in the chapters on the Athlone A and B editions above, some A-MSS may agree with the B-MSS in one reading, whereas a rival reading may be found in other A-MSS and some C-MSS. (Since Kane did not consult other versions when editing A, he does not give any account of this complex set of relationships, of which in many instances, as we have seen, he was apparently unaware.) In these circumstances, how does an editor decide what is an A reading, a B reading, or a C reading? And how does an editor determine whether variation in readings in manuscripts of different versions over equivalent text is to be ascribed to authorial revision or scribal transmission?

These points are significant in assessing the origin and character of the text found in Z. For example, many of the readings in Z are also found in B-MSS. If we accept the distinctions between the three versions established by Kane, we must suppose that the scribe of Z, although he predominantly followed an A-Text as his exemplar, periodically introduced B readings; the 'contaminated' quality of Z is one of the reasons Kane rejects this version as scribally corrupt. But most of the BZ readings are also found in other A-MSS as well, although not the A-MSS adopted by Kane as the basis of his edition of A, and in some of these cases Kane has now decided that he erred in his identification of the A-Text, and that these readings are indeed original to A.[28] As I have suggested in chapter 21, if Kane had scrutinised the relations between the different versions line by line when establishing his A-Text, he might have come up with a different A- (and B-) Text. And if he had known of Z when establishing his A-Text, instead of discovering it, like Skeat, *after* he had made up his mind about the manuscripts and versions, he might also have regarded the many agreements between Z, A-MSS, and B-MSS (and often C-MSS as well) as evidence for Z's authenticity. The point needs to be strongly made that if, like Chambers, and like Kane and Donaldson in their edition of B, you take the view that editing any one version of the poem entails consulting the other versions, and only coming to a

[28] See above, pp. 400–1.

conclusion in the light of consideration of all the manuscripts of all the versions, then the discovery of Z means that *all the editing of the poem carried out in ignorance of this version must be done again.* For if Z is an authentic witness to a fourth authorial version of the poem, then it too must be consulted for its equivalent test when editing each of the other three versions. Unlike Kane, Schmidt has now been able to carry out such simultaneous editing of all four versions in his parallel-text edition of the poem – an enterprise in many ways facilitated by Kane's own work. As we shall see below, he has come to very different conclusions.

Kane first mentions Z in a footnote to his edition of the B-Text, published in 1975. He claims he had 'rightly dismissed [Z] as worthless for editorial use, but should have formally rejected [it] in Vol. 1', i.e. his edition of A; in fact, the absence of any mention of the manuscript in his edition of A would appear to be strong evidence that Kane had been unaware of its existence. He now judged it to be a 'conflated and sophisticated text', contaminated by both C and (to a less extent) B. Its A-Text was disordered, producing 'an imperfect or wholly inconsequent exposition', and omitting much authentic A-Text material. It also included 'many lines not relatable to any version, thus presumably spurious'.[29] Kane put forward two suggestions for the existence of Z's curious version:

> One possibility is that the early part of Z was copied from a text produced by someone acquainted with all versions of the poem, literate and able to write tolerable long lines, who was restoring from memory, and occasionally by sophistication, a physically defective copy, very imperfect, or in many places defaced, or both, of the A version. The other possibility is that the whole of the 'A' component of the manuscript is merely a memorial reconstruction, the uneven quality of the text and the occasional coincidence of omission with sophistication being simply results of uneven recollection.[30]

This description stood until the publication of Rigg–Brewer in 1983. Their introduction took issue with many aspects of Kane's account of Z, claiming that the manuscript presented a coherent and self-sufficient version of the poem – albeit different from A, B, and C.

[29] Kane also claimed that 'some of the groups of "new" lines occur where approximate multiples of 20 or 40 lines are wanting (i.e. the presumptive contents of sides or leaves)'; this argument has been authoritatively demolished by Richard Firth Green in 'The Lost Exemplar of the Z-Text of *Piers Plowman*'.
[30] Kane–Donaldson, 14–15, n. 95.

Rigg and Brewer distinguished four different factors relevant in making a decision between Kane's hypothesis that Z represented a scribal rewriting of the poem, and the alternative hypothesis that Z was an authorial version of *Piers Plowman*, written by Langland before he wrote A, B, and C.

The first of these was textual. The presence in Z of B/C lines and readings, and the relationship of Z with the manuscript tradition of A, was, Rigg and Brewer believed, neutral: 'it can be used to support Kane's position or ours'. The present writer has now revised this opinion. Since 1983, examination of the relationship between A-MSS and the B-Text has brought to light the extensive degree of agreement between Z, the A-MSS rejected by Kane for his A-Text, and the B- (and sometimes C-)Text. The simplest explanation for this pattern of agreements is that Kane erred in his choice of reading for the A-Text, and that the authentic reading is that found in the other A-MSS, together with Z and B (C). This would then support the argument for Z's authenticity.[31]

The second factor is the version's literary quality. Here there is a strong case for preferring Z's authenticity. Rigg and Brewer adduce the overall coherence of the narrative, the quality of a number of Z's unique lines and readings (which has struck many readers as Langlandian to a degree beyond the likely capabilities of an imitator),[32] the fact that several of the key episodes in the poem can be seen to be present in germ form in Z (e.g. the debate between Meed and Conscience in Passus III, and the account of the Deadly Sins in Passus V),[33] and also the fact that there are no signs of 'patching' either where Z lacks passages found in A or where Z has material not in A. All these characteristics are hard to explain if the version is in origin scribal. (It should also be noted that no such claims could be

---

[31] See pp. 394–405 above. The B/C readings in Z and EAMH³ are taken by Ralph Hanna, in a brief discussion, to be unoriginal, and due to the contamination of these manuscripts by scribes who had previously copied B- and C-MSS ('The Manuscripts of *Piers Plowman*', 19–21). He thus rejects the hypothesis that Z could be an authorial version of the poem. His argument is made on the assumption that Kane's choice of A readings for his edition of A is beyond question, an assumption which is insecure. In particular, as we have seen above, Kane himself has changed his mind about a number of the EAMH³/Z/B/C readings he originally rejected for his A-Text, and now believes that they are original to the A tradition. Kane's revised view is endorsed by the choices of Schmidt's A-Text; see my forthcoming review article, 'Schmidt's Parallel-Text Edition of *Piers Plowman*'.

[32] The editors recognise that 'this is a subjective judgment, and cannot be proved one way or another'. Cf. Rigg–Brewer, 15–17, 26–7.

[33] On this point see further Brewer, 'Z and the A- B- C-Texts of *Piers Plowman*'.

made for versions of the poem found in the other contaminated or conflated manuscripts of the poem, e.g. Hm 114.)[34]

The third factor, Z's linguistic characteristics, also supports Rigg–Brewer's hypothesis. As they comment, 'the text of Z is linguistically totally coherent and uniform, in spelling, morphology, syntax and vocabulary: the lines and passages peculiar to Z show no signs of being alien to the parts shared with A. Such consistency goes deeper than would be expected from a sophisticated scribal pastiche.'[35]

The fourth factor is the date of the manuscript. Here Rigg–Brewer state, 'If Bodley 851 was written before 1388 [the date of the death of its probable compiler, John Wells of Ramsay][36] this seems a very early date for the diffusion of all versions in such a way as to produce conflation on this scale' (p. 12). But since the quires containing the *Piers Plowman* version were originally separate, it is impossible to prove that the manuscript had assumed its present form by 1388. Thus the dating evidence is in the last resort a neutral factor in the verdict on the origin of Z.

Rigg–Brewer's hypothesis has been variously received. Most notable was the review by George Kane published in *Speculum* in 1985, which condemned the edition without reserve.[37] Other reviewers have been less harsh.[38] Several have agreed on the 'Langlandian' quality of some of Z's unique lines and passages, while acknowledging that judgement of such a quality must be subjective. Some have stressed the equivocal nature of the evidence, and the difficulty of deciding whether it supports an argument for scribal or for authorial origin.[39] Others have argued that the metrical patterns of Z's unique lines are otherwise found only in the A-, B-, and C-Texts and hence are a strong indication that the same author was responsible for all four versions.[40] There has been a consensus that the date of the manuscript is difficult to fix with certainty, but also a recognition,

---

[34] See George Russell and Venetia Nathan, 'A *Piers Plowman* Manuscript in the Huntington Library'.

[35] Rigg–Brewer, 12; cf. 26–7 and 115–27.   [36] Cf. Rigg–Brewer, 2–5.

[37] His views were endorsed by Russell; see ' "As They Read It" ', 176 n. 4.

[38] E.g. Derek Pearsall, Richard Firth Green, Robert Adams, Hugh White.

[39] Cf. e.g. Derek Pearsall's comment that 'it has also to be acknowledged that every single argument in favour of the authority of Z as a pre-A version of the poem can be answered by arguments nearly as or equally good, or better, in favour of the traditional hypothesis' (review of Rigg–Brewer, 182).

[40] See A. V. C. Schmidt, 'The Authenticity of the Z Text of *Piers Plowman*'; Hoyt N. Duggan, 'The Authenticity of the Z-text of *Piers Plowman*'. Another advocate of Z's authenticity was persuaded by Langland's progressive use of the Psalter commentary of Hugh of St Cher; see Judson Boyce Allen, 'Langland's Reading and Writing'.

unfortunately less than general, that the argument for Z's authenticity is not contingent on date.[41] Z's claims have been strongly endorsed by Schmidt, whose new parallel-text edition of the poem prints Z alongside A, B, and C.

It has also been recognised that Rigg–Brewer's hypothesis on the origin of Z has damagingly undermined some of the implicit assumptions of the Athlone project headed by George Kane, principally that the manuscripts represent three original versions of the poem and three only. This assumption was vital to the Athlone project, for as one reviewer pointed out, 'the practical necessities of the editor of a critical text' are such that he or she 'can have no truck with the idea of a continuously evolving text' as implied by the existence of Z.[42] The consequence of this assumption, in another reviewer's opinion, was that 'Kane and Donaldson have made Langland appear a neater and more consistent poet than even the most benevolent reading of his spiritual odyssey might lead one to expect.' If it is discarded, then readers' intuitions about Langland's writing habits may be better satisfied, but 'for future editors of his poem ... the prospect it raises is truly daunting'.[43]

But that remark was written before 1991, when the first steps were taken towards 'the creation of a multi-level, hyper-textually linked electronic archive of the textual tradition of all three versions' of *Piers Plowman*. This visionary project, masterminded by Hoyt Duggan, has a claim to being the perfect solution to the dilemma confronting would-be editors and readers of the poem in the post-Kane–Donaldson era. For as Duggan says, 'Editors of electronic texts, unlike earlier editors of printed editions, need not suppress or conceal editorial agreement nor impose spurious notions of authority. They may, instead, exploit editorial agreement and embrace the provisional nature of scholarly editing.'[44] The electronic team (Duggan, Robert Adams, Eric Eliason, Ralph Hanna III, Thorlac Turville-Petre) intend

---

[41] See Ralph Hanna, 'The Manuscripts of *Piers Plowman*', 14–21, for a discussion of Rigg–Brewer which assumes, mistakenly, that 'the strongest apparent basis for Rigg–Brewer's claim that Z is a pre-1388 text is predicated upon the codicology of Bodley 851' (15). In fact, as is plain from a reading of our Introduction, our claim is predicated on the *internal* evidence of the version: its textual, literary, and linguistic characteristics. The same arguments for Z's authenticity would apply if the version was extant only in a manuscript dated a hundred years later.

[42] See Pearsall, review of Rigg–Brewer, 181–2.   [43] Green, review of Rigg–Brewer, 132.

[44] All quotations from Duggan relating to this project have been taken from *The Piers Plowman Electronic Archive* (1994), which has a site on the World Wide Web. See also Duggan, 'The Electronic *Piers Plowman*'.

to make accessible to their users the essential data which underlies a critical edition but is usually obscured by it: facsimiles and transcriptions of all the individual manuscripts, and the reconstructed archetypes of A, B, and C. In addition to this they will produce critical texts of A, B, and C.[45] (One respect in which such an endeavour may prove particularly useful is in the flexibility it should provide in the matters of paragraphing, punctuation, capitalisation, and the assignment of titles (rubrics) to the various parts of the poem. All these editorial elements are silently determined by the printed critical text, often with crucial effect upon its interpretation; the electronic text offers the means of indicating how provisional are such editorial readings of the text.)[46]

The revolutionary nature of such a project is fully acknowledged. Duggan points out that 'The extremely plastic nature of an electronic text is conducive to representing the actual textual tradition of *Piers Plowman*, one filled with an unusual degree of ambiguity and uncertainty'. And he goes on to say,

> An electronic edition can accommodate scholars who prefer a 'best text' documentary tradition as well as those who want the best possible modern editorial reconstruction. In the world enabled by electronic texts, theoretical differences formerly thought to be irreconcilable need no longer prevent dissemination of textual evidence ...
>
> We claim no permanently definitive status for our critical edition. Its construction will serve to exhibit many of the possibilities of the new technology. We can, nevertheless, make permanently available

---

[45] Adams' article 'Editing *Piers Plowman B*' gives some indication of the textual principles such a critical edition might adopt; it is clear that he occupies the same broadly 'eclecticist' camp as Kane (see 33). Cf. also Duggan, *The Piers Plowman Electronic Archive*: 'Real methodological issues divide eclecticists. The difference between George Kane's approach to the editing of *Piers Plowman* and ours reflects two of the most basic of those issues. The first is whether the evidence used to determine textual originality should be almost exclusively micro-linguistic (lexical and morphological issues affecting words and short phrases, with little regard to their origin in manuscripts of varying parentage and reliability) or whether editors instead should combine such considerations with evidence based on larger linguistic units (the sentence or paragraph) as well as that derived from what we know of the psychology of the composition process itself, the sociology of authorial dictional adjustment, and the transmission history of texts. In the particular case of *Piers Plowman*, it can often be shown that small, archetypal variations among the three versions of the poem, variations that Kane's narrowly philological eclecticism tends to screen out as scribal, correspond to subtle pressures emanating from macro-linguistic or paralinguistic sources and which are, therefore, quite likely to be authorial.'

[46] Cf. Pearsall, 'Theory and Practice in Middle English Editing', 122–3, for a brief account of the ways in which editorial punctuation, paragraphing, etc. are 'act[s] of appropriation' of the text.

in electronic form *all* the manuscript texts upon which critical texts must be based, thus facilitating the creation of yet other editions. As recent consideration of the metrical structure of the poem has revealed defects in early editions, so future discoveries will prompt other editors to construct different theories of the text.[47] The greatest part of our editorial work – transcriptions and collations in particular – will establish a data base permanently useful to both editors and literary critics. Such work – because it can be absorbed into future critical editions – need never be replaced. Students and critics of the future can interrogate such an *Archive* in ways unimagined by its creators.

This is heady stuff. And although the heart may sink at the prospect of 'yet other editions', the editorial history of the poem gives us clear cause to expect them. It would be extraordinary if the new medium of the electronic text did not initiate a major shift in the way that the textual problems of the poem have been conceptualised and tackled, although such a shift has been predictable for some time, in the aftermath of the disquiet generated by the Athlone edition of *Piers Plowman*. For the work of Kane and Donaldson, in particular, was so radical and bold that critics were bound to react strongly against it, proposing alternative editorial principles and practices in much the same way that critics reacted to Manly's disruption of Skeat.

Such reaction has fitted well with the trend in medieval studies identified earlier, the increased interest in scribes and the dissemination of texts, with many textual critics coming to see the processes by which texts were transmitted and received as at least as proper a focus of attention as the words and/or intentions of the author, difficult (or impossible) as the latter are to recover. This shift in critical attention is, evidently, linked to a similar shift in critical theory as applied to later texts. The passion and intensity with which Kane pursues his search for Langland's *ipsissima verba* has been attributed by a number of critics to a romantic notion of the author as sublime, producing poetry of unique character and quality beyond the imitation of scribes (and incidentally, unlikely to be subject to authorial revision).[48] An anti-heroic age is sceptical of this concept, and interested instead in seeing creative writing (and reading) as a product

---

47   Duggan refers to his metrical investigations of Langland; cf. e.g. 'Notes Toward a Theory of Langland's Meter'.

48   This observation has now become commonplace. For its most definitive statement in relation to Kane–Donaldson, see Lee Patterson, 'The Logic of Textual Criticism and the Way of Genius'. On the matter of revision, see Shelley, 'A Defence of Poetry', 294, col. 1.

of collaboration between a number of different social forces.[49] Taken to its extreme, this school of textual criticism, in its ties with a post-structuralist denial of the author function, removes the possibility of editing altogether, since it rejects the notion of authorial intention as a relevant factor in the production of texts. This is particularly disabling in the case of editing Langland, since the concept of authorial revision demands the positing of authorial intention as a way of making sense of the plethora of textual variants within and between the various versions. Remove that concept, and the editor is left powerless, with no justification for publishing anything other than manuscript facsimiles.[50]

Much of the criticism of Kane–Donaldson, however, has been made from a more traditional standpoint. Many of their critics have objected to their edition on the basis of individual readings, but a few have also queried the premises informing their editing. In particular, the order in which the versions were written, and the order of their dissemination, have come under scrutiny, with Robert Adams, Anne Hudson, Jill Mann, John Bowers, and Ralph Hanna III all inquiring within a few years of each other whether it is right to suppose that A precedes B, given the fact that almost all the extant A-MSS are later than the extant B-MSS.[51] As we saw in chapter 7 above, Skeat was responsible for settling the order A B C (acting on the hint by Price), and his justification for this order appealed to what he saw as common sense, rather than any more compelling form of logic or evidence.[52]

[49] Or as Stephen Nichols put it, in his introduction to the recent volume of *Speculum* devoted to essays on 'The New Philology', there is now an 'insistence that the language of texts be studied not simply as discursive phenomena but in the interaction of text language with the manuscript matrix and of both language and manuscript with the social context and networks they inscribe' ('Introduction: Philology in a Manuscript Culture', 9).

[50] These and other issues are discussed with clarity and insight by Derek Pearsall in 'Theory and Practice in Middle English Editing', where he surveys a wide range of recent Middle English editing and textual criticism in the light of his view 'that the record in the manuscripts of the practice of authorial revision and of the existence of authorial variants is evidence of kinds of text and compositional process that the modern critical edition misrepresents' (123). Cf also J. A. Burrow, 'The Sinking Island and the Dying Author', 14–18, and pp. 321–2 above.

[51] See Doyle, 'Remarks on Surviving Manuscripts of *Piers Plowman*', esp. 36. He recognises that the fact that early copies of A are now wanting does not necessarily imply that they did not once exist. Adams queries the order of publication, rather than composition, of the texts in 'Editing *Piers Plowman B*'; Bowers, like Hudson and Mann, queries order of composition in a paper delivered at the Cambridge Langland conference in 1993, to be published in *YLS* 9. Hanna, in 'The Manuscripts of *Piers Plowman*', 19ff., suggests that A was a 'coterie' text circulated after B and C.

[52] See pp. 111 and 159–60 above. For further justification see Kane–Donaldson, 70–4 and cf. Rigg–Brewer, 12–13.

Hudson, in the light of an examination of the rewriting of various Wycliffite works, asks whether

> it is too provocative ... to wonder whether the usual sequential account of the versions of *Piers Plowman* might be, at least in part, reversible? To ponder whether it is *demonstrably* impossible that A might be an abbreviated version of B, with Z an alternative and more drastic truncation? Or to speculate that perhaps C and B are two independent modifications of a lost hyparchetypal text, rather than members in a chronological sequence?[53]

Mann has developed the idea, independently conceived, by demonstrating that several of the salient characteristics of A – the smaller amount of Latin, the simpler and more cogent story-line, and the text's very brevity – point towards A's being a teaching version written by the poet after he wrote B.[54]

Set against the questioning and exploratory nature of such work has now come a remarkable confirmation of the print culture Duggan's project has giddily drawn us away from. The first volume of Schmidt's parallel-text edition of the four texts of the poem (Z, A, B, and C), a deliberate echoing of Skeat's edition of 1886, has appeared at the beginning of 1995. The outstanding achievement of this edition is the fact that it has been accomplished at all, for the history of editing the poem since Skeat is a sombre illustration of the extraordinary toll, in terms both of time and energy, which this defeatingly complex text has taken of its editors. Schmidt's parallel-text comprises a corrected text of Z, and critical texts, based on all the manuscripts, of A, B, and C. The second and final volume, which will provide the commentary justifying the textual decisions, is due before the end of the century. Meanwhile Schmidt has taken the text of B which he has established for this edition and used it to replace that of his first Everyman edition, grasping the opportunity to rework the Everyman edition almost in its entirety at the same time. The transformed Everyman paperback is thus conceived not (like the first) as an adjunct to Kane–Donaldson, but as an adjunct to Schmidt's parallel-text edition.[55]

---

[53] 'The Variable Text', 60.

[54] Skeat had regarded A's smaller quantity of Latin as an argument for the opposite view; see above, p. 115. Mann's paper, 'The Power of the Alphabet', was also originally delivered at the Cambridge 1993 Langland conference.

[55] The following description is necessarily brief, and interested readers are referred to my fuller analysis of Schmidt's new editions in a forthcoming review article, 'Schmidt's Parallel-Text Edition of *Piers Plowman*'.

The Introduction to the new Everyman is largely unchanged, with the signal exception that the section on the text of the poem has been expanded to twenty-five pages (from an original four and a half). The textual and lexical commentary has also been substantially rewritten, and the literary and historical commentary contracted (in anticipation of the fuller coverage to be provided in volume II of the parallel-text edition). The critical apparatus is now more extensive, and it makes far less reference to Kane–Donaldson, instead regularly citing the support of (Schmidt's) Z, A, and C for the readings Schmidt has now determined on for the B-Text.

The edition's peculiar interest is that it returns to the principle first established by Knott and by Chambers and Grattan, but disregarded by Kane in his edition of A, that the editing of the various versions of the poem must run concurrently. One of the striking consequences of the application of this principle, or so it would appear from a preliminary analysis of the four texts, is that many A-MS readings previously rejected by Kane, and some of the B-MS readings rejected by Schmidt, have been reinstated in the text. Often the reason for this is that they are also present in Z, of whose authenticity Schmidt is convinced, regarding its readings as 'part of the comparative evidence for the establishing of the B-text itself' (p. xii). Schmidt himself states that he has now

> reduced the number of emendations from some 750, about the same number as in *K-D*, to 476 (counting individual readings, of which there may be more than one in a line). If to these are added a number of readings from the individual MSS which are likely to be by contamination from A or C, the number rises to some 500.[56]

Schmidt's explanatory comments on the policies dictating this result are couched in far more tentative and cautious language than that found in the first edition. Thus he remarks that 'the step from discriminating between MS readings to "reconstructing" the readings of the lost sub-archetypes and archetype has now been, in many instances, more cautiously taken as a result of subsequent experience in editing both A and C' (p. lxxiv). This experience presumably dictated the editorial circumspection that is abundantly, and newly, evidenced throughout the Introduction to the second edition. For example, Schmidt acknowledges the 'mostly hypothetical' nature of

---

[56] lxxiv. It is not clear how these figures are to be reconciled with the ones Schmidt earlier gave in his first edition; see p. 415 above.

his reconstruction of the history of the B-Text, and the question 'whether a "critical" text of B is desirable or feasible' (p. lviii). He fully recognises the hazards involved in emending B from the evidence of Z, A, and C, as a consequence of his 'assumption of progressive or "linear" revision, i.e., revision without reversion to original readings'; such an assumption, he now recognises, 'may well prove impossible to demonstrate' (p. lxxvi). He proleptically defends himself against 'the reader of a "positivist" turn of mind, who objects in principle to heavily emended texts' (p. lxxv). And he warns us that he has retreated from the extremes of the Kane–Donaldson position that he once felt more inclined to accept:

> The principles invoked [in establishing his edition] have remained unchanged from those of fifteen years ago.[57] I find it still true, that 'in coming to different conclusions from Kane and Donaldson I have often used their methods and considered possibilities and approaches first suggested by them'. However, the number of differences between my conclusions and theirs has greatly increased. What this indicates about the validity of those 'methods' and 'approaches' must be left to the reader to decide. (p. lxxix)

It will be interesting to see how both editions – the second Everyman, and its parent parallel-text – stand up to critical scrutiny. Certainly they represent a heroic endeavour, for as this book has illustrated in its account of the achievements of previous editors of critical editions of *Piers Plowman*, the complexity of the textual problem presented by the poem's various forms has in the past overburdened the taxonomic capability of one or two brains alone. Westcott and Hort observed in 1882, 'No individual mind can ever act with perfect uniformity, or free itself completely from its own idiosyncrasies: the danger of unconscious caprice is inseparable from personal judgement.'[58] Duggan's adoption of the scientific model of a team of researchers, working with electronic aid, is more likely to result in something that may be fairly described as success, particularly since the plasticity of the electronic medium should escape the printed critical edition's inevitable foreclosing of editorial routes other than the one it has itself chosen. For the same reason, however, an electronic edition may be in practice difficult, or at least uncomfortable, to use – for the normal purposes of reading, that is, unless it

[57] The remarks quoted above suggest that this cannot be entirely the case.
[58] *The New Testament*, vol. II, 17. It should be noted that Westcott and Hort were claiming here that *two* minds – viz. their own – would be sufficient to overcome these problems.

turns out that readers avail themselves only of the critical texts which the editors promise as part of their multi-faceted project, and not the supporting material.

But many intractable problems remain for future editors of *Piers Plowman*, whether electronic or not. They will still have to wrestle with the theoretical and practical conundrums, possibly insoluble, presented by what we believe to be the fact of authorial revision. They will have to decide on the extent to which the principles of classical editing first applied to the poem by Chambers, a process subsequently brought to fruition by his pupil Kane, are necessarily helpful or valid in an analysis of the likely origin, scribal or authorial, of the thousands of manuscript variants of the authorially revised text of a highly popular alliterative poem. And they will have to edit the three, or four texts of the poem simultaneously, as Knott and particularly Chambers recognised only too well, and as Schmidt has now done, in order to avoid the errors of Skeat in 1866 and Kane in 1960. This will necessitate a long drawn-out and arduous process of editing and re-editing, with no certain hope of reaching a secure end point with which fellow readers of the poem will agree.

Works cited

I EDITIONS OF PIERS PLOWMAN

Crowley, Robert, ed., *The Vision of Pierce Plowman*. 3 editions. London, 1550. (Pepys' copy of one of the first editions has been reprinted in facsimile with an afterword by J. A. W. Bennett. London, 1976.).

Rogers, Owen, ed., *The Vision of Pierce Plowman, newlye imprynted after the authours olde copy*. London, 1561.

Whitaker, Thomas Dunham, ed., *Visio Willi de Petro Plouhman Item Visiones ejusdem de Dowel, Dobet, et Dobest or, The Vision of William Concerning Piers Plouhman*... London, 1813.

Wright, Thomas, ed., *The Vision and the Creed of Piers Ploughman*. 2 vols. London, 1842; revised edition 1856.

Skeat, W. W., ed., *The Vision of William Concerning Piers Plowman* ... *The 'Vernon' Text; or Text A.* EETS OS 28. London, 1867.

ed., *The Vision of William Concerning Piers Plowman* ... *The 'Crowley' Text; or Text B.* EETS OS 38. London, 1869.

ed., *The Vision of William Concerning Piers Plowman* ... *The 'Whitaker' Text; or Text C.* EETS OS 54. London, 1873.

ed., *The Vision of William Concerning Piers Plowman* ... *Notes to Texts A, B, and C.* EETS OS 67. London, 1877.

(Note: the above volume was also sometimes bound as EETS OS 81, i.e. with the following volume.)

ed., *The Vision of William Concerning Piers Plowman* ... *General Preface, Notes, and Indexes.* EETS OS 81. London, 1885.

ed., *The Vision of William Concerning Piers Plowman in Three Parallel Texts* ... 2 vols. Oxford, 1886. Reprinted with bibliography by J. A. W. Bennett, 1954.

Knott, T. A., and Fowler, David, eds., *Piers Plowman. A Critical Edition of the A Version.* Baltimore, 1952.

Kane, George, ed., *Piers Plowman: The A Version.* London, 1960. Second edition, 1988.

and Donaldson, E. T., eds., *Piers Plowman: The B Version.* London, 1975. Second edition, 1988.

Pearsall, Derek, ed., *Piers Plowman, by William Langland. An Edition of the C-Text.* London, 1978. Berkeley and Los Angeles, 1979. Reprinted, with corrections, Exeter 1994.

Schmidt, A. V. C., ed., *William Langland, The Vision of Piers Plowman. A Critical Edition of the B-Text.* London and New York, 1978. Reprinted, with revisions and corrections, 1982, 1984, 1987. Second edition, 1995.

434

Works cited

Rigg, A. G., and Brewer, Charlotte, eds., *Piers Plowman: The Z Version*. Toronto, 1983.

Schmidt, A. V. C., ed., *William Langland Piers Plowman. A Parallel-Text Edition of the A, B, C and Z Versions*. 2 volumes. London, 1995–

2 EDITIONS OF PORTIONS OF PIERS PLOWMAN

Cooper, Elizabeth, *The Muses Library; or a Series of English Poetry from the Saxons, to the Reign of Charles II* ... London, 1737.

Warton, Thomas, *The History of English Poetry, from the Close of the Eleventh to the Commencement of the Eighteenth Century*. 4 vols. (the fourth volume was not completed). London, 1774–81.

Ritson, Joseph., ed., *The English Anthology*. 3 vols. London, 1793–4.

Price, Richard, ed., *The History of English Poetry* ... *by Thomas Warton* ... *A New Edition Carefully Revised With Numerous Additional Notes* ... 4 vols. London, 1824.

Skeat, W. W., ed., *The Vision of William Concerning Piers the Plowman by William Langland (or Langley) According to the Version Revised and Enlarged by the Author about A. D. 1377*. Oxford, 1869 (frequently revised, the latest revision being the 10th edition, 1923, frequently reprinted).

Davis, J. F., ed., *Langland: Piers Plowman Prologue and Passus I–VII. Text B*. London, 1897.

Salter, Elizabeth, and Pearsall, Derek, eds., *Piers Plowman. Selections from the C-Text*. London, 1967.

Bennett, J. A. W., ed., *Langland, Piers Plowman Prologue and Passus I–VII of the B-Text as found in Bodleian MS. Laud Misc. 581*. Oxford, 1972.

3 TRANSLATIONS OF PIERS PLOWMAN

Goodridge, J. F., *Langland: Piers the Ploughman*. Harmondsworth, 1959.

Schmidt, A. V. C., *William Langland: Piers Plowman*. Oxford, 1992.

4 EDITIONS OF OTHER WORKS

Barr, Helen, ed., *The Piers Plowman Tradition. A Critical Edition of* Pierce the Ploughman's Crede, Richard the Redeless, Mum and the Sothsegger *and* The Crowned King. London, 1993.

Beatty, A., ed., *A New Ploughman's Tale. Chaucer Society*. Second series, vol. xxxix. London, 1902.

Benson, L. D. et al., eds., *The Riverside Chaucer*. Oxford, 1988.

Berthelette, Thomas, *Jo. Gower de Confessione Amantis*. London, 1532.

Cowper, J. M., *The Select Works of Robert Crowley*. EETS ES 15. London, 1872.

Forshall, Josiah, and Madden, Frederic, eds., *The Holy Bible: Containing the Old and New Testaments, with the Apocryphal Books, in the Earliest English Versions Made From the Latin Vulgate by John Wycliffe and his Followers*. 4 vols. Oxford, 1850.

Works cited

Furnivall, F. J., ed., *A Temporary Preface to the Six-Text Edition of Chaucer's Canterbury Tales, Part I*. London, 1868.

Political, Religious and Love Poems. EETS 15. London, 1866. Second edition, 1903.

Caxton's Book of Curtesye. EETS ES 3. London, 1868.

Furnivall, F. J. and Meyer, Paul, eds., *Caxton's Englishing of Alain Chartier's Curial*. EETS ES 54. London, 1888.

Furnivall, F. J. and Koch, John, eds., *Specimens of All The Accessible Unprinted Manuscripts of the Canterbury Tales*. Parts 4–9. Chaucer Society. London, 1897–1902.

Glauning, Otto, ed., *Lydgate's Minor Poems*. EETS ES 80. London, 1900.

Godden, Malcolm, ed., *Ælfric's Catholic Homilies*. EETS SS 5. Oxford, 1979.

Gollancz, Israeli, ed., *Hoccleve's Works, The Minor Poems in the Ashburnham MS*. EETS ES 73. 2 vols. London, 1925.

Grattan, J. H. G., and Sykes, G. F. H., eds., *The Owl and the Nightingale*. EETS ES 119. London, 1935.

Hales, John, and Furnivall, F. F., eds., *Bishop Percy's Folio MS*. 3 vols. London, 1867–8.

Herrtage, S. J., ed., *The English Charlemagne Romances Part 1. Sir Ferumbras*. EETS ES 34. London, 1879.

Sir Ferumbras. EETS ES 38. London, 1881.

Kemble, John Mitchell, ed., *The Anglo-Saxon Poems of Beowulf, The Travellers Song, and The Battle of Finnes-burh*. London, 1833–7.

Liddell, Mark, ed., *Chaucer: the Prologue to the Canterbury Tales; the Knightes Tale, the Nonnes Prestes Tale*. New York, 1901.

Lumiansky, R. M., and Mills, David, eds., *The Chester Mystery Cycle*. EETS SS 3 and 9. London, 1974 and 1986.

Macaulay, G. C., ed., *John Gower's English Works*. 2 vols. EETS ES 81–2. London, 1900–1.

McKnight, George, ed., *King Horn, Floris and Blauncheflur, The Assumption of our Lady*. EETS OS 14. London, 1901.

Madden, Frederic, ed., *Syr Gawayne, A Collection of Ancient Romance Poems*. The Bannatyne Club. London, 1839.

Laȝamon's Brut. 3 vols. London, 1847.

Manly, J. M., and Rickert, Edith, *The Text of the Canterbury Tales Studied on the Basis of All Known Manuscripts*. 8 vols. Chicago and London, 1940.

Morley, Henry, ed., *Tales of the Seven Deadly Sins: Being the Confessio Amantis of John Gower*. London, 1889.

Paris, Gaston and Pannier, Léopold, eds., *La Vie de saint Alexis*. Paris, 1872.

Pauli, Reinhold, ed., *Confessio Amantis of John Gower*. London, 1857.

Percy, Thomas, ed., *Reliques of Ancient Poetry*. 3 vols. London, 1765. Fourth edition, 3 vols., London, 1794.

Ritson, Joseph, ed., *Ancient Engleish Metrical Romances Selected and Publish'd by Joseph Ritson*. 3 vols. London, 1802.

Schick, J., ed., *Lydgate's Temple of Glas*. EETS ES 60. London, 1891.

Skeat, W. W., ed., *Lancelot of the Laik*. EETS OS 6. London, 1865.

The Lay of Havelok the Dane. EETS ES 4. London, 1868. Second edition, revised K. Sisam. Oxford, 1915.

Works cited

A Treatise on the Astrolabe. EETS ES 16. London, 1872.

Complete Works of Geoffrey Chaucer. 7 vols. Oxford, 1894–7.

Sweet, Henry, ed., *The Oldest English Texts*. EETS OS 83. London, 1885.

King Alfred's West-Saxon Version of Gregory's Pastoral Care. EETS OS 45. London, 1871.

Thorpe, Benjamin, ed., *Cædmon's Metrical Papaphrase of Parts of the Holy Scriptures*. London, 1832.

Analecta Anglo-Saxonica. London, 1834.

Tyrwhitt, Thomas, ed., *The Canterbury Tales of Chaucer*. 5 vols. London, 1775–8.

Westcott, B. F., and Hort, F. J., eds., *The New Testament*. 2 vols. Cambridge and London, 1881 and 1882.

Wright, Thomas, ed. *The Canterbury Tales of Geoffrey Chaucer*. 3 vols. London, 1847–51.

The Chester Plays. 2 vols. London, 1843 and 1847.

The Political Songs of England. Camden Society. London, 1839.

Wyatt, A. J., ed., *Beowulf and the Finnsburg Fragment*. New Edition revised, with Introduction and Notes, by R. W. Chambers. Cambridge, 1914.

5 SECONDARY SOURCES

Aarsleff, Hans, *The Study of Language in England 1780–1860*. Second edition. London, 1983.

'Scholarship and Ideology: Joseph Bédier's Critique of Romantic Medievalism'. *Historical Studies and Literary Criticism*, ed. Jerome J. McGann. Madison, 1985. 93–113.

Ackerman, R. W., 'Sir Frederic Madden and Medieval Scholarship'. *NM* 73 (1972): 1–14.

'Madden's Gawain Anthology'. *Medieval Studies in Honor of Lillian Herlands Hornstein*, eds. J. B. Bessinger and R. R. Raymo. New York, 1976. 5–18.

Adams, Robert, Review of Rigg–Brewer. *SAC* 7 (1985): 233–7.

'The Reliability of the Rubrics in the B-Text of *Piers Plowman*'. *MÆ* 54 (1985): 208–31.

'Langland's Theology'. *A Companion to Piers Plowman*, ed. John Alford. Berkeley and Los Angeles, 1988. 87–114.

'Editing and the Limitations of the *Durior Lectio*'. *YLS* 5 (1991): 7–15.

'Editing *Piers Plowman B*: The Imperative of an Intermittently Critical Edition'. *SB* 45 (1992): 31–68.

'Langland's *Ordinatio*: The *Visio* and *Vita* Once More'. *YLS* 8 (1994): 51–84.

Alford, John A., Review of Kane–Donaldson. *Speculum* 52 (1977): 1002–5.

Allen, Judson Boyce, 'Langland's Reading and Writing: *Detractor* and the Pardon Passus'. *Speculum* 59 (1984): 342–62.

Armstrong, Herbert B. J., ed., *A Norfolk Diary. Passages from the Diary of the Rev. Benjamin John Armstrong*. London, 1949.

Armstrong's Norfolk Diary. London, 1963.

Auden, W. H., *The Dyer's Hand*. London, 1963.

Baker, Donald C., 'The Evolution of Henry Bradshaw's Idea of the Order of *The Canterbury Tales*.' *Chaucer Newsletter* 3 (1981): 2–6.

'Frederick James Furnivall'. *Editing Chaucer: The Great Tradition*, ed. Paul G. Ruggiers. 157–69.

Baldwin, Anna, *The Theme of Government in Piers Plowman*. Cambridge, 1981.

Bale, John, *Scriptorum Illustrium Maioris Brytannie ... Catalogus*. Basel, 1557–9.

Index Britanniae Scriptorum ... John Bale's Index of British and Other Writers, eds., R. L. Poole and Mary Bateson. Oxford, 1902. Reissued, with an introduction by Caroline Brett and James P. Carley. Cambridge, 1990.

Barker, Nicolas, *The Publications of the Roxburghe Club 1814–1962*. Cambridge, 1964.

Barney, Peter, 'Line-Number Index to the Athlone Edition of *Piers Plowman*'. *YLS* 7 (1993): 97–114.

Barney, Stephen A., Review of Schmidt and Pearsall. *Speculum* 56 (1981): 161–5.

Bate, W. J., 'Percy's Use of His Folio-Manuscript'. *JEGP* 43 (1944): 336–7.

Bennett, J. A. W., 'A New Collation of a *Piers Plowman* Manuscript (Hm 137)'. *MÆ* 17 (1948) 21–31.

Review of Kane. *RES* 14 (1963): 68–71.

Review of Kane–Donaldson. *RES* 28 (1977): 323–6.

Benzie, William, *Dr. F. J. Furnivall: Victorian Scholar-Adventurer*. Norman, Oklahoma, 1983.

Blackman (formerly Chick), Elsie, 'Notes on the B-Text MSS of *Piers Plowman*'. *JEGP* 17 (1918): 489–545.

Review of F. A. R. Carnegy, *An Attempt to Approach the C-Text of Piers Plowman*. *MLR* 29 (1934): 492–3

Bloomfield, M. W., 'The Present State of *Piers Plowman* Studies'. *Speculum* 14 (1939): 215–32.

The Seven Deadly Sins: An Introduction to the History of a Religious Concept, with Special Reference to Medieval Literature. East Lansing, 1952.

Review of Kane. *Speculum* 36 (1961): 133–7.

Bowers, John, 'Hoccleve's Two Copies of *Lerne to Dye*: Implications for Textual Critics'. *Papers of the Bibliographical Society of America* (83) (1989): 437–72.

'*Piers Plowman* and the Police'. *YLS* 6 (1993): 1–50.

Boyd, Beverly, 'William Caxton'. *Editing Chaucer: The Great Tradition*. Ed. Paul Ruggiers. 13–34.

Bradley, Henry, 'The Misplaced Leaf of "Piers the Plowman"'. *Athenæum* 4095 (21 April 1906): 483. Reprinted in EETS OS 135B (1908).

'The Authorship of "Piers the Plowman"'. *MLR* 5 (1910): 202–7. Reprinted in EETS OS 139F (1910).

'Who was John But?' *MLR* 8 (1913): 88–9.

'Thomas Usk: The "Testament of Love"'. *Athenæum* (6 February 1897): 184. Reprinted in *The Collected Papers of Henry Bradley*, ed. Robert Bridges. Oxford, 1928. 229–32.

Brewer, Charlotte, 'Z and the A- B- and C-Texts of *Piers Plowman*'. *MÆ* 53 (1984): 194–219.

'The Textual Principles of Kane's A-Text'. *YLS* 3 (1989): 67–90.

'Editors of Piers Plowman'. *The Medieval Text. Editors and Critics*, eds. M. Borch, A. Haarder, and J. McGrew. Odense, 1990. 45–63.

Works cited

'Authorial vs. Scribal Writing in *Piers Plowman*'. *Medieval Literature*, ed. T. W. Machan. Binghamton, New York, 1991. 59–89.

'George Kane's Processes of Revision'. *Crux and Controversy*, eds. A. J. Minnis and Charlotte Brewer. Cambridge, 1992. 71–92.

'Schmidt's Parallel-Text Edition of *Piers Plowman*'. *MÆ*, forthcoming.

Brewer, Charlotte, and Rigg, A. G. (introd.). *Piers Plowman. A Facsimile of the Z-Text in Bodleian Library, Oxford, MS Bodley 851*. Cambridge, 1994.

Brewer, Derek, 'The Annual Chaucer Lecture. Furnivall & the Old Chaucer Society.' *The Chaucer Newsletter* 1, No. 2 (1979): 2–6.

Bright, A. H., *New Light on Piers Plowman*. London, 1928.

Bronson, Bertrand H., *Joseph Ritson: Scholar at Arms*. 2 vols. Berkeley, 1938.

Brooks, E. St John., 'The *Piers Plowman* Manuscripts in Trinity College, Dublin'. *The Library*, fifth series 6 (1951): 5–22.

Buckley, Vincent, 'George Russell as a Topic in his Own Right'. *Medieval English Religious and Ethical Literature*, eds. Geoffrey Kratzmann and James Simpson. Cambridge, 1986. 1–15.

Burrow, J. A., 'The Audience of *Piers Plowman*'. *Anglia* 75 (1957): 373–84. Reprinted, with a new postscript, in J. A. Burrow, *Essays on Medieval Literature*. Oxford, 1984. 102–116.

'The Sinking Island and the Dying Author: R. W. Chambers Fifty Years On'. Chambers Memorial Lecture. *Essays In Criticism* 40 (1990): 1–23.

Cargill, Oscar, 'The Langland Myth'. *PMLA* 50 (1935): 35–56.

Carnegy, F. A. R., *An Attempt to Approach the C-Text of Piers the Plowman*. London, 1934.

Chambers, R. W., 'The Authorship of "Piers Plowman"'. *MLR* 5 (1910): 1–32. Reprinted in EETS OS 139E (1910).

'The Original Form of the A-Text of "Piers Plowman"'. *MLR* 6 (1911): 302–23.

Widsith: A Study in Old English Heroic Legend. Cambridge, 1912.

'The "Shifted Leaf" in "Beowulf"'. *MLR* 10 (1915): 37–41.

'The Three Texts of "Piers Plowman" and Their Grammatical Forms'. *MLR* 14 (1919): 129–51.

Beowulf: An Introduction to the Study of the Poem. Cambridge, 1921.

'Long Will, Dante, and the Righteous Heathen'. *Essays and Studies* 9 (1924): 50–69.

'The Continuity of English Prose from Alfred to More and his School'. Part of Introduction, in N. Harpsfield, *The Life and Death of Sir Thomas Moore*, eds. E. V. Hitchcock and R. W. Chambers. EETS OS 186 (1932). Also published separately (London, 1932).

'The Manuscripts of *Piers Plowman* in the Huntington Library, and Their Value for Fixing the Text of the Poem'. *Huntington Library Bulletin* (1935): 1–27.

Thomas More. London, 1935.

(introd.) *Piers Plowman: The Huntington Library Manuscript (H. M. 143) reproduced in Photostat*. San Marino, 1936.

Man's Unconquerable Mind. London, 1939.

'A Piers Plowman Manuscript'. *National Library of Wales Journal* 2 (1941): 42–3.

'Incoherencies in the A- and B-Texts of *Piers Plowman* and their Bearing on the Authorship'. *London Mediæval Studies* 1 (1948 for 1937): 27–39.

'Robert or William Longland?' *London Mediæval Studies* 1 (1948 for 1939): 430–62.

Chambers, R. W., and Grattan, J. H. G., 'The Text of "Piers Plowman"'. *MLR* 4 (1909): 359–89.

'The Text of "Piers Plowman": Critical Methods'. *MLR* 11 (1916): 257–75.

'The Text of "Piers Plowman"'. *MLR* 26 (1931): 1–51.

Clarke, M. V., and Galbraith, V. H., 'The Deposition of Richard II'. *BJRL* 14 (1930): 125–81.

Coffman, G. R., 'The Present State of a Critical Edition of *Piers Plowman*'. *Speculum* 20 (1945): 482–3.

Coleridge, Herbert, *A Dictionary of the First, or Oldest Words in the English Language: from the Semi-Saxon Period of AD 1250 to 1300 . . .* London, 1862.

Cooper, Helen, 'Langland's and Chaucer's Prologues'. *YLS* 1 (1987): 71–81.

Craster, E., *History of the Bodleian Library, 1845–1945*. Oxford, 1952.

Dahl, Eric, '*Diverse Copies Have It Diverselye*: An Unorthodox Survey of *Piers Plowman* Textual Scholarship from Crowley to Skeat'. *Suche Werkis to Werche. Essays on Piers Plowman in Honor of David C. Fowler*, ed. Míceál F. Vaughan. East Lansing, 1993. 53–80.

Dain, Alphonse, *Les Manuscrits*. Second edition. Paris, 1964.

Day, Mabel, 'The Alliteration of the Versions of "Piers Plowman" in Its Bearing on Their Authorship'. *MLR* 17 (1922): 403–9.

'The Revisions of "Piers Plowman"'. *MLR* 23 (1928): 1–27.

'"Din" and "Doom" in "Piers Plowman". A, II, 183'. *MLR* 26 (1931): 336–8.

Dickins, Bruce, 'John Mitchell Kemble and Old English Scholarship'. *PBA* 25 (1939): 51–84.

DiMarco, Vincent, *Piers Plowman: A Reference Guide*. Boston, 1988.

'Eighteenth-Century Suspicions Regarding the Authorship of *Piers Plowman*'. *Anglia* 100 (1982): 124–9.

'Godwin on Langland'. *YLS* 6 (1992): 123–35.

D'Israeli, Isaac, *Amenities of Literature*. 3 vols. London, 1841.

Donaldson, E. T., *Piers Plowman: The C-Text and Its Poet*. New Haven, 1949.

'The Texts of *Piers Plowman*: Scribes and Poets'. *MP* 50 (1952–3): 269–73.

'MSS R and F in the B-Tradition of *Piers Plowman*'. *Transactions of the Connecticut Academy of Arts and Sciences* 39 (1955): 177–212.

'"Piers Plowman": Textual Comparison and the Question of Authorship'. *Chaucer und seine Zeit: Symposion für W. Schirmer*, ed. A. Esch. Tübingen, 1968. 241–7.

'The Psychology of Editors'. *Speaking of Chaucer*. London, 1970. 102–18.

Douglas, David, *English Scholars, 1660–1730*. Second Edition. London, 1951.

Doyle, A. I., Review of Kane. *English Studies* 43 (1962): 55–9.

'The Manuscripts'. *Middle English Alliterative Poetry and its Literary Background*, ed. David Lawton. Cambridge, 1982. 88–100.

'Remarks on Surviving Manuscripts of *Piers Plowman*'. *Medieval English Religious and Ethical Literature*, eds. Geoffrey Kratzmann and James Simpson. Cambridge, 1986. 35–48.

Duggan, Hoyt N., 'Notes Toward a Theory of Langland's Meter'. *YLS* 1 (1987): 41–70.

Works cited

'The Authenticity of the Z-text of *Piers Plowman*: Further Notes on Metrical Evidence'. *MÆ* 56 (1987): 25–45.

Review of A. V. C. Schmidt, *The Clerkly Maker: Langland's Poetic Art*. *YLS* 2 (1988): 167–74.

'The *Piers Plowman* Electronic Archive'. 1994. Mosaic (World Wide Web). http:// jefferson.village.virginia.edu/piers/report 94.html.

'The Electronic *Piers Plowman*: A New Diplomatic Critical Edition'. *Æstel* 1 (1993): 1–21.

Earle, John, *The Deeds of Beowulf*. Oxford, 1892.

Edwards, A. S. G., 'Walter W. Skeat'. *Editing Chaucer: The Great Tradition*, ed. Paul G. Ruggiers. 171–89.

'Observations on the History of Middle English Editing'. *Manuscripts and Text: Editorial Problems in Later Middle English Literature*, ed. Derek Pearsall. Cambridge, 1987. 34–48.

'*Piers Plowman* in the Seventeenth Century: Gerard Langbaine's Notes'. *YLS* 6 (1992): 141–4.

Ferguson, W. K., *The Renaissance in Medieval Thought*. Cambridge, Mass., 1948.

Firth, C. H., 'Joseph Wright 1855–1930'. *PBA* 18 (1932): 3–19.

Foulet, Alfred, and Speer, Mary Blakely, *On Editing Old French Texts*. Lawrence, Kansas, 1979.

Fowler, D. C., 'The Relationship of the Three Texts of *Piers the Plowman*'. *MP* 1 (1952–3): 269–73.

Review of Kane. *MP* 58 (1961): 115–16.

'A New Edition of the B Text of *Piers Plowman*'. *YES* 7 (1977): 23–42.

'Editorial "Jamming": Two New Editions of *Piers Plowman*'. *Review* 2 (1980): 211–69.

Frantzen, Allen, *Desire for Origins*. New Brunswick and London, 1990.

Ganz, Peter, *Jacob Grimm's Conception of German Studies*. Inaugural Lecture delivered before the University of Oxford on 18 May 1973. Oxford, 1973.

Garnett, James, Review of *Parallel-Text*. *American Journal of Philology* 8 (1887): 347–55.

Garnett, Richard, *The Philological Essays of the Late Rev. Richard Garnett Edited by his Son*. London, 1859.

Gill, Stephen, 'Wordsworth's Poems: the Question of Text'. *Romantic Revisions*, eds. Robert Brinkley and Keith Hanley. Cambridge, 1992. 43–63.

Godwin, William, *Life of Geoffrey Chaucer, the Early English Poet* ... 2 vols. London, 1803.

Görlach, Manfred, Review of Kane–Donaldson. *Archiv* 213 (1976): 396–9.

Görnemann, Gertrud, *Zur Verfasserschaft und Entstehungsgeschichte von 'Piers the Plowman'*. Heidelberg, 1916.

Gradon, Pamela, 'Langland and the Ideology of Dissent'. *PBA* 66 (1980): 179–205.

Grattan, J. H. G., 'The Text of "Piers Plowman": a Newly Discovered Manuscript and Its Affinities'. *MLR* 42 (1947): 1–8.

'The Text of *Piers Plowman*: Critical Lucubrations with Special Reference to the Independent Substitution of Similars'. *St Phil* 44 (1947): 593–604.

'The Critical Edition of *Piers Plowman*: Its Present Status'. *Speculum* 26 (1951): 582–3.

Works cited

Gray, Thomas, *The Works of Thomas Gray, with Memoirs of his Life and Writings by William Mason*. 2 vols. London, 1814.

Greg, W. W., *The Calculus of Variants. An Essay in Textual Criticism*. Oxford, 1929.

Green, Richard Firth, Review of Rigg–Brewer. *Analytical and Enumerative Bibliography* 8 (1984): 129–33.

'The Lost Exemplar of the Z-Text of *Piers Plowman* and its 20–Line Pages'. *MÆ* 61 (1987): 307–9.

Greetham, D. C., *Textual Scholarship: An Introduction*. New York and London, 1994.

Griffith, John G., 'Author-Variants in Juvenal: A Reconsideration'. *Festschrift Bruno Snell*, ed. H. Erbse. Munich, 1956. 101–11.

Haas, Renate, 'The Social Functions of F. J. Furnivall's Medievalism'. *The Living Middle Ages*, eds. Uwe Böker, Manfred Markus, and Rainer Schöwerling. Stuttgart and Regensburg, 1989. 319–32.

Hammond, Eleanor, *Chaucer: A Bibliographical Manual*. Chicago, 1908.

Hanna III, Ralph, 'The Manuscripts of *Piers Plowman*'. *YLS* 7 (1993): 1–25.

William Langland. Aldershot and Brookfield, 1993.

Haseldon, R. B., 'The Fragment of *Piers Plowman* in Ashburnham No. CXXX'. *Modern Philology* 29 (1932): 391–4.

Hewitt-Smith, Kathleen M., 'Revisions in the Athlone Editions of the A and B Versions of Piers Plowman'. *YLS* 4 (1990): 151–4.

Hickes, George, *Linguarum vett. septentrionalium thesaurus grammatico-criticus et archaeologicus*. 2 vols. Oxford, 1703–5.

Housman, A. E., *Selected Prose*, ed. J. Carter. Cambridge, 1961.

Hudson, Anne, 'Robert of Gloucester and the Antiquaries'. *N & Q* 214 (1969): 323–6.

'Middle English'. *Editing Medieval Texts*, ed. A. G. Rigg. New York and London, 1977. 34–57.

'The Legacy of *Piers Plowman*'. *A Companion to Piers Plowman*, ed. John A. Alford. Berkeley and Los Angeles, 1988. 251–66.

'The Variable Text'. *Crux and Controversy*, eds. A. J. Minnis and Charlotte Brewer. Cambridge, 1992. 49–60.

'*Piers Plowman* and the Peasants' Revolt: A Problem Revisited'. *YLS* 8 (1994): 85–106.

Hussey, S. S., ed., *Piers Plowman: Critical Approaches*. London, 1969.

James, Clive, 'George Russell: A Reminiscence'. *Medieval English Religious and Ethical Literature*, eds. Geoffrey Kratzmann and James Simpson. Cambridge, 1986. 16–18.

Jansen, Sharon L., 'Politics, Protest, and a New *Piers Plowman* Fragment: The Voice of the Past in Tudor England'. *RES* NS 40 (1989): 92–9.

Johnston, Arthur, *Enchanted Ground*. London, 1964.

Jusserand, J. J., '*Piers Plowman*, the Work of One or of Five'. *MP* 6 (1909): 271–327. Reprinted in EETS, OS 139B (1910).

'*Piers Plowman*, the Work of One or of Five: A Reply'. *MP* 7 (1910): 289–326. Reprinted in EETS OS 139D (1910).

Kane, George, ' "Piers Plowman": Problems and Methods of Editing the B-Text'. *MLR* 43 (1948): 1–25.

Works cited

'The Autobiographical Fallacy in Chaucer and Langland Studies'. Chambers Memorial Lecture. London, 1965.

Piers Plowman. The Evidence for Authorship. London, 1965.

'Conjectural Emendation'. *Medieval Literature and Civilization: Studies in Memory of G. N. Garmonsway*, eds. D. A. Pearsall and R. A. Waldron. London, 1969. 155–69.

'A Short Report on the Athlone Press Edition of *Piers Plowman*'. *Chaucer Newsletter* 2 (1980): 15.

'John M. Manly and Edith Rickert'. *Editing Chaucer: The Great Tradition*, ed. Paul Ruggiers. 207–30.

'The "Z Version" of *Piers Plowman*'. *Speculum* 60 (1985): 910–30.

'"Good" and "Bad" Manuscripts: Texts and Critics'. *SAC* 2 (1986): 137–45.

'The Text'. *A Companion to Piers Plowman*, ed. John A. Alford. Berkeley and Los Angeles, 1988. 175–200.

Kelly, Robert L., 'Hugh Latimer as Piers Plowman'. *SEL* 17 (1977): 13–26.

Kennedy, Edward Donald, and Wittig, Joseph, *Medieval English Studies Presented to George Kane.* Woodbridge, 1988.

Kenney, E. J., *The Classical Text.* Berkeley, Los Angeles, and London, 1974.

King, John N., 'Robert Crowley: A Tudor Gospelling Poet', *YES* 8 (1978): 220–37.

'Robert Crowley's Editions of *Piers Plowman*'. *MP* 73 (1976): 342–52.

English Reformation Literature. Princeton, 1982.

Knott, T. A., 'The "Lost Leaf" of "Piers the Plowman" '. *Nation* 88 (1909): 482–3.

'An Essay Toward the Critical Text of the A-Version of "Piers the Plowman" '. *MP* 12 (1915): 129–61.

'Observations on the Authorship of *Piers the Plowman*'. *MP* 14 (1916–17): 531–58; *MP* 15 (1916–17): 23–41.

Kron, Richard, *William Langleys Buch von Peter dem Plfüger.* Erlangen, 1885.

Kurath, Hans, et al. *The Middle English Dictionary. Plan and Bibliography.* Ann Arbor and London, 1954.

Lawler, Traugott, Review of Kane–Donaldson. *MP* 77 (1979–80): 66–71.

Lawton, David, 'Lollardy and the *Piers Plowman* Tradition'. *MLR* 76 (1981): 780–93.

Liddell, Mark, *An Introduction to the Scientific Study of English Poetry.* London, 1902.

Lounsbury, Thomas R., *Studies in Chaucer. His Life and Writings.* 3 vols. London, 1892.

Lye, Edward, *Dictionarium Saxonico et Gothico-Latinum.* 2 vols. London, 1772.

McGann, Jerome J., *A Critique of Modern Textual Criticism.* Chicago and London, 1983.

McKitterick, David, *A History of Cambridge University Press.* Cambridge, 1992.

Maas, Paul, *Textual Criticism.* Translated by Barbara Flower. Oxford, 1958.

Madan, Falconer, Craster, H. H. E., and Denholm-Young, N., eds., *A Summary Catalogue of the Western Manuscripts in the Bodleian Library.* Vol. II, Part 2. Oxford, 1937.

Manly, J. M., 'The Lost Leaf of "Piers the Plowman" '. *MP* 3 (1905–6): 359–66. Reprinted in EETS OS 135B (1908).

'*Piers the Plowman* and its Sequence'. Chapter 1 in *The Cambridge History of English Literature*, vol. II: *The End of The Middle Ages*, eds. A. W. Ward and A. R. Waller. Cambridge, 1908. 1–42. Reprinted in EETS OS 135B (1908).

Works cited

'The Authorship of *Piers Plowman*'. *MP* 7 (1909–10): 83–144. Reprinted in EETS OS 139C (1910).

Mann, Jill, 'The Power of the Alphabet: A Reassessment of the Relation between the A and B Versions of *Piers Plowman*'. *YLS* 8 (1994): 21–50.

Markham, Mrs [Elizabeth Penrose], *A History of England*. Twelfth edition. London, 1846.

Marsh, George P., *Lectures on the English Language (First Series)*. New York and London, 1860.

Mathew, Gervase, Review of Kane. *MÆ* 30 (1961): 126–8.

Mawer, Allen, Review of R. W. Chambers, *Beowulf. An Introduction to the Study of the Poem*. *MLR* 18 (1923): 96–8.

Mayhew, A. L., ed., *A Glossary of Tudor and Stuart Words ... Collected by Walter W. Skeat*. Oxford, 1914.

Middleton, Anne, 'The Audience and Public of "Piers Plowman"'. *Middle English Alliterative Poetry and its Literary Background*, ed. David Lawton. Cambridge, 1982. 103–23.

'*Piers Plowman*'. *A Manual of the Writings in Middle English 1050–1500*, ed. Albert E. Hartung. Vol. VII. New Haven, 1986. 2211–34, 2417–43.

'Making a Good End: John But as a Reader of *Piers Plowman*'. *Medieval English Studies Presented to George Kane*, eds. Edward Donald Kennedy, et al.. 243–63.

'The Critical Heritage'. *A Companion to Piers Plowman*, ed. John A. Alford. Berkeley and Los Angeles, 1988. 1–25.

'William Langland's "Kynde Name": Authorial Signature and Social Identity in Late Fourteenth-Century England'. *Literary Practice and Social Change in Britain, 1380–1530*, ed. Lee Patterson. Berkeley, Los Angeles, and London, 1990. 15–82.

'Life in the Margins, or, What's an Annotator to Do'. *New Directions in Textual Studies*, eds. Dave Oliphant and Robin Bradford. Austin, 1990. 167–83.

Milroy, James, *The Language of Gerard Manley Hopkins*. London, 1977.

Mitchell, A. G., 'The Text of *Piers Plowman* C Prologue l. 215'. *MÆ* 8 (1939): 118–20.

'A Newly-Discovered Manuscript of the C-Text of "Piers Plowman"'. *MLR* 36 (1941): 243–4.

'Worth Both His Ears'. *MLN* 59 (1944): 222.

'Notes on the C-text of *Piers Plowman*', *London Mediæval Studies* 1 (1948 for 1939): 483–92.

'Lady Meed and the Art of *Piers Plowman*'. Chambers Memorial Lecture. London, 1956.

Mitchell, A. G., and Russell, G. H., 'The Three Texts of "Piers the Plowman"'. *JEGP* 52 (1953): 445–56.

Moore, Edward, *Contributions to the Textual Criticism of the Divina Commedia*. Cambridge, 1889.

Morris, Richard, *Specimens of Early English*. Oxford, 1867.

Munby, A. N. L., *Phillipps Studies*. 5 vols. Cambridge, 1951–60.

Portrait of an Obsession: The Life of Sir Thomas Phillipps, the World's Greatest Book Collector, adapted by Nicolas Barker from the five volumes of Phillipps Studies. London, 1967.

Works cited

Munro, John, ed., *Frederick James Furnivall: A Volume of Personal Record*. London, 1911.

Murray, K. M. Elisabeth, *Caught in the Web of Words: James Murray and the Oxford English Dictionary*. Oxford, 1979.

Nichols, Stephen G., 'Introduction: Philology in a Manuscript Culture'. *Speculum* 65 (1990): 1–10.

Nicol, Henry, 'M. G. Paris's Method of Editing in his *Vie de Saint Alexis*'. *TPS* (1873–4): 332–45.

Norbrook, David, *Poetry and Politics in the English Renaissance*. London, 1984.

Oates, J. C. T., 'Young Henry Bradshaw'. *Essays in Honor of Victor Scholderer*, ed. D. E. Rhodes. Mainz, 1970.

Patterson, Lee C., 'The Logic of Textual Criticism and the Way of Genius: The Kane–Donaldson *Piers Plowman* in Historical Perspective'. *Textual Criticism and Literary Interpretation*, ed. Jerome J. McGann. Chicago, 1985, 55–91.

Pearsall, Derek, Review of Kane–Donaldson. *MÆ* 46 (1977): 1002–5.

'The Ilchester Manuscript of *Piers Plowman*'. *NM* 82 (1981): 181–93.

'Textual Criticism and Fifteenth-Century Manuscript Production'. *Fifteenth Century Studies*, ed. Robert F. Yeager. Hamden, Connecticut, 1984. 121–36.

Review of Rigg–Brewer. *Archiv* 222 (1985): 181–4.

'Editing Medieval Texts: Some Developments and Some Problems'. *Textual Criticism and Literary Interpretation*, ed. Jerome J. McGann. Chicago, 1985. 92–106.

An Annotated Critical Bibliography of Langland. Ann Arbor, 1990.

'Authorial Revision in Some Late-Medieval Texts'. *Crux and Controversy*, eds. A. J. Minnis and Charlotte Brewer. Cambridge, 1992. 39–48.

'Theory and Practice in Middle English Editing'. *Text* 7 (1995): 107–26.

Percival, Janet, *The Papers of Raymond Wilson Chambers (1874–1942). A Handlist*. The Library, University College London, Occasional Publications 4. London, 1978.

Pope, Alexander, *The Dunciad Variorum. The Dunciad*, ed. James Sutherland. Third edition. London and New Haven, 1963.

Preminger, Alex J., Warnke, Frank J., and Hardison Jr., O. B., eds., *Princeton Encyclopedia of Poetry and Poetics*. Princeton, 1974.

Prothero, G. W. *A Memoir of Henry Bradshaw*. London, 1888.

Quirk, Randolph, 'Langland's Use of Kind Wit and Inwit'. *JEGP* 52 (1953): 182–8.

'Vis Imaginativa'. *JEGP* 53 (1954): 81–3.

Rickert, Edith, 'John But, Messenger and Maker'. *MP* 11 (1913): 107–16.

Rigg, A. G., 'Medieval Latin Poetic Anthologies (I)'. *Medieval Studies* 39 (1977): 281–330.

'Medieval Latin Poetic Anthologies (II)'. *Medieval Studies* 40 (1978): 387–407.

'Medieval Latin Poetic Anthologies (III)'. *Medieval Studies* 41 (1979): 468–505.

Ritson, Joseph, *Bibliographia Poetica: a Catalogue of Engleish Poets of the Twelfth, Thirteenth, Fourteenth, Fifteenth, and Sixteenth Centurys, With a Short Account of their Works*. London, 1802.

Observations on the Three First Volumes of the History of English Poetry ... London, 1782.

Works cited

Rogers, Gillian, 'The Percy Folio Manuscript Revisited'. *Romance in Medieval England*, eds. Maldwyn Mills, Jennifer Fellows, and Carol Meale. Cambridge, 1991. 39–64.

Ross, Thomas, 'Thomas Wright. *Editing Chaucer: The Great Tradition*, ed. Paul Ruggiers. 145–56.

Ruggiers, Paul, ed., *Editing Chaucer: The Great Tradition*. Norman, Oklahoma, 1984.

Russell, George, 'The Evolution of a Poem: Some Reflections on the Textual Tradition of *Piers Plowman*'. *Arts*. The Proceedings of the Sydney University Arts Association 2 (1962): 33–46.

'Some Aspects of the Process of Revision in *Piers Plowman*'. *Piers Plowman: Critical Approaches*, ed. S. S. Hussey. 27–49.

'Editorial Theory and Practice in Middle English Texts: Some Observations'. *Iceland and the Medieval World: Studies in Honour of Ian Maxwell*, eds. G. Turville-Petre and J. S. Martin. Melbourne, 1972. 162–76.

'The Poet as Reviser: the Metamorphosis of the Confession of the Seven Deadly Sins in *Piers Plowman*'. *Acts of Interpretation: The Text in Its Contexts 700–1600. Essays on Medieval and Renaissance Literature in Honor of E. Talbot Donaldson*, eds. Mary J. Carruthers and Elizabeth D. Kirk. Norman, Oklahoma, 1982. 53–65.

'Some Early Responses to the C-Version of *Piers Plowman*'. *Viator* 15 (1984): 275–303.

'The Imperative of Revision in the C Version of *Piers Plowman*'. *Medieval English Studies Presented to George Kane*, eds. Edward Donald Kennedy, Ronald Waldron, and Joseph Wittig. Woodbridge, 1988. 233–44.

' "As They Read It": Some Notes on Early Responses to the C-Version of *Piers Plowman*'. *Leeds Studies in English* NS 20 (1989): 173–89.

and Nathan, Venetia, 'A *Piers Plowman* Manuscript in the Huntington Library'. *Huntington Library Quarterly* 26 (1963): 119–30.

Samuels, M. L., 'Langland's Dialect'. *MÆ* 54 (1985): 232–47.

'Dialect and Grammar'. *A Companion to Piers Plowman*, ed. John A. Alford. Berkeley and Los Angeles, 1988. 201–21.

Scase, Wendy, 'Two *Piers Plowman* C-Text Interpolations: Evidence for a Second Textual Tradition'. *Notes and Queries* 232 (1987): 456–63.

Schmidt, A. V. C., 'The Authenticity of the Z Text of *Piers Plowman*: A Metrical Examination'. *MÆ* 53 (1984): 295–300.

Shelley, Percy Bysshe, 'A Defence of Poetry'. *Shelley's Prose*, ed. David Lee Clark. London, 1988. 276–97.

Sherbo, Arthur, 'Samuel Pegge, Thomas Holt White, and *Piers Plowman*'. *YLS* 1 (1987): 122–8.

'Walter William Skeat in the *Cambridge Review*'. *YLS* 3 (1989): 109–30.

The Clerkly Maker: Langland's Poetic Art. Cambridge, 1987.

Sisam, Kenneth, ed., *Fourteenth Century Verse and Prose*. Oxford, 1921.

'Notes on Old English Poetry'. *RES* 22 (1946), 257–68. Reprinted as 'The Authority of Old English Poetical Mansucripts'. *Studies in the History of Old English Literature*. Oxford, 1953. 29–44.

Studies in the History of Old English Literature. Oxford, 1953.

Works cited

Sisson, C. J., 'Raymond Wilson Chambers. 1874–1942'. *PBA* 30 (1944): 427–39.

'R. W. Chambers. A Portrait of a Professor'. First Chambers Memorial Lecture. London, 1950.

Skeat, W. W., *Parallel Extracts from Twenty-nine Manuscripts of Piers Plowman ...* EETS OS 17. London, 1866.

Questions for Examination in English Literature. London, 1873.

ed., *Testimonials in Favour of the Rev. Walter W. Skeat.* Cambridge, 1878.

Etymological Dictionary of the English Language. 2 vols. Oxford, 1882–4. Revised and enlarged, 1910.

'First Editions'. *N&Q* 8th series, vol. 1. 24 (1892): 480.

A Student's Pastime: Being a Select Series of Articles Reprinted from 'Notes and Queries'. Oxford, 1896.

'A New "Havelok" MS'. *MLR* 6 (1911): 455–7.

Smith, A. H., 'Piers Plowman and the Pursuit of Poetry'. Inaugural Lecture at University College, London, 1950. Reprinted in *Style and Symbolism in Piers Plowman: A Modern Critical Anthology*, ed. Robert J. Blanch. Knoxville, 1969. 26–39.

Smith, David Nichol, and Brooks, Cleanth, eds., *The Percy Letters.* vol. III. *The Correspondence of Thomas Percy and Thomas Warton*, eds. M. G. Robinson and Leah Dennis. Louisiana, 1951.

Stafford, Fiona, *The Sublime Savage: a Study of James MacPherson and the Poems of Ossian.* Edinburgh, 1988.

Stanley, E. G., 'Unideal Editing of Old English Verse'. *PBA* 70 (1984): 231–73.

Review of Kane–Donaldson. *N &Q* 23 (1976): 435–7.

Steeves, H. R., *Learned Societies and English Literary Scholarship.* New York, 1913.

Stock, Brian, 'The Middle Ages as Subject and Object'. *NLH* 5 (1974): 527–47.

Stroud, T. A., 'Manly's Marginal Notes on the *Piers Plowman* Controversy'. *MLN* 64 (1949): 9–12.

Tashjian, Georgian R., Tashjian, David R., and Enright, Brian J., eds., *Richard Rawlinson: A Tercentenary Memorial.* Kalamazoo, 1990.

Taylor, Beverly, and Brewer, Elisabeth, *The Return of King Arthur.* Cambridge, 1983.

Teichmann, Eduard, 'Zum Texte von William Langland's Vision'. *Anglia* 15 (1893): 223–60.

Thorne, J. R., and Uhart, Marie-Claire, 'Robert Crowley's *Piers Plowman*'. *MÆ* 55 (1986): 248–53.

Thorpe, James, *Principles of Textual Criticism.* San Marino, 1972.

Trench, Richard Chenevix, 'Some Deficiencies in our English Dictionaries'. Two papers read to the Philological Society in November 1857. Second edition, London 1860, bound into *TPS* 1857.

Proposal for the Publication of A New English Dictionary by the Philological Society, bound into *TPS* 1857.

On the Study of Words. London, 1851. Eighth edition, 1858.

English Past and Present. London, 1855.

Turville-Petre, Thorlac, Review of Kane–Donaldson. *SN* 49 (1977): 153–5.

Review of Schmidt. *RES* 30 (1979): 454–7.

Works cited

Von Nolcken, Christina, '*Piers Plowman*, the Wycliffites, and *Pierce the Plowman's Creed*'. *YLS* 2 (1988): 71–102.

Warton, Thomas, *Observations on the Faerie Queene of Spenser*. London and Oxford, 1754. Second edition, 2 vols. London, 1862.

Wawn, Andrew, 'The Genesis of the *Plowman's Tale*'. *YES* 2 (1972): 21–40.

'Chaucer, *The Plowman's Tale* and Reformation Propaganda: The Testimonies of Thomas Godfray and *I Playne Piers*'. *BJRL* 57 (1973): 174–92.

Weldon, James, '*Ordinatio* and Genre in MS CCC 201'. *Florilegium* 12 (1993): 159–75.

Wenzel, Siegfried, 'Reflections on the (New) Philology'. *Speculum* 65 (1990): 11–18.

Whitaker, Thomas Dunham, *An History of the Original Parish of Whalley and Honour of Clitheroe*. London, 1801. Fourth edition, revised by J. G. Nichols and P. A. Lyons. 2 vols. London, 1872, 1876.

The History and Antiquities of the Deanery of Craven. London, 1805.

White, Helen C., *Social Criticism in Popular Religious Literature of the Sixteenth Century*. New York, 1944.

White, Hugh, Review of Rigg–Brewer. *MÆ* 53 (1984): 290–4.

Wiener, Martin J., *English Culture and the Decline of the Industrial Spirit 1850–1980*. Cambridge, 1981.

Wilks, John, 'The Influence of R. W. Chambers on the Development of University Libraries'. Chambers Memorial Lecture. London, 1953.

Williams, R. A., *The Finn Episode in Beowulf: an Essay in Interpretation*. Cambridge, 1924.

Windeatt, B. A., 'Thomas Tyrwhitt'. *Editing Chaucer: The Great Tradition*, ed. Paul Ruggiers. 117–43.

Wordsworth, Jonathan, 'Revision as Making: *The Prelude* and Its Peers'. *Romantic Revisions*, eds. Robert Brinkley and Keith Hanley. Cambridge, 1992. 18–42.

[Wright, Thomas,] 'The Visions of Piers Plowman'. *Gentleman's Magazine* n.s. 1 (1834): 385–91.

Zupitza, Julius, ed., *Specimens of All The Accessible Unprinted Manuscripts of the Canterbury Tales*. Parts 1–3. Chaucer Society. London, 1892–3.

6 UNPUBLISHED SOURCES

Archives

Athlone Press Papers, University of London Library.

Bradshaw Papers, Cambridge University Library.

Chambers Papers, University College London.

Early English Text Society Papers.

Oxford University Press archives, Bodleian Library, Oxford.

Skeat–Furnivall Library, Kings College, London.

Dissertations

Allen, B. F., 'The Genealogy of the C Text Manuscripts of *Piers Plowman*'. MA thesis. University of London, 1923.

Works cited

Brewer, Charlotte, 'Some Implications of the Z-Text for the Textual Tradition of *Piers Plowman*'. D.Phil. thesis. University of Oxford, 1986.

Carnegy, F. A. R., 'Problems Connected with the Three Texts of *Piers the Plowman*'. MA thesis. University of London, 1923.

Chick (later Blackman), Elsie, 'A Preliminary Investigation of the Pedigree of the B-text MSS of *Piers Plowman*'. MA thesis. University of London, 1914.

Crawford, William R., 'Robert Crowley's Editions of *Piers Plowman*: A Bibliographical and Textual Study'. Dissertation. Yale University, 1957.

Hussey, S. S., 'Eighty Years of *Piers Plowman* Scholarship: A Study of Critical Methods'. MA thesis. University of London, 1952.

Fowler, David, 'A Critical Text of Piers Plowman A-2'. Ph.D. dissertation. University of Chicago, 1949.

Kane, George, 'The B-text of Piers Plowman, Passus XVIII–XX'. Ph.D. thesis. University of London, 1946.

Mitchell, A. G., 'A Critical Edition of Piers Plowman, Context, Prologue, and Passus I–IV'. Ph.D. thesis. University of London, 1939.

Manuscripts of Piers Plowman

(See also Kane, 'The Text', 178–80; Hanna, *William Langland*, 37–42; Schmidt, *William Langland Piers Plowman. A Parallel-Text Edition of the A, B, C and Z Versions*, vol. I, x–xii.)

Z-Text

Z   Bodleian Library MS Bodley 851

A-Text

A	Bodleian Library MS Ashmole 1468
Ch	Chaderton MS, Liverpool University Library F. 4. 8 (conjoint A/C-Text; = C-MS Ch)
D	Bodleian Library MS Douce 323
E	Trinity College, Dublin, MS D.4.12 (= Knott–Fowler T^2)
H	British Library MS Harley 875
H^2	British Library MS Harley 6041 (conjoint A/C-Text; = C-MS H^2)
H^3	British Library MS Harley 3954 (conjoint B/A-Text; = B-MS H)
J	Ingilby MS, Pierpont Morgan Library of New York MS M 818 (= Knott–Fowler I)
K	Bodleian Library MS Digby 145 (= Knott–Fowler Di; conjoint A/C-Text; = C-MS D^2)
L	Lincoln's Inn MS no. 150
M	Society of Antiquaries of London MS no. 687 (formerly the Bright MS)
N	National Library of Wales MS no. 733 (conjoint A/C-Text; = C-MS N^2)
R	Bodleian Library MS Rawlinson Poetry 137
T	Trinity College, Cambridge, MS R.3.14 (conjoint A/C-Text; = C-MS T)
U	University College, Oxford, MS 45

Works cited

V   Vernon Manuscript, Bodleian Library MS English Poetry a.1

W   *olim* The Duke of Westminster's MS, Eaton Hall (conjoint A/C-Text; = C-MS W)

Note also:

Pembroke College, Cambridge, MS 312 C/6 (fragment containing parts of IV and VII. Not mentioned by Kane)

B-Text

Bm British Library MS Additional 10574 (conjoint C/A/B-Text; = C-MS L)

Bo   Bodleian Library MS Bodley 814 (conjoint C/A/B-Text; = C-MS B)

C   Cambridge University Library MS Dd.1.17

C^2 Cambridge University Library MS Ll.4.14

Cot British Library MS Cotton Caligula A XI (conjoint C/A/B-Text; = C-MS O)

F   Corpus Christi College, Oxford, MS 201

G   Cambridge University Library MS Gg.4.31

H   British Library MS Harley 3954 (conjoint B/A-Text; = A-MS H^3)

Hm Huntington Library MS Hm 128 (formerly Ashburnham 130)

Hm^2 Huntington Library MS Hm 128 (fragments of B II and III copied from the same archetype as that of Hm)

Ht   Huntington Library MS 114 (formerly MS Phillipps 8252, formerly Heber. A mixed text with A, B, and C elements. Rejected by Kane–Donaldson)

L   Bodleian Library MS Laud Misc. 581

M   British Library MS Additional 35287 (formerly Ashburnham 129)

O   Oriel College, Oxford, MS 79

R   Bodleian Library MS Rawlinson Poetry 38, four leaves of which are bound in British Library MS Lansdowne 398

S   *olim* Sion College MS Arc. L. 40. 2/E. 76 (now Tokyo, Toshiyuki Takamiya, MS 23. A B-Text with hundreds of unique variants. Rejected by Kane–Donaldson)

W   Trinity College, Cambridge, MS B.15.17

Y   Newnham College, Cambridge, Yates-Thompson MS

Note also:

Bodleian Library MS James 2 (see p. 20 n. 5 above. Unmentioned by Kane–Donaldson)

Bodleian Library MS Wood donat 7 (see A. S. G. Edwards, '*Piers Plowman* in the Seventeenth Century: Gerard Langbaine's Notes')

British Library MS Sloane 2578 (see Sharon L. Jansen, 'Politics, Protest, and a New *Piers Plowman* Fragment: The Voice of the Past in Tudor England', and p. 10 n. 12 above)

Gonville and Caius College, Cambridge, MS 201 (a transcript of Rogers' 1561 edition)

C-Text

A   University of London Library MS S.L. V.17 (formerly in the library of Sir Louis Sterling)

Works cited

B   Bodleian Library MS Bodley 814 (conjoint C/A/B-Text; = B-MS Bo)
Ch   Chaderton MS, Liverpool University Library F. 4. 8 (conjoint A/C-Text; = A-MS Ch)
D   Bodleian Library MS Douce 104
D^2 Bodleian Library MS Digby 145 (conjoint A/C-Text; = A-MS K)
E   Bodleian Library MS Laud Misc. 656
F   Cambridge University Library MS Ff.5.35
G   Cambridge University Library MS Dd.3.13
H^2 British Library MS Harley 6041 (conjoint A/C-Text; = A-MS H^2)
I   Ilchester Manuscript, University of London Library MS S.L. V.88
K   Bodleian Library MS Digby 171
L   British Library Additional 10574 (conjoint C/A/B-Text; = B-MS Bm)
M   British Library MS Cotton Vespasian B XVI
N   British Library MS Harley 2376
N^2 National Library of Wales MS no. 733 (conjoint A/C-Text; = A-MS N)
O   British Library MS Cotton Caligula A XI (conjoint C/A/B-Text; = B-MS Cot)
P   Huntington Library MS Hm 137 (formerly Phillipps 8231, formerly Heber)
P^2 British Library MS Additional 34779 (formerly Phillipps 9056, formerly Heber)
Q   Cambridge University Library Additional 4325
R   British Library MS Royal Library 18.B.XVII
S   Corpus Christi College, Cambridge, MS 293
T   Trinity College, Cambridge, MS R.3.14 (conjoint A/C-Text; = A-MS T)
U   British Library MS Additional 35157
V   Trinity College, Dublin, MS D.4.1
W   *olim* The Duke of Westminster's MS, Eaton Hall (conjoint A/C-Text; = A-MS W)
X   Huntington Library MS 143
Y   Bodleian Library MS Digby 102
Z   Bodleian Library MS Bodley 851 (conjoint Z/C-Text)

(There is some confusion about the sigils attached to the C portion of British Library Additional 10574 and to that of British Library MS Cotton Caligula A XI. Skeat did not assign these manuscripts separate sigils. Chambers listed the C portion of Add. 10574 as O, and the C portion of Cotton Caligula A XI as L. Donaldson followed suit in 1949, as did DiMarco in 1982. In 1988, however, Kane listed the C portion of Add. 10574 as L, and the C portion of Cotton Caligula as O; he was followed by Hanna in 1993 and by Schmidt in 1995. This is the listing I have adopted here.)

Note also:
Gonville and Caius College, Cambridge, MS 669/646, fol. 210 (a seventeen-line fragment; see Doyle, 'Remarks on Surviving Manuscripts of *Piers Plowman*', 45)
olim Cambridge, John Holloway, fragment

General index

452

Index of manuscripts

Note: additional discussions or mentions of the genetic relations of the various MSS of *Piers Plowman* appear at pp. 175 n.36, 138 ff., and 163ff. (Skeat's grouping of A-, B- and C-MSS respectively); 242ff. (Knott's grouping of A-MSS); 257ff. (Blackman's grouping of B-MSS); 266ff. (Allen's grouping of C-MSS); 330ff. (Knott–Fowler's grouping of A-MSS); 362 (Kane's grouping of A-MSS); 384–5, 386–7 (Kane–Donaldson's grouping of B-MSS); 413–14 (Schmidt's grouping of B-MSS).

CAMBRIDGE STUDIES IN MEDIEVAL LITERATURE

General Editor: Professor Alastair Minnis, Professor of Medieval Literature,
University of York

Editorial board
Professor Piero Boitani (Professor of English, Rome)
Professor Patrick Boyde, FBA (Serena Professor of Italian, Cambridge)
Professor John Burrow, FBA (Winterstoke Professor of English, Bristol)
Professor Alan Deyermond, FBA (Professor of Hispanic Studies, London)
Professor Peter Dronke, FBA (Professor of Medieval Latin Literature, Cambridge)
Dr Tony Hunt (St Peter's College, Oxford)
Professor Nigel Palmer (Professor of German Medieval and Linguistic Studies,
Oxford)
Professor Winthrop Wetherbee (Professor of English, Cornell)

Titles published